THE DELPHIAN COURSE

A SYSTEMATIC PLAN OF EDUCATION, EMBRACING THE WORLD'S PROGRESS AND DEVELOPMENT OF THE LIBERAL ARTS

COUNCIL OF REVIEW

VERY REV. J. K. BRENNAN	Missouri
GISLE BOTHNE, M. A.	University of Minnesota
CHAS. H. CAFFIN	New York
JAMES A. CRAIG, M.A., B.D., PH.D.	University of Michigan
MRS. SARAH PLATT DECKER	Colorado
ALCÉE FORTIER, D.LT.	Tulane University
ROSWELL FIELD	Chicago
BRUCE G. KINGSLEY	Royal College of Organists, England
D. D. LUCKENBILL, A.B., PH.D	University of Chicago
KENNETH MCKENZIE, PH.D	Yale University
FRANK B. MARSH, PH.D.	University of Texas
DR. HAMILTON WRIGHT MABIE	New York
W. A. MERRILL, PH.D., L.H.D.	University of California
T. M. PARROTT, PH.D.	Princeton University
GRANT SHOWERMAN, PH.D.	University of Wisconsin
H. C. TOLMAN, PH.D., D.D.	Vanderbilt University
I. E. WING, M.A.	Michigan

VOL. X

THE DELPHIAN SOCIETY

American History,
Art, Literature,
Poetry and Fiction, Expeditions
Part Ten
Plus Study Guide

Copyright © 2019 by Libraries of Hope. All rights reserved. No part of this publication may be reproduced, stored in a retrieval system, or transmitted in any form or by any means, electronic, mechanical, photocopying, recording or otherwise, without prior written permission of the publisher. International rights and foreign translations available only through permission of the publisher.

Copyright from:
The Delphian Course, by the Delphian Society. Chicago: The Delphian Society, (1913).

Study Guide, by the Delphian Society, Chicago" The Delphian Society, (1911).

Cover Image: Ribbons and Lace, by Edmund Blair Leighton, (1902), from Wikimedia Commons.

Libraries of Hope, Inc. Appomattox, Virginia 24522

Website: www.librariesofhope.com
Email: librariesofhope@gmail.com

Printed in the United States of America

TABLE OF CONTENTS
PART X

UNITED STATES HISTORY

Chapter I.
Age of Discovery and Exploration.................................... 2

Chapter II.
Age of Settlement 8

Chapter III.
Beginnings of a Nation.. 15

Chapter IV.
Establishment of an Efficient Government............................ 21

Chapter V.
The Early Republic 26

Chapter VI.
From Jackson to Lincoln... 33

Chapter VII.
The Latter Part of the Nineteenth Century........................... 39

FAMOUS HISTORICAL ADDRESSES.

Chapter VIII.
Call to Arms.. 45
Boston's Place in History... 48
Hayne-Webster Debate 51
Speech of Gettysburg.. 73
Lincoln's Second Inaugural Address.................................. 74
The Martyr President.. 76
The New South... 79

EXPOSITIONS AND PROGRESS

Chapter IX.
Early International Fairs... 83

Chapter X.
The Centennial 91

Chapter XI.
The Columbian Exposition 103

Chapter XII.
The World's Fair Congresses 111
    The Educated Woman 113
    The Kindergarten 115
    Women and Politics 118
    Self Government 121
    Woman's Suffrage 123
    The Right to Vote 125
    The Moral Initiative 129
    Marriage 131
    Domestic Service 134
    Salvation Army 138
    The Stage and Its Women 140
    Polish Women 144
    Women in Spain 147

Chapter XIII.
The Pan-American Exposition 152

Chapter XIV.
Louisiana Purchase Exposition 160

Chapter XV.
Lewis and Clark Exposition 168

Chapter XVI.
Jamestown Exposition 184

Chapter XVII.
Alaska-Yukon-Pacific Exposition 196

Chapter XVIII.
Panama-Pacific Exposition 201

AMERICAN PAINTING

Chapter XIX.
Early American Painters 207

Chapter XX.
Recent American Painters 214

Chapter XXI.
Art Centers in America 225

Chapter XXII.
Mural Painting in America 235

AMERICAN LITERATURE
Prefatory Chapter 247

Chapter I.
Colonial Literature 255

Chapter II.
Nineteenth Century Literature 279
Irving 283

Chapter III.
Cooper 304

Chapter IV.
Hawthorne 322

Chapter V.
Emerson 350

AMERICAN POETRY

Chapter VI.
Bryant 363

Chapter VII.
Longfellow 372

Chapter VIII.
Lowell; Holmes 396

Chapter IX.
Poe 412

Chapter X.
Whittier 421

Chapter XI.
Aldrich; Taylor 438

Chapter XII.
Recent Poets 445

Chapter XIII.
Recent Poems 458

Chapter XIV.
American Life in American Fiction........................... 466
    Howells 466
    Warner 473
    James 481
    Harte 489
    Jackson 498
Description of Illustrations....................................... 512

INDICES

FULL PAGE ILLUSTRATIONS

PART X

	PAGE
OXEN PLOUGHING (Water Color)	Frontispiece
A BUSY STREET AT THE NIJNI NOVGOROD FAIR	14
LANDSCAPE—COROT (Photogravure)	48
FOUR THOUSAND SHEEP CHANGING PASTURE	80
INDIAN GIRLS WEAVING BASKETS	112
COLUMBUS' FIRST LANDING PLACE	131
SMITHSONIAN INSTITUTE	168
AMONG THE HYDAH INDIANS	192
HELEN HUNT FALLS	224
OLD FAITHFUL—YELLOWSTONE	256
ROTUNDA GALLERY—CONGRESSIONAL LIBRARY	304
GARDEN OF THE SANTA BARBARA MISSION (Photogravure)	352
LOOKING DOWN THE CANON	416
A MEXICAN CATHEDRAL	464
MAP SHOWING UNITED STATES' GROWTH	VIII

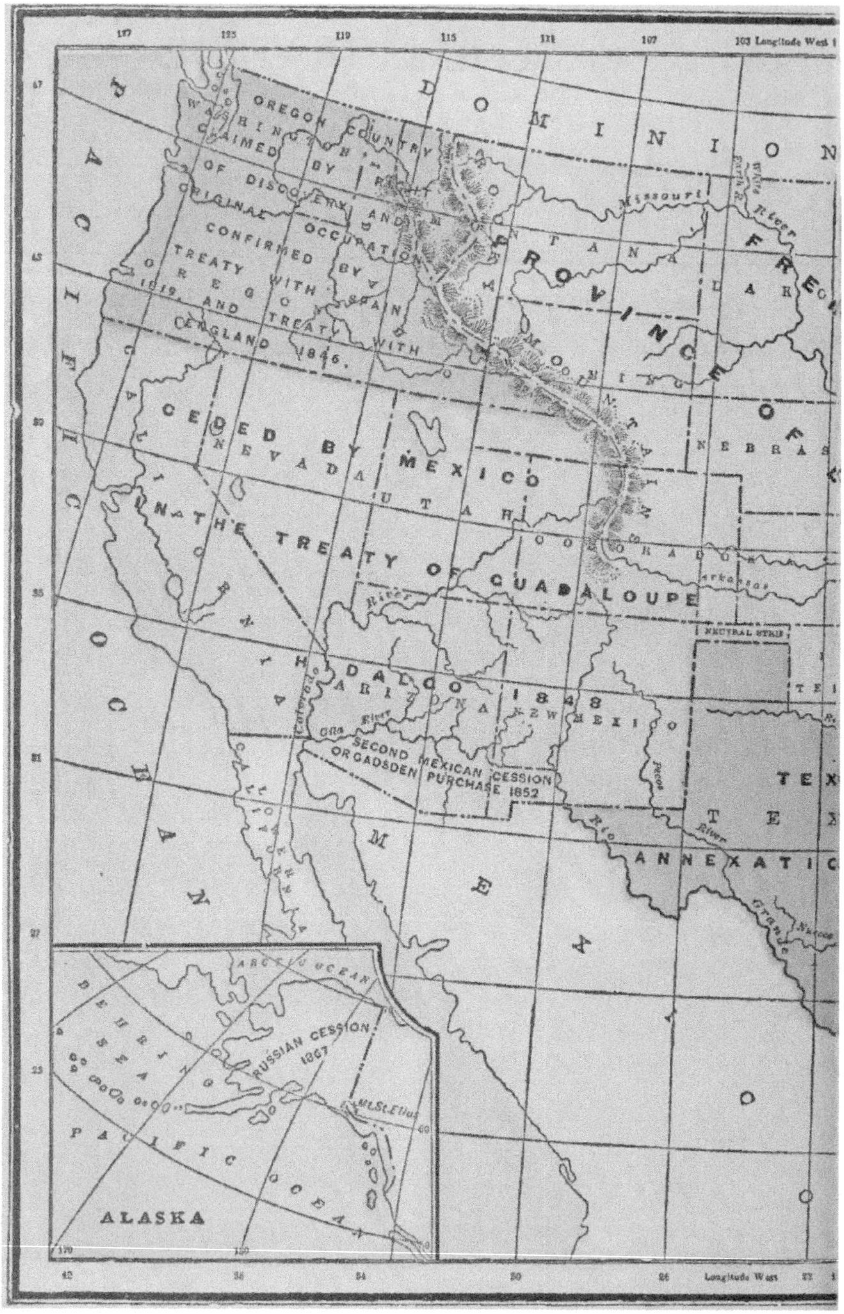

DOMINION
OREGON COUNTRY CLAIMED BY RIGHT OF DISCOVERY AND ORIGINAL OCCUPATION CONFIRMED BY TREATY WITH SPAIN 1819, AND TREATY WITH ENGLAND 1846.
WASHINGTON
OREGON
IDAHO
MONTANA
WYOMING
Missouri
River
CEDED BY MEXICO IN THE TREATY OF GUADALOUPE HIDALGO 1848
NEVADA
UTAH
COLORADO
Arkansas
NEBRASKA
CALIFORNIA
ARIZONA
NEW MEXICO
Colorado
Gila River
Pecos
SECOND MEXICAN CESSION OR GADSDEN PURCHASE 1852
NEUTRAL STRIP
TEXAS
Rio Grande
MEXICO
PACIFIC OCEAN
ARCTIC OCEAN
BEHRING SEA
RUSSIAN CESSION 1867
Mt.St.Elias
PACIFIC OCEAN
ALASKA
Longitude West

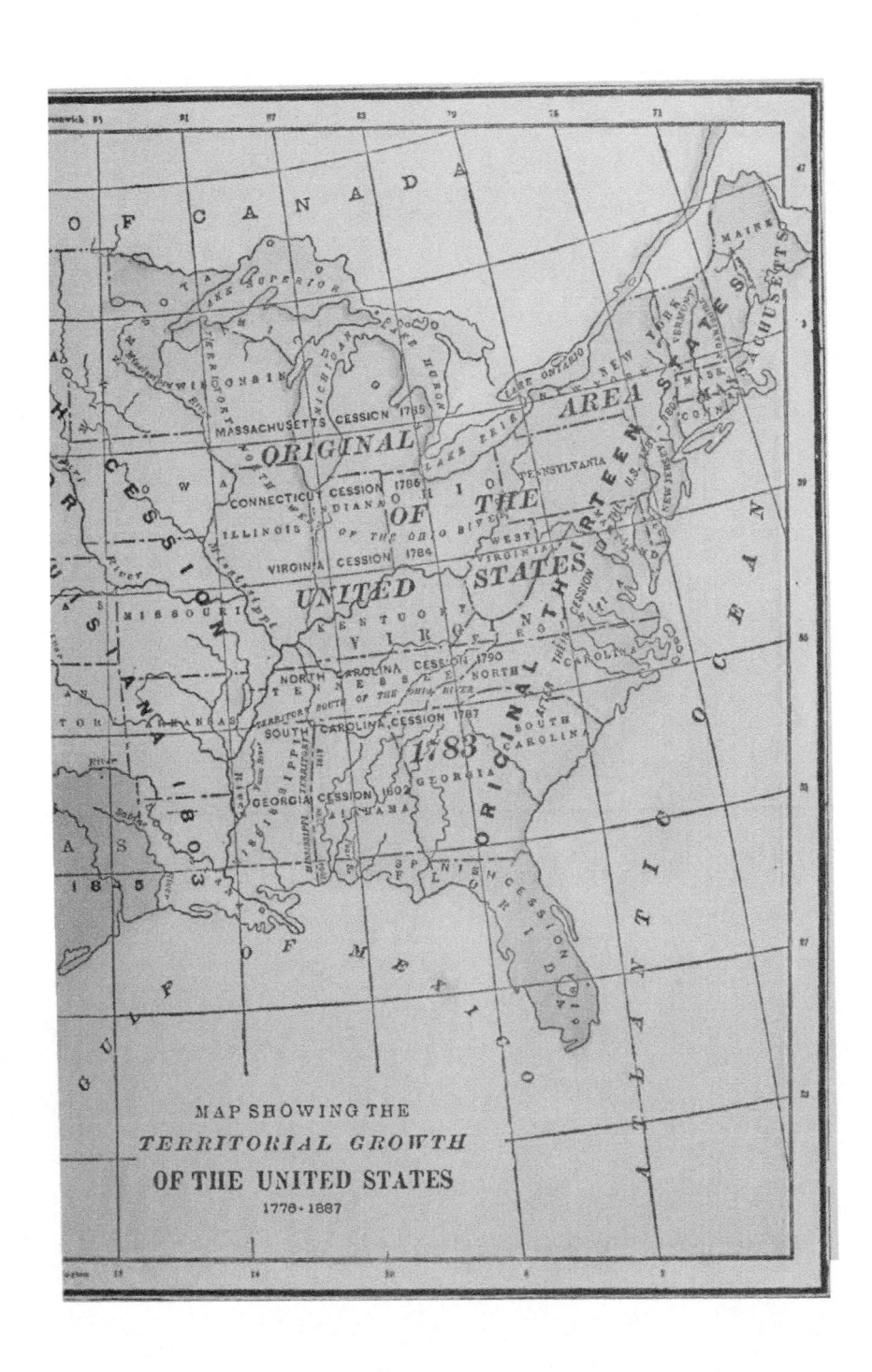

MAP SHOWING THE
TERRITORIAL GROWTH
OF THE UNITED STATES
1776-1887

I have seen the glories of art and architecture, and mountain and river; I have seen the sun set on Jungfrau, and the full moon rise over Mont Blanc; but fairest vision on which these eyes ever looked was the flag of my country in a foreign land. Beautiful as a flower to those who love it, terrible as a meteor to those who hate it, it is a symbol of the power and glory and the honor of ninety millions of Americans.

George F. Hoar.

RÉSUMÉ OF UNITED STATES HISTORY

CHAPTER I.

The Age of Discovery and Exploration.

The history of civilization, to a far greater degree than has been realized until recently, is the history of trade. For the last few centuries the wars that have been fought—whatever the causes set forth in formal proclamations—have been waged for commercial reasons; and the demands of trade, at the close of the fifteenth century, led to the discovery of a new world.

From very early times the luxuries of Europe had been imported from the East. Silks, spices, ivory, costly woods and incense were brought across the deserts of Asia by caravans and were reloaded upon vessels for various European ports. At best this was a costly undertaking, and only the wealthy could afford to buy the precious wares when at last they were displayed for sale. However, the Turks had gradually extended their territory westward, and after the fall of Constantinople, in 1453, the well-established caravan routes were no longer even moderately secure from marauding bands. As a consequence, it became apparent that if the profitable trade of the Orient were not to be wholly lost, some new way of reaching the desired land must be found.

The Renaissance had awakened the minds of men and set them thinking. Some read diligently the writings and philosophies of the ancients, and, under their inspiration, brought forth literary masterpieces of their own. Painters caught the spirit of the Greeks and created wonderful pictures which astonish and mystify the world today. Men of more practical bent applied their attention to matters of every day concern, and mariners, grown more venturesome, were much assisted by the invention of the compass and the astrolabe. The Portuguese produced many bold sailors and one of their number succeeded in circumnavigating Africa. Yet while this new waterway gave access to the East, it was so interminably long as to be hardly practical.

The Travels of Marco Polo had stimulated Europeans with a desire to know more of a land which had impressed the illustrious Venetian as so remarkable and full of resources. The invention of printing led to the more general diffusion of such literature, and, take it all in all, many were pondering upon various plans which might lead to the working out of a new route thither.

Christopher Columbus, a native of Genoa, Italy, studied the writings of Polo and all the maps and charts then available. He was persuaded that if one should sail due west, he must come at last to the countries visited by Polo on his prolonged journey to the Orient—to Cathay (China), and Cipango (Japan). The story of his weary striving to enlist the interest of kings in his enterprise is well known,—how he wandered from court to court, vainly trying to procure funds necessary for the fitting out of an expedition. The truth was that European monarchs were concerned with matters vitally affecting their kingdoms and had scant time for men like Columbus, who appeared to his contemporaries to be almost mentally unbalanced, so intense was he in promoting his scheme.

It was Isabella of Castile who finally offered to aid Columbus, and every child in America who has had even a few years in school remembers the names of the three small vessels at last placed at his command—the Pinta, the Niña and the Santa Maria. Slight, fragile crafts they were, in the like of which no one would attempt an ocean voyage today. And yet the discovery of two unknown continents fell to the share of those who sailed in the three light barks.

To understand the disappointment, neglect and shame that overtook Columbus' later life, one must ever keep in mind the object with which he first set out—*to find a new route to the Indies,* as the East was often called. On that memorable morning when he planted the Spanish flag on the new-found land and took possession of it in the name of the king and queen of Spain, Columbus firmly believed he had touched upon the shores of the country concerning which Marco Polo had written: Cathay, or possibly the islands which Polo had said skirted its eastern coast. Slight investigation, to be sure, did not reveal the much-desired riches, but it was quite enough to have given reality to a dream and, having taken such trophies as the region afforded, the vessels soon put about to carry the glad tidings back to Spain. High honors were accorded the great admiral upon his return, and the imaginations of Spanish adventurers were enkindled with wild fancies and extravagant hopes. The news of the great discovery was not heralded about very widely, for naturally Spain wished to keep her recently-found territory for herself.

Columbus made three later voyages. He visited some of the islands belonking to the West Indies group and coasted along South America and Central America. Because he supposed he had reached the Indies, the people found inhabiting the lands were called Indians. Thus we see that the name by which the American red man is commonly known was given him by mistake. In vain did Columbus search for the coveted wares of the Orient; in vain did he attempt to reach that portion of the country of which travellers had written. Then, dejected, reproached by the sovereigns who had made his great work possible, poor and broken-hearted, he died in 1506, never knowing what a boon he had conferred upon humanity.

For many years this mistaken idea of Columbus was kept alive. Spaniards, French and English came thither, not with the desire to learn of a strange country, but with the hope of being the first to reach the Orient and point the way to a new trade route. To be sure, the more they searched, the more they learned about the continent and at last the truth was borne in upon them that this was not Cathay. Even then the desire to get through a land which hindered their progress was paramount. We may read how the sixteenth century was filled with adventures made with the hope of finding an outlet to the land beyond. The St. Lawrence, Mississippi, Amazon, de la Plata, and many other rivers were traced with the vain purpose. Even Captain John Smith, of Virginia, thought that the little James river might be the way through the country to a western ocean.

And yet, as we read the strange story, and see how lives were wasted and fortunes spent with a mistaken purpose, it need not seem so remarkable that it took men at least one hundred years to believe what was long thought beyond credence: that a great, unappropriated world had been brought to light. It must ever seem marvellous, when reflected upon, that civilization after civilization had been born, kingdom after kingdom had risen and fallen, and the human race, whose progress is recorded since about 4777 B. C., remained for the most part in ignorance of a great undiscovered country. There were, to be sure, people living in the new land, but they dwelt apart from the great stream of human progress.

Spain had issued forth victorious in a terrible war with the Moors—a war which had been finally waged for life or death. Having driven the Mohammedans from Christian Spain, there were many devoted Spaniards who saw another religious mission opening before them: to convert the simple people of the newly found lands to the orthodox faith. For this reason, among others, the Pope was besought to make Spain a grant of the world discovered by Columbus. Alexander VI, utterly unscrupulous about important matters, was not likely to discern that in this comparatively unimportant matter—as it was then viewed—he was acting beyond any authority he possessed, when he gave to the king of Spain, and his heirs forever, such lands as lay west of an imaginary line drawn through the Atlantic ocean.

Now Spain entered upon a wonderful chapter of her development. Only in late years has the world awakened to the tremendous part she played in the early history of America. With a courage not exceeded by men at any time, her proud-hearted subjects threw themselves into the prodigious task of exploration and discovery. While other European nations still went their ways, as though no momentous change had taken place in the world, Spanish leaders and priests were pressing through the well-nigh impenetrable forests and deserts of America, making their conquests and founding their settlements.

"She was the only European nation that did not drowse. Her mailed explorers overran Mexico and Peru, grasped their incalculable riches, and made those kingdoms inalienable parts of Spain. Cortez had conquered and was colonizing a savage country a dozen times as large as England years before the first English-speaking expedition had ever seen the mere coast where it was to plant colonies in the New World; and Pizarro did a still greater work. Ponce de Leon had taken possession for Spain of what is now one of the States of our Union a generation before any of those regions were seen by Saxons. That first traveller in North America, Alvar Nuñez Cabeza de Vaca, had walked his unparalleled way across the continent from Florida to the Gulf of California half a century before the first foot of our ancestors touched our soil.

"They were Spaniards who first saw and explored the greatest gulf in the world; Spaniards who discovered the two greatest rivers; Spaniards who found the greatest ocean; Spaniards who first knew that there were two continents of America; Spaniards who first went round the world! There were Spaniards who had carved their way into the far interior of our own land, as well as of all to the south, and founded their cities a thousand miles inland long before the first Anglo-Saxon came to the Atlantic sea-board. That early Spanish spirit of *finding out* was fairly superhuman. Why, a poor Spanish lieutenant with twenty soldiers pierced an unspeakable desert and looked down upon the greatest natural wonder of America or of the world—the Grand Cañon of the Colorado—three full centuries before any 'American' eyes saw it! And so it was from Colorado to Cape Horn. Heroic, impetuous, imprudent Balboa had walked that awful walk across the Isthmus, and found the Pacific Ocean, and built on its shores the first ships that were ever made in the Americas, and sailed that unknown sea, and had been dead more than half a century before Drake and Hawkins saw it." [1]

The Spanish explored Florida, the Gulf of Mexico, found the great ocean,—called by them for some time the South Sea,—the Pacific, and crossed it. They traced the Father of Waters—the Mississippi—to its mouth, and from Florida crossed the continent to New Mexico, Arizona and California. Brazil was explored and the silver mines of Peru soon made to yield up their treasure.

The French joined in the search to the Indies. Following the St. Lawrence from its mouth, Cartier landed at the rapids, which he named Lachine (Chinese), and spent the winter at

---

[1] Lummis, The Spanish Pioneers, 20.

Mont Royal—Montreal. Soon after Columbus' great discovery, John and Sebastian Cabot sailed across the Atlantic from England and coasted along the shores of Newfoundland. For thus reaching the supposed "China" John Cabot was given ten pounds—about $500— and a yearly pension amounting to about $1,000.

By great injustice the new world was called America. It happened in this way: An Italian by the name of Amerigo Vespucci made several visits to the shores of Brazil. Upon his last return to Europe he wrote extensively of his voyages. He said that only three-quarters of the world had been known to the ancients and that the other fourth had now been found. A German map maker suggested that this fourth be called America, and so named Brazil on his map. In time the whole of South America was thus designated, and when it was at last understood that the two continents were connected, the whole of the new world came to be known by this name.

After the lapse of fifty years the coasts of the two continents had been quite generally visited. No permanent settlements had yet been made, and for fifty years longer the hope of finding an inside passage to China deterred men from making the most of their opportunities.

FROM A DRAWING MADE ABOUT
1450.

CHAPTER II.

THE AGE OF SETTLEMENT.

The great pioneers in America—the Spanish—were unceasing in their activities during the first two centuries after the discovery of the new world. For the first century they were almost alone here; during the second century they were still foremost. The Portuguese made some settlements in South America, but the Spanish made more, and still more numerous were their settlements in Mexico. In what is now the United States, fewer towns were founded, although the first permanent colony planted here was the one that grew up around the fort at St. Augustine—founded in 1565. Through New Mexico, Arizona, Texas and California their tremendous strength was felt and the later development of the southern Pacific slope was deeply affected by the Spanish. In 1769 the Franciscans landed near the present site of San Diego and began their tireless efforts to civilize the Indians. The final suppression of their work resulted disastrously indeed.

"That later times have reversed the situation; that Spain (largely because she was drained of her best blood by a conquest so enormous that no nation even now could give the men or the money to keep the enterprise abreast with the world's progress) has never regained her old strength, and is now a drone beside the young giant of nations that has grown, since her day, in the empire she opened—has nothing to do with the obligation of American history to give her justice for the past. Had there been no Spain four hundred years ago, there would be no United States today. It is a most fascinating story to every genuine American,—for every one worthy of the name admires heroism and loves fair-play everywhere, and is first of all interested in the truth about his own country." [1]

Spain's enormous profits from the mines of Peru soon aroused the lethargy of England. Adventurous spirits began

---
[1] Lummis, Spanish Pioneers in America, 90.

to intercept Spanish galleons on the seas, and, finding that their sovereign made slight inquiry as to the means by which they gained their wealth, they laid in wait for the stately ships that were returning with much treasure. The buccaneering of Hawkins, Drake and men of similar spirit, did much to stimulate a feeling of hostility between the two countries. Spain stood for a united Church; the Holy See found Spanish sovereigns among the staunchest supporters of Catholicism. England had shaken herself free from Rome, and for religious causes Spain wanted to strike a blow at the sturdy island. However, rivalry in trade has always been as potent a factor as religion in provoking a war—today it is the stronger of the two, but even in former ages its force was not to be despised. Spain laid claim to all the new world with the exception of certain districts in Brazil, settled by Portugal. Between England and Spain it was to be war to the death, and the resources of the latter were bountifully expended in preparing the Spanish Armada which was to strike at the heart of the rival country.

For many years Spain had been draining her country of its fighting strength in prosecuting wars on the continent. Recently her men of vigor had been plunging into the unknown world, and while the fact was not wholly realized by the king, Spain was ill prepared to enter upon a terrible struggle with sturdy England. When the ministers, filled with alarm for England's safety, called for soldiers, practically the whole island responded—Catholic and Protestant alike—ready to fight for native land.

Utterly defeated on the seas, both countries understood the meaning of Spain's defeat and England's victory. Henceforth Spain must hold what she could. Having attempted too much, she was doomed to lose everything. Confident of their strength, the English were now free to plant their colonies at will.

The attempts made by the English to establish colonies in Newfoundland and on the island of Roanoke failed. The early English settlements were managed by companies of merchants in London, who were looking for prompt returns for investments and did not comprehend the conditions prevailing in a remote wilderness. Those who responded to the call for men to go out into a new country were, as a rule, those who had failed at home. Successful business men were not likely to entertain the idea of beginning in a strange land. Men who had recently served in continental wars and were now without employment; men who found themselves out of work because land in England was being thrown into large holdings for sheep pastures; sons of nobles who wished to seek their fortunes but who knew nothing of actual work—such were the men who responded to the opportunity given by companies promoting colonies in America.

In 1907 there was held in Jamestown, Virginia, an exposition commemorating the three hundredth anniversary of the founding of that little town. In 1607, on the banks of the James river, the first permanent English settlement was made in America. Men of all sorts and conditions came hither, but one tendency characterized nearly all: a strong aversion to work. Even the ones who were willing did not know how to proceed, and lack of food, bad water, fevers and dissensions worked them woe. Had it not been for Captain John Smith the whole colony might have been destroyed. As it was, in 1610 the survivors had already set sail for England when they met Lord Delaware bringing food and other necessities, and were persuaded to turn back to the homes they had just abandoned.

In time prosperity came to Virginia. There were many rivers affording water and fertile soil. Along these streams great fields of tobacco soon were planted. This commodity found a ready sale in England, and the Virginian planters became the wealthy men of the eastern sea-board. The very conditions of life explain the political organization that sprang up among them almost unnoticed. Living far apart, rivers rather than roads afforded them means of communication. Ships came up to the planter's private wharf, loaded on his tobacco for shipment to England, and gave him in exchange such articles, commodities and products as he could not procure at home. A visit between planters involved quite a journey. As a natural result, towns were few, roads poor, and the political unit became, not the township, as in New England, but the county.

In 1619 three events significant for the future transpired

in Virginia: a goodly number of maidens were brought out to become the wives of the colonists and make possible the establishment of permanent homes; the first colored slaves were brought to Jamestown and sold to the planters; and the first legislative assembly convened in the little Jamestown church to make laws for the community. To be sure, the charter of Virginia was afterwards withdrawn and the colony became a royal province, but the spirit of representation, justice and freedom had been fostered and was destined to assert itself in the future.

In 1620 the Mayflower made its memorable voyage, bringing to the cold, inhospitable shores of New England that little company of brave men and women who came hither for the purpose of worshipping as they thought right. Even little children in America today know the story of their wanderings; how, persecuted in England, they found a place of refuge in Holland, but soon realized that in course of time their nationality would there be lost. Then with a mighty effort and a staunch courage they resolutely turned their faces toward the new world, hoping to be able there to remain Englishmen and enjoy freedom of religious thought and service. Among them the faults of idleness and indolence were not found, but they landed in the month of December and were ill prepared for the intense cold, miserable shelter and scanty food. Small wonder that more than half died before spring. Their difficulties with the Indians, their trials and dangers need no recital here. Like other stories of Colony Days, they are early implanted in the minds of all American citizens.

There was no single commodity to be grown here which would bring prosperity to New England. The soil of this section had been made poor and stony by great glaciers which spread over the whole region twice, at least, in ages long passed away. The deposits that were brought down by these rivers of ice filled up the old river beds and when the ice at length subsided, new streams set to work to cut down their channels. Young rivers are generally characterized by waterfalls, and these were especially plentiful in New England. As a result of its topography, then, this region became, not a farming section, but a manufacturing district. Towns sprang up everywhere. Roads led from one to another. Each locality possessed its own peculiar needs. Consequently the township, and not the county, became the political unit of New England.

Conditions in England accounted for the large migration westward during the latter part of the seventeenth century. Religious persecution affected in turn Catholics, Puritans, Dissenters and Quakers. Maryland was settled as a refuge for Catholics, and in 1649 the first act of religious toleration ever enacted in America was passed in this colony. William Penn founded Philadelphia—City of Brotherly Love—as a home for Quakers. Rhode Island was settled by people who were driven out of Puritan Massachusetts because they would not conform to the ideas of that sect. In the latter part of the century, political reasons were as potent as those pertaining to religion. The Stuarts were trying to give the theory of the Divine Right of kings a material reality in England. Many independent spirits found submission intolerable and migrated to other lands. Again, during the Commonwealth, the royalists did not feel safe at home, and they in turn looked across the ocean and felt that it was best to try their fortunes in the western land.

While the English were swarming to the Atlantic seaboard, other nations were not idle. As early as 1604 the French tried to plant colonies in Nova Scotia and Port Royal, but neither was successful. However, forts were established at Montreal and Quebec, and Jesuit Fathers, in company with French traders and explorers, journeyed all through the St. Lawrence basin, around the Great Lakes and down the Mississippi, founding a station near the mouth of the great river— New Orleans. From Quebec to the Gulf of Mexico they thus blocked out a highway through the continent. Conditions within France prevented a firm and aggressive policy in the new world at a time when this alone could have won lasting possessions.

The Dutch, who had become to a considerable extent the carriers for Europe on the high seas, looked eagerly toward the new world. In 1909 the Hudson-Fulton celebration in New York commemorated the three hundredth anniversary since Henry Hudson had sailed up the Hudson River in his vessel, the Half-Moon, in search for a passage to China. The

Dutch, like the French, found the fur trade with the Indians profitable. There was scarcely any limit to the number of pelts to be bought for a trifling amount from the natives. Simple-minded people, the Indians were satisfied to exchange the most valuable furs for gaudy scarfs or brightly colored beads.

To encourage settlement, the Dutch trading company offered any one who would take a little colony of fifty families to the new world at his own expense, sixteen miles along the bank of a river or eight miles along both banks, the tract to reach inland almost any distance. They were given rights corresponding in some respects to those exercised by feudal lords and were called Patroons. Even with such inducements the Dutch did not come thither in very large numbers. They early came into conflict with the Swedes in Delaware and were driven out of that colony. Their settlements at Fort Orange, Albany and New Amsterdam, New York, were very prosperous. However, Charles II granted all this region to his brother, the Duke of York, who came over to take possession of it. The Dutch were too wedded to their commerce to launch upon war. War destroys trade and their interest was to build it up; consequently, in 1664 the Dutch governor surrendered the colony to the English.

The dawn of the eighteenth century found thirteen English colonies stretching along the Atlantic coast. The French were strong to the north, and there was still a struggle to be waged for the Mississippi basin. However, in that struggle the English were destined to win. Spain, foremost in early discovery, had no part in the settlement of the East. Florida, to be sure, remained a Spanish province, but it was not strong enough to make itself felt.

From this time forward, save for the rivalry with France, interest in America was to center for years in the welfare of those colonies that reached from Massachusetts to Georgia. Considered geographically, they were distinguished as the New England, Middle and Southern Colonies. Classified according to their government, some were charter, some royal, some proprietary. The colonies of Massachusetts, Connecticut and Rhode Island were governed by charters which had been granted by English sovereigns and which designated certain provisions concerning the administration of each. Local affairs were left largely in the hands of the colonists. The royal colonies were provinces governed directly by the king; New Hampshire, New York, New Jersey, Virginia, North and South Carolina and Georgia being of this kind. Pennsylvania, Delaware and Maryland were proprietary colonies and were under the immediate control of the proprietors who had received these tracts as grants from the king. The township system, as has been noted, prevailed in the north; in the south the county system, and in the Middle colonies a combination of the two grew up.

A SPANISH GALLEON.

Copyright by Underwood and Underwood, N. Y.
A BUSY STREET AT THE NIJNI NOVGOROD FAIR.

CHAPTER III.

THE BEGINNINGS OF A NATION.

During the latter part of the seventeenth and the first half of the eighteenth centuries, England and France were at war with one another. Rivalries in trade and for imperial possessions were the real points of difficulty between them, although other reasons were set forth upon the various outbreaks of hostilities. This strife between the two countries invariably spread into the colonies and in America these wars became known as King William's, Queen Anne's or King George's war, according to the particular sovereign who chanced to be on the English throne at the time.

The French allied themselves with the Indians more firmly and more uniformly than did the English. For this reason war between the English colonies and the French in America meant Indian raids and massacres. The towns on the frontiers always suffered most. The Indians were semi-barbarous and, while they had been docile and kind in their attitude toward the first white explorers, the utter greed and injustice displayed by these men aroused feelings of deepest distrust and hatred on the part of the Red men. When outbreaks of war gave them confidence to fight at all, they shot out from behind trees, burned dwellings, scalped women and children and in every particular followed the same methods by which they had always fought each other.

For these reasons the recitals of Indian raids are invariably similar. Harrowing deeds, fiendish delight in causing suffering, lack of sympathy for the helpless, characterized the attacks made upon the little English hamlets along the eastern coast during these years and the ones made later upon settlers who pressed farther west, making them more fearful than ever of the natives and more determined to drive them back, away from their settlements. We today are sufficiently removed to view the matter fairly and to realize how mistaken has been the policy pursued toward the American Indians For that reason the government today is doing what it can to educate and protect the survivors of this fast disappearing race; but for the most part the blunders belong to the past and must remain a dark page on our history.

The French held New France—the St. Lawrence basin and the Great Lake region—together with the Mississippi basin, which was known as Louisiana. This territory they were determined to keep. By the last of the seventeenth century the English had made a long line of settlements along the Atlantic. Whenever war broke out between the French and English colonies, the English made what effort they could to get control of the region in the vicinity of Quebec, with the hope of ultimately gaining the mouth of the St. Lawrence; and the land west of the Appalachian range,—thus to have room for expansion. Success attended now one, now the other of the two nations. Finally the French began to build a chain of forts along the eastern Mississippi valley, the better to protect their possessions. Encouraged by success, they soon laid claim to the Ohio valley, the Ohio being a mighty tributary of their great water-way. At this the people of Virginia took alarm. A Virginian company had already formed for the purpose of controlling and settling this region. The governor of the colony sent word to the French to remove their forts in this vicinity. When the request was refused, hostilities broke out between the French and English colonies.

Heretofore the wars which had occurred in America had been started in Europe. This one, often called the French and Indian war, alone originated in the New World.

It is interesting at the start to see the relative situation of the two nations in America. The English had settled at points most convenient and accessible for themselves. Clinging at first to the coast, they built up an almost continuous line of towns and villages. They had been chartered by the king and local affairs were generally managed by representative bodies within the colonies themselves. The French were not so fortunate. With utter lack of understanding concerning life in this new land, an attempt was made by the French government to manage each detail of administration from the home-country. Colonists were sent out to settle in places designated before they left France. In order to hold a vast territory, these colonists were scattered apart, wide distances intervening between them. In case of war they were weak, for early forts were in the very necessity of the case simple affairs, unable to withstand serious attack. Again these Frenchmen in America had not become accustomed to meeting emergencies themselves. They were used to receiving instructions and to carrying them out. It was largely this mistaken policy of colonization that finally brought the French disappointment and loss of territory.

The English government deemed it necessary to send General Braddock with a detachment of regulars to resist the French in this last war waged against them by the colonies. George Washington, a young Virginian who had come into notice for efficient service, was chosen to assist him. In vain did Washington try to make plain the method of attack to be expected in the wilds of America. By adhering to tactics which had proved effectual in Europe, Braddock met with total defeat and was himself killed. The later movements of the war were better managed, owing to the fact that William Pitt was called to the head of English administration. The last great battle was fought at Quebec, where both French and English generals lost their lives.

Spain had been drawn into the struggle as an ally of France. When the formal treaty was signed in 1763 the French were obliged to withdraw from America, while Great Britain received New France and Louisiana, with the exception of New Orleans and vicinity, and some minor islands. Spain gave Florida up to Great Britain, while she herself was compensated by New Orleans and the region west of the Mississippi. How much this implied none understood at that time.

For some years after the conclusion of this struggle the English colonists were busy building roads, improving the means of internal communication and plying their trade. Nevertheless, while these years were prosperous, there was a growing discontent because of trade laws which greatly hampered commerce.

It must be remembered that a spirit of unity had been fostered among the English colonies by the recent war. The defeat of the French had been largely due to the colonists, who fought bravely and stubbornly. The outcome of the struggle had been highly gratifying to them and had given the first signal indication of their strength.

From this it would be possible to draw inferences that would be quite mislea ling. Virginia was one of the leaders through these years and no colony was ever more loyal. It was something of a cross to be forbidden to sell tobacco in any but English markets; nevertheless, the southern colonies adjusted themselves very well to this condition. Even New England, principally engaged in trade, conformed outwardly at least to the trade laws. To protect English manufacturers, the colonists were forbidden to manufacture steel, woolen goods and certain other articles for colonial or foreign trade. Sugar and molasses had to be imported from the British West Indies, or otherwise were subject to a heavy duty. Many productions of America were forbidden markets other than those of England, and all goods destined for the colonies from European ports had to be reshipped from England.

In every particular these regulations were enacted for the benefit of the mother-country; the welfare of colonial commerce was quite ignored. While bitter feeling was thus created, nothing immediately came of it, but the laws were systematically evaded. In 1764, consequently, notification was given that smuggling must cease and that special courts were to be established for punishing offenders. Furthermore, for protection against the Indians, it was purposed to send ten thousand regulars to be quartered in times of peace upon the colonies. To partly defray the expense of maintaining this army, in 1765 Parliament passed the notorious Stamp Act. This required all legal papers to bear government stamps according to the value represented by the documents, and all newspapers to be printed upon paper stamped by the government. This has been a very common method of raising an internal tax in times of special need as, for example, during our recent Spanish war, at which time not only legal papers but many drugs were required to bear a stamp, as means of raising a war fund.

The English colonies had been chartered by the king,— not by Parliament. While their foreign affairs had been managed in England, they had been accustomed to electing representatives to local assemblies for the consideration of their internal affairs. In the course of their deliberations, these legislative assemblies heard and approved of measures involving internal taxes. Long years before, the matter of taxation without representation had been fought out in England, and representation was a right dearly loved by all Britains. Now it had not seemed possible for English colonists so far remote to have representation in the Parliament of England, but they held that their local assemblies took the place of the general Parliament, for that reason. When, therefore, the Stamp Act was read in the House of Burgesses in Virginia, Patrick Henry delivered his famous oration from which the phrase "Give me liberty or give me death!" is so often quoted. A series of resolutions were passed, denying the right of Parliament to levy internal taxes upon the American colonies. It has well been said that as copies of these resolutions and Henry's address spread through the towns along the sea-board, none who read them could ever see matters in quite the same light again. A feeling of common interest once more permeated the land—this time not against a foreign nation, but against the attitude hitherto tolerated: that the trade of the colonies existed only for the convenience and benefit of England.

When we condemn the policy of England at this time it should be kept in mind that the members of Parliament were themselves divided on this question. There were many men in England who admitted that in taking their stand the colonists were but proving themselves true Englishmen. Some of the most influential speeches in favor of representation for the colonists were made by men who never saw our shores. Again, it should be recalled that the reigning sovereign, George III, was less an Englishman than he liked to believe. His policy, not alone in this matter, but in many others, brought manifold difficulties upon his kingdom.

The Stamp Act, with its attendant experiences and demonstrations, is well remembered by all Americans. So strenuous was the opposition against it that it was soon repealed. Yet it was impossible for members of Parliament generally to immediately grasp the real issue. They felt it unreasonable for the colonists to object to contribute toward the support of soldiers furnished for their own protection, losing sight of the fact that the colonists had not asked for the soldiers, resented their presence, and felt abundantly able to protect themselves. They thought it but right that the colonies should help to raise a needed sum of money, but failed to understand that it was the method of raising the money—not the amount—that was contested. Temporary good feeling was restored by the revocation of the Stamp Act, but this was again destroyed by the Townsend Acts of 1767. Victory here again tended to crystallize a general determination to stand together against any form of injustice or oppression. Men who had hewn their freedom out of a wilderness could not be expected to relinquish it on slight provocation. It happened to be a tax on tea that led to the final disruption. It might as well have been any other. The colonists had taken their stand on the platitude: "no taxation without representation," and it mattered not whether the tax was little or great, the commodity essential or not.

This is not a place for a rehearsal of the vicissitudes of the Revolution of 1775. All know the story of the final rupture that led to war; of the weary struggle that lasted almost beyond the strength of the colonists; of the courage born of necessity; and the ultimate recognition on the part of King George of the independence of the United States. Lexington, Bunker Hill, Valley Forge, Brandywine, Yorktown—how many stories are suggested by the mere enumeration of these names! In the trials of dark years filled with anxiety, distress and suffering, a consciousness of the great mission of a free country was borne upon the vision of a few noble, unselfish men and by it they were transformed into statesmen whose part it was to guide the infant republic. Today we give little heed to battles, and the array of soldiery on fields where differences long since were fought out is left to the student of military affairs; but it is wholesome to occasionally review the trials that have been endured, the burdens that have been borne by generous patriots in years gone by, in order that the freedom and liberty of the present time may be the better understood and appreciated. Only by a continued vigilance and loyal devotion to country can the structure raised by our forefathers be preserved.

CHAPTER IV.

The Establishment of an Efficient Government.

During the years of the Revolution (1775-1781) the general government of the thirteen states was vested in a Continental Congress. The powers and functions of this body were not defined, but the exigencies of war allowed the delegates, who convened from time to time, to take such measures as they thought best for the common good. However, it would be a mistake to suppose that the administration of affairs during the war was directed in the main by the Continental Congress. Each colony sent representatives to the different Congresses which assembled (each *state,* after the Declaration of Independence); but long intervals elapsed between the convocations of these bodies, and public opinion was largely molded by individuals. Washington in reality exercised general control, as his position of Commander-in-Chief of the Army allowed him to do. When money was urgently needed and could not be supplied by the Continental Congress, Washington, Robert Morris, and others borrowed on their personal accounts.

It had been understood that some new form of government would be necessary after the independence of the states was assured. To this end a convention was assembled and the Articles of Confederation framed. The system of federal administration that these provided could not go into effect until all the states signed them. Two years elapsed before the last state gave consent. Maryland was the one to hold out longest. With good reason, she, together with certain of the smaller states, refused to come into a union until the states which in the beginning had been given "sea-to-sea" grants should cede any claim upon lands west of the Appalachian Mountains to the general government. These states were Massachusetts, Connecticut, Virginia, North and South Carolina, and Georgia. So many complications had arisen concerning territories overlapping each other that any subsequent adjustment of them would have been impossible. It may be noted in this connection that this indefinite reach of country which thus became the property of the federal government, and so beneficial to all, supplied the one strong bond that held discordant states together when others failed.

We must repeatedly go back to the early situation of the English colonies in America if we would understand the problems that were involved in any union of them. Each had been settled for some particular reason, chartered by some English sovereign, or had started under the guidance of some proprietor who was the recipient of a royal grant. Maryland was founded as a refuge for Catholics; Georgia, as a home for debtors; Massachusetts was settled for the most part by men who desired religious freedom; political oppression had driven them thither. Pennsylvania had been a place of safety for Quakers; New York was founded by the Dutch. In like manner, one might recall the circumstances that led in the beginning to the peopling of the thirteen states. While in the course of one hundred and fifty years these original motives had been gradually lost from sight, still, each continued to be in many respects isolated. In time of danger the colonies had acted together. When the danger was passed, each turned again to its own concerns. Thus when the independence of the "United States" was declared, this meant little to the majority of the people. There were, to be sure, men who stood above provincial jealousies and saw far into the future. They realized that local feeling must give way to that of a national character. However, at the start such men were comparatively few.

The government provided by the Articles of Confederation was just such as might logically have been expected, past history of the states being taken into consideration. It was expressly stated that "each state retained its sovereignty, freedom and independence." A Congress composed of delegates from each state was provided, any state sending from two to seven, as it pleased. This Congress was to take measures for internal improvements, establish a postal system, etc. The regularity of trade was still left to the states; in the matter of foreign affairs Congress was to act freely, but the states must sanction its actions. Congress could advise, but not command; it could pass ordinances, but could not enforce them. It was even powerless to levy taxes for the payment of federal debts or the support of the federal government. Nine out of thirteen states had to approve of all measures before these became binding.

One who reads in detail the records of these years is appalled by the situation in which our country found itself. There was a debt of $92,000,000 that had been contracted by the Continental Congress and passed over to the new government; the states owed at least $21,000,000 more. It was impossible to pay the interest on the money, and the states would not tax their people for federal obligations. It was soon seen that Congress could only advise, and in time few heeded its counsel at all. There was always great anxiety to know what the states would do, since with them rested the ultimate decision of all matters. Trade was prostrated, having been ruined during the war. The future looked dark indeed to all who had the welfare of the young republic deeply at heart.

English troops were still quartered in America, for it was maintained, and with truth, that all the provisions of the peace treaty had not been met. One of these provisions was that those who had supported the king in the recent war, and whose property had been confiscated when they fled to Canada and other places of refuge, should be compensated by the United States for possessions thus lost. The people generally felt very bitter that this condition should have been allowed by the commissioners and had no intention of discharging such obligations.

While at home affairs were in such a precarious condition, foreign powers merely waited for the disruption of the states, hoping at that time to profit by the catastrophe.

"England, apparently, expected the weak structure presently to fall to pieces. She would not withdraw her troops from the western points because the debts of the British merchants were not paid and the property rights of the exiled Tories were not restored. Neither would she send a diplomatic representative to America, seeming to regard the Confederation as of no international importance. France, and Spain and Holland, seeing the Confederation utterly unable to repay the moneys they had loaned it, scarcely able to pay so much as the interest on its debts, alternated between anger and contempt in their treatment of it; and confidently expected to see it very soon in ruinous collapse and final disintegration. France and Spain were somewhat hopefully wondering, it was evident, what the spoils and plunder of the wreck would be, and to whom it would fall to do the plundering."[1]

By most delicate advances and tactful management, men like Washington, Hamilton, Jefferson, Madison and others, presented the idea of taking concerted action in the matter of trade and of revising the Articles of Confederation so that they might prove adequate; while the states generally approved they did not take sufficient interest to elect delegates. Finally it was agreed that a convention should be called for May, 1787. This was attended by delegates from all the states except Rhode Island—"the home of the otherwise-minded." This proved to be the famous Constitution Convention whose proceedings were kept secret until its work was finished.

Affairs had reached such a state that all seriously minded people feared for the new republic. In Massachusetts a man by the name of Shays had raised a rebellion to prevent the courts from trying suits for recovery of debts. It had required prompt action on the part of the state militia to put down this demonstration of anarchy. It looked as though certain of the states might seek the protection of European powers. For these reasons, the men who came together, carefully chosen by the various twelve states, firmly intended to do their utmost to save the union. It may well be believed that had their debates been made public at the time, no power could have brought order out of the chaos that would have followed. As it was, men from large states and small states, free states and slave states, from liberal-minded states and the more conservative, fought out their difficulties in hot debates and settled upon their compromises. In certain respects the views of Hamilton and Jefferson might be set over against one another as two extremes. Hamilton had small faith in any government which did not bear close resemblance to a monarchy; Jefferson was such an advocate of freedom and liberty that he jealously watched each movement lest it should curtail the rights of the people.

There were many public-spirited men who vigorously opposed the new constitution when drafts of it were brought home to each of the states. Patrick Henry had refused to attend the Convention because he had feared that an attempt

---
[1] Wilson: Hist. of the American People, v. 3, 56.

would be made to set aside the Articles of Confederation which he, with others, had framed. Mason of Virginia, Samuel Adams of Massachusetts and Lee thought the states would be endangered by the establishment of so strong a central government. We can easily see the force of this argument. The fact was that the time had come when the question was no longer the preservation of the rights of thirteen states, but the possibility of maintaining the integrity of one government in the face of almost overpowering obstacles.

It was evident, upon close study, that no strange or unusual features had been incorporated into this new instrument of government. A chief executive, two legislative houses and federal courts were plainly necessary. The small states were placed on an equality with the large ones in the upper legislative house;'the people retained their right of election. The powers of officers were clearly stated and their terms were to be short. The situation had to be relieved in some way and as speedily as possible. Delaware accepted the Constitution first and was soon followed by Pennsylvania. New York yielded last —July, 1788, and the new government went into operation. It was fortunate that Washington, who bore the confidence of the whole nation, could be at the helm for the next eight years and by his true statesmanlike qualities and strong personality give character and dignity to the United States, at home and abroad.

CHAPTER V.

The Early Republic.

The republic, newly organized under a strong centralized government, had need of clear-sighted, public-spirited men. Not only was it necessary to put the new machinery for federal administration into operation, but in each state reconstruction was required to meet the provisions of the federal constitution. States had hitherto regulated their own trade, levied import and export duties, coined money, and performed many of the functions surrendered now to the United States government. Bitter opposition was encountered when the new government assumed the old Continental indebtedness, together with the various state debts. Many felt that the obligation had been incurred by a government no longer existing, and that to saddle the new republic with such a heavy load was to place it at once in jeopardy. On the other hand, there were not lacking able financiers and men with a deep sense of responsibility who saw instantly that if our nation were to gain standing abroad it must discharge every legitimate claim against it, and that if, taking advantage of a discarded form of government, such claims were dishonored, European powers would have no assurance whatever that loans they might be asked to make in the future would be paid.

A site for the capital was secured, convenient and central for the states then making up the Union. It was not possible at that time to foresee a day when men would have to journey 3,000 miles and more through that republic in order to reach the District of Columbia.

Washington was a man of dignified and courtly manners and he imparted to the presidency a certain reserve and charm that gained for it respect in an age when conditions at best were primitive in a world still new. Many of the sensible rules he laid down have never been changed, such, for example, as that the President receives calls, but does not pay them; that he extends invitations, but does not accept them; that he must be approached by foreign representatives.

not directly, but through the Department of State. Kindly and courteous to all, deeply impressed with the consciousness that he was but serving the people, none have ever borne themselves with greater fortitude and patience than Washington, the Father of our Country. He wrote: "I walk upon untrodden ground. There is scarcely an action the motive of which may not be subjected to a double interpretation. There is scarcely any part of my conduct which cannot hereafter be drawn into precedent."

As it was, Jefferson and his followers, who had caught the spirit of equality which was being over-accentuated by the French during this age of revolution, accused Washington of introducing aristocratic manners into democratic America. They criticised the justices of the Supreme Court for wearing robes. They clamored for the maintenance of all institutions, political and social, on a common level. The Teutonic peoples are not capable of going to the extremes reached occasionally by the Latin peoples. In America this expression was but a faint demonstration of that feeling which in France went to the length of declaring the title "Citizen" too distinguishing, and suggesting that "Biped" be substituted.

There was another view of the case, not to be ignored. Just as the Romans of early days were ready to kill as a traitor any who should wish a king to again rule over them, so in the United States, having withdrawn from the kingdom of England, the people generally were determined to eliminate everything suggestive of royalty. After a few years the fear died out in America because there was nothing to keep it alive.

When Washington's first term expired the country turned to him as unanimously as it had at first. However, political parties were coming to be fairly well defined. Those who approved of the administration were called Federalists. John Adams, Alexander Hamilton, Robert Morris, and others of prominence were of this party. Those who disapproved of the administration were called Anti-Federalists, or Republicans. Thomas Jefferson was their leader. James Madison and Edmund Randolph were also found among them. These men disapproved of the salaries voted by Congress for various governmental officials; they did not believe that the United States should assume the state debts, and they disliked the "aristocratic" bearing of the President, his Secretaries and other officials.

One of the hardest problems with which Washington had to cope during his second term was that of preventing the country from taking sides in the French Revolution. As a young republic, it was natural that we should feel much sympathy with another nation which was trying to throw off the oppression of monarchical government. France had aided us somewhat in the Revolutionary war—less from a desire to help us than a hope of injuring Great Britain. It was now expected that we would be ready to repay our obligations. However, the situation of the United States was still precarious. She had won slight recognition abroad and at home her government was not yet firmly established. English troops were still stationed along the western frontier, waiting for developments. Were the United States to declare for France, war with England would be inevitable and none could foresee the issue. Our indebtedness was already too great to make it in the least prudent to embark upon such an uncertain course.

Popular feeling is always hard to withstand. Washington saw clearly that the United States must remain neutral. Even Jefferson realized this necessity. Nevertheless, when Genet landed upon our shores and enlisted popular sympathy for the French republic, prudence was cast to the winds and Jefferson, who loved the French nation, found himself carried along with the tide. These were trying days for the President. Popular sentiment condemned his attitude and he was grossly maligned. Having offered his life freely in the service of his country, he found it hard to bear the censure now heaped upon him. Jay was sent to England to make a treaty, and while he did the best he could, the result was far from satisfactory. That we should make a treaty of friendship with England at this time gave deep offense to France.

Declining to serve a third term, Washington delivered his Farewell Address and retired to his home at Mount Vernon, while John Adams became our second president. A war with France seemed inevitable, but the *coup d'état* of Napoleon reversed conditions there.

The Alien and Sedition laws, soon passed by the Federalists, who predominated in Congress, brought their party into odium. The first of these laws provided that foreigners must live here fourteen years before they could become citizens and also gave the President power to send out of the country any foreigner whom he deemed dangerous to the peace of the United States. The second law provided for the punishment of any who wrote, spoke, or printed anything that defamed the government or its officials.

An early Amendment to the Constitution had established free speech in our country, and this Sedition Act appeared to threaten it, particularly as Adams vigorously enforced the new law. Because of these two laws, the Kentucky and Virginia Resolutions were passed by the legislatures of the two states. While not in themselves important, they were the first links in a long chain of statecraft, which finally endangered the whole country and led on to civil war. For that reason it will be helpful to grasp at once their significance. The Kentucky Resolutions, passed by the legislature of Kentucky, held that the Constitution of the United States was a compact whereby the various states had created a general government, conceding to it certain definite and clearly expressed powers, reserving to themselves all others, that each state, as party to this compact, had the right to judge for itself whether or not the general government usurped rights not accorded it and to declare unconstitutional powers exercised in excess of those granted. These Resolutions declared that the Alien and Sedition laws were unconstitutional, judged by this test, and hence "null and void." The Virginia Resolutions, while more delicately worded, held that in case of dangerous exercise of power by the federal government, the states had the right to interfere.

These Resolutions, together with the addition made by the Kentucky legislature in 1799 "that nullification (by the states) of all unauthorized acts done under color of the constitution is the rightful remedy," sufficiently explain the doctrine of States Rights and Nullification. The clear mind of John C. Calhoun of South Carolina, so logical in all but his first premise, was to later give additional fire and force to the argument, but immediately many saw danger ahead. They knew the Federalist party had gone too far and were glad to have the objectionable laws forgotten.

Jefferson's administration is remembered for two events, prominent in our history. The first was the war waged against Great Britain for a free and unhampered commerce. With an unwarrantable boldness, she was impressing our seamen on the ground that "once an Englishman, always an Englishman," and was searching our vessels under the pretext of suspecting they carried contraband goods. The conditions became intolerable, and unprepared as we were for the exigencies of war, it became impossible to avoid it. Fighting on land was disastrous; in 1814 the eastern coast was blockaded and marching to Washington the British burned the Capitol and other public buildings. However, the victories of Perry and Lawrence on the seas did much to win us the respect of our adversaries. Strange to say, when peace was signed in December, 1814, nothing was said about those matters for which the nations had gone to war. Nevertheless, our commerce was no longer molested.

The second event of importance—far more significant for the future than this short war—was the purchase of Louisiana in 1803. Spain by a secret treaty had ceded Louisiana to France in 1800. In 1803 it became known that Napoleon was about to send an army thither to take possession of the Mississippi and close it to American commerce. This was not to be thought of and Monroe was sent to France to secure what territory and rights he could. Then it became known, to the surprise of all, that Napoleon, needing funds, would sell the entire territory. Although many objected to the purchase, it was finally made for $15,000,000. Inestimable advantage was thereby given to the United States. The territory was indefinite and none had any clear idea of its magnitude. Several entire states and portions of others have been blocked out of this wide-reaching land.

After the war of 1812, attention turned from the east to the west. Immediately after the Revolutionary war, migration across the mountains began. Once started it has never ceased. "To the West," the cry has been for generations. At first "the West" meant Kentucky and Tennessee, then Ohio, Indiana and Illinois. Farther and farther have the streams of humanity gone westward, until, reaching the coast at last, Alaska today lies open to those who wish to find homes in a new country. By 1821 the Union had expanded to include twenty-four states, Louisiana, Missouri and Illinois being the most western.

The "Era of Good Feeling" came in with Monroe, prosperity being the natural result of much that had gone before. In 1819, Spain, finding it impossible to hold Florida advantageously, hemmed in as it had come to be by the United States, ceded it for the sum of $5,000,000 to our government. Another matter of importance during the administration of Monroe was the promulgation of the Monroe Doctrine.

It may be recalled that the Congress of Vienna attempted to set aside the ideas of liberty inculcated by the revolutionary period of 1789 and the years following. Hoping to wipe out the results of Napoleon's quickly established republics, boundaries were set back as they had been before the outbreak of disturbance and rulers restored to their thrones. Under the direction of Prince Metternich of Austria, the Holy Alliance was formed between Austria, Russia and Prussia. Whatever the objects of this alliance as published to the world, its real object was to suppress any demonstration of independence on the part of European subjects. To be sure, the original motive of the three allies was to protect themselves, but they compelled the king of Naples to withdraw a constitution he had granted his people under threatened revolution, and lent their aid willingly for similar assistance wherever it was needed. Spain now besought the Holy Alliance to assist her in rewinning certain colonies in South America which had declared themselves free and independent. Their independence had already been recognized by the United States. It would be plainly a menace to have European powers open a war so near for the purpose of recovering lost territory. More particularly, Russia was making aggressive moves in the northwestern part of North America. Thereupon Monroe issued a proclamation to the effect that the new world was no longer open to colonization by European powers, and that any attempt on the part of such powers to interfere in the affairs of republics already recognized by our government would be interpreted by the United States to be an unfriendly act. This had an immediate effect. Spain gave up her plan for coercing her erstwhile possessions and Russia ceased to creep farther down the Pacific coast.

Throughout the eight years that Monroe served as President, and the term filled by John Quincy Adams—singularly uneventful—the growth of material prosperity and the westward expansion were most significant for the future. Five new states were admitted during Monroe's administration alone. The west was fairly teeming with activity.

"Every year the mere scale of affairs, if nothing more, was enlarged and altered, by the tidelike movement of population into the western country, the setting up of new states, the quick transfigurements of economic conditions, the incalculable shiftings and variations of a society always making and to be made. The restless, unceasing, adventurous movement of the nation made a deeper impression upon its politics than did its mere growth. The boatman's song on the long western rivers, the crack of the teamster's whip in the mountain passes, the stroke of the woodman's axe ringing out in the stillness of the forest, the sharp report of the rifle of huntsman, pioneer, and scout on the fast advancing frontier, filled the air as if with the very voices of change, and were answered by events quick with fulfillment of their prophecy."

CHAPTER VI.

From Jackson to Lincoln.

The election of Andrew Jackson in 1828 was indicative of the change which unnoticed had gradually come about in the United States. Although not a westerner, the West liked him, feeling that he was one of the people. John Quincy Adams had been a president whom all had found difficult to approach; the West had merely tolerated him. With patriotic intentions and tireless devotion to the round of duties encumbent upon the Chief Executive, he had nevertheless impressed men as belonging to an age already passed away. Jackson was in all senses of the term a self-made man. Self-educated, he had risen into prominence and won distinction in a war with the Indians. In the Seminole war he had acted in such a high-handed way that he had embarrassed the administration and nearly brought on serious trouble with Spain. Yet everyone knew that he had acted from the best motives. His election was hailed by the people generally as a triumph. At last they had a president whom they could understand—who was one of them.

With Jackson came in the "Spoils System," rotation in office, based on the theory that to the victor belongs the spoils. It was popularly believed that the man who had secured the presidency through the instrumentality of his party and his friends was in duty bound to favor the adherents of that party and those friends by dismissing all who held federal offices and giving the positions to his supporters. Accordingly, office holders great and small were summarily turned aside and their places taken by Jackson's friends and co-workers. Until recent years this policy, so extravagant for the country, was followed. Every four years inexperienced men were given federal offices left vacant by others who had just learned the routine of the positions. Thus the government was always educating men, then dismissing them when they had learned their work so they could perform it expeditiously. President Cleveland vigorously opposed the Spoils system, placing as many offices as possible upon the Civil Service list and allowing the office-holder to remain at his post during good behavior.

As has already been noted, the North had become a manufacturing section; the South, an agricultural region. The culture of cotton was becoming more extensive each year, while rice and tobacco were staple crops. It had been demonstrated that the colored people could thrive well in the warm, moist atmosphere of the southern states, while white laborers found the climate oppressive and often unhealthy. Consequently the South had built up on slave labor, while the North had almost entirely abolished it.

In 1828, congressmen of the North passed a new tariff bill, placing a high duty upon imports, which they wished to keep out of the country for the purpose of encouraging the manufactures of New England. This bill was strenuously fought by southerners, because it appeared to be ruinous to their section. When the bill went into effect its disastrous features were immediately apparent to the South. While cotton brought no more than before, the goods which the South had to buy in exchange cost much more. The condition seemed unbearable. Now it was that the afflicted states harked back to the theory of State Sovereignty and Nullification. South Carolina was foremost in the defense. John C. Calhoun resigned his position as Vice-President, went home and was returned to the United States Senate, there to debate the matter in the interests of his constituents who looked to him for help. Calhoun hoped to see a peaceful adjustment, but he went to the full length of his argument and showed that if one section of the country set up conditions unbearable to the other the afflicted states must seek redress. He held that the Constitution was a compact by which the states relegated certain of their functions to a federal government; that if this federal government usurped other functions, the states might nullify its exercise of power in these directions. He held that Congress had no authority to levy tariffs except for revenue, hence those levied for the fostering of home industries were unconstitutional. While the whole South shared these ideas, they are often spoken of as the Hayne or Calhoun doctrines because these men advocated them so strenuously.

Daniel Webster took the opposing side. He said that nullification on the part of a state of any act passed by Congress was nothing short of rebellion. The speeches made by Hayne, Calhoun and Webster are masterpieces of oratory, and have passed into our recorded history.

Clay came forward with a compromise, providing that the objectionable tariff should be reduced each year until 1842, and thereafter 20 per cent duty should be levied on articles which had been placed upon the dutiable list. This would not be sufficient to "protect" home industries, so the South acquiesced and harmony was again restored. Nevertheless, the theory of Nullification had been only set aside, not exploded.

Jackson opposed the idea of a national bank, so when the charter came up for renewal in 1836, he vetoed it. Instead, the deposits of the government were to be distributed among the various states. As collected, the revenue was deposited in a few favored banks which made such hazardous speculations that during the next administration the whole country was thrown into a serious panic. Plainly finance was a department in which this *man of the people* was not at home.

The great question which agitated the country from this time forward concerned the extension of slavery. To be sure, marked prosperity attended the United States after the effects of the great panic were passed. Inventions of various kinds opened the way for the utilization of the vast resources abounding in the new land. In spite of such material advancement, however, there was growing a momentous subject of contention, which, brushed aside for the time, asserted itself again and again, and finally expanded to such proportions that it overshadowed all else.

In 1619, it will be recalled, a Dutch trading vessel brought the first boat-load of Negro slaves to Virginia. They continued to be imported until the year 1808, that being the date specified in the Constitution to terminate such importation. Before the Revolutionary war the North, for the most part, had discontinued slave labor. The social and industrial order gave no such opportunity for slaves to be profitably used as was the case in the South. The Ordinance of 1789 forbade slavery in the Northwest Territory, but provided that fugitive slaves, taking refuge there, should be returned.

The westward migration of people from the seaboard and from the states that had grown up across the mountains, brought the subject up repeatedly. The South wanted to extend its territory; the North was gradually becoming opposed to the whole system. In 1819 there were twenty-two states in the Union—eleven free, eleven slave states. The Ohio river became the boundary between the two sections, and there were many who thought it advisable to keep the balance then existing. When Missouri applied for admission into the Union, therefore, as a slave state, violent opposition was encountered. The matter went over to the next session of Congress, whereupon Maine was ready for admission. Thus the two states came in together with the famous Compromise of 1820, which provided that slavery should not exist in the territory procured from France in 1803 north of the latitude 36° 30′, with the exception of Missouri. Thus was a sensitive problem settled for the time.

In 1833 the Antislavery Society was organized in Philadelphia. By the distribution of literature of various kinds this society did what it could to win sympathy for the slaves of the South and to create an anti-slavery sentiment. Slave owners were indignant and did all they could to prevent this society in accomplishing its ends. Violence frequently resulted, presses which printed these documents being destroyed and the mails searched for objectionable matter. The South tried in vain to have a law passed prohibiting the circulation of anti-slavery material through the mails, but succeeded in passing a bill which forbade Congress to receive petitions pertaining to slavery.

The Anti-slavery Society failed to enlist the aid of many thoughtful men who personally opposed the extension of slavery, even the very system, indeed. Such men saw that the Constitution had left the regulation of slavery to each state and believed that its abolition was not a question to be settled by Congress at all. Besides, they disliked the lawless methods of the anti-slavery men, who used any means to attain their ends.

In 1845 Texas was admitted as a state. The history of

our acquisition of this Mexican territory is more or less complicated. Many southerners had moved over the border line and settled. After Mexico declared herself free from Spain, quite a section of territory declared itself free from Mexico and formed a separate country. Those who had settled here desired to become a part of the United States and appealed to Congress for admission. To comply with this request, since Texas claimed much disputed land, was to precipitate war with Mexico. Popular feeling favored the acquirement of this territory and the war of 1848 brought a large tract of land into the possession of the country. Immediately the question arose as to whether this should be free or slave territory. Rumors of all kinds were afloat. It was said that the South would secede if it failed to gain some part of this acquisition. Finally the Compromise of 1850 settled once more the difficulties which were dividing the people. This provided that California was to be admitted as a free state, but that the remainder of the Mexican territory should be open for both free and slave settlers; that the slave trade should be abolished in the District of Columbia and a fugitive slave law should permit slave owners to recover slaves that escaped to free states.

To the surprise of all, when Congress assembled after the election of Pierce, Stephen A. Douglas brought forward a bill which provided for the formation of two territories: Kansas and Nebraska. Although both lay north of 36° 30', Douglas intended to satisfy the South, and declared that the Missouri Compromise had been unconstitutional at the outset, and secured its repeal. Kansas was to be free or slave, according to the will of the settlers.

Now men North and South rushed in to populate the new territory. Nebraska was too far north to make slavery profitable, but Kansas might become a prosperous slave state. For some time scenes of lawlessness were enacted in this new territory, as hot-headed partisans struggled for supremacy.

Abraham Lincoln came into prominence during these years in his debates with Douglas, while both were candidates for the United States Senate. Lincoln's clear, homely sentences went straight to the hearts of the northerners. "A house divided against itself cannot stand." So well understood was his position upon this question that when his election to the presidency was known South Carolina seceded from the Union. Six other states followed her example and the Confederacy of the South was organized. Many hold today that the South thought by thus withdrawing that she could exact better terms from the Union than if she remained within. It is said that it was still expected that a compromise might be made. Although secession had been argued about and threatened for many years, it came as a great surprise. Finally feeling ran so high that war seemed imminent. Four more states withdrew and in April of 1861 word reached the capital that an army of the Confederacy had fired upon Fort Sumter. From that day both sides realized that peace was no longer to be expected.

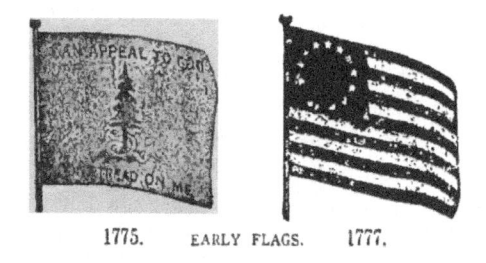

1775.   EARLY FLAGS.   1777.

CHAPTER VII.

The Latter Part of the Nineteenth Century.

The war which had divided North and South caused tremendous loss of life and property. It has been estimated that for each day during the four years that war waged, the lives of seven hundred men were sacrificed. The federal government poured out approximately $2,500,000 for each of those fearful days—about $34,000,000,000 in all—and was left with an additional debt of $2,600,000,000. The Confederacy gave lavishly of its stores and was still left with a debt of $1,400,-000,000. While the burden of debt was serious, the loss of life was more serious still. Up to 1861 the progress of civilization in America had gone steadily forward. By the elimination of a rising generation, progress received a back-set at this time, particularly as the population was soon increased by a large emigration from the more backward states of Europe. Through the seventies, eighties and nineties, Slavs, Lithuanians, Poles, etc., infiltrated into the social structure of this country in surprising numbers. "Defeated men of a defeated race," they have been called. Mentally and physically inferior, it was quite natural that their arrival just after the terrible loss of American blood should have been disastrous to continued advancement.

The first colossal task confronting the government at the close of the war was: what disposition should be made of the states which had seceded? Under what conditions were they to be received once more into the Union? Any fair and unbiased examination into the Reconstruction period must make convincingly plain the great calamity that the South received when Lincoln fell by the hand of a mad assassin. He, and he alone, was perhaps great enough to have guided the nation through the storm and stress of years characterized by intense sectional feeling. He was gifted with a generosity of heart and a delicacy of feeling seldom met. He was the leader of the entire nation—not a faction of it. Believing in the *sovereignty of the state*, the South had finally withdrawn from the Union and entered into a civil war to give reality to the theory. In the struggle made to preserve the Union, the North had lost much, but the South had lost more. In the North, affairs had gone on to some extent apart from the war; in the South the war had been the one engrossing matter. In the North, four men out of every nine of suitable age had enlisted; in the South, nine out of every ten had gone to the front. Again, destruction of property was greatest in the South, since the war was principally waged there; and finally, the slaves who were set free had been the property of their owners. The South had lost utterly.

Realizing all this, the President set to work to bind up the wounds of a nation. With a kindliness and nobility of spirit, he discouraged the idle arguments that were put forward: Were the states of the Confederacy out of the Union, or had they, in fact, been in it throughout? Lincoln went so far as to say that the welfare of the country would be better served if a solution of such problems were not attempted. However, his broad policy did not meet the wishes of the Republican leaders. Filled with exultation, now that the strain was over, with coarser instincts and shorter vision, they wished the defeated states to suffer still greater humiliation. It is possible that Lincoln, whose words in his second inaugural address rang clear and true: "With malice toward none, with charity for all, with firmness in the right, as God gives us to see the right, let us strive to finish the work we are in,   to do all which may achieve and cherish a just and lasting peace among ourselves," might have won opponents to his way of thinking and restored in briefer time peace and good will among men. This Johnson, who succeeded him, was wholly unable to do.

Provisional government was set up in the southern states until new constitutions should be prepared to meet the changes that had taken place. The whole country knew that some measures must be taken immediately concerning the negroes who might become a menace to society if they remained in idleness. The southern states brought forward regulations by which the colored people should be bound out to service, with wages fixed by law. Such disposition had been common in England at an earlier time and was not of necessity oppressive. However, the North, failing quite to understand the conditions in the South, found the idea astounding. Men away from the region involved, saw only in this movement an attempt on the part of southerners to withhold freedom from those whose sorry plight had moved the North to espouse their cause. Men of the North became imbued with the idea that with citizenship alone could the negro be protected in a country now hostile to him, and the crime of conferring the right of suffrage upon a race until now held in bondage was committed. It must be said to Johnson's credit that he violently opposed this measure but it was passed in spite of him.

While the ballot had been thus extended to a great ignorant mass of humanity, all the leaders of the South—all who were possessed of $20,000 worth of property—were for some time debarred from citizenship. While the most able, most experienced were thus disqualified, adventurers from the North hurried into the southern states and, having only personal profit at stake, did what they could to intensify the bitterness which was growing up between the franchised negro and the unfranchised southerner, meantime shaping matters so that they themselves filled all remunerative positions.

Month by month conditions became more unbearable in the South. It was useless to complain because each complaint was long misinterpreted. To be sure, there were men in the North who saw that the policy followed by Congress in regard to the South was mistaken, but they made small impression upon the sentiment of their day. The Constitution was amended by the Fifteenth Amendment, which gave the right of franchise to the negro, and no state could be received again into the Union until it recognized and conceded the same privilege.

Prevented from making use of regular methods for accomplishing their ends, southern men shortly resorted to unusual methods. In sport a band of young men had hit upon the idea of going about masked among the colored people, bent upon amusement. They found it easy to intimidate them so that they would yield to whatever was required of them. The spirit of jest soon gave way to earnestness. Here, apparently, was a means by which conditions might be made more endurable, and they made the most of it. The youths who originated the plan had styled themselves the Kuklos—meaning *the circle;* this was soon corrupted into Ku Klux, and Klan was added. Going about among the negroes in the night, on horses, masked and wrapped in sheets, the ignorant darkies were so frightened that they obeyed injunctions to remain away from political meetings, and to cease to meddle in affairs of which they knew practically nothing. This lawless method of attaining an end worked out differently, according to the neighborhood. Prudent men did not go too far; they confined themselves to threats which they had small intention of executing. Nevertheless, as will always happen under such circumstances, the more impassioned and fearless went to the full length of the opportunity thus offered and many crimes were committed in the name of the Ku Klux Klan. Northerners who were thought to believe in the right of suffrage for the negro were treated severely whenever they came into the territory where the secret society operated. It was remarkable to see how rapidly this lawless system spread. During Grant's administration the federal government was obliged to institute a regular crusade to stamp it out.

For its failure in the policy sustained toward the South, and for many other reasons, the Republican party, which had come out of the war with great prestige, fell into disfavor. The construction of western railroads was begun shortly after the war closed, and while these roads did much to open up the country, it was found that incredible graft was involved in the matter and while Congress censured those who were shown to have been involved, they still held their seats. Finally, in 1873, a serious panic swept over the country, due largely to the imprudent loans which had been negotiated in connection with western railroad building Grant's administration was a disappointment to many—most of all, to himself. Gradually the country came into a normal condition again, and with the opening of Hayes' administration the period of Reconstruction may be said to close.

In 1867 the territory of the United States was materially increased by the purchase of Alaska from Russia. The resources of that region were little appreciated at the time, and it was commonly declared that we had purchased merely icebergs and glaciers. Even today, when the wealth of the northern land has been shown to be rich in coal deposits, minerals and fisheries, many of the possibilities of Alaska are still to be revealed.

The last important encounter with the Indians occurred in 1876. Enraged by the steady advance of the white man toward their remaining tracts, Sitting Bull induced his tribesmen to make an attack upon them. The outbreak was soon quelled but General Custer and his soldiers perished, almost to a man, in one of the ambushes laid for them. Hope of victory being no longer possible, recent years have found the remnant of the Red men reconciled to their fate. While the government is doing much today to educate the young generation, disease frequently overtakes them as a result of radically changed life and makes heavy inroads upon their numbers.

We are still too near the events of the past forty years to view them in a wholly impartial way. The industrial growth of the country has been paramount, casting into secondary importance the political life of the nation. Inventions of many kinds have tended to eliminate distances; the telephone, telegraph cable, improved application of steam, and the discovery of the possibilities of electricity have transformed all enlightened lands, but especially have they wrought changes in a country so vast as this. New farm implements and machinery have given opportunity for the cultivation of wide tracts of prairies hitherto untilled; appliances for mining have led to the rapid accumulation of precious ores. Devices for facilitating manufactures have lessened the cost of production. Because the lot of the day-laborer is far better in America than in European countries, hundreds of thousands of emigrants have flocked to our shores every year. In spite of the steady influx, there is still room for all and work for those who wish it.

Only once since 1865 has the sturdy spirit for arbitrating difficulties given way before provocation for war. In 1898 a wave of hysterical feeling plunged the country into a brief war with Spain. Subsequent events showed that this war was no exception to the general statement—that modern wars have been fought for commercial purposes.

The United States celebrated its first centennial in 1876. That a century had witnessed a complete change in the relations existing between the two countries was sufficiently evident by the fact that Great Britain took a prominent part in the exposition held in Philadelphia. Many beneficial results of this first great exposition in America followed. Heretofore Americans had been too deeply engrossed in shaping a country for habitation to give special attention to the finer arts of living. Now for the first time beauty was emphasized; comparison of workmanship stimulated the people to put forth fresh efforts. Architecture which had previously been little more than an accident, became a study. From that year may be said to date a new era in the development of culture and refinement, and any particular study of American art must start from that time.

THIRTY-HORSE HARVESTER.

FAMOUS HISTORICAL ADDRESSES

CHAPTER VIII.

The Call to Arms.

PATRICK HENRY.

(1775)

No MAN thinks more highly than I do of the patriotism, as well as abilities, of the very worthy gentlemen who have just addressed the House. But different men often see the same subject in different lights; and, therefore, I hope it will not be thought disrespectful to those gentlemen, if, entertaining as I do opinions of a character very opposite to theirs, I shall speak forth my sentiments freely and without reserve. This is no time for ceremony.

The question before the House is one of awful moment to this country. For my own part, I consider it as nothing less than a question of freedom or slavery; and in proportion to the magnitude of the subject ought to be the freedom of the debate. It is only in this way that we can hope to arrive at truth, and fulfil the great responsibility which we hold to God and our country. Should I keep back my opinions at such a time, through fear of giving offense, I should consider myself as guilty of treason toward my country, and of an act of disloyalty toward the Majesty of Heaven, which I revere above all earthly kings.

Mr. President, it is natural to man to indulge in the illusions of hope. We are apt to shut our eyes against a painful truth, and listen to the song of that siren, till she transforms us into beasts. Is this the part of wise men, engaged in a great and arduous struggle for liberty? Are we disposed to be of the number of those, who, having eyes, see not, and having ears, hear not, the things which so nearly concern their temporal salvation? For my part, whatever anguish of spirit it may cost, I am willing to know the whole truth; to know the worst, and to provide for it.

I have but one lamp by which my feet are guided; and that is the lamp of experience. I know of no way of judging of the future but by the past. And judging by the past, I wish to know what there has been in the conduct of the British ministry, for the last ten years, to justify those hopes with which gentlemen have been pleased to solace themselves and the House? Is it that insidious smile with which our petition has been lately received? Trust it not, sir; it will prove a snare to your feet. Suffer not yourself to be betrayed with a kiss. Ask yourselves how this gracious reception of our petition comports with those warlike preparations which cover our waters and darken our land. Are fleets and armies necessary to a work of love and reconciliation? Have we shown ourselves so unwilling to be reconciled, that force must be called in to win back our love? Let us not deceive ourselves, sir. These are the implements of war and subjugation; the last arguments to which kings resort.

I ask gentlemen, sir, what means this martial array, if its purpose be not to force us to submission? Can gentlemen assign any other possible motive for it? Has Great Britain any enemy in this quarter of the world to call for all this accumulation of navies and armies? No, sir, she has none. They are meant for us: they can be meant for no other. They are sent over to bind and rivet upon us those chains, which the British ministry have been so long forging. And what have we to oppose to them? Shall we try argument? Sir, we have been trying that for the last ten years. Have we anything new to offer upon the subject? Nothing. We have held the subject up in every light of which it is capable; but it has been all in vain. Shall we resort to entreaty and humble supplication? What terms shall we find, which have not been already exhausted? Let us not, I beseech you, sir, deceive ourselves longer. Sir, we have done everything that could be done, to avert the storm which is now coming on. We have petitioned; we have remonstrated; we have supplicated; we have prostrated ourselves before the throne, and have implored its interposition to arrest the tyrannical hands of the ministry and Parliament. Our petitions have been slighted; our remonstrances have produced additional violence and insult; our supplications have been disregarded; and we have been spurned, with contempt, from the foot of the throne! In vain, after these things, may we indulge the fond hope of peace and reconciliation. There is no longer any room for hope. If we wish to be free— if we mean to preserve inviolate those inestimable privileges for which we have been so long contending—if we mean not basely to abandon the noble struggle in which we have been so long engaged, and which we have pledged ourselves never to abandon, until the glorious object of our contest shall be obtained—we must fight! I repeat it, sir, we must fight! An appeal to arms and to the God of Hosts is all that is left us!

They tell us, sir, that we are weak—unable to cope with so formidable an adversary. But when shall we be stronger? Will it be the next week, or the next year? Will it be when we are totally disarmed, and when a British guard shall be stationed in every house? Shall we gather strength by irresolution and inaction? Shall we acquire the means of effectual resistance by lying supinely on our backs and hugging the delusive phantom of hope, until our enemies shall have bound us hand and foot?

Sir, we are not weak if we make a proper use of those means which the God of nature has placed in our power. Three millions of people armed in the holy cause of liberty, and in such a country as that which we possess, are invincible by any force which our enemy can send against us. Besides, sir, we shall not fight our battles alone. There is a just God who presides over the destinies of nations, and who will raise up friends to fight our battles for us. The battle, sir, is not to the strong alone; it is to the vigilant, the active, the brave. Besides, sir, we have no election. If we were base enough to desire it, it is now too late to retire from the contest. There is no retreat but in submission and slavery! Our chains are forged! Their clanking may be heard on the plains of Boston! The war is inevitable—and let it come! I repeat it, sir, let it come!

It is in vain, sir, to extenuate the matter. Gentlemen may cry Peace, Peace—but there is no peace. The war is actually begun! The next gale that sweeps from the north will bring to our ears the clash of resounding arms! Our brethren are already in the field! Why stand we here idle? What is it that gentlemen wish? What would they have? Is life so dear, or peace so sweet, as to be purchased at the price of chains and slavery? Forbid it, Almighty God! I know not what course others may take; but as for me, give me liberty or give me death!

Boston's Place in History.
Edward Everett Hale.

Faneuil Hall is the cradle of liberty, and the child was born not far away. It was in the council chamber of the old Statehouse yonder that "American independence was born." These are the words of John Adams, whose features you are looking on. He assisted at the birth, and he has told for us the story.

He says, speaking of that day: "Otis was a flame of fire; Otis hurried everything before him. American independence was then and there born. In fifteen years the child grew up to manhood, and declared himself free."

When that moment came, the Congress of the United States was sitting in Philadelphia. It had been summoned two years before, on the seventeenth of June, 1774—St. Botolph's day, be it remembered, the Saint's day of Boston. On that day, Samuel Adams, of Boston, moved in the Provincial Assembly, sitting at Salem, that a Continental Congress should be called at Philadelphia—at Philadelphia, observe, because there was no English garrison there! Samuel Adams took the precaution to lock the door of the Salem Assembly chamber on the inside. While the motion was under discussion, the English governor, Gage's secretary, appeared at the outside of the door to dissolve the Assembly. But Sam Adams was stronger than he. The delegates were chosen—he was one; James Bowdoin, John Adams, Thomas Cushing, and Robert Treat Paine were the others. All these were from Boston.

Two years were to pass before the declaration was drawn and signed. When that time came, our delegation had been changed by the substitution of Hancock for Bowdoin, and Gerry for Cushing. Franklin, another Latin School boy, served with John Adams and Thomas Jefferson, Roger Sherman and Robert Livingston, on the committee which made the draft of the Declaration. And when the time came for its signature, John Hancock's name "stands at the top of freedom's roll."

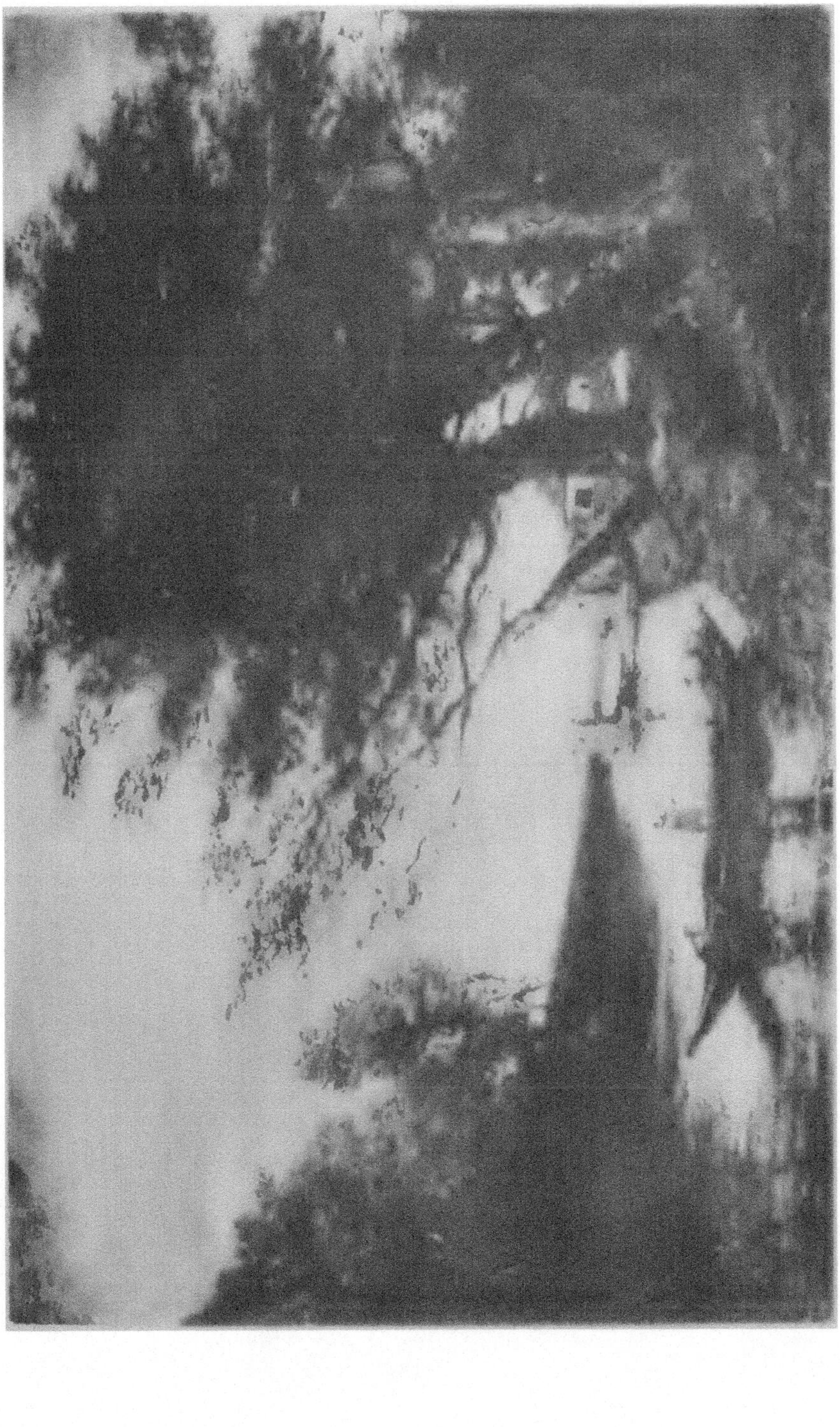

We need not be over-modest in Boston when we speak of such men and such times. American independence was born in our old Statehouse. Sam Adams was the father of American independence. Liberty was cradled in this hall. Franklin and Adams, of those who drew the Declaration, were born here. John Hancock was sent to preside over that Assembly, and accepted bravely the honors and the perils of his great position. I could not anywhere give any history, however succinct, of the Declaration; I could not account for the America of to-day without saying all this,—no, not if I were addressing the Shah of Persia in his palace in Ispahan.

I believe, if I were in your Honor's chair next January, on one of those holidays which nobody knows what to do with, I would commemorate the first great victory of 1775. To do this well, I would issue an order that any schoolboy in Boston who would bring his sled to School Street, might coast down hill all day there, in memory of that famous coasting in January, 1775, when the Latin School boys told the English general that to coast on School Street was their right "from time immemorial," and when they won that right from him.

We have made a pleasure park of the Old Fort Independence, thanks, I believe, to our friend Mr. O'Neil. Let no man take his sweetheart there, where sheep may be grazing between the useless cannon, without pointing out to her the birth of the Somerset on St. Botolph's day, the day democracy began her march around the world. Let him show her the bastions on Dorchester heights. Let him say to her: "It was here that Lord Percy gathered the flower of King George's army to storm the heights yonder. And it was from this beach that they left Boston forever."

When he takes her to his old schoolhouse he shall ask first to see the handwriting of some of our old boys—of Franklin, of Sam Adams, of John Hancock, of Paine, of Bowdoin, and of Hooper. They shall not stop the car at Hancock Street without a memory of the man who signed the Declaration. They shall cross the pavement on Lynde Street, and he shall say: "These stones have been red with blood from Bunker Hill." And when this day of days comes round, the first festival in our calendar, the best boy of our High School, or of our Latin School, shall always read to us the Declaration in which the fathers announced the truth to the world.

And shall this be no homage to the past—worship deaf and dumb? As the boy goes on his errand he shall say: "To such duty I, too, am born. I am God's messenger." As the young man tells the story to his sweetheart, he shall say: "We are God's children also, you and I, and we have our duties." They look backward only to look forward. "God needs me that this city may still stand in the forefront of his people's land. Here am I, God may draft me for some special duty, as he drafted Warren and Franklin. Present! Ready for service? Thank God I came from men who were not afraid in battle. Thank God I was born from women whose walk was close to him. Thank God, I am his son." And she shall say: "I am his daughter."

He has nations to call to his service. "Here am I."

He has causeways to build for the march forward of his people. "Here am I."

There are torrents to bridge, highways in deserts. "Here am I."

He has oceans to cross. He has the hungry world to feed. He has the wilderness to clothe in beauty. "Here am I."

God of heaven, be with us as thou wert with these fathers.

God of heaven, we will be with thee, as the fathers were.

WASHINGTON'S COAT OF ARMS.

THE HAYNE-WEBSTER DEBATE.

Speech of Mr. Hayne,

In the Senate, on Mr. Foote's Resolution, Thursday, January 21, and Monday, January 25, 1830.

WHEN I took occasion, Mr. President, two days ago, to throw out some ideas with respect to the policy of the government in relation to the public lands, nothing certainly could have been further from my thoughts than that I should be compelled again to throw myself upon the indulgence of the Senate. Little did I expect to be called upon to meet such an argument as was yesterday urged by the gentleman from Massachusetts [Mr. Webster]. Sir, I questioned no man's opinions, I impeached no man's motives, I charged no party, or State, or section of country with hostility to any other; but ventured, I thought in a becoming spirit, to put forth my own sentiments in relation to a great national question of public policy. Such was my course. The gentleman from Missouri [Mr. Benton], it is true, had charged upon the Eastern States an early and continued hostility toward the West, and referred to a number of historical facts and documents in support of that charge. Now, sir, how have these different arguments been met? The honorable gentleman from Massachusetts, after deliberating a whole night upon his course, comes into this chamber to vindicate New England; and, instead of making up his issue with the gentleman from Missouri on the charges which he had preferred, chooses to consider me as the author of those charges, and, losing sight entirely of that gentleman, selects me as his adversary and pours out all the vials of his mighty wrath upon my devoted head. Nor is he willing to stop there. He goes on to assail the institutions and policy of the South, and calls in question the principles and conduct of the State which I have the honor to represent. When I find a gentleman of mature age and experience, of acknowledged talents and profound sagacity, pursuing a course like this, declining the contest from the West and making war upon the unoffending South, I must believe, I am bound to believe, he has some object in view that he has not ventured to disclose. Mr. President, why is this? Has the gentleman discovered in former controversies with the gentleman from Missouri that he is overmatched by that Senator? And does he hope for an easy victory over a more feeble adversary? Has the gentleman's distempered fancy been disturbed by gloomy forebodings of "new alliances to be formed," at which he hinted? Has the ghost of the murdered Coalition come back, like the ghost of Banquo, to "sear the eyeballs" of the gentleman, and will it not "down at his bidding"? Are dark visions of broken hopes and honors lost forever still floating before his heated imagination? Sir, if it be his object to thrust me between the gentleman from Missouri and himself, in order to rescue the East from the contest it has provoked with the West, he shall not be gratified. Sir, I will not be dragged into the defense of my friend from Missouri. The South shall not be forced into a conflict not its own. The gentleman from Missouri is able to fight his own battles. The gallant West needs no aid from the South to repel any attack which may be made on them from any quarter. Let the gentleman from Massachusetts controvert the facts and arguments of the gentleman from Missouri if he can; and if he win the victory, let him wear its honors; I shall not deprive him of his laurels.

The gentleman from Massachusetts, in reply to my remarks on the injurious operations of our land system on the prosperity of the West, pronounced an extravagant eulogium on the paternal care which the government had extended toward the West, to which he attributed all that was great and excellent in the present condition of the new States. The language of the gentleman on this topic fell upon my ears like the almost forgotten tones of the Tory leaders of the British Parliament at the commencement of the American Revolution. They, too, discovered that the colonies had grown great under the fostering care of the mother country; and I must confess, while listening to the gentleman, I thought the appropriate reply to his argument was to be found in the remark of a celebrated orator, made on that occasion: "They have grown great in spite of your protection."

The gentleman, in commenting on the policy of the government in relation to the new States, has introduced to our notice a certain Nathan Dane of Massachusetts, to whom he attributes the celebrated Ordinance of '87, by which he tells us "slavery was forever excluded from the new States north of the Ohio." After eulogizing the wisdom of this provision in terms of the most extravagant praise, he breaks forth in admiration of the greatness of Nathan Dane; and great indeed he must be, if it be true, as stated by the Senator from Massachusetts, that "he was greater than Solon and Lycurgus, Minos, Numa Pompilius, and all the legislators and philosophers of the world," ancient and modern. Sir, to such high authority it is certainly my duty, in a becoming spirit of humility, to submit. And yet the gentleman will pardon me when I say that it is a little unfortunate for the fame of this great legislator that the gentleman from Missouri should have proved that he was not the author of the Ordinance of '87, on which the Senator from Massachusetts has reared so glorious a monument to his name. Sir, I doubt not the Senator will feel some compassion for our ignorance when I tell him that so little are we acquainted with the modern great men of New England that, until he informed us yesterday that we possessed a Solon and a Lycurgus in the person of Nathan Dane, he was only known to the South as a member of a celebrated assembly called and known by the name of "Hartford Convention." In the proceedings of that assembly, which I hold in my hand (at page 19), will be found, in a few lines, the history of Nathan Dane; and a little further on there is conclusive evidence of that ardent devotion to the interest of the new States which, it seems, has given him a just claim to the title of "Father of the West." By the second resolution of the "Hartford Convention" it is declared "that it is expedient to attempt to make provision for restraining Congress in the exercise of an unlimited power to make new States and admit them into this Union." So much for Nathan Dane of Beverly, Massachusetts.

In commenting upon my views in relation to the public lands, the gentleman insists that, it being one of the conditions of the grants that these lands should be applied to "the common benefit of all the States, they must always remain a fund for revenue;" and adds, "they must be treated as so much treasure." Sir, the gentleman could hardly find language strong enough to convey his disapprobation of the policy which I had ventured to recommend to the favorable consideration of the country. And what, sir, was that policy, and what is the difference between that gentleman and myself on this subject? I threw out the idea that the public lands ought not to be reserved forever as "a great fund for revenue;" that they ought not to be treated "as a great treasure;" but that the course of our policy should rather be directed toward the creation of new States, and building up great and flourishing communities.

We are ready to make up the issue with the gentleman as to the influence of slavery on individual and national character,—on the prosperity and greatness either of the United States or of particular States. Sir, when arraigned before the bar of public opinion on this charge of slavery, we can stand up with conscious rectitude, plead not guilty, and put ourselves upon God and our country. Sir, we will not consent to look at slavery in the abstract. We will not stop to inquire whether the black man, as some philosophers have contended, is of an inferior race, nor whether his color and condition are the effects of a curse inflicted for the offenses of his ancestors. We deal in no abstractions. We will not look back to inquire whether our fathers were guiltless in introducing slaves into this country. If an inquiry should ever be instituted into these matters, however, it will be found that the profits of the slave trade were not confined to the South. Southern ships and Southern sailors were not the instruments of bringing slaves to the shores of America, nor did our merchants reap the profits of that "accursed traffic." But, sir, we will pass over all this. If slavery, as it now exists in this country, be an evil, we of the present day found it ready made to our hands. Finding our lot cast among a people whom God had manifestly committed to our care, we did not sit down to speculate on abstract questions of theoretical liberty. We met it as a practical question of obligation and duty. We resolved to make the best of the situation in which Providence had placed us, and to fulfill the high trust which had devolved upon us as the owners of slaves, in the only way in which such a trust could be fulfilled without spreading misery and ruin throughout the land. We found that we had to deal with a people whose physical, moral, and intellectual habits and character totally disqualified them for the enjoyment of the blessings of freedom. We could not send them back to the shores from whence their fathers had been taken; their numbers forbade the thought, even if we did not know that their condition here is infinitely preferable to what it possibly could be among the barren sands and savage tribes of Africa; and it was wholly irreconcilable with all our notions of humanity to tear asunder the tender ties which they had formed among us, to gratify the feelings of a false philanthropy. What a commentary on the wisdom, justice, and humanity of the Southern slave-owner is presented by the example of certain benevolent associations and charitable individuals elsewhere! Shedding weak tears over sufferings which had existence only in their own sickly imaginations, these "friends of humanity" set themselves systematically to work to seduce the slaves of the South from their masters. By means of missionaries and political tracts, the scheme was in a great measure successful. Thousands of these deluded victims of fanaticism were seduced into the enjoyment of freedom in our Northern cities. And what has been the consequence? Go to these cities now and ask the question. Visit the dark and narrow lanes, and obscure recesses, which have been assigned by common consent as the abodes of those outcasts of the world, the free people of color. Sir, there does not exist, on the face of the whole earth, a population so poor, so wretched, so vile, so loathsome, so utterly destitute of all the comforts, conveniences, and decencies of life, as the unfortunate blacks of Philadelphia, and New York, and Boston. Liberty has been to them the greatest of calamities, the heaviest of curses. Sir, I have had some opportunities of making comparison between the condition of the free negroes of the North and the slaves of the South, and the comparison has left not only an indelible impression of the superior advantages of the latter, but has gone far to reconcile me to slavery itself. Never have I felt so forcibly that touching description, "the foxes have holes, and the birds of the air have nests, but the Son of man hath not where to lay his head," as when I have seen this unhappy race, naked and houseless, almost starving in the streets, and abandoned by all the world. Sir, I have seen in the neighborhood of one of the most moral, religious, and refined cities of the North a family of free blacks driven to the caves of the rock, and there obtaining a precarious subsistence from charity and plunder.

But, Mr. President, to be serious, what are we of the South to think of what we have heard this day? The Senator from Massachusetts tells us that the tariff is not an Eastern measure, and treats it as if the East had no interest in it. The Senator from Missouri insists it is not a Western measure, and that it has done no good to the West. The South comes in, and, in the most earnest manner, represents to you that this measure, which we are told "is of no value to the East or the West," is "utterly destructive of our interests." We represent to you that it has spread ruin and devastation through the land, and prostrated our hopes in the dust. We solemnly declare that we believe the system to be wholly unconstitutional, and a violation of the compact between the States and the Union; and our brethren turn a deaf ear to our complaints, and refuse to relieve us from a system "which not enriches them, but makes us poor indeed." Good God! Mr. President, has it come to this? Do gentlemen hold the feelings and wishes of their brethren at so cheap a rate that they refuse to gratify them at so small a price? Do gentlemen value so lightly the peace and harmony of the country that they will not yield a measure of this description to the affectionate entreaties and earnest remonstrances of their friends? Do gentlemen estimate the value of the Union at so low a price that they will not even make one effort to bind the States together with the cords of affection? And has it come to this? Is this the spirit in which this government is to be administered? If so, let me tell gentlemen, the seeds of dissolution are already sown, and our children will reap the bitter fruit.

Who then, Mr. President, are the true friends of the Union? Those who would confine the federal government strictly within the limits prescribed by the Constitution; who would preserve to the States and the people all powers not expressly delegated; who would make this a federal and not a national Union, and who, administering the government in a spirit of equal justice, would make it a blessing and not a curse. And who are its enemies? Those who are in favor of consolidation; who are constantly stealing power from the States, and adding strength to the federal government; who, assuming an unwarrantable jurisdiction over the States and the people, undertake to regulate the whole industry and capital of the country. But, sir, of all descriptions of men, I consider those as the worst enemies of the Union who sacrifice the equal rights which belong to every member of the Confederacy to combinations of interested majorities for personal or political objects. But the gentleman apprehends no evil from the dependence of the States on the federal government; he can see no danger of corruption from the influence of money or of patronage. Sir, I know that it is supposed to be a wise saying that "patronage is a source of weakness;" and in support of that maxim it has been said that "every ten appointments make a hundred enemies." But I am rather inclined to think, with the eloquent and sagacious orator now reposing on his laurels on the banks of the Roanoke, that "the power of conferring favors creates a crowd of dependents." He gave a forcible illustration of the truth of the remark when he told us of the effect of holding up the savory morsel to the eager eyes of the hungry hounds gathered around his door. It mattered not whether the gift was bestowed on Towser or Sweetlips, "Tray, Blanch, or Sweet-heart;" while held in suspense, they were governed by a nod, and, when the morsel was bestowed, the expectation of the favors of to-morrow kept up the subjection of to-day.

The Senator from Massachusetts, in denouncing what he is pleased to call the Carolina doctrine, has attempted to throw ridicule upon the idea that a State has any constitutional remedy, by the exercise of its sovereign authority, against "a gross, palpable, and deliberate violation of the Constitution." He called it "an idle" or "a ridiculous notion," or something to that effect, and added that it would make the Union a "mere rope of sand." Now, sir, as the gentleman has not condescended to enter into any examination of the question, and has been satisfied with throwing the weight of his authority into the scale, I do not deem it necessary to do more than to throw into the opposite scale the authority on which South Carolina relies; and there, for the present, I am perfectly willing to leave the controversy. The South Carolina doctrine, that is to say, the doctrine contained in an exposition reported by a committee of the Legislature in December, 1828, and published by their authority, is the good old Republican doctrine of '98,— the doctrine of the celebrated "Virginia Resolutions" of that year, and of "Madison's Report" of '99. It will be recollected that the Legislature of Virginia, in December, '98, took into consideration the Alien and Sedition laws, then considered by all Republicans as a gross violation of the Constitution of the United States, and on that day passed, among others, the following resolutions:—

"The General Assembly doth explicitly and peremptorily declare that it views the powers of the federal government, as resulting from the compact to which the States are parties, as limited by the plain sense and intention of the instrument constituting that compact; as no farther valid than they are authorized by the grants enumerated in that compact; and that, in case of a deliberate, palpable, and dangerous exercise of other powers not granted by the said compact, the States who are parties thereto have the right, and are in duty bound, to interpose for arresting the progress of the evil, and for maintaining, within their respective limits, the authorities, rights, and liberties appertaining to them."

Thus it will be seen, Mr. President, that the South Carolina doctrine is the republican doctrine of '98; that it was promulgated by the fathers of the faith; that it was maintained by Virginia and Kentucky in the worst of times; that it constituted the very pivot on which the political revolution of that day turned; that it embraces the very principles the triumph of which, at that time, saved the Constitution at its last gasp, and which New England statesmen were not unwilling to adopt when they believed themselves to be the victims of unconstitutional legislation. Sir, as to the doctrine that the federal government is the exclusive judge of the extent as well as the limitations of its powers, it seems to me to be utterly subversive of the sovereignty and independence of the States. It makes but little difference, in my estimation, whether Congress or the Supreme Court are invested with this power. If the federal government, in all or any of its departments, is to prescribe the limits of its own authority, and the States are bound to submit to the decision, and are not to be allowed to examine and decide for themselves when the barriers of the Constitution shall be overleaped, this is practically "a government without limitation of powers." The States are at once reduced to mere petty corporations, and the people are entirely at your mercy. I have but one word more to add. In all the efforts that have been made by South Carolina to resist the unconstitutional laws which Congress has extended over them, she has kept steadily in view the preservation of the Union by the only means by which she believes it can be long preserved,— a firm, manly, and steady resistance against usurpation. The measures of the federal government have, it is true, prostrated her interests, and will soon involve the whole South in irretrievable ruin. But even this evil, great as it is, is not the chief ground of our complaints. It is the principle involved in the contest, a principle which, substituting the discretion of Congress for the limitations of the Constitution, brings the States and the people to the feet of the federal government, and leaves them nothing they can call their own. Sir, if the measures of the federal government were less oppressive, we should still strive against this usurpation. The South is acting on a principle she has always held sacred,—resistance to unauthorized taxation. These, sir, are the principles which induced the immortal Hampden to resist the payment of a tax of twenty shillings. "Would twenty shillings have ruined his fortune? No! but the payment of a tax of twenty shillings, on the principle on which it was demanded, would have made him a slave." Sir, if, acting on these high motives,—if, animated by that ardent love of liberty which has always been the most prominent trait in the Southern character,—we should be hurried beyond the bounds of a cold and calculating prudence, who is there, with one noble and generous sentiment in his bosom, that would not be disposed, in the language of Burke, to exclaim, "You must pardon something to the spirit of liberty"?

Speech of Mr. Webster in Reply to Mr. Hayne,

In the Senate, on Foote's Resolution, Tuesday and Wednesday, January 26 and 27, 1830.

MR. PRESIDENT.—When the mariner has been tossed for many days in thick weather and on an unknown sea, he naturally avails himself of the first pause in the storm, the earliest glance of the sun, to take his latitude and ascertain how far the elements have driven him from his true course. Let us imitate this prudence, and, before we float farther on the waves of this debate, refer to the point from which we departed, that we may at least be able to conjecture where we now are. I ask for the reading of the resolution before the Senate.

The secretary read the resolution, as follows:—

"*Resolved*, That the committee on public lands be instructed to inquire and report the quantity of public lands remaining unsold within each State and Territory, and whether it be expedient to limit for a certain period the sales of the public lands to such lands only as have heretofore been offered for sale, and are now subject to entry at the minimum price. And, also, whether the office of surveyor-general, and some of the land offices, may not be abolished without detriment to the public interest; or whether it be expedient to adopt measures to hasten the sales and extend more rapidly the surveys of the public lands."

We have thus heard, sir, what the resolution is which is actually before us for consideration; and it will readily occur to every one that it is almost the only subject about which something has not been said in the speech, running through two days, by which the Senate has been entertained by the gentleman from South Carolina. Every topic in the wide range of our public affairs, whether past or present,—everything general or local, whether belonging to national politics or party politics,—seems to have attracted more or less of the honorable member's attention, save only the resolution before the Senate. He has spoken of everything but the public lands; they have escaped his notice. To that subject, in all his excursions, he has not paid even the cold respect of a passing glance.

When this debate, sir, was to be resumed on Thursday morning [January 21], it so happened that it would have been convenient for me to be elsewhere. The honorable member, however, did not incline to put off the discussion to another day. He had a shot, he said, to return, and he wished to discharge it. That shot, sir, which he thus kindly informed us was coming, that we might stand out of the way or prepare ourselves to fall by it and die with decency, has now been received. Under all advantages, and with expectation awakened by the tone which preceded it, it has been discharged and has spent its force. It may become me to say no more of its effect than that, if nobody is found, after all, either killed or wounded, it is not the first time in the history of human affairs that the vigor and success of the war have not quite come up to the lofty and sounding phrase of the manifesto.

The gentleman, sir, in declining to postpone the debate, told the Senate, with the emphasis of his hand upon his heart, that there was something rankling *here* which he wished to relieve. [Mr. Hayne rose and disclaimed having used the word *rankling,* but according to Gales and Seaton's "Register of Debates" the word was used.] It would not, Mr. President, be safe for the honorable member to appeal to those around him upon the question whether he did in fact make use of that word. But he may have been unconscious of it. At any rate, it is enough that he disclaims it. But still, with or without the use of that particular word, he had yet something *here,* he said, of which he wished to rid himself by an immediate reply. In this respect, sir, I have a great advantage over the honorable gentleman. There is nothing *here,* sir, which gives me the slightest uneasiness; neither fear, nor anger, nor that which is sometimes more troublesome than either, the consciousness of having been in the wrong. There is nothing, either originating *here,* or now received *here* by the gentleman's shot. Nothing originating here, for I had not the slightest feeling of unkindness towards the honorable member. Some passages, it is true, had occurred since our acquaintance in this body, which I could have wished might have been otherwise; but I had used philosophy and forgotten them. I paid the honorable member the attention of listening with respect to his first speech; and when he sat down, though surprised, and I must even say astonished, at some of his opinions, nothing was farther from my intention than to commence any personal warfare. Through the whole of the few remarks I made in answer, I avoided, studiously and carefully, everything which I thought possible to be construed into disrespect. And, sir, while there is thus nothing originating *here* which I wished at any time or now wish to discharge, I must repeat also, that nothing has been received *here* which *rankles,* or in any way gives me annoyance. I will not accuse the honorable member of violating the rules of civilized war; I will not say that he poisoned his arrows. But whether his shafts were or were not dipped in that which would have caused rankling if they had reached their destination, there was not, as it happened, quite strength enough in the bow to bring them to their mark. If he wishes now to gather up those snafts, he must look for them elsewhere; they will not be found fixed and quivering in the object at which they were aimed.

The honorable member complained that I had slept on his speech. I must have slept on it, or not slept at all. The moment the honorable member sat down, his friend from Missouri [Mr. Benton] rose, and, with much honeyed commendation of the speech, suggested that the impressions which it had produced were too charming and delightful to be disturbed by other sentiments or other sounds, and proposed that the Senate should adjourn. Would it have been quite amiable in me, sir, to interrupt this excellent good feeling? Must I not have been absolutely malicious if I could have thrust myself forward to destroy sensations thus pleasing? Was it not much better and kinder both to sleep upon them myself and to allow others also the pleasure of sleeping upon them? But, if it be meant by sleeping upon his speech that I took time to prepare a reply to it, it is quite a mistake. Owing to other engagements, I could not employ even the interval between the adjournment of the Senate and its meeting the next morning in attention to the subject of this debate. Nevertheless, sir, the mere matter of fact is undoubtedly true. I did sleep on the gentleman's speech and slept soundly. And I slept equally well on his speech of yesterday, to which I am now replying. It is quite possible that in this respect, also, I possess some advantage over the honorable member, attributable, doubtless, to a cooler temperament on my part; for, in truth, I slept upon his speeches remarkably well.

But the gentleman inquires why *he* was made the object of such a reply. Why was *he* singled out. If an attack has been made on the East he, he assures us, did not begin it; it was made by the gentleman from Missouri [Mr. Benton]. Sir, I answered the gentleman's speech because I happened to hear it; and because, also, I chose to give an answer to that speech which, if unanswered, I thought most likely to produce injurious impressions. I did not stop to inquire who was the original drawer of the bill. I found a responsible indorser before me, and it was my purpose to hold him liable, and to bring him to his just responsibility without delay. But, sir, this interrogatory of the honorable member was only introductory to another. He proceeded to ask me whether I had turned upon him in this debate from the consciousness that I should find an overmatch if I ventured on a contest with his friend from Missouri. If, sir, the honorable member, *modestiae gratiâ*, had chosen thus to defer to his friend and to pay him a compliment without intentional disparagement to others, it would have been quite according to the friendly courtesies of debate, and not at all ungrateful to my own feelings. I am not one of those, sir, who esteem any tribute of regard, whether light and occasional or more serious and deliberate, which may be bestowed on others, as so much unjustly withholden from themselves. But the tone and manner of the gentleman's question forbid me thus to interpret it. I am not at liberty to consider it as nothing more than a civility to his friend. It had an air of taunt and disparagement, something of the loftiness of asserted superiority, which does not allow me to pass it over without notice. It was put as a question for me to answer, and so put as if it were difficult for me to answer, whether I deemed the member from Missouri as overmatch for myself in debate here. It seems to me, sir, that this is extraordinary language and an extraordinary tone for the discussions of this body.

Matches and overmatches! Those terms are more applicable elsewhere than here, and fitter for other assemblies than this. Sir, the gentleman seems to forget where and what we are. This is a senate, a senate of equals, of men of individual honor and personal character and of absolute independence. We know no masters, we acknowledge no dictators. This is a hall for mutual consultation and discussion; not an arena for the exhibitions of champions. I offer myself, sir, as a match for no man; I throw the challenge of debate at no man's feet. But then, sir, since the honorable member has put the question in a manner that calls for an answer, I will give him an answer; and I tell him that, holding myself to be the humblest of the members here, I yet know nothing in the arm of his friend from Missouri, either alone or when aided by the arm of *his* friend from South Carolina, that need deter even me from espousing whatever opinions I may choose to espouse, from debating whenever I may choose to debate, or from speaking whatever I may see fit to say on the floor of the Senate. Sir, when uttered as matter of commendation or compliment, I should dissent from nothing which the honorable member might say of his friend. Still less do I put forth any pretensions of my own. But when put to me as matter of taunt, I throw it back, and say to the gentleman that he could possibly say nothing less likely than such a comparison to wound my pride of personal character. The anger of its tone rescued the remark from intentional irony, which otherwise, probably, would have been its general acceptation. But, sir, if it be imagined that by this mutual quotation and commendation; if it be supposed that, by casting the characters of the drama, assigning to each his part, to one the attack, to another the cry of onset; or if it be thought that by a loud and empty vaunt of anticipated victory, any laurels are to be won here; if it be imagined, especially, that any or all of these things will shake any purpose of mine,—I can tell the honorable member, once for all, that he is greatly mistaken, and that he is dealing with one of whose temper and character he has yet much to learn. Sir, I shall not allow myself on this occasion, I hope on no occasion, to be betrayed into any loss of temper; but if provoked, as I trust I never shall be, into crimination and recrimination, the honorable member may perhaps find that, in that contest, there will be blows to take as well as blows to give; that others can state comparisons as significant, at least, as his own; and that his impunity may possibly demand of him whatever powers of taunt and sarcasm he may possess. I commend him to a prudent husbandry of his resources.

We approach at length, sir, to a more important part of the honorable gentleman's observations. Since it does not accord with my views of justice and policy to give away the public lands altogether, as a mere matter of gratuity, I am asked by the honorable gentleman on what ground it is that I consent to vote them away in particular instances. How, he inquires, do I reconcile with these professed sentiments my support of measures appropriating portions of the lands to particular roads, particular canals, particular rivers, and particular institutions of education in the West? This leads, sir, to the real and wide difference in political opinion between the honorable gentleman and myself. On my part, I look upon all these objects as connected with the common good, fairly embraced in its object and its terms; he, on the contrary, deems them all, if good at all, only local good. This is our difference. The interrogatory, which he proceeded to put, at once explains this difference. "What interest," asks he, "has South Carolina in a canal in Ohio?" Sir, this very question is full of significance. It develops the gentleman's whole political system, and its answer expounds mine. Here we differ. I look upon a road over the Alleghanies, a canal round the falls of the Ohio, or a canal or railway from the Atlantic to the western waters, as being an object large and extensive enough to be fairly said to be for the common benefit. The gentleman thinks otherwise, and this is the key to his construction of the powers of the government. He may well ask what interest has South Carolina in a canal in Ohio. On his system, it is true, she has no interest. On that system, Ohio and Carolina are different governments and different countries, connected here, it is true, by some slight and ill-defined bond of union, but in all main respects separate and diverse. On that system, Carolina has no more interest in a canal in Ohio than in Mexico. The gentleman, therefore, only follows out his own principles; he does no more than arrive at the natural conclusions of his own doctrines; he only announces the true results of that creed which he has adopted himself, and would persuade others to adopt, when he thus declares that South Carolina has no interest in a public work in Ohio.

Sir, we narrow-minded people of New England do not reason thus. Our *notion* of things is entirely different. We look upon the States, not as separated, but as united. We love to dwell on that union, and on the mutual happiness which it has so much promoted, and the common renown which it has so greatly contributed to acquire. In our contemplation, Carolina and Ohio are parts of the same country; States united under the same general government, having interests common, associated, intermingled. In whatever is within the proper sphere of the constitutional powers of this government, we look upon the States as one. We do not impose geographical limits to our patriotic feeling or regard; we do not follow rivers and mountains and lines of latitude to find boundaries beyond which public improvements do not benefit us. We, who come here as agents and representatives of these narrow-minded and selfish men of New England, consider ourselves as bound to regard with an equal eye the good of the whole, in whatever is within our power of legislation. Sir, if a railroad or canal, beginning in South Carolina and ending in South Carolina, appeared to me to be of national importance and national magnitude, believing, as I do, that the power of government extends to the encouragement of works of that description, if I were to stand up here and ask, What interest has Massachusetts in a railroad in South Carolina? I should not be willing to face my constituents. These same narrow-minded men would tell me that they had sent me to act for the whole country, and that one who possessed too little comprehension, either of intellect or feeling, one who was not large enough, both in mind and in heart, to embrace the whole, was not fit to be intrusted with the interest of any part.

Sir, I do not desire to enlarge the powers of the government by unjustifiable construction, nor to exercise any not within a fair interpretation. But when it is believed that a power does exist, then it is, in my judgment, to be exercised for the general benefit of the whole. So far as respects the exercise of such a power, the States are one. It was the very object of the Constitution to create unity of interests to the extent of the powers of the general government. In war and peace we are one; in commerce one; because the authority of the general government reaches to war and peace, and to the regulation of commerce. I have never seen any more difficulty in erecting lighthouses on the lakes than on the ocean; to improving the harbors of inland seas than if they were within the ebb and flow of the tide; or in removing obstructions in the vast streams of the West, more than in any work to facilitate commerce on the Atlantic coast. If there be any power for one, there is power also for the other; and they are all and equally for the common good of the country.

I must now beg to ask, sir, Whence is this supposed right of the States derived? Where do they find the power to interfere with the laws of the Union? Sir, the opinion which the honorable gentleman maintains is a notion founded in a total misapprehension, in my judgment, of the origin of this government, and of the foundation on which it stands. I hold it to be a popular government, erected by the people; those who administer it responsible to the people; and itself capable of being amended and modified, just as the people may choose it should be. It is as popular, just as truly emanating from the people, as the State governments. It is created for one purpose; the State governments for another. It has its own powers; they have theirs. There is no more authority with them to arrest the operation of a law of Congress than with Congress to arrest the operation of their laws. We are here to administer a Constitution emanating immediately from the people, and trusted by them to our administration. It is not the creature of the State governments. It is of no moment to the argument that certain acts of the State legislatures are necessary to fill our seats in this body. That is not one of their original State powers, a part of the sovereignty of the State. It is a duty which the people, by the Constitution itself, have imposed on the State legislatures, and which they might have left to be performed elsewhere, if they had seen fit. So they have left the choice of President with electors; but all this does not affect the proposition that this whole government—President, Senate, and House of Representatives—is a popular government. It leaves it still all its popular character. The governor of a State (in some of the States) is chosen, not directly by the people, but by those who are chosen by the people for the purpose of performing, among other duties, that of electing a governor. Is the government of the State, on that account, not a popular government? This government, sir, is the independent offspring of the popular will. It is not the creature of State legislatures: nay, more, if the whole truth must be told, the people brought it into existence, established it, and have hitherto supported it for the very purpose, amongst others, of imposing certain salutary restraints on State sovereignties. The States cannot now make war; they cannot contract alliances; they cannot make, each for itself, separate regulations of commerce; they cannot lay imposts; they cannot coin money. If this Constitution, sir, be the creature of State legislatures, it must be admitted that it has obtained a strange control over the volitions of its creators.

The people, then, sir, erected this government. They gave it a Constitution, and in that Constitution they have enumerated the powers which they bestow on it. They have made it a limited government. They have defined its authority. They have restrained it to the exercise of such powers as are granted; and all others, they declare, are reserved to the States or the people. But, sir, they have not stopped here. If they had, they would have accomplished but half their work. No definition can be so clear as to avoid possibility of doubt; no limitation so precise as to exclude all uncertainty. Who, then, shall construe this grant of the people? Who shall interpret their will, where it may be supposed they have left it doubtful? With whom do they repose this ultimate right of deciding on the powers of the government? Sir, they have settled all this in the fullest manner. They have left it with the government itself, in its appropriate branches. Sir, the very chief end, the main design for which the whole Constitution was framed and adopted was to establish a government that should not be obliged to act through State agency, or depend on State opinion and State discretion. The people had had quite enough of that kind of government under the Confederation. Under that system, the legal action, the application of law to individuals, belonged exclusively to the States. Congress could only recommend; their acts were not of binding force till the States had adopted and sanctioned them. Are we in that condition still? Are we yet at the mercy of State discretion and State construction? Sir, if we are, then vain will be our attempt to maintain the Constitution under which we sit.

But, sir, the people have wisely provided, in the Constitution itself, a proper, suitable mode and tribunal for settling question of constitutional law. There are in the Constitution grants of powers to Congress, and restrictions on these powers. There are, also, prohibitions on the States. Some authority must, therefore, necessarily exist, having the ultimate jurisdiction to fix and ascertain the interpretation of these grants, restrictions, and prohibitions. The Constitution has itself pointed out, ordained, and established that authority. How has it accomplished this great and essential end? By declaring, sir, that *"the Constitution, and the laws of the United States made in pursuance thereof, shall be the supreme law of the land, anything in the Constitution or laws of any State to the contrary notwithstanding."*

This, sir, was the first great step. By this the supremacy of the Constitution and laws of the United States is declared. The people so will it. No State law is to be valid which comes in conflict with the Constitution, or any law of the United States passed in pursuance of it. But who shall decide this question of interference? To whom lies the last appeal? This, sir, the Constitution itself decides also, by declaring *"that the judicial power shall extend to all cases arising under the Constitution and laws of the United States."* These two provisions cover the whole ground. They are, in truth, the keystone of the arch! With these it is a government; without them it is a confederation. In pursuance of these clear and express provisions, Congress established, at its very first session, in the judicial act, a mode for carrying them into full effect, and for bringing all questions of constitutional power to the final decision of the Supreme Court. It then, sir, became a government. It then had the means of self-protection; and but for this, it would, in all probability, have been now among things which are past. Having constituted the government and declared its powers, the people have further said that, since somebody must decide on the extent of these powers, the government shall itself decide; subject always, like other popular governments, to its responsibility to the people. And now, sir, I repeat, how is it that a State legislature acquires any power to interfere? Who or what gives them the right to say to the people, "We, who are your agents and servants for one purpose, will undertake to decide that your other agents and servants, appointed by you for another purpose, have transcended the authority you gave them!" The reply would be, I think, not impertinent,—"Who made you a judge over another's servants? To their own masters they stand or fall."

Sir, I deny this power of State legislatures altogether. It cannot stand the test of examination. Gentlemen may say that, in an extreme case, a State government might protect the people from intolerable oppression. Sir, in such a case the people might protect themselves without the aid of the State governments. Such a case warrants revolution. It must make, when it comes, a law for itself. A nullifying act of a State legislature cannot alter the case, nor make resistance any more lawful. In maintaining these sentiments, sir, I am but asserting the rights of the people. I state what they have declared, and insist on their right to declare it. They have chosen to repose this power in the general government, and I think it my duty to support it, like other constitutional powers.

For myself, sir, I do not admit the competency of South Carolina, or any other State, to prescribe my constitutional duty, or to settle, between me and the people, the validity of laws of Congress for which I have voted. I decline her umpirage. I have not sworn to support the Constitution according to her construction of its clauses. I have not stipulated, by my oath of office or otherwise, to come under any responsibility, except to the people, and those whom they have appointed to pass upon the question whether laws supported by my votes conform to the Constitution of the country. And, sir, if we look to the general nature of the case, could anything have been more preposterous than to make a government for the whole Union, and yet leave its powers subject, not to one interpretation, but to thirteen or twenty-four interpretations? Instead of one tribunal, established by all, responsible to all, with power to decide for all, shall constitutional questions be left to four-and-twenty popular bodies, each at liberty to decide for itself, and none bound to respect the decisions of others; and each at liberty, too, to give a new construction on every new election of its own members? Would anything with such a principle in it, or rather with such a destitution of all principle, be fit to be called a government? No, sir. It should not be denominated a Constitution. It should be called, rather, a collection of topics for everlasting controversy; heads of debate for a disputatious people. It would not be a government. It would not be adequate to any practical good, or fit for any country to live under.

To avoid all possibility of being misunderstood, allow me to repeat again, in the fullest manner, that I claim no powers for the government by forced or unfair construction. I admit that it is a government of strictly limited powers; of enumerated, specified, and particularized powers; and that whatsoever is not granted is withheld. But notwithstanding all this, and however the grant of powers may be expressed, its limit and extent may yet, in some cases, admit of doubt; and the general government would be good for nothing, it would be incapable of long existing, if some mode had not been provided in which those doubts, as they should arise, might be peaceably but authoritatively solved.

The people have preserved this, their own chosen Constitution, for forty years, and have seen their happiness, prosperity, and renown grow with its growth and strengthen with its strength. They are now, generally, strongly attached to it. Overthrown by direct assault it cannot be; evaded, undermined, NULLIFIED, it will not be, if we and those who shall succeed us here as agents and representatives of the people shall conscientiously and vigilantly discharge the two great branches of our public trust,—faithfully to preserve and wisely to administer it.

Mr. President, I have thus stated the reasons of my dissent to the doctrines which have been advanced and maintained. I am conscious of having detained you and the Senate much too long. I was drawn into the debate with no previous deliberation, such as is suited to the discussion of so grave and important a subject. But it is a subject of which my heart is full, and I have not been willing to suppress the utterance of its spontaneous sentiments. I cannot, even now, persuade myself to relinquish it without expressing once more my deep conviction that, since it respects nothing less than the Union of the States, it is of most vital and essential importance to the public happiness. I profess, sir, in my career hitherto, to have kept steadily in view the prosperity and honor of the whole country, and the preservation of our Federal Union. It is to that Union we owe our safety at home and our consideration and dignity abroad. It is to that Union that we are chiefly indebted for whatever makes us most proud of our country. That Union we reached only by the discipline of our virtues in the severe school of adversity. It had its origin in the necessities of disordered finance, prostrate commerce, and ruined credit. Under its benign influences these great interests immediately awoke as from the dead, and sprang forth with newness of life. Every year of its duration has teemed with fresh proofs of its utility and its blessings; and although our territory has stretched out wider and wider, and our population spread farther and farther, they have not outrun its protection or its benefits. It has been to us all a copious fountain of national, social, and personal happiness.

I have not allowed myself, sir, to look beyond the Union, to see what might lie hidden in the dark recess behind. I have not coolly weighed the chances of preserving liberty when the bonds that unite us together shall be broken asunder. I have not accustomed myself to hang over the precipice of disunion, to see whether, with my short sight, I can fathom the depth of the abyss below; now could I regard him as a safe counselor in the affairs of this government whose thoughts should be mainly bent on considering, not how the Union may be best preserved, but how tolerable might be the condition of the people when it shall be broken up and destroyed. While the Union lasts, we have high, exciting, gratifying prospects spread out before us for us and our children. Beyond that I seek not to penetrate the veil. God grant that in my day, at least, that curtain may not rise! God grant that on my vision never may be opened what lies behind! When my eyes shall be turned to behold for the last time the sun in heaven, may I not see him shining on the broken and dishonored fragments of a once glorious Union; on States dissevered, discordant, belligerent; on a land rent with civil feuds, or drenched, it may be, in fraternal blood! Let their last feeble and lingering glance rather behold the gorgeous ensign of the republic, now known and honored throughout the earth, still full high advanced, its arms and trophies streaming in their original lustre, not a stripe erased or polluted nor a single star obscured, bearing for its motto no such miserable interrogatory as "What is all this worth?" nor those other words of delusion and folly, "Liberty first and Union afterwards;" but everywhere, spread all over in characters of living light, blazing on all its ample folds, as they float over the sea and over the land, and in every wind under the whole heavens, that other sentiment, dear to every true American heart,—Liberty *and* Union, now and forever, one and inseparable!

Address Delivered at the Dedication of the Cemetery at Gettysburg.

Fourscore and seven years ago our fathers brought forth upon this continent a new nation, conceived in liberty, and dedicated to the proposition that all men are created equal. Now we are engaged in a great civil war, testing whether that nation, or any nation so conceived and so dedicated, can long endure. We are met on a great battle-field of that war. We have come to dedicate a portion of that field, as a final resting-place for those who here gave their lives that that nation might live. It is altogether fitting and proper that we should do this. But, in a larger sense, we cannot dedicate—we cannot consecrate—we cannot hallow—this ground. The brave men, living and dead, who struggled here have consecrated it, far above our power to add or detract. The world will little note, nor long remember, what we say here, but it can never forget what they did here. It is for us the living, rather, to be dedicated here to the unfinished work which they who fought here have thus far so nobly advanced. It is rather for us to be here dedicated to the great task remaining before us,—that from these honored dead we take increased devotion to that cause for which they gave the last full measure of devotion—that we here highly resolve that these dead shall not have died in vain—that this nation, under God, shall have a new birth of freedom —and that government of the people, by the people, and for the people, shall not perish from the earth.

Abraham Lincoln.

November 19, 1863.

Letter to Horace Greeley.

Executive Mansion, Washington,
August 22, 1862.

Hon. Horace Greeley.—*Dear Sir:* I have just read yours of the 19th, addressed to myself through the *New York Tribune.* If there be in it any statements or assumptions of fact which I may know to be erroneous, I do not now and here controvert them. If there be in it any inferences which I may believe to be falsely drawn, I do not now and here argue against them. If there be perceptible in it an impatient and dictatorial tone, waive it in deference to an old friend, whose heart I have always supposed to be right.

As to the policy I "seem to be pursuing," as you say, I have not meant to leave any one in doubt.

I would save the Union. I would save it in the shortest way under the Constitution. The sooner the National authority can be restored, the nearer the Union will be "The Union as it was." If there be those who would not save the Union unless they could at the same time *destroy* Slavery, I do not agree with them. My paramount object in this struggle *is* to save the Union and is *not* either to save or destroy Slavery. If I could save the Union without freeing *any* slave, I would do it; and if I could save it by freeing *all* the slaves, I would do it; and if I could do it by freeing some and leaving others alone, I would also do that. What I do about Slavery and the colored race, I do because I believe it helps to save this Union; and what I forbear, I forbear because I do *not* believe it would help to save the Union. I shall do *less*, whenever I shall believe what I am doing hurts the cause; and I shall do *more*, whenever I shall believe doing more will help the cause. I shall try to correct errors when shown to be errors; and I shall adopt new views so fast as they shall appear to be true views. I have here stated my purpose according to my view of *official* duty, and I intend no modification of my oft-expressed *personal* wish that all men, everywhere, could be free.

Yours,

A. LINCOLN.

THE SECOND INAUGURAL ADDRESS.

FELLOW-COUNTRYMEN: At this second appearing to take the oath of the Presidential office, there is less occasion for an extended address than there was at the first. Then, a statement, somewhat in detail, of a course to be pursued, seemed fitting and proper. Now, at the expiration of four years, during which public declarations have been constantly called forth on every point and phase of the great contest which still absorbs the attention and engrosses the energies of the nation, little that is new could be presented. The progress of our arms, upon which all else chiefly depends, is as well known to the public as to myself; and it is, I trust, reasonably satisfactory and encouraging to all. With high hope for the future, no prediction in regard to it is ventured.

On the occasion corresponding to this four years ago, all thoughts were anxiously directed to an impending civil war. All dreaded it; all sought to avert it. While the inaugural address was being delivered from this place, devoted altogether to *saving* the Union without war, insurgent agents were in the city seeking to *destroy* it without war—seeking to dissolve the Union, and divide effects, by negotiation. Both parties deprecated war; but one of them would *make* war rather than let the nation survive; and the other would *accept* war rather than let it perish. And the war came.

One-eighth of the whole population were colored slaves, not distributed generally over the Union, but localized in the southern part of it. These slaves constituted a peculiar and powerful interest. All knew that this interest was, somehow, the cause of the war. To strengthen, perpetuate, and extend this interest was the object for which the insurgents would rend the Union, even by war; while the Government claimed no right to do more than to restrict the territorial enlargement of it. Neither party expected for the war the magnitude or the duration which it has already attained. Neither anticipated that the *cause* of the conflict might cease with, or even before, the conflict itself should cease. Each looked for an easier triumph, and a result less fundamental and astounding. Both read the same Bible, and pray to the same God; and each invokes His aid against the other. It may seem strange that any men should dare to ask a just God's assistance in wringing their bread from the sweat of other men's faces; but let us judge not, that we be not judged. The prayers of both could not be answered; that of neither has been answered fully. The Almighty has His own purposes. "Woe unto the world because of offenses! for it must needs be that offenses come; but woe to that man by whom the offense cometh." If we shall suppose American Slavery is one of those offenses which, in the providence of God, must needs come, but which, having continued through His appointed time, He now wills to remove, and that He gives to both North and South this terrible war, as the woe due to those by whom the offense came, shall we discern therein any departure from those divine attributes which the believers in a living God always ascribe to Him? Fondly do we hope, fervently do we pray, that this mighty scourge of war may speedily pass away. Yet, if God wills that it continue until all the wealth piled by the bondman's two hundred and fifty years of unrequited toil shall be sunk, and until every drop of blood drawn with the lash shall be paid by another drawn with the sword, as was said three thousand years ago, so still it must be said, "The judgments of the Lord are true and righteous altogether."

With malice toward none, with charity for all, with firmness in the right, as God gives us to see the right, let us strive

THE WHITE HOUSE IN 1861.

on to finish the work we are in; to bind up the nation's wounds; to care for him who shall have borne the battle, and for his widow, and his orphan; to do all which may achieve and cherish a just and a lasting peace among ourselves and with all nations.

THE MARTYR PRESIDENT.

HENRY WARD BEECHER.

(Brooklyn, April 15, 1865.)

THERE is no historic figure more noble than that of Moses, the Jewish law-giver. There is scarcely another event in history more touching than his death. He had borne the great burdens of state for forty years, shaped the Jews to a nation, filled out their civil and religious polity, administered their laws, guided their steps, or dwelt with them in all their journeyings in the wilderness; had mourned in their punishment, kept step with their march, and led them in wars, until the end of their labors drew nigh. The last stage was reached. Jordan only lay between them and the promised land. Then came the word of the Lord unto him, "Thou mayest not go over: Get thee up into the mountain, look upon it, and die."

From that silent summit, the hoary leader gazed to the north, to the south, to the west, with hungry eyes. The dim outlines rose up. The hazy recesses spoke of quiet valleys between the hills. With eager longing, with sad resignation, he looked upon the promised land. It was now to him a forbidden land. It was a moment's anguish. He forgot all his personal wants, and drank in the vision of his people's home. His work was done. There lay God's promise fulfilled.

Again a great leader of the people has passed through toil, sorrow, battle, and war, and come near to the promised land of peace, into which he might not pass over. Who shall recount our martyr's sufferings for this people? Since the November of 1860, his horizon has been black with storms. By day and by night he trod a way of danger and darkness. On his shoulders rested a government dearer to him than his own life. At its integrity millions of men were striking at home. Upon this government foreign eyes lowered. It stood like a lone island in a sea full of storms; and every tide and wave seemed eager to devour it. Upon thousands of hearts great sorrows and anxieties have rested, but not on one such, and in such measure, as upon that simple, truthful, noble soul, our faithful and sainted Lincoln. He wrestled ceaselessly, through four black and dreadful purgatorial years, wherein God was cleansing the sin of his people as by fire.

At last the watcher beheld the gray dawn for the country. The mountains began to give forth their forms from out the darkness; and the East came rushing toward us with arms full of joy for all our sorrows. Then it was for him to be glad exceedingly, that had sorrowed immeasurably. Peace could bring to no other heart such joy, such rest, such honor, such trust, such gratitude. But he looked upon it as Moses looked upon the promised land. Then the wail of a nation proclaimed that he had gone from among us. Not thine the sorrow, but ours, sainted soul.

Never did two such orbs of experience meet in one hemisphere, as the joy and the sorrow of the same week in this land. The joy was as sudden as if no man had expected it, and as entrancing as if it had fallen a sphere from heaven. In one hour it lay without a pulse, without a gleam, or breath. A sorrow came that swept through the land as huge storms sweep through the forest and field, rolling thunder along the sky, dishevelling the flowers, daunting every singer in thicket or forest, and pouring blackness and darkness across the land and up the mountains. Did ever so many hearts, in so brief a time, touch two such boundless feelings? It was the uttermost of joy; it was the uttermost of sorrow—noon and midnight, without a space between.

The blow brought not a sharp pang. It was so terrible that at first it stunned sensibility. Citizens were like men awakened at midnight by an earthquake, and bewildered to find everything that they were accustomed to trust wavering and falling. The very earth was no longer solid. The first feeling was the least. Men waited to get straight to feel. They wandered in the streets as if groping after some impending dread, or undeveloped sorrow, or some one to tell them what ailed them. They met each other as if each would ask the other, "Am I awake or do I dream?" There was a piteous helplessness. Strong men bowed down and wept. Other and common griefs belonged to some one in chief: this belonged to all. It was each and every man's. Every virtuous household in the land felt as if its first-born were gone. Rear to his name monuments, found charitable institutions, and write his name above their lintels; but no monument will ever equal the universal, spontaneous, and sublime sorrow that in a moment swept down lines and parties, and covered up animosities, and in an hour brought a divided people into unity of grief and indivisible fellowship of anguish.

And now the martyr is moving in triumphal march, mightier than when alive. The nation rises up at every stage of his coming. Cities and states are his pall-bearers, and the cannon beats the hours with solemn progression. Dead, dead, dead, he yet speaketh! Is Washington dead? Is Hampden dead? Is David dead? Is any man that ever was fit to live dead? Disenthralled of flesh, and risen in the unobstructed sphere where passion never comes, he begins his illimitable work. His life now is grafted upon the infinite, and will be fruitful as no earthly life can be. Pass on, thou that hast overcome! Your sorrows, or people, are his peace! Your bells, and bands, and muffled drums, sound triumph in his ear. Wail and weep here; God makes it echo joy and triumph there. Pass on!

Four years ago, oh Illinois, we took from your midst an untried man, and from among the people. We return him to you a mighty conqueror. Not thine any more, but the nation's; not ours, but the world's. Give him place, oh ye prairies! In the midst of this great continent his dust shall rest, a sacred treasure to myriads who shall pilgrim to that shrine to kindle anew their zeal and patriotism. Ye winds that move over the mighty places of the West, chant requiem! Ye people, behold a martyr whose blood, as so many articulate words, pleads for fidelity, for law, for liberty!

The New South.

HENRY W. GRADY.

"There was a South of slavery and secession—that South is dead. There is a South of union and freedom—that South, thank God, is living, breathing, growing every hour." These words, delivered from the immortal lips of Benjamin H. Hill, at Tammany Hall, in 1866, true then, and truer now, I shall make my text to-night.

In speaking to the toast with which you have honored me, I accept the term, "The New South," as in no sense disparaging to the old. Dear to me, sir, is the home of my childhood, and the traditions of my people. I would not, if I could, dim the glory they won in peace and war, or by word or deed take aught from the splendor and grace of their civilization, never equaled, and perhaps never to be equaled in its chivalric strength and grace. There is a new South, not through protest against the old, but because of new conditions, new adjustments, and, if you please, new ideas and aspirations.

Doctor Talmage has drawn for you, with a master's hand, the picture of your returning armies. He has told you how, in the pomp and circumstance of war, they came back to you, marching with proud and victorious tread, reading their glory in a nation's eyes! Will you bear with me while I tell you of another army that sought its home at the close of the late war—an army that marched home in defeat and not in victory—in pathos and not in splendor, but in glory that equaled yours, and to hearts as loving as ever welcomed heroes home? Let me picture to you the foot-sore Confederate soldier, as, buttoning up in his faded gray jacket the parole which was to bear testimony to his children of his fidelity and faith, he turned his face southward from Appomattox in April, 1865.

Think of him as ragged, half-starved, heavy-hearted, enfeebled by want and wounds, having fought to exhaustion, he surrenders his gun, wrings the hands of his comrades in silence, and lifting his tear-stained and pallid face for the last time to the graves that dot old Virginia hills, pulls his gray cap over his brow and begins the slow and faithful journey. What does he find—let me ask you who went to your homes eager to find, in the welcome you had justly earned, full payment for four years' sacrifice—what does he find when, having followed the battle-stained cross against overwhelming odds, dreading death not half so much as surrender, he reaches the home he left so prosperous and beautiful?

He finds his house in ruins, his farm devastated, his slaves free, his stock killed, his barns empty, his trade destroyed, his money worthless, his social system, feudal in its magnificence, swept away; his people without law or legal status, his comrades slain, and the burdens of others heavy on his shoulders. Crushed by defeat, his very traditions are gone. Without money, credit, employment, material, or training, and, besides all this, confronted with the gravest problem that ever met human intelligence,—the establishing of a status for the vast body of his liberated slaves.

What does he do—this hero in gray, with a heart of gold? Does he sit down in sullenness and despair? Not for a day. Surely God, who had stripped him of his prosperity, inspired him in his adversity. As ruin was never before so overwhelming, never was restoration swifter. The soldiers stepped from the trenches into the furrow; horses that had charged Federal guns marched before the plough; and the fields that ran red with human blood in April were green with the harvest in June.

Copyright by Underwood & Underwood, N. Y.
FOUR THOUSAND SHEEP CHANGING PASTURE.—AUSTRALIA.

From the ashes left us in 1864 we have raised a brave and beautiful city. Somehow or other we have caught the sunshine in the bricks and mortar of our homes, and have builded therein not one ignoble prejudice or memory.

The old South rested everything on slavery and agriculture, unconscious that these could neither give nor maintain healthy growth. The new South presents a perfect Democracy, the oligarchs leading in the popular movement—a social system compact and closely knitted, less splendid on the surface but stronger at the core; a hundred farms for every plantation, fifty homes for every palace, and a diversified industry that meets the complex needs of this complex age.

The new South is enamoured of her new work. Her soul is stirred with the breath of a new life. The light of a grander day is falling fair on her face. She is thrilling with the consciousness of a growing power and prosperity. As she stands upright, full-statured and equal among the people of the earth, breathing the keen air and looking out upon the expanding horizon, she understands that her emancipation came because in the inscrutable wisdom of God her honest purpose was crossed, and her brave armies were beaten.

This is said in no spirit of time-serving or apology. The South has nothing for which to apologize. She believes that the late struggle between the States was war and not rebellion, revolution and not conspiracy, and that her convictions were as honest as yours. I should be unjust to the dauntless spirit of the South and to my own convictions if I did not make this plain in this presence. The South has nothing to take back. In my native town of Athens is a monument that crowns its central hills—a plain, white shaft. Deep cut into its shining side is a name dear to me above the names of men, that of a brave and simple man who died in a brave and simple faith. Not for all the glories of New England—from Plymouth Rock all the way—would I exchange the heritage he left me in his soldier's death. To the feet of that shaft I shall send my children's children to reverence him who ennobled their name with his heroic blood. But, sir, speaking from the shadow of that memory, which I honor as I do nothing else on earth, I say that the cause in which he suffered and for which he gave his life was adjudged by higher and fuller wisdom than his or mine, and I am glad that the omniscient God held the balance of battle in His Almighty Hand, and that human slavery was swept forever from American soil—the American Union saved from the wreck of war.

This message, Mr. President, comes to you from consecrated ground. Every foot of the soil about the city in which I live is sacred as a battle-ground of the Republic. Every hill that invests it is hallowed to you by the blood of your brothers who died for your victory, and doubly hallowed to us by the blood of those who died hopeless, but undaunted, in defeat— sacred soil to all of us, rich with memories that make us purer and stronger and better, silent but stanch witnesses in its red desolation of the matchless valor of American hearts and the deathless glory of American arms—speaking an eloquent witness, in its white peace and prosperity, to the indissoluble union of American states and the imperishable brotherhood of the American people.

Now, what answer has New England to this message? Will she permit the prejudice of war to remain in the hearts of the conquerors when it has died in the hearts of the conquered? Will she transmit this prejudice to the next generation, that in their hearts, which never felt the generous ardor of conflict it may perpetuate itself? Will she withhold, save in strained courtesy, the hand which, straight from his soldier's heart, Grant offered to Lee at Appomattox? Will she make the vision of a restored and happy people, which gathered above the couch of your dying captain, filling his heart with grace, touching his lips with praise, and glorifying his path to the grave—will she make this vision on which the last sigh of his expiring soul breathed a benediction, a cheat and delusion? If she does, the South, never abject in asking for comradeship, must accept with dignity its refusal; but if she does not refuse to accept in frankness and sincerity this message of good-will and friendship, then will the prophecy of Webster, delivered in this very society forty years ago amid tremendous applause, become true, be verified in its fullest sense, when he said: "Standing hand to hand and clasping hands, we should remain united as we have been for sixty years, citizens of the same country, members of the same government, united, all united now and united forever."

EXPOSITIONS AND PROGRESS

CHAPTER IX.

Early International Fairs.

Exhibitions date far back in the world's history. Even the celebration of the Olympic Games might be considered in this light, for, outside the precinct sacred to the gods, wares were displayed and sold. Until modern facilities for convenient transportation were devised, markets could not be supported continuously; instead it was customary to hold periodic Fairs—the word *fair* being in all probability derived from the Latin *feria*, meaning holiday. Such gatherings for the benefits of trade were held in Asia and in southern Europe in early times and in the seventeenth century seem to have found their way into Gaul; hence into England in the age of Alfred the Great. By the tenth century they were well established throughout Europe. From the beginning they appear to have been associated with religious festivals—the gathering of unusual numbers of people doubtless first suggesting the advantage of such occasions for exhibiting wares and effecting sales.

The largest fair of this description perpetuated to this day in Europe is the one held yearly at Nijni Novgorod, located at the junction of the Oka and Volga, 715 miles from St. Petersburg. This is officially opened on the 27th of July, but owing to the uncertainty of travel, some do not arrive with their goods until later. Many of the transactions on these fair grounds are still conducted by barter. Tea is the chief commodity of commerce although silks, rugs, cloth, hides and morocco are greatly in evidence.

Persian rugs, tea, costly spices and other wares are sent by caravans from interior Asia to be transferred to boats when the chain of interlinking water ways giving final access to Nijni Novgorod is reached. Those who have sold their goods and are returning each year pass those en route for the coming fair before they arrive home.

The Russian government warns foreigners against remaining in this little town over night while the fair is continued, for it is impossible to provide police supervision for the numerous nationalities that camp in the vicinity. Tea to the value of more than a million dollars is frequently displayed at once and large sums of money constantly change hands.

On the Ganges a great fair is annually held and each year during the season when faithful pilgrims gather to visit the spot sacred to Mohamed, one of these prolonged markets is provided. Years ago, before shops existed in Mexico, upon the site of the present capital such a fair was regularly held and attracted more than fifty thousand people.

While fairs of this kind have been numerous in centuries past and are still observed in remote places, industrial expositions purely for the purpose of exhibit are of recent date—the first international exposition being held in London in 1851.

The London Exposition of 1851 resulted from a desire of Prince Albert to provide an exhibit which should illustrate British industrial development. Although but national as first conceived, it was later thought an excellent idea to invite other nations to coöperate and give the event international significance. Being the first undertaking of the kind, novelty and innovation attended all features. Having estimated the space required for such a showing, architects were asked to submit designs for a building which should be adequate to cover 700,000 and not exceed 900,000 square feet. While but one month was allowed for preparation, more than two hundred competitors offered plans. The one offered by Sir Joseph Paxton was adopted. He was a landscape gardener and the form and shape of the Crystal Palace is said to have been based on that of the giant leaf of the African water lily. The building was made 1851 feet long, to correspond with the year, and 450 feet broad. It was erected in about four months at an approximate cost of $1,000,000. It covered twenty acres.

The following lines from a speech made by the Prince Consort at a banquet given by the Lord Mayor of London in the interest of this coming event convey an excellent idea of the hopes which were entertained for the project by those most intimately associated with it.

"I conceive it to be the duty of every educated person closely to watch and study the time in which he lives, and, as far as in him lies, to add his humble mite of individual exertion to further the accomplishment of what he believes Providence to have ordained. Nobody, however, who has paid any attention to the particular features of our present era, will doubt for a moment that we are living at a period of most wonderful transition, which tends rapidly to accomplish that great end—to which, indeed, all history points—the realization of the unity of mankind; not a unity which breaks down the limits and levels the peculiar characteristics of the different nations of the earth, but rather a unity, the results and products of these very national varieties and antagonistic qualities. The distances which separated the different nations and parts of the globe are gradually vanishing before the achievements of modern invention and we can traverse them with incredible speed; the languages of all nations are known; and their acquirement placed within the reach of everybody; thought is communicated with the rapidity and even by the power of lightning. On the other hand, the great principle of the division of labor, which may be called the moving power of civilization, is being extended to all branches of science, industry and art. Whilst formerly the greatest mental energies strove at universal knowledge, and that knowledge was confined to few, now they are directed to specialties, and in these again even to the minutest points. Moreover, the knowledge now acquired becomes the property of the community at large. Whilst formerly discovery was wrapt in secrecy, it results from the publicity of the present day, that no sooner is a discovery or invention made, than it is already improved upon and surpassed by competing effort. . . . The exhibition of 1851 is to give us a true text and a living picture of the point of development at which the whole of mankind has arrived in this great task, and a new starting point, from which all nations will be able to direct their further exertions."

The Crystal Palace was opened on the first day of May by Queen Victoria, who from the beginning had manifested deep interest in the industrial exhibit, which was continued until the following October. The United States was offered 40,000 feet for display; France was accorded 65,000 feet. England and her colonies entered 7381 exhibits; the rest of the world, 6556. Five thousand people from the United States visited this remarkable showing and 499 exhibits were made from this country. In comparison with the splendid exhibits made by Great Britain in manufactured goods, the twelve samples of cotton and three of woolen goods from the United States were indeed meager but attention was won by the McCormick reapers, by wagons and racing sulkies and by the Chickering pianos, which excelled anything in these lines offered by European countries. Our metallic life-boats were then unknown in Europe, where wood alone was used. The American daguerreotypes were acknowledged to be better than those made abroad and Whipple displayed the first photograph of the moon, thus giving to this land the honor of having first applied the "new art" to astronomy.

The exhibits were grouped under four divisions: raw materials, which fell into four classes; manufactured articles, separated into nineteen groups; machinery, divided into six groups, and fine arts—but one group in thirty.

The average number of daily visitors to the Crystal Palace was 42,809, while the largest day swelled this number to 109,915. Financially, the undertaking was thoroughly successful, several million dollars being cleared. Of far greater importance was the impetus given the industrial world by interchange of ideas which resulted from a comparison of exhibits in London and the discussion of them in journals throughout the reading world. However, it has to be admitted that the hope of perpetuating peace by more intimate acquaintance between men of different nations was not realized—wars following the event seemingly as easily as they had preceded it.

While other fairs of national and slight international importance followed, the next one of note was held in France in 1867 in the city of Paris. The symmetrical form of the Crystal Palace had rendered it difficult to arrange the exhibits of several countries in a way to avoid confusion. The main building in Paris was designed to facilitate this end. It consisted of seven concentric ovals arranged in such a way that one might continue around one gallery or oval and see all exhibits of one kind made by the various competing nations, or might follow one avenue or radius and see all the exhibits entered by one nation alone. The building was 1550 feet long, 1250 feet wide and covered eleven acres. Around it were grouped other buildings of interest and minor importance—a Turkish mosque, a Swiss chalet, a Swedish cottage, an English lighthouse and an Egyptian temple.

The exposition was opened on the first day of April and continued until November. Probably no greater splendor has ever accompanied an exposition, for the court of Emperor Napoleon compared favorably with any in Europe and such distinguished rulers as the Czar of Russia, Sultan of Turkey, Khedive of Egypt, King of Germany, with Bismarck, and the kings of Denmark, Portugal and Sweden were invited thither and as honored guests of the French court witnessed the spectacle.

Thirty nations contributed 50,026 exhibits. These were arranged into seven groups in the main building, to correspond with the seven galleries. First came the Gallery of the History of Labor. This was designed to give a living picture of civilization. Beginning with the crude stone implements made by prehistoric man, the history of human labor was here set forth through stone, bronze, iron periods and our present steel age. Next came the Materials and Appliances in the Liberal Arts. This exhibition included the type and paper and books of the printer; the instruments of the medical profession; musical instruments and sundry other things. Third was shown Furniture and other objects used in dwellings. In addition to all kinds of furniture, glass, pottery, carpets and tapestries, apparatus for heating and lighting and watches and clocks were displayed. The fourth gallery was given over to Garments, tissues for clothing and other articles of Wearing Apparel—such as shawls, laces, ornaments of different varieties. The fifth group was comprised of Products, raw and manufactured, of Extracted Industries—mining, forestry particularly. Sixth, Instruments and process of Common Arts —apparatus in mining, whatever pertained to railroads, for example. The last group was comprised of Foods—fresh or preserved, in various stages of preparation.

In other buildings were to be seen live stock and agricultural implements, horticultural displays of plants and flowers, and, important from the standpoint of progress, the last class of exhibits: those whose special object was the improvement of the physical and moral conditions of people. Improved methods of education, sanitary houses and the like were here included.

This classification has been enumerated at length because it has generally been conceded to be one of the best groupings ever provided by any exposition.

The exhibits entered from the United States numbered 536. Grand prizes were awarded Cyrus W. Field for the Trans-Atlantic cable; David E. Hughes of New York for the printing telegraph; and C. H. McCormick for his harvester. By an imperial decree, McCormick was made Chevalier of the Imperial Order of the Legion of Honor. The exhibit of minerals sent from this country awakened considerable interest in Europe. American farm implements, pianos, sewing machines and locomotives were highly commended and American glass found to compare favorably with that shown by older countries.

Appreciating the wonderful opportunity such a display afforded workmen of various callings, the British Society of Art sent mechanics and artisans chosen by a system of careful selection to spend a week in Paris during this summer to study each his special work and upon return to report the result of his investigation to his less favored fellow-workmen.

The third great international exhibition to precede any in our own country was held in Austria in 1873. The city of Vienna had been undergoing a complete change in the ten years just passed and from an old town of almost mediæval appearance, had become a modern city with fine buildings and broad streets. It was thought fitting to celebrate this transformation, and, furthermore, the successful expositions previously held in Paris and elsewhere convinced ambitious Austrians that they would do well to emulate the example of their neighbors. Accordingly, nations were invited to participate in an exhibit "having for its object to represent the present state of modern civilization and the entire sphere of national economy, and to promote its further development and progress."

A park known as the Prater, including 286 acres, was set aside for the various uses of the fair. The buildings were more substantially made than those which had been previously used for purposes of this kind. In addition to the main building, known as the Palace of Industry, another building was provided for machinery and a third for agricultural purposes.

From the first it appeared as though the fates were not auspicious. The exposition was opened in May, when it was expected that the weather would be fine. On the contrary, for several weeks cold days, often dull and rainy, followed. Visitors were as a rule unfamiliar with the language spoken and had recourse to such French as they could command. Finding the number of guests materially affected by the inclement weather, innkeepers became exorbitant in their charges and so constant were the demands upon strangers for the veriest comforts that many who had intended to visit the fair were moved to change their plans and spend vacations elsewhere. Finally, before the summer was over, cholera broke out in Vienna, ending effectually any further tide of visitors thither.

About 50,000 exhibits were shown. Of these 654 were entered by the United States. They followed in the main the lines which had been shown in Paris and London. American farm implements and machinery aroused far more interest than manufactured cotton and wool—wherein the country was still weak. The extensive agricultural interests of Austria were emphasized by the showing of stock. Many breeds of cattle, horses and other domestic animals were entered, including grey oxen and 250 kinds of pigs—"deemed sufficient to represent the grunters of all nations"—among them the wild red pigs of the Don.

Financially this exposition was a failure. However, it brought to a land remote from western Europe a display of industrial activity and concerns which could not fail to bear fruit later.

THE CENTENNIAL

Welcome to All Nations.

Bright on the banners of lily and rose,
    Lo, the last sun of the century sets!
Wreathe the black cannon that scowled on our foes;
    All but her friendships the nation forgets!
All but her friends and their welcome forgets!
    These are around her, but where are her foes?
Lo, while the sun of the century sets,
    Peace with her garlands of lily and rose!

Welcome! a shout like the war-trumpet's swell,
    Wakes the wild echoes that slumber around!
Welcome! it quivers from Liberty's bell;
    Welcome! the walls of her temple resound!
Hark! the gray walls of her temple resound!
    Fade the far voices o'er river and dell;
Welcome! still whisper the echoes around;
    Welcome! still trembles on Liberty's bell!

Thrones of the continents! Isles of the sea!
    Yours are the garlands of peace we entwine!
Welcome once more to the land of the free,
    Shadowed alike by the palm and the pine.
Softly they murmur, the palm and the pine,
    "Hushed is our strife in the land of the free."
Over your children their branches entwine,
    Thrones of the continents! Isles of the sea!

        —*Oliver Wendell Holmes.*

CHAPTER XI.

The Centennial.

As the first hundred years of American independence were fast drawing to an end, it was generally conceded that some fitting celebration of so momentous an occasion should be undertaken. Just what form this should assume was long discussed. Patriotic meetings, to be held in every hamlet of the land, were suggested. Others thought that each state should provide some special celebration. Finally a national exhibition was talked about but when the idea was advanced that foreign nations as well be invited to join, there was a strong impression that England would be loathe to share in any commemoration of American independence, and that her attitude would influence other European states. However, this erroneous conception was soon dispelled when preliminary investigation was guardedly made. It was found that European countries would welcome an opportunity such as an exposition in America would afford.

No previous exhibition had commemorated an anniversary or historical event, and in those lands where international fairs had earlier been held, there had arisen no question as to where such exhibits should properly be made. The capitals of England, France and Austria were most appropriate in each case. But in the United States the situation was quite different. Several cities contested for the honor. New York maintained that its position on the country's threshold should insure it preference; although Washington was not then able to provide such accommodation for strangers as would be required there were many who felt that it was the most suitable place for the fair. However, when it was remembered that Philadelphia had been the seat of the Continental Congress, that it had once been the capital of the republic, and that it was midway between north and south, popular sentiment settled upon it as the most acceptable location. Accordingly, an act of Congress provided for "celebrating the One Hundredth

Anniversary of American Independence by holding an International Exhibition of Arts, Manufactures, and Products of the Soil and Mine, in the City of Philadelphia and State of Pennsylvania in the year 1876."

In 1853 New York had attempted to hold a fair modelled after that of London. This had not been successful, for while its promoters tried to advertise it as a national undertaking, it received no financial aid and little influence from the general government. Moreover, such an industrial showing in New York at this time aroused bitter antagonism in other states. Europeans were invited to enter exhibits, but knowing well that few from their own lands would visit our distant shores in those days of retarded travel, they exhibited only for American spectators.

A building in the form of a Greek cross was erected in what is now Bryant Park. It covered 170,000 square feet. Of the 4,100 exhibits entered, a considerable number were provided by the various states. Such farm implements and machinery as were brought from Europe proved to be far more clumsy than ours. In the departments of silks, broadcloths and glass there were no rivals for European products in this country. Little art was shown. The doubtful success of this project counted against New York when the site for the Centennial Exposition was under consideration.

Philadelphia generously raised $1,500,000 and the state of Pennsylvania $1,000,000. Congress appropriated $1,500,000 besides $500,000 for the erection of a Federal Building. The success of the fair was soon assured and in 1874 invitations were extended in the name of the President to the governments of foreign countries to participate—it being expressly stated that no expense should attach to the United States for any exhibits made by foreign nations. England immediately appropriated $250,000 for the purpose of making a creditable showing and little Japan $600,000.

The special event which this exhibition commemorated was not forgotten. In periodicals and various publications of the time the experiences that these hundred years had brought were summarized. This historic feature should be borne in mind in any study of this first world's fair held within our borders.

Dwelling at length upon the vicissitudes of our countrymen, one wrote: "They have reached their first resting-place, and pardonably enjoy the opportunity of looking back at the road they have traversed. They pause to contemplate its gloomy beginnings, the perilous precipices along which it wound, and the sudden quagmires that often interrupt it, all now softened by distance and by the consciousness of success. Opening with a forest-path, it has broadened and brightened with a highway of nations."

Fairmount Park, including 450 acres, was chosen for the exhibition grounds. The city of Philadelphia expended a considerable amount in providing good roads and a fine bridge to give access thither. In addition to the Main Building—1880 feet in length and 464 feet wide—Machinery Hall, Horticultural Hall, and Agricultural Building, Government Building, the Woman's Building and an Art Gallery were erected. Furthermore, twenty-six states provided each its own building and several foreign countries were represented. In comparison with buildings which subsequent expositions have been able to show, the state buildings of the Centennial were like dwellings of modest proportions. Twenty-one acres were roofed by the various structures.

The exhibits numbered 30,864 and were contributed by the various states and territories and by forty-nine foreign powers or their colonies. Spain and her colonies entered 3822; England and her dependencies 3584. The United States furnished 8525—excelling as before in her display of machinery. Five South American states were represented.

The lighting facilities of the age did not permit the buildings to be opened in the evening. Gas was piped to various parts of the grounds to accommodate night watchmen. In view of our present day conveniences, a smile is provoked by reading the self-congratulatory comment of that day to the effect that whereas in 1851 the Cornelius chandeliers for burning lard oil had been favorably received in London, "now that is the light of other days, thanks to our new riches in kerosene."

One of the new devices that interested Europeans was the signal service, which for the first time was shown in 1876, interpreting the weather and predicting storms. Unusual conditions in the United States, where one wire under the same control extended throughout the breadth of a continent, permitted the trial of this system as no European country could have done. It was the proud boast of this service at the Centennial that it was able to have daily observations made at one hundred stations scattered over the continent.

The Bell telephone was now for the first time exhibited and excited much interest because one was thereby enabled to speak with someone in a different portion of a building. Soon after the fair the American bicycle manufacture developed— this country having profited by the English cycles exhibited.

Among educational innovations, we note with interest the advent of the kindergarten—today everywhere regarded with favor and generally required. A journal of the times commented upon it thus: "Of the divers species of Garten—Blumen-, Thier-, Bier-, rife in Vaterland, the Kinder- is the latest selected for acclimation in America. If the mothers of our land take kindly to it, it will probably become something of an institution among us." That its efficiency might be demonstrated among people to whom it was wholly strange, children from an orphanage were brought each day to a little building and given kindergarten training for the entertainment of visitors.

This was the first time in the history of the world that any complete collection of women's work had been arranged. A woman designed the building and throughout plans for this exhibit were made by the women themselves. Again, the Centennial afforded the first opportunity for Japanese art and goods to become generally known in America.

It is difficult to estimate the exhilarating and educative influence of this exposition upon the life of the American people alone. Their fathers had hewn homes out of a wilderness; gradually a nation had been welded together. Before any marked degree of material prosperity had overtaken the country, it had been plunged into the horrors of civil war. Now came this great fair on the wave of material progress that followed the period of reconstruction.

Before the Centennial there had been little that was artistic. Houses had been made substantial and useful rather than attractive; there was little art to be seen. For the first time a large number of people at this exhibition discovered what means might provide when accompanied with cultivated taste. Nearly forty years of steady improvement in knowledge and culture enable us to view our earlier shortcomings with much indulgence and some amusement. That France and Vienna had both been compelled to close their doors on two or three occasions because zealots took exception to their "images," as they chose to call some of the statues, and smashed them, was denied quickly for reasons of expediency, but was nevertheless true. Critics commented that while the nude in art shocked the earlier visitors to the art gallery, yet before the summer had passed people had outgrown provincialism and become able to appreciate beauty wherever found— particularly beauty as revealed by the wonderful lines of the human body. It was found necessary to forbid people to take canes or umbrellas into the gallery because it happened on several occasions that with the best intentions enthusiasts insisted on pointing out features of canvases that pleased them, only to bring disaster and ruin upon the work of art when the pressure of the crowd forced these appurtenances through the pictures. Journals of the day commented upon the fact that those countries wherein Americans were least known sent the finest collection of pictures thither. Spain and England contributed their treasures; while Italy and France which attracted the greater number of travellers in those days by their mild winter climates, sent poor although numerous displays. However, this first opportunity to witness the art of many lands simultaneously was gratefully appreciated.

The Art Gallery, afterwards known as the Memorial Building, was erected at a cost of $1,500,000—which sum was contributed by Philadelphia and the state legislature to provide a permanent museum for the city.

Enthusiasm was sustained throughout the summer by various "state days" that were instituted. These brought delegations from remote sections of the country and receptions were held in the state buildings. The most successful of these occasions was the day assigned to Pennsylvania—September 28th. 250,000 people visited the grounds and at night were entertained by the finest fireworks up to that time ever displayed in the United States.

While the amusement concessions which have become such an important part of world's fairs were not yet thought of, much amazement was caused among the prudent when it was made known that a citizen of Dayton, Ohio, had paid $7,000 for the exclusive right to sell popcorn on the grounds. Moreover 450 roll chairs were taxed $40 each for the season and it was questioned as to whether this venture might prove safe for the syndicate providing them.

The following lines from one of the addresses made at the close of the exposition sets forth the results as seen by those who had been closely connected with the fair throughout:

"The exhibition has concentrated here specimens of the varied products of the United States and made better known to us our vast resources. It has brought to us the representatives of many nations,—men skilled, accomplished, and experienced,—and they have brought with them stores of treasures in all the forms given to them by long-practiced industry and art. And others are here from new lands, even younger than our own, giving full promise of a bright and glorious future. It has placed side by side, for comparison, the industries of the world. In viewing them the utilitarian revels in the realization that man is striving earnestly to make all things contribute to his convenience and comfort; the philosopher stands in awe at their contemplation as he dwells upon the cherished thought of the possible unity of nations; and he who looks at the grandeur of the scene from a spiritual standpoint is filled with the hope that the day is near 'when the glory of the Lord shall cover the earth as the waters cover the sea.'

"It has taught *us* in what *others* excel, and excited our ambition to strive to equal them. It has taught others that our first century has not been passed in idleness, and that at least in a few things we are already in the advance. It has proved to them as to us that national prejudices are as unprofitable as they are unreasonable; that they are hindrances to progress and to welfare, and that the arts of peace are most favorable for advancing the condition, the power, and the true greatness of a nation. It has been the occasion of a delightful union among the representatives of many nations, marked by an intelligent appreciation of each other, rich in instruction and fruitful in friendships. It has placed before our own people, as a school for their instruction, a display—vast and varied beyond precedent—comprising the industries of the world, including almost every product known to science and to art.

"The international exhibition is to be regarded as a reverential tribute to the century which has just expired. That century has been recalled. Its events have been reviewed. Its fruits are gathered. Its memories hallowed. Let us enter on the new century with a renewed devotion to our country, with the highest aims for its honor and for the purity, integrity, and welfare of its people."

Centennial Oration.

The event which today we commemorate supplies its own reflections and enthusiasms, and brings its own plaudits. They do not all hang on the voice of the speaker, nor do they greatly depend upon the contacts and associations of the place. The Declaration of American Independence was, when it occurred, a capital transaction in human affairs; as such it has kept its place in history; as such it will maintain itself while human interest in human institutions shall endure.

This day has now been celebrated by a great people, at each recurrence of its anniversary, for a hundred years, with every form of ostentatious joy, with every demonstration of respect and gratitude for the ancestral virtue which gave it its glory, and with the firmest faith that growing time should neither obscure its lustre nor reduce the ardor or discredit the sincerity of its observance.

In the great procession of nations, in the great march of humanity, we hold our place. Peace is our duty, peace is our policy. In its arts, its labors, and its victories, then, we find scope for all our energies, rewards for all our ambitions, renown enough for all our love of fame. In the august presence of so many nations, which, by their representatives, have done us the honor to be witnesses of our commemorative joy and gratulation, and in sight of the collective evidences of the greatness of their own civilization with which they grace our celebration, we may well confess how much we fall short, how much we have to make up, in the emulative competitions of the times. Yet, even in this presence, and with a just deference to the age, the power, the greatness of the other nations of the earth, we do not fear to appeal to the opinion of mankind whether, as we point to our land, our people, and our laws, the contemplation should not inspire us with a lover's enthusiasm for our country.

Time makes no pauses in his march. Even while I speak the last hour of the receding is replaced by the first hour of the coming century, and reverence for the past gives way to the joys and hopes, the activities and the responsibilities of the future. A hundred years hence the piety of that generation will recall the ancestral glory which we celebrate today, and crown it with the plaudits of a vast population which no man can number. By the mere circumstance of this periodicity our generation will be in the minds, in the hearts, on the lips of our countrymen at the next Centennial commemoration, in comparison with their own character and condition and with the great founders of the nation. What shall they say of us? How shall they estimate the part we bear in the unbroken line of the nation's progress? And so on, in the long reach of time, forever and forever, our place in the secular roll of the ages must always bring us into observation and criticism. Under this double trust, then, from the past and for the future, let us take heed to our ways, and, while it is called today, resolve that the great heritage we have received shall be handed down through the long line of the advancing generations, the home of liberty, the abode of justice, the stronghold of faith among men, "which holds the moral elements of the world together," and of faith in God, which binds that world to His throne.—*William M. Evarts.*

CENTENNIAL HYMN.

Our fathers' God! from out whose hand
The centuries fall like grains of sand,
We meet today, united, free,
And loyal to our land and Thee,
To thank Thee for the era done,
And trust Thee for the opening one.

Here, where of old, by Thy design,
The fathers spake that word of Thine,
Whose echo is the glad refrain
Of rended bolt and falling chain,
To grace our festal time, from all
The zones of earth our guests we call.

Be with us while the New World greets
The Old World thronging all its streets,
Unveiling all the triumphs won
By art or toil beneath the sun;
And unto common good ordain
This rivalship of hand and brain.

Thou, who hast here in concord furled
The war-flags of a gathered world,
Beneath our Western skies fulfill
The Orient's mission of good-will,
And, freighted with Love's Golden Fleece,
Send back the Argonauts of peace.

For art and labor met in truce,
For beauty made the bride of use
We thank Thee, while, withal, we crave
The austere virtues strong to save,
The honor proof to place our gold,
The manhood never bought nor sold!

O! make Thou us, through centuries long,
In peace secure, in justice strong;
Around our gift of freedom draw
The safeguards of Thy righteous law;
And, cast in some diviner mould,
Let the new cycle shame the old!

—*John Greenleaf Whittier.*

COLUMBIAN ODE.

COLUMBIA, on thy brow are dewy flowers
   Plucked from wide prairies and from mighty hills.
Lo! toward this day have led the steadfast hours.
   Now to thy hope the world its beaker fills.
The old earth hears a song of blessed themes,
And lifts her head from a deep couch of dreams.
Her queenly nations, elder-born of Time,
   Troop from high thrones to hear,
Clasp thy strong hands, tread with thee paths sublime,
   Lovingly bend the ear.

Spain, in the broidered robes of chivalry,
   Comes with slow foot and inward brooding eyes.
Bow to her banner! 'twas the first to rise
     Out of the dark for thee.
And England, royal mother, whose right hand
   Molds nations, whose white feet the ocean tread,
Lays down her sword on thy beloved strand
     To bless thy wreathèd head;
Hearing in thine her voice, bidding thy soul
Fulfill her dream, the foremost at the goal.
And France, who once thy fainting form upbore,
Brings beauty now where strength she brought of yore.
   France, the swift-footed, who with thee
   Gazed in the eyes of Liberty,
And loved the dark no more.

     Around the peopled world
     Bright banners are unfurled.
The long procession winds from shore to shore.
     The Norseman sails
     Through icy gales
To the green Vineland of his long-ago.
Russia rides down from realms of sun and snow.
     Germany casts afar
     Her iron robes of war,
And strikes her harp with thy triumphal song.
   Italy opens wide her epic scroll,
In bright hues blazoned, with great deeds writ long,
   And bids thee win the kingdom of the soul.
And the calm Orient, wise with many days,
   From hoary Palestine to sweet Japan
     Salutes thy conquering youth;

Bidding thee hush while all the nations praise,
  Know, though the world endure but for a span,
    Deathless is truth.
Lo! unto these the ever-living Past
  Ushers a mighty pageant, bids arise
Dead centuries, freighted with visions vast,
  Blowing dim mists into the Future's eyes,
    Their song is all of thee,
    Daughter of mystery.

    Alone! alone!
  Behind wide walls of sea!
And never a ship has flown
  A prisoned world to free.
Fair is the sunny day
  On mountain and lake and stream,
Yet wild men starve and slay
  And the young earth lies adream.
Long have the dumb years passed with vacant eyes,
  Bearing rich gifts for nations throned afar,
  Guarding thy soul inviolate as a star,
Leaving thee safe with God till man grow wise.
  At last one patient heart is born
  Fearless of ignorance and scorn;
His strong youth wasteth at the sealèd gate—
  Kings will not open to the untrod path.
His hope grows sear while all the angels wait,
  The prophet bows under the dull world's wrath;
    Until a woman fair
    As morning lilies are
    Brings him a jeweled key—
    And lo! a world is free.
Wide swings the portal never touched before,
Strange luring winds blow from an unseen shore.
    Toward dreams that cannot fail
    He bids the three ships sail,
While man's new song of hope rings out against the gale.

    Over the wide unknown,
      Far to the shores of Ind,
    On through the dark alone,
      Like a feather blown by the wind;

Into the west away,
  Sped by the breath of God,
Seeking the clearer day
  Where only his feet have trod:
From the past to the future we sail;
  We slip from the leash of kings.
Hail, spirit of freedom—hail!
  Unfurl thine impalpable wings!
Receive us, protect us, and bless
  Thy knights who brave all for thee.
Though death be thy soft caress
  By that touch shall our souls be free.
Onward and ever on,
  Till the voice of despair is stilled,
Till the haven of peace is won
  And the purpose of God fulfilled!
            —*Harriet Monroe.*

CHAPTER XI.

THE COLUMBIAN EXPOSITION.

SINCE the birth of Christ, no single event has had for subsequent history the importance of the discovery of 1492. Even today we can scarcely credit the fact that a populated eastern hemisphere could pass through several thousand years of recorded life while another in the west, embracing one-third the land surface of the earth, remained unknown. It is now generally acknowledged that our continent was visited at least once—perhaps several times—before Columbus landed upon its shores; but this does not in the slightest degree detract from his abiding glory. In spite of such possible early visits thither, resulting from chance or storm-driven barks, Europe remained in her long stupor regarding two continents. And Columbus died broken-hearted because his dream of reaching India was shattered, since he had but reached a continent which lay inconveniently in his path! Every school-boy knows for how many years the delusion inspired men to exploration, always with the hope that some water way might be found which should at last give access to coveted Cathay.

The first hundredth anniversary of the discovery of the New World found little attempted in it but exploration. By 1692 a chain of colonies were planted along the Atlantic seaboard. The third hundredth anniversary fell sixteen years after the little fringe of English colonies had declared themselves free from the mother country. Yet, notwithstanding that they were still suffering from privations resulting from the recent war and were struggling with problems of a newly organized government, it is gratifying to know that they did not permit this momentous event to pass unnoticed, but in so far as they were able, did honor to the great discoverer. Few newspapers were established in our land at that time, else it is probable that many hamlet celebrations would be recorded. We know that New York, Boston, Philadelphia and Baltimore observed the day and old files of their papers still preserved in the Congressional Library chronicle with some detail the commemoration ceremonies.

It is interesting to read some of the toasts drunk at the banquet held in New York. The first was appropriately given to the memory of "Christopher Columbus, the discoverer of the New World;" another "May peace and liberty ever pervade the United Columbian States." The third was prophetic: "May this be the last celebration of this discovery that finds a slave on this globe." The last quoted from quite a long list expressed a hope that "the fourth century be as remarkable for the improvement and knowledge of the rights of man as the first was for the development and improvement of nautic science."

The oration delivered in Boston in memory of the matchless discovery calls to mind the pervading religious tone of early New England. The speaker took a text found in Daniel, xii, 4, "Many shall run to and fro and knowledge shall be increased." Glanced at casually today the oration might be easily mistaken for a sermon.

In the late eighties the grateful duty of honoring the memory of Columbus at the four hundredth anniversary was discussed in papers and journals. An exposition that should adequately reveal the amazing progress of the last few years was conceded by general consent to be appropriate. It was commonly agreed that no ordinary effort would suffice but that it devolved upon our country to provide a creditable showing.

At first several cities contended for the exhibition but it shortly resolved itself into a contest between New York and Chicago—the two financial centers of the republic. It is amusing today to read the arguments pro and con, some being excellent and others farfetched. Citizens of the eastern metropolis felt that their city was most accessible and consequently more convenient to all European powers. They regarded Chicago somewhat in the light of an agricultural center and warmly maintained that if this was to be made an international event, it was mistaken counsel that argued in favor of making the fair accessible merely to western farmers. Those who regarded Chicago as the most desirable location pointed out that should we hold the fair on the Atlantic seaboard, little else would be seen by the majority of foreign visitors, whereas the journey inland could not fail to give some conception of a great and resourceful continent. They cited the advantages of their summer climate and their recent progress which justly asked recognition. Congress had indicated that $5,000,000 would have to be pledged by the city to which should be entrusted so much responsibility and the Chicago delegates were prepared to show that amount already subscribed. Suddenly one of the municipalities eager to secure the fair offered $10,000,000 when time for telegraphic communication with the interior was no longer available. Quickly the Chicago representatives offered the same amount and were upheld by their townsmen as soon as the matter became known. From the start the Lake City determined that it would surpass everything previously known in the history of expositions.

It was felt in the east, and with good reason, that there was likely to be "more material breadth than æsthetic height" in this center of successful packers and tradesmen, but the citizens of Chicago were themselves not unconscious of many crudities that had long provoked disparaging criticism and they reached out in every direction for the finest architects, and most gifted decorators to supervise their new undertaking.

The World's Columbian Exposition was placed under dual control, or as one commentator has happily expressed it, the two controlling bodies bore a relation similar to that of the business and editorial departments of a journal. Congress provided that a National Commission should be chosen, to consist of two delegates from each state and territory, these to be nominated by the respective governors and appointed by the President, with eight others appointed wholly by him. All matters between ours and foreign countries in so far as they pertained to the fair were settled by this Commission—all questions relative to the exhibits, their classification, selection and countless other relevant concerns. The financial affairs were vested in a board of forty-five Chicago citizens, whose responsibility it was to provide grounds, buildings and direct the general business of the fair. Besides these two governing bodies, a Board of Lady Managers was chosen in the same way as the National Commission and had control of woman's interests as involved in the Exposition, and finally the World's Congress Auxiliary was chosen, having nothing whatever to do with the exhibits or related matters, but created for the purpose of arranging a series of congresses to be held in Chicago during the exposition months,—these to consider all lines of mental endeavor.

Jackson Park, a triangular piece of ground embracing approximately 586 acres, and having a lake frontage of one and a half miles, was selected as a suitable site. It was simply a barren waste of sand and marsh and had nothing to commend it from the standpoint of scenic beauty. However, when Frederick Law Olmsted, the leading landscape gardener in the United States, was appointed to take charge of its improvement, he found possibilities for it previously undreamed. The proximity of the lake solved the problem. By dredging out canals and lagoons, the displaced sand used to create an island, later unsuspected "wooded" beauties began to appear.

It was quickly seen that if each building should exemplify some individual style of architecture, the final showing would be most heterogeneous and discordant. Consequently it was determined that all the important buildings should adhere to Renaissance and classic styles—these conceded by the best authorities to be the finest architectural expressions known. Moreover, the height of the buildings was limited to approximately sixty-five feet. These regulations insured the harmonious effect which so charmed the eye in the "White City."

The Manufactures and Liberal Arts was the largest and most important building. It covered nearly forty acres, was several times as large as the Coliseum and three times the area of the Great Pyramid's base. Its general style was modelled after the Temple of Jupiter Stator in Rome. More than twice as much steel was used in its construction as in the Brooklyn bridge and several carloads of nails were needed to put down the flooring. Its aisles were laid off as streets and illuminated by arc lights. Its very size determined that it must be simple and dignified, impressing more by its massiveness than it could by embellishment.

The Administration Building was placed in a central position, and, since it was little used for exhibition purposes, could be more elaborate in its decoration. With the exception of the Fine Arts Building, it was the most richly adorned.

Volumes might have been written simply on the progress of civilization as demonstrated in the Transportation Building. Romanesque in style, it had the general form of three large train sheds and covered nine and one-half acres. Its main entrance was an immense arch which was covered with gold-leaf and called the "golden door." Over one entrance was the quotation from Bacon: "There be three things which make a nation great and prosperous—a fertile soil, busy workshops, and easy conveyance for men and things from place to place." Over another, these lines from Macaulay: "Of all inventions, the alphabet and the printing press alone excepted, those inventions which abridge distance have done most for civilization." In this original and attractive structure were displayed whatever pertained to transporting men and things. Early mail stages might be contrasted with palace cars and ocean greyhounds. Canoes hollowed from the trunks of trees exemplified man's first feeble endeavors and models of present floating palaces and battleships the attainments of the nineteenth century.

The splendor of many of the exhibits in the Mines and Mining Building attracted spectators constantly. Here were shown whatever pertained to the extraction of ores themselves. The ends of the earth lent their riches. A large collection of gold nuggets from New South Wales was shown, not far away from 10,000 carats of uncut diamonds from the Kimberley diamond fields of South Africa. Mexico sent the model of the Castle of Chapultepec wrought in pure gold. A statue of Justice in silver represented a mine in Montana and a globe of copper, twelve feet in diameter, came from the Michigan copper region.

The Agricultural Building covered nineteen acres. It was pleasing as an example of classic Renaissance architecture, while its contents were probably exhausted by few. The very immensity defied minute examination.

Whereas at the Centennial a very small area had sufficed for the telegraphic display that was made in the field of electricity, in the fair of 1893 a large and effective building was needed to display the various uses to which this natural force had been applied.

The Fine Arts Building was the most beautiful on the grounds and in its classic simplicity might have been erected by the Greeks themselves had they known and used the dome. It afforded the most remarkable opportunity that has ever been given for Americans to see in their own borders the treasured works of art from other lands.

The Woman's Building, designed by a woman and managed throughout by the Board of Lady Managers, was worthy of place by the beautiful buildings surrounding it. Mrs. Alice Freeman Palmer pointed out in an article written somewhat later, that on this occasion women demonstrated beyond question their executive ability and power to cope with baffling and perplexing conditions; that having thus given evidence of their independent power, henceforth their work might well be placed on its merits by that of men, without further differentiation.

One of the innovations was the Children's Building—an after-thought, requiring strenuous effort on the part of the Board of Lady Managers, which in the press of time stood temporary sponsor for the requisite funds to insure it place. Children throughout the land were asked to contribute; private movements of one kind and another were initiated to raise money; states were called upon to help and finally a bazaar held at the home of Mrs. Potter Palmer, President of the Ladies' Board, realized the amount still needed. The building cost about $25,000. It was 150 feet long by 90 feet wide and its exterior was decorated by sixteen medallions of children of other lands in native costume. One hundred babies could be cared for in its crèche. A kindergarten was maintained and talks were given older children on foreign countries, then groups of them taken to see the exhibits made by nations previously discussed. Whatever pertained to the moral and physical welfare of the child was dealt with for the instruction of mothers. A collection of toys from many lands was displayed. On top of the building a model playground for the little ones was provided. The educational benefit of the undertaking was unquestioned. Moreover, weary mothers could leave children here in safety while they went about the grounds.

The President's invitation to foreign nations to participate in this world exposition, issued in December of 1890, elicited a hearty response. Forty-six entered exhibits and nineteen erected buildings. These with the various state buildings filled a wide area with exhaustless interest. Only natural products and relics were shown in these—the regular exhibits being entered in the buildings provided for them. Much variety was displayed in the foreign and state sections. Virginia copied the home of Washington at Mount Vernon, heirlooms of old Virginian families being displayed therein; Pennsylvania built an appropriate Colonial house; Massachusetts, a model of John Hancock's old home in Boston; New York, a restored Van Rensselaer mansion; Florida represented the oldest building in the United States—Fort Marion at St. Augustine; while California built a mission in the main following the one best preserved today, at Santa Barbara.

Historically the Convent La Rabida, erected at a cost of $25,000, and reproducing faithfully the actual convent where Columbus, disheartened and worn, sought shelter, and where hope for him dawned at last, held first place. In it were shown documents, maps, and relics of the Admiral.

To rest the eye and relax nerves strained by close attention to this wealth of industrial achievement and material gain, amusement was provided by a Bazaar of Nations. The Midway Plaisance was located on a strip of land comprising about 85 acres. A Street of Constantinople, Street in Cairo, a Moorish Palace, Villages of Laplanders, South Sea Islanders, Germans, and other nationalities, Indian Camps, a California Ostrich Farm, and the Ferris Wheel were among its numerous attractions. The amount realized from these concessions helped materially to defray exorbitant expenses of the fair.

It is impossible to convey the faintest impression of the transcendent beauty of the Columbian Exposition. In the day time it presented, as one well-known commentator said, "frozen history of the world's achievement." Its buildings amazed the beholder and the general effect was stupendous. But it was by night that the White City became a dream, a vision of loveliness. All imperfections shadowed by night, the glory of the Court of Honor, with its feathery sprays and gorgeous colors, fascinated and charmed. This was the first exposition to revel in electricity for illumination and the outlines of the buildings threaded with tiny lights created an impression which could not surprise the people so greatly today, so accustomed have we become to striking displays of light in all large cities.

A cry of dismay spread over the land that so much beauty should be eliminated by the termination of the fair, but it was convincingly shown that while these buildings charmed by their fresh appearance, they were only constructed for short duration and could not be perpetuated. However, the Fine Arts building, having been erected with an idea of permanency, was retained as a memorial and is known today as the Field Museum, Marshall Field having generously contributed $1,000,000 for its uses.

This memorable exposition was such an overwhelming success that it brought great credit upon the city which had so substantially contributed and worked to make it possible. That it has had a far-reaching influence upon our industries, art, education and life cannot be questioned.

CHAPTER XII.

The World's Fair Congresses.

The World's Congress Auxiliary arranged for twenty different Congresses to assemble in Chicago during the summer months of 1893. The first to hold its session was the Congress of Representative Women. Congresses of Art, Education, Music, Literature, Commerce and Finance, Peace and Arbitration, Social Reform and, most remarkable of all, a Parliament of Religions, which continued its meetings for seventeen days. For the first time in the world's history, Catholic and Protestant adherents of Christianity, Hebrews, Mohamedans, Buddhists, followers of Confucius, and such other religious sects as are found throughout the civilized world, sat down together to hear each belief explained sympathetically by one who loved it.

>"I dreamed
That stone by stone I reared a sacred fane,
A Temple, neither Pagod, Mosque nor Church,
But loftier, simpler, always open-doored
To every breath from Heaven; and Truth and Peace
And Love and Justice came and dwelt therein."

Akbar's vision seemed for a moment about to be fulfilled, and many a broad-minded religious teacher exclaimed that it seemed too good to be true.

It was explained that the place of assembly was no debating ground. Each was to state as clearly as possible his own views—not to quarrel with those of his neighbor. It was stated that all these religions were not for a moment assumed to be of equal importance in the world, but that as beliefs of devout worshippers, they were all interesting.

While it is impossible to say what influence this convention exerted, it is safe to assume that none who participated or listened to addresses by men inspired to give their own religion noblest expression, could ever find his spiritual outlook quite so circumscribed as before. Simple faith is always appealing and powerful. One minister exclaimed when invited to share in the program: "It is gratifying to know we are to have a chance to view religion as a whole—we are so accustomed to seeing fragments of it." Acquaintance among people tends to lessen misunderstanding and hostility, and when we finally come to be able to see all worshippers, however blindly, reaching toward one final goal we shall but approach the exalted attitude of Akbar, the great Asiatic ruler contemporaneous with the wise Elizabeth and worthy to rank with the broad visioned of all time. A Mohamedan by inheritance, the following was his favorite prayer—merely polished by the poet:

"O God, in every temple I see people that see Thee, and in every language
I hear spoken, people praise thee.
Polytheism and Islam feel after thee.
Each religion says, 'Thou art one, without equal.'
If it be a mosque, people murmur the holy prayer, and if it be a Christian Church, people ring the bell from love to Thee.

"Sometimes I frequent the Christian cloister, and sometimes the mosque,
But it is thee whom I seek from temple to temple.
Thy elect have no dealings with heresy or with orthodoxy: for neither of them stands behind the screen of thy truth.
Heresy for the heretic, and religion to the orthodox.
But the dust of the rose-petal belongs to the heart of the perfume-seller."

Never before in the world's history have been assembled more gifted and distinguished women than those who gathered from the quarters of the globe for the Congress of Representative Women. From across the seas came those talented from many lands, and in our own, women closely associated with various social movements as well as personally renowned. Madame Modjeska, Clara Morris and Julia Marlowe had something to say regarding women in their relation to the drama. Susan B. Anthony and Mrs. Elizabeth Cady Stanton advocated citizens' rights for their sex; Frances Willard was concerned in her life interest, temperance. The aged and venerated Mrs. Julia Ward Howe took the long

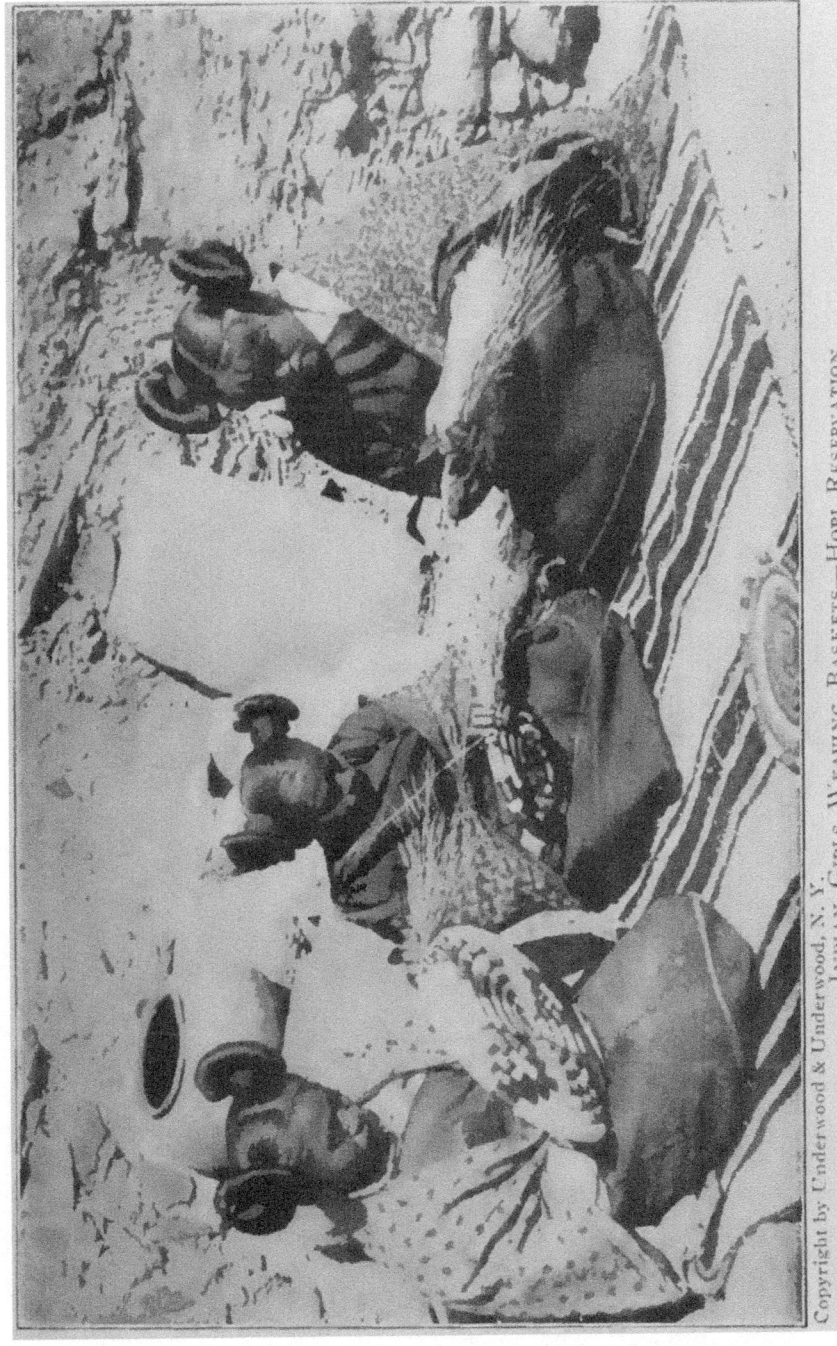

Copyright by Underwood & Underwood, N. Y.
INDIAN GIRLS WEAVING BASKETS—HOPI RESERVATION.

journey to be present at the illustrious meeting. Mrs. Maude Ballington Booth explained the hopes of that organization with which she has long been identified in her adopted country; and Miss Jane Addams, already a deep student of social science, advocated social reform.

Many of slight acquaintance outside their own localities save among people of allied work, whether educational or philanthropic, presented papers. The kindergarten, which had been accorded experimental trial at the Centennial, had become a strong force in education. Mrs. Potter Palmer, the efficient President of the Board of Lady Managers, carried the outlook of the educated woman into the dedicatory program of the Exposition.

Because of its significance as being the first movement of the kind, illustrative citations have been made from the most important addresses presented before the Congress of Representative Women. No one can reread them now without realizing how prophetic they were—how the thoughtful and discerning of the day already saw the dawn of light upon many a problem which is still vexing men and women of our country.

ADDRESS: THE EDUCATED WOMAN.

(Mrs. Potter Palmer on Dedication Day.)

OF all the changes that have resulted from the ingenuity and inventiveness of the race, there is none that equals in importance to woman the application of machinery to the performance of the never-ending tasks that have previously been hers. The removal from the household to the various factories where each work is now done of spinning, carding, dyeing, knitting, the weaving of the textile fabrics, sewing, the cutting and making of garments, and many other laborious occupations, has enabled her to lift her eyes from the drudgery that has oppressed her since prehistoric days.

The result is that women as a sex have been liberated. They now have time to think, to be educated, to plan and pursue courses of their own choosing. Consider the value to her race of one half its members being enabled to throw aside the intolerable bondage of ignorance that has always weighed them down! See the innumerable technical, professional, and art schools, academies, and colleges that have been suddenly called into existence by the unwonted demand! It is only about one hundred years since girls were first permitted to attend the free schools of Boston. They were then allowed to take the place of boys, for whom the schools were instituted, during the session when the latter were helping to gather in the harvest.

It is not strange that woman is drinking deeply of the long-denied fountain of knowledge. She had been told, until she almost believed it, by her physician, that she was too delicate and nervous an organization to endure the application and mental strain of the school room; by the scientist, that the quality of the grey matter of her brain would not enable her to grasp the exact sciences, and that its peculiar convolutions made it impossible for her to follow a logical proposition from premise to conclusion; by her anxious parents, that there was nothing man so abominated as a learned woman, nothing so unlovely as a bluestocking, and yet she comes smiling from her curriculum, with her honors fresh upon her, healthy and wise, forcing us to acknowledge that she is more than ever attractive, companionable, and useful.

What is to be done with this strong, self-poised creature of glowing imagination and high ideals, who evidently intends, as a natural inherent right, to pursue her self-development in her chosen line of work? Is the world ready to give her industrial and intellectual independence, and to open all doors before her? The human race is not so rich in talent, genius and useful creative energy that it can afford to allow any considerable proportion of these valuable attributes to be wasted or unproductive, even though they may be possessed by women.

The sex which numbers more than half the population of the world is forced to enter the keen competition of life, with many disadvantages both real and fictitious. Are the legitimate compensations and honors that should come as the result of ability and merit to be denied on the untenable ground of sex aristocracy? . . .

Even more important than the discovery of Columbus, which we are gathered together to celebrate, is the fact that the General Government has just discovered women. It has sent out a flash-light from its heights, so inaccessible to us, which we shall answer by a return signal when the Exposition is opened. What will be its next message to us?

The Kindergarten.

(Mrs. Sarah B. Cooper, President International Kindergarten Union.)

The kindergarten is the best agency for setting in motion the physical, mental and moral machinery of the little child, that it may do its own work in its own way. It is the rain, and dew, and sun that evoke the sleeping germ and bring it into self-activity and growth. It is teaching the little child to teach himself. The kindergarten devotes itself more to ideas than to words; more to things than to books. Children are taught words too much, while they fail to catch ideas. Give a child ideas. The world does not need fine rhetoric, valuable as that is, half so much as it needs practical, useful ideas. A famous inventor's counsel to a young man was: "Study to have ideas, my boy; study to have ideas. I have always found that if I had an idea I could express it on a shingle with a piece of chalk and let a draughtsman work it out handsomely and according to rule. I generally had ideas enough to keep three or four draughtsmen busy. You can always hire draughtsmen, but you can not hire ideas. Study to have ideas, my boy." The man should be the master, not the slave, of his learning, and whether he is the one or the other depends very largely on the way his knowledge has been gained. It is better to be the master of a little knowledge, with the capacity to use it creatively, than to be the unproductive carrier of all the learning in the libraries. Study to have ideas; life will give no end of opportunities for using them. That is exactly the aim of the kindergarten—to make the mind creative, to stimulate thought, to beget ideas. Habits of observation are cultivated. Observing is more than seeing. The child in the kindergarten is taught to observe— that is, to notice with attention, to see truly. What he learns in the schoolroom is calculated to make him keep his eyes wide open to the world about him. He is taught to think and that is the primary thing. The kindergarten makes the knowledge of ideas wait upon the knowledge of facts, just as it subordinates the cultivation of the memory to the development of faculty. . . .

Bodily vigor, mental activity, and moral activity are indispensable to a perfected life. All these are cherished and developed in the true kindergarten; all these make the man, and prepare him for efficient work in every department of life. Every child should have the privilege of making the most of himself by unfolding all that is in him. As one of the most noted among the disciples of the great Froebel, Miss Emily Sheriff, of London, says: "The poor man suffers wrong when his education is so defective that he can not use his faculties aright, when his senses are blunted, his observation and judgment insecure. This wrong to the poor may be avoided by early methodical training in the kindergarten, thus fitting them for industrial pursuits. As it is now," she goes on, "when boys and girls leave school to go to some trade, they go with hands and eyes absolutely uncultivated; they begin with clumsy fingers, with that untrue habit of vision which belongs to those who have never learned the difference between accurate and inaccurate impressions." Suppose these children had been first trained in the kindergarten—taught there to observe resemblances and differences of forms and colors, to reproduce accurately what they have observed accurately, to have acquired a certain sureness and delicacy of handling, which would be further cultivated by drawing at school,—then these boys and girls would enter an industrial apprenticeship, or any technical school, in a very different condition; they would be able to grapple at once with ordinary difficulties, instead of beginning the education of their hands and senses, and would in consequence reach much sooner the degree of proficiency that insures payment for work. When we withhold this cultivation of the senses and of manual dexterity, we actually maim children in the use of some of the most important faculties; we rob them of what nature designed for them. It is a fact that too little thought is given to boys and girls who upon leaving school will enter industrial ranks. Too large a share of training is paid to mere intellectual development; too little to practical morality and manual training. It is charged by some that our public schools tend to unfit our boys and girls for good, honest work. Is the charge true? do not believe it is. It ought not to be so. But a thoughtful observer and educator wisely says that four years of study without labor, wholly removed from sympathy with the laboring world, during the period of life when tastes and habits are rapidly formed, will almost inevitably produce disinclination, if not inability, to perform the work and duties of the shop or farm. There must be something wrong where such a feeling exists. That notable nation from which we have derived more good sense and more examples worthy of imitation than from all others, the Jewish nation, stands preëminent in this, that it has always honored labor. Every child was taught some manual craft, so that if his resources failed there should be no Jewish child who should not be able to do something, or make something. It is not necessary to be a drudge in order to be a workman. The kindergarten ennobles toil. It teaches the little child to work with his hand, but to control his work with his head. Let this purpose and spirit pervade industrial education until the child reaches manhood's estate, and his labor will be full, not only of manly quality, but of moral quality as well. The coördination of the work-shop and the school-house would be the emancipation of labor from present prejudices. . .

We must call the little children from the very earliest years, and prepare them for useful and honorable citizenship. I have tried to outline the plan. Let me briefly summarize. Take the very little child into the kindergarten and there begin the work of physical, mental, and moral training. Put the child in possession of his powers; develop his faculties; unfold his moral nature; cultivate mechanical skill in the use of the hands; give him a sense of symmetry and harmony, a quick judgment of number, measure, and size; stimulate his inventive faculties; make him familiar with the customs and usages of well-ordered lives; teach him to be kind, courteous, helpful, and unselfish; inspire him to love whatsoever things are true, and right, and kind, and noble; and thus equipped, physically, mentally, and morally, send him forth to the wider range of study, which should include within its scope some kind of industrial training. This training should put the boy or girl into the possession of the tools for technical employment, or for the cultivation of the arts of drawing and kindred employments; still further on the boy and girl should have a completed trade. Thus will they be prepared to solve the rugged problem of existence by earning their own living through honest, faithful work. Throw open the kindergarten and the schools for industrial and art training to every child, and, with the heart pure, the head clear, the hand skillful and ready, we shall hear no more of the mutterings of mob violence and internecine strife. Our fair land shall take its place in the very front ranks of nations distinguished for their industrial achievements. There must be more of genuine human sympathy between the top and the bottom of society. The prosperous and the happy must join hand and heart with the toilers and strugglers. The living, loving self is wanted. The heart must be the missionary. The life must be the sermon. All mankind must be brethren. The children must be taught these great principles, and aided in putting them into practice.

Women and Politics.

(Countess of Aberdeen.)

I WOULD like to explain from the outset that it is a mystery to me how any woman who has faced the matter can think it anything else but her plain matter-of-course duty to take an interest in politics, as far as she is able; and when one comes to look at the matter from a Christian point of view, the obligation becomes a hundredfold more imperative. So, in answer to the question, I reply, in words which I have often used on my own behalf and on behalf of hundreds and thousands of other women in our country who have taken up political work during the last six years,—"We are politicians because it has been shown to us that we can not do our duty, either to our own homes or to our country, without being so."

Friends and foes alike will often tell us that politics will always mean dirty work, and that fine sentiments and high aims are all very well for public platforms, but that they will not go down in practical daily life; and that this being so, we had better keep clear of what will inevitably tend to lower our standards of right and wrong. Our action in taking up politics is regarded in this light not only by those whose gibes and sneers we may very easily ignore, but it pains and grieves many good men and women—some, indeed, of the best men and women, and some of these may be very dear friends of our own. We have to meet their remonstrances. They tell us sadly that in their eyes we have come off our pedestal; that we have disappointed them; that a woman's influence and power were meant to be exerted at home, not in the din of public life; and that they can not bear the idea that any woman for whom they have any regard should be mixed up with the rough-and-tumble of politics. They want to keep us apart from all that; they want to build a temple for us where they can enshrine us apart from and above the world's rough ways and evils. And we, feeling to the full the value of their estimate of womanhood and their chivalrous feeling for us, shrink from their reproaches, and from the thought that we are becoming unwomanly in their sight and perhaps, indeed, taking away their ideal of womanhood. But we must face it out, and see on what these objections are founded. That they do point to a possible danger we must admit, and we must beware of it. But, as a rule, I think we may say that we shall find that the objections proceed principally from two sources: First, a very partial idea of what a woman's life should be; and second, a low estimate of politics. Let us look at the last first. When we go to political meetings—men's political meetings—we hear often a great deal of what politics should accomplish; that the end of all politics is the well-being of the people. We hear of all the good and noble things that such and such a policy has accomplished and will accomplish for the people—things that affect the lives and homes of the people, that make a vast difference to their happiness and to their power of living good and healthy lives. Many are the eloquent speeches we hear on the subject. And yet they come home and tell us that politics are not for women, that they would debase and degrade women; these politics which are to raise the whole people would contaminate us.

How do we reconcile these two statements? Do those who make the speeches believe in what they are saying publicly, or do they say it only to catch the ear of the people, and do they really believe in their hearts that political life as a matter of fact means only a race between men and between parties for power, influence, place and fame? With such an estimate of political life we can have nothing to do, and we do not wonder that any who incline toward such a view should use their best endeavor to keep us out of it. But we believe there are grand principles which may and which should inspire the government of the people, by the people, for the people; we believe implicitly in their power, when properly applied, to reform, and ennoble, and uplift; and that it is our duty as citizens to help forward such application. We desire to carry out these principles faithfully in our own lives, and we look upon those who follow politics for selfish and unworthy ends as traitors to the cause. And the reason why the vast majority of us who take up political work claim the suffrage, is because we believe we cannot do our duty in these directions until we have it.

Any of us who know anything of the lives of the poor, know how the social questions which we discuss backward and forward are living, pressing, realities to them. Questions about education, labor, the sweating system, licensing evils, the workhouse system, are all sternly real to them, and especially so to the women. We must so believe in our politics that we shall both believe and act as if politics must deal with these questions. We are not content to talk about these problems; we desire to understand them, and to help our fellow-women, who have such hard lives and so little leisure, to understand them too, so that they may decide what is to be done—they who will have the power when the time comes.

We must also believe in the power of right political thought in foreign politics. We must not give way to the idea that what is wrong in private life can ever be right in political life. We must not believe that what would be dishonorable or unjust in dealing one with another can be right and honorable in dealing with nations.

Then, as to the other misconception, which lies often at the root of the objections of which we have been speaking—a partial ideal for woman. A true standard for womanhood is a great need; for the good of both women and men it is needed. The ideal women in poetry and fiction are generally represented in their own homes, spreading a bright and holy influence as sister, daughter, wife and mother. Woman at her own fireside is enshrined as woman at her best. Far be it from me to disparage such an ideal. I only venture to say that it is an ideal which does not include the whole of a woman's life, and that true ideals are always expanding and enlarging. Woman is a human being as well as a woman, and must have duties as such toward human beings outside of her own home circle, and toward her country.

Self Government.

(Elizabeth Cady Stanton.)

The basic idea of the republic is the right of self government; the right of every citizen to choose his own representatives and to make the laws under which he lives; and as this right can be secured only by the exercise of the right of suffrage, the ballot in the hands of every qualified person indicates his true political status as a citizen in a republic.

The right of suffrage is simply the right to govern one's self. Every human being is born into the world with this right, and the desire to exercise it comes naturally with the responsibilities of life. "The highest earthly desire of a ripened mind," says Thomas Arnold, "is the desire to take an active share in the great work of government." Those only who are capable of appreciating this dignity can measure the extent to which women are defrauded as citizens of this great republic; neither can others measure the loss to the councils of the nation of the wisdom of representative women.

When men say that women do not desire the right of suffrage, but prefer masculine domination to self-government, they falsify every page of history, every fact of human nature. The chronic condition of rebellion, even of children against the control of nurses, elder brothers, sisters, parents, and teachers, is a protest in favor of the right of self government. Boys in schools and colleges find their happiness in disobeying rules, in circumventing and defying teachers and professors; and their youthful pranks are so many protests against a government in which they have no voice, and afford one of the most pleasing topics of conversation in after life.

The general unrest of the subjects of kings, emperors, and czars, expressed in secret plottings or open defiance against self-constituted authorities, shows the settled hatred of all people for governments to which they have not consented. But it is said that on this point women are peculiar, that they differ from all other classes, that being dependent they naturally prefer being governed by others. The facts of history contradict the assertion. These show that women have always been, as far as they dared, in a state of half-concealed resistance to fathers, husbands, and all self-constituted authorities; as far as good policy permitted them to manifest their real feelings they have done so. It has taken the whole power of the civil and canon law to hold woman in the subordinate position which it is said she willingly accepts. If woman had no will, no self-assertion, no opinions of her own to start with, what mean the terrible precautions of the sex in the past?

So persistent and merciless has been the effort to dominate the female element in humanity, that we may well wonder at the steady resistance maintained by woman through the centuries. She has shown all along her love of individual freedom, her desire for self-government; while her achievements in practical affairs and her courage in the great emergencies of life have vindicated her capacity to exercise this right.

These, one and all, are so many protests against absolute authority and so many testimonials in favor of self-government; and yet this is the only form of government that has never been fairly tried.

The few experiments that have been made here and there in some exceptional homes, schools, and territories have been only partially successful, because the surrounding influences have been adverse. When we awake to the fact that our schools are places for training citizens of a republic, the rights and duties involved in self-government will fill a larger place in the curriculum of our universities.

Woman suffrage means a complete revolution in our government, religion, and social life; a revision of our Constitution, an expurgated edition of our statute laws and codes, civil and criminal. It means equal representation in the halls of legislation and in the courts of justice; that woman may be tried by her own peers, by judges and advocates of her own choosing. It means light and sunshine, mercy and peace, in our dungeons, jails, and prisons; the barbarous idea of punishment superseded by the divine idea of reformation. It means police matrons in all our station-houses, that young girls when arrested during the night, intoxicated and otherwise helpless, may be under the watchful eye of judicious women, and not left wholly to the mercy of a male police.

In religion it means the worship of humanity rather than of an unknown God; a church in which the feminine element in Christianity will be recognized, in which the mother of the race shall be more sacred than symbols, sacraments, and altars; more worthy of reverence than bishops and priests.

A government and a religion that do not recognize the complete equality of woman are unworthy our intelligent support. And what does woman suffrage mean in social life? Health and happiness for women and children; one code of morals for men and women; love and liberty, peace and purity, in the home; cleanliness and order in the streets and alleys; good sanitary arrangements in the homes of the poor; good morals and manners taught in the schools; the crippling influence of fear of an angry God, a cunning devil, censorious teachers, severe parents, all lifted from the minds of children, so long oppressed with apprehensions of danger on every side. We can not estimate the loss to the world in this repression of individual freedom and development through childhood and youth.

Woman suffrage means a new and nobler type of men and women, with mutual love and respect for each other; it means equal authority in the home; equal place in the trades and professions; equal honor and credit in the world of work.

Our civilization today is simply masculine. Everything is carried by force, and violence, and war, and will be until the feminine element is fully recognized and has equal power in the regulation of human affairs.

Woman's Suffrage.

It has often been stated that if the majority of women wanted their civil rights they could have them. This is doubtless true, since a whole nation could not, in the nature of things, be decapitated, nor the combined and persistent claim of a whole class in a community be ignored.

But the majority of women do not as yet appear to desire civil and political privilege. It seems, in fact, that more men than women are in favor of granting such privilege. The men who are of this opinion believe in citizenship, and recognize that strength comes from the resolute shouldering of responsibility, as the long, slender stem of the date-palm grows steady when the leafy bough becomes heavy. They regard suffrage as an expression of the true republican sentiment that those who obey the law should understand it, and help to frame it. They believe that with the help of women civilization would move on with faster and longer strides.

What is the reason that so many women are indifferent or averse to the assumption of civic duties? I think their natural conservativeness and their conscientiousness stand in the way. They already find in the complexity of our life numberless demands upon thought and strength. Their aspirations for increased knowledge and culture, their æsthetic cravings, urge them to the limits of physical and mental endurance, and they feel that they can undertake nothing more. If man is a little world, woman is expected to be a little universe—"all things by turns and nothing long." A woman must be versatile, and ready to fill any niche at a moment's notice. She must sew on a button or write a poem, must roast herself in the kitchen or receive guests in a drawing-room. with equal grace and facility; and what with keeping up her geography and her accomplishments she will beg to be excused from what she thinks the dry and uninteresting subjects of business, current events, and politics.

It is easier under such circumstances to lead the natural, old-fashioned life of daughter, wife, and mother in a sheltered home than to strike out upon the sea of life as a bread-winner in business or profession.

The former course keeps us in the beaten track of precedent, and holds us in what is particularly agreeable to timid and conservative people, a goodfellowship with the majority. In Howell's "Undiscovered Country" we notice that the heroine gets tired of being phenomenal, and throws herself into the pleasures of dress and luxury with keen zest. It takes courage to go against the stream, to be independent and ahead of your generation; it needs a strong moral muscle to snap the withes of prejudice; it demands heroism to obey a law higher than the laws of sympathy and imitation; and if women, somewhat by nature and certainly by education, are lacking in such fiber, we can not be surprised by their slowness in rising to the emergencies of the hour.

Either obstacles must be removed or women must cultivate strength to overcome them; and, more than all, they must be made to see that they are of the people, and that the state belongs equally to them with men, and therefore must claim from them intellectual recognition and moral support.

The Right to Vote.

(Ida Harper.)

When the young people of the present generation read Uncle Tom's Cabin, and the speeches of Garrison and Phillips, and the history of ante-bellum days, they are filled with amazement. They are unable to comprehend that the monstrous evil of slavery existed and flourished in this beautiful country, and found its defenders among ministers and church members and the so-called best element of society. "And you named this the land of the free," they exclaim, "when three million human beings were held in bondage!" And we scarcely know how to explain to them the peculiar condition of public sentiment whose finer perceptions had become dulled by long familiarity with this crime. So indignant do they grow over the thought, we scarcely can persuade them that they owe any respect to ancestors who tolerated such an evil.

Just like this will it be, a few generations hence, as the youth of that age read of a time when the women of the nation were held in a state of political bondage. "Do you mean to say women were compelled to pay taxes and yet were refused all representation?" they will inquire. "Did they collect taxes from women to pay public officials and then not permit them to hold any of the offices or vote for those who did?" "Did they compel women to obey the laws and not let them help make the laws or select the lawmakers?" "Did they allow men who had no property to vote taxes on the property of women, to build railroads, sewers, etc., and not let the women express their wishes in respect to these improvements?" "Did the most ignorant and degraded foreigners, the lowest and most vicious of Americans, the paupers and vagrants, and saloon-keepers and drunkards, who happened to be men, have the privilege and the power of the ballot, while the hosts of church women, and the army of school-teachers, and all the wives and mothers were disfranchised because they were women?" And when all these questions are answered in the affirmative, these broad-minded and liberally educated young people will be filled with contempt for the generations that sanctioned this terrible injustice. Then they will begin to study the family history, and one will shout with triumphant joy, "My father and mother protested against these wrongs and fought long and bravely until they were abolished;" and another will discover, with deep humiliation and a shame which can never be eradicated, that his father voted against equal rights for women, and that his mother was a "remonstrant."

Future generations never can understand the social and political conditions which would not permit all citizens to have a voice in the municipal government of the city in which they lived, owned property, and paid taxes. Even we who are living under these conditions can not quite comprehend that absolute defiance of equity, justice, and right on the part of men who, having the power, refuse to grant to women the same privileges in the municipality which they themselves enjoy. There is not an interest which men have in the good government of the town or city that is not shared by women. Take, for instance, the question of street improvement, and we find women even more anxious for well-paved and cleanly kept streets. It is their dresses which must sweep up the débris; it is their thinly shod feet which must suffer from the cobble-stones between the street railroad-tracks, and from the inequalities of sidewalks and curbstones. Cleanliness is an essential characteristic of women, and if they were invested with the power to bring it about, the littered and dirty streets of our cities would be a thing of the past in a very short time. The woman who looks well to the ways of her own household would give equally as good attention to the ways of the city in which she and her family must live. There is a crying need for women in municipal housekeeping. In the making of parks, the building of fountains, the planting of shade-trees, women would feel even greater interest than do men.

Then we come to the subject of public health; here women are vitally interested. If sewers are defective, if drainage is bad, if water is impure, women and children, as well as men, must suffer; and it is highly probable that women, being less engrossed in business, would look into these things with more care than men. There is an idea that women are not deeply interested in these things, which would not be strange, as they have always been debarred from having any part in them, but facts do not bear out this theory. The Association of Collegiate Alumnæ, composed of a good many hundreds of the most highly educated women in the United States, with all the great questions of the day before them, selected the subject of drainage and sewerage for their investigations. They have brought forward a collection of valuable statistics and suggestions which have attracted the respectful attention of those best acquainted with these matters, and promise fruitful results. In New York, Indianapolis, Chicago, and a number of cities, the women have formed sanitary associations, and petitioned the boards of health to permit them to coöperate in the effort to keep the city clean and to enforce the rules of the board. This, at first, has been refused, or grudgingly granted, although after a trial their assistance has always been pronounced to be desirable. But here we have the spectacle, first, of women begging permission to do what is plainly their duty and right as citizens to do; second, performing without pay a work which men are receiving a salary for doing, and this salary women are taxed to pay. "But," they say, "women do not know how to construct sewers, lay off streets, build pavements, etc. Neither do men, except the few who have learned the business. But women have quite as much ability as men to select a good workman, to hold him to a contract, and to punish him for dishonesty.

JULIA WARD HOWE.

Her eyes have seen the glory of the presence of the Lord,
He was waiting in the garner where the fruits of life are stored:
He was mindful of the war song that was mightier than the sword:
  Of the Truth that marches on.

She had seen Him in the turning of her ninety golden years,
In the press of human struggle, human want and human tears;
She had seen His Kingdom growing in the midst of woes and fears—
  His day that marches on.

She had read a gracious gospel writ in many a gracious life—
Toiler, statesman, trader, poet: hero husband, hero wife—
She had found the peace eternal in the midst of mortal strife,
  Since God is marching on.

Where He sounded forth His trumpet, she would never call retreat:
Where he led his worn battalions in the weary dust and heat;
How swift her soul to answer him! How jubilant her feet!
  For God was marching on.

In the beauty of the autumn, by the shining of the sea,
She has found the great Enfranchisement; the Christ of Liberty.
As he died to make men holy, so she lived to make men free,
  Her soul is marching on.
  Oct. 18, 1910.   —*Amos R. Wells.*

The Moral Initiative as Related to Woman.
(Julia Ward Howe.)

This title indicates a topic which has come to me in hours of thought and of study, attracting me both by its philosophical and its practical aspect. The present century has seen great progress in these two departments. The old philosophies have been taken up, sometimes in a reverent, often in a sceptical spirit, and the critical procedure has acknowledged no barriers beyond which it is forbidden to pass. Rules of life, on the other hand, have also been sharply reviewed and amended. The salient points of morals have been distinctly sought out and emphasized, and the two great orders of thought, philosophy and ethics, have been brought into new relations of nearness and dearness. Religious teaching has passed from the observation of rites and the inculcation of metaphysical views and doctrines to the illustration of the intrinsic essence of Christianity; and the subtleties of mysticism, ritualism, and what not, have been forgotten in the sympathetic uprising of the heart of the multitude.

Now, what do I mean by this moral initiative as belonging to women? Is it a wise phrase that sounds metaphysical and means nothing? My thought of it is simply this: The world has had much good to say of its women, and much evil, and both with reason. The first woman has been credited with all the woes which have befallen humanity, and with all the sins into which it has fallen.

Buddhism considers the principle of evil in nature as resident in the female sex, and ascetics in all lands have held the same view. The legends of the mother of Christ have no doubt exercised a potent influence in elevating the moral position of the sex; yet in romance and stage-play today, as well as in ordinary society pleasantry, the question is common, Where is the woman who is at the bottom of the mischief? I think that wise people now ask the opposite question. When we meet with a man who is without fear and without reproach, whose blameless life seems to have gone on from strength to strength, upbuilding the community, and honoring humanity by his own noble image and conduct, we are apt to ask where the woman is. And our thoughts go back to the cradle in which his helpless infancy was tended,—even further, to the heart to which his own was the nearest thing on earth, to the breast from which he was fed with the essence of a pure life. Happy is the man whose mother has been a tower of strength to herself and her family. The first precious lessons it has been hers to give. No matter what storms may have raged without, how mean the home or how wild the street, he has first seen the light in an atmosphere of celestial purity. The mother love has watched at the gates of his childish Eden with a drawn sword. No evil counsel or influence has been allowed to come near him. And when in the necessary course of things he has passed out of her keeping, he has gone accompanied by the Christ-prayer, "I pray not that thou shouldst take him out of the world, but that thou shouldst keep him from the evil." This I call the moral initiative, the man's start in life. The nucleus of all that he is to believe, to aim at, and to do, has been delivered to him, like a sealed packet full of precious things, by a mother who honors supremely all that honors humanity, who dreads and despises all that dishonors and deforms it.

No one will deny that this type of woman is most precious. The question will rather be how we may maintain and multiply it. And here the whole horizon of the past confronts us, as well as the veiled heaven of the future. In this past we read that all that is slavish in human institutions is demoralizing; and that while discipline forms and exalts, despotism degrades and deforms, appealing back to the lower instincts, which have their place in animal life—fear, cunning, low self-love, and the low attachments of mere habit and interest. From the tyrannies of the old order into the liberty wherewith Christ has made us free the world is slowly passing, but all that detains humanity on its lower levels retards the progress of the race. Oh, that men, themselves enfranchised, should wish to detain their women in the bondage from which they themselves have been delivered! In true Christianity there is no moral distinction of sex, neither male nor female; but in the political life even of free America the man opens the door for himself and shuts it against his wife, opens the door for his son and shuts it upon his daughter. And this, I say, is demoralizing.

Copyright by Underwood & Underwood, N. Y.
COLUMBUS' FIRST LANDING PLACE.—PORTO RICA.

It compels one-half of the human race to look back toward the old barbarism, while the other insists upon looking forward to the new civilization. The man to whom the woman's freedom of soul is the first condition of his own, puts on that freedom a fatal barrier, and defrauds himself thereby. His mother should be his superior; his wife should be his equal and companion. He invites them to acquiesce in a lower position, to exercise a self-control which he does not dream of exacting from himself, but also to sacrifice the self-respect out of which should spring the very power of self-control, of self-sacrifice, of subordinating the pleasurable to the ethical, the caprice of self-indulgence to the steady purposes of duty. . . .

I believe in the political enfranchisement of women because I see in it the key to all that is rightly expected of them in the world's economy. I believe in it because I believe in logic; not so much in the short-sighted syllogisms which we teach as in the great logic which life teaches us, in which effects follow causes, and moral principles confirm themselves in moral results.

Marriage.

(Rev. Anna Shaw.)

The question before us is this, "What is marriage?" Is it a mere coming together of two people who have fallen in love? Do you know that love is the only thing people ever fall into? If a man undertakes any form of business in the world he deliberates upon the business, his attainments, his preparation to manage and master it, and the possibility of his success—the whole ground is studied over carefully; but when two people undertake to enter upon the most serious business in life—that from which they can not well ever be rescued—instead of deliberating they "fall" into it. A young man sees a young woman "with marvelous bangs," and that is the last of him. A young woman sees a young man with "a marvelous mustache," and that is the last of her. They have fallen in love. After they are married they find that marriage means something besides bangs and mustache. My idea of marriage is of the highest and holiest kind. I believe marriage, and the home that is the result of marriage, is the holy of holies this side of the throne of God; and that any two people who enter upon this sacred relation should be those who are fitted to found in this world a home which is a type of the home which awaits us all beyond. I believe that whatever broadens and enlarges woman, whatever develops any of the capacities which God has given her, fits her to become a founder of this kind of home. Anything which makes a woman free, anything which develops her physical, mental, moral, or spiritual life, makes her better fitted to be the founder of a home.

Now the whole thought upon this question is that women develop, but that during this age of development which has come to woman, men have remained stationary. As women grow broader, men are also growing broader, and I believe the man of the future will demand for his wife the woman of the future, as the man of today demands the woman of today. As our boys and girls are reared together, as they become educated in our institutions of learning together, as they go out in trades and professions together, our young men will never know any other kind of womanhood than that with which they are reared; and so I believe a woman's marriage prospect is equally good with a man's marriage prospect, for if a woman loses her prospect here a man must lose his prospect also. Since men will not give up marriage, women also, you see, can not give up marriage; so the marriage prospect of one sex is equally good with the marriage prospect of the other under any condition in life. But I believe the man of today is beginning to demand a nobler woman for his wife; and although in the past men considered that absolute ignorance and innocence and inability to do anything but entertain them were admirable traits in a sweetheart, it is marvelous how much good sense they expected of the woman after she became a wife. The difference between what a man demands of the woman with whom he is passing a few of his leisure hours and what he demands of her when she becomes his wife is wonderful; and I believe the man of the future will demand of the woman of the future that kind of training which will make her not only a good cook and a good housekeeper, but also his companion in all that interests and concerns him.

Why should we care for marriage unless it is the highest

state into which men and women can enter? Why should one seek marriage unless it is better to her than the unmarried state? If marriage offers nothing better than the conditions out of which one goes, unless marriage has something that it can hold up as an inducement over against these conditions, we can not expect the modern woman to give up her leisure, her independence, and all that comes to a woman outside of marriage.

I am not one who believes that motherhood is the highest crown of glory which a woman can wear. I must confess I have heard that poetry all my life. It is good poetry; it sounds well, and it comforts us, but it is not true. Woman is something more and greater than a mother. Woman is something more and greater than any of the external conditions of her life. The highest crown of glory that any woman can wear is pure, strong, noble, virtuous, dignified womanhood. After a woman has attained to that fullness of perfect womanhood, then let come to her what will, motherhood or spinsterhood, either will be equally with the other a crown of glory.

I say again that marriage must have something to offer to the average woman of today, the woman of culture, the woman of education, the woman able to earn a good salary and make for herself a beautiful home. Marriage must have something in it worthy of that woman, and worthy of the sacrifice which she shall make of her independence. I believe that marriage has much to offer. The ideal, the marriage which I believe God has in his mind when he conceives of home, is the marriage made by two who enter into the home as equal partners. So long as in the marriage ceremony of any church there remains the command on the part of one to obey, and of the other to compel or demand obedience, the home founded can not be the highest and best place for men and women. When public sentiment has arisen to that high plane which shall demand that no woman shall become subservient to her husband or commit perjury, we shall have the ideal marriage, and until we have ideal marriage we can not tell what effect any change in either business or social conditions can have upon woman's marriage prospect.

I believe that underlying the perfect marriage must be perfect equality of the two entering upon this estate; perfect equality everywhere and perfect respect; neither to rule as head over the other, neither to be submissive and subordinate to the other, but each to be the equal, the comrade and the friend of the other.

Now concerning this whole change in woman's life, I admit frankly that there may be some little harm, some little hurt, resulting from it. There has never been any great reformation without some harm in the transition period. In giving liberty to the slave some harm came to both slave and master. From any great movement we expect some evil to follow. There has never been a great revival of religion but some evil came in its train. So in this transition stage from subordination and dependence to self-respect and independence there will be some friction.

Domestic Service.
(Jane Addams.)

Ever since we entered upon the industrial revolution of the eighteenth century, factory labor—work done in factories—has been increasingly competing in the open market with household labor—work done in private houses. Taking out of account women with little children or invalids dependent upon them, to whom both factory and household labor are impossible and who are practically confined to the sewing trades, to all untrained women seeking employment a choice is open between these two forms of labor. There are few women so dull that they cannot paste labels on a box or do some form of factory work; few so dull that some perplexed housekeeper will not receive them, at least for a trial, into the household. Household labor, then, has to compete with factory labor not only in point of hours, in point of permanency of employment, in point of wages, but in point of the advantage it affords for family and social life; and all women seeking employment more or less consciously compare the two forms of labor in all these points.

The three points are easily disposed of. First: In regard to hours there is no doubt that the factory has the advantage. The average factory hours are from seven in the morning to six in the evening, with a chance of working over-time, which, in busy seasons, means until nine o'clock. This leaves most of the evenings and Sundays free. The average hours of household labor are from six in the morning to eight at night, with little difference in seasons. There is one afternoon a week, with an occasional evening, but Sunday is never wholly free.

Second: In regard to permanency of position the advantage is found clearly on the side of the household employé.

Third: In regard to wages the household is again fairly ahead, if we consider not alone the money received but also the opportunity offered for saving money. This is greater among household employés, because they do not pay board, the clothing required is simpler, and the temptation to spend money in recreation is less frequent. The average minimum wage paid an adult in household labor may be fairly put at two dollars and fifty cents a week; the maximum at six dollars, this excluding the comparatively rare opportunities for women to cook at forty dollars a month and the housekeeper's position at fifty dollars a month. The factory wages, viewed from the savings bank point of view, may be smaller in the average, but this I believe to be counterbalanced in the minds of the employés by the greater chance which the factory offers for increased wages. A girl over sixteen seldom works in a factory for less than four dollars a week, and she always cherishes the hope of being at last a forewoman with a permanent salary of from fifteen to twenty-five dollars a week. Whether she attains this or not she runs a fair chance, after serving a practical apprenticeship, of earning ten dollars a week as a skilled worker. A girl finds it easier to be content with four dollars a week when she pays for board, with a scale of wages rising toward ten dollars, than to be content with four dollars a week and board, the scale of wages rising toward six dollars; and the girl well knows that there are scores of liberally paid forewomen at fifteen dollars a week for one forty-dollar cook or fifty-dollar housekeeper. In many cases this position is well taken economically, for, although the opportunity for saving may be better for the employé in the household than in the factory, her family saves more when she works in a factory and lives with them. The rent is no more when she is at home. The two dollars and fifty cents which she pays into the family fund more than covers the cost of her actual food, and at night she can often contribute toward the family labor by helping her mother wash and sew.

This brings us easily to the fourth point of comparison, that of the possibilities afforded for family life. It is well to remember that women, as a rule, are devoted to their families; that they want to live with their parents, their brothers and sisters, and kinsfolk, and will sacrifice a good deal to accomplish this. This devotion is so universal that it is impossible to ignore it when we consider women as employés. Young unmarried women are not detached from family claims and requirements as young men are, and, so far as my observation goes, are more ready and steady in their response to the needs of the aged parents and helpless members of the family. But women performing labor in households have peculiar difficulties in enjoying family life, and are more or less dependent upon their employers for possibilities to see their relatives and friends. Curiously enough, the same devotion to the family life and quick response to its claims on the part of the employer operate against the girl in household labor, and places her in the unique position of isolation. The employer of household labor, to preserve her family life intact and free from intrusion, acts inconsistently in her zeal, and grants to her cook, for instance, but once or twice a week such opportunity for untrammeled association with her relatives as the employer's family claims constantly. So strongly is the employer imbued with the sanctity of her own family life that this sacrifice of the cook's family life seems to her perfectly justifiable. If one chose to be jocose one might say that it becomes almost a religious devotion, in which the cook figures as a burnt offering and the kitchen range as the patriarchal altar.

This devotion to family life the men of the family also share. A New York gentleman who lunches at Delmonico's, eats food cooked by a cook with a salary of five thousand dollars a year. He comes home hungry, and with a tantalizing memory of the lunch, to a dinner cooked by a cook who is paid at most forty dollars a month. The contrast between lunch and dinner is great, and the solace of the family is needed to make the dinner endurable, but the aforesaid gentleman quiets discontent with the reflection that in eating a dinner cooked by an individual cook they are in some occult manner cherishing the sanctity of the family life, though his keen business mind knows full well that in actual money he is paying more for his badly cooked dinner than for his well-cooked lunch.

To return from the digression—this peculiar isolation of the household. In addition to her isolation from her family, a woman finds all the conditions of her social life suddenly changed when she enters the service of a household. It is well to remember that the household employés for the better quarters of the city and the suburbs are largely drawn from the poorer quarters, which are nothing if not gregarious. The girl is born and reared in a tenement house full of children. She knows them almost as well as she knows her brothers and sisters, and plays with them almost as constantly. She goes to school, and there learns to march, to read, and to write in constant companionship with forty other children. If she lives at home until she is old enough to go to parties, those she goes to are mostly held in a public hall and are crowded with dancers. If she works in a factory she walks home with many other girls, in much the same spirit as she formerly walked to school with them. Most of the young men she knows are doing much the same sort of work, and she mingles with them in frank economic and social equality. If she is a cloak-maker, for instance, she will probably marry a cutter, who is a man with a good trade, and who runs a chance of some day having a shop of his own. In the meantime she remains at home, with no social break or change in her family and social life.

If she is employed in a household this is not true. Suddenly all the conditions of her life are changed. The individual instead of the gregarious instinct is appealed to. The change may be wholesome for her, but it is not easy; and the thought of the savings bank does not cheer us much when we are twenty. She is isolated from the people with whom she has been reared, with whom she has gone to school, with whom she has danced, and among whom she expects to live when she marries. She is naturally lonely and constrained.

Added to this is a social distinction, which she feels keenly, against her and in favor of the factory girls, in the minds of the young men of her acquaintance. A woman who has worked in households for twenty years told me that when she was a young and pretty nurse-girl the only young men who paid her attention were coachmen and unskilled laborers. The skill in the trades of her suitors increased as her position in the household increased in dignity. When she was a housekeeper, forty years old, skilled mechanics appeared, one of whom she married. Women seeking employment understand perfectly well this feeling, quite unjustifiable, I am willing to admit, among mechanics, and it acts as a strong inducement toward factory labor.

I have long since ceased to apologize for the views and opinions of working-people. I am quite sure that, on the whole, they are just about as wise and just about as foolish as the views and opinions of other people; but that this particularly foolish opinion of young mechanics is widely shared by the employing class can be demonstrated easily. It is only necessary to remind you of the number of Chicago night schools for instruction in stenography, in typewriting, telegraphy, bookkeeping, and all similar occupations, fitting girls for office work, and the meager number provided for acquiring skill in household work.

The contrast is further accentuated by the better social position of the office girl, and the advantages which she shares with factory girls, of lunch clubs, social clubs, and vacation homes, from which girls performing household labor are practically excluded by their hours of work, their geographical situation, and a curious feeling that they are not as interesting as factory girls.

Salvation Army.

(Maude Ballington Booth.)

Here, in this our dear country, during the last six years, the Army has forced itself into recognition by the public; and even those who care little for religion, or who dissent from our doctrines and object to our measures, have learned to hail us as a powerful social factor in the upraising of the criminal and almost hopeless classes. Among our officers we have a larger number of women than men.

That woman is especially fitted by God for this work

through the gifts of tenderness, affection, and persistency, is becoming more and more a recognized fact. We make no difference in our work between the man and the woman. We do not give her a separate sphere of the work, or organize her efforts as though she were in any way disqualified for standing shoulder to shoulder with man at the battle's front. Every position that can be held by man—every office and duty that can be performed by him—we throw open to her; and we have but one gauge by which to test the qualifications for responsibility, namely—success.

I have watched the field of labor, and I have seen much energy, much good talent thrown away—much good desire expended without result—until organization has put each worker into her right place and brought to all the one aim and object. Our women are organized for war. In the hardness of the struggle, the devotion and self-sacrifice needed can be understood only by those who have looked face to face with the great social and moral questions, and have wrestled hand to hand with the vice and sin which are our enemies and the enemies of our King. Daily are coming to my ears tributes of praise and admiration to the noble way our women, in the slums or on the street, in the saloons or in their ordinary corps work, are carrying this war—this battle—to the gates, and gaining the laurels of well-earned victory. The New York *Herald*, a little while ago, remarked that it had become an established fact in New York City that two wearers of the poke bonnet could quell a street riot more effectively than a squad of police; while a policeman himself acknowledged to our slum worker that she and her women could lead with ease a ruffian whom it would take six policemen to drag.

In connection with our slum and rescue work, we have found that it can be accomplished far more effectually by women than would ever be possible to the men of our organization. The very fact that women courageously and lovingly enter these strongholds of vice and iniquity unprotected, so far as the human eye can see—are fearless in the face of what many might consider danger—arouses in the hearts of these criminal and outcast men the little spark of chivalry and honor which lies dormant in their depraved nature. To take into such places our men warriors might indicate fear on the part of women—while courage is one of woman's most beautiful attributes, coupled as it is with less vigor and strength of muscle. It is women who must be organized into battalions to seek out the woman whose honor and purity have been trampled in the dust, for in their pure faces and loving words alone can the outcast woman read that there is hope for her; and they alone are qualified to kneel at the side of the abandoned one and plead with her whose life has been so embittered by wrong and shame. We have proved that women are not only capable of being thoroughly organized to lead, but also capable of being controlled and united to follow. Our opponents say that in organization each woman would want to be herself a leader, and that chaos would result from her inability to obey and follow. We find this absolutely incorrect; for the discipline of army organization has proved to us that woman, as a private, as an officer, or as a commander, can quite as well and methodically fill her place as any man that ever took the field.

The Stage and its Women.

(Georgia Cayvan.)

The terrible tension of stimulation, the restlessness and lack of repose which has come upon the American people through our rapid growth and formation as a nation, our intensity of interest and concentration of desire for the best of life, amounts to a disease which physicians call "Americanitis," and which makes essential a form of recreation which shall satisfy in the majority the intellectual craving at small expense of mental effort. Such recreation the stage supplies.

It is for us to take the tired men and women, to lift them out of the rush and struggle for a brief space, to help them forget the strife and ambition, the disappointment and sadness of their lives, in the world of the stage, where the glamour and romance bring restfulness, where ideal love and worthy deeds and noble sentiments are happily shown, and where griefs are only agreeably pathetic because they are not real agony, and everything comes out all right in the last act. And so we send them back to you, preachers and teachers and reformers, rested and refreshed, to take up the exactions of life.

And on these lines the stage becomes a popular educator, in that it presents to men and women who are too worn and weary, perhaps too indifferent and thoughtless, to read for themselves, literature in a form pleasing and easy of comprehension—gives them three volumes before eleven o'clock, tells whether he marries her or not in the last chapter, and sends them home satisfied.

It is not an ignoble mission to poetize the prose of simple things and lend a touch of romance to the practical for the inspiration of the masses too limited in mind, or too much occupied with the world's work, to grasp the splendor of great thoughts set in classical language. Remembering the drama's honorable service in the past, when it was the temple of art, the highest exponent of culture, perpetuating and disseminating the thought of the great teachers and philosophers before printing had made literature an inheritance of the common people, I claim for it also a place in the intellectual life of today, because it interprets for us in the classical drama the life of the past, which is the literature of the present, and presents to us with nice exactness in the modern play the life of today, which will be the literature of the future.

Moreover, the stage reaches a class of people which the pulpit cannot influence. Those most in need of ministration, the bitter, world-worn, pessimistic men and women, the heartbroken and hopeless, the gay and frivolous, as well as the immoral, come to us when they will not go to you. You seek out some of them with your vigilance and zeal; they come to us of their own accord. We speak to them in a language they understand; we appeal to their better natures by presenting pictures of true nobility of character, by making our villains more unfortunate and repulsive than the genuine article, and by always seeing to it that the hero marries a rich heiress, that the wronged wife is recompensed, and the betrayer of innocence is punished. Seriously, the influence of the stage upon the morals of the community is too valuable to be lightly considered. It should be guarded, and protected, and encouraged.

There is much talk of the elevation of the stage among some of those who devote themselves to it. But the real elevation of the stage must come from the people, not from the profession. It must come from a grander art-view, which shall refuse to narrow the art down to the personality of the artist. It must come from a purification of public sentiment which shall refuse to accept women whose only qualification for stars in the dramatic firmament is an appeal to morbid curiosity. It must come from a better understanding of the stage and its prerogatives, which shall demand and indorse legitimate drama rather than the sensational, the degrading, the sensual; which shall distinguish between talent and notoriety; and shall honor gifted womanliness rather than brainless beauty.

Pottery in the Household.

(M. Louise McLaughlin.)

WHETHER our sex can lay claim to the idea which resulted in the addition of household utensils to the home of primitive man, we do not know. The solution of that question is forever lost in the mists of antiquity. We know only that since prehistoric ages woman has figured largely as the maker and decorator of the vessels in which the food provided by her liege lord has been served. Now, when her rights and privileges have been increased in a measure undreamed of by her aboriginal predecessor, we find her still the conserver, and happily frequently the producer, of beauty in the household.

In the complication of modern life it is not given to every woman to devote herself to the pleasing task of providing with her own hands, and at the same time rendering beautiful, the household utensils. Let not the woman, however, who may be engaged in the practice of one of the learned professions, or busy in the reformation of the abuses which have become ingrained in the polish of this old world, look down upon her sister upon whom has descended the time-honored profession of her foremothers. In our time many a woman finds in the decoration of pottery, not only the gratification of her sense of beauty, but also the wherewithal for the support of her family. While from this point of view the practice of the art may be considered one of the lucrative occupations for women, it is from that of the household that we are to regard it. Viewed within the narrow circle of the home, the matter assumes almost paramount importance. From its more practical side, the ceramic art is seen to fill the necessity which was probably the first to arise, in furnishing the most satisfactory receptacle for food. In this capacity its importance in our households can scarcely be overestimated. Whatever may be said of the abuses of the table—the interference of high living with high thinking—the consumption of food is a daily necessity, and no substitute by which our civilized brains can be kept in good working order has been found. No change in the good old custom of families meeting around the common table has proved desirable, nor is there anything so delightful as the assembling of kindred spirits round the festal board.

Many refinements have been added since our forefathers gathered around the primitive bowl in which the household food was served, and helped themselves without other utensils than those which nature had provided them. Much of the grossness of the satisfaction of this natural appetite has been taken away. How much, we who are accustomed only to the manners of the latter part of the nineteenth century can scarcely realize.

Shorn of its grosser aspects, bounded with limits of temperance and common sense, this appetite for food should not be considered something which an intelligent being can pass over without consideration. Upon its proper gratification depends life itself, and during life the health of body and mind. Considered in this light, the art of the cook is the highest, and as an adjunct the ceramic art comes not far behind. That the palatableness of food has an actual influence upon its digestion and consequent benefit, is a fact acknowledged by medical authorities. How much of the benefit is derived from the tasteful serving of the viands has not been computed, but the effect is something of which people of refined tastes are keenly conscious. Good food served upon coarse ugly dishes loses half its savor. How much, then, does the art of cooking owe to the beautiful china in which its products may be presented? As a very essential aid in the serving of our daily food, decorated china plays a very important part, and thus may be considered a practically useful art.

Very early was the sense of beauty manifested in the

decoration of necessary utensils. We, following in the line of what should be progress, are inclined sometimes so to decorate these articles that the original use is lost sight of. In this, to our shame be it said, we fall behind our aboriginal models, who in their simplicity never lost sight of the fitness of things, and whose work consequently ranks high in true artistic beauty. The principle which underlies all good work—the abrogation of self—is applicable to this branch of art as well as to all others. The questions which must be answered by all decorative art are these: Is it suited to its purpose? Does it really beautify the object upon which it is applied?

To the decoration of household pottery these questions appeal with more than usual force. Here there is no room for the exhibition of skill unless it is subordinated to use. That is the all-important point of view, and from it all personal display becomes impertinent. We have much to learn upon this whole subject, but much has already been accomplished. In the light of the present exposition of woman's work it will be seen that a wonderful progress has been made. We can not here enter into the question of what constitutes the best decorative art, or what are the best means of developing the talent which, as has been demonstrated, woman has in her keeping.

Let us hope that the time will come when she will exercise this talent, freed from the shackles of custom and fashion; the time when she will not tie ribbons on jugs, paint pictures on plates, or transform her home into the likeness of a bric-a-brac shop. To paraphrase a well-known saying, let me decorate the homes of a people and I care not who teaches them.

POLISH WOMEN.

(Madame Helena Modjeska.)

First, I must ask your permission for a personal remark. When I was invited to appear in the congress as one of the representatives of women on the stage, I was not aware that two days later I should again step on the platform as a representative of Polish women.

This task fell to my share very unexpectedly, and found

me unprepared. The regular delegate was prevented at the last moment from arriving here, and as I am one of the members of the advisory Polish committee, I agreed to appear before you in her place, taking upon me the risk of coming before you unprepared, rather than suffering our Polish womanhood to remain unrepresented at this great gathering.

Being deprived of its political independence, Poland is hampered in every manifestation of its vitality. Those who have taken away from us our national existence try to make the whole world believe that there is not, that there never was, such a thing as a Polish nation. They endeavor to obliterate from the annals of humanity the history of Poland; to restrict, if not entirely prohibit, the use of our language; to hinder the development of every progress, be it economic, intellectual, or social.

In such conditions it is only natural that any organized movement of women toward improving their situation should be considered as a political crime, and punished accordingly. Whatever is done must be done in secret, and therefore I am prevented from giving you evidences of the work done by my countrywomen, and must confine myself to generalities, for fear that any personal allusion may bring on very serious consequences.

And yet we have in our country a splendid array of women, distinguished in every branch of human activity, with great minds and greater hearts, who work both individually and by combined efforts with the view of raising the level of Polish womanhood. Some of them would certainly be invited to figure on the Advisory Council lists of the divers empires to whose governments they are subjected, but they scorn to be enlisted otherwise than as Polish women. They would a hundred times prefer to have their names remain in oblivion, and left out of the golden book of deserving women, than to appear there as representatives of the nationality of their oppressors. The greater number of the Polish women who would be entitled to appear here are subjects of the Russian government.

In the present days the instruction and education of the Polish woman stand on a level equal to man—sometimes above it—and yet it is admitted that our men are distinguished by their encyclopedic knowledge. Our women are great readers, and, as may be proved by the statistics of our public libraries, their reading is not confined to novels, but to earnest books; and therefore scientific, literary, social, and political questions are familiar to them. Public lectures on serious subjects are a prominent feature of our city life, and certainly women make by far the larger part of their audiences.

Another element which tends to sharpen woman's intellect is the special character of Polish sociability. Probably social life is nowhere developed to such an extent as in Poland. Our men do not desert the house for the attractions of the club, the cafe, or the saloon. They remain at home, or gather together with women at the houses of their friends. Hospitality is essentially a virtue of the nation, but it is a hospitality free from any kind of display, as frequent in the humble abodes of the poor as in the palaces of aristocracy and plutocracy. The old Polish proverb is, "A guest in the house is God in the house." The main feature of these private reunions or parties is general conversation, directed by the lady of the house, but participated in equally by men and women—a conversation turning on serious topics, and where personal gossip is almost unknown.

This sociability, spread to all classes of our nation, has important advantages, as it reflects among other relations among them, as upon marriages. In other European countries it is only too often the case that the forming of marriages is purely a business transaction between two parties hardly known to each other. With us, on account of the frequent social intercourse, marriages are based on thorough acquaintance, and concluded through natural sympathy. While it can not be said that money considerations are always the moving cause, they yet figure in a small degree in the tying of matrimonial bonds. Thus it happens that in Poland the poor girl has suitors as well as the rich one; if the latter has the advantage as to their number, the former has a better chance in regard to the quality of her choice.

The unmarried girl in my country enjoys a position, if not so independent as in America, still much better than in the rest of the European continent.

In recent times especially there has been marked progress—

her social standing and her freedom of action are gaining ground every day. As a natural consequence there is a great movement among our unmarried girls to obtain independent livelihood, and not to look upon marriage as the ultimate goal of their ambition.

Our enemies are making a great mistake if they think that they can kill patriotism. As long as there is one Polish woman left alive Poland will not die, and the more they persecute us the better it is for us now. We may have deserved punishment for the faults and mistakes of the past; we must pay the penalty, and God only knows at what expense we pay it.

WOMEN IN SPAIN.

(Catalina D'Alcala.)

I salute all the women of this great republic, and their glorious flag, the stars and stripes, designed by a woman. In tracing the pages of the past we find that each nation has had some special mission for women to perform. To America has been intrusted the privilege of developing the highest qualities of womanly character and granting unrestrained action to them.

In carrying out the duty assigned me of reviewing the women of my country from the beloved Isabella's time, I must briefly notice the history of Spain previous to that illustrious reign and on down to the present day. For several hundred years after the great Saracen invasion Spain was broken up into a number of small but independent states, divided in their interests, and often in deadly hostility with one another. The country was inhabited by races the most dissimilar in their origin, religion, and government, the least important of which has exerted a sensible influence on the character and institutions of the present inhabitants. They regarded each other with a fiercer hatred than that with which they viewed the enemies of their faith. More Christian blood was wasted in these national feuds than in all their encounters with the infidels. The zeal which did at last unite them in a common warfare against the invaders was inevitably that of a religious fanaticism. The arts used by the ecclesiastical leaders to control the common people naturally resulted in giving Spain the deep tinge of superstition which has ever distinguished her among the nations of Europe. Yet our historians tell us that whatever were the vices of the Spaniards at that date they were not those of effeminate sloth. The privations which they had suffered at the hands of the spoilers had developed in them many hardy, sober qualities. It was under these conditions that the character of Isabella was formed. That with all her admirable virtues she had inherited some of the prevailing fanaticism is true. The fact that such a reign, so successful in bringing about the union of many conflicting elements, and stimulating special enterprises, was not followed by the permanent elevation of Isabella's own sex, points to some firmly fixed retarding influence in the economy of the nation. What the Spaniards have already accomplished in the way of learning and development of the higher mental and moral qualities is truly marvelous, in face of all the obstacles they have been forced to encounter.

It is well known that Isabella, as soon as she could bring order out of the chaos in which she found the government, devoted herself diligently to educational matters; and stimulated by her noble and intellectual influence, the women contributed much to the general illumination of that period. Female education embraced a broader field in the ancient languages than is common now. The learning of the women equaled their piety, and, far from contenting themselves with superficial attainments, they held professorships of Latin and rhetoric, and widened the domain of philosophical speculation. The queen's instructor in Latin was a woman, Doña Galinda. Another light was Isabel Losa. She mastered Greek, Latin, and Hebrew, and founded the hospital of Loretto. Sigea Aloysia of Toledo wrote letters to the pope in Latin, Greek, Hebrew, Arabic and Syrian. Even poetry and romance were not shunned by the gentler sex. Indeed, so strong became woman's position under this wonderful reign that Isabel de Rosores was permitted to preach in the great church in Barcelona. However, in this period, as ever since, a mistake was made in importing so many foreign teachers for the youth, thus bringing a mixture of ideas and influences, confusing national characteristics and depressing individual identity. Educational authorities everywhere claim the benefits of native instructors, the lack of whom truly has been a curse to Spain. With Isabella's death departed much of the wisdom of her administration, and the unstable rulers we have since had give rise to the saying that the royal palace became an insane asylum. Yet we find that many women of the time of Charles V. were noted for their political ability. All were eminently domestic in their homes—sewing, embroidering, and compounding home-made remedies for all known infirmities.

The Spaniard is a jealous being. He has suspiciously watched the late marvelous achievements of women in other nations. He is like a child, inclined to act contrary to the thing his attention is called to. In old times there were so many "woman's movements" he thought little about being excelled. Now in the present age of broad ideas he realizes the danger; that unless he strictly defines woman's position she may excel him, not only in intellectual attainments, but in political management.

The women of Spain are divided into four classes, those of the royal family, the nobility, the middle, and the lower class or peasantry. The daughters of the nobility as a rule are superficially educated, speak a little poor French and dabble in music and painting. Those of the middle class are great imitators of the nobility, although no amount of money will admit them to court society without the badge of a government office. A poor government clerk on two hundred a year can dance with a duchess, whereas the family of a millionaire without official position is excluded from the aristocracy. The women of this class are for the most part educated in convents. The peasant woman is truly a child of nature, with goodness of heart, caring for all who come within her reach, sharing her last morsel with Christian or heretic, and never accepting any remuneration. Be she rich or poor, the heart of the Spanish woman is a vast storehouse of Christian graces, cheerfulness, devotion, simplicity, and self-denial. The home influence is today what it always has been, pure and ennobling. Spanish women, so far as devotion is concerned, are model wives and mothers. When a woman once accepts a man's heart or his name she will die rather than be unfaithful.

Divorces are almost unknown. The uncertainty attending domestic life in some other nations is not felt in Spain. The family relation when once formed is permanent. Whatever may be said against the authority of the Church in affairs of State, all must admit that its control in family matters has a salutary effect on the social fabric. When even a member of the demimonde marries, which frequently occurs, she never returns to her previous life, but remains true to her family ties. I may say right here that this class of woman is not nearly so numerous in Spain as is generally supposed, and fewer still would be the departures from rectitude if there were as many avenues of self-support open to women there as in the United States. Women are taught from childhood to depend on their natural protectors. In Spain every man expects to provide for some woman of his household; if not for a wife or daughter, then for a mother or sister.

Necessity makes the opportunity. The fact that so many women are self-supporting in America does not argue favorably for the gallantry or ability of the men. The few Spanish women who are thrown upon their own resources scarcely know where to turn for an honest living. Housework and cigar-making are their principal occupations. Even sewing is not much of a public employment, as the majority of women, both of the wealthy and the poorer classes, make their own garments. They do not care for reading or any other mental improvement, so how else should they spend their time but in sewing? Much of the needlework is done by the nuns in the convents. There is no other country able to furnish such fine work in this particular.

Those who have not the health or inclination to become servants turn to the factories. The cigarette-makers are deserving of more sympathy than they receive. Many of them are true-hearted women with children to support, and they rock the cradle with grace and tenderness while they roll the cigars. The stage does not include as many classes of women as it does in almost any other country, for the reason that when a Spanish actress marries she always retires. The reports which have been circulated concerning our hospitals are sadly untrue. They have been for many years past conducted by women, and the Spanish Sister of Charity has proven herself to be a superior nurse. The prisons of Spain include one exclusively for women, which is said to be well managed by the sisters, and is never, I am glad to add, overcrowded.

A woman's resources are naturally limited in proportion as her education is restricted. The great need of Spain is widespread primary instruction. A compulsory law was enacted in 1877 for children between the ages of six and nine, free schooling being provided for the poor; but the law is not enforced, and even if it were, its provisions are too meager to meet the wants of a practical education. The universities are open only to men. Educated college women are the exception, not the rule, and the number of university-educated women is very small.

I do not wish to leave the impression that there is no longer any intellectual individuality or personal ambition among my countrywomen. Their meager advantages, their scanty education, their few chances to mingle on equal terms with the talented and good of the opposite sex have brought down upon them a long night of darkness. But we shall emerge from the shadows.

CHAPTER XIII.

THE PAN-AMERICAN EXPOSITION.

"Expositions are the time-keepers of progress. They record the world's advancement. They broaden and brighten the daily life of the people. They stimulate the energy, enterprise, and intellect of the people and quicken human genius. They open mighty storehouses of information to the student. Every exposition, great or small, has helped to some onward step. Friendly rivalry follows, which is the spur to wonderful improvement, to inspiration, to useful invention, and to high endeavor in all departments of human activity.
"These buildings will disappear, this creation of art and beauty and industry will perish from sight, but the influence will remain. Who can tell the new thoughts that may have been awakened, the ambitions fired, and the high achievements that will be wrought through this exposition?"—*From President McKinley's speech at Buffalo.*

Expositions have been happily called "new editions of a world encyclopedia." Every year adds its mite to the great fund of world knowledge and a decade finds industrial life noticeably modified and improved. Unlike the Centennial and Columbian exhibitions, this one did not commemorate a historical event but turned toward the future. Furthermore, while the commercial value of the two earlier fairs had not been lost sight of, it has to be acknowledged that in the Pan-American this feature was paramount.

The situation was that America had departed from her former policy and become involved in conflict with a European power. While it was afterwards shown conclusively that every advantage gained by the war might have been secured without it, the Spanish war is another story. Suffice it to say that it had been fought and that several Latin states to the south of us resented it and sympathized with Spain. This sentiment naturally did not prompt them to increase their trade with the United States; rather, they did their buying in

Europe. Expositions of national consequence had followed the Chicago triumph in several states, and at a dinner held in Buffalo in 1899, at which matters vital to the city were discussed, the conception of holding an exhibition simply for this hemisphere originated. Nearly a million dollars were subscribed before the banquet ended and the idea was eagerly adopted by townspeople.

Buffalo's situation on Lake Erie has given her remarkable advantage; on the other hand, she is ever overshadowed by the great metropolis of the state and union. Such a fair as the one which had recently been held in Omaha could not be expected to bring particular result, but when the novel notion of excluding the Old and accentuating the New World was discussed, great possibilities were immediately foreseen.

To hope to surpass the Chicago Fair in magnitude, imposing grandeur, or dignity was regarded as idle. It remained for the directors of this new undertaking to think of other ways in which they might create a worthy spectacle and win the approval of their countrymen. To their lasting credit it may be said that they were successful to an unexpected degree.

An undeveloped region embracing about 350 acres lay beyond Buffalo Park and this was taken for the exposition site, the beautiful Park furnishing a pleasing background. In a measure previously unknown in such an enterprise architects, decorators, landscape gardeners and sculptors worked together to produce unity. Instead of striving each to outdo his fellow worker, the contest was to see which could most perfectly merge his work into the unified plan. What is known in art as composition—the general design in which one portion is balanced against another—gave charm to the arrangement of buildings which was shortly evolved. "We must provide a beautiful spectacle," said the chief director, and that thought was never forgotten.

To convey a general conception of the plan, it was given the form of a cross, the transepts rather to the south of the center. At the entrance was erected the Triumphal Causeway—or bridge which was thrown across the canal which surrounded the grounds. At the opposite end was the Electric Tower. Around the fountain court at the end of the right transept were the Government buildings; around the corresponding left fountain court, the Horticultural group. Beyond the Electric Tower was a section known as the Plaza, bounded on the north by a circular peristyle, known as the Propylæum. This shut the cars which led thither from view. On the right of the Plaza was the Stadium, built in a few brief months, accommodating 12,000 people and given over to athletics, under the control of college men. The various exhibition buildings were artistically grouped throughout the grounds—the Ethnology and Agricultural and Liberal Arts Buildings on the right and north of the right transept offsetting the Temple of Music and Transportation Buildings on the left.

It is intended here to dwell upon those features which distinguished this exposition and gave it individuality which those who saw will never quite forget—not to enter upon any description of buildings commonly seen at exhibitions and described minutely in government reports. One peculiarity has already been noted: the harmonizing of many architectural efforts into a unified whole. The prevailing style exemplified in these buildings was Spanish Renaissance, out of delicate deference to the visitors from southern countries where this is so generally found.

The second feature which called forth surprise was the fact that color was used on the buildings. We today are accustomed to seeing public and business structures devoid of paint. On the other hand, in many parts of the country, an unpainted dwelling is rare. Even brick and cement residences are frequently painted. What is customary fails to arouse notice; whatever is unusual is likely to elicit disapproval. We fail to remember that the fact that a custom is observed among us does not signify that it has always been a custom. The Greeks, who have given us our most perfect models of beauty, did not leave their sculpture white and bare, as is the case today; they gave statues warm colors and made them lifelike. In the same way, they gave color to their buildings. However, these colorings disappeared long before the dawn of modern history.

The artist, Mr. Turner, who had general charge of decoration, determined to carry out a scheme of color, such having been considered in times past by architects but invariably abandoned. The entire Pan-American Exposition might be said to have had as its theme: Man's struggle with Nature. Man's triumph reached its climax in the Electric Tower, for which the mighty Falls of Niagara had been bridled. Associated with this idea, the entrance buildings were given deep and pronounced colors, to illustrate the ones used by primitive man; they modulated as one continued and in the Tower became mellow tints. It should not be inferred that a crude use of paint was employed; quite on the contrary. Miniature models of each building were painted again and again before the exact shades were attained. The body of the building was faintly tinted, deeper coloring used effectively around its adornments and trimmings. The warm colors that greeted the visitor were felt to bespeak welcome. The majority of those who witnessed the display accepted the plan provided as offered and found it agreeable. Others could not become accustomed to such an innovation. The green of the river was everywhere employed with gratifying results. Just what effect this experiment may have eventually in our land is something for future years to reveal.

A third feature was that sculpture more pronouncedly than before carried out the conception of the architects. To cite one or two examples, the Horticultural group of buildings stood as monuments to our natural resources, and taking the theme Nature's Bounty, the sculptor produced the Fountain of Wealth, with groups of Mineral Wealth, Floral Wealth and Animal Wealth. On the opposite side, the Government group glorified our institutions—man's creation—and on this side stood the Fountain of Man, with its statues portraying the savage age, age of despots and present enlightenment. It should not be implied that in times previous workers in stone and marble failed to conform to the underlying idea of buildings decorated else, but nowhere had this been so uniformly the case as at Buffalo.

And finally and by far most important, it remains to speak of the fourth innovation—the use of light. Chicago had shown the beauty of electrical light in making a night splendid. It remained for the Directors of the Pan-American, uniquely situated as they were with the mighty generating force of the Falls near at hand, to substitute living fire for lines of light. Instead of turning the full blaze on at once in the evening, it came more like a gorgeous dawn—first a blush of color, this deepening into richest red, and finally the full splendor of fire. Buildings were no longer outlined; they stood forth revealed; fountains tossed sprays that formed as lilies and sheaves of wheat. Children danced for joy and entreated their elders to tell whether or not it all was true, but these were quite as hopelessly bewildered. They no longer gazed upon a fairy scene; they actually stood and breathed and moved in a veritable fairy land as enchanting and unbelievable as they had known long ago when everything seemed possible. Nor did the wonder lessen by nightly repetition. Such a spectacle might have satisfied night-loving Whistler and given him an artist's rare joy. The poet's dream of "light that never was on land or sea" hovered for a few brief months as marvellously as perhaps it ever will on this terrestrial ball.

Congress appropriated $500,000 to provide an exhibition of its various departments at Buffalo. Those who object, as many always do, to having public funds thus expended forget that expositions supply almost the only opportunity the federal government has to bring home to the minds of the average citizen its various functions. All are taxed indirectly for national expenditures, but those dwelling in interior states have slight conceptions of harbor improvements or protection of human life at sea. There are states wherein Indian Reservations mean little, for while governmental reports of various descriptions are printed, comparatively few are read.

Of the amount provided for the Pan-American fair, $200,000 was expended in necessary buildings; the rest, in supplying a creditable display. The Board in charge of the federal exhibit was composed of twelve members, one from each of the eight Executive Departments, one from the Smithsonian, one from the Commission of Fish and Fisheries, one from the Bureau of American Republics and one from the Department of Labor. One of the novel features on this occasion was the collection procured at considerable expense from the Philippines, recently acquired, and from Hawaii. These probably attracted more spectators than other parts of the federal exhibit. The Bureau of Education for the first time used moving pictures to show military drills, the teaching of deaf mutes and other interesting features. The Department of the Interior showed voting machines, and the telautograph that transmits pictures by wire. On the lake in the Park a life-saving crew was stationed to give frequent demonstrations of its efficiency in time of wrecks. Imagination was needed to transform the placid lake into a storm-tossed sea. Whatever is newly acquired for such exhibits, as for example, the Philippine collection, is afterwards given permanent place in the National Museum.

It was early seen that the hope earnestly entertained for this fair was not to be largely realized in so far as it involved response from the Latin states to the south. Cuba, San Domingo, Ecuador, Chili, Honduras and Mexico erected buildings. Several other states were represented in the general exhibits.. The Director-General of the Exposition, Mr. Buchanan, had formerly been minister to Argentine Republic and by his wide acquaintance was able to arouse considerable interest. However, the Latin states have been accustomed to trade with European countries, partly because of our high tariff, and partly—as they have not hesitated to acknowledge— because they find the brusque manner predominating our commercial life intolerable. Marked courtesy in dealing with others has long been the heritage of the Latin race. One of the finest exhibits made by southern countries was a complete collection of food-plants, transported alive and throughout the summer growing to the edification of those who could never hope to see them in their native land.

The hope couched in the dedicatory panels on the Propylæum: "Here, by the great waters of the north, are brought together the peoples of the two Americas, in exposition of their resources, industries, products, inventions, arts and ideas"; and "May the century now begun unite in the bonds of peace, knowledge, goodwill, friendship and noble emulation all the dwellers in the Continents and Islands of the New World" may not have shown material realization as rapidly as had been expected. but there can be no doubt that some gain resulted from better understanding and acquaintance. The sentiment lately voiced by one of our educators: "The man I don't like is the man I don't know," is quite as applicable to nations, and it must never be forgotten that this flourishing nation in the north has overshadowed the younger and less experienced ones on the south and with characteristic assurance has not been hesitant to boast its superiority—a fact which is likely to be more quickly overlooked at home than abroad.

While Canada erected a building, her own journals criticised the slight showing she made, although to be sure certain provinces sent excellent specimens of their products.

Failing to receive as many foreign contributions as had been anticipated, exhibits of the United States filled every conceivable niche and much had to be turned away for lack of space. The Electrical Building contained the greatest promise for the future. Wireless telegraphy was demonstrated here for the first time in the history of expositions. X-ray machines were also first shown. Various appliances for utilizing this great and mysterious force in the household were displayed. The beautiful tower, 389 feet high, bore the inscription: "To those painters, sculptors and architects, tellers of tales, poets and creators of music, to those actors and musicians, who, in the New World, have cherished and increased the love of beauty."

The Art Building was erected in Buffalo Park by funds subscribed by loyal citizens, for the purpose of giving the city, after the Fair, a permanent home for the Buffalo Fine Arts Society. It was constantly visited by strangers—each succeeding exposition giving evidence of a growing love of pictures and statuary.

The Graphic Arts received greater attention than previously. Germany long surpassed us in the art of paper making but recently fine qualities have been forthcoming in the United States. Automatic typesetting machines were shown to have been cheapened and accelerated. A machine for folding, numbering, stitching, and covering magazines and pamphlets by one operation was for the first time displayed. Another printing 50,000 sixteen page forms of paper an hour in four colors filled the beholder with amazement.

The Machinery Building was dedicated "To those who in the deadly mine, on stormy seas, in the fierce breath of the furnace and in all perilous places, working ceaselessly, bring to their fellowmen comfort, sustenance and the grace of life." Three facts were impressed upon those who thoughfully gazed upon its wonders: That more and more hand labor is being replaced by machinery and no one can yet foresee to what lengths this may finally lead. That electricity is steadily encroaching upon the realm once dominated by steam and may some time supersede it. And finally, that speed is every year decreasing distance.

The Centennial was severely educational. There was less conscious strife for beauty and no attempt to amuse. One may judge how great a change time has wrought in this respect when he meditates upon the fact that the Pan-American Exposition cost $10,000,000 and that $3,000,000 were spent by the Directors on the Midway. Various new devices for entertainment were introduced which even now are antiquated. Life in America is strenuous and the populace turns for relief to places of amusement where it in turn is taken quite as strenuously.

The death of President McKinley, resulting from a shot fired by a fanatic as he was leaving the Temple of Music, threw the nation into mourning and cast into shadow the closing days of the exposition. While Buffalo was left with a deficit of $3,000,000, beyond this temporary financial burden, the Pan-American Exposition unquestionably taught the fair lake city many a useful lesson and gave it prestige. The legends graved on tablets and placed, where he who ran might read, embodied the spirit of the whole plan: that peace is better than war and its fruits alone worth gaining; that it is better for nations to forget prejudices and stand shoulder to shoulder in the forward march; that isolation engenders suspicion and acquaintance and understanding dispels it. "The brotherhood of man—the federation of nations—the peace of the world." "Between nation and nation, as between man and man, lives the one law of right."

CHAPTER XIV.

Louisiana Purchase Exposition.

It will be remembered that American settlements hugged the Atlantic coast for many years. When in the early nineteenth century men ventured over the Alleghenies to cut homes out of the wilderness, uninhabited save by roving tribes of Indians who retreated before them, these undertakings were regarded with misgivings by the less venturesome. Then settlements reached into the Mississippi basin, and there are men yet living who recall that the removal of a family from the New England states or New York to Michigan or Ohio, occasioned strong remonstrance on the part of relatives that they should thus leave civilization and go into the far west.

Trade usually precedes permanent location, and before homes were made beyond the mountains, the value of the Mississippi river for purposes of commerce was already plain to fur traders. Washington appreciated its significance as an artery to the sea and as early as 1790 said: "We must have and certainly shall have the full navigation of the Mississippi."

Spain claimed the territory west of the river and by the beginning of Jefferson's administration had practically placed an embargo upon it by forbidding Americans use of New Orleans as a shipping port. The anxiety and indignation of Americans whose trade was thus interrupted could not be ignored and the President found the situation of the country embarrassing. Relations with England were far from friendly and France had been offended by the refusal of the United States to accept the proposals made not long before by Genet. The new government was not situated to inspire confidence among the powers.

It so happened that Robert R. Livingston, our minister to France, learned that a secret treaty had been negotiated between France and Spain whereby Louisiana had been ceded to France in exchange for other territory less desired by Napoleon. The treaty was carefully guarded because France and England were on the verge of war and Napoleon foresaw that were it made public, the English would try to strike a blow at unprotected New Orleans. This information being communicated to Jefferson, he instructed Livingston to do all in his power to facilitate the acquisition of New Orleans, with the Floridas which were erroneously supposed to have been included in the treaty. He was authorized to pay $2,000,000 for this district and lest he might fail to accomplish this delicate task, Monroe was dispatched as special envoy to assist him. Livingston was offended by the insinuation that he might prove inadequate to meet the exigencies of the situation, but like a true patriot, put aside all personal consideration in face of his country's need. Approaching Talleyrand, the crafty French minister, the latter at first denied the existence of the treaty. Discovering that its terms were known, he became evasive. Others interviewed by Livingston were equally noncommital. Finally Livingston boldly stated that any attempt to cut the United States off from free use of the Mississippi would be met by force.

Napoleon's situation changed even from day to day. Although his dream of empire had included the New World, an uprising in San Domingo requiring him to send thither soldiers needed at home, led him suddenly to determine to be rid of all territories across the Atlantic. War with England was imminent, and in this gigantic game of chess which he played, he saw that pawns must be sacrificed. It was idle to attempt to protect Louisiana and so he decided to offer it to the United States. Livingston, wearied with two months' fruitless diplomacy, was suddenly bewildered by receiving a call from Talleyrand during which the Frenchman asked what the United States would give for Louisiana. The most our country had hope to attain was territory around the mouth of the river which would insure free use of its waters and the ambassador was deeply perplexed. He deliberated with Monroe, the two grasping some faint conception of what this territory might come to mean to the republic, and at the same time in doubt as to what would be the attitude of Congress toward negotiations made beyond the instructions given them. It was useless to wait for further direction in those days of belated travel and they resolved that here was a chance not to be lost. However, they showed marked coolness in refusing the first offer made to them—that the United States pay $20,000,000 and assume the payment of claims which had been entered by American citizens against French privateers. Thoroughly alarmed lest the scheme should fail, realizing that he could not hope to save the territory and needing money, Napoleon through his minister offered Louisiana for $15,000,000 from which amount the French claims might be deducted. These amounted to more than $4,000,000 and this offer was accepted, the formal transfer of Louisiana from France to the United States being made April 30, 1803.

No one realized what this would later mean to the nation in added resource. While Congress sanctioned the purchase and met the cost by an issue of six per cent bonds, there was strong outcry against money being thus expended. The region stretched away toward the Pacific coast. Rumor alone gave data regarding it. Jefferson was confident that it would prove advantageous because he had been told that a great salt region was included and this it was hoped Lewis and Clark would find on their expedition, undertaken later. Even astute statesmen failed utterly to grasp the wonderful significance of the newly acquired lands. These lines from an address by Daniel Webster indicate the utter lack of knowledge that long prevailed concerning the west:

"What do we want with this vast worthless area, this region of savages and wild beasts, of deserts, of shifting sands and whirlwinds of dust, of cactus, and prairie dogs? To what use could we ever hope to put those great deserts or those endless mountain ranges, impenetrable and covered to their very base with eternal snow? What can we ever hope to do with the western coast—a coast of 2,000 miles, rockbound, cheerless, uninviting, and not a harbor on it. What use have we for that country?"

From this area, including 864,944 square miles, twelve states and two territories have been carved, wholly or in part. Louisiana, named for Louis XIV., was the first state to be received into the Union from the tract. It was admitted in 1812. Missouri—Big Muddy—was admitted in 1821; Arkansas—bow of smoky water—in 1836; Minnesota—cloudy water—was received in 1858; Kansas—smoky water—in 1861, and the same year, Nebraska. Iowa came in in 1846; Colorado—red earth—was partly included in earlier Louisana and was admitted to statehood in 1876; Montana, North and South Dakota—united tribes—were all three admitted in 1899; Wyoming—broad plain—in 1890; Oklahoma—home of the red man—and Indian Territory were also formed from this great region. The sale of a single commodity in a very small portion of this district brings a larger price each year than was once paid for the entire tract.

On the 20th of December, 1803, the actual transfer of New Orleans and Lower Louisiana was made to the United States. At St. Louis, the center of Upper Louisiana, Spain made some pretense of opposing the sale. For that reason it was regarded as expedient to defer the transfer until the following spring. On the 9th of March, 1804, at the little fort there located, in the morning the Spanish flag was lowered and that of France raised; at noon the French flag came down and the stars and stripes were run up.

Although there was some discussion of commemorating this signal event in American history, until 1896 little was definitely considered. Finally it was agreed to hold an international exposition in memory of the purchase and Mr. Francis, formerly governor of the state, was made president of the directors of the Louisiana Purchase Exposition. Congress agreed to make an appropriation of $5,000,000 for this object provided $10,000,000 should be otherwise secured. $5,000,000 was raised by subscription in St. Louis and the city bonded for the other $5,000.000. Thus at the outset greater funds were available than had been in the case of any previous exposition.

Finding the response from the states rather feeble, delegates were sent to confer with the legislatures of twelve of them. Not content to trust to such co-operation as the usual invitation offered in the name of the President would elicit on the part of foreign governments, President Francis made a flying trip to Europe, was granted an interview with King Edward in England, President Loubet in France, Kaiser William in Germany, the king of Belgium and the ministers of Spain. He was invited to go to St. Petersburg but lack of time prevented. In each case he was successful in convincing rulers that this exposition was not intended to duplicate those previously held in our country, but had even a wider scope, and each of these countries made ample provision for the St. Louis Fair.

It gradually became plain that April 30, 1903 could not find the great exhibition ready and President Roosevelt announced to the world that it would be postponed until the following year. However, that momentous day was celebrated in St. Louis by fitting commemoration ceremonies by dignitaries from all participating nations.

Forest Park was decided upon for the exposition site. Unlike those earlier chosen, it had many natural beauties. Hills, ravines, lakes and fine groves supplied the landscape gardeners with much to develop. Including more than 1200 acres, it allowed still greater scope than the Chicago site. which it was long thought could scarcely be surpassed in point of magnitude. It was so vast that it was found necessary to provide electric cars to transfer visitors from one portion of the grounds to others.

It was determined to make Education the great feature of the exposition, it being fundamental to commerce and industry—the competitive fields between nations. For the first time in the history of expositions, Education was given a separate building and the most conspicuous place on the grounds. The exhibits were divided into sixteen departments which were highly commended—Education, Art, Liberal Arts; Varied Industries; Agriculture, Horticulture, Forestry, Mining; Manufactures, Machinery, Transportation, Electricity; Anthropology, Social Economy and Physical Culture.

To make the picture of human progress and recent improvement the more striking and evident, it was determined to show processes. Wherever possible, things were shown in the doing.

In the Educational exhibit, students were at work in the laboratories; classes in domestic science and manual arts were watched by spectators who found pleasure in witnessing the actual steps by which results were gained. Model schools for the blind and the deaf were conducted daily. Illustrated lectures were constantly given in Educational Hall.

In the building of Varied Industries, it was possible to see men at work tanning leather; see them cut soles for shoes; see others busy with other portions of the making and finally see the complete articles turned out ready for shipment. A similar plan was followed in other buildings. A ravine comprising several acres was given over to mining interests. Shafts were sunk and those wholly unacquainted with the various means employed for extracting the ore from the earth might watch men thus occupied.

The government had long furnished tanks for the observation of fish of every kind in the Fishery Buildings. Now for the first time a huge cage 300 feet by 150 feet in height was constructed to provide a place for every kind of bird available in the United States and many from other lands.

Festival Hall was devoted to music which was supplied liberally. For the first time in the history of expositions, a Temple of Fraternity was erected for members of all fraternal societies throughout the world. This was built by voluntary offerings from societies represented.

The Transportation Building at the Columbian Exposition had shown wonderful developments in methods for transporting people and freight. And yet, it is doubtful if in 1893 there was a single automobile in Chicago. In 1904 many fine motors were displayed. Electric cars had undergone marvellous change since the Fair of '93, and the fastest locomotive of that time would no longer be acceptable. While wood was largely used then for construction of cars, steel had superseded it almost entirely. Freight cars at that time carried as many as 20,000 pounds. In St. Louis they were shown to carry 100,000 pounds. Even more surprising, the first display of airships was now made. While the races arranged for dirigibles and aeroplanes were disappointing, still air navigation had to be accepted as a fact and no longer a dreamer's wild fancy.

In its display of new inventions, the Government showed means for photographing colors, although it must remain for a future fair to exhibit methods of accomplishing this with the cost sufficiently reduced to make it practical for general use. The telegraphone for the recording of sound waves was exhibited. This when sufficiently developed will make it possible for a telephone message delivered during one's absence to be recorded and reproduced at will. The telautograph, whereby the sender's own writing may be transmitted to the recipient was another of the remarkable inventions which succeeded the Columbian Exposition.

The Louisiana Purchase Exposition was very costly. In addition to the amount originally procured, that appropriated by the government for its own special exhibits, by the states, and by foreign governments, it was found necessary before the completion of the buildings to negotiate a loan of $4,600,000 from the general government, giving a lien on the gate receipts. This was a new expedient. However, the fact remains as was at the time pointed out: at such a remarkable showing of world concerns, one person may conceive a plan, invention or idea that may enrich the world beyond the entire expense involved. If this great undertaking demonstrated one fact more clearly than others it was that in those countries where education is most valued, there is to be found greatest commercial and industrial proficiency; that in countries that continue to compel classical training without the choice of scientific and modern courses, there is noticeable backwardness in commerce and industry.

The educational exhibit was particularly interesting in that it showed a unity in American educational training, although this is everywhere left to state provision. The National Educational Association which convenes each year has provided a channel through which whatever of advantage is discovered in one state becomes the property of all. In fact, in spite of many state systems, there was demonstrated greater similarity of work done in east and west of our wide country than in foreign countries where one system is maintained throughout.

It has long been conceded that the training of the young is vital to the well being of a country but this exposition went farther than that. It proved beyond the shadow of a doubt that supremacy among nations in the future will depend less upon their far reaching guns and well disciplined armies and more upon the general enlightenment and intelligence of their workmen; that the social problems that beset each land will be adequately understood and disposed of when each home is a cultural and educative center. Efficiency is the demand of the age and to develop efficient children, parents must be efficient. "The education of men and women within their homes is fully as important as the education of children," was said and demonstrated. It is gratifying to note that women's work found its place with that of men—placed not to arouse surprise at what mere woman hath wrought but to be judged solely on its merits.

Finally, it served to deepen the impression already made by the Pan-American Exposition, that when these tiny exposition cities can be made so beautiful by co-operation of trained architects and decorators, it is manifestly unnecessary for mankind to continue to dwell in such unsightly cities as fill our land. The average citizen constructs his own dwelling without a thought as to that of his neighbor, beside which it must stand. If it is painted, the color is chosen without regard to the surroundings; thus a red house may stand beside a yellow, green or white one, one often increasing the ugliness of the other. We have already grown to compel pleasing and unified spectacles inside the exposition gates and this idea needs only to be carried a little further to insure us pleasing and unified effects within the towns and cities which are our permanent abodes. Nor is it purely fanciful, as it would once have been considered, to predict that a time may come when it will be denied that a man has the right to erect a house that by its architectural form and color scheme is injurious to the effect of the neighborhood as a whole and repellent to the trained eye.

CHAPTER XV.

Lewis and Clark Exposition.

The Louisiana Purchase, as has been noted, occasioned much bitter criticism. The newly acquired territory was described as a region of jungle, swamp, desert, fit only for the habitation of savages, reptiles and fierce wild beasts. With a desire to modify some of the calumny that was heaped upon his head, but more particularly with a hope of ascertaining whether or not water connection with the Pacific might be found, President Jefferson determined to send out an expedition into the northwest. Accordingly, Congress appropriated $2,500 to defray the cost. This, at the time, was regarded as liberal provision.

Captain Meriweather Lewis, twenty-nine years of age, then acting as the President's private secretary, was eager to accompany the proposed expedition. Captain William Clark, another officer in the United States Army, and four years older, was appointed to share responsibilities with him. Having received full instruction to make a record of their experiences, to observe the nature of the country traversed, its vegetation, minerals where these could be discovered, and above all, to use the utmost diplomacy in dealing with the Indians, striving ever to win them by kindness, Lewis departed to meet Captain Clark in St. Louis. They arrived at this center of Upper Louisiana in December, 1803, and spent the winter in preparation and recruiting a party. Nine hardy young Kentuckians, fourteen volunteer soldiers, two French boatmen, an interpreter, a hunter and a negro servant made up the party proper, while to accompany them to the land of the Mandans—North Dakota—six additional soldiers, one corporal and nine rowers were also engaged.

The outfit when ready included a keel boat, fifty-five feet long, with cabin and forecastle, propelled by twenty-two oars and a square sail; two long skiffs, clothing, provisions, guns, powder and fourteen bales of gewgaws designed to attract the

SMITHSONIAN INSTITUTE.

Indians—tinkling bells, bright colored calicoes, and such other gay novelties as quickly appealed to these Forest Children.

On the 14th of May, 1804, the exploring party departed from St. Louis to laboriously ascend the Missouri. For weeks they proceeded through a region inhabited on either side the stream by semi-barbarous tribes. They landed at frequent intervals to cultivate the good will of the Indians and to make observations of the land surrounding the river. Herds of buffalo, many snakes, wolves, a few elk and plenty of deer were seen. There was no lack of fresh meat and wild fowl were abundant.

Council Bluff takes its name from the fact that near the site of that present city, Lewis and Clark met with representatives of the Ottoes and Missouri Indians; smoked the pipe of peace and presented gifts in the name of the great White Father of the United States. This meeting took place on the 3rd of August, 1804.

By the 25th of that month, they had ascended the stream to within twenty miles of Sioux City. Here a great mound held their attention. They found the Indians regarded it with superstitious fears, believing it to be inhabited by spirits. It measured nine hundred feet in length, two hundred in width and rose by steep elevation to a height of seventy feet. In this vicinity they saw many buffalo, prairie dogs, wild turkeys and ducks.

The first of November found the cold of winter closing in upon them and it seemed best to prepare winter quarters. The site of their camp was three miles below Bismarck, in North Dakota. Around them were villages of Mandans—Indians whom certain authorities have claimed to bear affinity to the Jewish race. Their remote connection to the Lost Tribes of Israel has been advocated. The tribe today is nearly extinct. Next to the Sioux, they were at that time the strongest in the northwest, being able to muster one thousand fighting warriors. They were friendly to the Lewis and Clark party and aided as they were able. The winter was very cold—the mercury often hovering around forty below zero. The leaders spent the months investigating the country to the slight extent they were able—covered as it was by its snowy blanket. They studied the habits of the Mandans, whose immorality they thought appalling; yet they themselves fared well among this nation, which was intelligent and thrifty.

April 7, 1805, they broke camp, sending back the keelboat to St. Louis with thirteen men. The rest began the ascent of the river in light canoes and skiffs. One important fact is to be noted: they engaged a French guide, Chaboneau, to accompany them. While he was cowardly and of slight use, his Indian wife, Sacajawea—Bird Woman—proved of invaluable assistance and time and again in his journal Lewis credits the success of the difficult passages to her instinctive guidance in discovering mountain passes and portages. Her child was born during the journey, she carrying him on her back during much of the way. She had been stolen from her own people and sold as a slave, having become one of the wives of this half-breed. While he continually complained about the difficulties of the way, never a murmur passed her lips and the little party found her undaunted courage and fearlessness inspiring.

By the 26th of April they reached the junction of the Missouri and Yellowstone Rivers. Great Falls was reached by the 16th of June and the Fourth of July was celebrated by a great feast of elk and bear meat. By September 12th the site of the present town of Missoula was gained. The Shoshones inhabited this region. They were poor but honest, and Lewis found them entirely trustworthy. The abundance of fresh berries and plants had made the entire party ill and for a time they were obliged to recuperate. By the first of November they had descended the Columbia to within one hundred miles of Portland. Six days later they gained sight of the great ocean and in December went into winter quarters near Astoria.

Having exhausted their supply of salt fish, several men were occupied during the winter months in evaporating ocean water to extract the salt and thus prepare a stock of dried fish to maintain them during the homeward journey. This proved to be somewhat slow and laborious work.

Eager to start back, now that they had accomplished their purpose they broke camp in March, gratifying the Indians by dividing among them the huts they had constructed. On the 23rd they began to retrace their way, with faces set toward home; the expedition party reached St. Louis September 23,

1806, having covered a journey of 2555 miles to the ocean and the same distance in return.

So long a time had passed without a word from them that the party had been given up as lost. When their successful exploration was made known, great rejoicing throughout the Union followed and the journals of the men were read with tremendous interest.

Faint conception of this remarkable undertaking is conveyed by a perusal of these bare facts. No expedition has ever been fraught with greater dangers or filled with more absorbing interest. A little handful of men set out to traverse an unknown land. Uncivilized tribes might at any step prevent their passage and overcome them. Instead, with but few occasions when it was necessary to fire among them, they accomplished this long trip and added three states of today by right of discovery: Idaho, Washington, Oregon. Many a time their very lives were threatened by unforeseen catastrophes. Once in the mountains Clark and several of his companions stepped into a cave to await the passage of a shower. Suddenly there was a cloudburst and water in this apparently protecting cave arose many feet in five minutes— forcing them to hurry for their lives. Only by reading their diaries can the numerous dangers of the way be conceived. Yet they reached civilization with the loss of but one member of the party, who died during the first part of the trip.

The Fair, held in Portland in 1905, commemorated this heroic and momentous expedition, particularly celebrating the discovery of Oregon and the great Northwest. It was the first exhibition to be held west of the Rockies and was the means of bringing a rich and resourceful district before the attention of those dwelling in the eastern and middle states. Even today the vast possibilities of this part of our country are unguessed by those most conversant with the Pacific Coast, and by the majority of American citizens they are not in the least realized.

The Lewis and Clark Exposition was not intended to rival the big fairs previously held in Chicago and St. Louis. In some respects it was more wonderful than either, but in others it did not even excite comparison. In the natural beauty of its location no exposition held away from the western coast could rival it. The exposition grounds lay at the foot of Willamette Heights, on the outskirts of Portland and over a dark fringe of trees the eternal snows of the Cascades towered majestically. Land and water were amply included, a long bridge joining the mainland with a peninsula that reaches far into the water. It was merely a question of clearing away underbrush, and developing natural beauty bountifully provided by a prodigal nature. The government assisted only by its own exhibit—made in five buildings which were grouped on the peninsula. One of these buildings was devoted to irrigation—the subject of such vital interest to the west. Only in recent years have the possibilities of irrigation been realized and the government has already expended large sums in reclaiming land that previously was regarded as valueless. It has now been conclusively proved that desert areas without fertilization can be made to blossom and yield fruit if they are but supplied with sufficient water. When the Federal government provided means for irrigation near Yuma, 105,000 acres of land, before a wilderness, were rendered arable and the yield since has been remarkable. Several other districts have been similarly dealt with and hundreds of thousands lie waste which will some day be converted into habitations for men. There is little doubt but that provision for saving the melting snow in Montana would supply adequate means for the cultivation of many of its present desolate regions.

For the first time in the history of expositions, irrigation was thoroughly displayed—dams, sluices, canals and irrigating ditches being shown in operation. This taught easterners more than volumes of wearisome treatises upon the subject could have ever done.

Foreign nations were invited to participate in this exhibition, their exhibits being shown largely in two buildings—the Foreign Exposition Building, devoted to European displays, and the Oriental Palace, in which several nations displayed their products liberally, but most completely were to be seen the products of Japan. It was said that the Mikado had not been satisfied with the exhibits made by his people at St. Louis and was determined that no effort should be spared to make their representation at Portland creditable.

No other structure excited greater interest than the For-

estry Building—a typical Oregon creation. Excepting Old
Faithful Inn, in the Yellowstone, it was the largest log building
ever erected. 205 feet in length, 108 feet wide and 50 feet
high, the fifty-two giant trees that, like columns, supported the
roof were worthy examples of western primeval forest. Not
a nail or bit of metal was used throughout; wooden pins
joined together portions of the building. In galleries lining
the interior, a large variety of woods, finished and unfinished,
were ready for examination. All trees used in the structure
were cut not very far from the exposition site, protected that
their bark might not be bruised, branches lopped off and
raised as they had recently stood for generations beneath the
skies.

For the edification of those unacquainted with the lumbering industry, this exposition afforded a chance to see logging and manufacture of lumber in the doing.

Many states put up buildings on the grounds. Far-away Maine reproduced the birthplace of Longfellow. Inside was a Hiawatha Room and an Evangeline Room. No elaborate exhibition was provided, but the house constituted the headquarters for Maine guests. The legislature made no appropriation for this effort; instead, lovers of the poet throughout the state raised the money necessary by popular subscription.

Illinois reproduced Lincoln's log cabin, where as a boy he read such books as he could procure before the firelight by the hearth. More elaborate state buildings were visited less frequently than this—beloved by a whole nation.

The Lewis and Clark Exposition was regarded as thoroughly successful. It furnished an excellent opportunity for pioneers to rally and compare their early experiences, when the matter of traveling from one part of a state to another was a greater undertaking than traversing a continent to-day. It called the attention of Americans everywhere to the expedition of two brave men, who were not alone in being animated with the spirit of adventure but were typical of an age when exploration was the consuming interest of the courageous. While our histories have hitherto passed over the work of western pathfinders as of slight concern, it is probable that those written in the future will give western history more attention, while not lessening the importance of historical development in the eastern and middle states. Various historical societies have already begun to mark the trails of the early explorers for the instruction of future generations. Finally, and most important, it riveted the attention for a few brief months upon the achievements of men in the west, showing the marvellous progress made in a single century and making known the fact that the days of the pioneer in the northwest are over. Thousands of acres in the states accruing to the Union by right of discovery on this occasion are ready for homeseekers today who would enjoy the opportunities the northwest offers and insure them for their children's children.

The amusement concessions were allotted space at the termination of the long bridge; this district was known as The Trail. While including the usual features found these days at amusement parks, a few were typically western. In one of these places, one could see men "panning" out metal, as they did in the Klondike.

Extracts from the Journals and Field Books of the Explorers.

The navigation is now very laborious. The river is deep, but with little current, and from 70 to 100 yards wide; the low grounds are very narrow, with but little timber, and that chiefly the aspen tree. The cliffs are steep, and hang over the river so much that often we could not cross them, but were obliged to pass and repass from one side of the river to the other, in order to make our way. In some places the banks are formed of dark black granite rising perpendicularly to a great height, through which the river seems, in the progress of time, to have worn its channel. On these mountains we see more pine than usual, but it is still in small quantities. Along the bottoms, which have a covering of high grass, we observed the sunflower blooming in great abundance. The Indians of the Missouri, more especially those who do not cultivate maize, make great use of the seed of this plant for bread, or in thickening their soup. They first parch and then pound it between two stones, until it is reduced to a fine meal. Sometimes they add a portion of water, and drink it thus diluted; at other times they add a sufficient portion of mar-row-grease to reduce it to the consistency of common dough, and eat it in that manner. This last composition we preferred to all the rest, and thought it at that time a very palatable dish. . . .

Being now very anxious to meet with the Shoshones or Snake Indians, for the purpose of obtaining the necessary information of our route, as well as to procure horses, it was thought best for one of us to go forward with a small party and endeavor to discover them, before the daily discharge of our guns, which is necessary for our subsistence, should give them notice of our approach. If by an accident they hear us, they will most probably retreat to the mountains, mistaking us for their enemies, who usually attack them on this side. . . .

July 22d. We set out at an early hour. The river being divided into so many channels, by both large and small islands, that it was impossible to lay down accurately by following in a canoe any single channel, Captain Lewis walked on shore, took the general courses of the river, and from the rising grounds laid down the situation of the islands and channels, which he was enabled to do with perfect accuracy, the view not being obstructed by much timber. At 1¼ miles we passed an island somewhat larger than the rest, and four miles further reached the upper end of another, on which we breakfasted. This is a large island, forming in the middle of a bend to the north a level fertile plain, ten feet above the surface of the water and never overflowed. Here we found great quantities of a small onion (Allium cernuum), about the size of a musket-ball, though some were larger; it is white, crisp, and as well flavoured as any of our garden onions (A. cepa); the seed is just ripening, and as the plant bears a large quantity to the square foot, and stands the rigors of the climate, it will no doubt be an acquisition to the settlers. From this production we called it Onion Island.

During the next 7¼ miles we passed several long circular bends, and a number of large and small islands which divide the river into many channels, and then reached the mouth of a creek on the north side (right hand, left bank). It is composed of three creeks, which unite in a handsome valley about four miles before they discharge into the Missouri, where it is about 15 feet wide and eight feet deep, with clear, transparent water. Here we halted for dinner, but as the canoes took different channels in ascending, it was some time before they all joined.

We were delighted to find that the Indian woman recognizes the country; she tells us that to this creek her countrymen make excursions to procure white paint on its banks, and we therefore call it White-earth Creek. She says also that the Three Forks of the Missouri are at no great distance—a piece of intelligence which has cheered the spirits of us all, as we hope soon to reach the head of that river. This is the warmest day, except one, we have experienced this summer. In the shade the mercury stood at 80°, which is the second time it has reached that height during this season. We camped on an island, after making 19¾ miles.

In the course of the day we saw many geese, cranes, small birds common to the plains, and a few pheasants. We also observed a small plover or curlew of a brown color, about the size of a yellow-legged plover or jack-curlew, but of a different species. It first appeared near the mouth of Smith's River, but is so shy and vigilant that we were unable to shoot it. Both the broad- and narrow-leaved willow continue, though the sweet willow has become very scarce. The rosebush, small honeysuckle, pulpy-leaved thorn, southern-wood, sage, box-elder, narrow-leaved cottonwood, redwood, and a species of sumach, are all abundant. So, too, are the red and black gooseberries, service-berry, choke-cherry, and the black, yellow, red, and purple currants, which last seems to be a favorite food of the bear. Before camping we landed and took on board Captain Clark, with the meat he had collected during this day's hunt, which consisted of one deer and an elk; we had, ourselves, shot a deer and an antelope. The mosquitoes and gnats were unusually fierce this evening. . . .

Sacajawea, our Indian woman, informs us that we are camped on the precise spot where her countrymen, the Snake Indians, had their huts five years ago, when the Minnetarres of Knife River first came in sight of them, and from which they hastily retreated three miles up the Jefferson, and concealed themselves in the woods. The Minnetarees, however, pursued and attacked them, killed four men, as many women and a number of boys, and made prisoners of four other boys and all the females, of whom Sacajawea was one. She does not, however, show any distress at these recollections, or any joy at the prospect of being restored to her country; for she seems to possess the folly or the philosophy of not suffering her feelings to extend beyond the anxiety of having plenty to eat and a few trinkets to wear.

July 30th. Captain Clark was this morning much restored; and, therefore, having made all the observations necessary to fix the longitude, we reloaded our canoes and begun to ascend Jefferson River. The river now becomes very crooked and forms bends on each side; the current is rapid, and cut into a great number of channels and sometimes shoals, the beds of which consist of coarse gravel. The islands are unusually numerous. On the right are high plains, occasionally forming cliffs of rocks and hills; while the left is an extensive low ground and prairie, intersected by a number of bayous or channels falling into the river. Captain Lewis, who had walked through it with Chaboneau, his wife, and two invalids, joined us at dinner, a few miles above our camp. Here the Indian woman said was the place where she had been made prisoner. The men being too few to contend with the Minnetarees, mounted their horses and fled as soon as the attack began. The women and children dispersed, and Sacajawea, as she was crossing at a shoal place, was overtaken in the middle of the river by her pursuers. As we proceeded, the low grounds were covered with cottonwood and thick underbrush; on both sides of the river, except where the high hills prevented it, the ground was divided by bayous; and these were dammed up by the beaver, which are very numerous here. We made 12¼ miles, and camped on the north side.

On our right is the point of a high plain, which our Indian woman recognizes as the place called the Beaver's Head, from a supposed resemblance to that object. This, she says, is not far from the summer retreat of her countrymen, which is on a river beyond the mountains, running to the west. She is therefore certain that we shall meet them either on this river, or on that immediately west of its source, which, judging from its present size, cannot be far distant. Persuaded of the absolute necessity of procuring horses to cross the mountains, it was determined that one of us should proceed in the morning to the head of the river, and penetrate the mountains till he found the Shoshones, or some other nation, who could assist us in transporting our baggage, the greater part of which we should be compelled to leave, without the aid of horses.

August 15th. Captain Lewis rose early, and having eaten nothing yesterday except his scanty meal of flour and berries, felt the inconveniences of extreme hunger. On inquiry (of McNeal) he found that his whole stock of provisions consisted of two pounds of flour. This he ordered to be divided into two equal parts, and one-half of it to be boiled with the berries into a sort of pudding. After presenting a large share to the chief, he and his three men breakfasted on the remainder. Cameahwait was delighted at this new dish; he took a little of the flour in his hand, tasted and examined it very narrowly, and asked if it was made of roots. Captain Lewis explained the process of preparing it, and the chief said it was the best thing he had eaten for a long time.

This being finished, Captain Lewis now endeavored to hasten the departure of the Indians, who still hesitated and seemed reluctant to move, although the chief addressed them twice for the purpose of urging them. On inquiring the reason, Cameahwait told him that some foolish person had suggested that he was in league with their enemies, the Pahkees, and had come only to draw them into ambuscade; but that he himself did not believe it. Captain Lewis felt uneasy at this insinuation; he knew the suspicious temper of the Indians, accustomed from their infancy to regard every stranger as an enemy, and saw that if this suggestion were not instantly checked, it might hazard the total failure of the enterprise. Assuming, therefore, a serious air, he told the chief that he was sorry to find they placed so little confidence in him, but that he pardoned their suspicions because they were ignorant of the character of white men, among whom it was disgraceful to lie, or entrap even an enemy by falsehood; that if they continued to think thus meanly of us, they might be assured no white man would ever come to supply them with arms and merchandise; that there was at this moment a party of white men waiting to trade with them at the forks of the river; and that, if the greater part of the tribe entertained any suspicion, he hoped there were still among them some who were men, who would go and see with their own eyes the truth of what he said, and who, if there was any danger, were not afraid to die. To doubt the courage of an Indian is to touch the tenderest string of his mind, and the surest way to rouse him to any dangerous achievement. Cameahwait instantly replied that he was not afraid to die, and mounting his horse, for the third time harangued the warriors. He told them that he was resolved to go if he went alone, or if he were sure of perishing; that he hoped there were among those who heard him some who were not afraid to die, and who would prove it by mounting their horses and following him. This harangue produced an effect on six or eight only of the warriors, who now joined their chief. With these Captain Lewis smoked a pipe; and then, fearful of some change in their capricious temper, set out immediately.

It was about twelve o'clock when his small party left the camp, attended by Cameahwait and the eight warriors. Their departure seemed to spread a gloom over the village; those who would not venture to go were sullen and melancholy, and the women were crying and imploring the Great Spirit to protect their warriors, as if they were going to certain destruction. Yet such is the wavering inconsistency of these savages, that Captain Lewis' party had not gone far when they were joined by ten or twelve more warriors; and before reaching the creek which they had passed on the morning of the thirteenth, all the men of the nation and a number of women had overtaken them, having changed, from the surly ill-temper in which they were two hours ago, to the greatest cheerfulness and gayety. When they arrived at the spring on the side of the mountain, where the party had camped on the 12th, the chief insisted on halting to let the horses graze; to which Captain Lewis assented, and smoked with them. They were excessively fond of the pipe, in which, however, they are not able to indulge much, as they do not cultivate tobacco themselves, and their rugged country affords them but few articles to exchange for it. Here they remained for about an hour, and on setting out, by arranging to pay four of the party, Captain Lewis obtained permission for himself and each of his men to ride behind an Indian. But he soon found riding without stirrups was much more tiresome than walking, and therefore dismounted, making the Indian carry his pack. About sunset they reached the upper part of the level valley, in the cove through which he had passed, and which they now called Shoshone Cove. The grass being burnt on the north side of the river, they crossed over to the south, and camped about four miles above the narrow pass between the hills, noticed as they traversed the cove before. The river was here about six yards wide, and frequently dammed up by the beaver.

Drewyer had been sent forward to hunt; but he returned in the evening unsuccessful, and their only supper therefore was the remaining pound of flour, stirred in a little boiling water, and then divided between the four white men and two of the Indians.

We soon drew near the camp, and just as we approached it a woman made her way through the crowd toward Sacajawea; recognizing each other, they embraced with the most tender affection. The meeting of these two young women had in it something peculiarly touching, not only from the ardent manner in which their feelings were expressed, but also from the real interest of their situation. They had been companions in childhood; in the war with the Minnetarees they had both been taken prisoners in the same battle; they had shared and softened the rigors of their captivity till one of them had escaped from the Minnetarees, with scarce a hope of ever seeing her friend relieved from the hand of her enemies. While Sacajawea was renewing among the women the friendships of former days, Captain Clark went on, and was received by Captain Lewis and the chief, who, after the first embraces and salutations were over, conducted him to a sort of circular tent or shade of willows. Here he was seated on a white robe, and the chief immediately tied in his hair six small shells resembling pearls, an ornament highly valued by these people, who procure them in the course of trade from the sea-coast. The moccasins of the whole party were then taken off, and after much ceremony the smoking began. After this the conference was to be opened. Glad of an opportunity of being able to converse more intelligibly, Sacajawea was sent for; she came into the tent, sat down, and was beginning to interpret, when, in the person of Cameahwait, she recognized her brother. She instantly jumped up, and ran and embraced him, throwing over him her blanket, and weeping profusely. The chief was himself moved, though not in the same degree. After some conversation between them she resumed her seat and attempted to interpret for us; but her new situation seemed to overpower her, and she was frequently interrupted by her tears. After the council was finished the unfortunate woman learned that all her family were dead except two brothers, one of whom was absent, and a son of her eldest sister, a small boy, who was immediately adopted by her.

The canoes arriving soon after, we formed a camp in a meadow on the left-hand side, a little below the forks, took out our baggage, and by means of our sails and willow-poles formed a canopy for our Indian visitors. About four o'clock the chiefs and warriors were collected and, after the customary ceremony of taking off the moccasins and smoking a pipe, we explained to them in a long harangue the purposes of our visit, making themselves the one conspicuous object of the good wishes of our government, on whose strength, as well as friendly disposition, we expatiated. We told them of their dependence on the will of our government for all their future supplies of whatever was necessary either for their comfort or defense; that, as we were sent to discover the best route by which merchandise could be conveyed to them, and no trade would be begun before our return, it was mutually advantageous that we should proceed with as little delay as possible; that we were under the necessity of requesting them to furnish us with horses to transport our baggage across the mountains, and a guide to show us the route; but that they should be amply remunerated for their horses, as well as for every other service they should render us. In the meantime our first wish was, that **they** should immediately collect as many horses as were necessary to transport our baggage to their village, where at our leisure we would trade with them for as many horses as they could spare.

The speech made a favorable impression. The chief, in reply, thanked us for our expressions of friendship toward himself and his nation, and declared their willingness to render us every service. He lamented that it would be so long before they should be supplied with firearms, but that till then they could subsist as they had heretofore done. He concluded by saying that there were not horses enough here to transport our goods, but that he would return to the village to-morrow, bring all his own horses, and encourage his people to come over with theirs. The conference being ended to our satisfaction, we now enquired of Cameahwait what chiefs were among the party, and he pointed out two of them. We then distributed our presents; to Cameahwait we gave a medal of small size, with a likeness of President Jefferson and on the reverse a figure of hands clasped with a pipe and tomahawk; to this was added an uniform coat, a shirt, a pair of scarlet leggings, a carrot of tobacco, and some small articles. Each of the other chiefs received a small medal struck during the presidency of General Washington, a shirt, handkerchief, leggings, knife, and some tobacco. Medals of the same sort were also presented to two young warriors, who, though not chiefs, were promising youths and very much respected in the tribe. These honorary gifts were followed by presents of paint, moccasins, awls, knives, beads, and looking-glasses. We also gave them all a plentiful meal of Indian corn, of which the hull is taken off by being boiled in lye; as this was the first they had ever tasted, they were very much pleased with it. They had, indeed, abundant sources of surprise in all they saw—the appearance of the men, their arms, their clothing, the canoes, the strange looks of the negro, and the sagacity of our dog, all in turn shared their admiration, which was raised to astonishment by a shot from the air-gun. This operation was instantly considered "great medicine," by which they, as well as the other Indians, mean something emanating directly from the Great Spirit, or produced by his invisible and incomprehensible agency. The display of all these riches had been intermixed with inquiries into the geographical situation of their country; for we had learned by experience that to keep savages in good temper their attention should not be wearied with too much business, but that serious affairs should be enlivened by a mixture of what is new and entertaining. Our hunters brought in, very seasonably, four deer and antelope, the last of which we gave to the Indians, who in a very short time devoured it.

November 7th. The morning was rainy, and the fog so

thick that we could not see across the river. We observed, however, opposite our camp, the upper point of an island (Puget's), between which and the steep hills on the right we proceeded for five miles (site of Cathlamet). Three miles lower is the beginning of an island separated from the right shore by a narrow channel; down this we proceeded under the direction of some Indians, whom we had just met going up the river, and who returned in order to show us their village. It consists of four houses only, situated on this channel behind several marshy islands formed by two small creeks. On our arrival they gave us some fish, and we afterward purchased some wappatoo-roots, fish, three dogs, and two otter-skins, for which we gave fish-hooks chiefly, that being an article of which they were very fond. . . .

We had not gone far from this village when the fog cleared off, and we enjoyed the delightful prospect of the ocean—that ocean, the object of all our labors, the reward of all our anxieties. This cheering view exhilarated the spirits of all the party, who were still more delighted on hearing the distant roar of the breakers. We went on with great cheerfulness under the high mountainous country which continued along the right bank (passing Three Tree and Jim Crow Points); the shore was, however, so bald and rocky, that we could not, until after going 14 miles from the last village, find any spot fit for a camp (opposite Pillar Rock). At that distance, having made during the day 34 miles, we spread our mats on the ground, and passed the night in the rain. Here we were joined by our small canoe, which had been separated from us during the fog this morning. Two Indians from the last village also accompanied us to the camp; but, having detected them in stealing a knife, they were sent off.

CHAPTER XVI.

The Jamestown Exposition.

In 1607 the first permanent English colony was successfully planted in Virginia, on the James River. The story of its trials and sufferings is known to every school boy. So little was the true nature of the new continent understood in the Old World that chevaliers and gentlemen, hoping to retrieve their fortunes, set out upon a voyage thither with the sole desire of becoming rich. Captain John Smith's arduous task in converting such a company into thrifty workers has been explained in every American history. Sickness, dissension and want so reduced the colony that they were about to return to the mother country when help arrived just in time to save the settlement for a future nation. The first and second hundredth anniversary had passed without particular attention and it was determined to celebrate the third centennial by holding an exposition as near the site of the original settlement as possible.

There was no attempt to rival the great expositions which this country had already produced. Rather, from the outset the idea of developing a kind of historical exposition which should set forth graphically the story of old colony days was emphasized. Believing that the strength of armies and battleships had been important in days bygone, it was stipulated in the beginning that "Such exposition should be adjacent to the waters of Hampton Roads, whereupon the navies of all nations may rendezvous in honor of the hardy mariner who braved the dangers of the deep to establish the first colony."

Congress appropriated approximately $1,700,000 for various exposition purposes and an invitation was extended in the name of the President to foreign nations to take part in a naval and military display which should be made in connection with the exhibition.

The district chosen for the exhibit included about 400 acres and was open to the view of Hampton Roads. The government constructed two huge piers out from the shore one-half mile, these being 200 feet in width. They were joined at the outer ends by a third, arched in the center to allow small boats to enter the area of water thus enclosed. These three piers were threaded with one million incandescent bulbs which, with searchlights, bathed the whole into white splendor at night.

The buildings were colonial in character. The Administration Building was centrally located and contained the auditorium—accommodating about six thousand people. Near it were the Twin Palaces—of History and Historic Art. This first was made fireproof and housed rare and valuable historical papers during the exposition months.

The two sides of the grounds not open to the water were enclosed by trellises of roses, honeysuckle, creepers and other vinery, supported by invisible wire to the height of eight feet, the top being capped by barbed wire to prevent intrusion. These two flowery walls were most effective. Moreover, all available space within the grounds was laid out in old-fashioned gardens.

A group of seven buildings constituted the Arts and Crafts Village—the Textile Building; Copper, Silver and Wooden Shops; Pottery Shop; Iron Shop; Model School; Mothers and Children's Building and the Pocahontas Hospital. These quaint, dignified, colonial buildings—like most of the others—were erected as permanent structures and have since been sold as residences, hotels, clubs and the like. In the Textile Building were set up looms and skilled workers carded wool, spun it and wove it into fabrics, after the fashion of long ago. In the workshops, furniture such as that used in the colonial houses of the seventeenth century was manufactured for the interest of visiting guests. Iron and copper kettles, pewter spoons, andirons, knockers, and every article of use in the early American home were reproduced as in the days gone by. Nails were pounded out; horse shoes wrought. Indeed, anyone who wished to study the social and industrial life of Old Colony days might here find it brought back for his leisurely study. Vessels came but rarely then from the Old World, and there was much that these must needs bring. The self-reliant colonist could not depend upon imported articles. It was necessary for him to become skillful in fashioning these for himself, or at least, in every settlement some one must be able to produce articles of various descriptions. It will be remembered that upon the Virginian plantation workshops of different kinds were maintained and the independent planter lived in a little world of his own—the ships that carried away his tobacco in many instances coming to his very wharf. However, all this came about somewhat later.

Nearly all the original thirteen states erected buildings—Pennsylvania reproducing Independence Hall. Four western states, Washington, Oregon, Idaho and Nevada, built one jointly, giving it the form of a maltese cross and each occupying one of the arms with its exhibits. Several of these buildings were also erected with the plan of later usefulness.

In the fireproof buildings devoted to old papers and other valuable historical evidence, fac-similes of the Declaration of Independence, Articles of Confederation and Constitution were shown, together with original papers of great value. Each state searched its archives for interesting matter to loan for the exhibit. One of the most interesting historical displays was the reproduced village of Jamestown, with its stockade, forts and Indian houses.

Due to the constant encroachments of the river, the site of early Jamestown is now a marsh. It lies about forty miles up the stream from the exposition grounds and many who visited the latter availed themselves of the day excursions offered by small crafts to see the spot thus identified with our early beginnings. The old church stands now in ruins and there is little else to distinguish the memorable spot.

In view of the splendid motives that led to this undertaking, it is almost a pity to touch upon the other side of the matter and show why this exposition failed to realize the hopes at first entertained for it. Intending to place only moderate stress upon military concerns, these soon were found to be wholly in the ascendency. Great Britain, Germany, France, Russia, Japan, Denmark, Belgium, Mexico, Costa Rica and other nations dispatched gunboats and troops thither. Some of the ones promoting the Fair, imbued with true American enterprise, sought to make each military pageant as imposing as possible and spread advertisements of this nature through the land. "This will be the greatest military display the world has ever seen;" "This will bring before the eyes of American citizens the greatest gathering of warships the world has ever known." "It will give us living pictures of war, with all its enticing splendors." And so extracts from flaming posters might be made indefinitely. In some countries such promises as these might have elicited great enthusiasm and joy, but in the United States where war is abhorred, they called out the condemnation of the discerning press and dismayed the thoughtful citizen. Many a man knew from personal experience that war has no attending splendors and many a household still mourns those whose lives went out in noble sacrifice for a great cause. It is all very well to rehearse the oft-repeated sentence that the greatest safeguard of peace is a large and well equipped army and navy. Many believe it, but nevertheless, the sight of a great fleet of battleships gives comfort and assurance far less than it inspires awe. These mighty contrivances are meant to destroy human life; the far penetration of their guns is the boast of the age. For two thousand years the doctrine of peace on earth, good will toward men has been preached, and in face of it manifestations of war must alway imply flat contradiction and inconsistency. It would be unsafe for one nation to disarm while its neighbors perfected their gunboats and armies, but at least long extended display of military pomp will find scant welcome in this country. Especially were the advertised mock battles commemorating critical times in our history resented.

It cannot help the popularity of a national exposition to have many of the nation's publications decrying some features of its plan—however they may seek to do justice to the rest— and it cannot be denied that this over-emphasizing military affairs alienated many who otherwise might have availed themselves of the chance to spend some time at Norfolk. Added to this was the disadvantage of summer climate in sultry Virginia from the last of April until fall. Furthermore, the effort seemed to demonstrate that however our nation may be at fault for not valuing highly historical things and relics of the past, the attention of the general public is won far more quickly by anything that points toward the future.

There was dearth of means for promoting the exposition

and the government was asked to loan $1,000,000 to the Jamestown Exposition Company, taking a lien upon the gate receipts, 40% of these to be reserved to make good this amount. The daily admissions during the fair were not allowed to become public, as has generally been the case. Various efforts were made to estimate them—all too high it turned out when the final showing to the government was made. The average daily admissions were only 1,500 and of the million loaned, $140,000 was returned. This occasioned some public discussion as to whether loans of this nature were justifiable or not.

For the first time in the history of expositions, the negroes made a separate showing. In a building designed by a negro architect and constructed by negro workmen, three thousand exhibits were made. The Fisk Jubilee Singers provided frequent concerts; the various schools for the colored children and older students made fine exhibits. The needlework done by the girls was excellent. Inventions made by them; books written by Booker T. Washington and other clever thinkers were to be seen. On one side of the entrance to their building was a windowless cabin of the kind provided for the slaves in 1860; on the other side, a pleasant wooden cottage commonly built by the enterprising among them to-day. Never in history has a race shown such remarkable progress in forty-five years. There are to-day in Virginia alone 47,000 homes owned by the colored people. August 3rd was observed as Negro Day, but while some six thousand of this race gathered in their building, other visitors to the grounds appeared to give slight attention to the occasion.

Someone recalling the early struggle with the Indians suggested the name The War-path for the amusement quarter and it clung to it. The shows were not all warlike in nature but were not patronized as constantly as they are in the north. The New South has had a great burden to meet in its reconstruction and money is not so plentiful among the middle class as in the north. Many found the expense of the trip thither and the admission all they cared to undertake.

The government set aside $50,000 for a permanent monument to be erected in memory of the first English settlement made in the United States. Built of light New Hampshire granite, it has the form of an obelisk, and rests upon a heavy base, approached from every side by a flight of stairs. The base bears but one inscription—a bit of advice of the London Company:

"Lastly and chiefly the way to prosper and achieve good success is to make yourselves all of one mind for the good of your country and your own, and to serve and fear God, the giver of all goodness, for every plantation which our Heavenly Father hath not planted shall be rooted out."—*Advice of London Council for Virginia to the Colony—1906.*

Low down on the obelisk, near the base on the four sides is an eagle carved in the granite, with wings outspread standing on a pedestal between two torches. Beneath is a scroll which on the south side, reads:

Jamestown
The First Permanent
Colony of the
English People
The Birthplace of
Virginia
and of
The United States
May 13, 1607.

In similar form are the other inscriptions: Virginia Colony of London, Chartered April 10, 1607, founded Jamestown and sustained Virginia 1607-1624. Another: Representative Government in America began in the First House of Burgesses assembled here July 30, 1619.

Finally, the commemoration inscription: This monument was erected by the United States, A. D. 1907, to commemorate the three hundredth anniversary of the settlement here.

The shaft is about 103 feet high above the base and is surmounted by an aluminum cap.

Exposition Oration.

We have met today to celebrate the opening of the Exposition which itself commemorates the first permanent settlement of men of our stock in Virginia, the first beginning of what has since become this mighty Republic. Three hundred years ago a handful of English adventurers, who had crossed the ocean in what we should now call cockle boats, as clumsy as they were frail, landed in the great wooded wilderness, the Indian-haunted waste, which then stretched down to the water's edge along the entire Atlantic coast. They were not the first men of European race to settle in what is now the United States, for there were already Spanish settlements in Florida and on the head waters of the Rio Grande; and the French, who at almost the same time were struggling up the St. Lawrence, were likewise destined to form permanent settlements on the Great Lakes and in the valley of the mighty Mississippi before the people of English stock went westward of the Alleghenies. Moreover, both the Dutch and the Swedes were shortly to found colonies between the two sets of English colonies, those that grew up around the Potomac, and those that grew up on what is now the New England coast. Nevertheless, this landing at Jamestown possesses for us of the United States an altogether peculiar significance and this without regard to our several origins. The men who landed at Jamestown and those who, thirteen years later, landed at Plymouth, all of English stock, and their fellow-settlers who during the next few decades streamed in after them, were those who took the lead in shaping the life history of this people in the Colonial and Revolutionary days. It was they who bent into definite shape our nation while it was still young enough most easily, most readily, to take on the characteristics which were to become part of its permanent life habit.

Yet let us remember that while this early English Colonial stock has left deeper than all others upon our national life the mark of its strong twin individualities, the mark of the Cavalier and of the Puritan, nevertheless this stock, not only from its environment but also from the presence with it of other stocks, almost from the beginning began to be differentiated strongly from any English people. As I have already said, about the time the first English settlers landed here the Frenchman and the Spaniard, the Swede and the Dutchman, also came hither as permanent dwellers, who left their seed behind them to help shape and partially to inherit our national life. The German, the Irishman, and the Scotchman came later, but still in Colonial times. Before the outbreak of the Revolution the American people, not only because of their surroundings, physical and spiritual, but because of the mixture of blood that had already begun to take place, represented a new and distinct ethnic type. This type has never been fixed in blood. All through the Colonial days new waves of immigration from time to time swept hither across the ocean, now from one country, now from another. The same thing has gone on ever since our birth as a nation; and for the last sixty years the tide of immigration has been at the full. The newcomers are soon absorbed into our eager national life, and are radically and profoundly changed thereby, the rapidity of their assimilation being marvellous. But each group of newcomers, as it adds to the life, also changes somewhat, and this change and growth and development have gone on steadily, generation by generation, throughout three centuries.

The pioneers of our people who first landed on these shores on that eventful day three centuries ago had before them a task which, during the early years, was of heartbreaking danger and difficulty. The conquest of a new continent is iron work. People who dwell in old civilizations and find that therein so much of humanity's lot is hard are apt to complain against the conditions as being solely due to man and to speak as if life could be made easy and simple if there were but a virgin continent in which to work. It is true that the pioneer life was simpler, but it was certainly not easier. As a matter of fact, the first work of the pioneers in taking possession of a lonely wilderness is so rough, so hard, so dangerous, that all but the strongest spirits fail. The early iron days of such a conquest search out alike the weak in body and the weak in soul. In the warfare against the rugged sternness of primeval nature only those can conquer who are themselves unconquerable. It is not until the first bitter years have passed that the life becomes easy enough to invite a mass of newcomers, and so great are the risk, hardship, and toil of the early years that there always exists a threat of lapsing back from civilization.

The history of the pioneers of Jamestown, of the founders of Virginia, illustrates the truth of all this. Famine and pestilence and war menaced the little band of daring men who had planted themselves alone on the edge of a frowning continent. Moreover, as men ever find, whether in the tiniest frontier community or in the vastest and most highly organized and complex civilized society, their worst foes were in their own bosoms. Dissension, distrust, the inability of some to work and the unwillingness of others, jealousy, arrogance and envy, folly and laziness; in short, all the shortcomings with which we have to grapple now were faced by those pioneers, and at moments threatened their whole enterprise with absolute ruin. It was some time before the ground on which they had landed supported them, in spite of its potential fertility, and they looked across the sea for supplies. At one moment so hopeless did they become, that the whole colony embarked, and was only saved from abandoning the country by the opportune arrival of help from abroad.

At last they took root in the land, and were already prospering when the Pilgrims landed at Plymouth. In a few years a great inflow of settlers began. Four of the present states of New England were founded. Virginia waxed apace. The Carolinas grew up to the south of it, and Maryland to the north of it. The Dutch colonies between, which had already absorbed the Swedish, were in their turn absorbed by the English. Pennsylvania was founded and, later still, Georgia. There were many wars with the Indians and with the dauntless captains whose banners bore the lilies of France. At last the British flag flew without a rival in all eastern North America. Then came the successful struggle for national independence.

For half a century after we became a separate nation there was comparatively little immigration to this country. Then the tide once again set hither, and has flowed in ever-increasing size until in each of the last three years a greater number of people came to these shores than had landed on them during the entire Colonial period. Generation by generation these people have been absorbed into the national life. Generally their sons, almost always their grandsons, are indistinguishable from one another and from their fellow-Americans descended from the Colonial stock. For all alike the problems of our existence are fundamentally the same, and for all alike these problems change from generation to generation.

Copyright by Underwood and Underwood, N. Y.
AMONG THE HYDAH INDIANS — ALASKA.

In the Colonial period, and for at least a century after its close, the conquest of the continent, the expansion of our people westward to the Alleghenies, then to the Mississippi, then to the Pacific, was always one of the most important tasks, and sometimes the most important, in our national life. Behind the first settlers the conditions grew easier, and in the older-settled regions of all the colonies life speedily assumed much of comfort and something of luxury; and though generally it was on a much more democratic basis than life in the Old World, it was by no means democratic when judged by our modern standards; and here and there, as in the tidewater regions of Virginia, a genuine aristocracy grew and flourished. But the men who first broke ground in the virgin wilderness, whether on the Atlantic coast or in the interior, fought hard for mere life. In the early stages the frontiersman had to battle with the savage, and when the savage was vanquished there remained the harder strain of war with the hostile forces of soil and climate, with flood, fever, and famine. There was sickness and bitter weather; there were no roads; there was a complete lack of all but the very roughest and most absolute necessaries. Under such circumstances the men and women who made ready the continent for civilization were able themselves to spend but little time in doing aught but the rough work which was to make smooth the ways of their successors. In consequence, observers whose insight was spoiled by lack of sympathy always found both the settlers and their lives unattractive and repellant. In Martin Chuzzlewit the description of America, culminating in the description of the frontier town of Eden, was true and life-like from the standpoint of one content to look merely at the outer shell; and yet it was a community like Eden that gave birth to Abraham Lincoln; it was men such as were therein described from whose loins Andrew Jackson sprang.

Hitherto each generation among us has had its allotted task, now heavier, now lighter. In the Revolutionary War the business was to achieve independence. Immediately afterwards there was an even more momentous task; that to achieve the national unity and the capacity for orderly development, without which our liberty, our independence, would have been a curse and not a blessing. In each of these two contests, while there were many great leaders from many different States, it is but fair to say that the foremost place was taken by the soldiers and the statesmen of Virginia; and to Virginia was reserved the honor of producing the hero of both movements, the hero of the war and of the peace that made good the results of the war—George Washington; while the two great political tendencies of the time can be symbolized by the names of two other great Virginians—Jefferson and Marshall —from one of whom we inherit the abiding trust in the people which is the foundation stone of democracy, and from the other the power to develop on behalf of the people a coherent and powerful government, a genuine and representative nationality.

The corner stone of the Republic lies in our treating each man on his worth as a man, paying no heed to his creed, his birthplace, or his occupation; asking not whether he is rich or poor; whether he labors with head or hand; asking only whether he acts decently and honorably in the various relations of his life, whether he behaves well to his family, to his neighbors, to the State. We base our regard for each man on the essentials and not the accidents. We judge him not by his profession, but by his deeds; by his conduct, not by what he has acquired of this world's goods. Other republics have fallen because the citizens gradually grew to consider the interests of a class before the interests of the whole; for when such was the case it mattered little whether it was the poor who plundered the rich or the rich who exploited the poor; in either event the end of the republic was at hand. We are resolute in our purpose not to fall into such a pit. This great Republic of ours shall never become the Government of plutocracy, and it shall never become the Government of a mob. God willing, it shall remain what our fathers who founded it meant it to be —a Government in which each man stands on his worth as a man, where each is given the largest personal liberty consistent with securing the well-being of the whole, and where. so far as in us lies, we strive continually to secure for each man such equality of opportunity that in the strife of life he may have a fair chance to show the stuff that is in him. We are proud of our schools and of the trained intelligence they give our children the opportunity to acquire. But what we care for most is the character of the average man; for we believe that if the average of character in the individual citizen is sufficiently high, if he possesses those qualities which make him worthy of respect in his family life and in his work outside, as well as the qualities which fit him for success in the hard struggle of actual existence—that if such is the character of our individual citizenship, there is literally no height of triumph unattainable in this vast experiment of government by, of, and for a free people.—*From President Roosevelt's speech at the opening of the Jamestown Exposition.*

PUBLIC LIBRARY, BOSTON, MASS.

CHAPTER XVII.

Alaska-Yukon-Pacific Exposition.

The exposition held in Seattle in 1909 commemorated no historical event. It was planned and undertaken wholly for commercial reasons, to emphasize the value of the Pacific trade and help to direct it into American channels, and to exploit the resources of Alaska and the Northwest.

When Secretary Seward bought Alaska for the sum of $7,200,000—which Russia asked to cede it to the United States—there was a general outcry against the expenditure of so much money for a region of glaciers and icefields. One member of Congress was aggressive in attempting to force an investigation as to what portion of the money Seward himself received from Russia for negotiating such a transaction, considering the whole affair insupportable. Since 1880 Alaskan commerce has amounted to $292,000,000. Not more than one person in a thousand in the United States comprehends the tremendous resources in this northern territory. Even those most familiar with the region cannot estimate them, for they lie for the most part untouched. The discovery of gold in the Klondike in 1896 and in Nome in 1899 started the tide of venturesome humanity northward, and while more returned spent and broken than realized their hopes, yet this constant journeying back and forth led to a more general understanding of the facts concerning Alaska. Since those astonishing years, several towns have sprung up along the southern coast and every year the number of people who choose to spend vacation weeks skirting along the inland passage or journeying up the Yukon, increases. Magnificent scenery, comparable only with that of Switzerland in point of mountains, and Scandinavia in point of fjords, repays the traveler. Primitive Indian villages. salmon fisheries, whaling stations and totem poles offer sufficiently novel features. Sitka, once the capital, rich in history and beautiful in setting, is worth going far to see. Juneau, nestling at the foot of a lofty mountain, is astir with importance as the political center of the territory. Skagway, "home of the north wind," is the most northern point visited by those who choose to cling to the shores rather than leave the comfort of their steamer for the inconveniences of inland travel in a new country.

However, it was not scenic advantages that the Exposition of 1909 attempted to reveal. This exhibition was directed by hard-headed business men who never lost sight of the objective point, to so graphically display the opportunities Alaska offers the homeseeker and capitalist that sturdy spirits might be prompted to settle there or to make investments.

Seattle was the natural place for the holding of such an exhibition. In the first place, her phenomenal growth resulted from the exodus to the gold-fields. Here the gold-seekers were fitted out for the exposures of their journey; here they returned, when successful, to spend some of the precious metal they had won. From a town of 40,000, within eight years Seattle became a city of 200,000, and the building carried on during that period amazed a nation. But the advantage of being the gateway to Alaska is but one of many possessed by this enterprising center. Its position is enviable. It stands on Puget Sound, the finest body of deep water in the western hemisphere. While many harbors have been created at great cost, Seattle possesses miles of natural wharfage adequate for the largest ocean vessels. At the present time the government is digging a canal which shall admit ships from the Sound to the fresh water lakes within the city itself, Lake Union and Lake Washington. When this was first begun, it was advocated that our battleships could thus come into fresh water and be freer of barnacles without the costly scraping. Far more important than that will be the fact that materials can thus be transported to the very factories and manufactures which will spring up around these lakes.

Furthermore, Seattle is convenient to the trade of the Orient. Ships from Japan and China are constantly in and out the harbor. The trade with Australia is already considerable and it was hoped to stimulate greater commercial intercourse with Central and South Americas.

It is doubtful whether an American city rivals Seattle in its situation. Built on a series of hills, it brings to mind

Scriptural phraseology that a city so placed cannot be hid. Its lights are visible many miles away. In front, the Sound; across this great sheet of quiet water, a line of firs against the sky and above them, the Cascades in eternal loveliness. In another direction lie the placid lakes and in the sky beyond Lake Washington, Mount Ranier, 14,500 feet high, suddenly appears, huge, round, like an inverted sugar-bowl.

The campus of the University of Washington was chosen for the exposition site. Nothing man could do to produce a beautiful spectacle could compare with what nature had already done. For this reason moderation characterized all adornment of grounds. The ones promoting the enterprise determined that funds expended should not be wasted but contribute to the permanent welfare of the state university. Several of the buildings erected were designed for future purposes when the fair should be concluded.

Twelve exhibit palaces were constructed: Government Building, Alaska Building, Yukon, Hawaii, and the Philippine Buildings; Forestry, Fine Arts, Agricultural and Horticultural, Mines, Fisheries, Manufactures and Machinery Buildings.

European nations were asked to exhibit whatever would illustrate their interest in Pacific trade. There was an earnest effort made to have every land that faces the Pacific Ocean represented. Save for its own exhibit and that of Alaska and the Philippines, the government contributed nothing. It was desired by the promoters that the exposition receive no outside aid.

Ground was broken on the 250-acre campus for the first building June 1, 1907. "Ready on Time" was the slogan. President Roosevelt sent the following message, being unable personally to take part in the celebration of the work actually begun: "You can say in strongest terms that I am a staunch believer in the great Pacific Northwest and the Alaska-Yukon country. It has a future of unlimited opportunity, backed up by limitless resources and possibilities. Seattle and other cities of Puget Sound and the Northwest are fortunate in facing the Pacific Ocean, with its vast commerce, and having everything to make them great and prosperous centers of population, trade and influence. The Alaska-Yukon-Pacific Exposition will be typical of the spirit and progress of the section it represents, and I wish it great success."

The center of the Alaska Building was the magnet that attracted all eyes. Upon black velvet and under a secure case was exhibited more than one million dollars worth of gold in nuggets. It was shown that in the last twelve years Alaska had produced enough gold to make a pile of twenty-dollar pieces ten miles high—twice as high as the Himalayas. Salmon exported in 1908 realized nearly $11,000,000; other fish reached half a million; copper is an important mineral and steadily increasing in annual yield.

British Columbia has unguessed resources. It is estimated that it could supply enough coal for the civilized world for one hundred years to come. Only one-tenth of its arable land has been taken up and but a small portion of that is under cultivation, yet its fruit yield amounts to $4,000,000 per year.

The government made special exhibits of its lighthouses, coast surveys and safeguards for navigation. These are important in view of merely Alaskan trade which amounts to $50,000,000 per year. The Philippine exhibit attracted many spectators. Fine and costly woods are here obtained. The pearl fisheries are important. Native huts were reproduced. A relief map of the islands was instructive.

Fresh pineapple was served by native girls in the Hawaiian Building at the slight charge of ten cents, made merely to defray the cost. Those who tasted the fruit which had ripened under favorable conditions can testify to how different it was from that gathered long before it is ready for general shipment. A sugar palace, reproducing in miniature the palace of native kings before the new government was instituted, attracted much attention and was sadly encroached upon before the summer ended. It was made entirely of native brown sugar. The rice industry was well illustrated.

The Forestry Building outdid the one built previously at Portland. This was 320 by 144 feet and the roof was supported by tree trunks forty feet in height and five in diameter. It would have been a simple thing to have procured immense trees for this purpose, but the promoters of the fair refused to consider such an idea. They wished to use logs the size of those cut every day into lumber at the Tacoma mills. The slogan, "The truth is good enough," was constantly seen at this exposition, and the moderation exercised elicited the admiration of those who saw it far more than any extravagant displays could have done. As a matter of fact, those who had contracted to supply the necessary number of logs found it hard to find enough whose diameter should not exceed five feet, but they were bound by their contract to eliminate all others. This building has since become the home of the Forestry Department of the University.

Machinery Hall was a place where great machines might be watched crushing rock to free the ore, or achieving some other end. It seemed unlike other buildings of a similar purpose in that it was a busy place where operations were in the doing. The lumber industry which employs one hundred thousand men in the state of Washington, was illustrated in all stages at this fair. The building has become the home of the engineering department. It was built of solid brick.

The Auditorium, a brick structure costing $300,000, has become the Assembly Hall of the campus. The Fine Arts Building, costing $200,000, has been taken over by the chemistry department. It was made fireproof. The Arctic Brotherhood Building is now a museum of Natural History and a fraternity house for Alaskan students.

The western states particularly made fine displays.

In every way the Alaska-Yukon-Pacific Exposition was successful. As at Portland, when all the bills were paid, there was still money remaining. More than 42,000 people were on the grounds daily and they have done much to make the wonders of the west known to those who could not be present. Although there is not likely to be any unnatural growth such as that which preceded 1909, there is a steady stream of people pressing westward to find new homes. The mining regions, agricultural centers, the apple districts of Idaho, Washington and Oregon, the citrus regions of California, all receive their share.

Of the trade of the Pacific, which amounts to $4,000,000,000, it was stated at this exposition that the United States has one-fifth. Commercial intercourse with Australia is very satisfactory, this country supplying an important lumber market. It is hoped to stimulate and extend the trade with South American countries as well as with the republics of Central America.

CHAPTER XVIII.

Panama-Pacific Exposition.

Aside from the Pan-American Exposition, the intent of which was to unite more closely the nations and peoples of the American continents, and the Alaskan-Yukon Exposition, which was intended to illustrate the vast resources of Alaska and the Northwest, all expositions held in the United States have commemorated some historical event of signal importance. The Panama-Pacific Exposition, on the contrary, commemorated a physical achievement, whose influence carried with it world-wide significance. By opening new trade routes and modifying old ones, the Panama Canal has affected the commerce of every nation, to a greater or less degree.

The history of the Canal, conceived as early as 1520 by Charles V. of Spain, seriously begun by a French company in 1878, has become a familiar story. During the years in which the United States government carried on the work of construction, and before this was actually begun—when, indeed, the Sanitary Commission was making the surrounding region suitable for habitation—questions of policy, expediency and safety were argued frequently before Congress and were discussed by the public press throughout the land. Suffice it to say that the cost of the Canal, approximating $400,000,000, was greater than any previous expenditure made by this nation for a single achievement.

Several cities contended for the honor of the international exposition which was to celebrate the Canal completed. It was due to the enterprise and activity of San Francisco's leading citizens that Congress accorded it to the metropolis of the Pacific Coast.

An area comprising six hundred and twenty-five acres, extending for more than two miles along the water front, was chosen as the site, and on the 14th of October, 1911, President Taft turned the first spade of earth on the grounds. On the 2d of February the year following the nations of the world were invited to participate in the great fair designed to give fitting observance to the triumph of man over nature in making the long-cherished dream of the Canal a reality.

The general plan for exposition buildings was entrusted to an Architectural Commission, which at once set aside earlier methods of treating each exhibit palace as a separate unit. Instead, eight of the fifteen palaces were designed almost as though comprising one structure. Some idea can be gained of this by mentally picturing a vast structure, one-half mile in length, one-quarter mile in width, its walls pierced by courts, one longitudinal and three lateral. At one end of this gigantic block the great Palace of Machinery was located; at the other end, separated by a beautiful lagoon, the Palace of Fine Arts. Near by were placed Transportation and Horticultural buildings and Festival Hall.

The outbreak of the war in Europe during the summer of 1914 caused various foreign countries to withdraw from participation; yet, in spite of the dubious situation, several countries erected buildings and supplied a wide variety of exhibits.

The series of courts which allowed visitors to pass from one Exhibit Palace to another without encountering the winds which in summer months are often disagreeable in San Francisco, added materially to the comfort of all, and their arrangement and decorations rendered them very pleasing to the eye. At the center of the great group of buildings first mentioned the Court of the Universe, six hundred by nine hundred feet in size, furnished seating capacity for seven thousand people. In its midst was a sunken garden, which, when the Exposition opened in February of 1915, was paved with rose-colored hyacinths. Their beauty and fragrance, together with the rose-colored vapor wafted from numerous urns around the Court, combined to make this a veritable dream when seen by evening lights.

To the right, and reached through a small court of access, was the Court of Ages—a Gothic shrine; to the left, the Court of the Four Seasons. The Tower of Jewels, rising to a height of 435 feet and surmounted by a huge sphere, gave accent to the architectural scheme.

To the east, somewhat removed from the Exhibit Palaces and the Pavilions of States and Nations, reached the Zone—

home of the amusement concessions, covering an area of sixty-five acres.

A carefully conceived color scheme, made to harmonize with sea, sky and landscape, enhanced the beauty of the Dream City. Even the sand sprinkled over drives and roadways was burned to give it the desired tone.

Were one to inquire what was the dominant note sounded by this Exposition, set by the rim of land upon which the setting sun gives his daily parting benediction, it might be answered that those who planned this City of Dreams harked back to the circumstances that first pointed westward—to the first ventures of the white race thither; to the aspirations which led to discovery; to the tragedies of exploration. The coming of the white man to America, his search for the fabled Fountain of Youth, and his vain quest for the fabulous wealth of the new land, mirrored in a play popular in Elizabethan days, wherein one enthusiast exclaims to another: "Why, man, in that country their very frying pans are made of gold!" The coming of the pioneers across the plains and over mountains—such and kindred themes suggested themselves immediately to the minds of those at work upon this Exposition. Sculptors exalted these stories in stone and painters put them on canvas. Pirates, buccaneers, priests, philosophers, explorers, pioneers—all who played a part in the movement which terminated in the union of the two oceans, were given prominent place.

The Fountain of Energy was immediately to be observed upon entering the main gate. The group set forth the unconquerable spirit in which the Canal was built. Energy, Lord of the Isthmian Way—a triumphant youth, mounted upon a charger, with arms extended as though to command a passage through the rugged backbone of the continent, rose from the pedestal of the fountain. From his shoulders sprang Fame and Valor, whose trumpets heralded his coming. In the basin of the fountain were four sculptured groups symbolizing the North and South Seas, and the Atlantic and Pacific Oceans.

From the Fountain of Energy, the way led direct to the Court of the Universe, above whose entrance rose the Tower of Jewels, Equestrian statues of Pizarro and Cortez placed in front. Within this Court were two noble mural fountains, of

El Dorado and Youth. El Dorado was a fabled king of the Aztecs; he was believed to rule a kingdom paved with gold. The Fountain of Youth recalled the search of Ponce de Leon. Surmounting arches which marked east and west entrances to this Court were the great sculptured groups—Nations of the East, the Orient, and Nations of the West, the Occident. A giant elephant, flanked by camel riders, priests and slaves and warriors, too, upon proud Arabian horses, lavish and ornate, conveyed a sense of Oriental power and a trace of its religious mysticism. Across the Court and contrasted strongly with this group was another—an ox team and prairie schooner, flanked by outriders, mounted American Indians, French and Spanish pioneers. This portrayed the westward march of the pioneer across the American continent.

In this Court were also appropriately placed the Fountains of Rising and Setting Sun. No figure was more loved than the female form with head drooped, and wings folded, suggesting repose at close of day. The Fountain of the Rising Sun symbolized aspiration, with which all things are possible.

The Court of Ages was a mighty epic poem expressing by medium of sculpture the theory of evolution. In its center was placed the Fountain of Earth, symbolizing the birth of life and its struggle upward and onward. In the Court of the Four Seasons, contrasting with the evolution of man, a bounteous nature was depicted bestowing her wealth upon him and ministering always to his needs. At the entrance stood the Fountain of Ceres, and four fountains of the seasons adorned the corners of the Court.

No other exposition has ever emphasized mural paintings to the extent that these were brought out at the San Francisco Exposition. Here were shown the finest conceptions of the foremost formal decorative painters of the age. Huge panels 125 feet long and from ten to fifteen feet in width ornamented the vast recesses of triumphal arches or formed the end of long colonnades.

The murals by Brangwyn were most striking. The subjects of these four famous productions were the elements—Earth, Air, Fire and Water. They revealed the elements in their relation to man, indicating the services which they render humanity. Two panels exemplified each subject, as for example, in treating Air, one of the panels depicted a huge windmill, rising amid a field of golden grain. The garments of workers are tossed to and fro; leaves are flying; the mill is being turned and grain ground for the harvesters. The other panel pictured hunters, whose arrows, together with the flight of birds, indicated the element of Air. Two panels devoted to Grapes and Fruit Pickers symbolized Earth, with its copious yield for mankind. Lavish nature is displayed. In treating the element Water, Brangwyn was able to show the muscled fishermen he adequately paints. They are hauling in their nets from the sea. Clouds above are about to pour down their moisture upon the earth. The companion panel revealed a fountain, whither people come to fill their jugs. Always the people in these murals are peasants—those of brawn who toil for their daily bread. The Brangwyn murals are now the possession of the Palace of Fine Arts in the Exposition city.

The largest and most significant murals, however, were those expressing the spirit of courage which led to the discovery of the western continent and made the triumphal waterway possible. They did honor to the endurance and toil which bequeathed so much to posterity. Two were devoted entirely to the Canal and the union of the two oceans.

"The Western race is indicated by pioneers and laborers who have wrested civilization from the wilderness, a vigorous group; but while they have accomplished this result, they have all but crowded the American Indian from his native land—in spite of his vain though courageous resistance. . . . In these Dodge murals we find the Herculean effort involved in the construction of the Panama Canal, with its record of disaster, death, strife against surpassing obstacles, spiritualized—almost immortalized. In the panel *Discovery*, for example, the figure of Balboa, booted and holding high the flag of Spain as he gazes toward a new ocean, and from an eminence confronts the figure of an Indian who, in the stern and taut personality of the adventurer, foresees as with a touch of impending prophecy the doom of his own race."

Mention should be made in any consideration, however cursory, of Childe Hassam's charming panel *Fruits and Flow-*

ers, placed over the entrance to the Palace of Education. It typifies the wealth of these in California.

"Vitality and exuberance, guided by a distinct sense of order, were the dominant notes of the Arts of the Exposition and pre-eminently of the sculpture. It proclaimed with no uncertain voice that 'all is well with this Western world'—it is not too much to claim that it supplied the humanizing ideality for which the Exposition stood—the daring, boastful, masterful spirits of enterprise and imagination—the frank enjoyment of physical beauty and effort—the fascination of danger; as well as the gentler, more reverent of our attributes, to this mysterious problem that is Life."

When we turn from the pleasing architecture, inspiring statuary and masterful painting to the exhibits which make up so large a part of any exposition, the opening of the war and its attendant absorption prevented these from being either as satisfying or as varied as would otherwise have been the case. The mighty strides of science were visible in the great Hall given over entirely to Motor Transportation. Ten years before scarcely any object there displayed could have been shown with any such degree of perfection and many were still unknown. Previous expositions have shown us every ore the veins of earth can yield, but in the machinery devised for obtaining and preparing gems and minerals for use, every ten years shows marked progress.

In manufactured articles, whatever the United States could furnish was widely exhibited. France made a heroic effort to send what she could hurriedly provide—her country invaded and the lives of her people in danger. Italy, Switzerland and the Scandinavian countries did what they were able and the Netherlands made a pleasing showing.

There is no question, however, that the abiding contributions to the future, and especially to the West, were in the realm of architecture and art. For the first time in the extreme West was an international exposition provided and the exquisite beauty of the Dream City will only be understood by those who saw. For years to come along the Pacific Slope effects of its lessons will be found, and upon a rising generation the rare opportunity it provided is certain to bear fruit a hundred fold.

AMERICAN PAINTING

CHAPTER XIX.

EARLY AMERICAN PAINTERS.

ART never timidly raised its head amid more austere and forbidding circumstances than in colonial America. It is idle to say that an untouched continent with limitless wilds peopled by naïve and dusky folk should have stimulated some latent genius to produce new and surprising pictures. The fact was that the early settlers did not look upon these sights with the sympathetic eye of painter or poet. Having sought religious freedom on the rocky shores of New England, the Puritans were soon absorbed in denying to others the privilege for which they had risked their all—that of worshipping as they desired. Their whole life became engrossed in a belief so exacting and prohibitive that it deemed all the gracious attributes of life worldly and hence reprehensible. Having torn away from the Established Church because of its ceremony and costly accessories, they abhorred these and looked upon pictures as allurements of Satan. Their reading was in the main confined to religious books and treatises, their music to religious hymns; while drama and art were regarded as insupportable. The Quakers, similarly, from whose sect the first American painter sprang, while less austere and certainly less inclined to judge their neighbors, were people of utmost simplicity. No better illustrations of their lack of indulgence could be cited than the stories told concerning West, who as a little child discovered by his Quaker mother with a crude sketch of his sleeping baby sister, feared to show her the paper lest he incur her deep displeasure; and again when a youth determined upon pursuing his beloved painting, the meeting of Friends held to consider his course wherein his parents struggled with the doubting villagers until these were inclined to accept the father's firm belief that the boy had a God-given gift and the right to exercise it.

Benjamin West (1738-1820) was born in Springfield,

Pennsylvania. Without contact whatsoever with pictures, he early gave indication of a strong gift for drawing. The amusing story of his first paint brush, made from the hairs he pulled from the kitten's fur and his paints, gathered from surprising sources—blue, for example, from the laundry indigo, has been many times related. Self-taught, he began as a boy to paint portraits in Philadelphia and later went to New York. An unusual opportunity to go to Europe as companion to young Allen gave him a chance to visit Italian art centers, where rumors of the gifted, self-instructed American painter won him much attention. Fortunately this did not unsettle his own ideas or conceptions. Taken to see the Apollo Belvedere by those who wished to watch its effect upon one untrammeled by conventional opinions, they were shocked to hear his first exclamation that it looked like a Mohawk Chief! Realizing how deeply he had perplexed his friends, he explained that with similar ease of motion and freedom of muscle the lithe and perfectly developed Red Men glide along and by his sincerity persuaded his friends that his criticism was justifiable as well as original.

Removing to England, West shortly fell under the king's patronage. It must always be granted that the story of his life reads like a fairy tale. The distance from the rough Quaker village on the American frontier to the position of Court painter was quickly spanned. Until the closing years of his life Fortune smiled upon the first American painter and favored him.

It was he who suggested to King George the advisability of establishing an Academy of Art under royal patronage and thus led to the founding of the Royal Academy in 1768. After the death of Reynolds, West succeeded as its president.

Primarily a portrait painter, West undertook several historical pieces. Best known among them is the Death of Wolfe. In painting this picture he called out warm criticism on every hand because instead of garbing his figures in classical drapery, he set them on canvas in costumes true to the age. This one innovation led ultimately to a revolution in art.

The needs of a new hospital founded in Philadelphia were presented to West who gave answer that he had no money, but would paint a picture for it. He took for his subject Christ

Healing the Sick. Such an alluring price was offered for it when completed that the struggling artist could not refuse, but he made a replica* for the hospital which was exhibited for some time, the admission fee accruing to the hospital fund and increasing it by several thousand pounds.

West's gallery in London was always open to American students and his kindly interest and advice widely sought. In the later years of his life the king's failing health caused the withdrawal of royal favor which seriously curtailed his resources. Loss of family, friends and fortune saddened his advanced life and hastened his death.

Today the art student finds more to avoid than emulate in West's pictures. His canvases were unwieldy in size, crowded with figures and his paint was too thin. Nevertheless, it would be difficult to cite a more successful career among modern painters and his influence in various directions was used on the side of progress. Particularly did his generous attitude towards struggling painters and the recognition of their work tend to stimulate this wholesale sentiment in England. His portraits are regarded as second only to those of Reynolds and Gainsborough, while superior to those of Romney.

John Singleton Copley (1737-1815) belonged to New England. It has often been stated that he also was self-taught, but this must be modified to the extent that his stepfather gave him such instruction as he was able, being an engraver who had himself painted several portraits. Moreover, Copley had opportunity to study such pictures as Boston then afforded. Upon the outbreak of the Revolution he went to Italy, where his family later joined him. Subsequently he removed to England. While never enjoying the popularity or good fortune of West, he was nevertheless in favor as a portrait painter. Although his tints were praised by West as equal to those of Titian, these have faded now to whiteness, thus changing entirely the former appearance of his work.

Copley did not leave America until after his thirtieth year, thus his work falls into two natural divisions; the portraits painted during his early life and his paintings after study of European models. Among the early portraits those of John Adams and John Hancock are best known. While in Italy

---
* The copy of a picture by the artist.

he executed a group of his own family which is pleasing today in spite of its stiffness and lack of flexibility. Among his historic pictures the Death of Lord Chatham and the Siege of Gibraltar are most important.

The third and last of these early portrait painters of first rank was Gilbert Stuart (1755-1828), born in Rhode Island. He was very different in temperament from the others. Copley was the aristocrat, West the broad-minded, kindly painter. Stuart was eccentric and lacking in what might be indefinitely termed moral responsibility. In financial matters he was as little to be depended upon as the playwright Sheridan. Perhaps no sentence summarizes his shortcomings better than one used by his biographer that he "would neither settle down nor settle up." Largely self taught, he tramped about in Europe from time to time, never relating to others his experiences. Finally induced to go to West's Gallery, he became his pupil for four years. The master recognized his native ability and overlooked his peculiarities. His particular strength lay in his power to divine the character of his sitter and to render the face true to life. So popular did he become in England that for a time he prospered. Thereupon he summoned his friends to dinner and informed them that his limited quarters forbade his usual entertainment of them simultaneously, but that he had contrived a method for making the matter entirely simple. Seven hat pegs would be placed in his hallway. When the eighth guest repaired thither he would find these filled and be careful to come earlier the next night. This plan was accepted and for some months Stuart dispensed hospitality to his own satisfaction. But life glided along far too smoothly now to gratify him and he set out for Ireland, where he is reported to have spent some time in jail, painting during his incarceration some of the noted of the land. Upon his return to America he produced the two portraits of Washington so well known that it was once humorously remarked should the Father of his Country reappear and fail to resemble the Stuart Portrait, he would be disowned by his countrymen.

Several other painters of this early period, while less eminent, deserve mention. Most of them studied art with West. Among these Charles Wilson Peale (1741-1827) did creditable work. Another pupil of West's was Robert Fulton, who after painting several portraits became more interested in boats and navigation. John Trumbull (1756-1843) is remembered for his pleasing portrait of Alexander Hamilton and more particularly perhaps for his four historical pictures produced to fill compartments in the Rotunda of the Capitol in Washington. It may well be doubted whether these would today bring the $32,000 he received for them.

Landscapes had been attempted by the first painters, but these were copies of European prints as a rule rather than sketches from nature. Among the first to catch the charm that natural beauty possesses and to put this upon canvas was Thomas Doughty (1793-1856). His view of the Hudson is gratifying today when landscape painting in America has become elevated beyond the dreams of those early years.

Durand and Thomas Cole were noteworthy among the earliest landscape painters. Durand worked first as an engraver, pounding out copper pennies for his plates and originating his own designs. After a sojourn in Europe he turned to portraits and afterwards to landscapes. Cole, though of English birth, became identified with the American school. He chose lofty themes: the rise and fall of nations, the swift passing of life, often producing several scenes to complete one series. In his Course of Empire he included five pictures, these showing the same general scene, a harbor and mountains protectingly near. A little village is founded, develops into a prosperous community, is pillaged by invaders and finally falls in ruins. The Voyage of Life was depicted in four pictures, these exemplifying childhood, youth, maturity, old age. Allegories of this description were much in favor and Cole's productions were quickly purchased. But it is in his simple sketches of the Catskills that he is best seen.

The early group of landscape painters became known as the Hudson River or White Mountain School. Among them were Rossiter, Kensett, Whittredge, Cropsey and Richards. Some of Whittredge's sketches of trees, with light piercing through them to moss-covered rocks, are particularly good. Richards made sketches around Lake George and in the White Mountains. Although his flowers are accurately done from a botanical standpoint, the harmony and sense of distance is sacrificed to that end.

The Hudson River School culminated in the work of Wyant, Martin and Inness. Wyant was limited in his scope, liking best to paint rolling country meadows flanked by tall, slender trees. Martin's best work was done in the Adirondacks. Greater than either was Inness, varied in his themes, versatile in his treatment.

George Inness (1825-1894) was born on the Hudson. As a child and youth he was delicate in health and for this reason the more easily gained his father's consent to his study of art. Although he was sent to a teacher for instruction he was never able to follow others or work in ways other than his own. He loved the meadows and lived for some time near the marshes of New Jersey, in sight of flat, moist districts frequented by wild fowl. He went to Europe several times, less to study than to compare methods and styles of painting and thus better arrive at conclusions regarding his own work. The second time he visited France he fell under the charm of the Barbizon painters, who influenced him, although he never imitated them.

Inness was a deep thinker and subject to the artist's moods of intense power and corresponding despair. When under the spell of his possibilities he could paint ceaselessly for fifteen hours together—talking often with congenial friends as he worked. At other times he was restless and at war with prevailing ideas of the age, scoffing at the folly of attaching value to medals and prizes bestowed by juries and committees.

"Work, work, do your best. If the world does not then appreciate you, what satisfaction can a diploma or a medal bring? They are only the recognition of a few men who appreciate you anyhow, and they go to so many who are not worthy of them that they do not carry any real significance to those who may deserve them. Pass your verdict upon yourself if you are capable of criticising yourself. The verdict of the world will be passed in due time, and it will be a just one, even if it does not sustain that of prize committees and juries of award."

This man of moods found his unfailing relief in nature, and his health was improved and his years prolonged by his tramps over hill and dale, by river and mountain. The public did not at once understand him and inferior ability was valued above his own. Yet before his life closed he had won his way and his pictures met a ready demand.

Just as he himself could not be taught by others, neither could he instruct those who would have chosen to come to him. Indeed, he did not believe in the teaching of art. He held that "the purpose of the painter is simply to reproduce in other minds the impression which a scene has made upon him. A work of art does not appeal to the intellect. It does not appeal to the moral sense. Its aim is not to instruct, not to edify, but to awaken an emotion."

A friend whose studio was near his own relates that upon many occasions Inness would drop in upon him, feverish in his attempt to fathom the mystery of art, or better, perhaps, the mystery of life. "What is it all about—art, painting? For what reason do men paint away their lives?" And then some ray of light would dawn upon him and thus did he once define art under similar circumstances. "Art is the endeavor on the part of Mind (Mind being the creative faculty) to express, through the senses, ideas of the great principles of unity."

Inness' work falls into two periods. In his earlier years he was painstaking and careful of details. Afterwards he strove for general effects. His later work is more generally prized, indicating deeper thought, broader knowledge and maturity.

While he painted in all seasons and every hour of the day, he was most fond of the rich colors of regal autumn. The names of his pictures give but slight indication of his work, being indefinite for the most part: An Old Roadway; A Summer Morning; A Sunset; A Day in June—these are important among them. Sometimes they are merely called A Landscape.

CHAPTER XX.

Recent American Painters.

There having been as yet no schools of art developed and generally recognized in this country, it is necessary to consider modern painters individually. Certain of them have been associated with others of lesser ability who have sympathized with their conceptions and adhered to their principles, but not in sufficient numbers to give rise to a school of painting. This is to be explained in part by the fact that several of our most gifted painters have felt obliged to spend their years in the art centers of the Old World, because these supplied an atmosphere stimulating to them, and unfortunately, too, because America has often been tardy in recognizing home talent and left her artists to seek commissions and patronage in other lands. Beyond these reasons, it must never be forgotten that the traditions and associations of old countries are lacking here and, although this is advantageous when viewed from certain standpoints, it presents corresponding disadvantages.

As the country becomes more settled and the pioneering of a continent belongs to the past instead of the present, beyond doubt the spirit of the American people will foster the fine arts to a degree unknown in the world for centuries. The last twenty-five years have witnessed a remarkable change in the general attitude toward the arts of peace and the next twenty-five are likely to show marked advance over anything so far indicated in our civilization. Generally diffused prosperity is likely to provide the means for home adornment and civic embellishment beyond that ordinarily found in European countries. Once the desire for such manifestations of culture be aroused, it may easily entail surprising results.

Elihu Vedder was born in New York in 1836, of Dutch parentage. It was expected that he would become a merchant, or perhaps follow the profession of his father—a dentist. However, the young Elihu gave evidence of no liking for either career. It was soon observed that he "chewed sticks into paint brushes" and invested all his spending money in paints. Finally his father reluctantly consented to his receiving instruction in drawing and he made fair progress. Thrown largely upon his own initiative by the death of his mother and withdrawal of his father to Cuba, as a youth Vedder traveled in Europe, spending several years in Italy. He returned home to enlist in the army upon the outbreak of the Civil War, but owing to a slight disability resulting from an accidental discharge of a gun in his arm years before, he was not accepted for field service.

His sketches and paintings did not attract particular attention until he painted the "Lair of the Sea-Serpent" during a visit to his father—then in Florida. The mysterious creature was felt by all who viewed it to be symbolic of the subtle ocean, unfathomable, direful, alluring. Another early and characteristic painting was the Questioner of the Sphinx, with a meaning but half revealed.

Perhaps his greatest work has been his illustrations for the Rubaiyat produced in 1884. Lacking color, merely drawings in black and white, these give proof of Vedder's originality and creative genius. They also possess the strange fascination peculiar to his work, always appealing to the mind, always as vague and mysterious as life itself. Never have illustrations blended more perfectly with the spirit of a production than his. First Omar, the Persian poet, is pictured with his friends, gazing down at the student, the theologian, the warrior, and the miser—these typifying humanity. Those insistent lines:

> "For some we loved, the loveliest and the best
> That from his Vintage rolling Time has prest,
>   Have drunk their Cup a Round or two before
> And one by one crept silently to rest!"

are accompanied by a figure sinking into unconsciousness deeper than that of sleep. The needless poppies fall from the lifeless hand, the lamps but one are all gone out. That last deep and unbreaking rest could scarcely be more eloquently symbolized.

All the vain searchings, the feverish, ceaseless study of philosopher and sage summarized by those potent words:

> "There was a Door for which I found no Key;
> There was a Veil through which I could not see.

Some little talk awhile of Me and Thee
There was, and then no more of Thee and Me."

—these are to be found as well in the illustration of the alchemist trying to find the secret of life; and in the skulls mingled with old tomes.

Finding no solace in learning, Omar gazes at the bowl fascinated, enchanted, and words are scarcely needed: the genius of the wine looks into his eyes and whispers to him:

"Then to the lip of the poor earthen Urn
I leaned, the Secret of my Life to learn:
 And Lip to Lip it murmured, 'While you live,
Drink!—for once dead, you never shall return!'"

The Present listening to the Past, a youth intently holding a seashell to his ear, suggests the inarticulate murmur—the futile questioning of what Eternity shall reveal.

"Strange, is it not, that of the myriads who
Before us passed the door of Darkness through
 Not one returns to tell us of the Road
Which to discover we must travel, too?"

Best known in America are the panels and the mosaic executed for the Congressional Library. The Enemy Sowing Tares, the Cumaean Sibyl, and the Keeper of the Threshold are conspicuous among his productions.

In late years Vedder has maintained his studio in Rome, but from its confines he loves well to escape to his old favorite, the sea, or to the spirit of the hills.

Utterly different has been the life of Winslow Homer. No painter has been more American, less influenced by European art, less imbued with European tenets.

Winslow Homer (1836-1910) was born in Boston. Like many another embryo artist, he spent more time in school decorating his books than in assimilating their contents. It is gratifying to find that he did not have to struggle against parental opposition before satisfying his soul for drawing. His father provided substitutes for the margins of his books and allowed him to expand as Nature prompted. It was thought best for him to learn engraving—from which he, like several other painters of note, have found it but a step to the brush. After a time this was set aside for free-hand drawing. Harper's Weekly was now in its beginnings and accepted some of Homer's first work. So promising did its promoters find him that a place on the staff was offered him, but this he declined, not wishing to bind himself to routine labor. However, when the war opened and the new magazine rallied its forces to meet the arduous demands now laid upon it, Homer was asked to go to the front and keep the paper supplied with scenes of the conflict. For two years he sent pictures from the battlefield, camp and hospital. Of all these sketches Prisoners from the Front is best known. It is said that many of the faces are portraits. The response it awakened is to be explained by the excitement of the times.

Besides his war illustrations, Winslow Homer made a study of the colored people and even aroused the antagonism of the more rabid by his genre pictures of them. The Visit from the Old Mistress, wherein the lady from the plantation house bestows a gracious call upon her former slaves, deferential in attention; The Carnival, representing several members of the family getting another ready for the festivity, and Sunday Morning in Virginia, wherein colored children with difficulty spell out their lesson, are best among them.

Homer never married, nor did he assume the slightest obligation that might even remotely interrupt his work. He was bound to his art with the most powerful ties of his life, leaving civilization and living for years at a time on the rocky, storm-swept coast of Maine. Some of his finest productions are pictures of the sea—found in all its moods among his canvases. He painted just what he saw, holding his canvas near the rocks to judge of its truthful colorings. No artist ever spent less time inquiring into the nature of art and its proper methods of expression. He simply painted prolifically. Some of his pictures tell a story—which critics would have us believe no artistic picture should do. But they tell it subtly and well; the story gives significance to the whole and is whatever one remembers when he views it. The Fog Warning, for example, depicts an old rugged fisherman in his dory; two or three large halibut are already beside him. A fog is rising over the waters, bringing a forecast of an enshrouding mist which ere long will endanger the little craft unless it puts in for shore.

The Life Line is a masterly production, showing little, but telling much. A strong cable, which holds the lifebuoy suspended from the invisible wreck to the shore, a sturdy old salt bearing a fainting woman in his arms, and the angry sea are all that is shown. Neither the water-tossed wreck nor the rescuers are included, yet the presence of both is felt. The Undertow shows a fortunate rescue just before it was too late. The Gulf Stream is a picture of horror. A waterspout is sweeping in from the distance. A colored man lies on the deck of a helpless craft, already disabled by the tempestuous sea. Frightened sea creatures have come to the surface because of the unusual conditions and the sharks are almost exulting over the impending misery. A vessel some distance away, which at first sight suggests hope, is found upon closer examination to be receding. High Seas, Eight Bells, West Wind—these and many others bring vividly before us the vast waters in their limitless extent, or the waves as they break upon the rocks. Homer spent months together in lighthouses, persuading the keepers to take him in, experiencing all the moods of the ocean and growing to understand its mysterious voice.

Few painters have ever shunned publicity more than Homer. He neither valued nor enjoyed the effusive praise which is lavished upon the successful artist. Strongly attached to his brothers and his friends, generous to everyone, he preferred solitude for the greater portion, emerging from it sometimes, but slipping back into it again without warning. Letters sent to his summer home after he returned to the city for the winter were found by him the following year—for he never troubled to have mail forwarded. Six months often passed before a friend might receive a reply to a matter of some special concern. His pictures were turned over to his dealer, for he would not suffer the annoyance of visitors around his studio. Few members of the Academy knew him even by sight. He founded no school, yet his influence upon American painting cannot be disputed.

John La Farge (1835-1910) was as thoroughly American as Winslow Homer. Here in America his life was largely spent and his fame established. His father as a young French soldier went to San Domingo, where he was made lieutenant. By dint of good fortune he escaped impending destruction in the island and took passage to the United States. Belonging to a well-established family, he soon found his place with the French colony in New York, composed of émigrés seeking safety from the horrors of the French Revolution and refugees from San Domingo. He married the daughter of a former San Domingo planter and settled in comfort in the growing metropolis, where his son was born.

As the boy grew older his grandfather, Binsse de St. Vistor, a miniature painter, instructed him in the rudiments of painting, although there was no thought of his pursuing the subject further. After finishing his law course he was sent abroad to visit his father's people and gain what he could from travel. While in Paris his father suggested his taking lessons in painting, and for a few weeks he went regularly to one of the studios. Upon his return he opened a law office in New York, but shortly after met William Hunt, then returning from extended art study abroad. La Farge was influenced by his enthusiasm to abandon law and go with him to the coast of Rhode Island. He soon discovered that his own ideas were broader than those of his teacher and he began to experiment for himself. Years after he explained his reluctance to undertake painting as his life-work, because he thought he might be better adapted to other work, and settled upon it only when he found it more appealing than anything else.

After a serious illness he went again to Europe, now meeting Rossetti and Burne-Jones. However, he was more interested in mural painting and in the study of stained glass windows.

When he returned to America he was commissioned to decorate a Boston church. He found it necessary to train painters to carry out his plans, and, wall decoration being wholly new in this country, was hampered on every hand. About this time he set up a furnace and began to manufacture opalescent glass. Battle Window, in Memorial Hall, Harvard, first called the attention of the general public to his skill in this direction. Later he produced the Watson Memorial Window in Trinity Church, Buffalo. This was exhibited in Paris in 1889 and won for him the insignia of the Legion of Honor.

This was especially gratifying to the artist, because it was an expression of appreciation from his father's countrymen.

Failing health led him to travel, first to Japan, later to the South Sea Islands. Often he was confined to his bed and frequently his burning genius impelled him to work when he was far from well. His fresco in the Church of the Ascension, New York, was executed immediately after his return from the Orient, and the refreshment of the voyage gave him unusual vigor for the undertaking, which is generally acknowledged as being his finest mural painting.

His work in the State Capitol of Minnesota is characteristic of his style and treatment.

Among mural decorations done for private persons, his Music and Drama, commissioned by Whitelaw Reid for his New York home, are excellent.

La Farge produced more than one thousand windows, the famous Peacock Window being most splendid; he painted flower pieces and figures as well as mural pictures. Furthermore, he is known for his writings concerning art and the ancient masters. He was a deep and insatiable scholar and surprised Chinese students by his acquaintance with Confucius and his teachings. In his treatment of Socrates he revealed his familiarity with Greek life and thought. More than most men he tried to analyze his opinions and the methods by which he reached them. He was an innovator and inventor, whose originality was remarkable. While his work was somewhat experimental, he has done much to give force to the doctrine of William Morris: that beauty might and should surround us. The recollection of bare walls in American churches led him to press on in his study of mural paintings. He discovered that decadence in mediæval windows was simultaneous with the separation of artist and his workmen. He saw that unless he would have the charm of individuality eliminated from his designs, he must remain with the work in its execution, imbuing those entrusted to do it with his spirit.

James McNeill Whistler (1834-1903) is classified with American painters simply from the fact that he happened to be born in this country. His art was developed in Europe, where his life was spent and his reputation won.

His father was a skillful engineer, who was commissioned

by the Russian government to lay out a railroad in that country. As a boy of nine Whistler was taken thither by his family, where he remained for some years. He received some instruction in drawing at St. Petersburg, and at the Hermitage had opportunity to study paintings of Velazquez and other artists of note. After his return to America he was sent to West Point, but was ill-fitted by Nature for the routine of a cadet's life. Even in his youth many of his eccentricities were manifest. He had grown up in the midst of luxury and was as sensitive as a girl about his appearance and apparel. He was uniformly late, regarding exact time as much too hampering for his temperament. Any rule was an intolerable restraint. Favor brought him an appointment in the office of the United States Coast Survey, but he adorned government sheets with heads and during the two months he remained, was fined by deducted time for constant tardiness and frequent absence. At the age of twenty-one he went abroad, never to return.

For years Whistler wrestled with poverty that hampers the average art student and struggling painter. His life was one prolonged protest and the world gives its ear grudgingly to messages set in this key. Realism was in the ascendancy: paint things as you see them; do not idealize; do not throw a haze about an object to enhance its beauty; paint all as it appears. This was the spirit of the day. Whistler believed that beauty might be everywhere seen, but not in all objects at all times. The attitude of the naturalist, that it is wrong for the painter to seek beauty, but rather that he should portray reality—the object as it is—was torture to this delicately poised genius. He felt that there are moments when Nature and men are at their best; those are the supreme moments that only the true artist sees and can portray.

Much has been made of Whistler's idiosyncrasies, and there is no doubt but that he was individual both by nature and cultivation. He liked to feel that he was the cynosure of all eyes. He denied the artificial demands of time as something too galling to his nature. When a director of an art association set a meeting for "four-thirty, precisely," Whistler replied that he never had nor ever would be able to attend any meeting at four-thirty, *precisely*. He never hesitated, after he became a lion, to keep dinner parties waiting hours at a time, if he became interested in his work. He forgot his age, and when his model questioned one day: "Mr. Whistler, where were you born?" he answered: "My child, I never was born; I came from on high." But nothing daunted came the reply from one who knew his moods: "How we mortals flatter ourselves. I should have imagined that you came from below." His friends were invited to his Sunday breakfasts, where such dishes as harmonized with his color schemes were served to them—in due time. His rooms were beautiful to look at, and if they lacked chairs and means of comfort, that did not in the slightest degree disturb the tranquillity of the designer. Beyond question his striving for effect and his egotism made him blind to the comfort of others, but his friends understood him and a wondering public found him all the more interesting because of his peculiarities.

Notes, Harmonies and Nocturnes he announced on exhibition, when his drawing and paintings were ready to be viewed. The Falling Rocket, called a Nocturne in black and gold, was the picture that precipitated Ruskin's wrath and led to the libel suit which Whistler brought against him wherein he received a verdict of damages to the amount of one farthing. This Whistler wore the remainder of his life on his watch chain.

A Symphony in Gray and Green—the Ocean; Harmony in Green and Rose; The Music Room—titles of this kind attracted attention; at first criticism was harsh indeed, but gradually it was seen that there was something in these pictures more than had at first been recognized and finally an enthusiastic coterie was ready for the artist's creations.

Whistler wrote as well as painted, and the following extract indicates his poetical conceptions:

"When the evening mist clothes the river-side with poetry as with a veil, and the poor buildings lose themselves in the dim sky and the tall chimneys become campanile, and the warehouses are palaces in the night, and the whole city hangs in the heavens, and the fairy land is before us—then the wayfarer hastens home, the workman and the cultured one, the wise and the one of pleasures ceased to understand as they have ceased to see, and Nature, who for once has sung in tune, sings her exquisite song to the artist alone, her son and her master; her son in that he loves her, and her master in that he knows her."

Of all his paintings, the Portrait of His Mother, in Luxembourg, is the one that the world at large has accepted. In it each finds the idea of mother, in a wholly different but quite as true a sense as it is found in Rembrandt's Mother. When once the mental attitude of the protesting painter is understood and the key to his art thus given, his pictures are less bewildering, less baffling. Of his work it may be truly felt that time alone can give the final verdict.

John Singer Sargent is included with American painters merely because his parents were Americans. He was born in Italy in 1856, was educated in Florence, studied painting in Paris and has for years maintained his studio in London. He has spent very little time in America; yet when Queen Victoria graciously offered him the privileges of citizenship, he delicately declined them.

His mother was skillful in water colors and there was no lack of sympathy with Sargent when his talent for drawing was indicated. Neither has he been obliged to struggle against poverty. He has been favored by fortune and his work was accepted from the start.

Quite as systematically as Winslow Homer evaded publicity, so has Sargent held himself aloof, watching humanity, studying them en masse, but not mingling with them. He is widely known as the greatest living portrait painter and when he visited New York in 1884 many flocked to him for portraits. Perhaps there is noticeable a lack of the kindly sympathy that Reynolds held for his subject, instantly putting one at his best. Sargent paints what he sees and views his subject as objectively and dispassionately as a scientist examining a specimen. His mural work in the Boston Public Library has made him well known in this country, his frieze of the Prophets being found in households from coast to coast. The exhibition of his paintings at the Exposition in Chicago was representative and gave him fame. Perhaps his rendering of Ellen Terry as Lady Macbeth is known best among his portraits.

Edwin Austin Abbey (1852-1911) might be called the story-teller among modern artists. As a boy his ambitious father was irritated by his lack of enthusiasm over his studies, since he wished him to follow one of the professions. Set to learn the printer's trade, he proved ill adapted for it and George W. Childs helped him to become an illustrator for Harper's Weekly. In 1883 he went abroad to study and after 1883 made his home in England. He was commissioned to decorate the delivery room of the Boston Public Library and is known today best by his pictures which tell the story of the Quest for the Holy Grail. After his successful work in this library he was appointed to paint the Coronation scene of Edward VII.

While as has been pointed out, the distance is considerable between the experiences of the boy set to learn typesetting to the man honored at home and the favorite of England's king, Abbey was the second among aspiring American youths to compass it. After his European study he abandoned his earlier illustrating to work in oils and his productions were favorably received among critics in foreign lands.

In contrast to those Americans who have found their interest in art centers of Europe, William Merritt Chase may be mentioned. No other modern painter has won such gratitude from American art students. He was born in 1849 and his father wished him to become a business man, like himself. However, when it developed that Chase had real ability, no opposition was put in his way and he was sent to Munich to study. He returned to America in 1879 and has since maintained his studio in New York, although his vacations have been spent largely abroad.

It is gratifying to note that his students provided a fund with which to have his portrait painted by Sargent. This excellent expression of appreciation hangs in the Metropolitan Museum.

He is known best as a portrait painter and among his best portraits are those of Whistler. Choate, Seth Low, and Rutherford Hayes. He paints landscapes occasionally and does both still-life and figure pieces.

Copyright by Underwood and Underwood, N. Y.
HELEN HUNT FALLS—NORTH CHEYENNE CAÑON.

CHAPTER XXI.

Art Centers of America.

ALTHOUGH the Metropolitan was by no means one of the earliest museums of art to be established in this country, it is usually mentioned first in any enumeration of American galleries. Its foundation was first suggested by John Hay and was seriously considered by a meeting of representative men held in New York in 1869. The first exhibition of pictures was held in 1871—some of them being loaned, others having been purchased in Europe for the Trustees. Funds were later raised for a new building to be erected in Central Park and this was opened to the public in 1880. Since that time it has been enlarged and remodeled.

In 1904 the late J. Pierpont Morgan was made President of the Board of Trustees. Himself a famous collector of rare art treasures, his private pictures have frequently been loaned to the Metropolitan. Various private collections have been bequeathed to this Museum, the Marquand and Hearn collections important among them. Sometimes collections have been given with the understanding that they should be kept intact, which has led to confusion attendant upon unrelated pictures of varying merit being shown together.

It is frequently deplored that our country should possess so few worthy examples of European art, but each year it becomes more difficult to acquire paintings by the masters. When private collections are sold, bidders for the great galleries are ready to pay large sums—often far in excess of the value of a canvas. A few generations ago when these conditions did not exist, Americans had little time and less means to procure works of art, nor had the desire for beautiful pictures found opportunity to develop in a new land where the winning of a livelihood demanded the attention of all. Moreover, it will be remembered that our earliest painters found scant encouragement in austere New England and in Quaker Pennsylvania for the production of pictures, although, to be sure, the vanity of our ancestors prompted them to have their portraits painted.

X—15

The Metropolitan owns no noteworthy example of early Italian painting. Among Flemish artists, Rubens is represented, though not always at his best. One of Van Dyck's best portraits, that of James Stuart, Duke of Richmond and Lenox, is here, and others less important. Several Dutch painters may be seen—Rembrandt in one excellent portrait, in his landscape The Mills, and in the Adoration of the Shepherds—a preliminary study for the picture by this name in the National Gallery. One of Ruysdael's, two by Cuyp and several by Frans Hals are fortunately here.

Holbein's portrait of the Archbishop Cranmer is one of the most valuable canvases in this gallery. Several paintings of Reynolds are found, but nearly all of them in the bad state of preservation common to his works. He used a kind of varnish to give added lustre to his pictures which has proved most disastrous. Gainsborough is represented; also Turner. Modern French painters are to be seen, among them notably Corot, Diaz, Daubigney, Breton, Troyon and Dupré, while Rosa Bonheur's great Horse Fair greets the visitor familiarly—it being widely reproduced in prints. It was presented to the Metropolitan by Vanderbilt, who paid over $50,000 for it.

Among early American painters, West is represented by two pictures—neither in his best style. Hagar and Ismael, a biblical painting, bears evidences of his Italian period. Portraits by Copley, one of Stuart's portraits of Washington and a replica of another and his excellent portraits of Don Josef de Jaudenes y Nebot and his wife, painted while this diplomat represented the Court of Spain in the United States, should be mentioned.

Thomas Doughty's On the Hudson and Thomas Cole's Valley of Vanchuse are included among the early landscapes; also Inness' Peace and Plenty and Autumn Oaks. Peace and Plenty portrays a wide reach of country, the trees riotous in autumn's rich tones. The fields lie wrapped in the silence of fall; the wheat stands in shocks. Flowing water indicates the cause of an abundant harvest. In the distance, farm buildings are visible.

In recent years the endowment of George A. Hearn has provided for the purchase of pictures by living American artists. It has too often been the case that struggling painters have been neglected until they have won recognition abroad, or have been obliged to turn from their chosen work for lack of appreciation. The United States was slow to recognize Whistler's unusual gifts, although the Metropolitan now possesses three of his paintings: A Lady in Gray, the Nocturne in Green and Gold, and the Nocturne in Black and Gold—this last one of the night scenes in Cremorne Gardens.

Winslow Homer, regarded by many as foremost among American painters, has been said to bear the relationship to our art that Walt Whitman does to our poetry or Lincoln to statesmanship. His Gulf Stream and Cannon Rock are here.

La Farge's wonderful skill in use of colors is apparent in a little Samoan Island scene—here with some of his flower pieces. Chase, having been identified with New York for years, is seen to advantage.

Sargent may be studied in five pictures: his portraits of Chase, of Marquand, former president of the Museum's Board of Trustees, and of Robert Louis Stevenson are best among them.

The Pennsylvania Academy of the Fine Arts was founded in 1805 and is the oldest institution of its kind in America. Its early foundation was largely due to the untiring efforts of Charles Wilson Peale to stimulate an interest for art and to provide opportunity for the training of the youth who manifested ability for drawing. There was in early times a lamentable dearth of pictures and statuary, but a series of casts was obtained from the Louvre and a cast of Venus de Medici from Italy. This Venus long constituted the greatest treasure and was kept concealed except on rare occasions—partly because it was regarded as very valuable and partly because it was hard for the early inhabitants of Philadelphia to grow accustomed to undraped statuary. In delicate consideration for feminine folk, Mondays were reserved for them alone.

The present building was completed in 1876, having cost more than five hundred thousand dollars. The Academy has been fortunate in its presidents, these having worked relentlessly for the furtherance of the plan which led originally to its establishment. While a portion of this sum was realized from the sale of the earlier site and a small sum left as a bequest, the greater part was raised through the tireless efforts of President Claghorn, who aroused sentiment and pride sufficiently to secure the new building. Since its completion it has been endowed by subscriptions and bequests.

The purpose of the Academy is best explained by quoting from the pledge of the association when organized: "To promote the cultivation of the Fine Arts, in the United States of America, by introducing correct and elegant copies from works of the first masters in sculpture and painting and by thus facilitating the access to such standards, and also by occasionally conferring moderate but honorable premiums, and otherwise assisting the studies and exciting the efforts of the artists gradually to unfold, enlighten and invigorate the talents of our countrymen." This it has accomplished and while not a repository of valuable canvases or marbles, by various private donations and bequests a few pictures by eminent painters have been acquired.

Van der Helst (1613-1670), like Hals a native of Haarlem, is represented by The Violinist, one of his best productions. Van der Helst fell under the influence of Frans Hals, his drawing being free and bold. One of Jan der Goyen's landscapes is found among the examples of Dutch painting.

There are no pictures illustrative of the best years of Italian art. For the decadent period, Guido Reni's beautiful Ganymede and five of Salvator Rosa's canvases may be seen, three being landscape with some mythological significance.

Ribera's style and characteristic treatment may be seen in his The Cid. Specimens of early Spanish and French paintings are lacking, but the Academy possesses several pictures by the recent painters of France—three of Corot's—the River Scene, South of France, and a Landscape,—a landscape by Rousseau, another by Dupré, Breton's Potato Harvester, and Rosa Bonheur's Highland Sheep, while with the Gibson Collection, Millet's Return of the Flock was secured. The chill of night having fallen, the shepherd is huddled in his heavy cloak, followed by the sheep that crowd together, while the faithful dog, ever alert, watches to see that none stray away.

The Academy is fortunate in having portraits by the early American School, these being more valuable from a historical than an artistic point of view. Stuart is here seen at his best, being adequately represented by twenty-four canvases. He maintained a studio in Philadelphia from 1785 to 1805 and many citizens came to him for their portraits. In many instances these have been donated in late years to the Academy. It has long been a matter of dispute as to whether the portrait of Washington which hangs in this gallery is an original or a replica.

Peale, an enthusiastic collector of curios, gathered together much of interest for his museum which was preserved in his home. His self-portrait standing in this museum is now in the Academy. Twelve portraits by Thomas Sully (1783-1872) are worthy of mention. One of these portrays George Frederick Cooke, an actor of some note, in his rôle of Richard III., and another represents Fanny Kemble as Beatrice.

West is seen to greater advantage here than at the Metropolitan. Three of his large canvases: Death on a Pale Horse, Paul and Barnabas, and the Rejected Christ being in the Academy. The last is regarded as one of his best productions. It was sold for three thousand guineas after his death and was presented in late years to this gallery. The artist caught the tension of the moment when Pilate caused Christ to be brought before the multitude that they might, should it so please them, exercise the privilege which custom had granted them—that of pardoning one prisoner on this holiday. Like so many of West's historical pictures, the canvas is crowded with people—all kinds and conditions of society being revealed in this particular case.

Death on a Pale Horse compels attention by its title. The painter conceived of Death, mounted on a horse, riding about and bringing destruction wherever he went. It is another version of the Mediaeval story of the Dance of Death.

Several excellent paintings by modern American artists are found. The Lady with the White Shawl, by William Merritt Chase is here; the Fox Hunt by Winslow Homer, before which the Adirondack guide who had glanced idly at other pictures paused to say: "By Jove, I've *seen* things that looked like that!", a portrait by Sargent and Phyllis, one of Walter MacEwen's old fashioned, charming, flowered-gowned maidens are here. Here also are two examples of William Hunt's work, one the original sketch of his Flight of Night—the subject of his mural painting in the New York Capitol. This is the more highly prized today because of the sad destruction of the beautiful painting executed so shortly before his death.

A board of Trustees was chosen in Boston in 1870 to consider the building of a museum which should furnish fire-proof quarters for several collections of various kinds, all allied with art. The Institute of Technology possessed a number of architectural casts which were not displayed to advantage; Harvard University could provide no suitable place for the Gray Collection of Prints; paintings owned by the Athenæum had been crowded out of their former gallery by increasing demands of books and the Lowell Institute had various possessions which needed housing. Without state or municipal aid, private funds were forthcoming for the erection of the first Museum, dedicated on the Fourth of July, 1876. Although enlarged in 1890, it became too crowded and the beautiful Boston Museum of today was begun in 1902. Its architectural plan has been widely commended, providing as it does for the best possible display of curios. It consists of a series of courts, off of which small rooms open. Thus large objects may be given desirable space and smaller ones studied at close range.

No American city affords the visitor better opportunities for the study of painting than Boston. Native painters are well represented and examples of various European schools are shown as well, in some instances, better, here than elsewhere.

Although the great Italian masters are wholly lacking, the Museum possesses work of obscure painters illustrative of several Italian schools. Even the style of Giotto is well portrayed in a small Giottoesque Nativity. A replica of St. Luke Painting the Virgin, now in Munich, illustrates the character of early Flemish painting. It is supposed to be the work of Roger van der Weyden. Rembrandt's portraits of Nicolas Tulp and his wife are the most valuable of the Dutch exhibits. Maes' Jealous Husband is here also.

El Greco, Goya, and best of all Velazquez, are represented —the last in a portrait of Philip IV., which has been the occasion of much discussion, some maintaining that it is genuine, others questioning it. At present the predominating opinion of conservative critics is that this is the work of Velazquez. Recently this great master's Don Baltasar Carlos and his Dwarf have most fortunately been acquired.

English canvases by Reynolds—in their usual state of partial ruin—, by Gainsborough, Constable and a landscape by Wilson—a View of Tivoli, are here. A head by Burne-Jones has found its way thither; but more renowned than any of these pictures is the Slave Ship, by Turner.

Modern French art is characteristically shown. The Death of Hector is ascribed to David. Chardin is represented by some of his still-life work. The modern landscape school is fittingly set forth in pictures by Rousseau, Diaz, Daubigny, Dupré, and Corot. Greatest of modern French painters, Millet is represented by The Shepherdess. Henri Regnault's painting, the Horses of Achilles, known well by reproductions, is here. This was painted when the artist was but twenty-four. His untimely death three years later prevented fulfilment of his early promise.

The early portrait school of America is well shown. Copley's Portrait of John Quincy Adams, of Dorothy Quincy and the Group of his own family give a fair idea of his labored style. West's Group of the Hope Family and Stuart's Washington, owned by the Athenæum and loaned to the Museum, may be seen by the side of Martha Washington's portrait. Another excellent Stuart is the portrait of General Knox. A landscape by Inness is illustrative of the early school.

The mysticism of Vedder is noticeable in his Sphynx and in the Sea Serpent. La Farge's Halt of the Wise Men, Winslow Homer's Fog Warning and two small panels by Whistler—the Blacksmith of Lyme Regis and the Little Rose of Lyme Regis—are exhibited. One of Chase's pieces of still life, Dead Fish, is here and William Hunt, well loved by Bostonians, may be seen in his self-portrait and the Fortune Teller. John A. Alexander, who has achieved fame in comparatively recent years, is to be seen in his Pot of Basil and Isabel. Nor should Edmund C. Tarbell, closely identified with the School of Art maintained in connection with this Museum, be forgotten. He was chosen to paint the portrait of General Loring who for thirty years was connected with the Boston Museum as a Trustee.

The Corcoran Gallery of Art was founded by William Wilson Corcoran, long a resident of Washington. He knew the Capital when it was a crude town, suffering in constant comparison with Philadelphia, the earlier center of government. He believed in the future of the city, in spite of the backsets it received during the Civil War, when all business buildings were appropriated by the government for temporary use and the place presented the appearance of a large military camp.

Mr. Corcoran was one of the first collectors of art in the United States and was interested in fostering native talent. His collection was largely composed of American paintings and he left this and an endowment of nine hundred thousand dollars "to be used solely for the purpose of encouraging Americans in the production of works pertaining to art."

The Corcoran Gallery was incorporated in 1870 and the first exhibition held in the old building in 1874. This in time proved to be insufficient and in 1893 the present building was begun. It was finished in 1897 and opened on the anniversary of Washington's Birthday. It is built in Neo-Grecian style, of white Georgian marble set on pink granite foundations. Two stories in height, the second story, used for the picture gallery, is lighted entirely from above.

In addition to providing an art repository for the city, it has a greater and far-reaching significance. Every two years exhibitions are held of paintings by living American artists. Over three hundred were entered for the first one, held in 1907. Sales that year from pictures purchased by patrons amounted to $49,000. Prizes are offered; Senator Clark has provided sums for these at the last three exhibits. There can be no doubt but that such exhibitions as these will grow to have a stimulating effect upon American art and will serve mutually the public, by developing a deeper love for artistic beauty and a cultivated sense for judging, and, at the same time, inspire painters to greater effort since they are assured fair-minded, appreciative audiences.

The pictures owned by the Corcoran Gallery give a very good idea of American painting as it developed, at first timidly and slowly, and recently with more rapid stride. There are but few examples of the early portrait school. Sully's Portrait of Andrew Jackson is here and Morse's paintings are to be seen as nowhere else. Samuel B. Morse (1791-1872) is so intimately associated with the telegraph today in the minds of people generally that his earlier work as an artist has been overshadowed. He painted many portraits and finally executed the large production, the House of Representatives, showing the room in the old Capitol with the representatives seated and occupied in various ways. The picture he hoped would be purchased by Congress, as indeed it should have been; this failing, Morse turned to electricity, although he never wholly broke his connections with art interests. West's Cupid and Psyche is here but does not show him at his best. One of the numerous replicas of Washington by Stuart belongs to this portrait collection.

The Hudson River School is well represented. Four canvases by Thomas Doughty are here: Autumn on the Hudson, a Landscape, Welsh Scenery, and Tintern Abbey. Durand is to be seen in the Edge of the Forest, and Cole's Departure and Return are true to the vein in which much of his work was done. The Departure shows a young knight, riding away in the morning of life with gay banners floating, nor little heeding the warning of the pious friar. The Return shows the conclusion of the story—he being borne home dead. Allegories of this kind were popular in Cole's generation.

The culmination of the early landscape school is found in the more finished paintings of Inness, whose Sunset in the Woods hangs in this gallery, near one by Wyant—his View from Mount Mansfield, one of his most perfect pictures.

Among figure painters of earlier years George Fuller (1822-1886) deserves mention. His Lorette is characteristic of his treatment.

Winslow Homer's Light on the Sea, English Cod—a still life study by Chase, and Edmund Tarbell's Josephine and Mercie merit admiration. One of the most recent artists to attract attention by the honors bestowed upon him at late exhibitions has been Edward W. Redfield—born in Delaware in 1869. His Delaware River belongs to this collection.

A few pictures by modern French artists have been donated to the Corcoran, but they are not extensive enough to form any important element in this Gallery established wholly in the interest of American painters. Indeed it is probable that as time goes on such canvases will be sent to the National Gallery, recently completed in Washington and designed by Congress as a respository for paintings by artists of every land.

Among American art centers, the Art Institute of Chicago deserves mention. It was incorporated in 1879 for the "founding and maintenance of schools of art and design, the formation and exhibition of collections of objects of art, and the cultivation and extension of the arts of design by any appropriate means."

The present building was opened to the public in 1893. Like the other Museums where schools of art are maintained, it provides exhibits from time to time that frequently have great merit and give the Institute an importance greater than that accorded it by pictures regularly shown.

A few valuable paintings are exhibited at the Art Institute—being in most cases loaned by the owners for this purpose. Among these is the Family Concert by Jan Steen; The Castle by Ruysdael; Rembrandt's Portrait of a Girl and Frans Hals' portrait of his son. Rubens is represented by his Portrait of Marquis Spinola, Van Dyck by the Portrait of Helena, and Hobbema by his Watermill, worth perhaps fifty thousand dollars today.

The modern French painters are several of them to be seen in one or more pictures. Landscapes by Rousseau, Dupré and three of Corot's; Breton's Song of the Lark and Millet's Woman Feeding Chickens and Bringing Home the Newborn Calf are most important among them. Troyon's Pasture in Normandy and Returning from Market both glow with the country life and spirit this painter subtly reveals.

There are but few pictures by the foremost American artists. Whistler's Nocturne—Southampton Water, Vedder's Storm in Umbria, landscapes by Inness and Wyant, and Alice, a bright charming girl by Chase, which brightens a sombre wall, are best among them.

CHAPTER XXII.

Mural Painting in America.

In 1817 Congress gave Trumbull a commission to paint four pictures for the adornment of the Capitol, these to commemorate important historical events. The subjects developed by the artist were the Declaration of Independence, Surrender of Burgoyne, Surrender of Cornwallis and the Resignation of Washington at Annapolis. Congress was prompted to appropriate $32,000 for these pictures more from a desire to give due importance to events of deep significance to the young republic than to adorn walls of the building.

Nearly sixty years later, La Farge was besought by the architect, Mr. Richardson, to decorate the walls of Trinity Church, which building he was then constructing in Boston. This was in the nature of an experiment, mural painting being almost unknown in the United States at the time. La Farge had long entertained the desire to undertake work of this description, but the mural painter must await the coming of commissions before resources or inspiration contribute to make his work a possibility. Although there were no trained painters to assist, although the time as stipulated was very limited, and, particularly, in spite of the fact that the work must be begun in an unfinished building in the severity of a New England winter, La Farge plunged into it with determination.

The church was built in Romanesque style, so La Farge appropriately chose subjects associated with the period when buildings formerly dedicated to pagan worship were used by followers of the new faith. Small scenes above the windows were chosen with this period in view. Two panels, Christ and Nicodemus and The Woman of Samaria were both done by La Farge and are indicative of his simplicity of composition. On the side walls were painted heroic figures of St. Peter and St. Paul and Moses, Jeremiah, Isaiah and Daniel. Over the arches scrolls were supported by child angels. In spite of discouraging obstacles, the artistic effect of the decoration when completed surprised even La Farge and had a far-reaching influence in the country. Order now followed order and the possibilities for this kind of decoration were brought home to many.

The Columbian Exposition gave a great impetus to mural painting in this country. Experiments of various kinds were tried and the results proved to be not only pleasing but stimulating. People from different parts of the United States witnessed the artistic effects of wall decoration and were led to take a more vital interest later when the question of beautifying public buildings arose in individual states. All the large undertakings in this field have been done since the Exposition of 1893, or have been completed since that time if already under way—consequently benefiting by the display of mural paintings there provided.

Boston was the first town in the United States to establish a public library. In recent years a new building has been erected to meet the needs of a growing municipality. Long recognized as one of the art centers of America, it was natural that unusual care should be taken to make the building artistic as well as serviceable.

Elmer E. Garnsey, who has been chosen to direct the interior decorations of so many public buildings, M. Puis de Chavannes, greatest of modern mural painters, Sargent and Abbey were commissioned to beautify Boston's new Library and it is today noteworthy among public buildings of this country. Puis was more than seventy years of age when this commission was received—too advanced in years and too delicate in health to justify his crossing the ocean to study the spaces allotted to him. Charts and photographs were used as guides instead, while the modern custom of having mural paintings done upon canvas and then "rolled" upon surfaces, enabled him to execute his work in his own studio in France. On the landing of the Grand Stairway his large painting, The Genius of Enlightenment, is seen to advantage. Under the general themes: Science and Letters, he provided eight panels to adorn the Staircase corridor. Grouped under the name of Science are represented Physics, Chemistry, History and Astronomy. A telegraph pole with its transmitting wires is seen in the lower corner of the panel representing Physics—America being the country to first develop uses of electricity; the inspiring figure floating through the air symbolizes Good News; the baneful creature with face concealed, Ill Tidings. The genius of Chemistry stands in a niche cut in living rock, watching an experiment, while winged boys gaze intently upon it. History, a classic figure, stands mournfully on the site of old ruins, trying to evoke the past; failing alone, she is accompanied by a youth—Science—bearing a torch in one hand, a book in the other. Puis was happily successful in his landscape backgrounds, this one being very pleasing. Astronomy is portrayed by primitive men gazing in bewildered earnestness at the heavens, while from a wattled hut a woman's face looks up. These are Chaldean shepherds who first studied the stars and conceived of influences exerted by them upon this planet. The four panels grouped under Letters include Philosophy and Poetry—Pastoral, Dramatic and Epic. Philosophy is represented by Plato, who stands in a garden discoursing to a pupil, while other disciples study in porticoes near by; Pastoral Poetry, by Virgil leaning against a tree with an expanse of blue ocean before him. Bee hives are conspicuous in the foreground and peaceful rural life is admirably portrayed.

Dramatic Poetry is perhaps the noblest of all these masterly pictures; it reveals Prometheus bound to a rock in the sea, the vulture hovering over him; moved by his sufferings, the Daughters of the Ocean rise from the waves, chanting soothing melodies. In the foreground Aeschylus is to be seen writing his great tragedy. Finally, Epic Poetry is shown in the person of Homer, accompanied by two figures symbolizing the Iliad and Odyssey. The Corridor wherein these panels are placed provided sufficient space for ocean and sweep of sky, hills and groves where Muses wander. Yellow marble was used in the construction of the Corridor and the colors of the paintings are subdued and gray.

The Pompeian Lobby has been so named because of Garnsey's exquisite Pompeian designs, covering its walls with bands and arabesques. This admits to the so-called Delivery Room, where books are brought to readers. This was entrusted to Abbey. The commission for its decoration was received by him just before his marriage and he held it in mind during a somewhat extended trip which followed. Various plans were considered, he particularly wishing to develop certain of the

Shakespeare stories. However, he decided that something of Anglo-Saxon origin would be most appropriate and determined upon the Quest of the Holy Grail—known in general outline by every school boy. The important scenes in the life of Galahad are depicted, beginning with the convent in which he was reared. In front of a wall tapestried in blue and gold, one of the nuns holds the babe in swaddling clothes, to whose vision an angel appears with the Holy Grail. The Oath of Knighthood is impressive. As the youth in a red robe kneels on the altar steps, Sir Launcelot and Sir Bors in full armor wait to fasten on his spurs. The sisters who have reared him watch the ceremony, bearing candles in their hands. The Court of King Arthur attracts with manifold interests. Evidently a banquet has just been served, for the Round Table is still covered with a white cloth. Crowds of people are engaged in conversation as the young knight is brought thither. The Departure for the Search for the Grail shows all the knights in full armor gathered in the chapel to receive the blessing of the Church before setting out on their adventures.

The Grail frieze consists in reality of a series of tableaux exemplifying Mediaeval life. The superb use of rich colors, the variety of costume, the trappings of knight-errantry and the inclusion of all classes of society, bewilder and fascinate. These people seem to live and to be even now engaged upon undertakings of the middle ages.

Finally, Sargent Hall—named in honor of its decorator, contains the splendid work of this greatest of modern portrait painters. He was originally commissioned to prepare decorations for both ends of the Hall. Later he was asked to unite these by ceiling decoration as well. The first finished portion exemplifies the Triumph of Religion. The gods of polytheism and idolatry are first shown, the figures of Moloch and Astarte being marvelously done. Sargent studied Egyptian and Assyrian art before undertaking this work until he was able to express himself admirably in Eastern forms. The confusion resulting from the strife between pagan worship and the faith of the Hebrews is revealed with masterly skill. Below is a lunette picturing the Hebrews in captivity and underneath this, the famous frieze of the Prophets—so widely known.

The painting which fills the opposite end was finished some

years later and is called the Dogma of Redemption. It is done in Byzantine style. The figure of Christ on the cross occupies the central portion of the scene; above are three figures exactly alike and representing the personages of the Trinity; the central one crowned like the pope, the others representing royalty and empire. Below the picture and corresponding to the frieze of Prophets is a frieze of the Angels of the Passion. This entire work, which had been highly commended by critics, is illustrative of religious belief of the Middle Ages.

The Congressional Library in Washington is the most beautiful library in America and among the finest in the world. It has only recently been completed and contains some of the best mural painting found in the United States. As in the Boston Library, Elmer E. Garnsey was given charge of all interior painting. He studied the available spaces and divisions of the building for three years before the various commissions were assigned.

The building consists of three stories: the ground floor, the second story, containing the Library, and the third, containing the Museum. In the lower story two corridors extend on either side of the Grand Stairway. One was decorated by Charles Sprague Pearce, and portrays the primitive Family. His drawing is weak, but the lunettes recall the story of prehistoric man. The one entitled religion is considered best. The corresponding corridor assigned to Henry Oliver Walker is pleasing, he having grouped his pictures under the general title of Lyric Poetry. Seven scenes compose the series. First is shown the Muse of Lyric Poetry, who is found attended by Passion, Beauty, Mirth, Pathos, Truth and Devotion. The second is entitled: Shakespeare's Adonis—slain by the wild boar; the third, Tennyson's Ganymede, borne to Olympus by Jove in the guise of an eagle. Keats' Endymion comes next—sleeping shepherd, on Mount Latmos. The fifth is Emerson's Uriel; the sixth, Wordsworth's Boy of Winander—at twilight by a gleaming lake, and last, Milton's Comus—listening to a song. Another corridor decorated by Edward Simmons contains the nine Muses—each shown in characteristic pose and surroundings. These are all excellent and Calliope perhaps the most impressive.

One of the corridors on the second floor was assigned to

John W. Alexander, who has portrayed six splendid paintings under the general title: Evolution of the Book. In the Building of the Cairn, primitive men are seen engaged in constructing a pile of boulders which shall serve as a memorial of some signal event. In the second, Egyptian Hieroglyphics, a maiden watches a workman while he cuts an inscription on a tomb; perhaps the most fascinating is the third—Oral Tradition, wherein hooded Arabs give close attention to one who relates a story for their edification; Picture Writing belongs to our own continent; an American Indian draws pictures on a hide to convey his meaning. The Manuscript Book is set back in a monastery of the Middle Ages, while the sixth and last of these graphic scenes commemorates the Invention of the Printing Press.

Another corridor is made beautiful by Walter McEwen's Stories of Greek Heroes. The first relates to Prometheus, who urges Epimetheus to beware of Pandora and her mysterious box; in the next, Orpheus lies in a woodland dying—slain by the Bacchantes. In the third, Perseus confronts Polydectes with the head of the Medusa; in the fourth, Theseus deserts the sleeping Ariadne. Hercules is to be seen with the distaff, spinning for Queen Omphale, and Bellerophon receives the winged Pegasus from Minerva. A picture of particular interest is the one wherein Jason seeks to enlist the attention of the Argonauts in his quest of the Golden Fleece; Paris—a doubtful hero—is shown at the home of Menelaus, whose hospitality he so shortly outrages. Last, Achilles, disguised as a school girl, is discovered by Ulysses.

The vestibule admitting to the Reading Room contains five pictures by Vedder. Their colors are subdued and well suited to this dimly lighted lobby. Government is the general subject of the series; Good Government is accompanied on the right by Peace and Prosperity. Corrupt Legislation by its attendant, Anarchy. The artist's fine drawing and sweeping lines prevail throughout.

The adornment of the rotunda was left to Edwin Blashfield. In the crown he painted the Human Understanding and in the collar of the dome twelve figures that make up the series illustrating the Evolution of Civilization. These seated figures symbolize twelve countries or periods, each having contributed to present civilization. Egypt contributes written records; Judea, religion; Rome, administration; Greece, philosophy; Islam, physics; Italy, the fine arts; Middle Ages, modern languages; Germany, art of printing; England, literature; France, emancipation; Spain, discovery; America, science—this last represented by a workman with a dynamo.

The task of making this beautiful rotunda a fitting crown to the whole lavishly decorated structure was not an easy one and it must always be a matter of gratification to his countrymen that Mr. Blashfield was able to discharge it admirably.

It is not possible to enter upon any exhaustive discussion of this remarkable building. Among its finest gems should be mentioned the two paintings by Kenyon Cox in the Museum. One represents The Arts. Poetry holding a large picture is enthroned; Sculpture, Painting, Architecture and Music attend. The other picture represents the Sciences. Astronomy in the center is flanked on the right by Botany and Zoology; on the left by Physics and Mathematics. The room is flooded with light and the artist has painted in a high key with faint shadows that his work might not appear too dark and heavy.

Every available space has been utilized by the ambitious painter for some picture or decorative scheme. These represent the different tendencies among present American painters. The Congressional Library in the matter of embellishment is true to the age in which it has been done and will be remembered as marking an important step in American decorative art.

In 1905 the largest commission for mural decoration ever given a single painter was assigned to John W. Alexander by the Trustees of the Carnegie Institute of Pittsburg.

This building was planned in the beginning as the municipal library for Pittsburg, from which branches were to be established later. With the intention of making the opening of the library the more agreeable and praiseworthy, those in charge of it engaged an orchestra to dispense music and provided for a loan exhibition of pictures for the occasion. Thereupon, the founder of the institute promptly provided the Trustees with a fund, the interest of which was to provide for the establishment of a School of Music and a Department of Fine Arts.

Unhampered by lack of funds, it has been possible for the Trustees to carry out ideas in connection with the practical administration of this Institute with a freedom unusual in educational institutions. As a result of enlarging the building to supply additional space, the redecorating of the Institute was necessary and this fell to Alexander, who strange to say, happened to be a native of Pittsburg. However, it was because of honors which he had already won at home and abroad and his recognized merit that led to his appointment as decorator. It was gratifying in addition to remember that Pittsburg was his native home.

It has often been noted that in spite of a continent filled with suggestive themes, our painters have preferred subjects found in classical tradition or at least in distant lands. This criticism can never be made regarding the decorations on the walls of Carnegie Institute. Recognizing keenly the fact that prosperity has overtaken Pittsburg because of her rich deposits, their removal from the earth and conversion into serviceable commodities, the entire scheme is shown as the city's triumph. Two series of pictures, one of them about ten feet above the entrance floor, the other higher up, are closely associated with her labor—the first containing fifteen scenes typifying the industries of the city, such as operations at the mills, foundries, work-shops, and coke-ovens. The smoke and steam that frequently envelop the workmen are shown in these pictures. Just as the murky brown smoke breaks above the foundries oftentimes, so in these pictures it scatters to reveal sturdy men at work, with muscles strong and minds alert. The union of mind and muscle is everywhere apparent. The city itself is typified as a man in armor—perhaps suggested by the abundance of steel ore—while to convey the idea that as a result of labor come prosperity, and all that wealth can bring, feminine forms approach this city symbol, bearing in their hands fruits of looms, and workshops of the world. Costly fabrics, beautiful works of art, graceful vases and costly urns—everything in short that may be found accompanying prosperity, they offer to the Spirit of the City.

The second series of pictures have to do with the means of approach to Pittsburg, by water and by land—these having been important in the past and still vital to its welfare.

The decorations in this thoroughly efficient Institute are both American and local in spirit. They accord dignity and honor to the brawn of strong, healthy men engaged in duties worthy of time and intelligence; they are local since they pertain to the region that has made such a monument of prosperity possible.

So general have mural decorations become that almost every large city can boast one or more buildings thus beautified. The Ponce de Leon at St. Augustine was one of the earlier hotels to engage the assistance of mural painters; today many through the country have followed a similar plan. Courthouses, schools, colleges and state capitols are not infrequently adorned by talented painters. Excellent mural painting can be found in the Appellate Courts Building in New York; banks in the east and middle west are appropriately decorated. The Capitol buildings in Iowa and in Pennsylvania both merit attention and praise, but the Capitol of Minnesota is mentioned here because it belongs to the north-west and thus far remains unsurpassed in interior beauty.

The legislature of Minnesota appropriated $250,000 for the mural decorations of its new Capitol at St. Paul. Garnsey, because of his splendid achievements elsewhere, was entrusted with them.

The first matter to be considered by a decorator is the style of architecture employed, that the interior adornment may seem, not something imposed upon it, but an integral part of the building itself. The quality and color of the marble, the stone, metal and woodwork are also questions of greatest importance. Color schemes must be carried out harmoniously if the eyes of future generations are not to be offended. The present method of having mural paintings done upon canvas and afterwards adhered to walls has lessened the risk of rapid destruction. The unfortunate fate of William Hunt's fine pictures in the New York Capitol, destroyed within ten years by the settling of the building, proved that precaution was necessary if public funds were to be forthcoming for such purposes.

The Governor's Reception Room is Venetian in style and contains six pictures, the subjects of which are closely associated with the history of the state. The Treaty of Traverse the Sioux was done by F. D. Millet; the Discovery of the Falls of St. Anthony by Douglas Volk. The other four pertain to Minnesota's part in the Civil War. Howard Pyle produced the one entitled the Minnesota Regiment at Nashville; Rufus Zogbaum, the First Regiment at Gettysburg; Millet, the First Regiment at Vicksburg, and Volk, the Second Regiment at Mission Ridge.

On the second floor are located the Senate Chamber, House of Representatives, and the Supreme Court. Over the entrance to the Senate Chamber, H. O. Walker painted the picture called: Yesterday, Today and Tomorrow, in which the torch of progress is being handed along, from one age to another. Over the entrance to the Supreme Court, Kenyon Cox produced another of similar proportions; Contemplation, Law and Letters. In the halls twelve small paintings give honor to twelve industries through which Minnesota has prospered: Milling, Stone-cutting, Winnowing, Commerce, Mining, Navigation, Hunting, Agriculture, Horticulture, Logging, Dairying, and Pioneering.

The Senate Chamber is finished in French Fleur de Peche marble, providing a creamy ground. Mahogany furniture is used and the decorations are in ivory, gold, and old blue. Two beautiful paintings by Blashfield are here. These are entitled Discoverers and Civilizers led to the Source of the Mississippi, and Minnesota the Grain State. Four others by Garnsey represent Courage, Freedom, Justice and Equality.

The room used by the Supreme Court is done in white Vermont marble. The paintings here are the work of La Farge and done in his best style. Over the Judge's bench is the first of the series pertaining to Law. It is called Moral and Divine Law and portrays Moses kneeling on Mount Sinai; the second, the Relation of the Individual to the State, is illustrated by Socrates discoursing to his friends on the Republic; the third, the Recording of Precedents, by Confucius reading from a scroll while pupils inscribe words of ancient wisdom; and the Adjustment of Conflicting Interest, by Count Raymond of Toulouse, swearing in the presence of state and ecclesiastical dignitaries to observe the liberties of the city.

The House of Representatives, also in white Vermont marble, is decorated by a frieze of green, red, and ivory. The ceiling is covered with designs of foliage, emblems and eagles.

Two paintings, Record and History, were done by Mackaye.

The building is crowned by a dome and in the large spandrels over its four arches are paintings by E. E. Simmons; The American Genius guarded by Wisdom following Hope; Wisdom banishing Savagery; Wisdom breaking the Ground; Wisdom as Minnesota distributing her products. Between the twelve windows of the dome are panels in deep blue, done by Garnsey.

Throughout the decorations are appropriate to Minnesota alone, and more and more is the thesis being accepted that subjects for decorations of public buildings in a great commonwealth should be found in local history and industrial conditions, without having to import to a new continent themes which have been repeatedly and more appropriately illustrated in foreign lands.

AMERICAN LITERATURE

Two Golden Days.

There are two days of the week upon which and about which I never worry. Two care-free days, kept sacredly free from fear and apprehension.

One of these days is yesterday. Yesterday, with all its cares and frets, with all its pains and aches, all its faults, its mistakes and blunders, has passed forever beyond the reach of my recall. I cannot undo an act that I wrought; I cannot unsay a word that I said on yesterday. All that it holds in my life, of wrongs, regret, and sorrow, is in the hands of the Mighty Love that can bring honey out of the rock, and sweet waters out of the bitterest desert—the love that can make the wrong things right, that can turn weeping into laughter, that can give beauty for ashes, the garment of praise for the spirit of heaviness, joy of the morning for woe of the night.

Save for the beautiful memories, sweet and tender, that linger like the perfume of roses in the heart of the day that is gone, I have nothing to do with yesterday. It was mine; it is God's.

And the other day I do not worry about is to-morrow. To-morrow, with all its possible adventures, its burdens, its perils, its large promise and poor performance, its failures and mistakes, is as far beyond the reach of my mastery as its dead sister, yesterday. It is a day of God's. Its sun will rise in roseate splendor, or behind a mask of weeping clouds. But it will rise. Until then—the same love and patience that hold yesterday and hold to-morrow, shining with tender promise into the heart of to-day—I have no possession in that unborn day of grace. All else is in the safe-keeping of the Infinite Love that holds for me the treasure of yesterday. The love that is higher than the stars, wider than the skies, deeper than the seas. To-morrow—it is God's day. It will be mine.

—Burdette.

PREFATORY CHAPTER.

AMERICAN literature may be regarded from two quite different points of view, either as a contributory stream to the great river of English literature, or as an independent organism, derived indeed from the old world, but mainly interesting because of its revelation of American life. Our estimate of American literature and the tests by which we arrive at such an estimate necessarily differ according to the point of view which we adopt. If we regard it from the first standpoint, we must apply neither the historical nor the personal test, but must compare American literature, man for man and book for book, with the authors and works of the corresponding period of English literature, Cooper with Scott, Longfellow and Poe with Browning, Tennyson, and Swinburne, the *Scarlet Letter* with *Vanity Fair, David Copperfield,* and *Adam Bede*. Such a comparison, we must frankly admit, American literature cannot sustain. Interesting and delightful as have been our contributions to the whole body of English literature, they have been, with a few exceptions, hardly of the first order of merit. A standard collection of the masterpieces of literature produced in English since the beginning of the seventeenth century would include comparatively few American works. We should outrank the other English settlements and conquests, Canada, Australia, and South Africa, but should still fall far behind the mother country. Yet, after all, this is only what is to be expected, and no American except one whose patriotism blinds his judgment would dream of making such a comparison.

There is, however, another test which we may apply to American literature and another reason for our interest and delight in it. American literature springs naturally from that of Great Britain, but almost from the beginning it has sought its themes in American life, and with the development of civilization on this continent our literature has developed in variety, in originality of subject and form, in ability to represent American life. We have a right, a duty even, to interest ourselves in American literature, simply because it is American—because it reflects for us the varied phases of our national existence.

This is especially true of the first period of our literature, the Colonial. The memoirs, histories, poems, and sermons of this time have for us Americans an interest which they can have for no others. The great revival in recent years of interest in American origins has called the attention of hundreds to these well-nigh forgotten works of our ancestors. Such a book as Cotton Mather's *Magnalia Christi Americana*, for example, has for us something of the interest which Bede's *Ecclesiastical History* has for the student of old English times. "It does," to quote Professor Trent's words, "for the early New England saints what Hakluyt and Purchas did for the Elizabethan seamen," and it has, for the average reader at least, the immense advantage of being written in quaint seventeenth century English, not in medieval Latin. Longfellow's poem, *The Phantom Ship*, is but one example of the many legends which it has furnished to later writers.

In the writings of Benjamin Franklin, scientist, statesman, philosopher, and man of letters, we find for the first time in American literature work which has an absolute value and makes its appeal to other than American readers. Franklin was the first great representative of the American spirit, industrious, practical, liberty-loving, humanitarian, and humorous. He was also a citizen of the world of the approved eighteenth century type. His works still live because they embody and reveal the man himself and the spirit of his age. His *Autobiography* is one of the masterpieces of this branch of literature and has been well styled a "cosmopolitan classic."

The stormy days of the Revolution and the hardly less troubled period that followed were not favorable to the production of pure literature. The genius of the new born nation turned toward war, diplomacy, and constitution-making rather than to humane letters. Yet it is precisely in this period that the first gleams of pure literature appear. A handful of lyrics by Freneau, a group of novels by Brockden Brown, give us the first evidence that the genius of literature, imaginative, poetic and creative, had flitted across the Atlantic to find an abiding place in the New World. There is nothing strikingly original in the work of either of these writers; in sentiment and form Freneau's poetry corresponds closely to the general run of mid-eighteenth century verse in England, and Brown's novels are strongly reminiscent of Mrs. Radcliffe and William Godwin. But the very titles of Freneau's best lyrics, *The Wild Honeysuckle, The Indian Burying-Ground, The Elegy on Those Who Fell at Eutaw*, show that he did not seek abroad for inspiration, and the most vivid passages in Brown's rather artificial romances are those that depict with startling realism the ravages of yellow fever in his native town and the horrors of an Indian raid along the Pennsylvania borders.

A great development of literary form, a still greater advance in range of action and positive achievement is seen in the work of three writers born toward the close of the eighteenth century. Washington Irving is the first American man of letters who was purely a man of letters, who owed his reputation solely to his writings. And his reputation, even in his own day, was world-wide, "the first ambassador," Thackeray calls him, "whom the New World of letters sent to the Old." An admirable literary artist, it might be said of him, as of his predecessor and model, Goldsmith, that he touched nothing which he did not adorn. His range, to be sure, was far less wide than Goldsmith's; he was neither a poet nor a dramatist, but he was a delightful essayist, a sunny humorist, and a picturesque historian. His supreme achievement, however, was the discovery, one might almost say the creation, of a new form of literature, the only form, perhaps, in which the work of American authors may fairly challenge comparison with the rest of the world—the short story. And Irving's most famous stories, *Rip Van Winkle* and *The Legend of Sleepy Hollow*, are genuinely American in subject, atmosphere, and temper.

Cooper presents in many ways a striking contrast to Irving. He lacks Irving's humor, his love of old romance, his charm of style. He was no literary artist, rather a country gentleman who almost by accident stumbled into literature. But he had a rich fund of experiences on sea and shore such as the quiet city-bred Irving quite lacked, and he had a still more important gift, the faculty of creation on a large scale. He was a born story-teller. In spite of his detestable prose style his great romances of the sea and the forest move swiftly and surely on their way. And in the highest sphere of all, that of character creation, Cooper's best work has been rarely equalled and never surpassed by any of his successors. "Leatherstocking, Uncas, Hardheart, Tom Coffin," says Thackeray, "are quite the equals of Scott's men; perhaps Leatherstocking is better than any one in Scott's lot. *La Longue Carabine* is one of the great prizemen of fiction. He ranks with your Uncle Toby, Sir Roger de Coverly, Falstaff—heroic figures all." Thackeray's praise may be, perhaps, a little high-pitched, but it is hardly becoming for an American to cavil at foreign praise of a writer whose works have made a triumphal procession through all European countries.

It is with a sense of disappointment that we turn from the work of Cooper's contemporary, William Cullen Bryant, the first American poet who obtained a hearing across the Atlantic. Bryant has nothing of Irving's easy grace or Cooper's creative power. He is limited in range, deficient in passion;

> If he stirs you at all, it is just, on my soul,
> Like being stirred up with the very North Pole

Lowell wrote mockingly, but not untruly in his *Fable for Critics*. In theme and manner Bryant seems by turns a young disciple of Wordsworth and a late survivor of the elegiac school of the eighteenth century. It is not easy at first to define the original and American element in his work. Yet Emerson was right when he called Bryant "this native, original and patriotic poet   a true painter of the face of this country and of the sentiment of his own people." Bryant's fame is largely due to his position as the father of American poetry. His sense of style, his gift of lyrical utterance, was far superior to that of any of his predecessors; and his work, from his precocious early poems to the fruit of his ripe old age, was singularly equable. He was at once accepted as the first real poet of America, and he never gave his followers cause to disavow him. But quite apart from the historic estimate of his position, we may note in Bryant the elements of simplicity, moral sincerity, devotion to Nature, particularly in her graver aspects, and sober love of liberty, which go far to justify Emerson's eulogy.

Lack of space forbids any detailed discussion of later phases of American literature. We can only touch briefly on the great movement to which the name of the New England Renaissance has been applied. In essence it was a spiritual and intellectual revolution, breaking the chains which for nearly two centuries had been imposed upon that region by Calvinistic theology and Puritanic convention. It asserted the right of the individual to judge and act for himself, to prove all things and hold fast that which was good. It threw open the long closed doors of the old world treasuries of Art, Music, and Literature. It dealt a shattering blow at the traditional system of education and introduced into our academic life that "free elective system" against which our colleges are only now beginning to react. Above all it gave birth to a noble body of literature of which Emerson is the prophet, Longfellow the poet, Hawthorne the romancer, and Lowell the scholar, critic, and representative citizen.

Two of the greatest figures of American literature stand altogether apart from this movement, Poe the Bohemian poet and romancer, Whitman the singer of democratic brotherhood. The two have little in common except their aloofness from the dominant New England intellectualism and didacticism of their day. Poe is the least American of our writers, a fact which goes far to explain the cold indifference of his contemporaries and the slight esteem which he enjoys even today in this country when compared with the generous recognition of his genius in foreign lands. He was from the beginning to the end of his unhappy life a Pegasus struggling in an ill-fitting harness. An artist first and last he had no "message" for his age, and his age was on the one side too clamorous for moral messages, and on the other too absorbed in material progress to open its heart to this rare artist of the grotesque and the beautiful, this poet of melancholy, madness, and death. Nor was the period of the Civil War and Reconstruction that followed more fitted to extend him its sympathy. It is only by degrees as we have shaken off our Puritan prejudice against the artist that we have learned to overcome our antipathy to the man, and to recognize the surpassing craftsmanship and power of his tales, the passion, pathos, and lyrical cry of his poems.

Of all American authors it is Whitman who has provoked

the most heated discussion at home and abroad. During his life he was pelted with all the hard and foul words of the vocabulary, and words were the mildest of the weapons employed against him. The law was invoked to prohibit the publication of his works; a persecuting bureaucrat stripped him of his scanty means of subsistence. To his lovers, on the other hand, "the good gray poet" seemed a super-human and almost sacred figure. This fierce clash of opinion, due in the first place to the freedom of speech with which the poet proclaimed a gospel that was as offensive to some as it was enlightening to others, goes back ultimately to the personality of the man. Just as Poe is an objective poet-artist whose work has a value altogether independent of his personality, so Whitman is essentially a subjective poet-prophet whose highest message was a revelation of his own personality. And his personality was a strange blend of strength with coarseness, fearlessness with brag, colossal egoism with a love for humanity that in action and speech often passed all bounds of convention. From his own personality sprang his gospel, a religion of humanity in which individualism joined hands with brotherly love in a triumphant march toward the goal of an all-embracing democracy. Some curious attempts have been made to show that Whitman's ideas are un-American. To me, at least, it seems quite plain both his personality and his message spring directly from his American environment and could nowhere else have taken just the form they did. Perhaps the most American thing about him is the joyous optimism with which he attempts to master, interpret, and spiritualize the vast surrounding materialism of America.

The great struggle of the Civil War produced curiously little permanent literature. Apart from a few fine lyrics, perhaps the only lasting contributions of that age to our literature are Lincoln's *Gettysburg Oration*, Lowell's *Commemoration Ode* and Whitman's *Drum Taps, Specimen Days* and the noble elegy on Lincoln, *When Lilacs Last in the Doorway Bloomed*. The literature produced since the Civil War is too varied, too large in bulk, and still too close to us to admit of wide generalization or impartial judgment. One thing seems clear, however, that it contains only one figure of the first class, he great humorist known and loved the world over under the name of Mark Twain. Some years before his death I attempted an appreciation of his work to which an editor prefixed the title, *Mark Twain—Made in America.* No phrase could more briefly and completely summarize the man and his work. He was American to the finger tips in his *naiveté,* his humor, his prejudices, his optimism, and his prose style, as American as Dickens, whom of all British writers he most closely resembles, was English. His very Americanism, while it endeared him to thousands of unsophisticated readers, went far to blind the eyes of the professional critic who sought in literature only a reflex of foreign models. It is too early as yet to affirm with certainty how much of Twain will live, but I believe that in his best work, *Roughing It, Life on the Mississippi* and the inimitable *Huckleberry Finn,* he has left us imperishable records of American life along the great river and upon the plains and mountains of the West.

A few words only are needed to summarize this brief review of American literature. It is plain that in some of the highest branches America has produced little or nothing. We have made no contribution to the drama of the world; we have no epic of the settlement, of the Civil War, or of the conquest of the West. Our best work has been done along lines indicated by our earliest writers, the lyric, the short story, and the novel, to which we should probably add the rhapsodies in prose and verse of Emerson and Whitman. Imagination of the highest creative type has been on the whole lacking; perfection of form has been oftener obtained than is generally supposed. From the beginning our literature has been marked by a didactic note. Our writers, with but few exceptions, have cherished the desire to instruct or to exhort. This is clearly apparent in our first great author, Franklin, and is not altogether wanting in Mark Twain. Twain himself realized this and like a true artist seems to have regretted it: "Information appears to stew out of me naturally," he says. "The more I calk up my sources and the tighter I get the more I leak wisdom."

Closely connected with this note is the popular, not to say the democratic character of American literature. It has little of the esoteric. No American author has wished, like Milton, for an audience "fit, though few." There is no literary caste in this country for every American is at least a potential reader, and it is to this not impossible everyman that our literature has been addressed.

This intimate connection between writer and reader is mainly responsible, I think, for the note of optimism so clearly heard in American literature. Cheerful confidence in the future has been from the beginning an American characteristic. Even in these days of "muck-raking" when every cheap magazine breaks out once a month with some fresh eruption of scandal, there seems to be a general feeling that all will be well in the end, that evils have only to be made known in order to be ended. 'Tis a consummation devoutly to be wished; whether it is in accord with the teachings of history or not is another question.

Finally American literature, making again a few necessary exceptions, has been realistic. Hampered as it has been by tradition and convention it has none the less sought its themes at home, not abroad, in the real present, not in the romantic past. From Franklin to Mark Twain is a long distance, but the way is filled with a series of works that picture the life of our countrymen, give voice to their thoughts, and record their aspirations. And if I may close where I began, I would repeat that the main value and chief interest of American literature consists in the fact that it is a true reflection of American life.

CHAPTER I.

Colonial Literature

COLONIAL AMERICA is divided historically into two periods. The first beginning with the settlement of Jamestown, Virginia, in 1607, ends with the date of Bacon's Rebellion and King Philip's War, in 1676. In those seventy years a section of the English people snatched from country towns and busy cities made new dwellings in a primitive and dangerous wilderness, where they were home-sick and yearning to keep in touch with absent friends; or, as in the case of the Puritans, in love with their freedom, perilous as it was, and anxious to coax and win others to try the dangers of the deep and of their environment, for sweet Liberty's sake. Naturally enough, their records were, at first, in the form of letters, the daily happenings, work, perils of the colonists, with accounts of strange fauna and flora, and descriptions of that horrible man-monster, the American Indian. Yet Captain John Smith wrote a book called "The True Relation of Virginia" (1608), enlarged later into "The General History of Virginia," mostly a compilation, vigorously colored with his own personality, and containing the rude germ of the charming legend of Pocahontas. In the second period Robert Berkeley wrote a "History of Virginia," published in London in 1705, less personal, full of observation of plants, animals and Indians, but not free from prejudice. The Virginians were churchmen and royalists, a wealthy, worldly, cheerful, gaming, hunting, and often illiterate set. Still the records of that colony, whether in letter, diary, or book, bear the impress of their surroundings, and were directly valuable in broadening and enriching the English literature of that day.

The Puritan colonies were theocracies, the mass of the people being men of the middle class, mechanics and farmers. But their leaders were clergymen, educated at the universities, who, to use the language of Mather, "felt that without a college these regions would have been mere unwatered places for the devil." Harvard College was accordingly founded in 1638, and a printing press set up in Cambridge in 1639, under the oversight of the university authorities.

The first English book issued in America was a collection of David's Psalms in metre, called "The Bay Psalm Book," and intended for singing in divine worship, public and private. Ere long new writers employed the press, mostly divines, famous and useful in their own congregations and town and time, whose themes were the vanity of life, impending doom and the immanence of sin; their names form the lists in forgotten catalogues; their books moulder in the dimness of attic libraries, or on the shelves of octaogenarian bibliophiles.

A different personality does stand out in this first Puritan period, that of Mrs. Anne Bradstreet, not because of the beauty of her verse, as we judge poetry nowadays, but because of the sweet and powerful influence it exerted during a long life, and by reason of the grief of her disciples, John Norton and John Rogers, who commenced the second colonial period of Puritan literature with graceful and mournful elegies on her death.

This second period began in 1676, and ended with the early struggles of the American Revolution. It contains such names as that of Michael Wigglesworth, "the explicit and unshrinking rhymer of the Five Points of Calvinism." The Puritan religion, as developed amid the hardships of the American wilderness, became narrow, intense, and gloomy; and these poems of anguish and of the wrath of God, were read and studied with the Bible and the Shorter Catechism.

The Mather family ruled intellectually in New England for three generations, the greatest of the great name being Cotton Mather, who was born in 1663, and died in 1728. He had an enormous memory, enormous industry, and enormous vanity. He was devout in all the minutiæ of life: poking the fire, wind-

Copyright by Underwood & Underwood, N. Y.
OLD FAITHFUL—YELLOWSTONE.

ing the clock, putting out the candle, washing his hands, and paring his nails, with appropriate religious texts and meditations. He knew Hebrew, Latin, Greek, French, Spanish, and one Indian tongue. He had the largest private library in America. He wrote many books, the names of some being as follows: "Boanerges. A Short Essay to Strengthen the Impressions Produced by Earthquakes;" "The Comforts of One Walking Through the Valley of the Shadow of Death;" "Ornaments for the Daughters of Zion;" "The Peculiar Treasure of the Almighty King Opened," etc. He also compiled the most famous book produced by any American during the colonial time: "Magnalia Christi Americana; or, The Ecclesiastical History of New England, from its first planting in the year 1620 unto the year of Our Lord, 1698." It is a history of the settlement of New England, with lives of its governors, magistrates and divines; a history of Harvard College and the churches; an account of the "Wars of the Lord," narrating the troubles of the New Englanders with "the Devil, Separatists, Familists, Antinomians, Quakers, clerical imposters, and Indians." It is an ill-digested mass of personal reminiscences, social gossip, snatches of conversation, touches of description, traits of character and life, that help us to paint for ourselves some living pictures of early New England.

Jonathan Edwards, the most acute and original thinker yet born in America, was graduated at Yale College in 1720, after a marvellous boyhood of intense and rigid intellectual discipline. As a student at college and afterwards as tutor there, his researches and discoveries in science were so great that had he not preferred theology he would have made a distinguished investigator in astronomy and physics. He was the pastor of a church at Northampton until he was dismissed on account of the strictness of his discipline, then missionary to the Indians near Stockbridge, and in 1758 was called to be president of Princeton College. As a man Jonathan Edwards was simple, meek, spiritual, gentle, and disinterested; as a metaphysician he was acute, profound, and remorselessly logical; as a theologian he was the massive champion of John Calvin and all the rigors of his creed.

There were many distinguished names in the various colonies during the second period—governors, divines, lawyers, professors, physicians, and college presidents. There were also forty-three newspapers and magazines in Philadelphia, Boston, and New York, together with the necessary and utilitarian almanac. But the only really renowned authors were Cotton Mather and Jonathan Edwards, and they contributed to ecclesiastical history and theology rather than to literature. Benjamin Franklin, whose literary work began in this period, became yet more distinguished in the next, and is reserved for later treatment. But colonial history, as reproduced in letters, diaries, and state and family records, and in Mather's book, has been the great storehouse from which Hawthorne, Whittier, and Longfellow drew the materials for their familiar romances, tales, or verse, and has thus formed the sturdy foundations of a purely American literature.

CAPTAIN JOHN SMITH.

No name is more indelibly impressed on the early history of Virginia than that of the adventurous Captain John Smith (1580-1631). He was a redoubtable warrior and experienced navigator, who has told his own story in such a way as to excite some doubts as to its truth. After abundance of adventures in the East of Europe, he took part in the English attempt to colonize Virginia. In exploring the country he was captured by the Indians, and, as he asserted, was saved by the intercession of Pocahontas. He was made president of the colony of Jamestown, but in 1609 was obliged to return to England, having been disabled by an explosion of gunpowder. Yet he afterwards resumed his explorations and was made Admiral of New England. Finally he settled down in his native land and wrote a number of books describing Virginia and New England, and reciting his own history. This humble successor of Sir Walter Raleigh is favorably mentioned by Fuller among the worthies of England.

Captain John Smith's Captivity.

Smith's "General History of Virginia, New England and the Summer Isles" (1624), gives an account of voyages, discoveries and settlements from 1584 to 1624. Book III., which was edited by the Rev. W. Simmonds, D. D., from Smith's account, gives the following narrative. The spelling is here modernized except in proper names.

But our comedies never endured long without a tragedy; some idle exceptions being muttered against Captain Smith for not discovering the head of Chickahamania River, and being taxed by the Council [of the Virginia Company] to be too slow in so worthy an attempt. The next voyage he proceeded so far that with much labor by cutting of trees asunder he made his passage; but when his barge could pass no farther, he left her in a broad bay, out of danger of shot, commanding none should go ashore till his return: himself with two English and two savages went up higher in a canoe; but he was not long absent, but his men went ashore, whose want of government gave both occasion and opportunity to the savages to surprise one George Cassen, whom they slew, and much failed not to have cut off the boat and all the rest.

Smith, little dreaming of that accident, being got to the marshes at the river's head, twenty miles in the desert, had his two men slain (as is supposed) sleeping by the canoe, whilst himself by fowling sought them victual: who finding he was beset with two hundred savages, two of them he slew, still defending himself with the aid of a savage, his guide, whom he bound to his arm with his garters, and used him as a buckler, yet he was shot in his thigh a little, and had many arrows that stuck in his clothes, but no great hurt, till at last they took him prisoner.

When this news came to Jamestown, much was their sorrow for his loss, few expecting what ensued.

Six or seven weeks those barbarians kept him prisoner, many strange triumphs and conjurations they made of him, yet he so demeaned himself amongst them, as he not only diverted them from surprising the Fort, but procured his own liberty, and got himself and his company such estimation amongst them, that those savages admired him more than their own Quiyouckosucks.

At last they brought him to Meronocomoco, where was Powhatan their Emperor. Here more than two hundred of those grim courtiers stood wondering at him, as he had been a monster; till Powhatan and his train had put themselves in their greatest braveries. Before a fire upon a seat like a bedstead, he sat covered with a great robe, made of rarowcun [raccoon] skins, and all the tails hanging by. On either hand did sit a young wench of sixteen or eighteen years, and along on each side the house, two rows of men, and behind them as many women, with all their heads and shoulders painted red: many of their heads bedecked with the white down of birds; but every one with something: and a great chain of white beads about their necks.

At his entrance before the king, all the people gave a great shout. The Queen of Appamotuck was appointed to bring him water to wash his hands, and another brought him a bunch of feathers, instead of a towel, to dry them: having feasted him after their best barbarous manner they could, a long consultation was held, but the conclusion was, two great stones were brought before Powhatan: then as many as could laid hands on him, dragged him to them, and thereon laid his head, and being ready with their clubs, to beat out his brains, Pocahontas, the King's dearest daughter, when no entreaty could prevail, got his head in her arms, and laid her own upon his to save him from death: whereat the Emperor was contented he should live to make him hatchets, and her bells, beads and copper; for they thought him as well of all occupations as themselves. For the King himself will make his own robes, shoes, bows, arrows, pots; plant, hunt, or do anything so well as the rest.

> They say he bore a pleasant show,
>   But sure his heart was sad,
> For who can pleasant be, and rest,
>   That lives in fear and dread:
> And having life suspected, doth
>   It still suspected lead?

Two days after, Powhatan having disguised himself in the most fearfullest manner he could, caused Captain Smith to be brought forth to a great house in the woods, and there upon a mat by the fire to be left alone. Not long after from behind a mat that divided the house, was made the most dolefullest noise he ever heard; then Powhatan more like a devil than a man, with some two hundred more as black as himself, came unto him and told him now they were friends, and presently he should go to Jamestown, to send him two great guns, and a grindstone, for which he would give him the country of Capahowosick, and forever esteem him as his son Nantaquoud.

So to Jamestown, with twelve guides, Powhatan sent him. That night they quartered in the woods, he still expecting (as he had done all this long time of his imprisonment) every hour to be put to one death or other: for all their feasting. But Almighty God (by His divine providence) had mollified the hearts of those stern barbarians with compassion. The next morning betimes they came to the Fort, where Smith having used the savages with what kindness he could, he showed Rawhunt, Powhatan's trusty servant, two demi-culverins and a millstone to carry [to] Powhatan: they found them somewhat too heavy; but when they did see him discharge them, being loaded with stones, among the boughs of a great tree loaded with icicles, the ice and branches came so tumbling down, that the poor savages ran away half dead with fear. But at last we regained some conference with them, and gave them such toys; and sent to Powhatan, his women, and children such presents, as gave them in general full content.

NEW ENGLAND.

REV. WILLIAM MORELL, an English clergyman, spent a year or two (1623) at Plymouth, and after his return wrote a Latin poem "Nova Anglia" to which he added an English version. The opening contains the following passage:

> FEAR not, poor Muse, 'cause first to sing her fame
> That's yet scarce known, unless by map or name;
> A grandchild to earth's Paradise is born,
> Well limb'd, well nerv'd, fair, rich, sweet, yet forlorn.
> Thou blest director, so direct my verse
> That it may win her people friends' commerce.
> Whilst her sweet air, rich soil, blest seas, my pen
> Shall blaze, and tell the natures of her men.
> New England, happy in her new, true style,
> Weary of her cause she's to sad exile

Exposed by hers unworthy of her land;
Entreats with tears Great Britain to command
Her empire, and to make her know the time,
Whose act and knowledge only makes divine.
A royal work well worthy England's king,
These natives to true truth and grace to bring;
A noble work for all these noble peers,
Which guide this State in their superior spheres.
You holy Aarons, let your censers ne'er
Cease burning till these men Jehovah fear.

MRS. ANNE BRADSTREET.

AMONG the earliest and therefore most honored verse writers of New England was Mrs. Anne Bradstreet (1612-1672). She was the daughter of Governor Thomas Dudley, and her husband, Simon Bradstreet, also became Governor of Massachusetts. When her poems were printed in London in 1650, the publishers prefixed the title, "The Tenth Muse, lately sprung up in America." They were didactic and meditative, treating of the Four Elements, the Seasons of the Year, and ended with a political dialogue between Old and New England. An enlarged edition, published at Boston in 1678, was superior to the first in literary merit. Mrs. Bradstreet was the mother of eight children, whom she commemorated in these homely lines:

> I had eight birds hatcht in the nest;
> Four cocks there were, and hens the rest.
> I nurst them up with pains and care,
> Nor cost nor labor did I spare;
> Till at the last they felt their wing,
> Mounted the trees, and learnt to sing.

A Love-Letter to her Husband.

Phœbus, make haste, the day's too long, begone,
The silent night's the fittest time for moan,
But stay this once unto my suit give ear,
And tell my griefs in either Hemisphere:
(And if the whirling of thy wheels don't drown
The woful accents of my doleful sound),
If in thy swift career thou canst make stay,
I crave this boon, this errand by the way:
Commend me to the man more loved than life,
Show him the sorrows of his widow'd wife,

My dumpish thoughts, my groans, my brackish tears,
My sobs, my longing hopes, my doubting fears
And if he love, how can he there abide?
My interest's more than all the world beside.
He that can tell the stars or ocean sand,
Or all the grass that in the meads do stand,
The leaves in the woods, the hail or drops of rain,
Or in a cornfield number every grain,
Or every mote that in the sunshine hops,
May count my sighs and number all my drops.
Tell him, the countless steps that thou dost trace,
That once a day thy spouse thou may'st embrace;
And when thou canst not treat by loving mouth,
Thy rays afar salute her from the south.

But for one month I see no day (poor soul),
Like those far situate under the pole,
Which day by day long wait for thy arise,
Oh, how they joy when thou dost light the skies!
O Phœbus, hadst thou but thus long from thine
Restrained the beams of thy beloved shrine,
At thy return, if so thou couldst or durst,
Behold a Chaos blacker than the first.
Tell him here's worse than a confused matter,
His little world's a fathom under water,
Nought but the fervor of his ardent beams,
Hath power to dry the torrent of these streams.
Tell him I would say more, but cannot well,
Oppresséd minds abrupted tales do tell.
Now post with double speed, mark what I say,
By all our loves conjure him not to stay.

MICHAEL WIGGLESWORTH.

This "little feeble shadow of a man" was the pastor of Meldon for about fifty years, though occasionally obliged by physical weakness to suspend preaching. He died in 1705, aged seventy-four. His poem "The Day of Doom," describing the last judgment, remains a monument of the severest Puritanical theology. Another of his poems "Meat out of the Eater," is a series of meditations on afflictions as useful to Christians. The following verses are given as an appendix to the former poem.

A Song of Emptiness.—Vanity of Vanities.

Vain, frail, short-lived, and miserable man,
   Learn what thou art, when thy estate is best,
A restless wave o' th' troubled ocean,
   A dream, a lifeless picture finely dressed.

A wind, a flower, a vapor and a bubble,
   A wheel that stands not still, a trembling reed,
A trolling stone, dry dust, light chaff and stuff,
   A shadow of something, but truly nought indeed.

Learn what deceitful toys, and empty things,
   This world and all its best enjoyments be:
Out of the earth no true contentment springs,
   But all things here are vexing vanity.

For what is beauty but a fading flower,
   Or what is pleasure but the devil's bait,
Whereby he catcheth whom he would devour,
   And multitudes of souls doth ruinate?

And what are friends, but mortal men as we,
   Whom death from us may quickly separate?
Or else their hearts may quite estranged be,
   And all their love be turned into hate.

And what are riches, to be doated on?
   Uncertain, fickle, and ensnaring things;
They draw men's souls into perdition,
   And when most needed, take them to their wings.

Ah, foolish man! that sets his heart upon
   Such empty shadows, such wild fowl as these,
That being gotten will be quickly gone,
   And whilst they stay increase but his disease.

COTTON MATHER.

No family was more prominent in the ecclesiastical history of New England than that of the Mathers. The non-conformist minister, Richard Mather, emigrated to Massachusetts in 1635. His son, Increase Mather, for a time resided in England, but returned to America and was made pastor of the North Church, Boston. He was also president of Harvard College and obtained from William III. a new charter for the colony. Still more famous was his son Cotton Mather (1663-1728), noted for his learning, industry and piety, yet full of vanity. His fluency in writing was shown in the production of nearly four hundred books. But his fatal delusion about witchcraft has affixed an indelible stigma on his name. He had written "Memorable Providences relating to Witchcraft" in 1685, and when the mania broke out in Salem in 1692 he eagerly promoted the agitation, and wrote his "Wonders of the Invisible World," which was controverted by Robert Calef's "More Wonders of the Invisible World," published in London in 1700. When the witch-hunting epidemic had passed away, it was found that Mather's reputation had suffered. He was unable to obtain the object of his ambition, the presidency of Harvard. His chief work, the ecclesiastical history of New England, he called "Magnalia Christi Americana."

BISHOP GEORGE BERKELEY.

America is indebted to Bishop Berkeley (1684-1753), not only for his gracious prophecy of her future importance, but for what he tried to do to bring about its fulfillment, though his residence in America did not last three years. George Berkeley, born near Kilkenny, Ireland, and educated at Trinity College, Dublin, early manifested a strong predilection for metaphysical speculation. His opposition to philosophic materialism led him to use arguments so subtle that he was popularly supposed to deny the existence of matter. But his aim was rather to establish the doctrine that a continual exercise of creative power is implied in the world presented to the senses. His views were set forth in a "Treatise on the Principles of Human Knowledge" (1710), and in "Dialogues between Hylas and Philonous" (1713). After publishing these works Berkeley went to London, where he enjoyed the society of the wits who gave literary fame to the reign of Queen Anne. Then he spent some years in travel on the Continent. After his return to Ireland he was made Dean of Derry, and married the daughter of the Speaker of the Irish House of Commons. Having received a bequest of nearly £4000 from Miss Vanhomrigh, Dean Swift's "Vanessa," he offered to devote his talents and fortune to the promotion of education in America. Relying on the promises of the king and his ministers, he crossed the ocean to found a college at Newport, Rhode Island. During his residence here he meditated and composed his "Alciphron, or the Minute Philosopher," a dialogue in defence of religion. Receiving no parliamentary grant, he was obliged to return, but transferred the library of 880 volumes he had brought for his own use to Yale College, where they had the startling effect of converting the president to Episcopacy. Berkeley was made Bishop of Cloyne in 1734, and held this position for nearly twenty years. Being subject to fits of melancholia, he had recourse to the use of tar water. This led to his writing "Siris, a Chain of Philosophical Reflections and Inquiries concerning the Virtues of Tar Water." He died at Oxford, where he had removed six months before in order to be near his son. This learned and liberal Irish clergyman was most warmly praised by his contemporaries, even the satirist Pope ascribing to him "every virtue under heaven."

America.

(On the Prospect of Planting Arts and Learning in America, A. D. 1732.)

The Muse, disgusted at an age and clime
    Barren of every glorious theme,
In distant lands now waits a better time,
    Producing subjects worthy fame.

In happy climes, where from the genial sun
    And virgin earth such scenes ensue,
The force of art by nature seems outdone,
    And fancied beauties by the true:

In happy climes, the seat of innocence,
    Where nature guides and virtue rules;
Where men shall not impose for truth and sense
    The pedantry of courts and schools.

There shall be sung another golden age,
    The rise of empires and of arts,
The good and great, inspiring epic rage,
    The wisest heads and noblest hearts.

Not such as Europe breeds in her decay,
    Such as she bred when fresh and young,
When heavenly flame did animate her clay,
    By future poets shall be sung.

Westward the course of empire takes its way;
    The four first acts already past,
A fifth shall close the drama with the day—
    Time's noblest offspring is the last.

From 1765-1800.

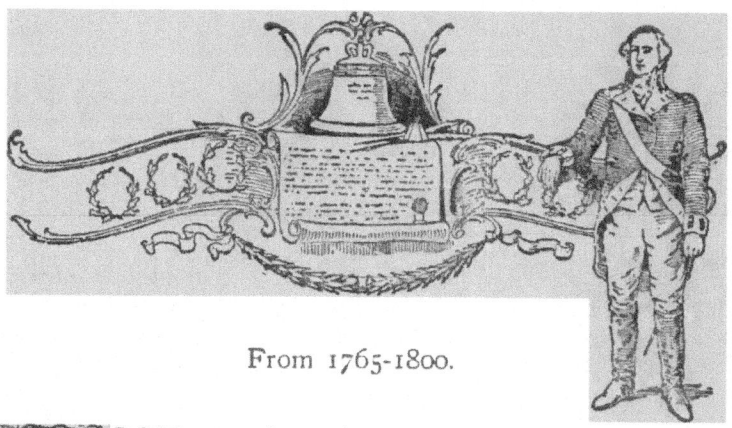

FROM the first English settlement in America, problems of government had occupied the colonists. In the cabin of the *Mayflower* the Pilgrim Fathers formed themselves into a body politic by a solemn compact. In several of the colonies constitutions were framed, which afterwards served as models for those of the States and of the Federal Government. In their town meetings, provisional assemblies and legislatures the people and their representatives discussed the fundamental principles of government. These earnest Christians found in the Bible directions for public affairs as well as for private conduct, and gladly adopted the Laws of Moses as far as they seemed applicable. In New England the people sympathized with the Parliament in its resistance to the arbitrary exercise of power by the Stuart kings. The same struggle was repeated on a smaller scale in the colonies when the assemblies sought to curb the royal and proprietary governors.

When George III. and his subservient Parliament sought to shift part of the burdens of the mother country on the colonies, now showing some degree of prosperity, they were amazed at the steadfast resistance of the Americans, who had become accustomed to regulate their public affairs. The colonies had been drawn closer together during the war with the French and Indians, and now made common cause against British injustice. Political discussion took the place that had once been occupied by theological controversy. Liberty and Union were the favorite themes of speakers and writers.

They produced the brilliant oratory of Patrick Henry, the state papers of Jefferson and Dickinson, and the elaborate defense of the new constitution by Hamilton and Madison. Most of these writings, admirable as they are in style and valuable as historical documents, lie outside of the domain of literature proper. But the progress of the Revolution was enlivened by satires and burlesques, and diversified by occasional poems. The careful student will note that the literary attempts of America closely corresponded to the style then prevailing in England, despite some attempts to give a native smack in words or facts.

Though Benjamin Franklin was a conspicuous actor in the public events of this period, his literary activity belonged rather to the earlier colonial time, yet his interesting "Autobiography" and his witty letters were written during his residence in France. Of the outburst of oratory which preceded the Revolution much has perished. Even the speeches on which rest the fame of James Otis and Patrick Henry and John Adams, were reconstructed by later writers from vague traditions. The "Pennsylvania Farmer's Letters," by John Dickinson, and the stirring pamphlet, "The Crisis," by Thomas Paine, stimulated the patriotism of the colonists. The satires of John Trumbull and the ballads of Francis Hopkinson gave zest to the Whigs and threw contempt on the Tories. The best poet of the period was the fluent Philip Freneau, who wrote odes, hymns, satires and ballads. Most of these writers continued to use the press after the national independence was acknowledged and the Federal government fully established. The *Federalist* was a series of essays by Hamilton, Madison and Jay, intended to explain and commend the proposed constitution to the people of New York for ratification. So ably were they written that they have since maintained their place as a valuable exposition of the aims and intentions of the founders of the Republic.

BENJAMIN FRANKLIN.

The public career and private life of Benjamin Franklin (1706-1790) are familiar throughout Europe as well as America. The early part is charmingly recorded with characteristic frankness in his entertaining "Autobiography," and later writers have taken pleasure in narrating the whole fully in various biographies. This work is concerned not with his honorable achievements as statesman and diplomatist, nor with his public-spirited activity as a citizen, nor with his discoveries in science and their practical applications to human convenience, but with his modest contributions to literature.

Benjamin Franklin, the youngest son in the large family of a Boston tallow-chandler, read every book he could lay his hands on, using for that purpose his infrequent leisure, and even his time of sleep. Early employed in his brother's printing-office, he began to write for the press. Subsequently, in Philadelphia, in his own paper, *The Pennsylvania Gazette*, he wrote articles month after month and year after year, notable for their clear and sprightly style, and their sentiments of liberality and good will. One of his jocular efforts is the "Drinker's Dictionary," a catalogue of slang words expressive of intoxication, of which some sound strangely modern and familiar, as *rocky, jag*, and the like.

In December, 1732, appeared the first issue of "The Pennsylvania Almanac, by Richard Saunders," afterwards known as "Poor Richard." It was full of humor, from the announcing advertisement, the exquisite fooling of the annual preface, the statements of eclipses and forecasts of the weather, to the verses and proverbs, inculcating industry and economy.

Some of the wisdom of "Poor Richard" is borrowed from Bacon, Rochefoucauld, and others; but most of it is the expression of Franklin's own shrewd, homely sense reduced to saws. For twenty-five years the annual sale of "Poor Richard" was not less than ten thousand copies. It was quoted all over the colonies, reprinted in England, and translated into French, Spanish, and even into modern Greek.

In 1741 Franklin founded the first literary periodical in America. It was called *The General Magazine and Historical Chronicle for all the British Provinces in America.* It lasted but six months, and is interesting only as marking a new development in this country.

When Franklin went to England in 1757 as agent for the colony, he made use of the press as before, and often wrote under an assumed name. An essay of his, published in the *Annual Register,* London, in 1760, and entitled, "Extract from a Piece written in Pennsylvania," gave Adam Smith arguments which he reproduced in his "Wealth of Nations." So likewise an important pamphlet, entitled, "The Interests of Great Britain Considered with regard to her Colonies and the Acquisition of Canada and Guadaloupe," had considerable influence on the policy of England, and helped to secure for that country the possession of Canada.

Franklin was deeply outraged by the fact that the English officers employed savages during the progress of the Revolutionary War, and while in Paris, in order to bring the horrors of Indian warfare home to the minds of the rulers of England he published what purported to be the supplement of a Boston newspaper, with all Defoe's minuteness of statement. This "Extract of a letter from Captain Gerrish of the New England Militia" contained an account of eight packs of scalps, taken from the inhabitants of the frontier colonies, "cured, dried, hooped, and painted, with all the Indian triumphal marks," and sent as a present to the Governor of Canada, to be by him transmitted to England. This hoax was widely scattered, and was soon quoted as a description of facts.

While in Paris, too, Franklin wrote to Madame Brillon his well known story of "Paying too dear for the Whistle," and the trifles—"Ephemera," "The Petition of the Left Hand," "The Handsome and Deformed Leg," "Morals of Chess," and the "Dialogue between Franklin and the Gout;" together with the celebrated "Letter to Madame Helvetius."

Franklin corresponded with the most learned men of his day, and all of his scientific discoveries were communicated in letters. These have been collected and published, together with his short, frank, and extremely interesting "Autobiography." When he left his father's home, he abandoned Puritanism in creed and conduct. He accepted the free-thinking tone then popular in England as well as France, yet he easily accommodated himself to the conventionalities of the society in which he lived.

Franklin's passion was a love of the useful. He brought to every subject—the homely business of the day, a scientific theory, or the tragic severance of a nation from its mother country—that clear sense which, stripping every proposition of disguising entanglements, revealed the naked ultimate for all to see and pass judgment upon. He had a luminous personality and a humorous tongue. Much of his power arose from an unfailing courtesy which chose to persuade rather than dominate.

Franklin's name was signed to four of the most important documents of American history—the Declaration of Independence, the Treaty of Alliance with France, the Treaty of Peace with Great Britain, the Federal Constitution.

For fifty years, on two Continents, social, scientific and political thought felt the impact of his shrewd and tolerant spirit. Count Mirabeau announced Franklin's death to the French nation in the following significant words: "The genius which has freed America and poured a flood of light over Europe, has returned to the bosom of Divinity."

Poor Richard's Almanac.

(From his "Autobiography.")

In 1732 [at the age of twenty-seven] I first published my *Almanac*, under the name of "Richard Saunders." It was continued by me about twenty-five years, and commonly called *Poor Richard's Almanac*. I endeavored to make it both entertaining and useful; and it accordingly came to be in such demand that I reaped considerable profit from it, vending annually near ten thousand. And observing that it was generally read—scarce any neighborhood in the Province being without it—I considered it a proper vehicle for conveying instruction among the common people, who bought scarcely any other books. I therefore filled all the little spaces that occurred between the remarkable days in the Calendar with proverbial sentences, chiefly such as inculcated industry and frugality as the means of procuring wealth, and thereby securing virtue; it being more difficult for a man in want to always act honestly, as, to use here one of those proverbs, "It is hard for an empty sack to stand upright."

These proverbs, which contained the wisdom of many ages and nations, I assembled and formed into a connected discourse prefixed to the *Almanac* of 1757, as the harangue of a wise old man to the people attending an auction. The bringing of all these scattered counsels thus into a focus enabled them to make greater impression. The piece being universally approved was copied in all the newspapers of the American continent, reprinted in Britain on a large sheet of paper to be stuck up in houses. Two translations were made of it in France; and great numbers of it were bought by the clergy and gentry, to distribute gratis among their poor parishioners and tenants. In Pennsylvania, as it discouraged useless expense in foreign superfluities, some thought it had its share of influence in producing that growing plenty of money which was observable several years after its publication.

The Way to Wealth.

(From "Poor Richard's Almanac.")

Courteous reader, I have heard that nothing gives an author so great pleasure as to find his works respectfully quoted by others. Judge, then, how much I must have been gratified by an incident I am going to relate to you. I stopped my horse lately where a great number of people were collected at an auction of merchants' goods. The hour of the sale not being come, they were conversing on the badness of the times; and one of the company called to a plain, clean old man, with white locks;—"Pray, Father Abraham, what think you of the times? Will not these heavy taxes quite ruin the country? How shall we ever be able to pay them? What would you advise us to?" Father Abraham stood up and replied, "If you would have my advice, I will give it you in short; for *A word to the wise is enough,* as Poor Richard says." They joined in desiring him to speak his mind, and, gathering round him, he proceeded as follows:

"Friends," said he, "the taxes are indeed very heavy, and. if those laid on by the government were the only ones we had to pay, we might more easily discharge them; but we have many others, and much more grievous to some of us. We are taxed twice as much by our idleness, three times as much by our pride, and four times as much by our folly; and from these taxes the commissioners cannot ease or deliver us, by allowing an abatement. However, let us harken to good advice, and something may be done for us; *God helps them that help themselves,* as Poor Richard says.

"It would be thought a hard government that should tax its people one-tenth part of their time, to be employed in its service; but idleness taxes many of us much more; sloth, by bringing on diseases, absolutely shortens life. *Sloth, like rust, consumes faster than labor wears; while the used key is always bright,* as Poor Richard says. *But dost thou love life? Then do not squander time, for that is the stuff life is made of,* as Poor Richard says. How much more than is necessary do we spend in sleep, forgetting that *The sleeping fox catches no poultry,* and that *There will be sleeping enough in the grave,* as Poor Richard says.

"*If time be of all things the most precious, wasting time must be,* as Poor Richard says, *the greatest prodigality;* since, as he elsewhere tells us, *Lost time is never found again; and what we call time enough always proves little enough.* Let us then up and be doing, and doing to the purpose; so by diligence shall we do more with less perplexity.

"But with our industry we must likewise be steady, settled and careful, and oversee our own affairs, with our own eyes, and not trust too much to others; for, *Three removes are as bad as a fire;* and again, *Keep thy shop, and thy shop will keep thee;* and again, *If you would have your business done, go; if not, send.*

"So much for industry, my friends, and attention to one's

own business; but to these we must add frugality, if we would make our industry more certainly successful. A man may, if he knows not how to save as he gets, keep his nose all his life to the grindstone, and die not worth a groat at last. *A fat kitchen makes a lean will.*

"Away, then, with your expensive follies, and you will not then have so much cause to complain of hard times, heavy taxes, and chargeable families.

"And further, *What maintains one vice would bring up two children.* You may think, perhaps, that a little tea or a little punch now and then, diet a little more costly, clothes a little finer, and a little entertainment now and then, can be no great matter; but remember, *Many a little makes a mickle.* Beware of little expenses: *A small leak will sink a great ship,* as Poor Richard says; and again, *Who dainties love, shall beggars prove;* and moreover, *Fools make feasts, and wise men eat them.*

"Here you are all got together at this sale of fineries and knickknacks. You call them *goods;* but, if you do not take care, they will prove *evils* to some of you. You expect they will be sold cheap, and perhaps they may for less than they cost; but, if you have no occasion for them, they must be dear to you. Remember what Poor Richard says: *Buy what thou hast no need of, and ere long thou shalt sell thy necessaries.* And again, *At a great pennyworth pause a while.* He means, that perhaps the cheapness is apparent only, and not real; or the bargain, by straitening thee in thy business, may do thee more harm than good. For in another place he says, *Many have been ruined by buying good pennyworths.* Again, *It is foolish to lay out money in a purchase of repentance;* and yet this folly is practised every day at auctions, for want of minding the Almanac. Many a one, for the sake of finery on the back, have gone with a hungry belly and half-starved their families. *Silks and satins, scarlet and velvets, put out the kitchen fire,* as Poor Richard says.

"But what madness must it be to *run in debt* for these superfluities! We are offered, by the terms of this sale, six months' credit; and that, perhaps, has induced some of us to attend it, because we cannot spare the ready money, and hope now to be fine without it. But, ah! think what you do when you run in debt; you give to another power over your liberty. If you cannot pay at the time, you will be ashamed to see your creditor; you will be in fear when you speak to him; you will make poor, pitiful, sneaking excuses; and, by degrees, come to lose your veracity, and sink into base, downright lying; for *The second vice is lying, the first is running in debt,* as Poor Richard says; and again, to the same purpose, *Lying rides upon Debt's back;* whereas a free-born Englishman ought not to be ashamed nor afraid to see or speak to any man living. But poverty often deprives a man of all spirit and virtue. *It is hard for an empty bag to stand upright.*

"What would you think of that prince, or of that government, who should issue an edict forbidding you to dress like a gentleman or gentlewoman, on pain of imprisonment or servitude? Would you not say that you were free, have a right to dress as you please, and that such an edict would be a breach of your privileges, and such a government tyrannical? And yet you are about to put yourself under such tyranny, when you run in debt for such dress! Your creditor has authority, at his pleasure, to deprive you of your liberty, by confining you in jail till you shall be able to pay him. When you have got your bargain, you may perhaps think little of payment; but, as Poor Richard says, *Creditors have better memories than debtors; creditors are a superstitious sect, great observers of set days and times.* The day comes round before you are aware, and the demand is made before you are prepared to satisfy it; or, if you bear your debt in mind, the term, which at first seemed so long, will, as it lessens, appear extremely short. Time will seem to have added wings to his heels as well as his shoulders. *Those have a short Lent, who owe money to be paid at Easter.* At present, perhaps, you may think yourselves in thriving circumstances, and that you can bear a little extravagance without injury; but,

For age and want save while you may;
No morning sun lasts a whole day.

Gain may be temporary and uncertain, but ever, while you live, expense is constant and certain; and *It is easier to build two chimneys, than to keep one in fuel,* as Poor Richard says; so, *Rather go to bed supperless, than rise in debt.*

"This doctrine, my friends, is reason and wisdom; but, after all, do not depend too much upon your own industry, and frugality, and prudence, though excellent things; for they may all be blasted, without the blessing of Heaven; and, therefore, ask that blessing humbly, and be not uncharitable to those that at present seem to want it, but comfort and help them. Remember, Job suffered, and was afterwards prosperous."

Thus the old gentleman ended his harangue. I resolved to be the better for it; and though I had at first determined to buy stuff for a new coat, I went away resolved to wear my old one a little longer. Reader, if thou wilt do the same, thy profit will be as great as mine. I am, as ever, thine to serve thee.

RICHARD SAUNDERS.

Turning the Grindstone.

When I was a little boy, I remember, one cold winter's morning, I was accosted by a smiling man with an axe on his shoulder. "My pretty boy," said he, "has your father a grindstone?" "Yes, sir," said I. "You are a fine little fellow," said he; "will you let me grind my axe on it?" Pleased with the compliment of "fine little fellow," "Oh yes, sir," I answered: "it is down in the shop." "And will you, my man," said he, patting me on the head, "get me a little hot water?" How could I refuse? I ran, and soon brought a kettleful. "How old are you? and what's your name?" continued he, without waiting for a reply: "I am sure you are one of the finest lads that ever I have seen: will you just turn a few minutes for me?"

Tickled with the flattery, like a little fool, I went to work, and bitterly did I rue the day. It was a new axe, and I toiled and tugged till I was almost tired to death. The school-bell rang, and I could not get away; my hands were blistered, and the axe was not half ground. At length, however, it was sharpened; and the man turned to me with, "Now, you little rascal, you've played truant: scud to the school, or you'll rue it!" "Alas!" thought I, "it is hard enough to turn a grindstone this cold day; but now to be called a little rascal is too much."

It sank deep in my mind; and often have I thought of it since. When I see a merchant over-polite to his customers,— begging them to take a little brandy, and throwing his goods on the counter,—thinks I, That man has an axe to grind. When I see a man flattering the people, making great professions of attachment to liberty, who is in private life a tyrant, methinks, Look out, good people! that fellow would set you turning grindstones. When I see a man hoisted into office by party spirit, without a single qualification to render him either respectable or useful,—alas! methinks, deluded people, you are doomed for a season to turn the grindstone for a booby.

AN AMERICAN CAMPUS.

NINETEENTH CENTURY LITERATURE

CHAPTER II.

GENERAL SURVEY; IRVING.

AMERICAN literature could not properly exist until the American nation had entered on its independent career. During the colonial period the people were occupied in subduing the wilderness and adapting themselves to new conditions of life. Few but the scholarly preachers of the gospel had inclination or leisure for writing, and the chief printed productions of the times were religious and theological. For books of other kinds the people looked to the mother country. In the Revolutionary period questions of human rights and government were urgent and drew forth treatises of marked ability. Yet there were some evidences of literary activity in other directions. Newspapers, now struggling into existence, furnished a ready means for circulating satires and occasional verses.

With the beginning of the new century the turbulence of war had ceased, a stable government was formed, and the minds of Americans were turned from their former dependence on the writers of England. There came an original tone of thought, a deep reflection on the new aspects of the world, a wholesome independence of mind. For a time Philadelphia seemed likely to become the literary centre, as it was the capital, of the nation. Charles Brockden Brown was the first American novelist, and Joseph Dennie, the editor of the *Portfolio*, was hailed as the American Addison, but his writings are now forgotten. Philadelphia continued to be the place of publication even for New England authors, and *Graham's Magazine* was the medium through which Longfellow and others reached the public.

But the pioneers of the new era of American literature belonged to New York, if not by birth, by choice of residence. Three men stand forth as representatives of this class—Irving, Cooper and Bryant. Widely different in their nature and training, as in their finished work, they were yet all distinctively American. The cheerful Irving began as a playful satirist and delineator of oddities, and became a skillful sketcher of the pleasant features of merry England and picturesque Spain, as well as of his beloved Hudson. In much of his work he exhibits the contrast of the past with the present, producing sometimes humorous, and sometimes pathetic scenes. Cooper belonged to that lake region of New York where the Indians and whites came into closest contact and unequal conflict. He revealed to Europe the romance of the American forest. Again, as an officer in the navy, he acquired such familiarity with sea-life, as to make him the foremost sea-novelist of the language. Excellent in description and well furnished with material, he yet rated his own abilities too highly, and wrote much which may readily be ignored. Bryant early displayed his power as a meditative poet on nature, but the duties of active life summoned him to quite different work in New York City. As editor of a daily newspaper, he battled strenuously and honorably for righteousness until in old age he received the loving veneration of his fellow-citizens. But in literature he remains the author of "Thanatopsis" and a translator of Homer.

The influence of Harvard College as a promoter of learning tended to give Boston a supremacy in literature. Here the *North American Review* was early established, and the study of German and other foreign literatures was promoted. The Unitarian movement, apart from its theological effects, had a distinct uplifting effect on American culture. Channing and Emerson, Longfellow and Lowell, assisted, each in his own way, in broadening and elevating the minds of their countrymen. As an outgrowth of this humanitarian tendency came the anti-slavery movement, which stirred some of these writers to passionate outbursts, but could not draw them from their literary pursuits. At a later period, the civil war left a more lasting impression on their characters and work, yet when it had passed, the survivors made still nobler contributions to literature. Whittier, the Quaker poet and anti-slavery lyrist, wrote the most popular ballad of the war, and afterwards showed his best art in peaceful themes. So also Mrs. Harriet Beecher Stowe was able to present the wrongs of slavery in a popular romance, and thus urge on the war, yet later contented herself with mild pictures of domestic life. Apart from most of the foregoing, and by a method peculiarly his own, Hawthorne studied the spiritual facts of New England life, and unveiled its mysteries and romance. Others more quickly won recognition; his subtler genius required longer time for correct appreciation. Gradually his true worth has been discerned, and now he is acknowledged to be the chief representative of American romance.

In remarkable contrast with Hawthorne in life and character and work stands the brilliantly gifted, but miserably unfortunate, Edgar A. Poe. He not only proved himself the greatest metrical artist of the English language, weaving words into music at his pleasure, but he was the skillful producer of weird romances and cunningly devised tales, usually gloomy and terrible, sometimes extravagant. His erratic course and untimely death have drawn the pity of the world. His melodious verses have been models for Tennyson and Swinburne, as well as French poets. W. G. Simms was the prolific romanticist of the South, seeking to rival Cooper in the delineation of the Indians, and in reproducing the Revolutionary scenes of his native State. John P. Kennedy wrote also a novel of the Revolution, and sketched country life in Virginia.

Of American poets Longfellow has been the most popular, partly from his choice of subjects easily understood by all, and partly from his artistic treatment of them. His sympathetic heart and his generous culture have enabled him to give adequate expression to the common human emotions.

Lowell is distinctly the most cultured of American poets, and has excelled as essayist and critic. Yet he has not reached the popularity of Longfellow or Whittier, and is perhaps most widely known as a humorist and writer of Yankee dialect. In his later years he was a noble representative of America in foreign courts.

Dr. O. W. Holmes was noted as a skillful writer of occasional verses before his peculiar merits as a prose-writer were displayed in the *Atlantic Monthly*. Here his "Autocrat of the Breakfast-Table" was a brilliant combination of humor, satire and scholarship, and interspersed were some of his best poems. He was devoted to Boston, which he celebrated as "the hub of the solar system."

The size of the present work has not afforded sufficient room for the adequate treatment of history and historians. But the work of Americans in this department must at least be mentioned, as they have attained special fame and are truly representative of the country. William H. Prescott (1796-1859), in spite of the affliction of blindness, devoted his life to historical studies, and produced standard works on the history of Spain, Mexico, and Peru. Written in a stately and dignified style, they have stood the test of time and the investigation of later students. George Bancroft (1800-1891), after studying in German universities and teaching a classical school in Massachusetts, undertook to prepare an exhaustive history of the United States down to the adoption of the Constitution. The many public positions, which he held, partly helped and partly hindered the completion of his great work. Almost fifty years elapsed before the twelfth and final volume appeared. While the whole forms a lasting monument to the author's industry, its very length has prevented it from attaining the highest success.

Most successful in securing popular attention and applause was John Lothrop Motley (1814-77), who, after ten years of patient research, published in 1856, "The Rise and Fall of the Dutch Republic." Other works connected with the history of the Netherlands occupied his later years, except so far as he was engaged in diplomatic service. His thorough mastery of his subject and his power of pictorial presentation of the past make vivid the men and events of a critical period in European history.

WASHINGTON IRVING.

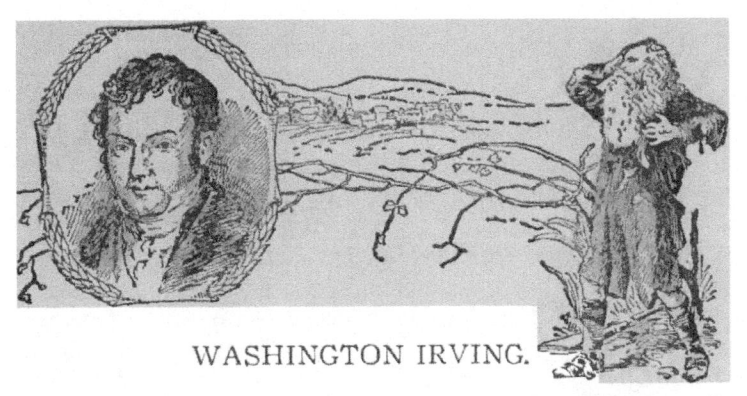

WASHINGTON IRVING was born in New York City in 1783 and died in 1859, at the age of seventy-six. His books are still so popular, and in feeling so modern, that it is hard to realize that his birth immediately followed the close of the Revolution, and that he did not see even the beginnings of the present generation. To read some of his stories, one might think they were written yesterday—were there any one competent to write them.

He was the son of a rigid Scotch Presbyterian and of a gentle English woman; his childhood and youth were delicate, but his enjoyment of life was unfailing, and the indulgence which he always received never hurt him. His aspect and manners were refined, graceful and charming; by organization he was an aristocrat, though he was democratic in intention. At the outset of his career he amused himself in society, and satirized it in good-natured sketches in the *Spectator* vein, as the pages of the brilliant but short-lived *Salmagundi* still bear witness. His first important work was the famous "Knickerbocker's History of New York," a permanent piece of humor, the fairy godchild, so to say, of Rabelais and Swift. The author went to Europe for a pleasure trip. In the midst of his social successes in London the firm with which he was connected failed, and he turned to literature, which hitherto had been the diversion of his leisure, as the means of livelihood. In 1819, Washington, then six-and-thirty, sat seriously down and produced the book of tales called "The Sketch Book," containing that "primal story"—"Rip Van Winkle." His success was immediate, great and lasting; but he was too modest to admit that it could be fully deserved. He remained alone in that opinion; his work was like himself, and, like himself, was nearly perfect in its degree. During the forty remaining years of his life he continued to delight his contemporaries and build up his fortunes with imaginative and historical work, much of it with a Spanish background. From 1826 to 1829 he lived in Spain writing "The Alahambra," the "Life of Columbus," and other books. In the latter year he returned to London as secretary of legation; but two years later homesickness brought him back to New York and he fixed his residence at Sunnyside. During the next ten years he wrote five volumes on American and English subjects, of which the collection of tales, "Wolfert's Roost," is the best known. In 1842 he was appointed American Minister to Spain, and the duties of his office chiefly occupied him during his four years' sojourn at Madrid. On his return home he began the "Life of Washington," which was the chief work of his declining life, the last volume appearing in the year of his death.

Irving's personal character and history were as delightful as are his works. His mental constitution was serene and harmonious; nothing was in excess; he was at peace with himself and optimistic towards the world; he had no theories to ventilate, and was averse to contentions and strife of every kind. The easy amiability of his nature and his strong social tendencies might have formed an element of weakness, had he not been assailed and strengthened by bereavement and misfortune, which developed the man in him. The girl to whom he was betrothed died, and he lived a bachelor all his life. Irving was manly with men; with women, refined and chivalrous; and sincere and sane in literature. He regarded his species with a humorous tenderness; saw the good and slighted the evil in life; hence sunshine, abiding, but not intense, radiates from all he wrote.

Altogether nearly a third of Irving's life was passed abroad, where he was as much loved and appreciated as here. But no more patriotic American lived than he. In him the human and the literary instincts made a rounded whole. His style is clear, easy and flexible; his standpoint, tranquil; his humor, ever smiling; his pathos, true; his sentiment, sometimes thin, but never sickly. The generous impulses and moral beauty of his character warm and vitalize his work. So long as taste, repose, and simplicity please the mind, Irving's contribution to our literature will be remembered and valued.

Death of Peter Stuyvesant.

(From "Knickerbocker's History of New York.")

In process of time, the old governor, like all other children of mortality, began to exhibit tokens of decay. Like an aged oak, which, though it long has braved the fury of the elements, and still retains its gigantic proportions, yet begins to shake and groan with every blast—so was it with the gallant Peter; for, though he still bore the port and semblance of what he was in the days of his hardihood and chivalry, yet did age and infirmity begin to sap the vigor of his frame—but his heart, that most unconquerable citadel, still triumphed unsubdued. With matchless avidity would he listen to every article of intelligence concerning the battles between the English and Dutch—still would his pulse beat high whenever he heard of the victories of De Ruyter—and his countenance lower, and his eyebrows knit, when fortune turned in favor of the English. At length, as on a certain day he had just smoked his fifth pipe, and was napping after dinner in his arm-chair, conquering the whole British nation in his dreams, he was suddenly aroused by a fearful ringing of bells, rattling of drums, and roaring of cannon, that put all his blood in a ferment. But when he learnt that these rejoicings were in honor of a great victory obtained by the combined English and French fleets over the brave De Ruyter and the younger Von Tromp, it went so much to his heart that he took to his bed, and in less than three days was brought to death's door by a violent cholera morbus! But, even in this extremity, he still displayed the unconquerable spirit of Peter *the Headstrong;* holding out to the last gasp with the most inflexible obstinacy against the whole army of old women, who were bent upon driving the enemy out of his bowels, after a true Dutch mode of defence, by inundating the seat of war with catnip and pennyroyal.

While he thus lay, lingering on the verge of dissolution, news was brought to him that the brave De Ruyter had suffered but little loss—had made good his retreat—and meant once more to meet the enemy in battle. The closing eye of the old warrior kindled at the words—he partly raised himself in bed— a flash of martial fire beamed across his visage—he clinched his withered hand, as if he felt within his gripe that sword which waved in triumph before the walls of Fort Christina, and, giving a grim smile of exultation, sunk back upon his pillow and expired.

Thus died Peter Stuyvesant, a valiant soldier—a loyal subject—an upright governor, and an honest Dutchman—who wanted only a few empires to desolate to have been immortalized as a hero!

His funeral obsequies were celebrated with the utmost grandeur and solemnity. The town was perfectly emptied of its inhabitants, who crowded in throngs to pay the last sad honors to their good old governor. All his sterling qualities rushed in full tide upon their recollections, while the memory of his foibles and his faults had expired with him. The ancient burghers contended who should have the privilege of bearing the pall; the populace strove who should walk nearest to the bier—and the melancholy procession was closed by a number of gray-headed negroes, who had wintered and summered in the household of their departed master for the greater part of a century.

With sad and gloomy countenances the multitude gathered around the grave. They dwelt with mournful hearts on the sturdy virtues, the signal services, and the gallant exploits of the brave old worthy. They recalled with secret upbraidings their own factious opposition to his government—and many an ancient burgher, whose phlegmatic features had never been known to relax, nor his eyes to moisten—was now observed to puff a pensive pipe, and the big drop to steal down his cheek—while he muttered with affectionate accent and melancholy shake of the head—"Well den!—Hardkoppig Peter ben gone at last!"

Rip Van Winkle.

WHOEVER has made a voyage up the Hudson must remember the Kaatskill Mountains. They are a dismembered branch of the great Appalachian family, and are seen away to the west of the river, swelling up to a noble height, and lording it over the surrounding country. Every change of season, every change of weather, indeed every hour of the day, produces some change in the magical hues and shapes of these mountains, and they are regarded by all the good wives, far and near, as perfect barometers. When the weather is fair and settled, they are clothed in blue and purple, and print their bold outlines on the clear evening sky; but sometimes, when the rest of the landscape is cloudless, they will gather a hood of gray vapors about their summits, which, in the last rays of the setting sun, will glow and light up like a crown of glory.

At the foot of these fairy mountains the voyager may have descried the light smoke curling up from a village, whose shingle-roofs gleam among the trees, just where the blue tints of the upland melt away into the fresh green of the nearer landscape. It is a little village of great antiquity, having been founded by some of the Dutch colonists in the early times of the province, just about the beginning of the government of the good Peter Stuyvesant (may he rest in peace!), and there were some of the houses of the original settlers standing within a few years, built of small yellow bricks brought from Holland, having latticed windows and gable fronts. surmounted with weathercocks.

In that same village, and in one of these very houses, (which, to tell the precise truth, was sadly time-worn and weather-beaten,) there lived many years since, while the country was yet a province of Great Britain, a simple, good-natured fellow, of the name of Rip Van Winkle. He was a descendant of the Van Winkles who figured so gallantly in the chivalrous days of Peter Stuyvesant, and accompanied him to the siege of Fort Christina. He inherited, however, but little of the martial character of his ancestors. I have observed that he was a simple, good-natured man; he was, moreover, a kind neighbor, and an obedient henpecked husband. Indeed, to the latter circumstance might be owing that meekness of spirit which gained him such universal popularity; for those men are most apt to be obsequious and conciliating abroad, who are under the discipline of shrews at home. Their tempers, doubtless, are rendered pliant and malleable in the fiery furnace of domestic tribulation, and a curtain lecture is worth all the sermons in the world for teaching the virtues of patience and longsuffering. A termagant wife may, therefore, in some respects, be considered a tolerable blessing; and if so, Rip Van Winkle was thrice blessed.

Certain it is, that he was a great favorite among all the good wives of the village, who, as usual with the amiable sex, took his part in all family squabbles; and never failed, whenever they talked those matters over in their evening gossipings, to lay all the blame on Dame Van Winkle. The children of the village, too, would shout with joy whenever he approached. He assisted at their sports, made their playthings, taught them to fly kites and shoot marbles, and told them long stories of ghosts, witches, and Indians. Whenever he went dodging about the village, he was surrounded by a troop of them, hanging on his skirts, clambering on his back, and playing a thousand tricks on him with impunity; and not a dog would bark at him throughout the neighborhood.

The great error in Rip's composition was an insuperable aversion to all kinds of profitable labor. It could not be from the want of assiduity or perseverance; for he would sit on a wet rock, with a rod as long and heavy as a Tartar's lance, and fish all day without a murmur, even though he should not be encouraged by a single nibble. He would carry a fowling-piece on his shoulder for hours together, trudging through woods and swamps, and up hill and down dale, to shoot a few squirrels or wild pigeons. He would never refuse to assist a neighbor even in the roughest toil, and was a foremost man at all country frolics for husking Indian corn, or building stone fences: the women of the village, too, used to employ him to run their errands, and to do such little odd jobs as their less obliging husbands would not do for them. In a word, Rip was ready to attend to anybody's business but his own; but as to doing family duty, and keeping his farm in order, he found it impossible.

In fact, he declared it was of no use to work on his farm; it was the most pestilent little piece of ground in the whole country; everything about it went wrong, and would go wrong, in spite of him. His fences were continually falling to pieces; his cow would either go astray, or get among the cabbages; weeds were sure to grow quicker in his fields than anywhere else; the rain always made a point of setting in just as he had some outdoor work to do; so that though his patrimonial estate had dwindled away under his management, acre by acre, until there was little more left than a mere patch of Indian corn and potatoes, yet it was the worst conditioned farm in the neighborhood.

His children, too, were as ragged and wild as if they belonged to nobody. His son Rip, an urchin begotten in his own likeness, promised to inherit the habits, with the old clothes of his father. He was generally seen trooping like a colt at his mother's heels, equipped in a pair of his father's cast-off galligaskins, which he had much ado to hold up with one hand, as a fine lady does her train in bad weather.

Rip Van Winkle, however, was one of those happy mortals, of foolish, well-oiled dispositions, who take the world easy, eat white bread or brown, whichever can be got with least thought or trouble, and would rather starve on a penny than work for a pound. If left to himself, he would have whistled life away in perfect contentment; but his wife kept continually dinning in his ears about his idleness, his carelessness, and the ruin he was bringing on his family. Morning, noon, and night her tongue was incessantly going, and everything he said or did was sure to produce a torrent of household eloquence. Rip had but one way of replying to all lectures of the kind, and that, by frequent use, had grown into a habit. He shrugged his shoulders, shook his head, cast up his eyes, but said nothing. This, however, always provoked a fresh volley from his wife, so that he was fain to draw off his forces, and take to the outside of the house,—the only side which, in truth, belongs to a henpecked husband.

Rip's sole domestic adherent was his dog Wolf, who was as much henpecked as his master; for Dame Van Winkle regarded them as companions in idleness, and even looked upon Wolf with an evil eye, as the cause of his master's going so often astray. True it is, in all points of spirit befitting an honorable dog, he was as courageous an animal as ever scoured the woods; but what courage can withstand the ever-during and all-besetting terrors of a woman's tongue? The moment Wolf entered the house his crest fell, his tail drooped to the ground or curled between his legs, he sneaked about with a gallows air, casting many a sidelong glance at Dame Van Winkle, and at the least flourish of a broomstick or ladle, he would fly to the door with yelping precipitation.

Times grew worse and worse with Rip Van Winkle as years of matrimony rolled on; a tart temper never mellows with age, and a sharp tongue is the only edged tool that grows keener with constant use. For a long while he used to console himself, when driven from home, by frequenting a kind of perpetual club of the sages, philosophers, and other idle personages of the village, which held its sessions on a bench before a small inn, designated by a rubicund portrait of his Majesty George the Third. Here they used to sit in the shade through a long lazy summer's day, talking listlessly over village gossip, or telling endless sleepy stories about nothing. But it would have been worth any statesman's money to have heard the profound discussions that sometimes took place, when by chance an old newspaper fell into their hands from some passing traveler. How solemnly they would listen to the contents, as drawled out by Derrick Van Bummel, the schoolmaster, a dapper, learned little man, who was not to be daunted by the most gigantic word in the dictionary; and how sagely they would deliberate upon public events some months after they had taken place!

The opinions of this junto were completely controlled by Nicholas Vedder, a patriarch of the village, and landlord of the inn, at the door of which he took his seat from morning till night, just moving sufficiently to avoid the sun and keep in the shade of a large tree; so that the neighbors could tell the hour by his movements as accurately as by a sun-dial. It is true he was rarely heard to speak, but smoked his pipe incessantly. His adherents, however (for every great man has his adherents), perfectly understood him, and knew how to gather his opinions. When anything that was read or related displeased him, he was observed to smoke his pipe vehemently, and to send forth short, frequent, and angry puffs; but when pleased, he would inhale the smoke slowly and tranquilly, and emit it in light and placid clouds; and sometimes, taking the pipe from his mouth, and letting the fragrant vapor curl about his nose, would gravely nod his head in token of perfect approbation.

From even this stronghold the unlucky Rip was at length routed by his termagant wife, who would suddenly break in upon the tranquillity of the assemblage and call the members all to naught; nor was that august personage, Nicholas Vedder himself, sacred from the daring tongue of this terrible virago, who charged him outright with encouraging her husband in habits of idleness.

Poor Rip was at last reduced almost to despair; and his only alternative, to escape from the labor of the farm and clamor of his wife, was to take gun in hand and stroll away into the woods. Here he would sometimes seat himself at the foot of a tree, and share the contents of his wallet with Wolf, with whom he sympathized as a fellow-sufferer in persecution. "Poor Wolf," he would say, "thy mistress leads thee a dog's life of it; but never mind, my lad, whilst I live thou shalt never want a friend to stand by thee!" Wolf would wag his tail, look wistfully in his master's face, and if dogs can feel pity, I verily believe he reciprocated the sentiment with all his heart.

In a long ramble of the kind on a fine autumnal day, Rip had unconsciously scrambled to one of the highest parts of the Kaatskill Mountains. He was after his favorite sport of squirrel shooting, and the still solitudes had echoed and re-echoed with the reports of his gun. Panting and fatigued, he threw himself, late in the afternoon, on a green knoll, covered with mountain herbage, that crowned the brow of a precipice. From an opening between the trees he could overlook all the lower country for many a mile of rich woodland. He saw at a distance the lordly Hudson, far, far below him, moving on its silent but majestic course, with the reflection of a purple cloud, or the sail of a lagging bark, here and there sleeping on its glassy bosom, and at last losing itself in the blue highlands.

On the other side he looked down into a deep mountain glen, wild, lonely, and shagged, the bottom filled with fragments from the impending cliffs, and scarcely lighted by the reflected rays of the setting sun. For some time Rip lay musing on this scene; evening was gradually advancing; the mountains began to throw their long blue shadows over the valleys; he saw that it would be dark long before he could reach the village, and he heaved a heavy sigh when he thought of encountering the terrors of Dame Van Winkle.

As he was about to descend, he heard a voice from a distance, hallooing, "Rip Van Winkle! Rip Van Winkle!" He looked round, but could see nothing but a crow winging its solitary flight across the mountain. He thought his fancy must have deceived him, and turned again to descend, when he heard the same cry ring through the still evening air: "Rip Van

Winkle! Rip Van Winkle!"—at the same time Wolf bristled up his back, and, giving a loud growl, skulked to his master's side, looking fearfully down into the glen. Rip now felt a vague apprehension stealing over him; he looked anxiously in the same direction, and perceived a strange figure slowly toiling up the rocks, and bending under the weight of something he carried on his back. He was surprised to see any human being in this lonely and unfrequented place, but supposing it to be some one of the neighborhood in need of his assistance, he hastened down to yield it.

On nearer approach he was still more surprised at the singularity of the stranger's appearance. He was a short, square-built old fellow, with thick bushy hair and a grizzled beard. His dress was of the antique Dutch fashion,—a cloth jerkin strapped round the waist, several pairs of breeches, the outer one of ample volume, decorated with rows of buttons down the sides, and bunches at the knees. He bore on his shoulder a stout keg, that seemed full of liquor, and made signs for Rip to approach and assist him with the load. Though rather shy and distrustful of this new acquaintance, Rip complied with his usual alacrity; and mutually relieving one another, they clambered up a narrow gully, apparently the dry bed of a mountain torrent. As they ascended, Rip every now and then heard long rolling peals, like distant thunder, that seemed to issue out of a deep ravine, or rather cleft, between lofty rocks, toward which their rugged path conducted. He paused for an instant, but supposing it to be the muttering of one of those transient thunder-showers which often take place in mountain heights, he proceeded. Passing through the ravine, they came to a hollow, like a small amphitheatre, surrounded by perpendicular precipices, over the brinks of which impending trees shot their branches, so that you only caught glimpses of the azure sky and the bright evening cloud. During the whole time Rip and his companion had labored on in silence; for though the former marveled greatly what could be the object of carrying a keg of liquor up this wild mountain, yet there was something strange and incomprehensible about the unknown, that inspired awe and checked familiarity.

On entering the amphitheatre, new objects of wonder presented themselves. On a level spot in the center was a company of odd-looking personages playing at ninepins. They were dressed in a quaint outlandish fashion; some wore short doublets, others jerkins, with long knives in their belts, and most of them had enormous breeches, of similar style with that of the guide's. Their visages, too, were peculiar: one had a large beard, broad face, and small piggish eyes; the face of another seemed to consist entirely of nose, and was surmounted by a white sugar-loaf hat, set off with a little red cock's tail. They all had beards, of various shapes and colors. There was one who seemed to be the commander. He was a stout old gentleman, with a weather-beaten countenance; he wore a laced doublet, broad belt and hanger, high-crowned hat and feather, red stockings, and high-heeled shoes, with roses in them. The whole group reminded Rip of the figures in an old Flemish painting, in the parlor of Dominie Van Shaick, the village parson, and which had been brought over from Holland at the time of the settlement.

What seemed particularly odd to Rip was, that though these folks were evidently amusing themselves, yet they maintained the gravest faces, the most mysterious silence, and were, withal, the most melancholy party of pleasure he had ever witnessed. Nothing interrupted the stillness of the scene but the noise of the balls, which, whenever they were rolled, echoed along the mountains like rumbling peals of thunder.

As Rip and his companion approached them, they suddenly desisted from their play, and stared at him with such fixed statue-like gaze, and such strange, uncouth, lacklustre countenances, that his heart turned within him, and his knees smote together. His companion now emptied the contents of the keg into large flagons, and made signs to him to wait upon the company. He obeyed with fear and trembling; they quaffed the liquor in profound silence, and then returned to their game.

By degrees Rip's awe and apprehension subsided. He even ventured, when no eye was fixed upon him, to taste the beverage, which he found had much of the flavor of excellent Hollands. He was naturally a thirsty soul, and was soon tempted to repeat the draught. One taste provoked another; and he reiterated his visits to the flagon so often that at length his senses were overpowered, his eyes swam in his head, his head gradually declined, and he fell into a deep sleep.

Rip Van Winkle's Return.

On *waking*, Rip found himself on the green knoll from whence he had first seen the old man of the glen. He rubbed his eyes—it was a bright sunny morning. The birds were hopping and twittering among the bushes, and the eagle was wheeling aloft, and breasting the pure mountain breeze. "Surely," thought Rip, "I have not slept here all night." He recalled the occurrences before he fell asleep. The strange man with the keg of liquor—the mountain ravine—the wild retreat among the rocks—the woe-begone party at nine-pins—the flagon—"Oh! that wicked flagon!" thought Rip—"what excuse shall I make to Dame Van Winkle?"

He looked round for his gun, but in place of the clean well-oiled fowling-piece, he found an old fire-lock lying by him, the barrel encrusted with rust, the lock falling off, and the stock worm-eaten. He now suspected that the grave roysterers of the mountain had put a trick upon him, and having dosed him with liquor, had robbed him of his gun. Wolf, too, had disappeared, but he might have strayed away after a squirrel or partridge. He whistled after him, and shouted his name, but all in vain; the echoes repeated his whistle and shout, but no dog was to be seen.

He determined to revisit the scene of the last evening's gambol, and if he met with any of the party, to demand his dog and gun. As he rose to walk, he found himself stiff in the joints, and wanting in his usual activity. "These mountain beds do not agree with me," thought Rip, "and if this frolic should lay me up with a fit of rheumatism, I shall have a blessed time with Dame Van Winkle." With some difficulty he got down into the glen; he found the gully up which he and his companion had ascended the preceding evening; but to his astonishment a mountain stream was now foaming down it, leaping from rock to rock, and filling the glen with babbling murmurs. He, however, made shift to scramble up its sides, working his toilsome way through thickets of birch, sassafras, and witch-hazel; and sometimes tripped up or entangled by the wild grape vines that twisted their coils and tendrils from tree to tree, and spread a kind of network in his path.

At length he reached to where the ravine had opened through the cliffs to the amphitheatre; but no traces of such opening remained. The rocks presented a high impenetrable wall, over which the torrent came tumbling in a sheet of feathery foam, and fell into a broad deep basin, black from the shadows of the surrounding forest. Here, then, poor Rip was brought to a stand. He again called and whistled after his dog; he was only answered by the cawing of a flock of idle crows, sporting high in the air about a dry tree that overhung a sunny precipice; and who, secure in their elevation, seemed to look down and scoff at the poor man's perplexities. What was to be done? The morning was passing away, and Rip felt famished for want of his breakfast. He grieved to give up his dog and gun; he dreaded to meet his wife; but it would not do to starve among the mountains. He shook his head, shouldered the rusty firelock, and, with a heart full of trouble and anxiety, turned his steps homeward.

As he approached the village, he met a number of people, but none whom he knew, which somewhat surprised him, for he had thought himself acquainted with every one in the country round. Their dress, too, was of a different fashion from that to which he was accustomed. They all stared at him with equal marks of surprise, and whenever they cast eyes upon him, invariably stroked their chins. The constant recurrence of this gesture induced Rip, involuntarily, to do the same, when, to his astonishment, he found his beard had grown a foot long.

He had now entered the skirts of the village. A troop of strange children ran at his heels, hooting after him, and pointing at his gray beard. The dogs, too, not one of which he recognized for an old acquaintance, barked at him as he passed. The very village was altered: it was larger and more populous. There were rows of houses which he had never seen before, and those which had been his familiar haunts had disappeared. Strange names were over the doors—strange faces at the windows—everything was strange. His mind now misgave him; he began to doubt whether both he and the world around him were not bewitched. Surely this was his native village, which he had left but a day before. There stood the Kaatskill mountains—there ran the silver Hudson at a distance—there was every hill and dale precisely as it had always been—Rip was sorely perplexed—"That flagon last night," thought he, "has addled my poor head sadly!".

It was with some difficulty that he found the way to his own house, which he approached with silent awe, expecting every moment to hear the shrill voice of Dame Van Winkle. He found the house gone to decay—the roof fallen in, the windows shattered, and the doors off the hinges. A half-starved dog, that looked like Wolf, was skulking about it. Rip called him by name, but the cur snarled, showed his teeth, and passed on. This was an unkind cut indeed.—"My very dog," sighed poor Rip, "has forgotten me!"

He entered the house, which, to tell the truth, Dame Van Winkle had always kept in neat order. It was empty, forlorn, and apparently abandoned. This desolateness overcame all his connubial fears—he called loudly for his wife and children—the lonely chambers rang for a moment with his voice, and then all again was silence.

He now hurried forth, and hastened to his old resort, the village inn—but it too was gone. A large rickety wooden building stood in its place, with great gaping windows, some of them broken, and mended with old hats and petticoats, and over the door was painted, "The Union Hotel, by Jonathan Doolittle." Instead of the great tree that used to shelter the quiet little Dutch inn of yore, there now was reared a tall naked pole, with something on the top that looked like a red night-cap, and from it was fluttering a flag, on which was a singular assemblage of stars and stripes—all this was strange and incomprehensible. He recognized on the sign, however, the ruby face of King George, under which he had smoked so many a peaceful pipe, but even this was singularly metamorphosed. The red coat was changed for one of blue and buff, a sword was held in the hand instead of a sceptre, the head was decorated with a cocked hat, and underneath was painted in large characters, GENERAL WASHINGTON.

There was, as usual, a crowd of folk about the door, but none that Rip recollected. The very character of the people seemed changed. There was a busy, bustling, disputatious tone about it, instead of the accustomed phlegm and drowsy tranquillity. He looked in vain for the sage Nicholas Vedder, with his broad face, double chin, and fair long pipe, uttering clouds of tobacco smoke, instead of idle speeches; or Van Bummel, the schoolmaster, doling forth the contents of an ancient newspaper. In place of these a lean, bilious-looking fellow, with his pockets full of handbills, was haranguing vehemently about the rights of citizens—election—members of Congress—liberty—Bunker's hill—heroes of seventy-six—and other words, that were a perfect Babylonish jargon to the bewildered Van Winkle.

The appearance of Rip, with his long, grizzled beard, his rusty fowling-piece, his uncouth dress, and the army of women and children that had gathered at his heels, soon attracted the attention of the tavern politicians. They crowded round him, eying him from head to foot with great curiosity. The orator bustled up to him, and drawing him partly aside, inquired, "on which side he voted?" Rip stared in vacant stupidity. Another short but busy little fellow pulled him by the arm, and rising on tiptoe, inquired in his ear, "whether he was Federal or Democrat." Rip was equally at a loss to comprehend the question; when a knowing, self-important old gentleman, in a sharp cocked hat, made his way through the crowd, putting them to the right and left with his elbows as he passed, and planting himself before Van Winkle, with one arm a-kimbo, the other resting on his cane, his keen eyes and sharp hat penetrating, as it were, into his very soul, demanded in an austere tone, "what brought him to the election with a gun on his shoulder, and a mob at his heels, and whether he meant to breed a riot in the village?"

"Alas! gentlemen," cried Rip, somewhat dismayed, "I am a poor, quiet man, a native of the place, and a loyal subject of the King, God bless him!"

Here a general shout burst from the bystanders—"A tory! a tory! a spy! a refugee! hustle him! away with him!"

It was with great difficulty that the self-important man in the cocked hat restored order; and having assumed a tenfold austerity of brow, demanded again of the unknown culprit, what he came there for, and whom he was seeking. The poor man humbly assured him that he meant no harm, but merely came there in search of some of his neighbors, who used to keep about the tavern.

"Well—who are they?—name them."

Rip bethought himself a moment and inquired, "Where's Nicholas Vedder?"

There was a silence for a little while, when an old man replied, in a thin, piping voice, "Nicholas Vedder? why, he is dead and gone these eighteen years. There was a wooden tomb-stone in the church-yard that used to tell all about him, but that's rotten and gone too."

"Where's Brom Dutcher?"

"Oh, he went off to the army in the beginning of the war; some say he was killed at the storming of Stony Point—others say he was drowned in the squall, at the foot of Antony's Nose. I don't know—he never came back again."

Where's Van Bummel, the schoolmaster?"

"He went off to the wars, too; was a great militia general and is now in Congress."

Rip's heart died away, at hearing of these sad changes in his home and friends, and finding himself thus alone in the world. Every answer puzzled him, too, by treating of such enormous lapses of time, and of matters which he could not understand: war—Congress—Stony Point!—he had no courage to ask after any more friends, but cried out in despair, "Does nobody here know Rip Van Winkle?"

"Oh, Rip Van Winkle!" exclaimed two or three. "Oh to be sure! that's Rip Van Winkle yonder, leaning against the tree."

Rip looked and beheld a precise counterpart of himself as he went up the mountain; apparently as lazy, and certainly as ragged. The poor fellow was now completely confounded. He doubted his own identity, and whether he was himself or another man. In the midst of his bewilderment, the man in the cocked hat demanded who he was, and what was his name?

"God knows," exclaimed he, at his wit's end; "I'm not myself—I'm somebody else—that's me yonder—no—that's somebody else, got into my shoes—I was myself last night, but I fell asleep on the mountain, and they've changed my gun, and everything's changed, and I'm changed, and I can't tell what's my name, or who I am!"

Ichabod Crane and Katrina Van Tassel.

In this by-place of nature there abode, in a remote period of American history, that is to say, some thirty years since, a worthy wight of the name of Ichabod Crane, who sojourned, or, as he expressed it, "tarried," in Sleepy Hollow, for the purpose of instructing the children of the vicinity. He was a native of Connecticut, a State which supplies the Union with pioneers for the mind as well as for the forest, and sends forth yearly its legions of frontier woodsmen and country schoolmasters. The cognomen of Crane was not inapplicable to his person. He was tall, but exceedingly lank, with narrow shoulders, long arms and legs, hands that dangled a mile out of his sleeves, feet that might have served for shovels, and his whole frame most loosely hung together. His head was small, and flat at top, with huge ears, large green, glassy eyes, and a long snipe nose, so that it looked like a weathercock perched upon his spindle neck, to tell which way the wind blew. To see him striding along the profile of a hill on a windy day, with his clothes bagging and fluttering about him, one might have mistaken him for the genius of famine descending upon the earth, or some scare-crow eloped from a cornfield.

The school-house was a low building of one large room, rudely constructed of logs; the windows partly glazed, and partly patched with leaves of copybooks. It was most ingeniously secured at vacant hours, by a withe twisted in the handle of the door, and stakes set against the window-shutters; so that though a thief might get in with perfect ease, he would find some embarrassment in getting out;—an idea most probably borrowed by the architect, Yost Van Houten, from the mystery of an eelpot. The school-house stood in a rather lonely but pleasant situation, just at the foot of a woody hill, with a brook running close by, and a formidable birch-tree growing at one end of it. From hence the low murmur of his pupils' voices, conning over their lessons, might be heard of a drowsy summer's day, like the hum of a beehive; interrupted now and then by the authoritative voice of the master, in the tone of menace or command; or, peradventure, by the appalling sound of the birch, as he urged some tardy loiterer along the flowery path of knowledge. Truth to say, he was a conscientious man, that ever bore in mind the golden maxim, "spare the rod and spoil the child."—Ichabod Crane's scholars certainly were not spoiled.

Among the musical disciples who assembled, one evening in each week, to receive his instructions in psalmody, was Katrina Van Tassel, the daughter and only child of a substantial Dutch farmer. She was a blooming lass of fresh eighteen, plump as a partridge; ripe and melting and rosy-cheeked as one of her father's peaches, and universally famed, not merely for her beauty, but her vast expectations. She was withal a little of a coquette, as might be perceived even in her dress, which was a mixture of ancient and modern fashions, as most suited to set off her charms. She wore the ornaments of pure yellow gold, which her great-great-grandmother had brought over from Saardam; the tempting stomacher of the olden time, and withal a provokingly short petticoat, to display the prettiest foot and ankle in the country round.

Ichabod Crane had a soft and foolish heart toward the sex; and it is not to be wondered at, that so tempting a morsel soon found favor in his eyes, more especially after he had visited her in her paternal mansion. Old Baltus Van Tassel was a perfect picture of a thriving, contented, liberal-hearted farmer. He seldom, it is true, sent either his eyes or his thoughts beyond the boundaries of his own farm; but within these, everything was snug, happy and well-conditioned. He was satisfied with his wealth, but not proud of it; and piqued himself upon the hearty abundance, rather than the style, in which he lived. His stronghold was situated on the banks of the Hudson, in one of those green, sheltered, fertile nooks, in which the Dutch farmers are so fond of nestling. A great elm-tree spread its broad branches over it; at the foot of which bubbled up a spring of the softest and sweetest water, in a little well, formed of a barrel; and then stole sparkling away through the grass, to a neighboring brook, that babbled along among alders and dwarf willows. Hard by the farm-house was a vast barn, that might have served for a church; every window and crevice of which seemed bursting forth with the treasures of the farm; the flail was busily resounding within it from morning to night; swallows and martins skimmed twittering about the eaves; and rows of pigeons, some with one eye turned up, as if watching the weather, some with their heads under their wings, or buried in their bosoms, and others, swelling and cooing and bowing about their dames, were enjoying the sunshine on the roof. Sleek, unwieldy porkers were grunting in the repose and abundance of their pens, from whence sallied forth, now and then, troops of sucking pigs, as if to snuff the air. A stately squadron of snowy geese were riding in an adjoining pond, convoying whole fleets of ducks; regiments of turkeys were gobbling through the farm-yard, and guinea-fowls fretting about it like ill-tempered housewives, with their peevish, discontented cry. Before the barn door strutted the gallant cock, that pattern of a husband, a warrior, and a fine gentleman; clapping his burnished wings and crowing in the pride and gladness of his heart —sometimes tearing up the earth with his feet, and then generously calling his ever-hungry family of wives and children to enjoy his rich discovery.

The pedagogue's mouth watered, as he looked upon this sumptuous promise of luxurious winter fare. In his devouring mind's eye, he pictured to himself every roasting pig running about, with a pudding in its belly, and an apple in its mouth; the pigeons were snugly put to bed in a comfortable pie, and tucked in with a coverlet of crust; the geese were swimming in their own gravy; and the ducks pairing cosily in dishes, like snug married couples, with a decent competency of onion sauce. In the porkers he saw carved out the future sleek side of bacon, and juicy relishing ham; not a turkey, but he beheld daintily trussed up, with its gizzard under its wing, and, peradventure, a necklace of savory sausages; and even bright chanticleer himself lay sprawling on his back, in a side dish, with uplifted claws, as if craving that quarter which his chivalrous spirit disdained to ask while living.

As the enraptured Ichabod fancied all this, and as he rolled his great green eyes over the fat meadow lands, the rich fields of wheat, of rye, of buckwheat, and Indian corn, and the orchards burthened with ruddy fruit, which surrounded the warm tenement of Van Tassel, his heart yearned after the damsel who was to inherit these domains, and his imagination expanded with the idea, how they might be readily turned into cash, and the money invested in immense tracts of wild land, and shingle palaces in the wilderness. Nay, his busy fancy already realized his hopes, and presented to him the blooming Katrina, with a whole family of children, mounted on the top of a wagon loaded with household trumpery, with pots and kettles dangling beneath; and he beheld himself bestriding a pacing mare, with a colt at her heels, setting out for Kentucky, Tennessee—or the Lord knows where!

When he entered the house, the conquest of his heart was complete. It was one of those spacious farm-houses, with high-ridged, but lowly-sloping roofs, built in the style handed down from the first Dutch settlers, the low projecting eaves forming a piazza along the front, capable of being closed up in bad weather. Under this were hung flails, harness, various utensils of husbandry, and nets for fishing in the neighboring river. Benches were built along the sides for summer use; and a great spinning-wheel at one end, and a churn at the other, showed the various uses to which this important porch might be devoted. From this piazza the wonderful Ichabod entered the hall, which formed the centre of the mansion, and the place of usual residence. Here, rows of resplendent pewter, ranged on a long dresser, dazzled his eyes. In one corner stood a huge bag of wool, ready to be spun; in another, a quantity of linsey-woolsey just from the loom; ears of Indian corn, and strings of dried apples and peaches, hung in gay festoons along the walls, mingled with the gaud of red peppers; and a door left ajar, gave him a peep into the best parlor, where the claw-footed chairs and dark mahogany tables shone like mirrors, andirons with their accompanying shovel and tongs, glistened from their covert of asparagus tops; mock-oranges and conch shells decorated the mantelpiece; strings of various-colored birds' eggs were suspended above it; a great ostrich egg was hung from the centre of the room, and a corner cupboard, knowingly left open, displayed immense treasures of old silver and well-mended china.

From the moment Ichabod laid his eyes upon these regions of delight, the peace of his mind was at an end, and his only study was how to gain the affections of the peerless daughter of Van Tassel.

INDIANS OF ARIZONA.

CHAPTER III.

JAMES FENIMORE COOPER.

DISTINCTIVELY American in theme and spirit was the lasting work of James Fenimore Cooper; his attempts to portray European scenes and characters are justly neglected. But he is still the most prominent of American romancers of the old frontier and the sea. He was born at Burlington, New Jersey, September 15th, 1789, but his boyhood was spent at Cooperstown, New York, a village founded by his father, Judge Cooper, in 1790, when that portion of the state was a veritable wilderness, inhabited chiefly by Indians, trappers and pioneers. Cooper's early education was conducted by his father, a man of strong character and some attainments, and the boy entered Yale College at the early age of thirteen. Leaving college after three years of study, he entered the navy as a midshipman, and remained in the service until a short time after his marriage in 1811.

Observation and experience on the New York frontier and in the naval service had given him a mass of material available for fiction, but he did not attempt authorship until he was thirty years of age. His first romance, "Precaution," which attempted to portray polite society, was a failure. Two years later, however, "The Spy," based upon experiences of one of Washington's secret agents in New York during the Revolutionary War, made Cooper famous throughout his own country and soon afterward in Europe.

In 1823 appeared "The Pioneers," an exciting story of life at the outposts of civilization, and also "The Pilot," his first sea story. These books were the forerunners of two series, in their widely differing veins. Yet three years passed before

ROTUNDA GALLERY—CONGRESSIONAL LIBRARY.

the appearance of "The Last of the Mohicans," abounding in sharp contrasts of Indians, pioneers and British and French soldiers in the time of the French and Indian war. Cooper is now charged with having greatly idealized his Indian characters, but his contemporaries commended him for fidelity to the types he had studied.

After publishing "The Red Rover," his second sea story, Cooper went to Europe, where he remained six years, residing in different cities. Intensely patriotic, as well as easily offended, he was greatly irritated by European comment on his country and its people. He therefore printed in English newspapers and reviews some vigorous corrections of misstatements regarding America, and he also published a book with the same purpose. His manner was so combative that the controversy he provoked continued for years. Meanwhile he was earnestly observant of European politics and published three novels abounding in political speculation and action, which have fallen into the background.

His first prominent work after his return to his native country was a "Naval History of the United States;" after which he wrote novels in rapid succession, as well as his "Lives of Distinguished American Naval Officers." But unfortunately he became again involved in useless controversy, attacking New England and the Puritans. Always interested and active in politics, he was an object of severe newspaper criticism. Cooper, combative and proud, had some legal ability, and instituted many libel suits, all of which were successful, and yet wasted his time and talents. He died at Cooperstown, September 14th, 1851.

In Europe, Cooper has often been termed "the Walter Scott of America," and the comparison is apt to the extent that he, like Scott, took patriotic, passionate interest in embodying in literature such interesting characters and experiences of his native land as were vanishing. The value of his work becomes apparent when the reader now notes how small is the remaining fiction of the periods treated by Cooper. The accuracy of Cooper's descriptions of men and scenes was sufficiently attested in his own day, when there still survived participators in wars with the Indians, French and British, and when the war of 1812-15 was recent history. Cooper was weak in construction and had little sense of humor. His style is formal and he indulges too much in detail. Though he created such apparently real characters as Natty Burapo and Long Tom Coffin, he was unable generally to individualize his characters by appropriate speech. In chapters descriptive of incidents, however, he is almost equal to Scott, and was as highly admired by the elder Dumas and other European writers of exciting romance.

The Deerslayer.

The ark, as the floating habitation of the Hutters was generally called, was a very simple contrivance. A large flat, or scow, composed the buoyant part of the vessel; and in its center, occupying the whole of its breadth, and about two-thirds of its length, stood a low fabric, resembling the castle in construction, though made of materials so light as barely to be bullet-proof. As the sides of the scow were a little higher than usual, and the interior of the cabin had no more elevation than was necessary for comfort, this unusual addition had neither a very clumsy nor a very obtrusive appearance. It was, in short, little more than a modern canal-boat, though more rudely constructed, of greater breadth than common, and bearing about it the signs of the wilderness, in its bark-covered posts and roof. The scow, however, had been put together with some skill, being comparatively light, for its strength, and sufficiently manageable. The cabin was divided into two apartments, one of which served for a parlor, and the sleeping-room of the father, and the other was appropriated to the uses of the daughters. A very simple arrangement sufficed for the kitchen, which was in one end of the scow, and removed from the cabin, standing in the open air; the ark being altogether a summer habitation.

The "and-bush," as Hurry in his ignorance of English termed it, is quite as easily explained. In many parts of the lake and river, where the banks were steep and high, the smaller trees and larger bushes, as has been already mentioned, fairly overhung the stream, their branches not infrequently dipping into the water. In some instances they grew out in nearly horizontal lines, for thirty or forty feet. The water being uniformly deepest near the shores, where the banks were highest and the nearest to a perpendicular, Hutter had found no difficulty in letting the ark drop under one of these covers, where it had been anchored with a view to conceal its position; security requiring some such precautions, in his view of the case. Once beneath the trees and bushes, a few stones fastened to the ends of the branches had caused them tô bend sufficiently to dip into the river; and a few severed bushes, properly disposed, did the rest. The reader has seen that this cover was so complete as to deceive two men accustomed to the woods, and who were actually in search of those it concealed; a circumstance that will be easily understood by those who are familiar with the matted and wild luxuriance of a virgin American forest, more especially in a rich soil.

The discovery of the ark produced very different effects on our two adventurers. As soon as the canoe could be got round to the proper opening, Hurry leaped on board, and in a minute was closely engaged in a gay, and a sort of recriminating discourse with Judith, apparently forgetful of the existence of all the rest of the world. Not so with Deerslayer. He entered the ark with a slow, cautious step, examining every arrangement of the cover with curious and scrutinizing eyes. It is true, he cast one admiring glance at Judith, which was extorted by her brilliant and singular beauty; but even this could detain him but a single instant from the indulgence of his interest in Hutter's contrivances. Step by step did he look into the construction of the singular abode, investigate its fastenings and strength, ascertain its means of defense, and make every inquiry that would be likely to occur to one whose thoughts dwelt principally on such expedients. Nor was the cover neglected. Of this he examined the whole minutely, his commendation escaping him more than once, in audible comments. Frontier usages admitting of this familiarity, he passed through the rooms as he had previously done at the castle; and, opening a door, issued into the end of the scow opposite to that where he had left Hurry and Judith. Here he found the other sister, employed on some coarse needlework, seated beneath the leafy canopy of the cover.

As Deerslayer's examination was by this time ended, he dropped the butt of his rifle, and, leaning on the barrel with both hands, he turned toward the girl with an interest the singular beauty of her sister had not awakened. He had gathered from Hurry's remarks that Hetty was considered to have less intellect than ordinarily falls to the share of human beings; and his education among Indians had taught him to treat those who were thus afflicted by Providence, with more than common tenderness. Nor was there anything in Hetty Hutter's appearance, as so often happens, to weaken the interest her situation excited. An idiot she could not properly be termed, her mind being just enough enfeebled to lose most of those traits that are connected with the more artful qualities, and to retain its ingenuousness and love of truth. It had often been remarked of this girl, by the few who had seen her, and who possessed sufficient knowledge to discriminate, that her perception of the right seemed almost intuitive, while her aversion to the wrong formed so distinctive a feature of her mind, as to surround her with an atmosphere of pure morality; peculiarities that are not infrequent with persons who are termed feeble-minded; as if God had forbidden the evil spirits to invade a precinct so defenseless, with the benign purpose of extending a direct protection to those who have been left without the usual aids of humanity. Her person, too, was agreeable, having a strong resemblance to that of her sister, of which it was a subdued and humble copy. If it had none of the brilliancy of Judith's, the calm, quiet, almost holy expression of her meek countenance, seldom failed to win on the observer; and few noted it long, that did not begin to feel a deep and lasting interest in the girl. She had no color, in common, nor was her simple mind apt to present images that caused her cheek to brighten; though she retained a modesty so innate, that it almost raised her to the unsuspecting purity of a being superior to human infirmities. Guileless, innocent, and without distrust, equally by nature and from her mode of life, Providence had, nevertheless, shielded her from harm by a halo of moral light, as it is said "to temper the wind to the shorn lamb."

"You are Hetty Hutter," said Deerslayer, in the way one puts a question unconsciously to himself, assuming a kindness of tone and manner that were singularly adapted to win the confidence of her he addressed. "Hurry Harry has told me of you, and I know you must be the child?"

"Yes, I'm Hetty Hutter," returned the girl, in a low, sweet voice, which nature, aided by some education, had preserved from vulgarity of tone and utterance: "I'm Hetty; Judith Hutter's sister, and Thomas Hutter's youngest daughter."

"I know your history, then, for Hurry Harry talks considerable, and he is free of speech, when he can find other people's consarns to dwell on. You pass most of your life on the lake, Hetty?"

"Certainly. Mother is dead; father is gone a-trapping, and Judith and I stay at home. What's *your* name?"

"That's a question more easily asked than it is answered, young woman; seeing that I'm so young, and yet have borne more names than some of the greatest chiefs in all America."

"But you've *got* a name—you don't throw away one name before you come honestly by another?"

"I hope not, gal—I hope not. My names have come nat'rally; and I suppose the one I bear now will be of no great lasting, since the Delawares seldom settle on a man's r'al title, until such time as he has opportunity of showing his true natur', in the council or on the war-path; which has never behappened me; seeing, firstly, because I'm not born a redskin, and have no right to sit in *their* councilings, and am much too humble to be called on for opinions from the great of my own color; and, secondly, because this is the first war that has befallen in my time, and no inimy has yet inroaded far enough into the colony to be reached by an arm even longer than mine."

"Tell me your names," added Hetty, looking up at him artlessly, "and, maybe, I'll tell you your character."

"There is some truth in that, I'll not deny, though it often fails. Men are deceived in other men's characters, and frequently give 'em names they by no means desarve. You can see the truth of this in Mingo names, which, in their own tongue, signify the same things as the Delaware names,—at least, so they tell me, for I know little of that tribe, unless it be by report,—and no one can say they are as honest or as upright a nation. I put no great dependence, therefore, on names."

"Tell me *all* your names," repeated the girl, earnestly, for her mind was too simple to separate things from professions, and she *did* attach importance to a name; "I want to know what to think of you."

"Well, sartain; I've no objection, and you shall hear them

all. In the first place, then, I'm Christian, and white-born, like yourself, and my parents had a name that came down from father to son, as is a part of their gifts. My father was called Bumppo; and I was named after him, of course, the given name being Nathaniel, or Natty, as most people saw fit to tarm it."

"Yes, yes—Natty—and Hetty"—interrupted the girl quickly, and looking up from her work again, with a smile: "You are Natty, and I'm Hetty—though you are Bumppo, and I'm Hutter. Bumppo isn't as pretty as Hutter, is it?"

"Why, that's as people fancy. Bumppo has no lofty sound, I admit; and yet men have bumped through the world with it. I did not go by this name, howsoever, very long; for the Delawares soon found out, or thought they found out, that I was not given to lying, and they called me, firstly, 'Straight-tongue.'"

"That's a *good* name," interrupted Hetty, earnestly, and in a positive manner; "don't tell me there's no virtue in names!"

"I do not say *that,* for perhaps I desarved to be so called, lies being no favorites with me, as they are with some. After a while they found out that I was quick of foot, and then they called me 'The Pigeon'; which, you know, has a swift wing, and flies in a direct line."

"*That* was a *pretty* name!" exclaimed Hetty; "pigeons are pretty birds!"

"Most things that God has created are pretty in their way, my good gal, though they get to be deformed by mankind, so as to change their natur's, as well as their appearance. From carrying messages, and striking blind trails, I got at last to following the hunters, when it was thought I was quicker and surer at finding the game than most lads, and then they called me the 'Lap-ear'; as, they said, I partook of the sagacity of a hound."

"That's not so pretty," answered Hetty; "I hope you didn't keep *that* name long."

"Not after I was rich enough to buy a rifle," returned the other, betraying a little pride through his usually quiet and subdued manner; "*then* it was seen I could keep a wigwam in ven'son; and in time I got the name of 'Deerslayer,' which is that I now bear; homely as some will think it, who set more valie on the scalp of a fellow-mortal than on the horns of a buck."

"Well, Deerslayer, I'm not one of them," answered Hetty, simply; "Judith likes soldiers, and flary coats, and fine feathers; but they're all naught to me. *She* says the officers are great, and gay, and of soft speech; but they make me shudder, for their business is to kill their fellow-creatures. I like your calling better; and your last name is a very good one—better than Natty Bumppo."

"This is nat'ral in one of your turn of mind, Hetty, and much as I should have expected. They tell me your sister is handsome—oncommon, for a mortal; and beauty is apt to seek admiration."

"Did you never see Judith?" demanded the girl, with quick earnestness; "if you never have, go at once and look at her. Even Hurry Harry isn't more pleasant to look at; though *she* is a woman, and *he* is a man."

Deerslayer regarded the girl for a moment with concern. Her pale face had flushed a little, and her eye, usually so mild and serene, brightened as she spoke, in the way to betray the inward impulses.

"Ay, Hurry Harry," he muttered to himself, as he walked through the cabin towards the other end of the boat; "this comes of good looks, if a light tongue has had no consarn in it. It's easy to see which way that poor creatur's feelin's are leanin', whatever may be the case with your Jude's."

But an interruption was put to the gallantry of Hurry, the coquetry of his mistress, the thoughts of Deerslayer, and the gentle feelings of Hetty, by the sudden appearance of the canoe of the ark's owner, in the narrow opening among the bushes that served as a sort of moat to his position. It would seem that Hutter, or Floating Tom, as he was familiarly called by all the hunters who knew his habits, recognized the canoe of Hurry, for he expressed no surprise at finding him in the scow. On the contrary, his reception was such as to denote not only gratification, but a pleasure, mingled with a little disappointment at his not having made his appearance some days sooner.

"I looked for you last week," he said, in a half-grumbling, half-welcoming manner; "and was disappointed uncommonly that you didn't arrive. There came a runner through, to warn all the trappers and hunters that the colony and the Canadas were again in trouble; and I felt lonesome, up in these mountains, with three scalps to see to, and only one pair of hands to protect them."

"That's reasonable," returned March; "and 'twas feeling like a parent. No doubt, if I had two such darters as Judith and Hetty, my exper'ence would tell the same story, though in gin'ral I am just as well satisfied with having the nearest neighbor fifty miles off, as when he is within call."

"Notwithstanding, you didn't choose to come into the wilderness alone, now you knew that the Canada savages are likely to be stirring," returned Hutter, giving a sort of distrustful, and at the same time inquiring, glance at Deerslayer.

"Why should I? They say a bad companion, on a journey, helps to shorten the path; and this young man I account to be a reasonably good one. This is Deerslayer, old Tom, a noted hunter among the Delawares, and Christian-born, and Christian-edicated, too, like you and me. The lad is not parfect, perhaps, but there's worse men in the country that he came from, and it's likely he'll find some that's no better, in this part of the world. Should we have occasion to defend our traps, and the territory, he'll be useful in feeding us all; for he's a reg'lar dealer in ven'son."

"Young man, you are welcome," growled Tom, thrusting a hard, bony hand towards the youth, as a pledge of his sincerity; "in such times, a white face is a friend's, and I count on you as a support. Children sometimes make a stout heart feeble, and these two daughters of mine give me more concern than all my traps, and skins, and rights in the country."

"That's nat'ral!" cried Hurry. "Yes, Deerslayer, you and I don't know it yet by experience; but, on the whole, I consider that as nat'ral. If we *had* darters, it's more than probable we should have some such feelin's; and I honor the man that owns 'em. As for Judith, old man, I enlist, at once, as her soldier, and here is Deerslayer to help you to take care of Hetty."

"Many thanks to you, Master March," returned the beauty, in a full, rich voice, and with an accuracy of intonation and utterance that she shared in common with her sister, and which showed that she had been better taught than her father's life and appearance would give reason to expect; "many thanks to you; but Judith Hutter has the spirit and the experience that will make her depend more on herself than on good-looking rovers like you. Should there be need to face the savages, do you land with my father, instead of burrowing in the huts, under the show of defending us females, and—"

"Girl—girl," interrupted the father, "quiet that glib tongue of thine, and hear the truth. There are savages on the lake shore already, and no man can say how near to us they may be at this very moment, or when we may hear more from them!"

"If this be true, Master Hutter," said Hurry, whose change of countenance denoted how serious he deemed the information, though it did not denote any unmanly alarm, "if this be true, your ark is in a most misfortunate position, for, though the cover did deceive Deerslayer and myself, it would hardly be overlooked by a full-blooded Injin, who was out seriously in s'arch of scalps!"

"I think as you do, Hurry, and wish, with all my heart, we lay anywhere else, at this moment, than in this narrow, crooked stream, which has many advantages to hide in, but which is almost fatal to them that are discovered. The savages are near us, moreover, and the difficulty is, to get out of the river without being shot down like deer standing at a lick!"

"Are you sartain, Master Hutter, that the redskins you dread are ra'al Canadas?" asked Deerslayer, in a modest but earnest manner. "Have you seen any, and can you describe their paint?"

"I have fallen in with the signs of their being in the neighborhood, but have seen none of 'em. I was down stream a mile or so, looking to my traps, when I struck a fresh trail, crossing the corner of a swamp, and moving northward. The man had not passed an hour; and I know'd it for an Indian footstep, by the size of the foot, and the intoe, even before I found a worn moccasin, which its owner had dropped as useless. For that matter, I found the spot where he halted to make a new one, which was only a few yards from the place where he had dropped the old one."

"That doesn't look much like a redskin on the warpath?" returned the other, shaking his head. "An exper'enced warrior, at least, would have burned, or buried, or sunk in the river such signs of his passage; and your trail is, quite likely, a peaceable trail. But the moccasin may greatly relieve my mind, if you bethought you of bringing it off. I've come here to meet a young chief myself; and his course would be much in the direction you've mentioned. The trail may have been his'n."

"Hurry Harry, you're well acquainted with this young man, I hope, who has meetings with savages in a part of the country where he has never been before?" demanded Hutter, in a tone and in a manner that sufficiently indicated the motive of the question; these rude beings seldom hesitating, on the score of delicacy, to betray their feelings. "Treachery is an Indian virtue; and the whites, that live much in their tribes, soon catch their ways and practices."

"True—true as the Gospel, old Tom; but not personable to Deerslayer, who's a young man of truth, if he has no other ricommend. I'll answer for his *honesty*, whatever I may do for his valor in battle."

"I should like to know his errand in this strange quarter of the country."

"That is soon told, Master Hutter," said the young man, with the composure of one who kept a clean conscience. "I think, moreover, you've a *right* to ask it. The father of two such darters, who occupies a lake, after your fashion, has just the same right to inquire into a stranger's business in his neighborhood, as the colony would have to demand the reason why the Frenchers put more rijiments than common along the lines. No, no, I'll not deny your right to know why a stranger comes into your habitation or country, in times as serious as these."

"If such is your way of thinking, friend, let me hear your story without more words."

"'Tis soon told, as I said afore; and shall be honestly told. I'm a young man, and, as yet, have never been on a war-path; but no sooner did the news come among the Delawares, that wampum and a hatchet were about to be sent in to the tribe, than they wished me to go out among the people of my own color, and get the exact date of things for 'em. This I did, and, after delivering my talk to the chiefs, on my return, I met an officer of the crown on the Schoharie, who had moneys to send to some of the friendly tribes, that live farther west. This was thought a good occasion for Chingachgook, a young chief who had never struck a foe, and myself, to go on our first war-path in company; and an app'intment was made for us, by an old Delaware, to meet at the rock near the foot of this lake. I'll not deny that Chingachgook has *another* object in view, but it has no consarn with any here, and is his secret, and not mine; therefore I'll say no more about it."

"'Tis something about a young woman," interrupted Judith, hastily; then laughing at her own impetuosity, and even having the grace to color a little at the manner in which she had betrayed her readiness to impute such a motive. "If 'tis neither war nor a hunt, it must be love."

"Ay, it comes easy for the young and handsome, who hear so much of them feelin's, to suppose that they lie at the bottom of most proceedin's; but, on that head, I say nothin'. Chingachgook is to meet me at the rock an hour afore sunset to-morrow evening, after which we shall go our way together, molesting none but the king's inimies, who are lawfully our own. Knowing Hurry of old, who once trapped in our hunting-grounds, and falling in with him on the Schoharie, just as he was on the p'int of starting for his summer ha'nts, we agreed to journey in company; not so much from fear of the Mingos as from good fellowship, and, as he says, to shorten a long road."

"And you think the trail I saw may have been that of your friend, ahead of his time?" said Hutter.

"That's my idee; which may be wrong, but which may be right. If I saw the moccasin, however, I could tell in a minute whether it is made in the Delaware fashion or not."

"Here it is, then," said the quick-witted Judith, who had already gone to the canoe in quest of it; "tell us what it says; friend or enemy. You look honest; and *I* believe all you say, whatever father may think."

"That's the way with you, Jude; forever finding out friends, where I distrust foes," grumbled Tom; "but speak out, young man, and tell us what you think of the moccasin."

"That's not Delaware-made," returned Deerslayer, examining the worn and rejected covering for the foot with a cautious eye; "I'm too young on a war-path to be positive, but I should say that moccasin has a northern look, and comes from beyond the great lakes."

"If such is the case, we ought not to lie here a minute longer than is necessary," said Hutter, glancing through the leaves of his cover, as if he already distrusted the presence of an enemy on the opposite shore of the narrow and sinuous stream. "It wants but an hour or so of night, and to move in the dark will be impossible, without making a noise that would betray us. Did you hear the echo of a piece in the mountains, half-an-hour since?"

"Yes, old man, and heard the piece itself," answered Hurry, who now felt the indiscretion of which he had been guilty, "for the last was fired from my own shoulder."

"I feared it came from the French Indians; still it may put them on the look-out, and be a means of discovering us. You did wrong to fire in war-time, unless there was good occasion."

"So I began to think myself, Uncle Tom; and yet, if a man can't trust himself to let off his rifle in a wilderness that is a thousand miles square, lest some inimy should hear it, where's the use in carrying one?"

Hutter now held a long consultation with his two guests, in which the parties came to a true understanding of their situation. He explained the difficulty that would exist in attempting to get the ark out of so swift and narrow a stream, in the dark, without making a noise that could not fail to attract Indian ears. Any strollers in their vicinity would keep near the river or the lake; but the former had swampy shores in many places, and was both so crooked and so fringed with bushes, that it was quite possible to move by daylight without incurring much danger of being seen. More was to be apprehended, perhaps, from the ear than from the eye, especially as long as they were in the short, straitened, and canopied reaches of the stream.

"I never drop down into this cover, which is handy to my traps, and safer than the lake, from curious eyes, without providing the means of getting out ag'in," continued this singular being; "and that is easier done by a pull than a push. My anchor is now lying above the suction, in the open lake; and here is a line, you see, to haul us up to it. Without some such help, a single pair of hands would make heavy work in forcing a scow like this up stream. I have a sort of crab, too, that lightens the pull, on occasion. Jude can use the oar astarn as well as myself; and when we fear no enemy, to get out of the river gives us but little trouble."

"What should we gain, Master Hutter, by changing the position?" asked Deerslayer, with a good deal of earnestness; "this is a safe cover, and a stout defense might be made from the inside of this cabin. I've never fou't unless in the way of tradition; but it seems to me we might beat off twenty Mingos, with palisades like them afore us."

"Ay, ay; you've never fought except in traditions, that's plain enough, young man? Did you ever see as broad a sheet of water as this above us, before you came in upon it with Hurry?"

"I can't say that I ever did," Deerslayer answered, modestly. "Youth is the time to l'arn; and I'm far from wishing to raise my voice in counsel, afore it is justified by exper'ence."

"Well, then, I'll teach you the disadvantage of fighting in this position, and the advantage of taking to the open lake. Here, you may see, the savages will know where to aim every shot; and it would be too much to hope that *some* would not find their way through the crevices of the logs. Now, on the other hand, *we* should have nothing but a forest to aim at. Then we are not safe from fire, here, the bark of this roof being little better than so much kindling-wood. The castle, too, might be entered and ransacked in my absence, and all my possessions overrun and destroyed. Once in the lake, we can be attacked only in boats or on rafts—shall have a fair chance with the enemy—and can protect the castle with the ark. Do you understand this reasoning, youngster?"

"It sounds well—yes, it has a rational sound; and I'll not gainsay it."

"Well, old Tom," cried Hurry, "if we are to move, the sooner we make a beginning, the sooner we shall know whether we are to have our scalps for nightcaps, or not."

As this proposition was self-evident, no one denied its justice. The three men, after a short preliminary explanation, now set about their preparations to move the ark in earnest. The slight fastenings were quickly loosened; and, by hauling on the ine, the heavy craft slowly emerged from the cover. It was no sooner free from the encumbrance of the branches, than it swung into the stream, sheering quite close to the western shore, by the force of the current. Not a soul on board heard the rustling of the branches, as the cabin came against the bushes and trees of the western bank, without a feeling of uneasiness; for no one knew at what moment, or in what place, a secret and murderous enemy might unmask himself. Perhaps the gloomy light that still struggled through the impending canopy of leaves, or found its way through the narrow, ribbon-like opening, which seemed to mark, in the air above, the course of the river that flowed beneath, aided in augmenting the appearance of the danger; for it was little more than sufficient to render objects visible, without giving up all their outlines at a glance. Although the sun had not absolutely set, it had withdrawn its direct rays from the valley; and the hues of evening were beginning to gather around objects that stood uncovered, rendering those within the shadows of the woods still more sombre and gloomy.

No interruption followed the movement, however, and, as the men continued to haul on the line, the ark passed steadily ahead, the great breadth of the scow preventing its sinking into the water, and from offering much resistance to the progress of the swift element beneath its bottom. Hutter, too, had adopted a precaution suggested by experience, which might have done credit to a seaman, and which completely prevented any of the annoyances and obstacles which otherwise would have attended the short turns of the river. As the ark descended, heavy stones, attached to the line, were dropped in the center of the stream, forming local anchors, each of which was kept from dragging by the assistance of those above it, until the uppermost of all was reached, which got its "backing" from the anchor, or grapnel, that lay well out in the lake. In consequence of this expedient the ark floated clear of the incumbrances of the shore, against which it would otherwise have been unavoidably hauled at every turn, producing embarrassments that Hutter, single-handed, would have found it very difficult to overcome.

Favored by this foresight, and stimulated by the apprehension of discovery, Floating Tom and his two athletic companions hauled the ark ahead with quite as much rapidity as comported with the strength of the line. At every turn in the stream a stone was raised from the bottom, when the direction of the scow changed to one that pointed towards the stone that lay above. In this manner, with the channel buoyed out for him, as a sailor might term it, did Hutter move forward, occasionally urging his friends, in a low and guarded voice, to increase their exertions, and then, as occasions offered, warning them against efforts that might, at particular moments, endanger all by too much zeal. In spite of their long familiarity with the woods, the gloomy character of the shaded river added to the uneasiness that each felt; and when the ark reached the first bend in the Susquehanna, and the eye caught a glimpse of the broader expanse of the lake, all felt a relief, that perhaps none would have been willing to confess. Here the last stone was raised from the bottom, and the line led directly towards the grapnel, which, as Hutter had explained, was dropped above the suction of the current.

"Thank God!" ejaculated Hurry, "*there* is daylight, and we shall soon have a chance of *seeing* our inimies, if we are to *feel* 'em."

"That is more than you or any man can say," growled Hutter. "There is no spot so likely to harbor a party as the shore around the outlet, and the moment we clear these trees and get into open water, will be the most trying time, since it will leave the enemy a cover, while it puts us out of one. Judith, girl, do you and Hetty leave the oar to take care of itself, and go within the cabin; and be mindful not to show your faces at a window; for they who will look at them won't stop to praise their beauty. And now, Hurry, we'll step into this outer room ourselves, and haul through the door, where we shall all be safe, from a surprise, at least. Friend Deerslayer, as the current is lighter, and the line has all the strain on it that is prudent, do you keep moving from window to window, taking care not to let your head be seen, if you set any value on life. No one knows when or where we shall hear from our neighbors."

Deerslayer complied, with a sensation that had nothing in common with fear, but which had all the interest of a perfectly novel and a most exciting situation. For the first time in his life he was in the vicinity of enemies, or had good reason to think so; and that, too, under all the thrilling circumstances of

Indian surprises and Indian artifices. As he took his stand at the window, the ark was just passing through the narrowest part of the stream, a point where the water first entered what was properly termed the river, and where the trees fairly interlocked overhead, causing the current to rush into an arch of verdure; a feature as appropriate and peculiar to the country, perhaps, as that of Switzerland, where the rivers come rushing literally from chambers of ice.

The ark was in the act of passing the last curve of this leafy entrance, as Deerslayer, having examined all that could be seen of the eastern bank of the river, crossed the room to look from the opposite window, at the western. His arrival at this aperture was most opportune, for he had no sooner placed his eye at a crack than a sight met his gaze that might well have alarmed a sentinel so young and inexperienced. A sapling overhung the water, in nearly half a circle, having first grown towards the light, and then been pressed down into this form by the weight of the snows; a circumstance of common occurrence in the American woods. On this no less than six Indians had already appeared, others standing ready to follow them, as they left room; each evidently bent on running out on the trunk, and dropping on the roof of the ark as it passed beneath. This would have been an exploit of no great difficulty, the inclination of the tree admitting of an easy passage, the adjoining branches offering ample support for the hands, and the fall being too trifling to be apprehended. When Deerslayer first saw this party, it was just unmasking itself, by ascending the part of the tree nearest to the earth, or that which was much the most difficult to overcome; and his knowledge of Indian habits told him at once that they were all in their war paint, and belonged to a hostile tribe.

"Pull, Hurry," he cried; "pull for your life, and as you love Judith Hutter! Pull, man, pull!"

This call was made to one that the young man knew had the strength of a giant. It was so earnest and solemn, that both Hutter and March felt it was not idly given, and they applied all their force to the line simultaneously, and at a most critical moment. The scow redoubled its motion, and seemed to glide from under the tree as if conscious of the danger that was impending overhead. Perceiving that they were discovered, the

Indians uttered the fearful war whoop, and running forward on the tree, leaped desperately towards their fancied prize. There were six on the tree, and each made the effort. All but their leader fell into the river more or less distant from the ark, as they came, sooner or later, to the leaping-place. The chief, who had taken the dangerous post in advance, having an earlier opportunity than the others, struck the scow just within the stern. The fall proving so much greater than he had anticipated, he was slightly stunned, and for a moment he remained half bent and unconscious of his situation. At this instant Judith rushed from the cabin, her beauty heightened by the excitement that produced the bold act, which flushed her cheek to crimson, and, throwing all her strength into the effort, she pushed the intruder over the edge of the scow, headlong into the river. This decided feat was no sooner accomplished than the woman resumed her sway; Judith looked over the stern to ascertain what had become of the man, and the expression of her eyes softened to concern, next, her cheek crimsoned between shame and surprise, at her own temerity, and then she laughed in her own merry and sweet manner. All this occupied less than a minute, when the arm of Deerslayer was thrown around her waist, and she was dragged swiftly within the protection of the cabin. This retreat was not effected too soon. Scarcely were the two in safety, when the forest was filled with yells, and bullets began to patter against the logs.

The ark being in swift motion all this while, it was beyond the danger of pursuit by the time these little events had occurred; and the savages, as soon as the first burst of their anger had subsided, ceased firing, with the consciousness that they were expending their ammunition in vain. When the scow came up over her grapnel, Hunter tripped the latter, in a way not to impede the motion; and being now beyond the influence of the current, the vessel continued to drift ahead, until fairly in the open lake, though still near enough to the land to render exposure to a rifle-bullet dangerous. Hutter and March got out two small sweeps, and, covered by the cabin, they soon urged the ark far enough from the shore to leave no inducement to their enemies to make any further attempt to injure them.

CHAPTER IV.

NATHANIEL HAWTHORNE.

THE story of Hawthorne's life is a simple one. He was born in Salem, Mass., in 1804, and as a boy was brought up partly in that ancient town, and partly on the shores of Sebago Lake, in Maine, where his uncle, Richard Manning, had an estate. His father, who died of fever in Surinam, when Nathaniel was four years old, was an East India merchant, and captained his own vessel; an uncle, Daniel, had commanded a privateer in the Revolution; an ancestor, John Hathorne (as the name was then spelled), had been a judge in the witch trials; and the first emigrant, William, the elder son of the English family, was a man of note in the Province, and a major in the Indian wars. His mother was a woman of intellect and refinement; but Nathaniel was the first of the Hawthornes to evince literary proclivities.

He was an active, outdoor boy, though fond of reading and with thoughts of his own. As a student he was not distinguished, either before or during his Bowdoin college career; but he graduated well in the class of 1824; Longfellow was a classmate, and Franklin Pierce was in the class ahead of him. After graduating he lived in seclusion at his home in Salem for twelve years, writing, meditating, and occasionally publishing short sketches in Annuals and similar publications, uniformly over a pseudonym. Before 1840 he met, and in 1842 he married Sophia Peabody of Salem, and lived with her in "The Old Manse" at Concord, Mass. He had already tried the Brook Farm community life, and decided it was not suited to his requirements. He obtained an appointment in the Salem Custom House, and supported himself on the salary derived therefrom, and by writing sketches and stories. These were collected under the title of "Mosses from an Old Manse," and "The Snow Image and Other Stories." He was rotated out of office, and in 1850 wrote "The Scarlet Letter," which brought him fame here and abroad. Removing to Lenox, Mass., he produced "The House of the Seven Gables," "The Blithedale Romance," evolved from his Brook Farm observations, and "The Wonder-Book" and "Tanglewood Tales"—stories for children based on classic mythology. Taking up his residence for the second time in Concord, at "The Wayside," he wrote a campaign biography of his friend Franklin Pierce, and the latter, on his election to the Presidency of the United States, appointed Hawthorne consul at Liverpool, England. Shortly before the end of his term he resigned the office and sojourned for two or three years on the Continent. Returning in 1859 to England, he wrote "The Marble Faun" (published in England under the title of "Transformation"), and came back to America in 1860. The outbreak of the Civil War the following year interrupted his imaginative work; but he published a volume of English studies, "Our Old Home," and the first chapters of a new romance, "The Dolliver Romance," in the *Atlantic Monthly*. He died suddenly in Plymouth, New Hampshire, on a journey for health undertaken with Franklin Pierce, and was buried in Concord, May 23d, 1864.

The story of Hawthorne's mind and opinions may be gathered from his writings, especially from the shorter pieces contained in "Twice-Told Tales" and "The Mosses." These appear on the surface to be merely imaginative tales, exquisitely wrought; but they embody profound, radical and sometimes revolutionary views on all subjects of society and morals. He probed deeply into the mystery of human sin; the revelations thus evolved cast a tinge of sadness over much that he wrote; but Hawthorne was at heart an optimist, and his most searching analyses result in conclusions the most hopeful. The more he is studied, the more is the student impressed with his truth, justice and sanity. Common sense and the sense of humor existed in him side by side with the keenest insight and the finest imaginative gifts; and all that he wrote is rendered fascinating by the charm of a translucent, nearly perfect literary style. Everything that he produced was in its degree a work of art.

The four romances on which his reputation chiefly rests

belong in a class by themselves. No other writer has succeeded in mastering the principle on which they are composed. There is in them a living spirit which creates its own proper form. They are wrought from within outwards, like the growths of nature. The interest of outward events is in them subordinated to that of the vicissitudes of mind and soul of the characters, which are penetratingly interpreted. There is nothing arbitrary in Hawthorne's treatment; but in the end he has placed clearly before the reader the elements of the problem, and has suggested the solution. We rise from his books knowing more of life and man than when we took them up, and with better hopes of their destiny. The years which have passed since they were written have confirmed and exalted their value; and Hawthorne is now held to be the foremost—instead of, as he once wrote, "the obscurest"—man of letters in America.

Several studies of romances were published posthumously; and also the "Note-Books" which he kept all his life, and which reveal the care with which he studied nature and mankind. Their quality is objective, not subjective.

Personally Hawthorne was just short of six feet in height, broad-shouldered and active and strikingly handsome, with a large, dome-like head, black hair and brows, and dark blue eyes. His disposition, contrary to the general impression of him, was cheerful and full of sunny humor. His nature was social and genial, but he avoided bores, and disliked to figure in promiscuous society. His domestic life was entirely happy, and the flowering of his genius is largely due to the love and appreciation and creative criticism which he received from his wife. His friends were the men of his time most eminent in letters and art; but perhaps the most intimate of all—Franklin Pierce, Horatio Bridge and Albert Pike—were all workers on other than literary lines. They were men whom he loved for their manly and human qualities, and who were faithful to him to the end.

The Ambitious Guest.

ONE September night a family had gathered round their hearth, and piled it high with the driftwood of mountain streams, the dry cones of the pine, and the splintered ruins of great trees that had come crashing down the precipice. Up the chimney roared the fire, and brightened the room with its broad blaze. The faces of the father and mother had a sober gladness; the children laughed; the eldest daughter was the image of Happiness at seventeen; and the aged grandmother, who sat knitting in the warmest place, was the image of Happiness grown old. They had found the "herb, heart's-ease," in the bleakest spot of all New England. This family were situated in the Notch of the White Hills, where the wind was sharp throughout the year, and pitilessly cold in the winter,—giving their cottage all its fresh inclemency before it descended on the valley of the Saco. They dwelt in a cold spot and a dangerous one; for a mountain towered above their heads, so steep, that the stones would often rumble down its sides and startle them at midnight.

The daughter had just uttered some simple jest that filled them all with mirth, when the wind came through the Notch and seemed to pause before their cottage—rattling the door, with a sound of wailing and lamentation, before it passed into the valley. For a moment it saddened them, though there was nothing unusual in the tones. But the family were glad again when they perceived that the latch was lifted by some traveler, whose footsteps had been unheard amid the dreary blast which heralded his approach, and wailed as he was entering, and went moaning away from the door.

Though they dwelt in such a solitude, these people held daily converse with the world. The romantic pass of the Notch is a great artery, through which the life-blood of internal commerce is continually throbbing between Maine, on one side, and the Green Mountains and the shores of the St. Lawrence, on the other. The stage-coach always drew up before the door of the cottage. The wayfarer, with no companion but his staff, paused here to exchange a word, that the sense of loneliness might not utterly overcome him ere he could pass through the cleft of the mountain, or reach the first house in the valley. And here the teamster, on his way to Portland market, would put up for the night; and, if a bachelor, might sit an hour beyond the usual bedtime, and steal a kiss from the mountain maid at parting. It was one of those primitive taverns where the traveler pays only for food and lodging, but meets with a homely kindness beyond all price. When the footsteps were heard, therefore, between the outer door and the inner one, the whole family rose up, grandmother, children, and all, as if about to welcome some one who belonged to them, and whose fate was linked with theirs.

The door was opened by a young man. His face at first wore the melancholy expression, almost despondency, of one who travels a wild and bleak road, at nightfall and alone, but soon brightened up when he saw the kindly warmth of his reception. He felt his heart spring forward to meet them all, from the old woman, who wiped a chair with her apron, to the little child that held out its arms to him. One glance and smile placed the stranger on a footing of innocent familiarity with the eldest daughter.

"Ah, this fire is the right thing!" cried he, "especially when there is such a pleasant circle around it. I am quite benumbed; for the notch is just like the pipe of a great pair of bellows; it has blown a terrible blast in my face all the way from Bartlett."

"Then you are going towards Vermont?" said the master of the house, as he helped to take a light knapsack off the young man's shoulders.

"Yes; to Burlington, and far enough beyond," replied he. "I meant to have been at Ethan Crawford's to-night; but a pedestrian lingers along such a road as this. It is no matter; for, when I saw this good fire, and all your cheerful faces, I felt as if you had kindled it on purpose for me, and were waiting my arrival. So I shall sit down among you, and make myself at home."

The frank-hearted stranger had just drawn his chair to the fire when something like a heavy footstep was heard without rushing down the steep side of the mountain, as with long and rapid strides, and taking such a leap in passing the cottage as to strike the opposite precipice. The family held their breath, because they knew the sound, and their guest held his by instinct.

"The old mountain has thrown a stone at us, for fear we should forget him," said the landlord, recovering himself. "He sometimes nods his head and threatens to come down; but we are old neighbors, and agree together pretty well upon the whole. Besides we have a sure place of refuge hard by if he should be coming in good earnest."

Let us now suppose the stranger to have finished his supper of bear's meat; and, by his natural felicity of manner, to have placed himself on a footing of kindness with the whole family so that they talked as freely together as if he belonged to their mountain brood. He was of a proud, yet gentle spirit—haughty and reserved among the rich and great; but ever ready to stoop his head to the lowly cottage door, and be like a brother or a son at the poor man's fireside. In the household of the Notch he found warmth and simplicity of feeling, the pervading intelligence of New England, and a poetry of native growth, which they had gathered when they little thought of it from the mountain peaks and chasms, and at the very threshold of their romantic and dangerous abode. He had traveled far and alone; his whole life, indeed, had been a solitary path; for, with the lofty caution of his nature, he had kept himself apart from those who might otherwise have been his companions. The family, too, though so kind and hospitable, had that consciousness of unity among themselves, and separation from the world at large, which, in every domestic circle, should still keep a holy place where no stranger may intrude. But this evening a prophetic sympathy impelled the refined and educated youth to pour out his heart before the simple mountaineers, and constrained them to answer him with the same free confidence. And thus it should have been. Is not the kindred of a common fate a closer tie than that of birth?

The secret of the young man's character was a high and abstracted ambition. He could have borne to live an undistinguished life, but not to be forgotten in the grave. Yearning desire had been transformed to hope, and hope, long cherished, had become like certainty that, obscurely as he journeyed now, a glory was to beam on all his pathway,—though not, perhaps, while he was treading it. But when posterity should gaze back into the gloom of what was now the present, they would trace the brightness of his footsteps, brightening as meaner glories faded, and confess that a gifted one had passed from his cradle to his tomb with none to recognize him.

"As yet," cried the stranger—his cheek glowing and his eye flashing with enthusiasm—"as yet, I have done nothing. Were I to vanish from the earth to-morrow, none would know so much of me as you: that a nameless youth came up at nightfall from the valley of the Saco, and opened his heart to you in the evening, and passed through the Notch by sunrise, and was seen no more. Not a soul would ask, 'Who was he? Whither did the wanderer go?' But I cannot die till I have achieved my destiny. Then, let Death come! I shall have built my monument!"

There was a continual flow of natural emotion, gushing forth amid abstracted reverie, which enabled the family to understand this young man's sentiments, though so foreign from their own. With quick sensibility of the ludicrous, he blushed at the ardor into which he had been betrayed.

"You laugh at me," said he, taking the eldest daughter's hand, and laughing himself. "You think my ambition as nonsensical as if I were to freeze myself to death on the top of Mount Washington, only that people might spy at me from the country round about. And, truly, that would be a noble pedestal for a man's statue!"

"It is better to sit here by this fire," answered the girl, blushing, "and be comfortable and contented, though nobody thinks about us."

"I suppose," said her father, after a fit of musing, "there is something natural in what the young man says; and if my mind had been turned that way, I might have felt just the same. It is strange, wife, how his talk has set my head running on things that are pretty certain never to come to pass."

"Perhaps they may," observed the wife. "Is the man thinking what he will do when he is a widower?"

"No, no!" cried he, repelling the idea with reproachful kindness. "When I think of your death, Esther, I think of mine, too. But I was wishing we had a good farm in Bartlett, or Bethlehem, or Littleton, or some other township round the White Mountains; but not where they could tumble on our heads. I should want to stand well with my neighbors and be called Squire, and sent to General Court for a term or two; for a plain, honest man may do as much good there as a lawyer. And when I should be grown quite an old man, and you an old woman, so as not to be long apart, I might die happy enough in my bed, and leave you all crying around me. A slate gravestone would suit me as well as a marble one—with just my name and age, and a verse of a hymn, and something to let people know that I lived an honest man and died a Christian."

"There now!" exclaimed the stranger; "it is our nature to desire a monument, be it slate or marble, or a pillar of granite, or a glorious memory in the universal heart of man."

"We're in a strange way, to-night," said the wife, with tears in her eyes. "They say it's a sign of something, when folks' minds go a wandering so. Hark to the children!"

They listened accordingly. The younger children had been put to bed in another room, but with an open door between, so that they could be heard talking busily among themselves. One and all seemed to have caught the infection from the fireside circle, and were outvying each other in wild wishes, and childish projects of what they would do when they came to be men and women. At length a little boy, instead of addressing his brothers and sisters, called out to his mother.

"I tell you what I wish, mother," cried he. "I want you and father and grandma'm, and all of us, and the stranger too, to start right away, and go and take a drink out of the basin of the Flume!"

Nobody could help laughing at the child's notion of leaving a warm bed, and dragging them from a cheerful fire, to visit the basin of the Flume,—a brook which tumbles over the precipice, deep within the Notch. The boy had hardly spoken when a wagon rattled along the road, and stopped a moment before the door. It appeared to contain two or three men, who were cheering their hearts with the rough chorus of a song, which resounded, in broken notes, between the cliffs, while the singers hesitated whether to continue their journey or put up here for the night.

"Father," said the girl, "they are calling you by name."

But the good man doubted whether they had really called him, and was unwilling to show himself too solicitous of gain by inviting people to patronize his house. He therefore did not hurry to the door; and the lash being soon applied, the travelers plunged into the Notch, still singing and laughing, though their music and mirth came back drearily from the heart of the mountain.

"There, mother!" cried the boy, again. "They'd have given us a ride to the Flume."

Again they laughed at the child's pertinacious fancy for a

night ramble. But it happened that a light cloud passed over the daughter's spirit; she looked gravely into the fire, and drew a breath that was almost a sigh. It forced its way, in spite of a little struggle to repress it. Then starting and blushing, she looked quickly round the circle, as if they had caught a glimpse into her bosom. The stranger asked what she had been thinking of.

"Nothing," answered she, with a downcast smile. "Only I felt lonesome just then."

"Oh, I have always had a gift of feeling what is in other people's hearts," said he, half seriously. "Shall I tell the secrets of yours? For I know what to think when a young girl shivers by a warm hearth, and complains of lonesomeness at her mother's side. Shall I put these feelings into words?"

"They would not be a girl's feelings any longer if they could be put into words," replied the mountain nymph, laughing, but avoiding his eye.

"All this was said apart. Perhaps a germ of love was springing in their hearts, so pure that it might blossom in Paradise, since it could not be matured on earth; for women worship such gentle dignity as his; and the proud, contemplative, yet kindly soul is oftenest captivated by simplicity like hers. But while they spoke softly, and he was watching the happy sadness, the lightsome shadows, the shy yearnings of a maiden's nature, the wind through the Notch took a deeper and drearier sound. It seemed, as the fanciful stranger said, like the choral strain of the spirits of the blast, who in old Indian times had their dwelling among these mountains, and made their heights and recesses a sacred region. There was a wail along the road, as if a funeral were passing. To chase away the gloom, the family threw pine branches on their fire, till the dry leaves crackled and the flame arose, discovering once again a scene of peace and humble happiness. The light hovered about them fondly, and caressed them all. There were the little faces of the children, peeping from their bed apart, and here the father's frame of strength, the mother's subdued and careful mien, the high-browed youth, the budding girl, and the good old grandam, still knitting in the warmest place. The aged woman looked up from her task, and, with fingers ever busy, was the next to speak.

"Old folks have their notions," said she, "as well as young ones. You've been wishing and planning; and letting your heads run on one thing and another, till you've set my mind a wandering too. Now what should an old woman wish for, when she can go but a step or two before she comes to her grave? Children, it will haunt me night and day till I tell you."

"What is it, mother?" cried the husband and wife at once.

Then the old woman, with an air of mystery which drew the circle closer round the fire, informed them that she had provided her grave-clothes some years before,—a nice linen shroud, a cap with a muslin ruff, and everything of a finer sort than she had worn since her wedding day. But this evening an old superstition had strangely recurred to her. It used to be said, in her younger days, that if anything were amiss with a corpse, if only the ruff were not smooth, or the cap did not set right, the corpse in the coffin and beneath the clods would strive to put up its cold hands and arrange it. The bare thought made her nervous.

"Don't talk so, grandmother!" said the girl, shuddering.

"Now,"—continued the old woman, with singular earnestness, yet smiling strangely at her own folly,—"I want one of you, my children—when your mother is dressed and in the coffin—I want one of you to hold a looking-glass over my face. Who knows but I may take a glimpse at myself, and see whether all's right?"

"Old and young, we dream of graves and monuments," murmured the stranger youth. "I wonder how mariners feel when the ship is sinking, and they, unknown and undistinguished, are to be buried together in the ocean—that wide and nameless sepulchre?"

For a moment, the old woman's ghastly conception so engrossed the minds of her hearers that a sound abroad in the night, rising like the roar of a blast, had grown broad, deep, and terrible, before the fated group were conscious of it. The house and all within it trembled; the foundations of the earth seemed to be shaken, as if this awful sound were the peal of the last trump. Young and old exchanged one wild glance, and remained an instant, pale, affrighted, without utterance, or power to move. Then the same shriek burst simultaneously from all their lips.

"The Slide! The Slide!"

The simplest words must intimate, but not portray, the unutterable horror of the catastrophe. The victims rushed from their cottage, and sought refuge in what they deemed a safer spot—where, in contemplation of such an emergency, a sort of barrier had been reared. Alas! they had quitted their security, and fled right into the pathway of destruction. Down came the whole side of the mountain, in a cataract of ruin. Just before it reached the house, the stream broke into two branches—shivered not a window there, but overwhelmed the whole vicinity, blocked up the road, and annihilated everything in its dreadful course. Long ere the thunder of the great Slide had ceased to roar among the mountains, the mortal agony had been endured, and the victims were at peace. Their bodies were never found.

The next morning, the light smoke was seen stealing from the cottage chimney up the mountain side. Within, the fire was yet smouldering on the hearth, and the chairs in a circle round it, as if the inhabitants had but gone forth to view the devastation of the Slide, and would shortly return, to thank Heaven for their miraculous escape. All had left separate tokens, by which those who had known the family were made to shed a tear for each. Who has not heard their name? The story has been told far and wide, and will forever be a legend of these mountains. Poets have sung their fate.

There were circumstances which led some to suppose that a stranger had been received into the cottage on this awful night, and had shared the catastrophe of all its inmates. Others denied that there were sufficient grounds for such a conjecture. Woe for the high-souled youth, with his dream of Earthly Immortality! His name and person utterly unknown; his history, his way of life, his plans, a mystery never to be solved, his death and his existence equally a doubt! Whose was the agony of that death moment?

The Old Pyncheon Family.

HALF-WAY down a side-street of one of our New England towns stands a rusty wooden house, with seven acutely peaked gables, facing towards various points of the compass, and a huge, clustered chimney in the midst. The street in Pyncheon Street; the house is the old Pyncheon House; and an elm-tree, of wide circumference, rooted before the door, is familiar to every town-born child by the title of the Pyncheon Elm. On my occasional visits to the town aforesaid I seldom failed to turn down Pyncheon Street, for the sake of passing through the shadow of these two antiquities,—the great elm-tree and the weather-beaten edifice.

The aspect of the venerable mansion has always affected me like a human countenance, bearing the traces not merely of outward storm and sunshine but expressive also of the long lapse of mortal life, and accompanying vicissitudes that have passed within. Were these to be worthily recounted, they would form a narrative of no small interest and instruction, and possessing, moreover, a certain remarkable unity, which might always seem the result of artistic arrangement. But the story would include a chain of events extending over the better part of two centuries, and, written out with reasonable amplitude, would fill a bigger folio volume, or a longer series of duodecimos, than could prudently be appropriated to the annals of all New England during a similar period. It consequently becomes imperative to make short work with most of the traditionary lore of which the old Pyncheon House, otherwise known as the House of the Seven Gables, has been the theme. With a brief sketch, therefore, of the circumstances amid which the foundation of the house was laid, and a rapid glimpse at its quaint exterior, as it grew black in the prevalent east wind,—pointing, too, here and there, at some spot of more verdant mossiness on its roof and walls,—we shall commence the real action of our tale at an epoch not very remote from the present day. Still, there will be a connection with the long past,—a reference to forgotten events and personages, and to manners, feelings, and opinions, almost or wholly obsolete—which, if adequately translated to the reader, would serve to illustrate how much of old material goes to make up the freshest novelty of human life. Hence, too, might be drawn a weighty lesson from the little-regarded truth, that the act of the passing generation is the germ which may or must produce good or evil fruit in a far-distant time; that, together with the seed of the merely temporary crop, which mortals term expediency, they evidently sow the acorns of a more enduring growth, which may darkly overshadow their posterity.

The House of the Seven Gables, antique as it now looks, was not the first habitation erected by civilized man on precisely the same spot of ground. Pyncheon Street formerly bore the humbler appellation of Maule's Lane, from the name of the original occupant of the soil, before whose cottage-door it was a cow-path. A natural spring of soft and pleasant water—a rare treasure on the sea-girt peninsula, where the Puritan settlement was made—had early induced Matthew Maule to build a hut, shaggy with thatch, at this point, although somewhat too remote from what was then the center of the village. In the growth of the town, however, after some thirty or forty years, the site covered by this rude hovel had become exceedingly desirable in the eyes of a prominent and powerful personage, who asserted plausible claims to the proprietorship of this, and a large adjacent tract of land, on the strength of a grant from the legislature. Colonel Pyncheon, the claimant, as we gather from whatever traits of him are preserved, was characterized by an iron energy of purpose. Matthew Maule, on the other hand, though an obscure man, was stubborn in the defense of what he considered his right; and, for several years, he succeeded in protecting the acre or two of earth, which, with his own toil, he had hewn out of the primeval forest, to be his garden-ground and homestead. No written record of this dispute is known to be in existence. Our acquaintance with the whole subject is derived chiefly from tradition. It would be bold, therefore, and possibly unjust, to venture a decisive opinion as to its merits; although it appears to have been at least a matter of doubt, whether Colonel Pyncheon's claim was not unduly stretched, in order to make it cover the small metes and bounds of Matthew Maule. What greatly strengthens such a suspicion is the fact that this controversy between two ill-matched antagonists—at a period, moreover, laud it as we may, when personal influence had far more weight than now—remained for years undecided, and came to a close only with the death of the party occupying the disputed soil. The mode of his death, too, affects the mind differently, in our day, from what it did a century and a half ago. It was a death that blasted with strange horror the humble name of the dweller in the cottage, and made it seem almost a religious act to drive the plow over the little area of his habitation, and to obliterate his place and memory from among men.

Old Matthew Maule, in a word, was executed for the crime of witchcraft. He was one of the martyrs to that terrible delusion, which should teach us, among its other morals, that the influential classes, and those who take among themselves to be leaders of the people, are fully liable to all the passionate error that has ever characterized the maddest mob. Clergymen, judges, statesmen,—the wisest, calmest, holiest persons of their day,—stood in the inner circle roundabout the gallows, loudest to applaud the work of blood, latest to confess themselves miserably deceived. If any one part of their proceedings can be said to deserve less blame than another, it was the singular indiscrimination with which they persecuted, not merely the poor and aged, as in former judicial massacres, but people of all ranks; their own equals, brethren, and wives. Amid the disorder of such various ruin, it is not strange that a man of inconsiderable note, like Maule, should have trodden the martyr's path to the hill of execution almost unremarked in the throng of his fellow-sufferers. But, in after days, when the frenzy of that hideous epoch had subsided, it was remembered how loudly Colonel Pyncheon had joined in the general cry, to purge the land from witchcraft; nor did it fail to be whispered that there was an invidious acrimony in the zeal with which he had sought the condemnation of Matthew Maule. It was well known that the victim had recognized the bitterness of personal enmity in his persecutor's conduct towards him, and that he declared himself hunted to death for his spoil. At the moment of execution—with the halter about his neck, and while Colonel Pyncheon sat on horseback, grimly gazing at the scene—Maule had addressed him from the scaffold, and uttered a prophecy, of which history, as well as fireside tradition, has preserved the very words. "God," said the dying man, pointing his finger, with a ghastly look, at the undismayed countenance of his enemy, "God will give him blood to drink!"

After the reputed wizard's death, his humble homestead had fallen an easy spoil into Colonel Pyncheon's grasp. When it was understood, however, that the Colonel intended to erect a family mansion—spacious, ponderously framed of oaken timber, and calculated to endure for many generations of his posterity—over the spot first covered by the log-built hut of Matthew Maule, there was much shaking of the head among the village gossips. Without absolutely expressing a doubt whether the stalwart Puritan had acted as a man of conscience and integrity, throughout the proceedings which have been sketched, they, nevertheless, hinted that he was about to build his house over an unquiet grave. His home would include the home of the dead and buried wizard, and would thus afford the ghost of the latter a kind of privilege to haunt its new apartments, and the chambers into which future bridegrooms were to lead their brides, and where children of the Pyncheon blood were to be born. The terror and ugliness of Maule's crime, and the wretchedness of his punishment, would darken the freshly plastered walls, and infect them early with the scent of an old and melancholy house. Why, then,—while so much of the soil around him was to be strewn with the virgin forest-leaves,—why should Colonel Pyncheon prefer a site that had already been accursed?

But the Puritan soldier and magistrate was not a man to be turned aside from his well-considered scheme, either by dread of the wizard's ghost, or by flimsy sentimentalities of any kind, however specious. Had he been told of a bad air, it might have moved him somewhat; but he was ready to encounter an evil spirit on his own ground. Endowed with common sense, as massive and hard as blocks of granite, fastened together with stern rigidity of purpose, as with iron clamps, he followed out his original design, probably without so much as imagining an objection to it. On the score of delicacy, or any scrupulousness which a finer sensibility might have taught him, the Colonel, like most of his breed and generation, was impenetrable. He, therefore, dug his cellar, and laid the deep foundations of his mansion on the square of earth whence Matthew Maule, forty years before, had first swept away the fallen leaves. It was a curious and, as some people thought, an ominous fact that, very soon after the workmen began their operations, the spring of water, above mentioned, entirely lost the deliciousness of its pristine quality. Whether its sources were disturbed by the depth of the new cellar, or whatever subtler cause might lurk at the bottom, it is certain that the water of Maule's Well, as it continued to be called, grew hard and brackish. Even such we find it now; and any old woman of the neighborhood will certify that it is productive of intestinal mischief to those who quench their thirst there.

The reader may deem it singular that the head carpenter of the new edifice was no other than the son of the very man from whose dead grip the property of the soil had been wrested. Not improbably he was the best workman of his time; or, perhaps, the Colonel thought it expedient, or was impelled by some better feeling, thus openly to cast aside all animosity against the race of his fallen antagonist. Nor was it out of keeping with the general coarseness and matter-of-fact character of the age that the son should be willing to earn an honest penny, or, rather, a weighty amount of sterling pounds from the purse of his father's deadly enemy. At all events, Thomas Maule became the architect of the House of the Seven Gables, and performed his duty so faithfully that the timber framework, fastened by his hands, still holds together.

Thus the great house was built. Familiar as it stands in the writer's recollection,—for it has been an object of curiosity with him from boyhood, both as a specimen of the best and stateliest architecture of a long-past epoch, and as the scene of events more full of human interest, perhaps, than those of a gray feudal castle,—familiar as it stands, in its rusty old age, it is therefore only the more difficult to imagine the bright novelty with which it first caught the sunshine. The impression of its actual state, at this distance of a hundred and sixty years, darkens inevitably, through the picture which we would fain give of its appearance on the morning when the Puritan magnate bade all the town to be his guests. A ceremony of consecration, festive as well as religious, was now to be performed. A prayer and discourse from the Rev. Mr. Higginson, and the outpouring of a psalm from the general throat of the community, was to be made acceptable to the grosser sense by ale, cider, wine, and brandy, in copious effusion, and, as some authorities aver, by an ox, roasted whole, or, at least, by the weight and substance of an ox, in more manageable joints and sirloins. The carcass of a deer, shot within twenty miles, had supplied material for the vast circumference of a pasty. A codfish of sixty pounds, caught in the bay, had been dissolved into the rich liquid of a chowder. The chimney of the new house, in short, belching forth its kitchen-smoke, impregnated the whole air with the scent of meats, fowls, and fishes, spicily concocted with odoriferous herbs and onions in abundance. The mere smell of such festivity, making its way to everybody's nostrils, was at once an invitation and an appetite.

Maule's Lane, or Pyncheon Street, as it were now more decorous to call it, was thronged, at the appointed hour, as with a congregation on its way to church. All, as they approached, looked upward at the imposing edifice, which was henceforth to assume its rank among the habitations of mankind. There it rose, a little withdrawn from the line of the street, but in pride, not modesty. Its whole visible exterior was ornamented with quaint figures, conceived in the grotesqueness of a Gothic fancy, and drawn or stamped in the glittering plaster, composed of lime, pebbles, and bits of glass, with which the woodwork of the walls was overspread. On every side the seven gables pointed sharply towards the sky, and presented the aspect of a whole sisterhood of edifices, breathing through the spiracles of one great chimney. The many lattices, with their small, diamond-shaped panes, admitted the sunlight into hall and chamber, while, nevertheless, the second story, projecting far over the base, and itself retiring beneath the third, threw a shadowy and thoughtful gloom into the lower rooms. Carved globes of wood were affixed under the jutting stories. Little spiral rods of iron beautified each of the seven peaks. On the triangular portion of the gable, that fronted next the street, was a dial, put up that very morning, and on which the sun was still marking the passage of the first bright hour in a history that was not destined to be all so bright. All around were scattered shavings, chips, shingles, and broken halves of bricks; these, together with the lately turned earth, on which the grass had not begun to grow, contributed to the impression of strangeness and novelty proper to a house that had yet its place to make among men's daily interests.

The principal entrance, which had almost the breadth of a church-door, was in the angle between the two front gables, and was covered by an open porch, with benches beneath its shelter. Under this arched doorway, scraping their feet on the unworn threshold, now trod the clergymen, the elders, the magistrates, the deacons, and whatever of aristocracy there was in town or county. Thither, too, thronged the plebeian classes, as freely as their betters, and in larger numbers. Just within the entrance, however, stood two serving-men, pointing some of the guests to the neighborhood of the kitchen, and ushering others into the statelier rooms,—hospitable alike to all, but still with a scrutinizing regard to the high or low degree of each. Velvet garments, somber but rich, stiffly plaited ruffs and bands, embroidered gloves, venerable beards, the mien and countenance of authority, made it easy to distinguish the gentleman of worship, at that period, from the tradesman, with his plodding air, or the laborer, in his leather jerkin, stealing awe-stricken into the house which he had perhaps helped to build.

One inauspicious circumstance there was, which awakened a hardly concealed displeasure in the breasts of a few of the more punctilious visitors. The founder of this stately mansion —a gentleman noted for the square and ponderous courtesy of his demeanor—ought surely to have stood in his own hall, and to have offered the first welcome to so many personages as here presented themselves in honor of his solemn festival. He was as yet invisible; the most favored of the guests had not beheld him. This sluggishness on Colonel Pyncheon's part became still more unaccountable, when the second dignitary of the province made his appearance and found no more ceremonious a reception. The lieutenant-governor, although his visit was one of the anticipated glories of the day, had alighted from his horse, and assisted his lady from her side-saddle, and crossed the Colonel's threshold, without other greeting than that of the principal domestic.

This person—a gray-headed man, of quiet and most respectful deportment—found it necessary to explain that his master still remained in his study, or private apartment; on entering which, an hour before, he had expressed a wish on no account to be disturbed.

"Do you not see, fellow," said the high-sheriff of the county, taking the servant aside, "that this is no less a man than the lieutenant-governor? Summon Colonel Pyncheon at once! I know that he received letters from England this morning; and, in the perusal and consideration of them, an hour may have passed away without his noticing it. But he will be ill-pleased, I judge, if you suffer him to neglect the courtesy due to one of our chief rulers, and who may be said to represent King William, in the absence of the governor himself. Call your master instantly!"

"Nay, please your worship," answered the man, in much perplexity, but with a backwardness that strikingly indicated the hard and severe character of Colonel Pyncheon's domestic rule. "My master's orders were exceeding strict; and, as your worship knows, he permits of no discretion in the obedience of those who owe him service. Let who list open yonder door; I dare not, though the governor's own voice would bid me do it!"

"Pooh, pooh, Master High-Sheriff!" cried the lieutenant-governor, who had overheard the foregoing discussion, and felt himself high enough in station to play a little with his dignity. "I will take the matter into my own hands.' It is time that the good Colonel came forth to greet his friends; else we shall be apt to suspect that he has taken a sip too much of his Canary wine, in his extreme deliberation which cask it were best to broach in honor of the day! But since he is so much behind-hand, I will give him a remembrancer myself!"

Accordingly, with such a tramp of his ponderous riding-boots as might of itself have been audible in the remotest of the seven gables, he advanced to the door, which the servant pointed out, and made its new panels re-echo with a loud, free knock. Then, looking round, with a smile, to the spectators, he awaited a response. As none came, however, he knocked again, but with the same unsatisfactory result as at first. And now, being a trifle choleric in his temperament, the lieutenant-governor uplifted the heavy hilt of his sword, wherewith he so beat and banged upon the door that, as some of the bystanders whispered, the racket might have disturbed the dead. Be that as it might, it seemed to produce no awakening effect on Colonel Pyncheon. When the sound subsided the silence through the house was deep, dreary, and oppressive, notwithstanding that the tongues of many of the guests had already been loosened by a surreptitious cup or two of wine or spirits.

"Strange, forsooth!—very strange!" cried the lieutenant-governor, whose smile was changed to a frown. "But seeing that our host sets us the good example of forgetting ceremony,

I shall likewise throw it aside and make free to intrude on his privacy!"

He tried the door, which yielded to his hand, and was flung wide open by a sudden gust of wind that passed, as with a loud sigh, from the outermost portal through all the passages and apartments of the new house. It rustled the silken garments of the ladies, and waved the long curls of the gentlemen's wigs, and shook the window-hangings and the curtains of the bed-chambers; causing everywhere a singular stir, which yet was more like a hush. A shadow of awe and half-fearful anticipation—nobody knew wherefore, nor of what—had all at once fallen over the company.

They thronged, however, to the now open door, pressing the lieutenant-governor, in the eagerness of their curiosity, into the room in advance of them. At the first glimpse they beheld nothing extraordinary; a handsomely furnished room, of moderate size, somewhat darkened by curtains; books arranged on shelves; a large map on the wall, and likewise a portrait of Colonel Pyncheon, beneath which sat the original Colonel himself, in an oaken elbow-chair, with a pen in his hand. Letters, parchments and blank sheets of paper were on the table before him. He appeared to gaze at the curious crowd, in front of which stood the lieutenant-governor; and there was a frown on his dark and massive countenance, as if sternly resentful of the boldness that had impelled them into his private retirement.

A little boy—the Colonel's grandchild, and the only human being that ever dared to be familiar with him—now made his way among the guests and ran towards the seated figure; then, pausing half-way, he began to shriek with terror. The company, tremulous as the leaves of a tree, when all are shaking together, drew nearer, and perceived that there was an unnatural distortion in the fixedness of Colonel Pyncheon's stare; that there was blood on his ruff, and that his hoary beard was saturated with it. It was too late to give assistance. The iron-hearted Puritan, the relentless persecutor, the grasping and strong-willed man, was dead! Dead, in his new house! There is a tradition, only worth alluding to, as lending a tinge of superstitious awe to a scene perhaps gloomy enough without it, that a voice spoke loudly among the guests, the tones of which were like those of old Matthew Maule, the executed wizard, "God hath given him blood to drink!"

Thus early had that one guest,—the only guest who is certain, at one time or another, to find his way into every human dwelling,—thus early had Death stepped across the threshold of the House of the Seven Gables!

Colonel Pyncheon's sudden and mysterious end made a vast deal of noise in its day. There were many rumors, some of which have vaguely drifted down to the present time, how that appearances indicated violence; that there were the marks of fingers on his throat, and the print of a bloody hand on his plaited ruff; and that his peaked beard was disheveled, as if it had been fiercely clutched and pulled. It was averred, likewise, that the lattice-window, near the Colonel's chair, was open; and that, only a few minutes before the fatal occurrence, the figure of a man had been seen clambering over the garden-fence, in the rear of the house. But it were folly to lay any stress on stories of this kind, which are sure to spring up around such an event as that now related, and which, as in the present case, sometimes prolong themselves for ages afterwards, like the toadstools that indicate where the fallen and buried trunk of a tree has long since mouldered into the earth. For our own part, we allow them just as little credence as to that other fable of the skeleton hand which the lieutenant-governor was said to have seen at the Colonel's throat, but which vanished away as he advanced farther into the room. Certain it is, however, that there was a great consultation and dispute of doctors over the dead body. One—John Swinnerton by name—who appears to have been a man of eminence, upheld it, if we have rightly understood his terms of art, to be a case of apoplexy. His professional brethren, each for himself, adopted various hypotheses, more or less plausible, but all dressed out in a perplexing mystery of phrase, which, if it do not show a bewilderment of mind in these erudite physicians, certainly causes it in the unlearned peruser of their opinions. The coroner's jury sat upon the corpse, and, like sensible men, returned an unassailable verdict of "Sudden Death"!

It is indeed difficult to imagine that there could have been a serious suspicion of murder, or the slightest grounds for implicating any particular individual as the perpetrator. The rank, wealth, and eminent character of the deceased must have insured the strictest scrutiny into every ambiguous circumstance. As none such is on record, it is safe to assume that none existed. Tradition,—which sometimes brings down truth that history has let slip, but is often the wild babble of the time, such as was formerly spoken at the fireside, and now congeals in newspapers,—tradition is responsible for all contrary averments. In Colonel Pyncheon's funeral sermon, which was printed, and is still extant, the Rev. Mr. Higginson enumerates, among the many felicities of his distinguished parishioner's earthly career, the happy seasonableness of his death. His duties all performed, —the highest prosperity attained,—his race and future generations fixed on a stable basis, and with a stately roof to shelter them for centuries to come,—what other upward step remained for this good man to take, save the final step from earth to the golden gate of heaven! The pious clergyman surely would not have uttered words like these had he in the least suspected that the Colonel had been thrust into the other world with the clutch of violence upon his throat.

The family of Colonel Pyncheon, at the epoch of his death, seemed destined to as fortunate a permanence as can anywise consist with the inherent instability of human affairs. It might fairly be anticipated that the progress of time would rather increase and ripen their prosperity than wear away and destroy it. For not only had his son and heir come into immediate enjoyment of a rich estate, but there was a claim, through an Indian deed, confirmed by a subsequent grant of the General Court, to a vast and as yet unexplored and unmeasured tract of Eastern lands. These possessions—for as such they might almost certainly be reckoned—comprised the greater part of what is now known as Waldo County, in the State of Maine, and were more extensive than many a dukedom, or even a reigning prince's territory on European soil. When the pathless forest, that still covered this wild principality, should give place —as it inevitably must, though perhaps not till ages hence— to the golden fertility of human culture, it would be the source of incalculable wealth to the Pyncheon blood. Had the Colonel survived only a few weeks longer, it is probable that his great political influence, and powerful connections, at home and abroad, would have consummated all that was necessary to render the claim available. But, in spite of good Mr. Higginson's congratulatory eloquence, this appeared to be the one thing which Colonel Pyncheon, provident and sagacious as he was, had allowed to go at loose ends. So far as the prospective territory was concerned, he unquestionably died too soon. His son lacked not merely the father's eminent position, but the talent and force of character to achieve it: he could, therefore, effect nothing by dint of political interest; and the bare justice or legality of the claim was not so apparent, after the Colonel's decease, as it had been pronounced in his lifetime. Some connecting link had slipped out of the evidence and could not anywhere be found.

Efforts, it is true, were made by the Pyncheons, not only then, but at various periods for nearly a hundred years afterwards, to obtain what they stubbornly persisted in deeming their right. But, in course of time, the territory was partly regranted to more favored individuals, and partly cleared and occupied by actual settlers. These last, if they ever heard of the Pyncheon title, would have laughed at the idea of any man's asserting a right—on the strength of mouldy parchments, signed with the faded autographs of governors and legislators long dead and forgotten—to the lands which they or their fathers had wrested from the wild hand of Nature, by their own sturdy toil. This impalpable claim, therefore, resulted in nothing more solid than to cherish, from generation to generation, an absurd delusion of family importance, which all along characterized the Pyncheons. It caused the poorest member of the race to feel as if he inherited a kind of nobility, and might yet come into the possession of princely wealth to support it. In the better specimens of the breed, this peculiarity threw an ideal grace over the hard material of human life, without stealing away any truly valuable quality. In the baser sort its effect was to increase the liability to sluggishness and dependence, and induce the victim of a shadowy hope to remit all self-effort while awaiting the realization of his dreams. Years and years after their claim had passed out of the public memory, the Pyncheons were accustomed to consult the Colonel's ancient map, which had been projected while Waldo County was still an unbroken wilderness. Where the old land-surveyor had put down woods, lakes and rivers, they marked out the cleared spaces, and dotted the villages and towns, and calculated the progressively increasing value of the territory, as if there were yet a prospect of its ultimately forming a princedom for themselves.

In almost every generation, nevertheless, there happened to be some one descendant of the family gifted with a portion of the hard, keen sense, and practical energy, that had so remarkably distinguished the original founder. His character, indeed, might be traced all the way down, as distinctly as if the Colonel himself, a little diluted, had been gifted with an intermittent sort of immortality on earth. At two or three epochs, when the fortunes of the family were low, this representative of hereditary qualities had made his appearance, and caused the traditionary gossips of the town to whisper among themselves,—"Here is the old Pyncheon come again! Now the Seven Gables will be new shingled!" From father to son, they clung to the ancestral house with singular tenacity of home attachment. For various reasons, however, and from impressions often too vaguely founded to be put on paper, the writer cherishes the belief that many, if not most, of the successive proprietors of this estate were troubled with doubts as to their moral right to hold it. Of their legal tenure there could be no question; but old Matthew Maule, it is to be feared, trode downward from his own age to a far later one, planting a heavy footstep, all the way, on the conscience of a Pyncheon. If so, we are left to dispose of the awful query, whether each inheritor of the property—conscious of wrong, and failing to rectify it—did not commit anew the great guilt of his ancestor, and incur all its original responsibilities. And supposing such to be the case, would it not be a far truer mode of expression to say, of the Pyncheon family, that they inherited a great misfortune, than the reverse?

We have already hinted, that it is not our purpose to trace down the history of the Pyncheon family, in its unbroken connection with the house of the Seven Gables; nor to show, as in a magic picture, how the rustiness and infirmity of age gathered over the venerable house itself. As regards its interior life, a large, dim looking-glass used to hang in one of the rooms, and was fabled to contain within its depths all the shapes that had ever been reflected there,—the old Colonel himself, and his many descendants, some in the garb of antique babyhood, and others in the bloom of feminine beauty or manly prime, or saddened with the wrinkles of frosty age. Had we the secret of that mirror, we would gladly sit down before it, and transfer its revelations to our page. But there was a story, for which it is difficult to conceive any foundation, that the posterity of Matthew Maule had some connection with the mystery of the looking-glass, and that, by what appears to have been a sort of mesmeric process, they could make its inner region all alive with the departed Pyncheons; not as they had shown themselves to the world nor in their better and happier hours, but in doing over again some deed of sin, or in the crisis of life's bitterest sorrow. The popular imagination, indeed, long kept itself busy with the affair of the old Puritan Pyncheon and the wizard Maule; the curse, which the latter flung from his scaffold, was remembered, with the very important addition, that it had become a part of the Pyncheon inheritance. If one of the family did but gurgle in his throat, a bystander would be likely enough to whisper, between jest and earnest,—"He has Maule's blood to drink!" The sudden death of a Pyncheon, about a hundred years ago, with circumstances very similar to what have been related of the Colonel's exit, was held as giving additional probability to the received opinion on this topic. It was considered, moreover, an ugly and ominous circumstance, that Colonel Pyncheon's picture—in obedience, it was said, to a provision of his will —remained affixed to the wall of the room in which he died. Those stern immitigable features seemed to symbolize an evil influence, and so darkly to mingle the shadow of their presence with the sunshine of the passing hour, that no good thoughts or purpose could ever spring up and blossom there. To the thoughtful mind, there will be no tinge of superstition in what we figuratively express, by affirming that the ghost of a dead progenitor—perhaps as a portion of his own punishment—is often doomed to become the Evil Genius of his family.

The Pyncheons, in brief, lived along, for the better part of two centuries, with perhaps less of outward vicissitude than has attended most other New England families, during the same period of time. Possessing very distinctive traits of their own, they nevertheless took the general characteristics of the little community in which they dwelt; a town noted for its frugal, discreet, well-ordered, and home-loving inhabitants, as well as for the somewhat confined scope of its sympathies; but in which, be it said, there are odder individuals, and, now and then, stranger occurrences, than one meets with almost anywhere else. During the Revolution, the Pyncheon of that epoch, adopting the Royal side, became a refugee; but repented, and made his reappearance, just at the point of time to preserve the House of the Seven Gables from confiscation. For the last seventy years, the most noted event in the Pyncheon annals had been likewise the heaviest calamity that ever befell the race; no less than the violent death—for so it was adjudged—of one member of the family, by the criminal act of another. Certain circumstances, attending this fatal occurrence, had brought the deed irresistibly home to a nephew of the deceased Pyncheon. The young man was tried and convicted of the crime; but either the circumstantial nature of the evidence, and possibly some lurking doubt in the breast of the executive, or, lastly,—an argument of greater weight in a republic than it could have been under a monarchy,—the high respectability and political influence of the criminal's connections, had availed to mitigate his doom from death to perpetual imprisonment. This sad affair had chanced about thirty years before the action of our story commences. Latterly, there were rumors (which few believed, and only one or two felt greatly interested in) that this long-buried man was likely, for some reason or other, to be summoned forth from his living tomb.

RALPH WALDO EMERSON.

EMERSON, dying in 1882, a few months after Longfellow, had lived seventy-nine years; his first essay, "Nature," the matrix of all the subsequent ones, was published as early as 1836; his literary activity continued till within a few years of the end, yet his published works at the time of his death would have filled little more than a dozen volumes, and much of them was practically repetition of leading ideas in his philosophy. That philosophy, however, had made him the leader of elevated thought in this country; and he stands to-day as one of the few really original figures in the literature of modern times.

Mary Moody Emerson, his aunt, and Miss Sarah Bradford prepared him for college; but he would have his own way with books, and was never remarkable as a student; nor did outdoor exercise attract him. From a long line of New England Puritan clergymen he inherited a refined and sinless nature and extraordinary spiritual insight; his value to his fellow-men lay not in worldly experience nor in logic, but in his luminous intuitions; he comprehended without effort a large and lofty region of thought or perception, and caused glimpses of it to irradiate others. But his faculty lay in stating what he perceived, not in explaining it; he could not successfully argue or draw deductions, and as soon as he attempts to do so he becomes obscure and ceases to convince us. He was not fully understood, partly because he did not understand himself—he did not realize how different from other men he was. Men who came to him for counsel were impressed and exalted, but not definitely instructed; Emerson gave them what he had, but what he had was significant rather to the disincarnate intelligence than to the incarnate, every-day human being. Thus we finally recognize a certain disappointment in Emerson; but for youth he is a stimulating and invaluable companion. Contemplating the conceivable powers of the ideal man, he exaggerates the faculty of the actual individual; hopes thus aroused may help the young to rise higher than otherwise they might, but do not console age for failure.

Emerson read Plato and Swedenborg, and studied the lives of great men; he looked at modern science broadly and synthetically, catching its drift and its relations to spiritual life. He placed the goal of civilization at a high point, yet flattered man by regarding him as the potential peer of Christ, to whom he denied special divinity. Some of his insights have never been surpassed by a mortal intelligence; but some of his errors, proceeding, generally, from attempts to reason upon premises intuitively attained, are dreary lapses from his proper level. He made his impression upon the world by his essays; they are unique structures. They are not a woven tissue of consistent argument, but a collection of separate sayings upon given subjects, arranged in such order as seemed to their author naturally consecutive. There is no gradual induction into comprehension of the topic, but you begin and end on the same plane. Emerson was a seer, but not an artist. You may start at any point in his prose writings, and understand as much or as little as if you had commenced with the first page of "Nature."

It is probable that Emerson's poems, few comparatively though they are, will outlive his prose, and the poetry of most of his contemporaries. In these, in spite of their ruggedness of outward form, there is inspiration of the finest sort, and a spiritual music of ineffable beauty and purity. They present the essence of his best philosophy in terse and profound metrical form; they thrill with divine vitality. Strange to say, Emerson distrusted his own faculty in this direction: his ideal was too high, and he recognized his occasional failure to give perfect incarnation to his thought. But the thought is so exquisite and uplifting that the outward roughness is a relief, enabling us to endure the better what would else be almost intolerable beauty.

Emerson was twice married, his second wife surviving him. He twice visited Europe, and the friendship between him and Carlyle is historical. One of his most interesting books to the ordinary reader is "English Traits," in which he gives a singularly just and keen account of English character. His life was spent in Concord, near Boston; and he, during his lifetime, and his memory since his death, have helped to make it the Mecca of all travelers who regard whatever is purest and worthiest in human life and thought.

The American Scholar.

Mr. President and Gentlemen,

I GREET you on the recommencement of our literary year. Our anniversary is one of hope, and, perhaps, not enough of labor. We do not meet for games of strength or skill, for the recitation of histories, tragedies, and odes, like the ancient Greeks; for parliaments of love and poesy, like the Troubadours, nor for the advancement of science, like our contemporaries in the British and European capitals. Thus far, our holiday has been simply a friendly sign of the survival of the love of letters amongst a people too busy to give to letters any more. As such it is precious as the sign of an indestructible instinct. Perhaps the time is already come when it ought to be, and will be, something else; when the sluggard intellect of this continent will look from under its iron lids and fill the postponed expectation of the world with something better than the exertions of mechanical skill. Our day of dependence, our long apprenticeship to the learning of other lands, draws to a close. The millions that around us are rushing into life, cannot always be fed on the sere remains of foreign harvests. Events, actions arise, that must be sung, that will sing themselves. Who can doubt that poetry will revive and lead in a new age, as the star in the constellation Harp, which now flames in our zenith, astronomers announce, shall one day be the pole-star for a thousand years?

In this hope I accept the topic which not only usage but the nature of our association seem to prescribe to this day,— the AMERICAN SCHOLAR. Year by year we come up hither to read one more chapter of his biography. Let us inquire what light new days and events have thrown on his character and his hopes.

It is one of those fables which out of an unknown antiquity convey an unlooked-for wisdom, that the gods, in the beginning, divided Man into men, that he might be more helpful to himself; just as the hand was divided into fingers, the better to answer its end.

The old fable covers a doctrine ever new and sublime; that there is One Man,—present to all particular men only partially, or through one faculty; and that you must take the whole society to find the whole man. Man is not a farmer, or a professor, or an engineer, but he is all. Man is priest, and scholar, and statesman, and producer and soldier. In the *divided* or social states these functions are parceled out to individuals, each of whom aims to do his stint of the joint work, whilst each other performs his. The fable implies that the individual, to possess himself, must sometimes return from his own labor to embrace all the other laborers. But, unfortunately, this original unit, this fountain of power has been so distributed to multitudes, has been so minutely subdivided and peddled out, that it is spilled into drops, and cannot be gathered. The state of society is one in which the members have suffered amputation from the trunk, and strut about so many walking monsters,—a good finger, a neck, a stomach, an elbow, but never a man.

Man is thus metamorphosed into a thing, into many things. The planter, who is Man sent out into the field to gather food, is seldom cheered by any idea of the true dignity of his ministry. He sees his bushel and his cart, and nothing beyond, and sinks into the farmer, instead of Man on the farm. The tradesman scarcely ever gives an ideal worth to his work, but is ridden by the routine of his craft, and the soul is subject to dollars. The priest becomes a form; the attorney a statute-book; the mechanic a machine; the sailor a rope of the ship.

In this distribution of functions the scholar is the delegated intellect. In the right state he is *Man Thinking*. In the degenerate state, when the victim of society, he tends to become a mere thinker, or still worse, the parrot of other men's thinking.

In this view of him, as Man Thinking, the theory of his

office is contained. Him Nature solicits with all her placid, all her monitory pictures; him the past instructs; him the future invites. Is not indeed every man a student, and do not all things exist for the student's behoof? And, finally, is not the true scholar the only true master? But the old oracle said, "All things have two handles: beware of the wrong one." In life, too often, the scholar errs with mankind and forfeits his privilege. Let us see him in his school, and consider him in reference to the main influences he receives.

I. The first in time and the first in importance of the influences upon the mind is that of Nature. Every day, the sun; and, after sunset, Night and her stars. Ever the winds blow; ever the grass grows. Every day, men and women, conversing, beholding and beholden. The scholar is he of all men whom this spectacle most engages. He must settle its value in his mind. What is Nature to him? There is never a beginning, there is never an end, to the inexplicable continuity of this web of God, but always circular power returning into itself. Therein it resembles his own spirit, whose beginning, whose ending, he never can find,—so entire, so boundless. Far too as her splendors shine, system on system shooting like rays, upward, downward, without center, without circumference,—in the mass and in the particle, Nature hastens to render account of herself to the mind. Classification begins. To the young mind everything is individual, stands by itself. By and by, it finds how to join two things and see in them one nature; then three, then three thousand; and so, tyrannized over by its own unifying instinct, it goes on tying things together, diminishing anomalies, discovering roots running under ground whereby contrary and remote things cohere and flower out from one stem. It presently learns that since the dawn of history there has been a constant accumulation and classifying of facts. But what is classification but the perceiving that these objects are not chaotic, and are not foreign, but have a law which is also a law of the human mind? The astronomer discovers that geometry, a pure abstraction of the human mind, is the measure of planetary motion. The chemist finds proportions and intelligible method throughout matter; and science is nothing but the finding of analogy, identity, in the most remote parts. The ambitious soul sits down before

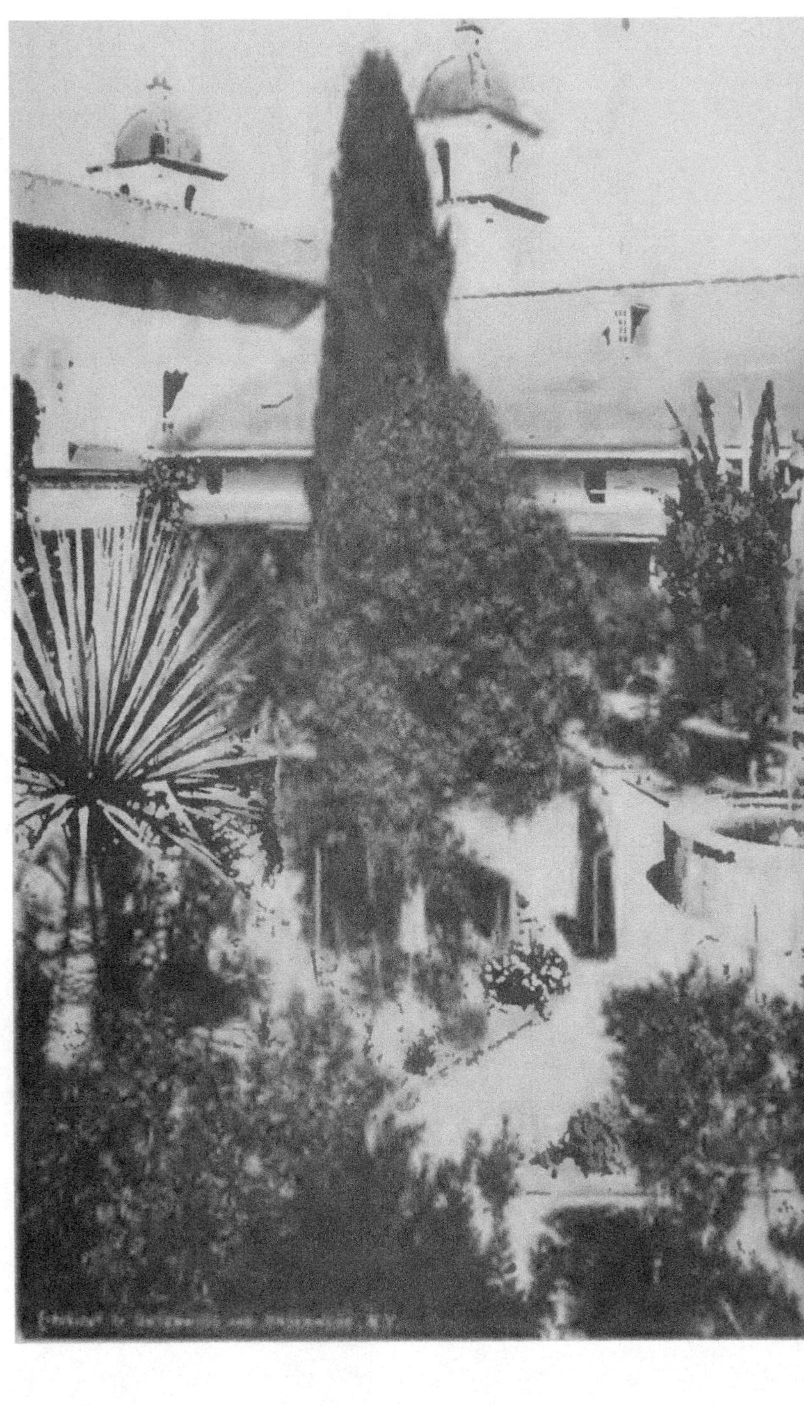

each refractory fact; one after another reduces all strange constitutions, all new powers, to their class and their law, and goes on forever to animate the last fiber of organization, the outskirts of Nature, by insight.

Thus to him, to this schoolboy under the bending dome of day, is suggested that he and it proceed from one root; one is leaf and one is flower; relation, sympathy, stirring in every vein. And what is that root? Is not that the soul of his soul? A thought too bold; a dream too wild. Yet when this spiritual light shall have revealed the law of more earthly natures,—when he has learned to worship the soul, and to see that the natural philosophy that now is, is only the first gropings of its gigantic hand, he shall look forward to an ever expanding knowledge as to a becoming creator. He shall see that nature is the opposite of the soul, answering to it part for part. One is seal and one is print. Its beauty is the beauty of his own mind. Its laws are the laws of his own mind. Nature then becomes to him the measure of his attainments. So much of Nature as he is ignorant of, so much of his own mind does he not yet possess. And, in fine, the ancient precept, "Know thyself," and the modern precept, "Study Nature," become at last one maxim.

II. The next great influence into the spirit of the scholar is the mind of the Past,—in whatever form, whether of literature, of art, of institutions, that mind is inscribed. Books are the best type of the influence of the past, and perhaps we shall get at the truth,—learn the amount of this influence more conveniently,—by considering their value alone.

The theory of books is noble. The scholar of the first age received into him the world around; brooded thereon; gave it the new arrangement of his own mind, and uttered it again. It came into him life; it went out from him truth. It came to him short-lived actions; it went out from him immortal thoughts. It came to him business; it went from him poetry. It was dead fact; now, it is quick thought. It can stand, and it can go. It now endures, it now flies, it now inspires. Precisely in proportion to the depth of mind from which it issued, so high does it soar, so long does it sing.

Or, I might say, it depends on how far the process had gone, of transmuting life into truth. In proportion to the completeness of the distillation, so will the purity and imperishableness of the product be. But none is quite perfect. As no air-pump can by any means make a perfect vacuum, so neither can any artist entirely exclude the conventional, the local, the perishable from his book, or write a book of pure thought, that shall be as efficient, in all respects, to a remote posterity, as to contemporaries, or rather to the second age. Each age, it is found, must write its own books; or rather, each generation for the next succeeding. The books of an older period will not fit this.

Yet hence arises a grave mischief. The sacredness which attaches to the act of creation, the act of thought, is transferred to the record. The poet chanting was felt to be a divine man: henceforth the chant is divine also. The writer was a just and wise spirit: henceforward it is settled the book is perfect; as love of the hero corrupts into worship of his statue. Instantly the book becomes noxious: the guide is a tyrant. The sluggish and perverted mind of the multitude, slow to open to the incursions of Reason, having once so opened, having once received this book, stands upon it, and makes an outcry if it is disparaged. Colleges are built on it. Books are written on it by thinkers, not by Man Thinking; by men of talent, that is, who start wrong, who set out from accepted dogmas, not from their own sight of principles. Meek young men grow up in libraries, believing it their duty to accept the views from Cicero, which Locke, which Bacon, have given; forgetful that Cicero, Locke, and Bacon were only young men in libraries when they wrote these books.

Hence, instead of Man Thinking, we have the bookworm. Hence the book-learned class, who value books, as such; not as related to Nature and the human constitution, but as making a sort of Third Estate with the world and the soul. Hence the restorers of readings, the emendators, the bibliomaniacs of all degrees.

Books are the best of things, well used; abused, among the worst. What is the right use? What is the one end which all means go to effect? They are for nothing but to inspire. I had better never see a book than to be warped by its attraction clean out of my own orbit, and made a satellite instead of a system. The one thing in the world, of value, is the active soul. This every man is entitled to; this every man contains within him, although in almost all men obstructed, and as yet unborn. The soul active sees absolute truth and utters truth, or creates. In this action it is genius; not the privilege of here and there a favorite, but the sound estate of every man. In its essence it is progressive. The book, the college, the school of art, the institution of any kind, stop with some past utterance of genius. This is good, say they,—let us hold by this. They pin me down. They look backward and not forward. But genius looks forward: the eyes of man are set in his forehead, not in his hindhead, man hopes: genius creates. Whatever talents may be, if the man create not, the pure efflux of the Deity is not his;—cinders and smoke there may be, but not yet flame. There are creative manners, there are creative actions, and creative words; manners, actions, words, that is, indicative of no custom or authority, but springing spontaneous from the mind's own sense of good and fair.

On the other part, instead of being its own seer, let it receive from another mind its truth, though it were in torrents of light, without periods of solitude, inquest, and self-recovery, and a fatal disservice is done. Genius is always sufficiently the enemy of genius by overinfluence. The literature of every nation bears me witness. The English dramatic poets have Shakespearized now for two hundred years.

Undoubtedly there is a right way of reading, so it be sternly subordinated. Man Thinking must not be subdued by his instruments. Books are for the scholar's idle times. When he can read God directly, the hour is too precious to be wasted in other men's transcripts of their readings. But when the intervals of darkness come, as come they must,—when the sun is hid and the stars withdraw their shining,—we repair to the lamps which were kindled by their ray, to guide our steps to the East again, where the dawn is. We hear, that we may speak. The Arabian proverb says, "A fig tree, looking on a fig tree, becometh fruitful."

It is remarkable the character of the pleasure we derive from the best books. They impress us with the conviction that one Nature wrote and the same reads. We read the verses of one of the great English poets, of Chaucer, of Marvell, of Dryden, with the most modern joy,—with a pleasure, I mean, which is in great part caused by the abstraction of all *time* from their verses. There is some awe mixed with the joy of our surprise, when this poet, who lived in some past world, two or three hundred years ago, says that which lies close to my own soul, that which I also had well-nigh thought and said. But for the evidence thence afforded to the philosophical doctrine of the identity of all minds, we should suppose some pre-established harmony, some foresight of souls that were to be, and some preparation of stores for their future wants, like the fact observed in insects, who lay up food before death for the young grub they shall never see.

I have now spoken of the education of the scholar by nature, by books, and by action. It remains to say somewhat of his duties.

They are such as become Man Thinking. They may all be comprised in self-trust. The office of the scholar is to cheer, to raise, and to guide men by showing them facts amidst appearances. He plies the slow, unhonored, and unpaid task of observation. Flamsteed and Herschel, in their glazed observatories, may catalogue the stars with the praise of all men, and the results being splendid and useful, honor is sure. But he, in his private observatory, cataloguing obscure and nebulous stars of the human mind, which as yet no man has thought of as such,—watching days and months sometimes for a few facts; correcting still his old records;—must relinquish display and immediate fame. In the long period of his preparation he must betray often an ignorance and shiftlessness in popular arts, incurring the disdain of the able who shoulder him aside. Long he must stammer in his speech; often forego the living for the dead. Worse yet, he must accept,—how often! poverty and solitude. For the ease and pleasure of treading the old road, accepting the fashions, the education, the religion of society, he takes the cross of making his own, and, of course, the self-accusation, the faint heart, the frequent uncertainty and loss of time, which are the nettles and tangling vines in the way of the self-relying and self-directed; and the state of virtual hostility in which he seems to stand to society, and especially to educated society. For all this loss and scorn, what offset? He is to find consolation in exercising the highest functions of human nature. He is one who raises himself from private considerations and breathes and lives on public and illustrious thoughts. He is the world's eye. He is the world's heart. He is to resist the vulgar prosperity that retrogrades ever to barbarism, by preserving and communicating heroic sentiments, noble biographies, melodious verse, and the conclusions of history. Whatsoever oracles the human heart, in all emergencies, in all solemn hours, has uttered as its commentary on the world of actions,—these he shall receive and impart. And whatsoever new verdict Reason from her inviolable seat pronounces on the passing men and events of to-day,—this he shall hear and promulgate.

These being his functions, it becomes him to feel all confidence in himself, and to defer never to the popular cry. He and he only knows the world. The world of any moment is the merest appearance. Some great decorum, some fetish of a government, some ephemeral trade, or war, or man, is cried up by half mankind and cried down by the other half, as if all depended on this particular up or down. The odds are that the whole question is not worth the poorest thought which the scholar has lost in listening to the controversy. Let him not quit his belief that a popgun is a popgun, though the ancient and honorable of the earth affirm it to be the crack of doom. In silence, in steadiness, in severe abstraction, let him hold by himself; add observation to observation, patient of neglect, patient of reproach, and bide his own time,—happy enough if he can satisfy himself alone that this day he has seen something truly. Success treads on every right step. For the instinct is sure, that prompts him to tell his brother what he thinks. He then learns that in going down into the secrets of his own mind he has descended into the secrets of all minds. He learns that he who has mastered any law in his private thoughts is master to that extent of all men whose language he speaks, and of all into whose language his own can be translated. The poet, in utter solitude remembering his spontaneous thoughts and recording them, is found to have recorded that which men in crowded cities find true for them also. The orator distrusts at first the fitness of his frank confessions, his want of knowledge of the persons he addresses, until he finds that he is the complement of his hearers;—that they drink his words because he fulfils for them their own nature; the deeper he dives into his privatest, secretest presentiment, to his wonder he finds this is the most acceptable, most public, and universally true. The people delight in it; the better part of every man feels, This is my music; this is myself.

In self-trust all the virtues are comprehended. Free should the scholar be,—free and brave. Free even to the definition of freedom, "without any hindrance that does not arise out of his own constitution." Brave; for fear is a thing which a scholar by his very function puts behind him. Fear always springs from ignorance. It is a shame to him if his tranquillity, amid dangerous times, arise from the presumption that like children and women his is a protected class; or if he seek a temporary peace by the diversion of his thoughts from politics or vexed questions, hiding his head like an ostrich in the flowering bushes, peeping into microscopes, and turning rhymes, as a boy whistles to keep his courage up. So is the danger a danger still; so is the fear worse. Manlike let him turn and face it. Let him look into its eye and search its nature, inspect its origin, —see the whelping of this lion,—which lies no great way back; he will then find in himself a perfect comprehension of its nature and extent; he will have made his hands meet on the other side, and can henceforth defy it and pass on superior. The world is his who can see through its pretension. What deafness, what stone-blind custom, what overgrown error you behold is there only by sufferance,—by your sufferance. See it to be a lie, and you have already dealt it its mortal blow.

Yes, we are the cowed,—we the trustless. It is a mischievous notion that we are come late into nature; that the world was finished a long time ago. As the world was plastic and fluid in the hands of God, so it is ever to so much of his attributes as we bring to it. To ignorance and sin, it is flint. They adapt themselves to it as they may; but in proportion as a man has anything in him divine, the firmament flows before him and takes his signet and form. Not he is great who can alter matter, but he who can alter my state of mind. They are the kings of the world who give the color of their present thought to all nature and all art, and persuade men by the cheerful serenity of their carrying the matter, that this thing which they do is the apple which the ages have desired to pluck, now at last ripe, and inviting nations to the harvest. The great man makes the great thing. Wherever Macdonald sits, there is the head of the table. Linnæus makes botany the most alluring of studies, and wins it from the farmer and the herb-woman; Davy, chemistry, and Cuvier, fossils. The day is always his who works in it with serenity and great aims. The unstable estimates of men crowd to him whose mind is filled with a truth, as the heaped waves of the Atlantic follow the moon.

For this self-trust, the reason is deeper than can be fathomed,—darker than can be enlightened. I might not carry with me the feeling of my audience in stating my own belief. But I have already shown the ground of my hope, in adverting to the doctrine that man is one. I believe man has been wronged; he has wronged himself. He has almost lost the light that can lead him back to his prerogatives. Men are become of no account. Men in history, men in the world of today, are bugs, are spawn, and are called "the mass" and "the herd." In a century, in a millennium, one or two men; that is to say, one or two approximations to the right state of every man. All the rest behold in the hero or the poet their own green and crude being,—ripened; yes, and are content to be less, so *that* may attain to its full stature. What a testimony, full of grandeur, full of pity, is borne to the demands of his own nature, by the poor clansman, the poor partisan, who rejoices in the glory of his chief. The poor and the low find some amends to their immense moral capacity, for their acquiescence in a political and social inferiority. They are content to be brushed like flies from the path of a great person, so that justice shall be done by him to that common nature which it is the dearest desire of all to see enlarged and glorified. They sun themselves in the great man's light, and feel it to be their own element. They cast the dignity of man from their downtrod selves upon the shoulders of a hero, and will perish to add one drop of blood to make that great heart beat, those giant sinews combat and conquer. He lives for us, and we live in him.

Men such as they are, very naturally seek money or power; and power because it is as good as money,—the "spoils," so called, "of office." And why not? for they aspire to the highest, and this, in their sleep-walking, they dream is highest. Wake them and they shall quit the false good and leap to the true, and leave governments to clerks and desks. This revolution is to be wrought by the gradual domestication of the idea of Culture. The main enterprise of the world for splendor, for extent, is the upbuilding of a man. Here are the materials strewn along the ground. The private life of one man shall be a more illustrious monarchy, more formidable to its enemy, more sweet and serene in its influence to its friend, than any kingdom in history. For a man, rightly viewed, comprehendeth the particular natures of all men. Each philosopher, each bard, each actor has only done for me, as by a delegate, what one day I can do for myself. The books which once we valued more than the apple of the eye, we have quite exhausted. What is that but saying that we have come up with the point of view which the universal mind took through the eyes of one scribe; we have been that man, and have passed on. First one, then another, we drain all cisterns, and waxing greater by all these supplies, we crave a better and more abundant food. The man has never lived that can feed us ever. The human mind cannot be enshrined in a person who shall set a barrier on any one side to this unbounded, unboundable empire. It is one central fire, which, flaming now out of the lips of Etna, lightens the capes of Sicily, and now out of the throat of Vesuvius, illuminates the towers and vineyards of Naples. It is one light which beams out of a thousand stars. It is one soul which animates all men.

There is one man of genius who has done much for this philosophy of life, whose literary value has never yet been rightly estimated;—I mean Emanuel Swedenborg. The most imaginative of men, yet writing with the precision of a mathematician, he endeavored to engraft a purely philosophical Ethics on the popular Christianity of his time. Such an attempt of course must have difficulty which no genius could surmount. But he saw and showed the connection between nature and the affections of the soul. He pierced the emblematic or spiritual character of the visible, audible, tangible world. Especially did his shade-loving muse hover over and interpret the lower parts of nature; he showed the mysterious bond that allies moral evil to the foul material forms, and has given in epical parables a theory of insanity, of beasts, of unclean and fearful things.

Another sign of our times, also marked by an analogous

political movement, is the new importance given to the single person. Everything that tends to insulate the individual,—to surround him with barriers of natural respect, so that each man shall feel the world is his, and man shall treat with man as a sovereign state with a sovereign state,—tends to true union as well as greatness. "I learned," said the melancholy Pestalozzi, "that no man in God's wide earth is either willing or able to help any other man." Help must come from the bosom alone. The scholar is that man who must take up into himself all the ability of the time, all the contributions of the past, all the hopes of the future. He must be an university of knowledges. If there be one lesson more than another which should pierce his ear, it is, The world is nothing, the man is all; in yourself is the law of all nature, and you know not yet how a globule of sap ascends; in yourself slumbers the whole of Reason; it is for you to know all; it is for you to dare all. Mr. President and Gentlemen, this confidence in the unsearched might of man belongs, by all motives, by all prophecy, by all preparation, to the American Scholar. We have listened too long to the courtly muses of Europe. The spirit of the American freeman is already suspected to be timid, imitative, tame. Public and private avarice make the air we breathe thick and fat. The scholar is decent, indolent, complaisant. See already the tragic consequence. The mind of this country, taught to aim at low objects, eats upon itself. There is no work for any but the decorous and the complaisant. Young men of the fairest promise, who begin life upon our shores, inflated by the mountain winds, shined upon by all the stars of God, find the earth below not in unison with these, but are hindered from action by the disgust which the principles on which business is managed inspire, and turn drudges, or die of disgust, some of them suicides. What is the remedy? They did not yet see, and thousands of young men as hopeful now crowding to the barriers for the career do not yet see, that if the single man plant himself indomitably on his instincts, and there abide, the huge world will come round to him. Patience,—patience; with the shades of all the good and great for company; and for solace the perspective of your own infinite life; and for work the study and the communication of principles, the making those instincts prevalent, the conversion of the world. Is it not the chief disgrace in the world, not to be an unit;—not to be reckoned one character;—not to yield that peculiar fruit which each man was created to bear, but to be reckoned in the gross, in the hundred, or the thousand, of the party, the section, to which we belong; and our opinion predicted geographically, as the north, or the south? Not so, brothers and friends,—please God, ours shall not be so. We will walk on our own feet; we will work with our own hands; we will speak our own minds. The study of letters shall be no longer a name for pity, for doubt, and for sensual indulgence. The dread of man and the love of man shall be a wall of defense and a wreath of joy around all. A nation of men will for the first time exist, because each believes himself inspired by the Divine Soul which also inspires all men.

AMERICAN POETRY

CHAPTER VI.

WILLIAM CULLEN BRYANT.

BRYANT was born of good New England stock, in Cummington, Massachusetts, in 1794. His father, Peter Bryant, was a village physician of more than ordinary culture, carefully educated, a student of English and French poetry, and had a respectable talent for rhyming. His mother was descended from John and Priscilla Alden. She was a pious, dignified, sensible woman, to whom her son alludes, in one of his poems, as the "stately lady." The boy was named William Cullen from a celebrated physician in Edinburgh, and his father meant that he should be of that profession, but the son showed such a decided aversion to it that the matter was dropped. The rugged and picturesque hill-country around the Bryant homestead seems to have developed in the boy that absorbing love of nature which, in after life, was one of his distinguishing characteristics. His grandfather, Ebenezer Snell, was the resident terror of the household. He gloried in his Puritan ancestors; and, as a magistrate, sent offenders, with fierce willingness, to the whipping-post,—then a common institution in Massachusetts; and his home rule was hardly less rigorous. From his harsh and severe discipline the boy fled to the hills and woods to be soothed by "the love of nature." He took refuge, in after life, in Unitarianism, and, as he grew to manhood, and beyond, he developed a coldness of manner and of mind that made him appear, outside of his intimates, and the intimate expression of a few poems—somewhat austere.

After a good preparatory education, Bryant entered Williams College, but some family losses prevented his taking a degree. One was afterwards conferred upon him, that of A. M.; and his name is enrolled as an alumnus of the College. After leaving college he studied law for three years, and, in 1815, he was admitted to the bar and commenced the practice of his profession in Great Barrington, Massachusetts. Here also he married.

In 1825 Bryant removed to New York and began his real life work, that of journalism; becoming, after some preliminary literary skirmishing, editor of the *Evening Post*. As head of that singularly elevated and reliable paper he made his mark as the foremost journalist of the United States; the Puritan austerity of his mind showing itself in his choice of words, his exclusion of slang, trivialities, sensationalism, and crude jokes, and in the intellectual clear-cut precision of his editorials. He gave sixty years of his life to newspaper work; became rich and influential; was celebrated as a critic; crossed the ocean several times, and allied himself to the best everywhere. While at home he spent the year between his house in New York, and his beautiful estate at Roslyn, Long Island.

The management of the *Evening Post* was Bryant's lifework; poetry was his recreation. The lad began to compose verse when he was ten years old, and to publish in his early teens. He wrote his most celebrated poem, "Thanatopsis," when not yet eighteen years of age. The first draft of the poem lay among the author's private papers for nearly five years, was discovered by his father, and sent by him to the *North American Review*, which accepted and published it in September, 1817. It was received with a sort of rapture here and on the other side of the Atlantic; it was the best poem yet written in America. It was and is unique. It placed Bryant in that goodly company, with Wordsworth and his fellows, who opened to men the life of Nature and the truth of Nature's God.

In 1874 Mr. Bryant was honored with an exquisite silver vase, symbolical of his life and writings, procured by public subscription, presented with appropriate ceremonies, and placed in the Metropolitan Museum of New York. He died suddenly, in June, 1878, after reciting, with marvelous fire and enthusiasm, a passage from Dante, at the unveiling of the bust of Mazzini, in Central Park. He was in the eighty-fourth year of his age.

Bryant wrote altogether one hundred and seventy-one original poems; one hundred of these treat exclusively of Nature, the others, whatever their subject, include expressions of the charms of Nature. He sings little of love, little of humanity, nothing of the wrongs of mankind. Poetry is his retreat, his temple, almost his religion; and many of his verses give that still sense of seclusion as of distant nut-dropping woods. Bryant's best known poems, after "Thanatopsis," are "The Death of the Flowers," "A Forest Hymn," "The Fringed Gentian," "The West Wind," "The Wind and the Stream," "Autumn Woods," "The Flood of Ages," and the hymn, "Blessed are they that Mourn." In his old age he made a noble translation of Homer's Iliad and Odyssey in blank verse.

Thanatopsis.

To him who in the love of Nature holds
Communion with her visible forms, she speaks
A various language; for his gayer hours
She has a voice of gladness and a smile
And eloquence of beauty, and she glides
Into his darker musings, with a mild
And healing sympathy, that steals away
Their sharpness ere he is aware. When thoughts
Of the last bitter hour come like a blight
Over thy spirit, and sad images
Of the stern agony, and shroud, and pall,
And breathless darkness, and the narrow house,
Make thee to shudder and grow sick at heart,
Go forth under the open sky, and list
To Nature's teachings, while from all around—
Earth and her waters, and the depths of air—
Comes a still voice—Yet a few days, and thee
The all-beholding sun shall see no more
In all his course; nor yet in the cold ground,
Where thy pale form was laid with many tears,
Nor in the embrace of ocean, shall exist
Thy image. Earth, that nourished thee, shall claim
Thy growth, to be resolved to earth again,

And, lost each human trace, surrendering up
Thine individual being, shalt thou go
To mix forever with the elements,
To be a brother to the insensible rock
And to the sluggish clod, which the rude swain
Turns with his share and treads upon. The oak
Shall send his roots abroad, and pierce thy mould.

Yet not to thine eternal resting-place
Shalt thou retire alone,—nor couldst thou wish
Couch more magnificent. Thou shalt lie down
With patriarchs of the infant world—with kings,
The powerful of the earth—the wise, the good,
Fair forms, and hoary seers of ages past,
All in one mighty sepulchre. The hills
Rock-ribbed, and ancient as the sun; the vales
Stretching in pensive quietness between;
The venerable woods; rivers that move
In majesty, and the complaining brooks
That make the meadows green; and, poured round all,
Old ocean's gray and melancholy waste,—
Are but the solemn decorations all
Of the great tomb of man. The golden sun,
The planets, all the infinite host of heaven,
Are shining on the sad abodes of death,
Through the still lapse of ages. All that tread
The globe are but a handful to the tribes
That slumber in its bosom. Take the wings
Of morning, traverse Barca's desert sands,
Or lose thyself in the continuous woods
Where rolls the Oregon, and hears no sound
Save his own dashings—yet—the dead are there:
And millions in those solitudes, since first
The flight of years began, have laid them down
In their last sleep—the dead reign there alone.
So shalt thou rest, and what if thou withdraw
In silence from the living, and no friend
Take note of thy departure? All that breathe
Will share thy destiny. The gay will laugh
When thou art gone, the solemn brood of care

Plod on, and each one as before will chase
His favorite phantom; yet all these shall leave
Their mirth and their employments, and shall come
And make their bed with thee. As the long train
Of ages glide away, the sons of men,
The youth in life's green spring, and he who goes
In the full strength of years, matron and maid,
And the sweet babe, and the gray-headed man,—
Shall one by one be gathered to thy side,
By those who in their turn shall follow them.

So live, that when thy summons comes to join
The innumerable caravan, which moves
To that mysterious realm, where each shall take
His chamber in the silent halls of death,
Thou go not, like the quarry-slave at night,
Scourged to his dungeon, but, sustained and soothed
By an unfaltering trust, approach thy grave
Like one who wraps the drapery of his couch
About him, and lies down to pleasant dreams.

THE DEATH OF THE FLOWERS.

THE melancholy days are come, the saddest of the year,
Of wailing winds, and naked woods, and meadows brown and
    sere.
Heaped in the hollows of the groves, the withered leaves lie dead:
They rustle to the eddying gust, and to the rabbit's tread.
The robin and the wren are flown, and from their shrubs the jay,
And from the wood-top calls the crow, through all the gloomy
    day.

Where are the flowers, the fair young flowers, that lately sprang
    and stood
In brighter light and softer airs—a beauteous sisterhood?
Alas! they are all in their graves: the gentle race of flowers
Are lying in their beds, with the fair and good of ours.
The rain is falling where they lie; but the cold November rain
Calls not from out the gloomy earth the lovely ones again.

The wind-flower and the violet, they perished long ago:
And the briar-rose and the orchis died amid the summer glow:
But on the hill the golden-rod, and the aster in the wood,
And the yellow sun-flower by the brook in autumn beauty stood,
Till fell the frost from the clear cold heaven, as falls the plague on men,
And the brightness of their smile was gone from upland, glade, and glen.

And now when comes the calm mild day—as still such days will come—
To call the squirrel and the bee from out their winter home,
When the sound of dropping nuts is heard, though all the trees are still,
And twinkle in the smoky light the waters of the rill,
The south wind searches for the flowers whose fragrance late he bore,
And sighs to find them in the wood and by the stream no more.

And then I think of one who in her youthful beauty died,
The fair meek blossom that grew up and faded by my side:
In the cold moist earth we laid her, when the forest cast the leaf;
And we wept that one so lovely should have a life so brief.
Yet not unmeet it was that one, like that young friend of ours,
So gentle and so beautiful, should perish with the flowers.

Waiting by the Gate.

Beside a massive gateway, built up in years gone by,
Upon whose top the clouds in eternal shadow lie,
While streams the evening sunshine on quiet wood and lea,
I stand and quietly wait till the hinges turn for me.

The tree-tops faintly rustle beneath the breeze's flight,
A soft and soothing sound, yet it whispers of the night:
I hear the wood-thrush piping one mellow descant more,
And scent the flowers that blow when the heat of day is o'er.

Behold the portals open, and o'er the threshold now
There steps a weary one with a pale and furrowed brow;
His count of years is full, his allotted task is wrought:
He passes to his rest from a place that needs him not.

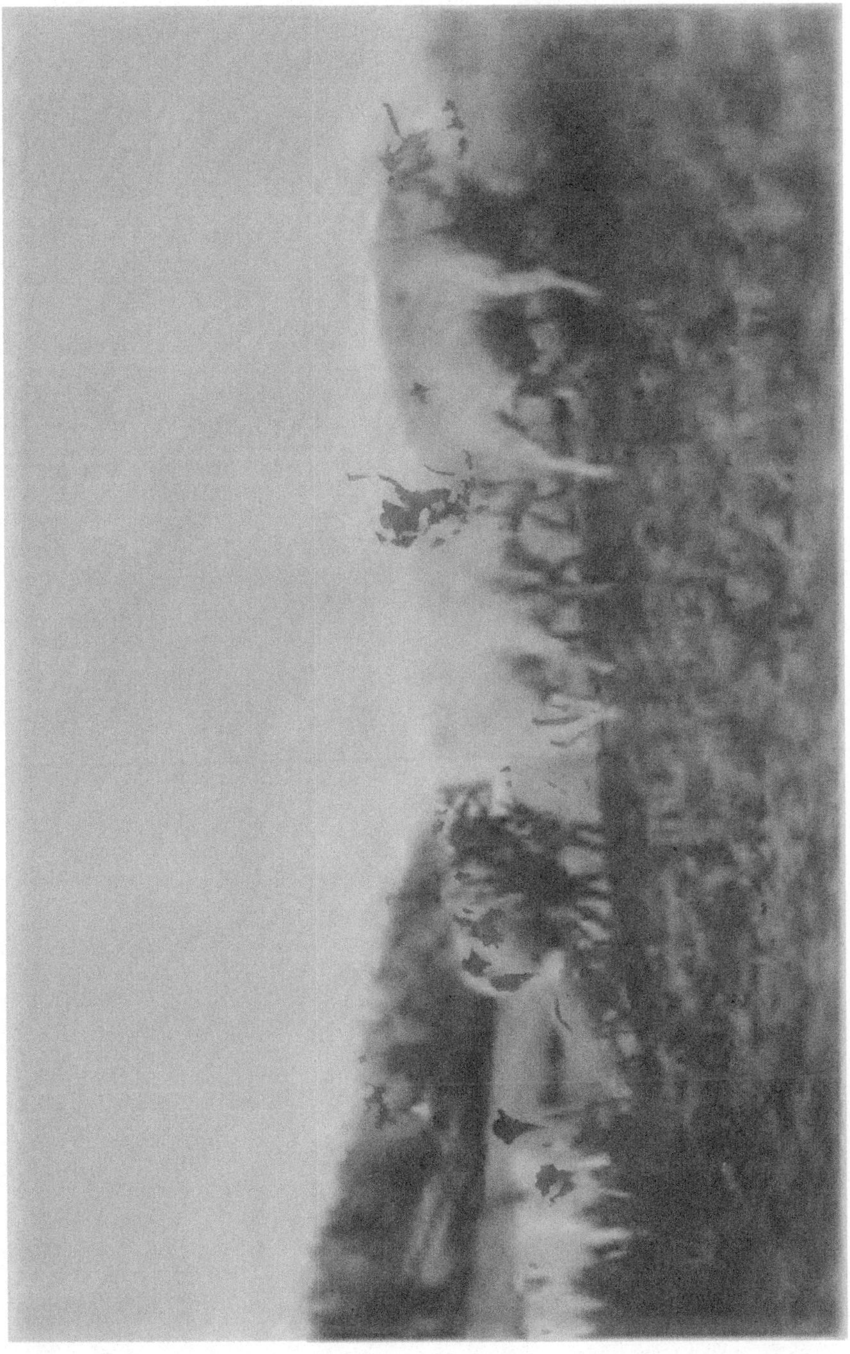

In sadness then I ponder, how quickly fleets the hour
Of human strength and action, man's courage and his power.
I muse while still the wood-thrush sings down the golden day,
And as I look and listen the sadness wears away.

Again the hinges turn, and a youth, departing, throws
A look of longing backward, and sorrowfully goes:
A blooming maid, unbinding the roses from her hair,
Moves mournfully away from amidst the young and fair.

O glory of our race that so suddenly decays!
O crimson flush of morning that darkens as we gaze!
O breath of summer blossoms that on the restless air
Scatters a moment's sweetness, and flies we know not where!

I grieve for life's bright promise, just shown and then withdrawn,
But still the sun shines round me; the evening bird sings on,
And I again am soothed, and, beside the ancient gate,
In this soft evening sunlight, I calmly stand and wait.

Once more the gates are open; an infant group go out,
The sweet smile quenched forever, and stilled the sprightly shout.
O frail, frail tree of Life, that upon the green sward strows
Its fair young buds unopened, with every wind that blows!

So come from every region, so enter, side by side,
The strong and faint of spirit, the meek and men of pride,
Steps of earth's great and mighty, between those pillars gray,
And prints of little feet mark the dust along the way.

And some approach the threshold whose looks are blank with fear,
And some whose temples brighten with joy in drawing near,
As if they saw dear faces, and caught the gracious eye
Of Him, the Sinless Teacher, who came for us to die.

I mark the joy, the terror; yet these, within my heart,
Can neither wake the dread nor the longing to depart;
And, in the sunshine streaming on quiet wood and lea,
I stand and calmly wait till the hinges turn for me.

The Battlefield.

Once this soft turf, this rivulet's sands,
    Were trampled by a hurrying crowd,
And fiery hearts and armed hands
    Encountered in the battle-cloud.

Ah! never shall the land forget
    How gushed the life-blood of her brave—
Gushed, warm with hope and courage yet,
    Upon the soil they fought to save.

Now all is calm, and fresh, and still,
    Alone the chirp of flitting bird,
And talk of children on the hill,
    And bell of wandering kine are heard.

No solemn host goes trailing by
    The black-mouthed gun and staggering wain;
Men start not at the battle-cry;
    Oh, be it never heard again!

Soon rested those who fought; but thou
    Who minglest in the harder strife
For truths which we receive not now,
    Thy warfare only ends with life.

A friendless warfare! lingering long
    Through weary day and weary year.
A wild and many-weaponed throng
    Hang on thy front, and flank, and rear.

Yet nerve thy spirit to the proof,
    And blench not at thy chosen lot;
The timid good may stand aloof,
    The sage may frown—yet faint thou not.

Nor heed the shaft too surely cast,
    The foul and hissing bolt of scorn;
For with thy side shall dwell, at last,
    The victory of endurance born.

Truth, crushed to earth, shall rise again:
  The eternal years of God are hers;
But Error, wounded, writhes in pain,
  And dies among his worshippers.

Yea, though thou lie upon the dust,
  When they who helped thee flee in fear,
Die full of hope and manly trust,
  Like those who fell in battle here.

Another hand thy sword shall wield,
  Another hand thy standard wave,
Till from the trumpet's mouth is pealed
  The blast of triumph o'er thy grave.

THE KENTUCKY LOG CABIN IN WHICH LINCOLN WAS BORN ON
FEBRUARY 12TH, 1809.

CHAPTER VII.

HENRY W. LONGFELLOW.

LONGFELLOW, born in 1807 and dying in 1882, lived through the period of the first and, so far, the best American literature. A New Englander of excellent family, he graduated in a famous class at the old New England college of Bowdoin, and spent his life in one of the most renowned New England towns, as Professor in Harvard for seventeen years, and thenceforward as the most widely known of New England poets. Twice—in 1831 and in 1843—he was happily married; four times, with an interval of forty years between the first and last visit, he sojourned in Europe. Though not rich, he never knew poverty; he was orthodox in his social and moral views; with the exception of the terrible tragedy of the burning of his second wife in 1861, his life was a studious, uneventful peace. He contemplated with intelligence and sympathy the life around him, and it is reflected in his poetry, enriched and enlarged with the tints and chiaroscuro derived from catholic culture. Without a trace of vulgarity, without stooping to the arts of the demagogue or falling into the crudity of didacticism, he is the poet of the people. The abiding perception of the disproportion between human facts and universal truths, which we call humor, was lacking in him; but he was always sincere and often eloquent and elevated. Imagination he had, gently romantic rather than grand and creative; but his success was due to the harmony of his nature, in which was nothing discordant or out of measure; poetry was his normal utterance. During his long career he produced much that lacks permanent value, but much also that is true and lasting poetry. His translations from the German and other foreign languages attest his scholarship, but do not illustrate his faculty; his "Dante's Divine Comedy," in spite of its dignity and frequent felicities, is not as a poem within measurable distance of the original. His prose books—"Outre-Mer," in 1834, "Hyperion" in 1839, and "Kavanagh," ten years later, are amiable but feeble books; "The Spanish Student" (1843) and "The Golden Legend" (1851) are essays in drama which indicate the limitations of the writer. The lyric, the ballad and the narrative poems are Longfellow's true field, and to them he thenceforward restricted himself. In each of them he touched high levels. During the Abolition epoch he wrote effective poems against slavery, and the Civil War elicited such fine ballads as "The Cumberland" and "Paul Revere," the latter aiming to stimulate the soldier of to-day by recalling the simple heroism of the night-rider of the past. But in general he preferred to moralize on life, and to depict its homely pathos and familiar charms and picturesqueness. "Excelsior," "The Psalm of Life," "The Day is Done," "The Open Window," "The Old Clock on the Stairs," "The Village Blacksmith" and many another, have entered into the language, and deservedly. But occasionally he showed, as in "Pegasus in Pound," that he could make pure allegory vibrate with tenderest life; and ever and anon he would summon his energies and achieve such long and lofty flights as "Evangeline" or "Hiawatha," which contain poetry to be long remembered among the honorable achievements of American literature.

In "Evangeline" the two Acadian lovers, parted by the edict of exile, seek each other for years, sometimes passing, unknowing, almost within arm's reach; and meet at last only when Gabriel, dying in the hospital, is found by Evangeline, who, for the sake of her lost lover, had dedicated herself to the succor of the suffering. This beautiful story suited the writer's genius, and the long, unrhymed verses gave opportunity for the music of words which was among his fortunate gifts. There are many passages of exquisite and haunting loveliness; that describing the lovers' meeting is Longfellow's best work; and the character of the Acadian maiden herself, gentle, faithful and strong, is the finest he ever drew.

"Hiawatha" has the short meter and quaint simplicity of the Norse eddas; it unites in an artistic group the most picturesque of our Indian legends. Nature and wild animals play their parts with men, women and supernatural creatures, as personages in the drama; the Indian spirit is preserved throughout, and in this strange world nothing is familiar but the beating of the universal human heart, which harmonizes and reconciles all. The figure of Hiawatha is noble, impressive and lovable, and Minnehaha wins our affections as she won his. The canto in which her death is described (The Famine) is deeply moving and beautiful. The poem, ridiculed at its first appearance, has conquered respect; it is a bold and unique achievement, and, of itself, secures the author's renown. Longfellow is one of the least pretentious of poets, but his importance may be estimated by imagining the gap which would be caused by the absence of his blameless and gracious figure.

The Open Window.

The old house by the lindens
   Stood silent in the shade,
And on the gravelled pathway
   The light and shadow played.

I saw the nursery windows
   Wide open to the air;
But the faces of the children,
   They were no longer there.

The large Newfoundland house-dog
   Was standing by the door;
He looked for his little playmates,
   Who would return no more.

They walked not under the lindens,
   They played not in the hall;
But shadow, and silence, and sadness,
   Were hanging over all.

The birds sang in the branches,
   With sweet, familiar tone;
But the voices of the children
   Will be heard in dreams alone!

And the boy that walked beside me,
  He could not understand
Why closer in mine, ah! closer,
  I pressed his warm, soft hand!

My Lost Youth.

Often I think of the beautiful town
  That is seated by the sea;
Often in thought go up and down
The pleasant streets of that dear old town,
  And my youth comes back to me.
    And a verse of a Lapland song
    Is haunting my memory still:
    "A boy's will is the wind's will,
And the thoughts of youth are long, long thoughts."

I can see the shady lines of its trees,
  And catch, in sudden gleams,
The sheen of the far-surrounding seas,
And islands that were the Hesperides
  Of all my boyish dreams.
    And the burden of that old song,
    It murmurs and whispers still:
    "A boy's will is the wind's will,
And the thoughts of youth are long, long thoughts."

I remember the black wharves and the slips,
  And the sea-tides tossing free;
And Spanish sailors with bearded lips,
And the beauty and mystery of the ships,
  And the magic of the sea.
    And the voice of that wayward song
    Is singing and saying still:
    "A boy's will is the wind's will,
And the thoughts of youth are long, long thoughts."

I remember the bulwarks by the shore,
  And the fort upon the hill;
The sunrise gun, with its hollow roar,
The drum-beat repeated o'er and o'er,

And the bugle wild and shrill.
    And the music of that old song
    Throbs in my memory still:
    "A boy's will is the wind's will,
And the thoughts of youth are long, long thoughts."

I remember the sea-fight far away,
    How it thundered o'er the tide!
And the dead captains, as they lay
In their graves, o'erlooking the tranquil bay
    Where they in battle died.
    And the sound of that mournful song
    Goes through me with a thrill:
    "A boy's will is the wind's will,
And the thoughts of youth are long, long thoughts."

I can see the breezy dome of groves,
    The shadows of Deering's Woods;
And the friendships old and the early loves
Come back with a Sabbath sound, as of doves
    In quiet neighborhoods.
    And the verse of that sweet old song,
    It flutters and murmurs still:
    "A boy's will is the wind's will,
And the thoughts of youth are long, long thoughts."

I remember the gleams and glooms that dart
    Across the school boy's brain;
The song and the silence in the heart,
That in part are prophecies, and in part
    Are longings wild and vain.
    And the voice of that fitful song
    Sings on, and is never still:
    "A boy's will is the wind's will,
And the thoughts of youth are long, long thoughts."

There are things of which I may not speak;
    There are dreams that cannot die;
There are thoughts that make the strong heart weak,
And bring a pallor to the cheek,

And a mist before the eye.
    And the words of that fateful song
    Come over me like a chill;
    "A boy's will is the wind's will,
And the thoughts of youth are long, long thoughts."

Strange to me now are the forms I meet
    When I visit the dear old town;
But the native air is pure and sweet,
And the trees that o'ershadow each well-known street,
    As they balance up and down,
    Are singing the beautiful song,
    Are sighing and whispering still:
    "A boy's will is the wind's will,
And the thoughts of youth are long, long thoughts."

And Deering's Woods are fresh and fair,
    And with joy that is almost pain
My heart goes back to wander there,
And among the dreams of the days that were,
    I find my lost youth again.
    And the strange and beautiful song,
    The groves are repeating again:
    "A boy's will is the wind's will,
And the thoughts of youth are long, long thoughts."

CHAUCER.

An old man in a lodge within a park;
    The chamber walls depicted all around
    With portraitures of huntsmen, hawk, and hound,
And the hurt deer. He listeneth to the lark,
Whose song comes with the sunshine through the dark
    Of painted glass in leaden lattice bound;
    He listeneth and he laugheth at the sound,
Then writeth in a book like any clerk.
He is the poet of the dawn, who wrote
    The Canterbury Tales, and his old age
    Made beautiful with song; and as I read
I hear the crowing cock, I hear the note
    Of lark and linnet, and from every page
    Rise odors of ploughed field or flowery mead.

Paul Revere's Ride.

MEANWHILE, impatient to mount and ride,
Booted and spurred with a heavy stride
On the opposite shore walked Paul Revere.
Now he patted his horse's side,
Now gazed at the landscape far and near,
Then, impetuous, stamped the earth,
And turned and tightened his saddle girth;
But mostly he watched with eager search
The belfry-tower of the Old North Church,
As it rose above the graves on the hill,
Lonely and spectral and sombre and still.
And lo! as he looks, on the belfry's height
A glimmer, and then a gleam of light!
He springs to the saddle, the bridle he turns,
But lingers and gazes, till full on his sight
A second lamp in the belfry burns!

A hurry of hoofs in a village street,
A shape in the moonlight, a bulk in the dark,
And beneath, from the pebbles, in passing a spark
Struck out by a steed flying fearless and fleet:
That was all! And yet, through the gloom and the light,
The fate of a nation was riding that night;
And the spark struck out by that steed in his flight
Kindled the land into flame with its heat.

He has left the village and mounted the steep,
And beneath him, tranquil and broad and deep,
Is the Mystic, meeting the ocean tides;
And under the alders, that skirt its edge,
Now soft on the sand, now loud on the ledge,
Is heard the tramp of his steed as he rides.
It was twelve by the village clock
When he crossed the bridge into Medford town.
He heard the crowing of the cock,
And the barking of the farmer's dog,
And felt the damp of the river fog,
That rises after the sun goes down.

It was one by the village clock,
When he galloped into Lexington.
He saw the gilded weathercock
Swim in the moonlight as he passed,
And the meeting-house windows, blank and bare,
Gaze at him with a spectral glare,
As if they already stood aghast
At the bloody work they would look upon.

It was two by the village clock,
When he came to the bridge in Concord town.
He heard the bleating of the flock,
And the twitter of birds among the trees,
And felt the breath of the morning breeze
Blowing over the meadows brown.
And one was safe and asleep in his bed
Who at the bridge would be first to fall,
Who that day would be lying dead,
Pierced by a British musket ball.

You know the rest. In the books you have read,
How the British Regulars fired and fled,—
How the farmers gave them ball for ball,
From behind each fence and farmyard wall,
Chasing the red-coats down the lane,
Then crossing the fields to emerge again
Under the trees at the turn of the road,
And only pausing to fire and load.

So through the night rode Paul Revere;
And so through the night went his cry of alarm
To every Middlesex village and farm,—
A cry of defiance and not of fear,
A voice in the darkness, a knock at the door,
And a word that shall echo for evermore!
For, borne on the night-wind of the Past,
Through all our history, to the last,
In the hour of darkness and peril and need,
The people will waken and listen to hear
The hurrying hoof-beats of that steed,
And the midnight message of Paul Revere.

WALTER VON DER VOGELWEID.

Vogelweid the Minnesinger,
  When he left this world of ours,
Laid his body in the cloister,
  Under Wurtzburg's minster towers.

And he gave the monks his treasures,
  Gave them all with this behest:
They should feed the birds at noontide
  Daily on his place of rest;

Saying, "From these wandering minstrels
  I have learned the art of song;
Let me now repay the lessons
  They have taught so well and long."

Thus the bard of love departed;
  And, fulfilling his desire,
On his tomb the birds were feasted
  By the children of the choir.

Day by day, o'er tower and turret,
   In foul weather and in fair,
Day by day, in vaster numbers,
   Flocked the poets of the air.

On the tree whose heavy branches
   Overshadowed all the place,
On the pavement, on the tombstone,
   On the poet's sculptured face.

On the cross-bars of each window,
   On the lintel of each door,
They renewed the War of Wartburg,
   Which the bard had fought before.

There they sang their merry carols,
   Sang their lauds on every side;
And the name their voices uttered
   Was the name of Vogelweid.

Till at length the portly abbot
   Murmured, "Why this waste of food?
Be it changed to loaves henceforward
   For our fasting brotherhood."

Then in vain o'er tower and turret,
   From the walls and woodland nests,
When the minster bells rang noontide,
   Gathered the unwelcome guests.

Then in vain, with cries discordant,
   Clamorous round the Gothic spire,
Screamed the feathered Minnesingers
   For the children of the choir.

Time has long effaced the inscriptions
   On the cloister's funeral stones,
And tradition only tells us
   Where repose the poet's bones.

But around the vast cathedral,
  By sweet echoes multiplied,
Still the birds repeat the legend,
  And the name of Vogelweid.

TWILIGHT.

The twilight is sad and cloudy,
  The wind blows wild and free,
And like the wings of sea-birds
  Flash the white caps of the sea.

But in the fisherman's cottage
  There shines a ruddier light,
And a little face at the window
  Peers out into the night.

Close, close it is pressed to the window,
  As if those childish eyes
Were looking into the darkness
  To see some form arise.

And a woman's waving shadow
  Is passing to and fro,
Now rising to the ceiling,
  Now bowing and bending low.

What tale do the roaring ocean,
  And the night-wind, bleak and wild,
As they beat at the crazy casement,
  Tell to that little child?

And why do the roaring ocean,
  And the night-wind, wild and bleak,
As they beat at the heart of the mother
  Drive the color from her cheek?

NUREMBERG.

In the valley of the Pegnitz, where across broad meadow-lands
Rise the blue Franconian mountains, Nuremberg, the ancient, stands.

Quaint old town of toil and traffic, quaint old town of art and song,
Memories haunt thy pointed gables, like the rocks that round them throng:

Memories of the Middle Ages, when the emperors, rough and bold,
Had their dwelling in thy castle, time-defying, centuries old;

And thy brave and thrifty burghers boasted, in their uncouth rhyme,
That their great imperial city stretched its hand through every clime.

In the court-yard of the castle, bound with many an iron band,
Stand the mighty linden planted by Queen Cunigunde's hand;

On the square the oriel window, where in old heroic days
Sat the poet Melchior singing Kaiser Maximilian's praise.

Everywhere I see around me rise the wondrous world of Art:
Fountains wrought with richest sculpture standing in the common mart;

And above cathedral doorways saints and bishops carved in stone,
By a former age commissioned as apostles to our own.

In the church of sainted Sebald sleeps enshrined his holy dust,
And in bronze the Twelve Apostles guard from age to age their trust;

In the church of sainted Lawrence stand a pix of sculpture rare,
Like the foamy sheaf of fountains, rising through the painted air.

Here, when Art was still religion, with a simple reverent heart,
Lived and labored Albrecht Dürer, the Evangelist of Art;

Hence in silence and in sorrow, toiling still with busy hand,
Like an emigrant he wandered, seeking for the Better Land.

Emigravit is the inscription on the tombstone where he lies;
Dead he is not, but departed,—for the artist never dies.

Fairer seems the ancient city, and the sunshine seems more fair,
That he once has trod its pavement, that he once has breathed its air.

EVANGELINE.

I.

MANY a weary year had passed since the burning of Grand-Pré,
When on the falling tide the freighted vessels departed,
Bearing a nation, with all its household gods, into exile,
Exile without an end, and without an example in story.
Far asunder, on separate coasts, the Acadians landed;
Scattered were they, like flakes of snow, when the wind from the northeast
Strikes aslant through the fogs that darken the Banks of Newfoundland.
Friendless, homeless, hopeless, they wandered from city to city,
From the cold lakes of the North to sultry Southern savannas—
From the bleak shores of the sea to the lands where the Father of Waters
Seizes the hills in his hands, and drags them down to the ocean,
Deep in their sands to bury the scattered bones of the mammoth.
Friends they sought and homes; and many, despairing, heart-broken,
Asked of the earth but a grave, and no longer a friend nor a fireside.
Written their history stands on tablets of stone in the churchyards.
Long among them was seen a maiden who waited and wandered,
Lowly and meek in spirit, and patiently suffering all things.
Fair was she and young; but, alas! before her extended,
Dreary and vast and silent, the desert of life, with its pathway
Marked by the graves of those who had sorrowed and suffered before her,
Passions long extinguished, and hopes long dead and abandoned,

As the emigrant's way o'er the Western desert is marked by
Camp-fires long consumed, and bones that bleach in the sunshine.
Something there was in her life incomplete, imperfect, unfinished;
As if a morning of June, with all its music and sunshine,
Suddenly paused in the sky, and, fading, slowly descended
Into the east again, from whence it late had arisen.
Sometimes she lingered in towns, till, urged by the fever within her,
Urged by a restless longing, the hunger and thirst of the spirit,
She would commence again her endless search and endeavor;
Sometimes in churchyards strayed, and gazed on the crosses and tombstones,
Sat by some nameless grave, and thought that perhaps in its bosom
He was already at rest, and she longed to slumber beside him.
Sometimes a rumor, a hearsay, an inarticulate whisper,
Came with its airy hand to point and beckon her forward.
Sometimes she spake with those who had seen her beloved and known him,
But it was long ago, in some far-off place or forgotten.
"Gabriel Lajeunesse!" they said; "Oh, yes! we have seen him.
He was with Basil the blacksmith, and both have gone to the prairies;
Coureurs-des-bois are they, and famous hunters and trappers."
"Gabriel Lajeunesse!" said others; "Oh, yes! we have seen him.
He is a voyageur in the lowlands of Louisiana."
Then would they say, "Dear child! why dream and wait for him longer?
Are there not other youths as fair as Gabriel? others
Who have hearts as tender and true, and spirits as loyal?
Here is Baptiste Leblanc, the notary's son, who has loved thee
Many a tedious year; come, give him thy hand and be happy!
Thou art too fair to be left to braid St. Catherine's tresses."
Then would Evangeline answer, serenely but sadly, "I cannot!
Whither my heart has gone, there follows my hand, and not elsewhere.
For when the heart goes before, like a lamp, and illumines the pathway,
Many things are made clear, that else lie hidden in darkness."
Thereupon the priest, her friend and father confessor,
Said, with a smile, "O daughter! thy God thus speaketh within thee!
Talk not of wasted affection, affection never was wasted;
If it enrich not the heart of another, its waters, returning

Back to their springs, like the rain, shall fill them full of refreshment;
That which the fountain sends forth returns again to the fountain.
Patience; accomplish thy labor; accomplish thy work of affection!
Sorrow and silence are strong, and patient endurance is godlike.
Therefore accomplish thy labor of love, till the heart is made godlike,
Purified, strengthened, perfected, and rendered more worthy of heaven!"
Cheered by the good man's words, Evangeline labored and waited.
Still in her heart she heard the funeral dirge of the ocean,
But with its sound there was mingled a voice that whispered, "Despair not!"
Thus did that poor soul wander in want and cheerless discomfort,
Bleeding, barefooted, over the shards and thorns of existence.
Let me essay, O Muse! to follow the wanderer's footsteps:—
Not through each devious path, each changeful year of existence;
But as a traveler follows a streamlet's course through the valley:
Far from its margin at times, and seeing the gleam of its water
Here and there, in some open space, and at intervals only;
Then drawing nearer its banks, through sylvan glooms that conceal it,
Though he behold it not, he can hear its continuous murmur;
Happy, at length, if he find a spot where it reaches an outlet.

II.

It was the month of May. Far down the Beautiful River,
Past the Ohio shore and past the mouth of the Wabash,
Into the golden stream of the broad and swift Mississippi,
Floated a cumbrous boat, that was rowed by Acadian boatmen.
It was a band of exiles: a raft, as it were, from the shipwrecked
Nation, scattered along the coast, now floating together,
Bound by the bonds of a common belief and a common misfortune;
Men and women and children, who, guided by hope or by hearsay,
Sought for their kith and their kin among the few-acred farmers
On the Acadian coast, and the prairies of fair Opelousas.
With them Evangeline went, and her guide, the Father Felician.
Onward o'er sunken sands, through a wilderness sombre with forests,
Day after day they glided adown the turbulent river:
Night after night, by their blazing fires, encamped on its borders.
Now through rushing chutes, among green islands, where plumelike

Cotton-trees nodded their shadowy crests, they swept with the current,
Then emerged into broad lagoons, where silvery sandbars
Lay in the stream, and along the wimpling waves of their margin,
Shining with snow-white plumes, large flocks of pelicans waded.
Level the landscape grew, and along the shores of the river,
Shaded by china-trees, in the midst of luxuriant gardens,
Stood the houses of planters, with negro cabins and dove-cots.
They were approaching the region where reigns perpetual summer,
Where through the Golden Coast, and groves of orange and citron,
Sweeps with majestic curve the river away to the eastward.
They, too, swerved from their course; and, entering the Bayou of Plaquemine,
Soon were lost in a maze of sluggish and devious waters,
Which, like a network of steel, extended in every direction.
Over their heads the towering and tenebrous boughs of the cypress
Met in a dusky arch, and trailing mosses in midair
Waved like banners that hang on the walls of ancient cathedrals.
Deathlike the silence seemed, and unbroken, save by the herons
Home to their roosts in the cedar-trees returning at sunset,
Or by the owl, as he greeted the moon with demoniac laughter.
Lovely the moonlight was as it glanced and gleamed on the water,
Gleamed on the columns of cypress and cedar sustaining the arches,
Down through whose broken vaults it fell as through chinks in a ruin.
Dreamlike, and indistinct, and strange were all things around them;
And o'er their spirits there came a feeling of wonder and sadness,—
Strange forebodings of ill, unseen and that cannot be compassed.
As, at the tramp of a horse's hoof on the turf of the prairies,
Far in advance are closed the leaves of the shrinking mimosa,
So, at the hoof-beats of fate, with sad forebodings of evil,
Shrinks and closes the heart, ere the stroke of doom has attained it.
But Evangeline's heart was sustained by a vision, that faintly
Floated before her eyes, and beckoned her on through the moonlight.
It was the thought of her brain that assumed the shape of a phantom.

Through those shadowy aisles had Gabriel wandered before her,
And every stroke of the oar now brought him nearer and nearer.

 Then in his place, at the prow of the boat, rose one of the oarsmen,
And, as a signal sound, if others like them peradventure
Sailed on those gloomy and midnight streams, blew a blast on his bugle.
Wild through the dark colonnades and corridors leafy the blast rang,
Breaking the seal of silence and giving tongues to the forest.
Soundless above them the banners of moss just stirred to the music.
Multitudinous echoes awoke and died in the distance,
Over the watery floor, and beneath the reverberant branches;
But not a voice replied; no answer came from the darkness;
And when the echoes had ceased, like a sense of pain was the silence.
Then Evangeline slept; but the boatmen rowed through the midnight,
Silent at times, then singing familiar Canadian boat-songs,
Such as they sang of old on their own Acadian rivers,
While through the night were heard the mysterious sounds of the desert,
Far off,—indistinct,—as of wave or wind in the forest,
Mixed with the whoop of the crane and the roar of the grim alligator.

 Thus ere another noon they emerged from the shades; and before them
Lay, in the golden sun, the lakes of the Atchafalaya.
Water-lilies in myriads rocked on the slight undulations
Made by the passing oars, and, resplendent in beauty, the lotus
Lifted her golden crown above the heads of the boatmen.
Faint was the air with the odorous breath of magnolia blossoms,
And with the heat of noon; and numberless sylvan islands,
Fragrant and thickly embowered with blossoming hedges of roses,
Near to whose shores they glided along, invited to slumber.
Soon by the fairest of these their weary oars were suspended.
Under the boughs of Wachita willows, that grew by the margin,
Safely their boat was moored; and scattered about on the greensward,
Tired with their midnight toil, the weary travellers slumbered.

Over them vast and high extended the cope of a cedar.
Swinging from its great arms, the trumpet-flower and the grape-vine
Hung their ladder of ropes aloft like the ladder of Jacob,
On whose pendulous stairs the angels ascending, descending,
Were the swift humming-birds, that flitted from blossom to blossom.
Such was the vision Evangeline saw as she slumbered beneath it.
Filled was her heart with love, and the dawn of an opening heaven
Lighted her soul in sleep with the glory of regions celestial.

Nearer, ever nearer, among the numberless islands,
Darted a light, swift boat, that sped away o'er the water,
Urged on its course by the sinewy arms of hunters and trappers.
Northward its prow was turned, to the land of the bison and beaver.
At the helm sat a youth, with countenance thoughtful and care-worn.
Dark and neglected locks overshadowed his brow, and a sadness
Somewhat beyond his years on his face was legibly written.
Gabriel was it, who, weary with waiting, unhappy and restless,
Sought in the Western wilds oblivion of self and of sorrow,
Swiftly they glided along, close under the lee of the island,
But by the opposite bank, and behind a screen of palmettos;
So that they saw not the boat, where it lay concealed in the willows;
All undisturbed by the dash of their oars, and unseen, were the sleepers;
Angel of God was there none to awaken the slumbering maiden.
Swiftly they glided away, like the shade of a cloud on the prairie.
After the sound of their oars on the tholes had died in the distance,
As from a magic trance the sleepers awoke, and the maiden
Said with a sigh to the friendly priest, "O Father Felician!
Something says in my heart that near me Gabriel wanders.
Is it a foolish dream, an idle and vague superstition?
Or has an angel passed, and revealed the truth to my spirit?"
Then, with a blush, she added, "Alas for my credulous fancy!
Unto ears like thine such words as these have no meaning."
But made answer the reverend man, and he smiled as he answered,—
"Daughter, thy words are not idle; nor are they to me without meaning,

Feeling is deep and still; and the word that floats on the surface
Is as the tossing buoy, that betrays where the anchor is hidden.
Therefore trust to thy heart, and to what the world calls illusions.
Gabriel truly is near thee; for not far away to the southward,
On the banks of the Têche, are the towns of St. Maur and St. Martin.
There the long-wandering bride shall be given again to her bridegroom,
There the long-absent pastor regain his flock and his sheepfold.
Beautiful is the land, with its prairies and forests of fruit trees;
Under the feet a garden of flowers, and the bluest of heavens
Bending above, and resting its dome on the walls of the forest.
They who dwell there have named it the Eden of Louisiana."

With these words of cheer they arose and continued their journey.
Softly the evening came. The sun from the western horizon
Like a magician extended his golden wand o'er the landscape;
Twinkling vapors arose; and sky and water and forest
Seemed all on fire at the touch, and melted and mingled together.
Hanging between two skies, a cloud with edges of silver,
Floated the boat, with its dripping oars, on the motionless water.
Filled was Evangeline's heart with inexpressible sweetness.
Touched by the magic spell, the sacred fountains of feeling
Glowed with the light of love, as the skies and waters around her.
Then from a neighboring thicket, the mocking-bird, wildest of singers,
Swinging aloft on a willow spray that hung o'er the water,
Shook from his little throat such floods of delirious music,
That the whole air and the woods and the waves seemed silent to listen.
Plaintive at first were the tones and sad; then soaring to madness
Seemed they to follow or guide the revel of frenzied Bacchantes.
Single notes were then heard, in sorrowful, low lamentation;
Till, having gathered them all, he flung them abroad in derision,
As when, after a storm, a gust of wind through the treetops
Shakes down the rattling rain in a crystal shower on the branches.
With such a prelude as this, and hearts that throbbed with emotion,
Slowly they entered the Têche, where it flows through the green Opelousas,
And, through the amber air, above the crest of the woodland,

Saw the column of smoke that arose from a neighboring dwelling;—
Sounds of a horn they heard, and the distant lowing of cattle.

III.

Near to the bank of the river, o'ershadowed by oaks from whose branches
Garlands of Spanish moss and of mystic mistletoe flaunted,
Such as the Druids cut down with golden hatchets at Yuletide,
Stood, secluded and still, the house of the herdsman. A garden
Girded it round about with a belt of luxuriant blossoms,
Filling the air with fragrance. The house itself was of timbers
Hewn from the cypress tree, and carefully fitted together.
Large and low was the roof; and on slender columns supported,
Rose-wreathed, vine-encircled, a broad and spacious veranda,
Haunt of the humming bird and the bee, extended around it.
At each end of the house, amid the flowers of the garden,
Stationed the dove-cotes were, as love's perpetual symbol,
Scenes of endless wooing, and endless contentions of rivals.
Silence reigned o'er the place. The line of shadow and sunshine
Ran near the tops of the trees; but the house itself was in shadow,
And from its chimney top, ascending and slowly expanding
Into the evening air, a thin blue column of smoke rose.
In the rear of the house, from the garden gate, ran a pathway
Through the great groves of oak to the skirts of the limitless prairie,
Into whose sea of flowers the sun was slowly descending.
Full in his track of light, like ships with shadowy canvas
Hanging loose from their spars in a motionless calm in the tropics,
Stood a cluster of trees, with tangled cordage of grapevines.

Just where the woodlands met the flowery surf of the prairie,
Mounted upon his horse, with Spanish saddle and stirrups,
Sat a herdsman, arrayed in gaiters and doublet of deerskin.
Broad and brown was the face that from under the Spanish sombrero
Gazed on the peaceful scene, with the lordly look of its master.
Round about him were numberless herds of kine that were grazing
Quietly in the meadows, and breathing the vapory freshness
That uprose from the river, and spread itself over the landscape.

Slowly lifting the horn that hung at his side, and expanding
Fully his broad, deep chest, he blew a blast, that resounded
Wildly and sweet and far, through the still damp air of the evening.
Suddenly out of the grass the long white horns of the cattle
Rose like flakes of foam on the adverse currents of ocean.
Silent a moment they gazed, then bellowing rushed o'er the prairie,
And the whole mass became a cloud, a shade in the distance.
Then, as the herdsman turned to the house, through the gate of the garden
Saw he the forms of the priest and the maiden advancing to meet him.
Suddenly down from his horse he sprang in amazement, and forward
Pushed with extended arms and exclamations of wonder;
When they beheld his face, they recognized Basil the blacksmith.
Hearty his welcome was, as he led his guests to the garden.
There in an arbor of roses with endless question and answer
Gave they vent to their hearts, and renewed their friendly embraces,
Laughing and weeping by turns, or sitting silent and thoughtful.
Thoughtful, for Gabriel came not; and now dark doubts and misgivings
Stole o'er the maiden's heart; and Basil, somewhat embarrassed,
Broke the silence and said, "If you came by the Atchafalaya,
How have you nowhere encountered my Gabriel's boat on the bayous?"
Over Evangeline's face at the words of Basil a shade passed.
Tears came into her eyes, and she said, with a tremulous accent,
"Gone? is Gabriel gone?" and, concealing her face on his shoulder,
All her o'erburdened heart gave way, and she wept and lamented.
Then the good Basil said,—and his voice grew blithe as he said it,—
"Be of good cheer, my child; it is only today he departed.
Foolish boy! he has left me alone with my herds and my horses.
Moody and restless grown, and tried and troubled, his spirit
Could no longer endure the calm of this quiet existence.
Thinking ever of thee, uncertain and sorrowful ever,
Ever silent, or speaking only of thee and his troubles,
He at length had become so tedious to men and to maidens.
Tedious even to me, that at length I bethought me, and sent him

Unto the town of Adayes to trade for mules with the Spaniards.
Thence he will follow the Indian trails to the Ozark Mountains,
Hunting for furs in the forests, on rivers trapping the beaver.
Therefore be of good cheer; we will follow the fugitive lover;
He is not far on his way, and the Fates and the streams are against him.
Up and away tomorrow, and through the red dew of the morning,
We will follow him fast, and bring him back to his prison."

Then glad voices were heard, and up from the banks of the river,
Borne aloft on his comrades' arms, came Michael the fiddler.
Long under Basil's roof had he lived, like a god on Olympus,
Having no other care than dispensing music to mortals.
Far renowned was he for his silver locks and his fiddle.
"Long live Michael," they cried, "our brave Acadian minstrel!"
As they bore him aloft in triumphal procession; and straightway
Father Felician advanced with Evangeline, greeting the old man
Kindly and oft, and recalling the past, while Basil, enraptured,
Hailed with hilarious joy his old companions and gossips,
Laughing loud and long, and embracing mothers and daughters.
Much they marveled to see the wealth of the ci-devant blacksmith,
All his domains and his herds, and his patriarchal demeanor;
Much they marveled to hear his tales of the soil and the climate,
And of the prairies, whose numberless herds were his who would take them;
Each one thought in his heart, that he, too, would go and do likewise.
Thus they ascended the steps, and, crossing the breezy veranda,
Entered the hall of the house, where already the supper of Basil
Waited his late return; and they rested and feasted together.

Over the joyous feast the sudden darkness descended.
All was silent without, and, illuming the landscape with silver,
Fair rose the dewy moon and the myriad stars; but within doors,
Brighter than these, shone the faces of friends in the glimmering lamplight.
Then from his station aloft, at the head of the table, the herdsman
Poured forth his heart and his wine together in endless profusion.
Lighting his pipe, that was filled with sweet Natchitoches tobacco.
Thus he spake to his guests, who listened, and smiled as they listened:—

"Welcome once more, my friends, who long have been friendless
 and homeless,
Welcome once more to a home, that is better perchance than the
 old one!
Here no hungry winter congeals our blood like the rivers;
Here no stony ground provokes the wrath of the farmer;
Smoothly the ploughshare runs through the soil, as a keel through
 the water.
All the year round the orange groves are in blossom; and grass
 grows
More in a single night than a whole Canadian summer.
Here, too, numberless herds run wild and unclaimed in the
 prairies;
Here, too, lands may be had for the asking, and forests of timber
With a few blows of the axe are hewn and framed into houses.
After your houses are built, and your fields are yellow with
 harvests,
No King George of England shall drive you away from your
 homesteads,
Burning your dwellings and barns, and stealing your farms and
 your cattle."
Speaking these words, he blew a wrathful cloud from his nostrils,
While his huge, brown hand came thundering down on the table,
So that the guests all started; and Father Felician, astounded,
Suddenly paused, with a pinch of snuff half-way to his nostrils.
But the brave Basil resumed, and his words were milder and
 gayer:—
"Only beware of the fever, my friends, beware of the fever!
For it is not like that of our cold Acadian climate,
Cured by wearing a spider hung round one's neck in a nutshell!"
Then there were voices heard at the door, and footsteps
 approaching
Sounded upon the stairs and the floor of the breezy veranda.
It was the neighboring Creoles and small Acadian planters,
Who had been summoned all to the house of Basil the herdsman.
Merry the meeting was of ancient comrades and neighbors:
Friend clasped friend in his arms; and they who before were as
 strangers,
Meeting in exile, became straightway as friends to each other,
Drawn by the gentle bond of a common country together.
But in the neighboring hall a strain of music, proceeding
From the accordant strings of Michael's melodious fiddle,
Broke up all further speech. Away, like children delighted,

All things forgotten beside, they gave themselves to the maddening
Whirl of the dizzy dance, as it swept and swayed to the music,
Dreamlike, with beaming eyes and the rush of fluttering garments.

 Meanwhile, apart at the head of the hall, the priest and the herdsman
Sat, conversing together of past and present and future;
While Evangeline stood like one entranced, for within her
Olden memories rose, and loud in the midst of the music
Heard she the sound of the sea, and an irrepressible sadness
Came o'er her heart, and unseen she stole forth into the garden.
Beautiful was the night. Behind the black wall of the forest,
Tipping its summit with silver, arose the moon. On the river
Fell here and there through the branches a tremulous gleam of the moonlight,
Like the sweet thoughts of love on a darkened and devious spirit.
Nearer and round about her, the manifold flowers of the garden
Poured out their souls in odors, that were their prayers and confessions
Unto the night, as it went its way, like a silent Carthusian.

CONGRESSIONAL LIBRARY, WASHINGTON.

CHAPTER VIII.
LOWELL; HOLMES.

"IN a liberal sense," wrote Mr. Edmund Clarence Stedman some years ago, "and somewhat as Emerson stands for American thought, the poet Lowell has become our representative man of letters." Lowell still stands as America's representative man of letters, not because he has struck the highest note, but because he has the greatest breadth and versatility, and has woven into his prose and verse more of the warp and woof of American life and thought than any one else. It is a far cry from the noble and lofty strain of the "Commemoration Ode" to the quaint humor and shrewdness of Hosea Biglow, and yet both have made a strong appeal in widely different ways, not only to America, but to all the English-speaking world.

James Russell Lowell was born in Cambridge, Mass., on February 22, 1819. His father was the Rev. Charles Lowell, and his grandfather was the Judge John Lowell who founded the Lowell Institute in Boston. He graduated at Harvard College in 1838, and was admitted to the bar in Boston in 1840. He never practiced law, however, but began his career as an author shortly after his admission to the bar, by publishing a volume of poems under the title of "A Year's Life." His first book was never republished, though a few of the poems in it were preserved by the author. In 1844 Lowell married Maria White, the gifted woman who had inspired "A Year's Life." Being an ardent abolitionist, she influenced Lowell into becoming a warm advocate of this cause, which he espoused with his whole heart and soul, and advocated with glowing words and flaming pen.

Indignation at the Mexican War and hatred of slavery were the direct inspiration of the humorous but caustic "Biglow papers," which Lowell began in 1846 and continued till 1848. A second, but less successful series appeared during the Civil War, in 1864. In both his mastery of the Yankee dialect and insight into the Yankee mind contributed to the effect intended.

Notwithstanding his intense interest in the issues of the day, slavery and the Civil War, Lowell found time for general literary work. As early as 1845 appeared one of the most beautiful of his poems, "The Vision of Sir Launfal," a poem on the quest of the Holy Grail. In another vein was the "Fable for Critics," which appeared anonymously, and keenly criticised the writers of the day, including himself.

In 1851 Lowell and his second wife traveled in Europe, remaining for over a year, the fruits of this residence abroad being essays on Italian art and literature and studies of Dante. In 1855 Lowell was appointed Professor of Modern Languages and Belles-Lettres at Harvard University; he was the first editor of the *Atlantic Monthly,* founded in 1857, and for ten years he was joint editor of the *North American Review.* His critical and miscellaneous essays in these periodicals he subsequently collected and published under the titles of "Among my Books" and "My Study Windows." On July 21, 1865, he delivered his noble "Commemoration Ode," in honor of the graduates of Harvard University who had fallen in the Civil War. This is Lowell's greatest poetical achievement, and immeasurably the finest poem called forth by the war. In 1869 appeared "Under the Willows and other Poems," and in 1870 "The Cathedral," one of the highest expressions of the poet's genius. In 1877 Lowell was appointed by President Hayes American Minister to Spain, and afterwards he was transferred to the Court of St. James, where he remained until 1885. During his residence in England, Oxford and Cambridge conferred upon him the degrees of D. C. L. and LL. D. On returning to the United States, he took up his residence at Cambridge, where he died August 12, 1891. Three years before his death he published "Heartsease and Rue," and "Political Essays," "American Ideas for English Readers," "Latest Literary Essays and Addresses," and "Old English Dramatists," were issued posthumously in 1892.

THE VISION OF SIR LAUNFAL.

Prelude to Part First.

Over his keys the musing organist,
   Beginning doubtfully and far away,
First lets his fingers wander as they list,
   And builds a bridge from Dreamland for his lay:
Then, as the touch of his loved instrument
   Gives hope and fervor, nearer draws his theme,
First guessed by faint auroral flushes sent
   Along the wavering vista of his dream.

      Not only around our infancy
        Doth heaven with all its splendors lie;
      Daily, with souls that cringe and plot,
        We Sinais climb and know it not.

Over our manhood bend the skies;
   Against our fallen and traitor lives
The great winds utter prophecies;
   With our faint hearts the mountain strives;
Its arms outstretched, the Druid wood
   Waits with its benedicite;
And to our age's drowsy blood
   Still shouts the inspiring sea.

Earth gets its price for what Earth gives us;
   The beggar is taxed for a corner to die in,
The priest hath his fee who comes and shrives us,
   We bargain for the graves we lie in;
At the Devil's booth are all things sold,
Each ounce of dross costs its ounce of gold;
   For a cap and bells our lives we pay,
Bubbles we buy with a whole soul's tasking:
   'T is heaven alone that is given away,
'T is only God may be had for the asking;
No price is set on the lavish summer;
June may be had by the poorest comer.

And what is so rare as a day in June?
    Then, if ever, come perfect days;
Then Heaven tries earth if it be in tune,
    And over it softly her warm ear lays:
Whether we look, or whether we listen,
We hear life murmur, or see it glisten;
Every clod feels a stir of might,
    An instinct within it that reaches and towers,
And, groping blindly above it for light,
    Climbs to a soul in grass and flowers;
The flush of life may well be seen
    Thrilling back over hills and valleys;
The cowslip startles in meadows green,
    The buttercup catches the sun in its chalice,
And there's never a leaf nor a blade too mean
    To be some happy creature's palace;
The little bird sits at his door in the sun,
    Atilt like a blossom among the leaves,
And lets his illumined being o'errun
    With the deluge of summer it receives;
His mate feels the eggs beneath her wings,
And the heart in her dumb breast flutters and sings;
He sings to the wide world, and she to her nest,—
In the nice ear of Nature which song is the best?

Now is the high-tide of the year,
    And whatever of life hath ebbed away
Comes flooding back with a ripply cheer,
    Into every bare inlet and creek and bay;
Now the heart is so full that a drop overfills it,
We are happy now because God wills it;
No matter how barren the past may have been,
'T is enough for us now that the leaves are green;
We sit in the warm shade and feel right well
How the sap creeps up and the blossoms swell;
We may shut our eyes, but we cannot help knowing
That skies are clear and grass is growing;
The breeze comes whispering in our ear,
That dandelions are blossoming near,
    That maize has sprouted, that streams are flowing,

That the river is bluer than the sky,
That the robin is plastering his house hard by;
And if the breeze kept the good news back,
For other couriers we should not lack;
   We could guess it all by yon heifer's lowing,—
And hark! how clear bold chanticleer,
Warmed with the new wine of the year,
   Tells all in his lusty crowing!
Joy comes, grief goes, we know not how;
Everything is happy now,
   Everything is upward striving;
'T is as easy now for the heart to be true
As for grass to be green or skies to be blue,—
   'T is the natural way of living:
Who knows whither the clouds have fled?
   In the unscarred heaven they leave no wake;
And the eyes forget the tears they have shed,
   The heart forgets its sorrow and ache;
The soul partakes the season's youth,
   And the sulphurous rifts of passion and woe
Lie deep 'neath a silence pure and smooth,
   Like burnt-out craters healed with snow.
What wonder if Sir Launfal now
Remembered the keeping of his vow?

PART FIRST

   "My golden spurs now bring to me,
     And bring to me my richest mail,
   For tomorrow I go over land and sea
     In search of the Holy Grail;
   Shall never a bed for me be spread,
   Nor shall a pillow be under my head,
Till I begin my vow to keep;
Here on the rushes will I sleep,
And perchance there may come a vision true
Ere day create the world anew."
   Slowly Sir Launfal's eyes grew dim,
   Slumber fell like a cloud on him,
And into his soul the vision flew.

II

The crows flapped over by twos and threes,
In the pool drowsed the cattle up to their knees,
　　The little birds sang as if it were
　　The one day of summer in all the year,
And the very leaves seemed to sing on the trees:
The castle alone in the landscape lay
Like an outpost of winter, dull and gray:
'T was the proudest hall in the North Countree,
　　And never its gates might opened be,
Save to lord or lady of high degree;
Summer besieged it on every side,
But the churlish stone her assaults defied;
She could not scale the chilly wall,
Though around it for leagues her pavilions tall
Stretched left and right,
Over the hills and out of sight;
　　Green and broad was every tent,
　　And out of each a murmur went
Till the breeze fell off at night.

III

The drawbridge dropped with a surly clang,
And through the dark arch a charger sprang,
Bearing Sir Launfal, the maiden knight,
In his gilded mail, that flamed so bright
It seemed the dark castle had gathered all
Those shafts the fierce sun had shot over its wall
　　In his siege of three hundred summers long,
And, binding them all in one blazing sheaf,
　　Had cast them forth: so, young and strong,
And lightsome as a locust-leaf,
Sir Launfal flashed forth in his maiden mail,
To seek in all climes for the Holy Grail.

IV

It was morning on hill and stream and tree,
　　And morning in the young knight's heart;
Only the castle moodily
Rebuffed the gifts of the sunshine free,
　　And gloomed by itself apart;

The season brimmed all other things up
Full as the rain fills the pitcher-plant's cup.

V

As Sir Launfal made morn through the darksome gate,
   He was 'ware of a leper, crouched by the same,
Who begged with his hand and moaned as he sate;
And a loathing over Sir Launfal came;
The sunshine went out of his soul with a thrill,
   The flesh 'neath his armor 'gan shrink and crawl,
And midway its leap his heart stood still
   Like a frozen waterfall;
For this man, so foul and bent of stature,
Rasped harshly against his dainty nature,
And seemed the one blot on the summer morn,—
So he tossed him a piece of gold in scorn.

VI

The leper raised not the gold from the dust:
"Better to me the poor man's crust,
Better the blessing of the poor,
Though I turn me empty from his door;
That is no true alms which the hand can hold;
He gives nothing but worthless gold
   Who gives from a sense of duty;
But he who gives but a slender mite,
And gives to that which is out of sight,
   That thread of the all-sustaining Beauty
Which runs through all and doth all unite,—
The hand cannot clasp the whole of his alms,
The heart outstretches its eager palms,
For a god goes with it and makes it store
To the soul that was starving in darkness before."

PRELUDE TO PART SECOND

Down swept the chill wind from the mountain peak,
    From the snow five thousand summers old;
On open wold and hilltop bleak
    It had gathered all the cold,
And whirled it like sleet on the wanderer's cheek;
It carried a shiver everywhere
From the unleafed boughs and pastures bare;
The little brook heard it and built a roof
'Neath which he could house him, winter-proof;
All night by the white stars' frosty gleams
He groined his arches and matched his beams;
Slender and clear were his crystal spars
As the flashes of light that trim the stars;
He sculptured every summer delight
In his halls and chambers out of sight;
Sometimes his tinkling waters slipt
Down through a frost-leaved forest-crypt,
Long, sparkling aisles of steel-stemmed trees
Bending to counterfeit a breeze;
Sometimes the roof no fretwork knew
But silvery mosses that downward grew;
Sometimes it was carved in sharp relief
With quaint arabesques of ice-fern leaf;
Sometimes it was simply smooth and clear
For the gladness of heaven to shine through, and here
He had caught the nodding bulrush-tops
And hung them thickly with diamond-drops,
That crystalled the beams of moon and sun,
And made a star of every one:
No mortal builder's most rare device
Could match this winter-palace of ice;
'T was as if every image that mirrored lay
In his depths serene through the summer day,
Each fleeting shadow of earth and sky,
    Lest the happy model should be lost,
Had been mimicked in fairy masonry
    By the elfin builders of the frost.

Within the hall are song and laughter,
  The cheeks of Christmas grow red and jolly,
And sprouting is every corbel and rafter
  With lightsome green of ivy and holly;
Through the deep gulf of the chimney wide
Wallows the Yule-log's roaring tide;
The broad flame-pennons droop and flap
  And belly and tug as a flag in the wind;
Like a locust shrills the imprisoned sap,
  Hunted to death in its galleries blind;
And swift little troops of silent sparks,
  Now pausing, now scattering away as in fear,
Go threading the soot-forest's tangled darks
  Like herds of startled deer.

But the wind without was eager and sharp,
Of Sir Launfal's gray hair it makes a harp,
    And rattles and wrings
    The icy strings,
  Singing, in dreary monotone,
  A Christmas carol of its own,
  Whose burden still, as he might guess,
  Was "Shelterless, shelterless, shelterless!"
The voice of the seneschal flared like a torch
As he shouted the wanderer away from the porch,
And he sat in the gateway and saw all night
  The great hall-fire, so cheery and bold,
  Through the window-slits of the castle old,
Build out its piers of ruddy light
  Against the drift of the cold.

PART SECOND

There was never a leaf on bush or tree,
The bare boughs rattled shudderingly;
The river was dumb and could not speak,
  For the weaver Winter its shroud had spun;
A single crow on the tree-top bleak
  From his shining feathers shed off the cold sun;

Again it was morning, but shrunk and cold,
As if her veins were sapless and old,
And she rose up decrepitly
For a last dim look at earth and sea.

II

Sir Launfal turned from his own hard gate,
For another heir in his earldom sate;
An old, bent man, worn out and frail,
He came back from seeking the Holy Grail;
Little he recked of his earldom's loss,
No more on his surcoat was blazoned the cross,
But deep in his soul the sign he wore,
The badge of the suffering and the poor.

III

Sir Launfal's raiment thin and spare
Was idle mail 'gainst the barbed air,
For it was just at the Christmas time;
So he mused, as he sat, of a sunnier clime,
And sought for a shelter from cold and snow
In the light and warmth of long-ago;
He sees the snake-like caravan crawl
O'er the edge of the desert, black and small,
Then nearer and nearer, till, one by one,
He can count the camels in the sun,
As over the red-hot sands they pass
To where, in its slender necklace of grass,
The little spring laughed and leapt in the shade,
And with its own self like an infant played,
And waved its signal of palms.

IV

" For Christ's sweet sake, I beg an alms;"—
The happy camels may reach the spring,
But Sir Launfal sees only the grewsome thing,
The leper, lank as the rain-blanched bone,
That cowers beside him, a thing as lone
And white as the ice-isles of Northern seas
In the desolate horror of his disease.

V

And Sir Launfal said, "I behold in thee
An image of Him who died on the tree;
Thou also hast had thy crown of thorns,
Thou also hast had the world's buffets and scorns,
And to thy life were not denied
The wounds in the hands and feet and side:
Mild Mary's Son, acknowledge me;
Behold, through him, I give to Thee!"

VI

Then the soul of the leper stood up in his eyes
    And looked at Sir Launfal, and straightway he
Remembered in what a haughtier guise
    He had flung an alms to leprosie,
When he girt his young life up in gilded mail
And set forth in search of the Holy Grail.
The heart within him was ashes and dust;
He parted in twain his single crust,
He broke the ice on the streamlet's brink,
And gave the leper to eat and drink:
'T was a mouldy crust of coarse brown bread,
    'T was water out of a wooden bowl,—
Yet with fine wheaten bread was the leper fed,
    And 't was red wine he drank with his thirsty soul.

VII

As Sir Launfal mused with a downcast face,
A light shone round about the place;
The leper no longer crouched at his side,
But stood before him glorified,
Shining and tall and fair and straight
As the pillar that stood by the Beautiful Gate,—
Himself the Gate whereby men can
Enter the temple of God in Man.

VIII

His words were shed softer than leaves from the pine,
And they fell on Sir Launfal as snows on the brine,
    That mingle their softness and quiet in one

With the shaggy unrest they float down upon;
And the voice that was calmer than silence said,
"Lo, it is I, be not afraid!
In many climes, without avail,
Thou hast spent thy life for the Holy Grail;
Behold, it is here,—this cup which thou
Didst fill at the streamlet for Me but now;
This crust is My body broken for thee,
This water His blood that died on the tree;
The Holy Supper is kept, indeed,
In whatso we share with another's need:
Not what we give, but what we share,—
For the gift without the giver is bare;
Who gives himself with his alms feeds three,—
Himself, his hungering neighbor, and Me."

IX

Sir Launfal awoke as from a swound:—
" The Grail in my castle here is found!
Hang my idle armor up on the wall,
Let it be the spider's banquet-hall;
 He must be fenced with stronger mail
Who would seek and find the Holy Grail."

X

The castle gate stands open now,
 And the wanderer is welcome to the hall
As the hangbird is to the elm-tree bough;
 No longer scowl the turrets tall,
The Summer's long siege at last is o'er;
When the first poor outcast went in at the door,
She entered with him in disguise,
And mastered the fortress by surprise;
There is no spot she loves so well on ground,
She lingers and smiles there the whole year round;
The meanest serf on Sir Launfal's land
Has hall and bower at his command;
And there's no poor man in the North Countree
But is lord of the earldom as much as he.

OLIVER WENDELL HOLMES.

HOLMES, born in 1809 and dying in 1894, was the descendant of a scholarly New England ancestry. After graduating at Harvard, he began life as a professor and practitioner in medicine; he was married in 1840, and lived all hi life in Boston. He twice visited Europe, first as a young fellow of one-and-twenty, and again, after more than half century, as a veteran of letters, known and loved in both hemispheres. Of all our writers, he is the sunniest, the wittiest and most discursive, and one of the least uneven.

Until 1857, Holmes had written nothing beyond occasional poems, excellent of their kind, but not of themselves sufficient to make a reputation. But in that year, the *Atlantic Monthly* was started and Holmes contributed to it a serie of unique essays entitled, "The Autocrat of the Breakfas Table." They had the form of familiar dialogues between group of diverse but common types in a boarding-house, upo all manner of topics. They immediately caught the fancy o all readers, and lifted Holmes to a literary altitude where h ever after remained. Two years later "Elsie Venner," h first novel, a study in heredity and in American village character, was published; it is good, but not in the same class wit the best imaginative work. The same criticism must be passe on "The Guardian Angel," his second effort in fiction, whic appeared in 1867. Both have so much merit that one wonder not to find them better. But they make it plain that Holmes' proper field was the discursive essay and the occasional poem and here his fame is solid and secure.

Wit rather than humor characterizes Holmes; yet he ha the tenderness which usually accompanies only the latter. Hi mind is swift in movement, and catches remote, analogies; he brings together the near and the far, with the effect of a pleasing surprise. His thought tends to shape itself in epigram: he says more "good things"—which are not merely good, but often wise—than any of his contemporaries. The habit of his mind was discursive and independent, rather than deeply original; he had opinions on all subjects; he stated them so brightly and aptly that they often seemed new; but in truth Holmes is orthodox. His quick sympathies and excellent taste, combined with the harmony of nature which creates the synthetic attitude, make him a poet whose productions not seldom reach a high plane, as for example in "The Chambered Nautilus." He is an optimist, and a moralizer, and turns both characteristics to sound literary advantage. The comic bias of his general outlook upon life leads him to be so constantly funny and acute, that the reader is in some danger of losing the fine edge of appreciation; the writer becomes his own rival. Once in a while, however, as in "Old Ironsides," the fervor of his patriotism, or of some other high emotion, thrills him into seriousness, and then he strikes a pure and lofty note. There is something lovable in all that he has done; and no man of letters among us has been the object of more widespread personal affection than has Holmes.

We return from other appreciations to the Autocrat series —for he wrote a number of books of a character similar to these first essays. The untrammeled plan of them suits his genius; he can spring here and there as chance or humor suggests, and entertain us in a hundred different ways one after another. He preaches charming lay sermons, on a score of texts at once, and unless unintermittent entertainment can be tedious, tediousness is impossible to Holmes. He opens no unknown worlds, but he makes us see the world we know better. He penetrates beneath the surface of human nature, though he falls short of creative insight. After reading him, we rise with a kindlier feeling towards men and things, and a wiser understanding of them.

The Chambered Nautilus.

This is the ship of pearl, which, poets feign,
   Sails the unshadow'd main,—
   The venturous bark that flings
On the sweet summer wind its purpled wings
  In gulfs enchanted, where the siren sings,
   And coral reefs lie bare,
Where the cold sea-maids rise to sun their streaming hair.

Its webs of living gauze no more unfurl;
   Wrecked is the ship of pearl!
   And every chambered cell,
Where its dim dreaming life was wont to dwell,
As the frail tenant shaped his growing shell,
   Before thee lies revealed,—
Its irised ceiling rent, its sunless crypt unsealed!

Year after year beheld the silent toil
   That spread his lustrous coil;
   Still, as the spiral grew,
He left the past year's dwelling archway through,
   Built up its idle door,
Stretched in his last-found home, and knew the old no more.

Thanks for the heavenly message brought by thee,
   Child of the wandering sea,
   Cast from her lap, forlorn!
From thy dead lips, a clearer note is born
Than ever Triton blew from wreathèd horn!
   While on mine ear it rings,
Through the deep caves of thought I hear a voice that sings:—

Build thee more stately mansions, O my soul,
   As the swift seasons roll!
   Leave thy low-vaulted past!
Let each new temple, nobler than the last,
Shut thee from heaven with a dome more vast,
   Till thou at length art free,
Leaving thine outgrown shell by life's unresting sea!

CONTENTMENT.

Little I ask; my wants are few;
   I only wish a hut of stone
(A *very plain* brown stone will do)
   That I may call my own;
And close at hand is such a one,
In yonder street that fronts the sun.

Plain food is quite enough for me;
   Three courses are as good as ten;—
If Nature can subsist on three,
   Thank Heaven for three. Amen!
I always thought cold victual nice;—
My *choice* would be vanilla ice.

I care not much for gold or land;—
   Give me a mortgage here and there,—
Some good bank-stock,—some note of hand,
   Or trifling railroad share;—
I only ask that Fortune send
A *little* more than I can spend.

Honors are silly toys, I know,
   And titles are but empty names;—
I would, *perhaps,* be Plenipo,—
   But only near St. James;—
I'm very sure I should not care
To fill our Gubernator's chair.

Jewels are baubles; 'tis a sin
   To care for such unfruitful things;—
One good-sized diamond in a pin,—
   Some, *not so large,* in rings,—
A ruby, and a pearl, or so,
Will do for me,—I laugh at show.

My dame should dress in cheap attire
   (Good, heavy silks are never dear);
I own, perhaps I *might* desire
   Some shawls of true cashmere,—
Some marrowy crapes of China silk,
Like wrinkled skins on scalded milk.

CHAPTER IX.

Edgar Allen Poe.

After more than fifty years, Poe is still something of a riddle; he was unfortunate in his biographers, who were either eulogists or enemies. He was more unfortunate in himself; he had not the capacity of truth, and mystified the events of his career. The son of actors, his inherited histrionic instinct prompted him to act many parts, until he lost the sense of his own individuality. He applied the great force of his imagination not only to the production of stories, but to the facts of real life; and his morbid vanity accented the distortion thus produced. In him a small and selfish nature was ever at war with a powerful and curious intellect; his character was a medley, fickle, weak and inconsistent. His career is a story of petty vicissitudes and ignoble misfortunes; of brilliant successes counteracted by perverse and unworthy follies. He was unfaithful to his friends and rancorous against his enemies; an unhappy man, driven to and fro by storms largely of his own raising. A congenital tendency to intemperance, ever confirming its hold upon him, darkened his life and hastened his death, which occurred in 1849, in his forty-first year. His wife, "Annabel Lee," had died two years before. So far as his personal acts and passions are concerned, Poe might be pronounced insane; but in the domain of intellect as applied to literature he was a unique and towering genius, author of some of the most exquisite and fascinating poetry, and of many of the most original and ingenious tales ever written in this country. His fame traveled far beyond his own country, and he is to-day more read in France than any other American author.

He was born in Boston in 1809; his parents both died in Richmond, Va., in 1815. He was then adopted by Mr. Allan, a rich Virginian. From the age of six to twelve he was at school in England; he attended the University of Virginia for a year, lost money by gambling, and then disappeared for a year. According to his own story, he went to aid Greece, but he probably never got further than London. In 1827 he published, at Boston, his first volume of poems, "Tamerlane." He enlisted as a private in the army, then was for nine months a cadet at West Point, but was dismissed for bad conduct.

Mr. Allan had hitherto supported Poe; but they now quarreled, and the young man of twenty-one set out to make a living by literature. A prize story, "A Manuscript Found in a Bottle," gained him the friendship of J. P. Kennedy, who made him editor of a Southern literary paper at a salary of $10 a week. The circulation of the magazine increased under his care, and he married his young cousin, Virginia Clemm. He soon after resigned his position and went to Philadelphia. He had already written "Hans Pfaal" and "Arthur Gordon Pym," and he now published the "Tales of the Grotesque and Arabesque," which confirmed his fame. He was also fitfully connected with two or three other periodicals. He wrote the "Murders in the Rue Morgue" in 1841, and two years later his "Gold Bug" won another prize of $100. At the age of five and thirty he was back in New York, writing for N. P. Willis's *Mirror* and other magazines; and in 1845 he wrote his famous poem "The Raven." He also lectured and wrote critiques, generally of a scathing character, but many of which posterity has justified. After his wife's death, his only work of importance was "Eureka," a speculative analysis of the universe.

Poe's stories fall into two classes, the analytical, of which the "Gold Bug" is an example, and the supernatural, such as "Ligeia." In many of his tales, however, these qualities are commingled. He was neither a humorist nor a character-painter, and none of his stories touch the heart; the man was deficient in human sympathies. They are to a high degree strange, impressive and ingenious, faultless in workmanship and structure, and masterpieces of art. They are finished, like gems, and of permanent literary worth: yet they can hardly be called works of inspiration: they are gems, not flowers. Poe's style is clear, succinct and polished, but self-conscious and artificial. The stories are by no means all of equal merit; Poe lacked good taste, and frequently overstepped the boundaries between the terrible and the revolting, the commonplace and the simple, fun and buffoonery. All his humorous tales are dismal failures. But when he is at his best, no writer can surpass him; we may say that he is unrivalled. In poetry, Poe is if possible more original and solitary than in his prose. The eerie and elfin beauty of some of his verses is magical; one is enchanted one knows not how. He had theories in poetry, as in prose; but it is probable that he squared his theories with his compositions, more often than the opposite. But there is more of art than of heart even in Poe's poetry; and we find that we go to him to be entertained and stimulated, but not for the needs of the deeper soul. His career was pathetic; but his genius is triumphant.

The Bells.

Hear the sledges with the bells—
Silver bells—
What a world of merriment their melody foretells!
How they tinkle, tinkle, tinkle,
In the icy air of night!
While the stars that oversprinkle
All the heavens, seem to twinkle
With a crystalline delight;
Keeping time, time, time,
In a sort of Runic rhyme
To the tintinnabulation that so musically wells
From the bells, bells, bells, bells,
Bells, bells, bells,—
From the jingling and the tinkling of the bells.

Hear the mellow wedding bells—
Golden bells!
What a world of happiness their harmony foretells!
Through the balmy air of night
How they ring out their delight!
From the molten-golden notes,
And all in tune,
What a liquid ditty floats
To the turtle-dove that listens while she gloats
On the moon!
Oh, from out the sounding cells,
What a gush of euphony voluminously wells!
How it swells!
How it dwells!
On the future! How it tells
Of the rapture that impels
To the swinging and the ringing

Of the bells, bells, bells,
Of the bells, bells, bells, bells,
Bells, bells, bells—
To the rhyming and the chiming of the bells!

Hear the loud alarum-bells—
Brazen bells!
What a tale of terror now their turbulency tells!
On the startled ear of night
How they scream out their affright!
Too much horrified to speak,
They can only shriek, shriek,
Out of tune,
In a clamorous appeal to the mercy of the fire,
In a mad expostulation with the deaf and frantic fire,
Leaping higher, higher, higher,
With a desperate desire,
And a resolute endeavor
Now—now to sit, or never,
By the side of the pale-faced moon.
Oh, the bells, bells, bells!
What a tale their terror tells
Of despair!
How they clang, and clash, and roar!
What a horror they outpour
On the bosom of the palpitating air!
Yet the ear, it fully knows,
By the twanging
And the clanging,
How the danger ebbs and flows;
Yet the ear distinctly tells,
In the jangling and the wrangling,
How the danger sinks and swells,
By the sinking or the swelling in the anger of the bells—
Of the bells, bells, bells, bells,
Bells, bells, bells—
In the clamor and the clangor of the bells!

Hear the tolling of the bells—
Iron bells!

What a world of solemn thought their melody compels!
In the silence of the night,
How we shiver with affright
At the melancholy menace of their tone;
For every sound that floats
From the rust within their throats
Is a groan.
And the people—ah, the people,
They that dwell up in the steeple,
All alone,
And who, tolling, tolling, tolling,
In that muffled monotone,
Feel a glory, in so rolling
On the human heart a stone:
They are neither man nor woman—
They are neither brute nor human—
They are Ghouls;
And their king it is who tolls;
And he rolls, rolls, rolls,
Rolls
A pæan from the bells!
And his merry bosom swells
With the pæan of the bells!
And he dances and he yells;
Keeping time, time, time,
In a sort of Runic rhyme,
To the pæans of the bells;
Keeping time, time, time,
In a sort of Runic rhyme
To the throbbing of the bells—
Of the bells, bells, bells—
To the sobbing of the bells!
Keeping time, time, time,
As he knells, knells, knells,
In a happy Runic rhyme,
To the rolling of the bells—
Of the bells, bells, bells;
To the tolling of the bells—
Of the bells, bells, bells, bells,
Bells, bells, bells—
To the moaning and the groaning of the bells.

Copyright by Underwood and Underwood, N. Y.
LOOKING DOWN THE CAÑON FROM INSPIRATION POINT.

The Raven.

Once upon a midnight dreary, while I pondered, weak and weary,
Over many a quaint and curious volume of forgotten lore;
While I nodded, nearly napping, suddenly there came a tapping,
As of some one gently rapping, rapping at my chamber door.
" 'Tis some visitor," I muttered, "tapping at my chamber door—
  Only this and nothing more."

Ah, distinctly I remember, it was in the bleak December,
And each separate dying ember wrought its ghost upon the floor.
Eagerly I wished the morrow; vainly I had sought to borrow
From my books surcease of sorrow—sorrow for the lost Lenore—
For the rare and radiant maiden whom the angels name Lenore—
  Nameless here forever more.

And the silken, sad, uncertain rustling of each purple curtain
Filled me with fantastic terrors never felt before;
So that now, to still the beating of my heart, I stood repeating,
" 'Tis some visitor entreating entrance at my chamber door;
Some late visitor entreating entrance at my chamber door;
  This it is, and nothing more."

Presently my soul grew stronger; hesitating then no longer,
"Sir," said I, "or Madam, truly your forgiveness I implore;
But the fact is, I was napping, and so gently came your rapping,
And so faintly you came tapping, tapping at my chamber door,
That I scarce was sure I heard you"—here I opened wide the door:—
  Darkness there and nothing more!

Deep into that darkness peering, long I stood there, wondering, fearing,
Doubting, dreaming dreams no mortal ever dared to dream before;
But the silence was unbroken, and the stillness gave no token,
And the only word there spoken was the whispered word "Lenore!"
This I whispered, and an echo murmured back the word "Lenore!"
  Merely this, and nothing more.

Back into my chamber turning, all my soul within me burning,
Soon again I heard a tapping somewhat louder than before.
"Surely," said I, "surely that is something at my window lattice;
Let me see, then, what thereat is, and this mystery explore—
Let my heart be still a moment, and this mystery explore;
        'Tis the wind, and nothing more!"

Open here I flung the shutter, when, with many a flirt and flutter,
In there stepped a stately Raven of the saintly days of yore;
Not the least obeisance made he; not an instant stopped or stayed he;
But, with mien of lord or lady, perched above my chamber door—
Perched upon a bust of Pallas just above my chamber door—
        Perched, and sat, and nothing more.

Then this ebony bird beguiling my sad fancy into smiling,
By the grave and stern decorum of the countenance it wore,
"Though thy crest be shorn and shaven, thou," I said, "art sure no craven,
Ghastly, grim and ancient Raven, wandering from the Nightly shore—
Tell me what thy lordly name is on the Night's Plutonian shore!"
        Quoth the Raven, "Nevermore!"

Much I marvelled this ungainly fowl to hear discourse so plainly,
Though its answer little meaning—little relevancy bore;
For we cannot help agreeing that no living human being
Ever yet was blest with seeing bird above his chamber door—
Bird or beast upon the sculptured bust above his chamber door,
        With such name as "Nevermore."

But the Raven, sitting lonely on the placid bust, spoke only,
That one word, as if his soul in that one word he did outpour.
Nothing further then he uttered—not a feather then he fluttered—
Till I scarcely more than muttered, "Other friends have flown before—
On the morrow *he* will leave me, as my hopes have flown before."
        Then the bird said, "Nevermore."

Startled at the stillness broken by reply so aptly spoken,
"Doubtless," said I, "what it utters is its only stock and store,
Caught from some unhappy master whom unmerciful Disaster
Followed fast and followed faster till his songs one burden bore—
Till the dirges of his Hope that melancholy burden bore
        Of 'Never—nevermore.'"

But the Raven still beguiling all my sad soul into smiling,
Straight I wheeled a cushioned seat in front of bird, and bust, and door;
Then, upon the velvet sinking, I betook myself to linking
Fancy unto fancy, thinking what this ominous bird of yore—
What this grim, ungainly, ghastly, gaunt and ominous bird of yore
        Meant in croaking "Nevermore."

Thus I sat engaged in guessing, but no syllable expressing
To the fowl whose fiery eyes now burned into my bosom's core;
This, and more, I sat divining, with my head at ease reclining
On the cushion's velvet lining that the lamp-light gloated o'er,
But whose violet velvet lining with the lamp-light gloating o'er,
        She shall press, ah, never more!

Then, methought, the air grew denser, perfumed from an unseen censer
Swung by seraphim whose footfalls tinkled on the tufted floor.
"Wretch," I cried, "thy God hath lent thee—by those angels he hath sent thee
Respite—respite and nepenthe from thy memories of Lenore!
Quaff, oh, quaff this kind nepenthe, and forget this lost Lenore!"
        Quoth the Raven, "Nevermore."

"Prophet!" said I, "thing of evil!—prophet still, if bird or devil!—
Whether Tempter sent, or whether tempest tossed thee here ashore,
Desolate, yet undaunted, on this desert land enchanted—
On this home by Horror haunted—tell me truly, I implore—
Is there—*is* there balm in Gilead?—tell me—tell me, I implore!"
        Quoth the Raven. 'Nevermore."

"Prophet!" said I, "thing of evil—prophet still, if bird or devil!"
By that Heaven that bends above us—by that God we both
    adore—
Tell this soul with sorrow laden if, within the distant Aidenn,
It shall clasp a sainted maiden whom the angels call Lenore—
Clasp a rare and radiant maiden, whom the angels name Lenore."
        Quoth the Raven, "Nevermore."

"Be that word our sign of parting, bird or fiend!" I shrieked
    upstarting—
"Get thee back into the tempest, and the Nights Plutonian shore!
Leave no black plume as a token of that lie thy soul hath spoken!
Leave my loneliness unbroken! quit the bust above my door!
Take thy beak from out my heart, and take thy form from off my
    door!"
        Quoth the Raven, "Nevermore."

And the Raven, never flitting, still is sitting, still is sitting
On the pallid bust of Pallas just above my chamber door;
And his eyes have all the seeming of a demon's that is dreaming,
And the lamplight o'er him streaming throws his shadow on the
    floor;
And my soul from out that shadow that lies floating on the floor
        Shall be lifted—nevermore!

CHAPTER X.

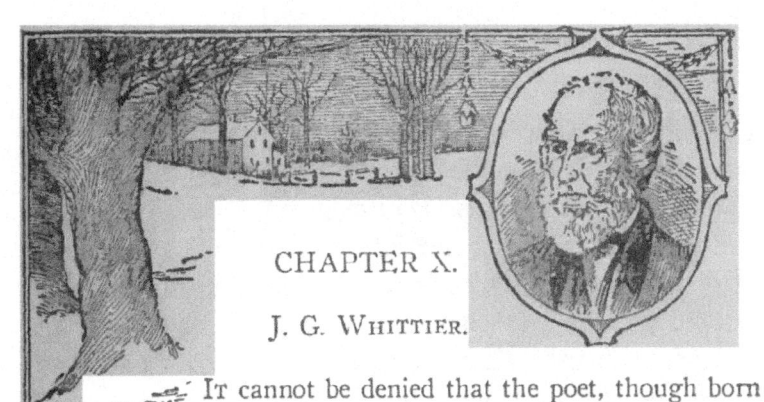

J. G. WHITTIER.

It cannot be denied that the poet, though born and not made, must be strongly influenced by his early surroundings. John Greenleaf Whittier was but little indebted to scholarly culture or to art or to literary companionship; he was self-made and largely self-taught. Born near Haverhill, Mass., on December 17th, 1807, he worked on his father's farm and received the rudiments of education at home. After he was seventeen years old, he attended the Haverhill Academy for two terms, and at nineteen he began to contribute anonymous poems to the *Free Press*, edited by Wm. Lloyd Garrison. Then began a friendship between the editor and the young poet which was cemented by their joint activity in the great Abolition Contest. Whittier wrote fervid anti-slavery lyrics, edited newspapers in Boston, Haverhill and Hartford, and was for a year a member of the Massachusetts legislature. In 1831, he published his first collection of poems, "Legends of New England," a number of Indian traditions, and shortly afterwards a poetical tale, "Mogg Megone." In 1836 he was appointed secretary of the American Anti-Slavery Society, and later became editor of the *Pennsylvania Freeman,* in Philadelphia. But the abolition cause was intensely unpopular; the printing office was at one time sacked and burned, and the editor was forced many times to face enraged mobs. In the *Freeman* appeared some of Whittier's best anti-slavery lyrics. There was crude force in these scornfully indignant lyrics, for though Whittier inherited Quaker blood, and adhered to the Quaker practice, he was a fiery apostle of human brotherhood. His health was always delicate, which he attributed to the "toughening" process, common when he was a boy. In 1840, he settled down at

Amesbury, Mass., where his sister and afterwards his niece abode with him. But for the last twenty years of his life he was deprived of the campanionship of relatives.

Poems inspired by the passion of political events as a rule are not of a lasting quality,—they pass away when the political questions that evoked them have been settled. Few readers to-day dip into the anti-slavery lyrics. But in writing them Whittier thought of other things than literary fame. He himself said that though he was not insensible to literary reputation, he set a higher value on his "name as appended to the anti-slavery declaration of 1833 than on the title page of any book."

Whittier wrote with ease and freedom and was a voluminous author. Among his best known books are, "Voices of Freedom," "Songs of Labor," "National Lyrics," "Snow-Bound," "Ballads of New England," "The Pennsylvania Pilgrim," "The King's Missive" and "At Sundown." A complete collection of the poet's writings in prose and verse revised by himself appeared a few years previous to his death, which took place on September 7th, 1892.

Whittier will always be best remembered for his charming New England idyl "Snow-Bound," into which his own early life and experiences on the farm were woven, and for such poems as "Maud Muller," "Barbara Fritchie," "In School Days," "Skipper Ireson's Ride" and "Telling the Bees." He is at his best in depicting peaceful and simple country scenes and characters. He lived close to the homely heart and life of the New England country people, and was to them a kind of lesser Robert Burns, not a writer of songs, yet a laureate of the woodlands, and of farm life, and of inland lakes and streams. His life was as simple and sweet as is most of his poetry. There was a harmony rarely found that intimately blended the poet's life with his poems.

The Worship of Nature.

The harp at Nature's advent strung
    Has never ceased to play;
The song the stars of morning sung
    Has never died away.

And prayer is made, and praise is given,
    By all things near and far;
The ocean looketh up to heaven,
    And mirrors every star.

Its waves are kneeling on the strand,
    As kneels the human knee,
Their white locks bowing to the sand,
    The priesthood of the sea!

They pour their glittering treasures forth,
    Their gifts of pearl they bring,
And all the listening hills of earth
    Take up the song they sing.

The green earth sends her incense up
    From many a mountain shrine;
From folded leaf and dewy cup
    She pours her sacred wine.

The mists above the morning rills
    Rise white as wings of prayer;
The altar curtains of the hills
    Are sunset's purple air.

The winds with hymns of praise are loud,
    Or low with sobs of pain,—
The thunder-organ of the cloud,
    The dropping tears of rain.

With drooping head and branches crossed
    The twilight forest grieves,
Or speaks with tongues of Pentecost
    From all its sunlit leaves.

The blue sky is the temple's arch,
  Its transept earth and air,
The music of its starry march
  The chorus of a prayer.

So Nature keeps the reverent frame
  With which her years began,
And all her signs and voices shame
  The prayerless heart of man.

The Grave by the Lake.

At the mouth of the Melvin River, which empties into Moultonboro Bay in Lake Winnipesaukee, is a great mound. The Ossipee Indians had their home in the neighborhood of the bay, which is plentifully stocked with fish, and many relics of their occupation have been found.

Where the Great Lake's sunny smiles
Dimple round its hundred isles,
And the mountain's granite ledge
Cleaves the water like a wedge,
Ringed about with smooth, gray stones,
Rest the giant's mighty bones.

Close beside, in shade and gleam,
Laughs and ripples Melvin stream;
Melvin water, mountain-born,
All fair flowers its banks adorn;
All the woodland's voices meet,
Mingling with its murmurs sweet.

Over lowlands forest-grown,
Over waters island-strown,
Over silver-sanded beach,
Leaf-locked bay and misty reach,
Melvin stream and burial-heap,
Watch and ward the mountains keep.

Who that Titan cromlech fills?
Forest-kaiser, lord o' the hills?
Knight who on the birchen tree
Carved his savage heraldry?
Priest o' the pine-wood temples dim,
Prophet, sage, or wizard grim?

Rugged type of primal man,
Grim utilitarian,
Loving woods for hunt and prowl,
Lake and hill for fish and fowl,
As the brown bear blind and dull
To the grand and beautiful:

Not for him the lesson drawn
From the mountains smit with dawn.
Star-rise, moon-rise, flowers of May,
Sunset's purple bloom of day,—
Took his life no hue from thence,
Poor amid such affluence?

Haply unto hill and tree
All too near akin was he:
Unto him who stands afar
Nature's marvels greatest are;
Who the mountain purple seeks
Must not climb the higher peaks.

Yet who knows in winter tramp,
Or the midnight of the camp,
What revealings faint and far,
Stealing down from moon and star,
Kindled in that human clod
Thought of destiny and God?

Stateliest forest patriarch,
Grand in robes of skin and bark,
What sepulchral mysteries,
What weird funeral-rites, were his?
What sharp wail, what drear lament,
Back scared wolf and eagle sent?

Now, whate'er he may have been,
Low he lies as other men;
On his mound the partridge drums,
There the noisy blue-jay comes;
Rank nor name nor pomp has he
In the grave's democracy.

Part thy blue lips, Northern lake!
Moss-grown rocks, your silence break!
Tell the tale, thou ancient tree!
Thou, too, slide-worn Ossipee!
Speak, and tell us how and when
Lived and died this king of men!

Wordless moans the ancient pine;
Lake and mountain give no sign;
Vain to trace this ring of stones;
Vain the search of crumbling bones:
Deepest of all mysteries,
And the saddest, silence is.

Nameless, noteless, clay with clay
Mingles slowly day by day;
But somewhere, for good or ill,
That dark soul is living still;
Somewhere yet that atom's force
Moves the light-poised universe.

Strange that on his burial sod
Harebells bloom, and golden-rod,
While the soul's dark horoscope
Holds no starry sign of hope!
Is the Unseen with sight at odds?
Nature's pity more than God's?

Thus I mused by Melvin's side,
While the summer eventide
Made the woods and inland sea
And the mountains mystery;
And the hush of earth and air
Seemed the pause before a prayer,—

Prayer for him, for all who rest,
Mother Earth, upon thy breast,—
Lapped on Christian turf, or hid
In rock-cave or pyramid:
All who sleep, as all who live,
Well may need the prayer, "Forgive!"

SNOW-BOUND.
A WINTER IDYL.

The sun that brief December day
Rose cheerless over hills of gray,
And, darkly circled, gave at noon
A sadder light than waning moon.
Slow tracing down the thickening sky
Its mute and ominous prophecy,
A portent seeming less than threat,
It sank from sight before it set.
A chill no coat, however stout,
Of homespun stuff could quite shut out,
A hard, dull bitterness of cold,
That checked, mid-vein, the circling race
Of life-blood in the sharpened face,
The coming of the snow-storm told.
The wind blew east; we heard the roar
Of Ocean on his wintry shore,
And felt the strong pulse throbbing there
Beat with low rhythm our inland air.

Meanwhile we did our nightly chores,—
Brought in the wood from out of doors,
Littered the stalls, and from the mows
Raked down the herd's-grass for the cows:
Heard the horse whinnying for his corn;
And, sharply clashing horn on horn,
Impatient down the stanchion rows
The cattle shake their walnut bows;
While, peering from his early perch
Upon the scaffold's pole of birch,
The cock his crested helmet bent
And down his querulous challenge sent.
Unwarmed by any sunset light
The gray day darkened into night,
A night made hoary with the swarm
And whirl-dance of the blinding storm,
As zigzag wavering to and fro
Crossed and recrossed the wingèd snow:
And ere the early bedtime came
The white drift piled the window frame,
And through the glass the clothes line posts
Looked in like tall and sheeted ghosts.

So all night long the storm roared on:
The morning broke without a sun;
In tiny spherule traced with lines
Of Nature's geometric signs,
In starry flake and pellicle
All day the hoary meteor fell;
And, when the second morning shone,
We looked upon a world unknown,
On nothing we could call our own.
Around the glistening wonder bent
The blue walls of the firmament,
No cloud above, no earth below,—
A universe of sky and snow!
The old familiar sights of ours
Took marvelous shapes; strange domes and towers
Rose up where sty or corn-crib stood,
Or garden wall or belt of wood;
A smooth white mound the brush pile showed,
A fenceless drift what once was road;
The bridle post an old man sat
With loose flung coat and high cocked hat;
The well-curb had a Chinese roof;
And even the long sweep, high aloof,
In its slant splendor, seemed to tell
Of Pisa's leaning miracle.

A prompt, decisive man, no breath
Our father wasted: "Boys, a path!"
Well pleased (for when did farmer boy
Count such a summons less than joy?)
Our buskins on our feet we drew;
With mittened hands, and caps drawn low,
To guard our necks and ears from snow,
We cut the solid whiteness through;
And, where the drift was deepest, made
A tunnel walled and overlaid
With dazzling crystal: we had read
Of rare Aladdin's wondrous cave,
And to our own his name we gave,
With many a wish the luck were ours
To test his lamp's supernal powers.
We reached the barn with merry din,
And roused the prisoned brutes within.

The old horse thrust his long head out,
And grave with wonder gazed about;
The cock his lusty greeting said,
And forth his speckled harem led;
The oxen lashed their tails, and hooked,
And mild reproach of hunger looked;
The hornèd patriarch of the sheep,
Like Egypt's Amun roused from sleep,
Shook his sage head with gesture mute,
And emphasized with stamp of foot.

All day the gusty north wind bore
The loosening drift its breath before;
Low circling round its southern zone,
The sun through dazzling snow-mist shone.
No church bell lent its Christian tone
To the savage air, no social smoke
Curled over woods of snow-hung oak.
A solitude made more intense
By dreary-voicèd elements,
The shrieking of the mindless wind,
The moaning tree boughs swaying blind,
And on the glass the unmeaning beat
Of ghostly finger tips of sleet.
Beyond the circle of our hearth
No welcome sound of toil or mirth
Unbound the spell, and testified
Of human life and thought outside.
We minded that the sharpest ear
The buried brooklet could not hear,
The music of whose liquid lip
Had been to us companionship,
And, in our lonely life, had grown
To have an almost human tone.

As night drew on, and, from the crest
Of wooded knolls that ridged the west,
The sun, a snow-blown traveler, sank
From sight beneath the smothering bank,
We piled with care our nightly stack
Of wood against the chimney back,—
The oaken log, green, huge, and thick,
And on its top the stout back-stick;

The knotty forestick laid apart,
And filled between with curious art
The ragged brush; then, hovering near,
We watched the first red blaze appear,
Heard the sharp crackle, caught the gleam
On whitewashed wall and sagging beam,
Until the old, rude-furnished room
Burst, flower-like, into rosy bloom;
While radiant with a mimic flame
Outside the sparkling drift became,
And through the bare-boughed lilac tree
Our own warm hearth seemed blazing free.
The crane and pendent trammels showed,
The Turks' heads on the andirons glowed;
While childish fancy, prompt to tell
The meaning of the miracle,
Whispered the old rhyme: *"Under the tree
When fire outdoors burns merrily,
There the witches are making tea."*

The moon above the eastern wood
Shone at its full; the hill-range stood
Transfigured in the silver flood,
Its blown snows flashing cold and keen,
Dead white, save where some sharp ravine
Took shadow, or the somber green
Of hemlocks turned to pitchy black
Against the whiteness of their back.
For such a world and such a night
Most fitting that unwarming light,
Which only seemed where'er it fell
To make the coldness visible.

Shut in from all the world without,
We sat the clean-winged hearth about,
Content to let the north wind roar
In baffled rage at pane and door,
While the red logs before us beat
The frost-line back with tropic heat;
And ever, when a louder blast
Shook beam and rafter as it passed,
The merrier up its roaring draught
The great throat of the chimney laughed,

The house dog on his paws outspread
Laid to the fire his drowsy head,
The cat's dark silhouette on the wall
A couchant tiger's seem to fall;
And, for the winter fireside meet,
Between the andirons' straddling feet,
The mug of cider simmered slow,
The apples sputtered in a row,
And, close at hand, the basket stood
With nuts from brown October's wood.

What matter how the night behaved?
What matter how the north wind raved?
Blow high, blow low, not all its snow
Could quench our hearth fire's ruddy glow.
O Time and Change!—with hair as gray
As was my sire's that winter day,
How strange it seems, with so much gone
Of life and love, to still live on!
Ah, brother! only I and thou
Are left of all that circle now,—
The dear home faces whereupon
That fitful firelight paled and shone.
Henceforward, listen as we will,
The voices of that hearth are still;
Look where we may, the wide earth o'er,
Those lighted faces smile no more.
We tread the paths their feet have worn,
   We sit beneath their orchard trees,
   We hear, like them, the hum of bees
And rustle of the bladed corn;
We turn the pages that they read,
   Their written words we linger o'er,
But in the sun they cast no shade,
No voice is heard, no sign is made,
   No step is on the conscious floor!
Yet Love will dream and Faith will trust
(Since He who knows our need is just)
That somehow, somewhere, meet we must.
Alas for him who never sees
The stars shine through his cypress trees!
Who, hopeless, lays his dead away,
Nor looks to see the breaking day

Across the mournful marbles play!
Who hath not learned, in hours of faith,
  The truth to flesh and sense unknown,
That Life is ever lord of Death,
  And Love can never lose its own!

We sped the time with stories old,
Wrought puzzles out, and riddles told,
Or stammered from our school-book lore
"The chief of Gambia's golden shore."
How often since, when all the land
Was clay in Slavery's shaping hand,
As if a far-blown trumpet stirred
The languorous, sin-sick air, I heard
"Does not the voice of reason cry,
  Claim the first right which Nature gave,
From the red scourge of bondage fly
  Nor deign to live a burdened slave!"
Our father rode again his ride
On Memphremagog's wooded side;
Sat down again to moose and samp
In trapper's hut and Indian camp;
Lived o'er the old idyllic ease
Beneath St. François' hemlock trees;
Again for him the moonlight shone
On Norman cap and bodiced zone;
Again he heard the violin play
Which led the village dance away,
And mingled in its merry whirl
The grandam and the laughing girl.
Or, nearer home, our steps he led
Where Salisbury's level marshes spread
Mile-wide as flies the laden bee;
Where merry mowers, hale and strong,
Swept, scythe on scythe, their swaths along
  The low green prairies of the sea.
We shared the fishing off Boar's Head,
  And round the rocky Isles of Shoals
The hake-broil on the driftwood coals;
The chowder on the sand-beach made,
Dipped, by the hungry, steaming hot,
With spoons of clam-shell from the pot.
We heard the tales of witchcraft old,

And dream and sign and marvel told
To sleepy listeners as they lay
Stretched idly on the salted hay,
Adrift along the winding shores,
    When favoring breezes deigned to blow
    The square sail of the gundalow,
And idle lay the useless oars.
Our mother, while she turned her wheel
Or run the new-knit stocking heel,
Told how the Indian hordes came down
At midnight on Cochecho town,
And how her own great-uncle bore
His cruel scalp-mark to fourscore.
Recalling, in her fitting phrase,
    So rich and picturesque and free
    (The common unrhymed poetry
Of simple life and country ways),
The story of her early days,—
She made us welcome to her home;
Old hearths grew wide to give us room;
We stole with her a frightened look
At the gray wizard's conjuring-book,
The fame whereof went far and wide
Through all the simple countryside;
We heard the hawks at twilight play,
The boat-horn on Piscataqua,
The loon's weird laughter far away;
We fished her little trout-brook, knew
What flowers in wood and meadow grew,
What sunny hillsides autumn-brown
She climbed to shake the ripe nuts down,
Saw where in sheltered cove and bay
The ducks' black squadron anchored lay,
And heard the wild geese calling loud
Beneath the gray November cloud.
Then, haply, with a look more grave,
And soberer tone, some tale she gave
From painful Sewel's ancient tome,
Beloved in every Quaker home,
Of faith fire-winged by martyrdom,
Or Chalkey's Journal, old and quaint,—
Gentlest of skippers, rare sea-saint!—
Who, when the dreary calms prevailed,

And water-butt and bread-cask failed,
And cruel, hungry eyes pursued
His portly presence, mad for food,
With dark hints muttered under breath
Of casting lots for life or death,
Offered, if Heaven withheld supplies,
To be himself the sacrifice.
Then, suddenly, as if to save
The good man from his living grave,
A ripple on the water grew,
A school of porpoise flashed in view.
"Take, eat," he said, "and be content;
These fishes in my stead are sent
By Him who gave the tangled ram
To spare the child of Abraham."

Our uncle, innocent of books,
Was rich in lore of fields and brooks,
The ancient teachers never dumb
Of Nature's unhoused lyceum.
In moons and tides and weather wise,
He read the clouds as prophecies,
And foul or fair could well divine,
By many an occult hint and sign,
Holding the cunning-warded keys
To all the woodcraft mysteries;
Himself to Nature's heart so near
That all her voices in his ear
Of beast or bird had meanings clear,
Like Apollonius of old,
Who knew the tales the sparrows told,
Or Hermes, who interpreted
What the sage cranes of Nilus said;
A simple, guileless, childlike man,
Content to live where life began;
Strong only on his native grounds,
The little world of sights and sounds
Whose girdle was the parish bounds,
Whereof his fondly partial pride
The common features magnified,
As Surrey hills to mountains grew
In White of Selborne's loving view.—
He told how teal and loon he shot.

And how the eagle's eggs he got,
The feats on pond and river done,
The prodigies of rod and gun;
Till, warming with the tales he told,
Forgotten was the outside cold,
The bitter wind unheeded blew,
From ripening corn the pigeons flew,
The partridge drummed i' the wood, the mink
Went fishing down the river brink.
In fields with bean or clover gay,
The woodchuck, like a hermit gray,
  Peered from the doorway of his cell;
The muskrat plied the mason's trade,
And tier by tier his mud-walls laid;
And from the shagbark overhead
  The grizzled squirrel dropped his shell.

Next, the dear aunt, whose smile of cheer
And voice in dreams I see and hear,—
The sweetest woman ever Fate
Perverse denied a household mate,
Who, lonely, homeless, not the less
Found peace in love's unselfishness,
And welcome wheresoe'er she went,
A calm and gracious element,
Whose presence seemed the sweet income
And womanly atmosphere of home,—
Called up her girlhood memories,
The huskings and the apple-bees,
The sleigh-rides and the summer sails,
Weaving through all the poor details
And homespun warp of circumstance
A golden woof-thread of romance.
For well she kept her genial mood
And simple faith of maidenhood;
Before her still a cloud-land lay,
The mirage loomed across her way;
The morning dew, that dried so soon
With others, glistened at her noon;
Through years of toil and soil and care,
From glossy tress to thin gray hair,
All unprofaned she held apart
The virgin fancies of the heart.

Be shame to him of woman born
Who had for such but thought of scorn.

There, too, our elder sister plied
Her evening task the stand beside;
A full, rich nature, free to trust,
Truthful and almost sternly just,
Impulsive, earnest, prompt to act,
And make her generous thought a fact,
Keeping with many a light disguise
The secret of self-sacrifice.
O heart sore-tried! thou hast the best
That Heaven itself could give thee,—rest,
Rest from all bitter thoughts and things!
  How many a poor one's blessing went
  With thee beneath the low green tent
Whose curtain never outward swings!

As one who held herself a part
Of all she saw, and let her heart
  Against the household bosom lean,
Upon the motley-braided mat
Our youngest and our dearest sat,
Lifting her large, sweet, asking eyes,
Now bathed within the fadeless green
And holy peace of Paradise.
Oh, looking from some heavenly hill,
  Or from the shade of saintly palms,
  Or silver reach of river calms,
Do those large eyes behold me still?
With me one little year ago:—
The chill weight of the winter snow
  For months upon her grave has lain;
And now, when summer south winds blow
  And brier and harebell bloom again,
I tread the pleasant paths we trod,
I see the violet-sprinkled sod,
Whereon she leaned, too frail and weak
The hillside flowers she loved to seek,
Yet following me where'er I went
With dark eyes full of love's content.
The birds are glad; the brier-rose fills
The air with sweetness; all the hills

Stretch green to June's unclouded sky;
But still I wait with ear and eye
For something gone which should be nigh,
A loss in all familiar things,
In flower that blooms, and bird that sings.
And yet, dear heart! remembering thee,
   Am I not richer than of old?
Safe in thy immortality,
   What change can reach the wealth I hold?
   What chance can mar the pearl and gold
Thy love hath left in trust with me?
   And while in life's late afternoon,
   Where cool and long the shadows grow,
I walk to meet the night that soon
   Shall shape and shadow overflow,
I cannot feel that thou art far,
Since near at need the angels are;
And when the sunset gates unbar,
   Shall I not see thee waiting stand,
And, white against the evening star,
   The welcome of thy beckoning hand?

CHAPTER XI.

Aldrich; Taylor.

ALDRICH has been an editor, novelist, and writer of travels. but is properly classed as a poet. In spite of his dainty verse and mildly humorous prose, he has not attained popularity, though his tender "Ballad of Babie Bell" and his short story of "Marjorie Daw," have been widely circulated.

Thomas Bailey Aldrich was born at Portsmouth, New Hampshire, in 1837. He removed to New York at the age of seventeen, and while employed in a publishing house began to write for newspapers and magazines. In 1866 he was called to Boston to become editor of *Every Saturday*, which position he held for eight years. After a year of travel in Europe he returned to Boston, but later fixed his residence at Ponkapog in the vicinity. From 1881 to 1890 he was editor of the *Atlantic Monthly*.

Aldrich's poems are usually short and carefully wrought, subdued in tone and suggestive rather than strongly picturesque. They exhibit a single phase or contrast of life, yet sometimes they run on in longer varied course, as in "Babie Bell," which relates sympathetically the advent and death of a child. In some of his pieces he describes aspects of his native New England, while others seem to belong to the remote East or realms of pure fancy. He has occasionally used blank verse, as in "Judith," and has even written a drama in prose. His short stories have been more successful than his novels, and his "Story of a Bad Boy," to some extent autobiographical, has been widely accepted as a fair picture of an average American boy.

Two Moods

I.

BETWEEN the budding and the falling leaf
Stretch happy skies;
With colors and sweet cries
Of mating birds in uplands and in glades
The world is rife.
Then on a sudden all the music dies,
The color fades.
How fugitive and brief
Is mortal life

Between the budding and the falling leaf!
O short-breathed music, dying on the tongue
Ere half the mystic canticle be sung!
O harp of life, so speedily unstrung!
Who, if 'twere his to choose, would know again
The bitter sweetness of the lost refrain,
Its rapture, and its pain?

II.

Though I be shut in darkness and become
Insentient dust blown idly here and there,
I count oblivion a scant price to pay
For having once had held against my lip
Life's brimming cup of hydromel and rue—
For having once known woman's holy love
And a child's kiss, and for a little space
Been boon companion to the Day and Night,
Fed on the odors of the summer dawn,
And folded in the beauty of the stars.
Dear Lord, though I be changed to senseless clay,
And serve the potter as he turns his wheel,
I thank Thee for the gracious gift of tears!

At Nijnii-Novgorod

"A crafty Persian set this stone;
    A dusk Sultana wore it;
  And from her slender finger, sir,
    A ruthless Arab tore it.

"A ruby, like a drop of blood—
    That deep-in tint that lingers
  And seems to melt, perchance was caught
    From those poor mangled fingers!

"A spendthrift got it from the knave,
    And tost it, like a blossom,
  That night into a dancing-girl's
    Accurst and balmy bosom.

"And so it went. One day a Jew
    At Cairo chanced to spy it
  Amid a one-eyed peddler's pack
    And did not care to buy it—

"Yet bought it all the same. You see,
　The Jew he knew a jewel.
He bought it cheap to sell it dear:
　The ways of trade are cruel.

"But I—be Allah's all the praise!—
　Such avarice, I scoff it!
If I buy cheap, why, I sell cheap,
　Content with modest profit.

"This ring—such chasing! Look, milord,
　What workmanship! By Heaven,
The price I name you makes the thing
　As if the thing were given!

"A stone without a flaw! A queen
　Might not disdain to wear it.
Three hundred roubles buys the stone;
　No kopeck less, I swear it!"

Thus Hassan, holding up the ring
　To me, no eager buyer.—
A hundred roubles was not much
　To pay so sweet a liar!

The Undiscovered Country

Forever am I conscious, moving here,
That should I step a little space aside
I pass the boundary of some glorified
Invisible domain—it lies so near!
Yet nothing know we of that dim frontier
Which each must cross, whatever fate betide,
To reach the heavenly cities where abide
(Thus Sorrow whispers) those that were most dear,
Now all transfigured in celestial light!
Shall we indeed behold them, thine and mine,
Whose going hence made black the noonday sun?—
Strange is it that across the narrow night
They fling us not some token, or make sign
That all beyond is not Oblivion.

Books and Seasons

BECAUSE the sky is blue; because blithe May
Masks in the wren's note and the lilac's hue;
Because—in fine, because the sky is blue
I will read none but piteous tales today.
Keep happy laughter till the skies be gray,
And the sad season cypress wears, and rue;
Them when the wind is moaning in the flue,
And ways are dark, bid Chaucer make us gay.
But now a little sadness! All too sweet
This springtide riot, this most poignant air,
This sensuous sphere of color and perfume!
So listen, love, while I the woes repeat
Of Hamlet and Ophelia, and that pair
Whose bridal bed was builded in a tomb.
—T. B. ALDRICH.

Bayard Taylor.

BAYARD TAYLOR was born in Chester County, Pennsylvania, on January 11th, 1825. His father was a farmer, belonging to the Society of Friends, and Bayard was apprenticed to a printing office. He soon began to contribute verses to the papers, and a collection of these early poems entitled "Ximena" was published in 1844. Then he made a pedestrian tour through Europe, and his vivacious account of his travels and experiences, entitled "Views Afoot; or Europe Seen with Knapsack and Staff" (1846), gained him a position on the staff of the *New York Tribune* in whose columns many of his sketches of travel first appeared.

It is as a lyric poet that Bayard Taylor shows his best qualities. Some of his songs, his Oriental idyls, and his Pennsylvania ballads are sure of an abiding place in American literature. His more elaborate poetical works are "The Poet's Journal" (1862), "The Picture of St. John" (1866), "The Masque of the Gods" (1872), "Lars" (1873), and "The Prophet" (1874), "Home Pastorals" (1875), and "Prince Deukalion" (1878).

NAPOLEON AT GOTHA.

We walk amid the currents of actions left undone,
The germs of deeds that wither before they see the sun.
For every sentence uttered, a million more are dumb:
Men's lives are chains of chances, and History their sum.

Not he, the Syracusan, but each impurpled lord
Must eat his banquet under the hair-suspended sword;
And one swift breath of silence may fix or change the fate
Of him whose force is building the fabric of a state.

Where o'er the windy uplands the slated turrets shine,
Duke August ruled at Gotha, in Castle Friedenstein,—
A handsome prince and courtly, of light and shallow heart,
No better than he should be, but with a taste for Art.

The fight was fought at Jena, eclipsed was Prussia's sun,
And by the French invaders the land was overrun;
But while the German people were silent in despair,
Duke August painted pictures, and curled his yellow hair.

Now, when at Erfurt gathered the ruling royal clan,
Themselves the humble subjects, their lord the Corsican,
Each bade to ball and banquet the sparer of his line:
Duke August with the others, to Castle Friedenstein.

Then were the larders rummaged, the forest-stags were slain,
The tuns of oldest vintage showered out their golden rain;
The towers were bright with banners,—but all the people said:
"We, slaves, must feed our master,—would God that he were dead!"

They drilled the ducal guardsmen, men young and straight and tall,
To form a double column, from gate to castle-wall;
And as there were but fifty, the first must wheel away,
Fall in beyond the others, and lengthen the array.

"*Parbleu!*" Napoleon muttered: "Your Highness' guards I prize,
So young and strong and handsome, and all of equal size."
"You, Sire," replied Duke August, "may have as fine, if you
Will twice or thrice repeat them, as I am forced to do!"

Now, in the Castle household, of all the folk, was one
Whose heart was hot within him, the Ducal Huntsman's son;
A bright and proud-eyed stripling; scarce fifteen years he had,
But free of hall and chamber; Duke August loved the lad.

He saw the forceful homage: he heard the shouts that came
From base throats, or unwilling, but equally of shame:
He thought: "*One* man has done it,—*one* life would free the land,
But all are slaves and cowards, and none will lift a hand!

"My grandsire hugged a bear to death, when broke his hunting-spear,
And has this little Frenchman a muzzle I should fear?
If kings are cowed, and princes, and all the land is scared,
Perhaps a boy can show them the thing they might have dared!"

Napoleon, on the morrow, was coming once again,
(And all the castle knew it) without his courtly train;
And, when the stairs were mounted, there was no other road
But one long, lonely passage, to where the Duke abode.

None guessed the secret purpose the silent stripling kept:
Deep in the night he waited, and, when his father slept,
Took from the rack of weapons a musket old and tried,
And cleaned the lock and barrel, and laid it at his side.

He held it fast in slumber, he lifted it in dreams
Of sunlit mountain-forests and stainless mountain-streams;
And in the morn he loaded—the load was bullets three:
"For Deutschland—for Duke August—and now the third for me!"

"What! ever wilt be hunting?" the stately Marshall cried;
"I'll fetch a stag of twenty!" the pale-faced boy replied,
As, clad in forest color, he sauntered through the court,
And said, when none could hear him: "Now, may the time be short!"

The corridor was vacant, the windows full of sun;
He stole within the midmost, and primed afresh his gun:
Then stood, with all his senses alert in ear and eye
To catch the lightest signal that showed the Emperor nigh.

A sound of wheels: a silence: the muffled sudden jar
Of guards their arms presenting: a footstep mounting far,
Then nearer, briskly nearer,—a footstep, and alone!
And at the farther portal appeared Napoleon!

Alone, his hands behind him, his firm and massive head
With brooded plans uplifted, he came with measured tread:
And yet, those feet had shaken the nations from their poise,
And yet, that will to shake them depended on the boy's!

With finger on the trigger, the gun held counter-wise,
His rapid heart-beats sending the blood to brain and eyes,
The boy stood, firm and deadly,—another moment's space,
And then the Emperor saw him, and halted, face to face.

A mouth as cut in marble, an eye that pierced and stung
As might a god's, all-seeing, the soul of one so young:
A look that read his secret, that lamed his callow will,
That inly smiled, and dared him his purpose to fulfil!

As one a serpent trances, the boy, forgetting all,
Felt but that face, nor noted the harmless musket's fall;
Nor breathed, nor thought, nor trembled: but, pale and cold as stone,
Saw pass, nor look behind him, the calm Napoleon.

And these two kept their secret; but from that day began
The sense of fate and duty that made the boy a man;
And long he lived to tell it,—and, better, lived to say:
"God's purposes were grander: He thrust me from His way!"

CHAPTER XII.

Recent Poets.

EDWIN MARKHAM was born in the state of Oregon in 1852. While yet a child his father died and the family removed to California. In very limited circumstances, his mother was unable to give him the early opportunities which she desired, but he developed an unusual fondness for nature and a free, out-of-door life. Added to this liking for woods and meadows and all living things was an insatiable love of reading. This last was hard to satisfy, because of the scarcity of reading material in a new country. Deprived of books in boyhood, as soon as fortune permitted, Markham became a book collector and acquired a fine private library.

By dint of hard effort, the future poet received first a Normal, then a college education. Nevertheless he felt that in many ways school life was less free and independent than he might have wished. Believing that manual labor should constitute a part of each one's work-a-day life, he applied himself to blacksmithing. However, during months passed as a smithy, he dreamed out poems for leisure hours.

For some time Markham has made his home in New York. His poems are known in many lands, for they have appealed particularly to those who have the welfare of humanity at heart and who look for some adjustment of present social wrongs. The *fraternity of man* is Markham's watchword, and in his *Man with a Hoe* and *The Sower* he has sought to bring home the misery of unceasing toil to those who remain deaf to all prayers and care for self alone. *Inasmuch* has been compared to Lowell's Vision of Sir Launfal. In lines like these the western poet continues to sing his songs for the world:

> There is a destiny that makes us brothers:
>   None goes his way alone:
> All that we send into the lives of others
>   Comes back into our own.

Brotherhood.

The crest and crowning of all good,
Life's final star, is Brotherhood;
For it will bring again to Earth
Her long-lost Poesy and Mirth;
Will send new light on every face,
A kingly power upon the race.
And till it come, we men are slaves,
And travel downward to the dust of graves.

Come, clear the way, then, clear the way;
Blind creeds and kings have had their day.
Break the dead branches from the path:
Our hope is in the aftermath—
Our hope is in heroic men,
Star-led to build the world again.
To this Event the ages ran:
Make way for Brotherhood—make way for Man.

The Butterfly.

O wingèd brother on the harebell, stay—
  Was God's hand very pitiful, the hand
  That wrought thy beauty at a dream's demand?
Yea, knowing I love so well the flowery way,
He did not fling me to the world astray—
  He did not drop me to the weary sand,
  But bore me gently to a leafy land:
Tinting my wings, He gave me to the day.

Oh, chide no more my doubting, my despair!
  I will go back now to the world of men.
Farewell, I leave thee to the world of air,
  Yet thou hast girded up my heart again;
For He that framed the impenetrable plan,
And keeps His word with thee, will keep with man.

THE GOBLIN LAUGH.

When I behold how men and women grind
   And grovel for some place of pomp or power,
   To shine and circle through a crumbling hour,
Forgetting the large mansions of the mind,
That are the rest and shelter of mankind;
   And when I see them come with wearied brains
   Pallid and powerless to enjoy their gains,
I seem to hear a goblin laugh unwind.

And then a memory sends upon its billow
   Thoughts of a singer wise enough to play,
   Who took life as a lightsome holiday:
Oft have I seen him make his arm a pillow,
Drink from his hand, and with a pipe of willow
   Blow a wild music down a woodland way.

IN POPPY FIELDS.

Here the poppy hosts assemble:
How they startle, how they tremble!
All their royal hoods unpinned
Blow out lightly in the wind.
Here is gold to labor for;
Here is pillage worth a war.

Men that in the cities grind,
Come! before the heart is blind.

EUGENE FIELD.

Of New England descent, but born in St. Louis in 1850, Eugene Field was a curious mixture of classical culture, roving fancy and wild West humor. He studied at more than one college, and after graduating from the University of Michigan in 1871, traveled in Europe. On his return he became a journalist, and was thus employed in several places before he settled in Chicago. Here for years Field filled a column daily with such whims and fancies, prose and verse, as entertained a host of readers. But this journalistic joker was an indefatigable collector of works and curios, and his last volume was "The Love Affairs of a Bibliomaniac." His fondness for children was shown not only in writing numerous lullabies and little folk's stories, but in his collection of their toys and trinkets. Field wrote some notable poems in Western dialect, and then varied his work by exquisite translations from Horace. During his life he issued a dozen volumes, and after his death, in 1895, his works were collected (10 vols., New York, 1896) with affectionate tributes from his friends.

Little Boy Blue.

The little toy dog is covered with dust,
    But sturdy and staunch he stands;
And the little toy soldier is red with rust,
    And his musket moulds in his hands.
Time was when the little toy dog was new,
    And the soldier was passing fair,
And that was the time when our Little Boy Blue
    Kissed them and put them there.

"Now, don't you go till I come," he said,
    "And don't you make any noise!"
So toddling off to his trundle-bed
    He dreamt of the pretty toys.
And as he was dreaming, an angel song
    Awakened our Little Boy Blue—
Oh, the years are many, the years are long,
    But the little toy friends are true.

Ay, faithful to Little Boy Blue they stand,
    Each in the same old place,
Awaiting the touch of a little hand,
    The smile of a little face.
And they wonder, as waiting these long years through,
    In the dust of that little chair,
What has become of our Little Boy Blue
    Since he kissed them and put them there.

WYNKEN, BLYNKEN AND NOD.

Wynken, Blynken, and Nod one night
    Sailed off in a wooden shoe,—
Sailed off on a river of misty light
    Into a sea of dew.
"Where are you going, and what do you wish?"
    The old moon asked the three.
"We have come to fish for the herring-fish
    That live in the beautiful sea;
    Nets of silver and gold have we,"
        Said Wynken,
        Blynken,
        And Nod.

The old moon laughed and sang a song,
    As they rocked in the wooden shoe;
And the wind that sped them all night long
    Ruffled the waves of dew;
The little stars were the herring-fish
    That lived in the beautiful sea.
"Now cast your nets wherever you wish,
    But never afeared are we!"
    So cried the stars to the fishermen three,
        Wynken,
        Blynken,
        And Nod.

All night long their nets they threw
    For the fish in the twinkling foam,
Then down the sky came the wooden shoe,
    Bringing the fishermen home;
'Twas all so pretty a sail, it seemed
    As if it could not be;
And some folks thought 'twas a dream they dreamed
    Of sailing that beautiful sea;
    But I shall name you the fishermen three;
        Wynken,
        Blynken,
        And Nod.

Wynken and Blynken are two little eyes,
  And Nod is a little head,
And the wooden shoe that sailed the skies
  Is the wee one's trundle-bed!
So shut your eyes while mother sings
  Of wonderful sights that be,
And you shall see the beautiful things
  As you rock on the misty sea
    Where the old shoe rocked the fishermen three,
      Wynken,
      Blynken,
      And Nod.

Joaquin Miller.

Joaquin Miller (1841-1913)—Cincinnatus Hiner Miller—was born in Indiana, but while yet a child his parents removed to Oregon. He studied law and shortly became identified with newspaper work.

Joaquin Miller traveled quite extensively in his later life, always attracting attention by the cow-boy costume he invariably wore. He is perhaps the boldest and most original of all the western poets. With serious faults that he never corrected, Miller displayed a certain spontaneity and freshness that gave his poems a welcome wherever they went. It is safe to say that they belong to a distinct stage of western civilization and as a product of that civilization alone will retain a place in the annals of American life.

Columbus.

  Behind him lay the gray Azores,
Behind the gates of Hercules;
Before him not the ghost of shores;
Before him only shoreless seas.
The good mate said: "Now must we pray,
For lo! the very stars are gone.
Brave Adm'r'l, speak; what shall I say?"
"Why, say: 'Sail on! sail on! and on!'"

"My men grow mutinous day by day;
My men grow ghastly wan and weak."
The stout mate thought of home; a spray
Of salt wave washed his swarthy cheek.
"What shall I say, brave Adm'r'l, say,
If we sight naught but seas at dawn?"
"Why, you shall say at break of day:
'Sail on! sail on! and on!'"

They sailed and sailed, as winds might blow,
Until at last the blanched mate said:
"Why, now not even God would know
Should I and all my men fall dead.
These very winds forget their way,
For God from these dread seas is gone.
Now speak, brave Adm'r'l; speak and say—"
He said: "Sail on! and on!"

They sailed. They sailed. Then spake the mate:
"This mad sea shows his teeth to-night.
He curls his lip, he lies in wait,
With lifted teeth, as if to bite!
Brave Adm'r'l, say but one good word:
What shall we do when hope is gone?"
The words leapt like a leaping sword:
"Sail on! sail on! sail on! and on!"

Then, pale and worn, he kept his deck,
And peered through darkness. Ah, that night
Of all dark nights! And then a speck—
A light! A light! A light! A light!
It grew, a starlit flag unfurled!
It grew to be Time's burst of dawn.
He gained a world; he gave that world
Its grandest lesson: "On! sail on!"

By the Balboa Seas.

The golden fleece is at our feet,
Our hills are girt in sheen of gold;
Our golden flower-fields are sweet
With honey hives. A thousand-fold
More fair our fruits on laden stem
Than Jordan tow'rd Jerusalem.

Behold this mighty sea of seas!
The ages pass in silence by.
Gold apples of Hesperides
Hang at our God-land gates for aye.
Our golden shores have golden keys
Where sound and sing the Balboa seas.

WALT WHITMAN.

WALT WHITMAN was born at West Hills, Long Island, on May 31, 1819. He was first a printer, then a teacher in country schools, and subsequently learned the carpenter's trade. He also contributed to newspapers and magazines and was at intervals connected with various papers in an editorial capacity. In 1849 he traveled through the western States, and afterwards took up his residence in New York City, where he frequented the society of newspaper men and litterateurs. In 1855 he published his notable work, "Leaves of Grass," in which he preaches the gospel of democracy and the natural man. It is a series of poems without rhyme or metrical form, dealing with moral, social and political problems. It was a new departure in literature, an unwonted method of conveying frank and untrammeled utterances. The book at first attracted but little attention, though it at once found some staunch admirers. Ralph Waldo Emerson said of it: "I find it the most extraordinary piece of wit and wisdom that America has yet contributed." This book Walt Whitman elaborated and added to for thirty years, and several editions have been published. It has excited bitter denunciation and warm approval. Original and forceful, Whitman cannot be judged by ordinary literary standards. His scornful trampling upon all metrical rules, and his freedom in treating of matters usually passed in silence, have so far been a decided barrier to the approval of his work.

During the war, Whitman became an hospital nurse at Washington. His experiences were wrought into a volume called "Drum Taps," since embodied with "Leaves of Grass." After the war he was for some years in the Government employ at Washington. He moved to Camden, New Jersey, in 1873. Besides adding to "Leaves of Grass," he published "Specimen Days and Collects" in 1883, "November Boughs" in 1885, "Sands at Seventy" in 1888, "Good-bye, my Fancy!" 1890.

Whitman died on March 26, 1892. His ambition was to be something more than a mere singer; a prophet and seer to his country and time. He has not yet been accepted by the people at large. He has won the approbation of some great minds, but so far he has not won the hearts of the people, to whom he dedicated his labors.

In All, Myself.

I am the poet of the Body and I am the poet of the Soul,
The pleasures of heaven are with me, and the pains of hell are with me;
The first I graft upon myself, the latter I translate into a new tongue.

I am the poet of the woman the same as the man,
And I say it is as great to be a woman as to be a man,
And I say there is nothing greater than the mother of men.

I chant the chant of dilation or pride,
We have had ducking and deprecation about enough,
I show that size is only development.

Have you outstript the rest? are you the President?
It is a trifle, they will more than arrive there everyone, and still pass on.
I am he that walks with the tender and growing night,
I call to the earth and sea, half-held by the night.
Press close bare-bosom'd night—press close magnetic nourishing night!
Night of South winds—night of the large few stars!
Still nodding night—mad naked summer night.

Smile, O voluptuous cool-breathed earth!
Earth of the slumbering and liquid trees!
Earth of departed sunset—earth of the mountains misty-topt!
Earth of the vitreous pour of the full moon just tinged with blue!
Earth of shine and dark mottling the tide of the river!
Earth of the limpid gray of clouds brighter and clearer for my sake!
Far-swooping elbow'd earth—rich apple-blossom'd earth!
Smile, for your lover comes.
Prodigal, you have given me love—therefore to you I give love!
O unspeakable passionate love.

The Pæan of Joy.

Now, trumpeter! for thy close,
Vouchsafe a higher strain than any yet;
Sing to my soul!—renew its languishing faith and hope;
Rouse up my slow belief—give me some vision of the future;
Give me, for once, its prophecy and joy.
O glad, exulting, culminating song!
A vigor more than earth's is in thy notes!
Marches of victory—man disenthralled—the conqueror at last!
Hymns to the universal God from universal Man—all joy!
A re-born race appears—a perfect world—all joy!
Women and men in wisdom, innocence, and health—all joy!
Riotous laughing bacchanals, filled with joy!
War, sorrowing, suffering gone—the rank earth purged—nothing but joy left!
The ocean filled with joy—the atmosphere all joy!
Joy! joy! in freedom, worship, love! Joy in the ecstasy of life!
Enough to merely be! Enough to breathe!
Joy! joy! all over joy!

There Was a Child Went Forth.

There was a child went forth every day;
And the first object he look'd upon, that object he became;
And that object became part of him for the day, or a certain part of the day, or for many years, or stretching cycles of years.
The early lilacs became part of this child,
And grass, and white and red morning-glories, and white and red clover, and the song of the phoebe-bird,

And the Third-month lambs, and the sow's pink-faint litter, and the mare's foal, and the cow's calf,
And the noisy brood of the barn-yard, or by the mire of the pond-side,
And the fish suspending themselves so curiously below there—and the beautiful curious liquid,
And the water-plants with their graceful flat heads—all became part of him.
The field-sprouts of Fourth-month and Fifth-month became part of him;
Winter-grain sprouts, and those of the light yellow corn, and the esculent roots of the garden,
And the apple-trees cover'd with blossoms, and the fruit afterward, and wood-berries, and the commonest weeds by the road;
And the old drunkard staggering home from the out-house of the tavern, whence he had lately risen,
And the school-mistress that pass'd on her way to the school,
And the friendly boys that pass'd—and the quarrelsome boys,
And the tidy and fresh-cheek'd girls—and the barefoot negro boy and girl,
And all the changes of city and country, wherever he went.
His own parents,
He that had father'd him, and she that had conceiv'd him in her womb, and birth'd him,
They gave this child more of themselves than that;
They gave him afterward every day—they became part of him.
The mother at home, quietly placing the dishes on the supper-table;
The mother with mild words—clean her cap and gown, a wholesome odor falling off her person and clothes as she walks by;
The father, strong, self-sufficient, manly, mean, anger'd, unjust;
The blow, the quick loud word, the tight bargain, the crafty lure,
The family usages, the language, the company, the furniture—the yearning and swelling heart,
Affection that will not be gainsay'd—the sense of what is real—the thought if, after all, it should prove unreal,
The doubts of day-time and the doubts of night-time—the curious whether and how,
Whether that which appears so is so, or is it all flashes and specks?
Men and women crowding fast in the streets—if they are not flashes and specks, what are they?

The streets themselves, and the façades of houses, and goods in
   the windows,
Vehicles, teams, the heavy-plank'd wharves—the huge crossing
   at the ferries,
The village on the highland, seen from afar at sunset—the river
   between,
Shadows, aureola and mist, the light falling on roofs and gables
   of white or brown, three miles off,
The schooner near by, sleepily dropping down the tide—the little
   boat slack-tow'd astern,
The hurrying tumbling waves, quick-broken crests, slapping,
The strata of color'd clouds, the long bar of maroon-tint, away
   solitary by itself—the spread of purity it lies motionless in,
The horizon's edge, the flying sea-crow, the fragrance of salt
   marsh and shore mud;
These became part of that child who went forth every day, and
   who now goes, and will always go forth every day.

One's-Self I Sing—

One's-Self I sing—a simple, separate Person;
Yet utter the word Democratic, the word *en masse*.
Of Physiology from top to toe I sing;
Not physiognomy alone, nor brain alone, is worthy for the muse—
   I say the Form complete is worthier far;
The Female equally with the male I sing.
Of Life immense in passion, pulse, and power,
Cheerful—for freest action form'd, under the laws divine,
The Modern Man I sing.

I think I could turn and live with animals, they are so placid and
   self-contain'd;
I stand and look at them long and long.
They do not sweat and whine about their condition;
They do not lie awake in the dark and weep for their sins;
They do not make me sick discussing their duty to God;
Not one is dissatisfied—not one is demented with the mania of
   owning things;
Not one kneels to another, nor to his kind that lived thousands of
   years ago;
Not one is respectable or industrious over the whole earth.
                                             —*Walt Whitman.*

O Captain! My Captain!

O Captain! my Captain! our fearful trip is done;
The ship has weather'd every rack, the prize we sought is won;
The port is near, the bells I hear, the people all exulting,
While follow eyes the steady keel, the vessel grim and daring:

    But O heart! heart! heart!
      O the bleeding drops of red,
    Where on the deck my Captain lies,
      Fallen cold and dead.

O Captain! my Captain! rise up and hear the bells;
Rise up—for you the flag is flung—for you the bugle trills;
For you bouquets and ribbon'd wreaths—for you the shores a-crowding;
For you they call, the swaying mass, their eager faces turning;

    Here Captain! dear father!
      This arm beneath your head;
    It is some dream that on the deck,
      You've fallen cold and dead.

My Captain does not answer, his lips are pale and still;
My father does not feel my arm, he has no pulse nor will;
The ship is anchor'd safe and sound, its voyage closed and done;
From fearful trip, the victor ship, comes in with object won:

    Exult, O shores, and ring, O bells!
      But I, with mournful tread,
    Walk the deck my Captain lies,
      Fallen cold and dead.

CHAPTER XIII.

Recent Poems.

Toujours Amour.

Prithee tell me, Dimple Chin,
At what age does love begin?
Your blue eyes have scarcely seen
Summers three, my fairy queen,
But a miracle of sweets,
Soft approaches, sly retreats,
Show the little archer there,
Hidden in your pretty hair;
When didst learn a heart to win?
Prithee tell me, Dimple Chin!

    "Oh!" the rosy lips reply,
      "I can't tell you if I try.
    'Tis so long I can't remember:
      Ask some younger lass than I!"

Tell, O tell me, Grizzled-Face,
Do your heart and head keep pace?
When does hoary Love expire,
When do frosts put out the fire?
Can its embers burn below
All that chill December snow?
Care you still soft hands to press,
Bonny heads to soothe and bless?
When does Love give up the chase?
Tell, O tell me, Grizzled-Face!

    "Ah!" the wise old lips reply,
      "Youth may pass and strength may die;
    But of Love I can't foretoken:
      Ask some older sage than I!"

"The Undiscovered Country."

    Could we but know
The land that ends our dark, uncertain travel,
  Where lie those happier hills and meadows low—
Ah, if beyond the spirit's inmost cavil,
  Aught of that country could we surely know,
    Who would not go?

    Might we but hear
The hovering angels' high imagined chorus,
 Or catch, betimes, with wakeful eyes and clear,
One radiant vista of the realm before us—
  With one rapt moment given to see and hear,
    Ah, who would fear?

    Were we quite sure
To find the peerless friend who left us lonely,
 Or there, by some celestial stream as pure,
To gaze in eyes that here were lovelit only—
  This weary mortal coil, were we quite sure,
    Who would endure?
        —*C. E. Stedman.*

The Symphony.

"O Trade! O Trade! would thou wert dead!
The Time needs heart—'tis tired of head:
We're all for love," the violins said.
"Of what avails the rigorous tale
Of bill for coin and box for bale?
Grant thee, O Trade! thine uttermost hope:
Level red gold with blue sky-slope,
And base it deep as devils grope:
When all's done, what hast thou won
Of the only sweet that's under the sun?
Ay, canst thou buy a single sigh
Of true love's least, least ecstasy?"
Then, with a bridegroom's heart-beats trembling,
All the mightier strings assembling
Ranged them on the violins' side
As when the bridegroom leads the bride,
And, heart in voice, together cried:
"Yea, what avail the endless tale
Of gain by cunning and plus by sale?
Look up the land, look down the land
The poor, the poor, the poor, they stand
Wedged by the pressing of Trade's hand
Against an inward-opening door
That pressure tightens evermore:
They sigh a monstrous foul-air sigh
For the outside leagues of liberty,
Where Art, sweet lark, translates the sky

Into a heavenly melody.
'Each day, all day' (these poor folks say),
'In the same old year-long, drear-long way,
We weave in the mills and heave in the kilns,
We sieve mine-meshes under the hills,
And thieve much gold from the Devil's bank tills,
To relieve, O God, what manner of ills?—
The beasts, they hunger, and eat, and die;
And so do we, and the world's a sty;
Rush, fellow-swine: why nuzzle and cry?
Swinehood hath no remedy
Say many men, and hasten by,
Clamping the nose and blinking the eye.
But who said once, in the lordly tone,
Man shall not live by bread alone
But all that cometh from the Throne?
          Hath God said so?
          But Trade saith *No*:
And the kilns and the curt-tongued mills say *Go!*
There's plenty that can, if you can't: we know.
Move out, if you think you're underpaid.
The poor are prolific; we're not afraid;
          Trade is trade.'"
Thereat this passionate protesting
Meekly changed, and softened till
It sank to sad requesting
And suggesting sadder still:
"And oh, if men might some time see
How piteous false the poor decree
That trade no more than trade must be!
Does business mean, *Die, you—live, I?*
Then 'Trade is trade' but sings a lie:
'Tis only war grown miserly.
If business is battle, name it so:
War-crimes less will shame it so,
And widows less will blame it so.
Alas, for the poor to have some part
In yon sweet living lands of Art,
Makes problem not for head, but heart.
Vainly might Plato's brain revolve it:
Plainly the heart of a child could solve it."

—*Sidney Lanier.*

The Rain.

The rain sounds like a laugh to me—
A low laugh poured out limpidly.
My very soul smiles as I listen to
  The low, mysterious laughter of the rain,
  Poured musically over heart and brain
Till sodden care, soaked with it through and through,
Sinks; and, with wings wet with it as with dew,
  My spirit flutters up, with every stain
  Rinsed from its plumage, and as white again
As when the old laugh of the rain was new.
  Then laugh on, happy Rain! laugh louder yet!—
Laugh out in torrent-bursts of watery mirth;
  Unlock thy lips of purple cloud, and let
Thy liquid merriment baptize the earth,
  And wash the sad face of the world, and set
The universe to music dripping-wet!

The Fishing Party.

Wunst we went a-fishin'—Me
An' my Pa an' Ma, all three,
When they wuz a picnic, 'way
Out to Hanch's Woods, one day.

An' they wuz a crick out there,
Where the fishes is, an' where
Little boys 't ain't big an' strong
Better have their folks along!

My Pa he ist fished an' fished!
An' my Ma she said she wished
Me an' her was home; an' Pa
Said he wished so worse'n Ma

Pa said ef you talk, er say
Anything, er sneeze, er play,
Hain't no fish, alive er dead,
Ever go' to bite! he said.

Purt' nigh dark in town when we
Got back home; an' Ma; says she,
Now she'll have a fish fer shore!
An' she buyed one at the store.

Nen at supper, Pa he won't
Eat no fish, an' says he don't
Like 'em.—An' he pounded me
When I choked! . . Ma, didn't he?

—*J. W. Riley.*

ODIUM THEOLGICUM.

I.

They met and they talked where the cross-roads meet,
  Four men from the four winds come,
And they talked of the horse, for they loved the theme,
  And never a man was dumb.
And the man from the North loved the strength of the horse,
  And the man from the East his pace,
And the man from the South loved the speed of the horse,
  The man from the West his grace.

So these four men from the four winds come,
  Each paused a space in his course
And smiled in the face of his fellow-man
  And lovingly talked of the horse.
Then each man parted and went his way
  As their different courses ran;
And each man journeyed with peace in his heart
  And loving his fellow-man.

II.

They met the next year where the cross-roads meet,
  Four men from the four winds come;
And it chanced as they met that they talked of God,
  And never a man was dumb.
One imaged God in the shape of a man,
  A spirit did one insist;
One said that Nature itself was God,
  One said that He didn't exist.

But they lashed each other with tongues that stung,
  That smote as with a rod:
Each glared in the face of his fellow-man,
  And wrathfully talked of God.
Then each man parted and went his way,
  As their different courses ran:
And each man journeyed with war in his heart,
  And hating his fellow-man.

MIRACLES.

Since I have listened to the song
    The melted snow-bank sings,
I've roamed the earth a credulous man,
    Believing many things.
The snow which made the mountains white
    Made green the babbling lea;
And since that day have miracles
    Been commonplace to me.

Sprung from the slime of sluggish streams,
    Inert, and dark, and chilly,
Have I not seen the miracle
    And glory of the lily?
Have I not seen, when June's glad smile
    Upon the earth reposes,
The cosmic impulse in the clod
    Reveal itself in roses?

Have I not seen the frozen hill,
    Where snowy chaos tosses,
Smile back upon the smiling sun
    With violets and mosses?
Have I not seen the dead old world
    Rise to a newer birth,
When fragrance from the lilac blooms
    Rejuvenates the earth?

Have I not seen the rolling earth,
    A clod of frozen death,
Burst from its grave-clothes of the snow
    Touched by an April breath?
Have I not seen the bareboughed tree,
    That from the winter shrinks,
Imparadised in apple blooms
    And loud with bobolinks?

Now who can riddle me this thing?
    Or tell me how or where
The tulip stains its crimson cup
    From the transparent air?
So from the wonder-bearing day
    I take the gifts it brings,
And roam the earth a credulous man,
    Believing many things.

—S. W. Foss.

I.

I asked no other thing,
  No other was denied.
I offered Being for it;
  The mighty merchant smiled.

Brazil? He twirled a button,
  Without a glance my way:
"But, madam, is there nothing else
  That we can show today?"

II.

Will there really be a morning?
  Is there such a thing as day?
Could I see it from the mountains
  If I were as tall as they?

Has it feet like water-lilies?
  Has it feathers like a bird?
Is it brought from famous countries
  Of which I have never heard?

Oh, some scholar! Oh, some sailor!
  Oh, some wise man from the skies!
Please to tell a little pilgrim
  Where the place called morning lies!

III.

Have you a brook in your little heart,
  Where bashful flowers blow,
And blushing birds go down to drink,
  And shadows tremble so?

And nobody knows, so still it flows,
  That any brook is there;
And yet your little draught of life
  Is daily drunken there.

A MEXICAN CATHEDRAL.

Then look out for the little brook in March,
    When the rivers overflow,
And the snows come hurrying from the hills,
    And the bridges often go.

And later, in August it may be,
    When the meadows parching lie,
Beware, lest this little brook of life
    Some burning noon go dry!
                  —*Emily Dickinson.*

AMERICAN FICTION

CHAPTER XIV.

American Life in American Fiction.

The Rise of Silas Lapham.

Lapham had the pride which comes of self-making, and he would not openly lower his crest to the young fellow he had taken into his business. He was going to be obviously master in his own place to every one; and during the hours of business he did nothing to distinguish Corey from the half dozen other clerks and bookkeepers in the outer office, but he was not silent about the fact that Bromfield Corey's son had taken a fancy to come to him. "Did you notice that fellow at the desk facing my typewriter girl? Well, sir, that's the son of Bromfield Corey—old Phillips Corey's grandson. And I'll say this for him, that there isn't a man in the office that looks after his work better. There isn't anything he's too good for. He's right here at nine every morning, before the clock gets in the word. I guess it's his grandfather coming out in him. He's got charge of the foreign correspondence. We're pushing the paint everywhere." He flattered himself that he did not lug the matter in. He had been warned against that by his wife, but he had the right to do Corey justice, and his brag took the form of illustration. "Talk about training for business. I tell you it's all in the man himself! I used to believe in what old Horace Greeley said about college graduates being the poorest kind of horned cattle, but I've changed my mind a little. You take that fellow Corey. He's been through Harvard, and he's had about every advantage that a fellow could have. Been everywhere, and talks half a dozen languages like English. I suppose he's got money enough to live without lifting a hand, any more than his father does; son of Bromfield Corey, you know. But the thing was in him. He's a natural born business man; and I've had many a fellow with me that had come up out of the street, and worked hard all his life, without ever losing his original opposition to the thing. But Corey likes it. I believe the fellow would like to stick at that desk of his night and day. I don't know where he got it. I guess it must be his grandfather, old Phillips Corey; it often skips a generation, you know. But what I say is, a thing has got to be born in a man; and if it ain't born in him, all the privations in the world won't put it there, and if it is, all the college training won't take it out."

Sometimes Lapham advanced these ideas at his own table, to a guest whom he brought to Nantasket for the night. Then he suffered exposure and ridicule at the hands of his wife, when opportunity offered. She would not let him bring Corey down to Nantasket at all.

"No, indeed!" she said. "I am not going to have them think we're running after him. If he wants to see Irene, he can find out ways of doing it for himself."

"Who wants him to see Irene?" retorted the Colonel angrily.

"I do," said Mrs. Lapham. "And I want him to see her without any of your connivance, Silas. I'm not going to have it said that I put my girls *at* anybody. Why don't you invite some of your other clerks?"

"He ain't just like other clerks. He's going to take charge of a part of the business. It's quite another thing."

"Oh, indeed!" said Mrs. Lapham vexatiously. "Then you *are* going to take a partner."

"I shall ask him down if I choose!" retorted the Colonel. disdaining her insinuation.

His wife laughed with the fearlessness of a woman who knows her husband.

"But you won't choose when you've thought it over, Si." Then she applied an emollient to his chafed surface. "Don't you suppose I feel as you do about it? I know just how proud you are, and I'm not going to have you do anything that will make you feel meeching afterward. You just let things take their course. If he wants Irene, he's going to find out some way of seeing her; and if he don't, all the plotting and planning in the world isn't going to make him."

"Who's plotting?" again retorted the Colonel, shuddering at the utterance of hopes and ambitions which a man hides with shame, but a woman talks over as freely and coolly as if they were items of a milliner's bill.

"Oh, not *you!*" exulted his wife. "I understand what *you* want. You want to get this fellow, who is neither partner nor clerk, down here to talk business with him. Well, now, you just talk business with him at the office."

The only social attention which Lapham succeeded in offering Corey was to take him in his buggy, now and then, for a spin out over the Milldam. He kept the mare in town, and on a pleasant afternoon he liked to knock off early, as he phrased it, and let the mare out a little. Corey understood something about horses, though in a passionless way, and he would have preferred to talk business when obliged to talk horse. But he deferred to his business superior with the sense of discipline which is innate in the apparently insubordinate American nature. If Corey could hardly help feeling the social difference between Lapham and himself, in his presence he silenced his traditions, and showed him all the respect that he could have exacted from any of his clerks. He talked horse with him, and when the Colonel wished he talked house. Besides himself and his paint Lapham had not many other topics, and if he had a choice between the mare and the edifice on the water side of Beacon street, it was just now the latter. Sometimes, in driving in or out, he stopped at the house, and made Corey his guest there, if he might not at Nantasket; and one day it happened that the young man met Irene there again. She had come up with her mother alone, and they were in the house, interviewing the carpenter as before, when the Colonel jumped out of his buggy and cast anchor at the pavement. More exactly, Mrs. Lapham was interviewing the carpenter, and Irene was sitting in the bow-window on a trestle, and looking out at the driving. She saw him come up with her father, and bowed and blushed. Her father went on upstairs to find her mother, and Corey pulled up another trestle which he found in the back part of the room. The first floorings had been laid throughout the house, and the partitions had been lathed so that one could realize the shape of the interior.

"I suppose you will sit at this window a good deal," said the young man.

"Yes, I think it will be very nice. There's so much more going on than there is in the Square."

"It must be very interesting to you to see the house grow."

"It is. Only it doesn't seem to grow so fast as I expected."

"Why, I'm amazed at the progress your carpenter has made every time I come."

The girl looked down, and then lifting her eyes she said, with a sort of timorous appeal:

"I've been reading that book since you were down at Nantasket."

"Book?" repeated Corey, while she reddened with disappointment. "Oh, yes. *Middlemarch*. Did you like it?"

"I haven't got through with it yet. Pen has finished it."

"What does she think of it?"

"Oh, I think she likes it very well. I haven't heard her talk about it much. Do you like it?"

"Yes; I liked it immensely. But it's several years since I read it."

"I didn't know it was so old. It's just got into the Seaside Library," she urged, with a little sense of injury in her tone.

"Oh, it hasn't been out such a great while," said Corey politely. "It came a little before *Daniel Deronda*."

The girl was again silent. She followed the curl of a shaving on the floor with the point of her parasol.

"Do you like that Rosamond Vincy?" she asked, without looking up.

Corey smiled in his kind way.

"I didn't suppose she was expected to have any friends. I can't say I liked her. But I don't think I disliked her so much as the author does. She's pretty hard on good-looking"—he was going to say girls, but as if that might have been rather personal, he said—"people."

"Yes, that's what Pen says. She says she doesn't give her any chance to be good. She says she should have been just as bad as Rosamond if she had been in her place."

The young man laughed. "Your sister is very satirical, isn't she?"

"I don't know," said Irene, still intent upon the convolutions of the shaving. "She keeps us laughing. Papa thinks that there's nobody that can talk like her." She gave the shaving a little toss from her, and took the parasol up across her lap. The unworldliness of the Lapham girls did not extend to their dress; Irene's costume was very stylish, and she governed her head and shoulders stylishly. "We are going to have the back room upstairs for a music-room and library," she said abruptly.

"Yes?" returned Corey. "I should think that would be charming."

"We expected to have book-cases, but the architect wants to build the shelves in."

The fact seemed to be referred to Corey for his comment.

"It seems to me that would be the best way. They'll look like part of the room then. You can make them low, and hang your pictures above them."

"Yes, that's what he said." The girl looked out of the window in adding, "I presume with nice bindings it will look very well."

"Oh, nothing furnishes a room like books."

"No. There will have to be a good many of them."

"That depends upon the size of your room and the number of your shelves."

"Oh, of course! I presume," said Irene, thoughtfully, "we shall have to have Gibbon."

"If you want to read him," said Corey, with a laugh of sympathy for an imaginable joke.

"We had a great deal about him at school. I believe we had one of his books. Mine's lost, but Pen will remember."

The young man looked at her, and then said, seriously: "You'll want Greene, of course, and Motley, and Parkman."

"Yes. What kind of writers are they?"

"They're historians, too."

"Oh, yes; I remember now. That's what Gibbon was. Is it Gibbon or Gibbons?"

The young man decided the point with apparently superfluous delicacy. "Gibbon, I think."

"There used to be so many of them," said Irene gaily. "I used to get them mixed up with each other, and I couldn't tell them from the poets. Should you want to have poetry?"

"Yes; I suppose some edition of the English poets."

"We don't any of us like poetry. Do you like it?"

"I'm afraid I don't very much," Corey owned. "But, of course, there was a time when Tennyson was a great deal more to me than he is now."

"We had something about him at school, too. I think I remember the name. I think we ought to have *all* the American poets."

"Well, not all. Five or six of the best: you want Longfellow and Bryant and Whittier and Holmes and Emerson and Lowell."

The girl listened attentively, as if making mental note of the names.

"And Shakespeare," she added. "Don't you like Shakespeare's plays?"

"Oh, yes, very much."

"I used to be perfectly crazy about his plays. Don't you think 'Hamlet' is splendid? We had ever so much about Shakespeare. Weren't you perfectly astonished when you found out how many other plays of his there were? I always thought there was nothing but 'Hamlet' and 'Romeo and Juliet' and 'Macbeth' and 'Richard III' and 'King Lear,' and that one that Robeson and Crane have—Oh, yes! 'Comedy of Errors.'"

"Those are the ones they usually play," said Corey.

"I presume we shall have to have Scott's works," said Irene, returning to the question of books.

"Oh, yes."

"One of the girls used to think he was *great*. She was always talking about Scott." Irene made a pretty little amiably contemptuous mouth. "He isn't American, though?" she suggested.

"No," said Corey; "he's Scotch, I believe."

Irene passed her glove over her forehead. "I always get him mixed up with Cooper. Well, papa has got to get them. If we have a library, we have got to have books in it. Pen says it's perfectly ridiculous having one. But papa thinks whatever the architect says is right. He fought him hard enough at first. I don't see how anyone can keep the poets and the historians and novelists separate in their mind. Of course papa will buy them if we say so. But I don't see how I am ever going to tell him which ones." The joyous light faded out of her face and left it pensive.

"Why, if you like," said the young man, taking out his pencil, "I'll put down the names we've been talking about."

He clapped himself on his breast pockets to detect some lurking scrap of paper.

"Will you?" she cried delightedly. "Here! take one of my cards," and she pulled out her card-case. "The carpenter writes it on a three-cornered block and puts it into his pocket, and it's so uncomfortable he can't help remembering it. Pen says she's going to adopt the three-cornered-block plan with papa."

"Thank you," said Corey. "I believe I'll use your card." He crossed over to her, and after a moment sat down on the trestle beside her. She looked over the card as he wrote. "Those are the ones we mentioned, but perhaps I'd better add a few others."

"Oh, thank you," she said, when he had written the card full on both sides. "He has got to get them in the nicest binding, too. I shall tell him about their helping to refurnish the room, and then he can't object." She remained with the card, looking at it rather wistfully.

Perhaps Corey divined her trouble of mind. "If he will take that to any bookseller, and tell him what bindings he wants, he will fill the order for him."

"Oh, thank you very much," she said, and put the card back into her card-case with great apparent relief. Then she turned her lovely face toward the young man, beaming with the triumph a woman feels in any bit of successful maneuvering, and began to talk with recovered gayety of other things, as if, having got rid of a matter annoying out of all proportion to its importance, she was now going to indemnify herself.

—*W. D. Howells.*

A Little Journey in the World.

Our lives are largely made up of the things we do not have. In May, the time of the apple blossom—just a year from the swift wooing of Margaret—Miss Forsythe received a letter from John Lyon. It was in a mourning envelope. The Earl of Chisholm was dead, and John Lyon was Earl of Chisholm. The information was briefly conveyed, but with an air of profound sorrow. The letter spoke of the change that this loss brought to his own life, and the new duties laid upon him, which would confine him more closely to England. It also contained congratulations—which circumstances had delayed—upon Mrs. Henderson's marriage, and a simple wish for her happiness. The letter was longer than it need have been for these purposes; it seemed to love to dwell upon the little visit to Brandon and the circle of friends there, and it was pervaded by a tone, almost affectionate, towards Miss Forsythe, which touched her very deeply. She said it was such a manly letter.

America, the earl said, interested him more and more. In all history, he wrote, there never had been such an opportunity for studying the formation of society, for watching the working out of political problems; the elements meeting were so new, and the conditions so original, that historical precedents were of little service as guides. He acknowledged an almost irresistible impulse to come back, and he announced his intention of another visit as soon as circumstances permitted.

I had noticed this in English travelers of intelligence before. Crude as the country is, and uninteresting according to certain established standards, it seems to have a "drawing" quality, a certain unexplained fascination. Morgan says that it is the social unconventionality that attracts, and that the American women are the lodestone. He declares that when an Englishman secures and carries home with him an American wife, his curiosity about the country is sated. But this is generalizing on narrow premises.

There was certainly in Lyon's letter a longing to see the country again, but the impression it made upon me when I read it—due partly to its tone towards Miss Forsythe, almost a family tone—was that the earldom was an empty thing without the love of Margaret Debree. Life is so brief at the best, and has so little in it when the one thing that the heart desires is denied. That the earl should wish to come to America again without hope or expectation was, however, quite human nature. If a man has found a diamond and lost it, he is likely to go again and again and wander about the field where he found it, not perhaps in any defined hope of finding another, but because there is a melancholy satisfaction in seeing the spot again. It was some such feeling that impelled the earl to wish to see again Miss Forsythe, and perhaps to talk to Margaret, but he certainly had no thought that there were two Margaret Debrees in America.

To her aunt's letter conveying the intelligence of Mr. Lyon's loss, Margaret replied with a civil message of condolence. The news had already reached the Eschelles, and Carmen, Margaret said, had written to the new earl a most pious note, which contained no allusion to his change of fortune, except an expression of sympathy with his now enlarged opportunity for carrying on his philanthropic plans—a most unworldly note. "I used to think," she had said, when confiding what she had done to Margaret, "that you would make a perfect missionary countess, but you have done better, my dear, and taken up a much more difficult work among us fashionable sinners. Do you know," she went on, "that I feel a great deal less worldly than I used to."

Margaret wrote a most amusing account of this interview, and added that Carmen was really very good-hearted, and not half as worldly-minded as she pretended to be; an opinion with which Miss Forsythe did not at all agree. She had spent a fortnight with Margaret after Easter, and she came back in a dubious frame of mind. Margaret's growing intimacy with Carmen was one of the sources of her uneasiness. They appeared to be more and more companionable, although Margaret's clear perception of character made her estimate of Carmen very nearly correct. But the fact remained that she found her company interesting. Whether the girl tried to astonish the country aunt, or whether she was so thoroughly a child of her day as to lack certain moral perceptions, I do not know, but her candid conversation greatly shocked Miss Forsythe.

"Margaret," she said one day, in one of her apparent bursts of confidence, "seems to have had such a different start in life from mine. Sometimes, Miss Forsythe, she puzzles me. I never saw anybody so much in love as she is with Mr. Henderson; she doesn't simply love him, she is *in* love with him. I don't wonder she is fond of him—any woman might be that—but, do you know, she actually believes in him."

"Why shouldn't she believe in him?" exclaimed Miss Forsythe, in astonishment.

"Oh, of course, in a way," the girl went on. "I like Mr. Henderson—I like him very much—but I don't believe in him. It isn't the way now to believe in anybody very much. We don't do it, and I think we get along just as well—and better. Don't you think it's nicer not to have any deceptions?"

Miss Forsythe was too stunned to make any reply. It seemed to her that the bottom had fallen out of society.

"Do you think Mr. Henderson believes in people?" the girl persisted.

"If he does not he isn't much of a man. If people don't believe in each other, society is going to pieces. I am astonished at such a tone from a woman."

"Oh, it isn't any tone in me, my dear Miss Forsythe," Carmen continued, sweetly. 'Society is a great deal pleasanter when you are not anxious and don't expect too much."

Miss Forsythe told Margaret that she thought Miss Eschelle was a dangerous woman. Margaret did not defend her, but she did not join, either, in condemning her; she appeared to have accepted her as part of her world. And there were other things that Margaret seemed to have accepted without that vigorous protest which she used to raise at whatever crossed her conscience. To her aunt she was never more affectionate, never more solicitous about her comfort and her pleasure, and it was almost enough to see Margaret happy, radiant, expanding day by day in the prosperity that was illimitable, only there was to her a note of unreality in all the whirl and hurry of the busy life. She liked to escape to her room with a book, and be out of it all, and the two weeks away from her country life seemed long to her. She couldn't reconcile Margaret's love of the world, her tolerance of Carmen, and other men and women whose lives seemed to be based on Carmen's philosophy, with her devotion to the church services, to the city missions, and the dozens of charities that absorb so much of the time of the leaders of society.

"You are too young, dear, to be so good and devout," was Carmen's comment on the situation.

To Miss Forsythe's wonder, Margaret did not resent this impertinence, but only said that no accumulation of years was likely to bring Carmen into either of these dangers. And the reply was no more satisfactory to Miss Forsythe than the remark that provoked it.

That she had had a delightful visit, that Margaret was more lovely than ever, that Henderson was a delighted host, was the report of Miss Forsythe when she returned to us. In a confidential talk with my wife she confessed, however, that she couldn't tell whither Margaret was going.

One of the worries of modern life is the perplexity where to spend the summer. The restless spirit of change affects those who dwell in the country, as well as those who live in the city. No matter how charming the residence is, one can stay in it only a part of the year. He actually needs a house in town, a villa by the sea, and a cottage in the hills. When these are secured—each one an establishment more luxurious year by year—then the family is ready to travel about, and is in a greater perplexity than before whether to spend the summer in Europe or in America, the novelties of which are beginning to excite the imagination. This nomadism, which is nothing less than society on wheels, cannot be satirized as a whim of fashion; it has a serious cause in the discovery of the disease called nervous prostration, which demands for its cure constant change of scene, without any occupation. Henderson recognized it, but he said that personally he had no time to indulge in it. His summer was to be a very busy one. It was impossible to take Margaret with him on his sudden and tedious journey from one end of the country to the other, but she needed a change. It was therefore arranged that after a visit to Brandon she should pass the warm months with the Arbusers in their summer home at Lenox, with a month—the right month—in the Eschelle villa at Newport; and he hoped never to be long absent from one place or the other.

Margaret came to Brandon at the beginning of June, just at the season when the region was at its loveliest, and just when its society was making preparations to get away from it to the sea, or the mountains, or to any place that was not home. I could never understand why a people who have been grumbling about snow and frost for six months, and longing for genial weather, should flee from it as soon as it comes. I had made the discovery, quite by chance—and it was so novel that I might have taken out a patent on it—that if one has a comfortable home in our northern latitude he cannot do better than to stay in it when the hum of the mosquito is heard in the land, and the mercury is racing up and down the scale between fifty and ninety. This opinion, however, did not extend beyond our little neighborhood, and we may be said to have had the summer to ourselves.

I fancied that the neighborhood had not changed, but the coming of Margaret showed me that this was a delusion. No one can keep in the same place in life simply by standing still, and the events of the past two years had wrought a subtle change in our quiet. Nothing had been changed to the eye, yet something had been taken away, or something had been added, a door had been opened into the world. Margaret had come home, yet I fancied it was not the home to her that she had been thinking about. Had she changed?

She was more beautiful. She had the air—I should hesitate to call it that of the fine lady—of assured position, something the manner of that greater world in which the possession of wealth has supreme importance, but it was scarcely a change of manner so much as of ideas about life and of the things valuable in it gradually showing itself. Her delight at being again with her old friends was perfectly genuine, and she had never appeared more unselfish or more affectionate. If there was a subtle difference, it might very well be in us, though I find it impossible to conceive of her in her former role of teacher and simple maiden, with her heart in the little concerns of our daily life. And why should she be expected to go back to that stage? Must we not all live our lives?

Miss Forsythe's solicitude about Margaret was mingled with a curious deference, as to one who had a larger experience of life than her own. The girl of a year ago was now the married woman, and was invested with something of the dignity that Miss Forsythe in her pure imagination attached to that position. Without yielding any of her opinions, this idea somehow changed her relations to Margaret: a little, I thought to the amusement of Mrs. Fletcher and the other ladies, to whom marriage took on a less mysterious aspect. It arose doubtless from a renewed sense of the incompleteness of her single life, long as it had been, and enriched as it was by observation.

In that June there were vexatious strikes in various parts of the country, formidable combinations of laboring-men, demonstrations of trades-unions, and the exhibition of a spirit that sharply called attention to the unequal distribution of wealth. The discontent was attributed in some quarters to the exhibition of extreme luxury and reckless living by those who had been fortunate. It was even said that the strikes, unreasonable and futile as they were, and most injurious to those who indulged in them, were indirectly caused by the railway manipulation, in the attempt not only to crush out competition, but to exact excessive revenues on fictitious values. Resistance to this could be shown to be blind, and the strikers technically in the wrong, yet the impression gained ground that there was something monstrously wrong in the way great fortunes were accumulated, in total disregard of individual rights, and in a materialistic spirit that did not take into account ordinary humanity. For it was not alone the laboring class that was discontented, but all over the country those who lived upon small invested savings, widows and minors, found their income imperilled by the trickery of rival operators and speculators in railways and securities, who treated the little private accumulations as mere counters in the games they were playing. The loss of dividends to them was poorly compensated by reflections upon the development of the country, and the advantage to trade of great consolidations, which inured to the benefit of half a dozen insolent men.

In discussing these things in our little parliament we were not altogether unprejudiced, it must be confessed. For, to say nothing of interests of Mr. Morgan and my own, which seemed in some danger of disappearing for the "public good," Mrs. Fletcher's little fortune was nearly all invested in that sound "rock-bed" railway in the Southwest that Mr. Jerry Hollowell had recently taken under his paternal care. She was assured, indeed, that dividends were only reserved pending some sort of reorganization, which would ultimately be of great benefit to all the parties concerned; but this was much like telling a hungry man that if he would possess his appetite in patience, he would very likely have a splendid dinner next year. Women are not constituted to understand this sort of reasoning. It is needless to say that in our general talks on the situation these personalities were not referred to, for although Margaret was silent, it was plain to see that she was uneasy.

Morgan liked to raise questions of casuistry, such as that whether money dishonestly come by could be accepted for good purposes.

"I had this question referred to me the other day," he said. "A gambler—not a petty cheater in cards, but a man who has a splendid establishment in which he has amassed a fortune, a man known for his liberality and good-fellowship and his interest in politics—offered the president of a leading college a hundred thousand dollars to endow a professorship. Ought the president to take the money, knowing how it was made?"

"Wouldn't the money do good—as much good as any other hundred thousand dollars?" asked Margaret.

"Perhaps. But the professorship was to bear his name, and what would be the moral effect of that?"

"Did you recommend the president to take the money, if he could get it without using the gambler's name?"

"I am not saying yet what I advised. I am trying to get your views on a general principle."

"But wouldn't it be a sneaking thing to take a man's money, and refuse him the credit of his generosity?"

"But was it generosity? Was not his object, probably, to get a reputation which his whole life belied, and to get it by obliterating the distinction between right and wrong?"

"But isn't it a compromising distinction," my wife asked, "to take his money without his name? The president knows that it is money fraudulently got, that really belongs to somebody else; and the gambler would feel that if the president takes it, he cannot think very disapprovingly of the manner in which it was acquired. I think it would be more honest and straightforward to take his name with the money."

"The public effect of connecting the gambler's name with the college would be debasing," said Morgan; "but, on the contrary, is every charity or educational institution bound to scrutinize the source of every benefaction? Isn't it better that money, however acquired, should be used for a good purpose than a bad one?"

"That is a question," I said, "that is a vital one in our present situation, and the sophistry of it puzzles the public. What would you say to this case? A man notoriously dishonest, but within the law, and very rich, offered a princely endowment to a college very much in need of it. The sum would have enabled it to do a great work in education. But it was intimated that the man would expect, after a while, to be made one of the trustees. His object, of course, was social position."

"I suppose, of course," Margaret replied, "that the college couldn't afford that. It would look like bribery."

"Wouldn't he be satisfied with an LL.D.?" Morgan asked.

"I don't see," my wife said, "any difference between the two cases stated and that of the stock gambler, whose unscrupulous operations have ruined thousands of people, who founds a theological seminary with the gains of his slippery transactions. By accepting his seminary the public condones his conduct. Another man, with the same shaky reputation, endows a college. Do you think that religion and education are benefited in the long run by this? It seems to me that the public is gradually losing its power of discrimination between the value of honesty and dishonesty. Real respect is gone when the public sees that a man is able to buy it."

This was a hot speech for my wife to make. For a moment Margaret flamed up under it with her old-time indignation. I could see it in her eyes, and then she turned red and confused, and at length said:

"But wouldn't you have rich men do good with their money?"

"Yes, dear; but I would not have them think they can blot out by their liberality the condemnation of the means by which many of them make money. That is what they are doing, and the public is getting used to it."

"Well," said Margaret, with some warmth, "I don't know that they are any worse than the stingy saints who have made their money by saving, and act as if they expected to carry it with them."

"Saints or sinners, it does not make much difference to me," now put in Mrs. Fletcher, who was evidently considering the question from a practical point of view, "what a man professes, if he founds a hospital for indigent women out of the dividends that I never received."

Morgan laughed. "Don't you think, Mrs. Fletcher, that it is a good sign of the times that so many people who make money rapidly are disposed to use it philanthropically?"

"It may be for them, but it does not console me much just now."

"But you don't make allowance enough for the rich. Perhaps they are under a necessity of doing something. I was reading this morning in the diary of old John Ward, of Stratford-on-Avon, this sentence: 'It was a saying of Navisson, a lawyer, that no man could be valiant unless he hazarded his body, nor rich unless he hazarded his soul!'"

"Was Navisson a modern lawyer?" I asked.

"No; the diary is dated 1648-1679."

"I thought so."

There was a little laugh at this, and the talk drifted off into a consideration of the kind of conscience that enables a professional man to espouse a cause he knows to be wrong as zealously as one he knows to be right; a talk that I should not have remembered at all, except for Margaret's earnestness in insisting that she did not see how a lawyer could take up the dishonest side.

Before Margaret went to Lenox, Henderson spent a few days with us. He brought with him the abounding cheerfulness, and the air of a prosperous, smiling world, that attended him in all circumstances. And how happy Margaret was! They went over every foot of the ground on which their brief courtship had taken place, and Heaven knows what joy there was to her in reviving all the tenderness and all the fear of it! Busy as Henderson was, pursued by hourly telegrams and letters, we could not but be gratified that his attention to her was that of a lover. How could it be otherwise, when all the promise of the girl was realized in the bloom and the exquisite sensibility of the woman. Among other things, she dragged him down to her mission in the city, to which he went in a laughing and bantering mood. When he had gone away, Margaret ran over to my wife, bringing in her hand a slip of paper.

"See that!" she cried, her eyes dancing with pleasure. It

was a check for a thousand dollars. "That will refurnish the mission from top to bottom," she said, "and run it for a year."

"How generous he is!" cried my wife. Margaret did not reply, but she looked at the check, and there were tears in her eyes.

—*Charles Dudley Warner.*

The Bostonians.

WHAT Basil Ransom actually perceived was that Miss Chancellor was a signal old maid. That was her quality, her destiny; nothing could be more distinctly written. There are women who are unmarried by accident, and others who are unmarried by option; but Olive Chancellor was unmarried by every implication of her being. She was a spinster as Shelley was a lyric poet, or the month of August is sultry. She was so essentially a celibate that Ransom found himself thinking of her as old, though when he came to look at her (as he said to himself) it was apparent that her years were fewer than his own. He did not dislike her, she had been so friendly; but, little by little, she gave him an uneasy feeling—the sense that you could never be safe with a person who took things so hard. It came over him that it was because she took things hard she had sought his acquaintance; it had been because she was strenuous, not because she was genial; she had had in her eye—and what an extraordinary eye it was!—not a pleasure, but a duty. She would expect him to be strenuous in return; but he couldn't—in private life, he couldn't; privacy for Basil Ransom consisted entirely in what he called "laying off." She was not so plain on further acquaintance as she had seemed to him at first; even the young Mississippian had culture enough to see that she was refined. Her white skin had a singular look of being drawn tightly across her face; but her features, though sharp and irregular, were delicate in a fashion that suggested good breeding. Their line was perverse, but it was not poor. The curious tint of her eyes was a living color; when she turned it upon you, you thought vaguely of the glitter of green ice. She had absolutely no figure, and presented a certain appearance of feeling cold. With all this, there was something very modern and highly developed in her aspect; she had the advantage as well as the drawbacks of a nervous organization. She smiled constantly at her guest, but from the beginning to the end of dinner, though he made several remarks that he thought might prove amusing, she never once laughed. Later, he saw that she was a woman without laughter; exhilaration, if it ever visited her, was dumb. Once only, in the course of his subsequent acquaintance with her, did it find a voice; and then the sound remained in Ransom's ear as one of the strangest he had heard.

She asked him a great many questions, and made no comment on his answers, which only served to suggest to her fresh inquiries. Her shyness had quite left her, it did not come back; she had confidence enough to wish him to see that she took a great interest in him. Why should she? he wondered. He couldn't believe he was one of *her* kind; he was conscious of much Bohemianism—he drank beer, in New York, in cellars, knew no ladies, and was familiar with a "variety" actress. Certainly, as she knew him better, she would disapprove of him, though, of course, he would never mention the actress, nor even, if necessary, the beer. Ransom's conception of vice was purely as a series of special cases of explicable accidents. Not that he cared; if it were a part of the Boston character to be inquiring, he would be to the last a courteous Mississippian. He would tell her about Mississippi as much as she liked; he didn't care how much he told her that the old ideas in the South were played out. She would not understand him any the better for that; she would not know how little his own views could be gathered from such a limited admission. What her sister imparted to him about her mania for "reform" had left in his mouth a kind of unpleasant after-taste; he felt, at any rate, that if she had the religion of humanity—Basil Ransom had read Comte, he had read everything—she would never understand him. He, too, had a private vision of reform, but the first principle of it was to reform the reformers. As they drew to the close of a meal which, in spite of all latent incompatibilities, had gone off brilliantly, she said to him that she should have to leave him after dinner, unless perhaps he should be inclined to accompany her. She was going to a small gathering at the house of a friend who had asked a few people, "interested in new ideas," to meet Mrs. Farrinder.

"Oh, thank you," said Basil Ransom. "Is it a party? I haven't been to a party since Mississippi seceded."

"No; Miss Birdseye doesn't give parties. She's an ascetic."

"Oh, well, we have had our dinner," Ransom rejoined, laughing.

His hostess sat silent a moment, with her eyes on the ground; she looked at such times as if she were hesitating greatly between several things she might say, all so important that it was difficult to choose.

"I think it might interest you," she remarked, presently. "You will hear some discussion, if you are fond of that. Perhaps you wouldn't agree," she added, resting her strange eyes on him.

"Perhaps I shouldn't—I don't agree with everything," he said, smiling and stroking his leg.

"Don't you care for human progress?" Miss Chancellor went on.

"I don't know—I never saw any. Are you going to show me some?"

"I can show you an earnest effort towards it. That's the most one can be sure of. But I am not sure you are worthy."

"Is it something very Bostonian? I should like to see that," said Basil Ransom.

"There are movements in other cities. Mrs. Farrinder goes everywhere; she may speak tonight."

"Mrs. Farrinder, the celebrated—?"

"Yes, the celebrated; the great apostle of the emancipation of women. She is a great friend of Miss Birdseye."

"And who is Miss Birdseye?"

"She is one of our celebrities. She is the woman in the world, I suppose, who has labored most for every wise reform. I think I ought to tell you," Miss Chancellor went on in a moment, "she was one of the earliest, one of the most passionate, of the old Abolitionists."

She had thought, indeed, she ought to tell him that, and it threw her into a little tremor of excitement to do so. Yet, if she had been afraid he would show some irritation at this news, she was disappointed at the geniality with which he exclaimed:

"Why, poor old lady—she must be quite mature!"

It was therefore with some severity that she rejoined:

"She will never be old. She is the youngest spirit I know. But if you are not in sympathy, perhaps you had better not come," she went.

"In sympathy with what, dear madam?" Basil Ransom asked, failing still, to her perception, to catch the tone of real seriousness. "If, as you say, there is to be a discussion, there will be different sides, and of course one can't sympathize with both."

"Yes, but every one will, in his way—or in her way—plead the cause of the new truths. If you don't care for them, you won't go with us."

"I tell you I haven't the least idea what they are! I have never yet encountered in the world any but old truths—as old as the sun and moon. How can I know? But *do* take me; it's such a chance to see Boston."

"It isn't Boston—it's humanity!" Miss Chancellor, as she made this remark, rose from her chair, and her movement seemed to say that she consented. But before she quitted her kinsman to get ready, she observed to him that she was sure he knew what she meant; he was only pretending he didn't.

"Well, perhaps, after all, I have a general idea," he confessed; "but don't you see how this little reunion will give me a chance to fix it."

She lingered an instant, with her anxious face. "Mrs. Farrinder will fix it," she said; and she went to prepare herself.

It was in this poor young lady's nature to be anxious, to have scruple within scruple and to forecast the consequences of things. She returned in ten minutes, in her bonnet, which she had apparently assumed in recognition of Miss Birdseye's asceticism. As she stood there drawing on her gloves—her visitor had fortified himself against Mrs. Farrinder by another glass of wine—she declared to him that she quite repented of having proposed to him to go; something told her that he would be an unfavorable element.

"Why, is it going to be a spiritual séance?" Basil Ransom asked.

"Well, I have heard at Miss Birdseye's some inspirational speaking." Olive Chancellor was determined to look him straight in the face as she said this; her sense of the way it might strike him operated as a cogent, not as a deterrent, reason.

"Why, Miss Olive, it's just got up on purpose for me!"

cried the young Mississippian, radiant, and clasping his hands. She thought him very handsome as he said this, but reflected that unfortunately men didn't care for the truth, especially the new kinds, in proportion as they were good-looking. She had, however, a moral resource that she could always fall back upon; it had already been a comfort to her, on occasions of acute feeling, that she hated men, as a class, anyway. "And I want so much to see an old Abolitionist; I have never set eyes on one," Basil Ransom added.

"Of course you couldn't see one in the South; you were too afraid of them to let them come there!" She was now trying to think of something she might say that would be sufficiently disagreeable to make him cease to insist on accompanying her; for, strange to record—if anything, in a person of that intense sensibility, be stranger than any other—her second thought with regard to having asked him had deepened with the elapsing moments into an unreasoned terror at the effects of his presence. "Perhaps Miss Birdseye won't like you," she went on, as they waited for the carriage.

"I don't know; I reckon she will," said Basil Ransom, good humoredly. He evidently had no intention of giving up his opportunity.

From the window of the dining-room, at that moment, they heard the carriage drive up. Miss Birdseye lived at the South End; the distance was considerable, and Miss Chancellor had ordered a hackney coach, it being one of the advantages of living in Charles Street that stables were near. The logic of her conduct was none of the clearest; for if she had been alone she would have proceeded to her destination by the aid of the streetcar; not from economy (for she had the good fortune not to be obliged to consult it to that degree), and not from any love of wandering about Boston at night (a kind of exposure she greatly disliked), but by reason of a theory she devotedly nursed, a theory which bade her put off invidious differences and mingle in the common life. She would have gone on foot to Boylston Street, and there she would have taken the public conveyance (in her heart she loathed it) to the South End. Boston was full of poor girls who had to walk about at night and to squeeze into horse-cars in which every sense was displeased; and why should she hold herself superior to these?

Olive Chancellor regulated her conduct on lofty principles, and this is why, having tonight the advantage of a gentleman's protection, she sent for a carriage to obliterate that patronage. If they had gone together in the common way she would have seemed to owe it to him that she should be so daring, and he belonged to a sex to which she wished to be under no obligations. Months before, when she wrote to him, it had been with the sense, rather, of putting *him* in debt. As they rolled toward the South End, side by side, in a good deal of silence, bouncing and bumping over the railway-tracks very little less, after all, than if their wheels had been fitted to them, and looking out at either side at rows of red houses, dusky in the lamplight, with protuberant fronts, approached by ladders of stone; as they proceeded, with these contemplative undulations, Miss Chancellor said to her companion, with a concentrated desire to defy him, as a punishment for having thrown her (she couldn't tell why) into such a tremor:

"Don't you believe, then, in the coming of a better day—in its being possible to do something for the human race?"

Poor Ransom perceived the defiance, and he felt rather bewildered; he wondered what type, after all, he *had* got hold of, and what game was being played with him. Why had she made advances, if she wanted to pinch him this way? However, he was good for any game—that one as well as another—and he saw that he was "in" for something of which he had long desired to have a nearer view. "Well, Miss Olive," he answered, putting on again his big hat, which he had been holding in his lap, "what strikes me most is that the human race has got to bear its troubles."

"That's what men say to women, to make them patient in the position they have made for them."

"Oh, the position of women!" Basil Ransom exclaimed. "The position of women is to make fools of men. I would change my position for yours any day," he went on. "That's what I said to myself as I sat there in your elegant home."

He could not see, in the dimness of the carriage, that she had flushed quickly, and he did not know that she disliked to be reminded of certain things, which, for her, were mitigations of the hard feminine lot. But the passionate quaver with which, a moment later, she answered him sufficiently assured him that he had touched her at a tender point.

"Do you make it a reproach to me that I happen to have a little money? The dearest wish of my heart is to do something with it for others—for the miserable."

Basil Ransom might have greeted this last declaration with the sympathy it deserved, might have commended the noble aspirations of his kinswoman. But what struck him, rather, was the oddity of so sudden a sharpness of pitch in an intercourse, which, an hour or two before, had begun in perfect amity, and he burst once more into an irrepressible laugh. This made his companion feel, with intensity, how little she was joking. "I don't know why I should care what you think," she said.

"Don't care—don't care. What does it matter? It is not of the slightest importance."

He might say that, but it was not true; she felt that there were reasons why she should care. She had brought him into her life, and she should have to pay for it. But she wished to know the worst at once. "Are you against our emancipation?" she asked, turning a white face on him in the momentary radiance of a street lamp.

"Do you mean your voting and preaching and all that sort of thing?" He made this inquiry, but seeing how seriously she would take his answer, he was almost frightened and hung fire. "I will tell you when I have heard Mrs. Farrinder."

They had arrived at the address given by Miss Chancellor to the coachman, and their vehicle stopped with a lurch. Basil Ransom got out; he stood at the door with an extended hand to assist the young lady. But she seemed to hesitate; she sat there with her spectral face. "You hate it!" she exclaimed, in a low tone.

"Miss Birdseye will convert me," said Ransom, with intention; for he had grown very curious, and he was afraid that now, at the last, Miss Chancellor would prevent his entering the house. She alighted without his help, and behind her he ascended the high steps of Miss Birdseye's residence. He had grown very curious, and among the things he wanted to know was why in the world this ticklish spinster had written to him.

—*Henry James.*

Barker's Luck.

A BIRD twittered! The morning sun shining through the open window was apparently more potent than the cool mountain air, which had only caused the sleeper to curl a little more tightly in his blankets. Barker's eyes opened instantly upon the light and the bird on the window ledge. Like all healthy young animals he would have tried to sleep again, but with his momentary consciousness came the recollection that it was *his* turn to cook the breakfast that morning, and he regretfully rolled out of his bunk to the floor. Without stopping to dress he opened the door and stepped outside, secure in the knowledge that he was overlooked only by the Sierras, and plunged his head and shoulders in the bucket of cold water that stood by the door. Then he began to clothe himself, partly in the cabin and partly in the open air, with a lapse between the putting on of his trousers and coat which he employed in bringing in wood. Raking together the few embers on the adobe hearth, not without a prudent regard to the rattlesnake which had once been detected in haunting the warm ashes, he began to prepare breakfast. By this time the other sleepers, his partners Stacy and Demorest, young men of about his own age, were awake, alert, and lazily critical of his progress.

"I don't care about my quail on toast being underdone for breakfast," said Stacy, with a yawn; "and you needn't serve with red wine. I'm not feeling very peckish this morning."

"And I reckon you can knock off the fried oysters after the Spanish mackerel for *me*," said Demorest, gravely. "The fact is, that last bottle of Veuve Clicquot we had for supper wasn't as dry as I am this morning."

Accustomed to these regular Barmecide suggestions, Barker made no direct reply. Presently, looking up from the fire, he said, "There's no more saleratus, so you mustn't blame me if the biscuit is extra heavy. I told you we had none when you went to the grocery yesterday."

"And I told you we hadn't a red cent to buy any with," said Stacy, who was also treasurer. "Put these two negatives together and you make the affirmative—saleratus. Mix freely and bake in a hot oven."

Nevertheless, after toilette as primitive as Barker's they

sat down to what he had prepared, with the keen appetite begotten of the mountain air and the regretful fastidiousness born of the recollection of better things. Jerked beef, frizzled with salt pork in a frying-pan, boiled potatoes, biscuit, and coffee composed the repast. The biscuits, however, proving remarkably heavy after the first mouthful, were used as missiles, thrown through the open door at an empty bottle, which had previously served as a mark for revolver practice, and a few moments later pipes were lit to counteract the effects of the meal and take the taste out of their mouths. Suddenly they heard the sound of horses' hoofs, saw the quick passage of a rider in the open space before the cabin, and felt the smart impact upon the table of some small object thrown by him. It was the regular morning delivery of the county newspaper!

"He's getting to be a mighty sure shot," said Demorest, approvingly, looking at his upset can of coffee as he picked up the paper, rolled into a cylindrical wad as tightly as a cartridge, and began to straighten it out. This was no easy matter, as the sheet had evidently been rolled while yet damp from the press; but Demorest eventually opened it and ensconced himself behind it.

"Nary news?" asked Stacy.

"No. There never is any," said Demorest, scornfully. "We ought to stop the paper."

"You mean the paper man ought to. *We* don't pay him," said Barker, gently.

"Well, that's the same thing, smarty. No news, no pay. Hallo!" he continued, his eyes suddenly riveted on the paper. Then, after the fashion of ordinary humanity, he stopped short and read the interesting item to himself. When he had finished he brought his fist and the paper, together, violently down upon the table. "Now look at this! Talk of luck, will you? just think of it. Here are *we*—hard-working men with lots of *sabe*, too—grubbin' away on this hillside like niggers, glad to get enough at the end of the day to pay for our soggy biscuits and horse-bean coffee, and just look what falls into the lap of some lazy sneakin' greenhorn who never did a stroke of work in his life! Here are *we*, with no foolishness, no airs nor graces, and yet men who would do credit to twice that amount of luck—and seem born to it, too—and we're set aside for some long, lank, pen-wiping scrub who just knows enough to sit down on his office stool and hold on to a bit of paper."

"What's up now?" asked Stacy, with a carelessness begotten of familiarity with his partner's extravagance.

"Listen," said Demorest, reading. "Another unprecedented rise has taken place in the shares of the 'Yellow Hammer First Extension Mine' since the sinking of the new shaft. It was quoted yesterday at ten thousand dollars a foot. When it is remembered that scarcely two years ago, the original shares, issued at fifty dollars per share, had dropped to only fifty cents a share, it will be seen that those who were able to hold on have got a good thing."

"What mine did you say?" asked Barker, looking up meditatively from the dishes he was already washing.

"The Yellow Hammer First Extension," returned Demorest, shortly.

"I used to have some shares in that, and I think I have them still," said Barker, musingly.

"Yes," said Demorest, promptly: "the paper speaks of it here. 'We understand,'" he continued, reading aloud, 'that our eminent fellow-citizen, George Barker, otherwise known as "Get Left Barker" and "Chucklehead" is one of these fortunate individuals.'"

"No," said Barker, with a slight flush of innocent pleasure, "it can't say that. How could it know?"

Stacy laughed, but Demorest coolly continued: "You didn't hear all. Listen! 'We say *was* one of them; but having already sold his apparently useless certificates to our popular druggist, Jones, for corn plasters, at a reduced rate, he is unable to realize.'"

"You may laugh, boys," said Barker, with simple seriousness; "but I really believe I have got 'em yet. Just wait. I'll see!" He rose and began to drag out a well-worn valise from under his bunk. "You see," he continued, "they were given to me by an old chap in return"—

"For saving his life by delaying the Stockton boat that afterwards blew up," returned Demorest, briefly. "We know it all! His hair was white, and his hand trembled slightly as he laid these shares in yours, saying, and you never forgot the words, 'Take 'em young man—and'"—

"For lending him two thousand dollars, then," continued Barker with a simple ignoring of the interruption, as he quietly brought out the valise.

"*Two thousand dollars!*" repeated Stacy. "When did *you* have two thousand dollars?"

"When I first left Sacramento—three years ago," said Barker, unstrapping the valise.

"How long did you have it?" said Demorest, incredulously.

"At least two days, I think," returned Barker, quietly. "Then I met that man. He was hard up, and I lent him my pile and took those shares. He died afterwards."

"Of course he did," said Demorest, severely. "They always do. Nothing kills a man more quickly than an action of that kind." Nevertheless the two partners regarded Barker rummaging among some loose clothes and papers with a kind of paternal toleration. "If you can't find them, bring out your government bonds," suggested Stacy. But the next moment, flushed and triumphant, Barker rose from his knees, and came towards them carrying some papers in his hands. Demorest seized them from him, opened them, spread them on the table, examined hurriedly the date, signatures, and transfers, glanced again quickly at the newspaper paragraph, looked wildly at Stacy and then at Barker, and gasped,—

"By the living hookey! it is *so!*"

"B' gosh! he has got 'em!" echoed Stacy.

"Twenty shares," continued Demorest, breathlessly, "at ten thousand dollars a share—even if it's only a foot—is two hundred thousand dollars! Jerusalem!"

"Tell me, fair sir," said Stacy, with sparkling eyes, "hast still left in yonder casket any rare jewels, rubies, sarcenet, or links of fine gold? Peradventure a pearl or two may have been overlooked!"

"No—that's all," returned Barker, simply.

"You hear him! Rothschild says 'that's all.' Prince Esterhazy says he hasn't another red cent—only two hundred thousand dollars."

"What ought I to do, boys?" asked Barker, timidly glancing from one to the other. Yet he remembered with delight all that day, and for many a year afterwards, that he only saw in their faces unselfish joy and affection at that supreme moment.

"Do?" said Demorest, promptly. "Stand on your head and yell! No! Stop! Come here!" he seized both Barker and Stacy by the hand, and ran out into the open air. Here they danced violently with clasped hands around a small buckeye, in perfect silence, and then returned to the cabin, grave but perspiring.

"Of course," said Barker, wiping his forehead, "we'll just get some money on these certificates and buy up that next claim which belongs to old Carter—where you know we thought we saw the indication."

"We'll do nothing of the kind," said Demorest, decidedly. "*We* ain't in it. That money is yours, old chap—every cent of it—property acquired before marriage, you know; and the only thing we'll do is to be d——d before we see you drop a dime of it into this God-forsaken hole. No!"

"But we're partners," gasped Barker.

"Not in *this!* The utmost we can do for you, opulent sir,—though it ill becomes us horney-handed sons of toil to rub shoulders with Dives,—is perchance to dine with you, to take a pasty and glass of Malvoisie, at some restaurant in Sacramento, when you've got things fixed, in honor of your return to affluence. But more would ill become us!"

"But what are *you* going to do?" said Barker, with a half-hysteric, half-frightened smile.

"We have not yet looked through our luggage," said Demorest, with invincible gravity, "and there's a secret recess—a double *fond*—to my portmanteau, known only to a trusty page, which has not been disturbed since I left my ancestral home in Faginia. There may be a few First Debentures of Erie or what not still there."

"I felt some strange, disk-like protuberance in my dress suit the other day, but belike they are but poker chips," said Stacy, thoughtfully.

An uneasy feeling crept over Barker. The color which had left his fresh cheek returned to it quickly, and he turned his eyes away. Yet he had seen nothing in his companions' eyes but affection—with even a certain kind of tender commiseration that deepened his uneasiness. "I suppose," he said desperately, after a pause, "I ought to go over to Boomville and make some inquiries."

"At the bank, old chap; at the bank!" said Demorest, emphatically. "Take my advice and don't go *anywhere else*. Don't breathe a word of your luck to anybody. And don't, whatever you do, be tempted to sell just now; you don't know how high that stock's going to jump yet."

"I thought," stammered Barker, "that you boys might like to go over with me."

"We can't afford to take another holiday on grub wages, and we're only two to work today," said Demorest, with a slight increase of color and the faintest tremor in his voice. "And it won't do, old chap, for us to be seen bumming round with you on the heels of your good fortune. For everybody knows we're poor, and sooner or later everybody'll know you *were* rich even when you first came to us."

"Nonsense!" said Barker, indignantly.

"Gospel, my boy!" said Demorest, shortly.

"The frozen truth, old man!" said Stacy.

Barker took up his hat with some stiffness and moved towards the door. Here he stopped irresolutely, an irresolution that seemed to communicate itself to his partners. There was a moment's awkward silence. Then Demorest suddenly seized him by the shoulders with a grip that was half a caress, and walked him rapidly to the door. "And now don't stand foolin' with us, Barker boy; but just trot off like a little man, and get your grip on that fortune; and when you've got your hooks in it hang on like grim death. You'll"—he hesitated for an instant only, possibly to find the laugh that should have accompanied his speech—"you're sure to find *us* here when you get back."

Hurt to the quick, but restraining his feelings, Barker clapped his hat on his head and walked quickly away. The two partners stood watching him in silence until his figure was lost in the underbrush. Then they spoke.

"Like him—wasn't it?" said Demorest.

"Just him all over," said Stacy.

"Think of him having that stock stowed away all these years and never even bothering his dear old head about it!"

"And think of his wanting to put the whole thing into this rotten hillside with us!"

"And he'd have done it, by gosh! and never thought of it again. That's Barker."

"Dear old man!"

"Good old chap!"

"I've been wondering if one of us oughtn't to have gone with him? He's just as likely to pour his money into the first lap that opens for it," said Stacy.

"The more reason why we shouldn't prevent him, or seem to prevent him," said Demorest, almost fiercely. "There will be knaves and fools enough who will try and put the idea of our using him into his simple heart without that. No! Let him do as he likes with it—but let him be himself. I'd rather have him come back to us even after he's lost the money— his old self and empty-handed—than try to change the stuff God put into him and make him more like others."

But when he reached the hotel, a strange trepidation overcame him. The dining-room was at its slack water, between the ebb of breakfast and before the flow of the preparation for the midday meal. He could not have his interview with Kitty in that dreary waste of reversed chairs and bare trestle-like tables, and she was possibly engaged in her household duties. But Miss Kitty had already seen him cross the road, and had lounged into the dining-room with an artfully simulated air of casually examining it. At the unexpected vision of his hopes, arrayed in the sweetest and freshest of rosebud sprigged print, his heart faltered. Then, partly with the desperation of a timid man, and partly through the working of a half-formed resolution, he met her bright smile with a simple inquiry for her father. Miss Kitty bit her pretty lip, smiled slightly, and preceded him with great formality to the office. Opening the door, without raising her lashes to either her father or the visitor, she said, with a mischievous accenting of the professional manner, "Mr. Barker to see you on business," and tripped sweetly away.

And this slight incident precipitated the crisis. For Barker instantly made up his mind that he must purchase the next claim for his partners of this man Carter, and that he would be obliged to confide to him the details of his good fortune, and, as a proof of his sincerity and his ability to pay for it, he did so bluntly. Carter was a shrewd business man, and the well-known simplicity of Barker was a proof of his truthfulness, to say nothing of the shares that were shown to him. His selling price for his claim had been two hundred dollars, but here was a rich customer who, from a mere foolish sentiment, would be no doubt willing to pay more. He hesitated with a bland but superior smile. "Ah, that was my price at my last offer, Mr. Barker," he said suavely; "but, you see, things are going up since then."

The keenest duplicity is apt to fail before absolute simplicity. Barker, thoroughly believing him, and already a little frightened at his own presumption—not for the amount of the money involved, but from the possibility of his partners refusing his gift utterly—quickly took advantage of this *locus penitentiae*. "No matter, then," he said, hurriedly; "perhaps I had better consult my partners first; in fact," he added, with a gratuitous truthfulness all his own, "I hardly know whether they will take it of me so I think I'll wait."

Carter was staggered; this would clearly not do! He recovered himself with an insinuating smile. "You pulled me up too short, Mr. Barker; I'm a business man, but hang it all! what's that among friends? If you reckoned I *gave my word* at two hundred—why, I'm there! Say no more about it—the claim's yours. I'll make you out a bill of sale at once."

"But," hesitated Barker, "you see I haven't got the money yet, and"—

"Money!" echoed Carter, bluntly, "what's that among friends? Gimme your note at thirty days—that's good enough for *me*. An' we'll settle the whole thing now,—nothing like finishing a job while you're about it." And before the bewildered and doubtful visitor could protest, he had filled up a promissory note for Barker's signature and himself signed a bill of sale for the property. "And I reckon, Mr. Barker, you'd like to take your partners by surprise about this little gift of yours," he added, smilingly. "Well, my messenger is starting for the Gulch in five minutes; he's going by your cabin, and he can just drop this bill o' sale, as a kind o' settled fact, on 'em afore they can say anything, see! There's nothing like actin' on the spot in these sort of things. And don't you hurry 'bout them either! You see, you sorter owe us a friendly call—havin' always dropped inter the hotel only as a customer—so ye'll stop here over luncheon, and I reckon, as the old woman is busy, why Kitty will try to make the time pass till then by playin' for you on her new pianner."

"Everything's up," gasped the breathless Barker. "It's all up about these stocks. It's all a mistake; all an infernal lie of that newspaper. I never had the right kind of shares. The ones I have are worthless rags;" and the next instant he had blurted out his whole interview with the bank manager.

The two partners looked at each other, and then, to Barker's infinite perplexity, the same extraordinary convulsion that had seized Miss Kitty fell upon them. They laughed, holding on each other's shoulders; they laughed, clinging to Barker's struggling figure; they went out and laughed with their backs against a tree. They laughed separately and in different corners. And then they came up to Barker with tears in their eyes, dropped their heads on his shoulder, and murmured, exhaustedly :—

"You blessed ass!"

"But," said Stacy, suddenly, "how did you manage to buy the claim?"

"Ah! that's the most awful thing, boys. I've *never paid for it,*" groaned Barker.

"But Carter sent us the bill of sale," persisted Demorest, "or we shouldn't have taken it."

"I gave my promissory note at thirty days," said Barker, desperately, "and where's the money to come from now? But," he added, wildly, as the men glanced at each other—"you said 'taken it.' Good heavens! you don't mean to say that I'm *too late*—that you've—you've touched it?"

"I reckon that's pretty much what we *have* been doing," drawled Demorest.

"It looks uncommonly like it," drawled Stacy.

Barker glanced blankly from the one to the other. "Shall we pass our young friend in to see the show?" said Demorest to Stacy.

"Yes, if he'll be perfectly quiet and not breathe on the glasses," returned Stacy.

They each gravely took one of Barker's hands and led him to the corner of the cabin. There, on an old flour barrel, stood a large tin prospecting pan, in which the partners also occasionally used to knead their bread. A dirty towel covered it. Demorest whisked it dexterously aside, and disclosed three large fragments of decomposed gold and quartz. Barker started back.

"Heft it!" said Demorest, grimly.

Barker could scarcely lift the pan!

"Four thousand dollars' weight if a penny!" said Stacy, in short staccato sentences. "In a pocket! Brought it out the second stroke of the pick! We'd been awfully blue after you left. Awfully blue, too, when that bill of sale came, for we thought you'd been wasting your money on *us*. Reckoned we oughtn't to take it, but send it straight back to you. Messenger gone! Then Demorest reckoned as it was done it couldn't be undone, and we ought to make just one 'prospect' on the claim, and strike a single stroke for you. And there it is. And there's more on the hillside."

"But it isn't *mine!* It isn't yours! It's Carter's. I never had the money to pay for it—and I haven't got it now."

"But you gave the note—and it is not due for thirty days."

A recollection flashed upon Barker. "Yes," he said, with thoughtful simplicity, "that's what Kitty said."

"Oh, Kitty said so," said both partners, gravely.

"Yes," stammered Barker, turning away with a heightened color, "and, as I didn't stay there to luncheon, I think I'd better be getting it ready." He picked up the coffee-pot and turned to the hearth as his two partners stepped beyond the door.

"Wasn't it exactly like him?" said Demorest.

"Him all over," said Stacy.

"And his worry over that note?" said Demorest.

"And 'what Kitty said,'" said Stacy.

"Look here! I reckon that wasn't *all* that Kitty said."

"Of course not."

"What luck!"
—*Bret Harte.*

RAMONA.

The wild mustard in Southern California is like that spoken of in the New Testament, in the branches of which the birds of the air may rest. Coming up out of the earth, so slender a stem that dozens can find starting-point in an inch, it darts up, a slender straight shoot, five, ten, twenty feet, with hundreds of fine feathery branches locking and interlocking with all the other hundreds around it, till it is an inextricable network like lace. Then it bursts into yellow bloom still finer, more feathery and lace-like. The stems are so infinitesimally small, and of so dark a green, that at a short distance they do not show, and the cloud of blossoms seems floating in the air; at times it looks like golden dust. With a clear blue sky behind it, as it is often seen, it looks like a golden snow-storm. The plant is a tyrant and a nuisance,—the terror of the farmer; it takes riotous possession of a whole field in a season; once in, never out; for one plant this year, a million the next; but it is impossible to wish that the land were freed from it. Its gold is as distinct a value to the eye as the nugget gold is in the pocket.

Father Salvierderra soon found himself in a veritable thicket of these delicate branches, high above his head, and so interlaced that he could make headway only by slowly and patiently disentangling them, as one would disentangle a skein of silk. It was a fantastic sort of dilemma, and not unpleasing. Except that the Father was in haste to reach his journey's end, he would have enjoyed threading his way through the golden meshes. Suddenly he heard faint notes of singing. He paused,—listened. It was the voice of a woman. It was slowly drawing nearer, apparently from the direction in which he was going. At intervals it ceased abruptly, then began again; as if by a sudden but brief interruption, like that made by question and answer. Then, peering ahead through the mustard blossoms, he saw them waving and bending, and heard sounds as if they were being broken. Evidently some one entering on the path from the opposite end had been caught in the fragrant thicket as he was. The notes grew clearer, though still low and sweet as the twilight notes of the thrush; the mustard branches waved more and more violently; light steps were now to be heard. Father Salvierderra stood still as one in a dream, his eyes straining forward into the golden mist of blossoms. In a moment more came, distinct and clear to his ear, the beautiful words of the second stanza of Saint Francis's inimitable lyric, "The Canticle of the Sun":

"Praise be to thee, O Lord, for all thy creatures, and especially for our brother the Sun,—who illuminates the day, and by his beauty and splendor shadows forth unto us thine."

"Ramona!" exclaimed the Father, his thin cheeks flushing with pleasure. "The blessed child!" And as he spoke, her face came into sight, set in a swaying frame of the blossoms, as she parted them lightly to right and left with her hands, and half crept, half danced through the loop-hole openings thus made. Father Salvierderra was past eighty, but his blood was not too old to move quicker at the sight of this picture. A man must be dead not to thrill at it. Ramona's beauty was of the sort to be best enhanced by the waving gold which now framed her face. She had just enough of olive tint in her complexion to underlie and enrich her skin without making it swarthy. Her hair was like her Indian mother's, heavy and black, but her eyes were like her father's, steel-blue. Only those who came very near to Ramona knew, however, that her eyes were blue, for the heavy black eye-brows and long black lashes so shaded and shadowed them that they looked black as night. At the same instant that Father Salvierderra first caught sight of her face, Ramona also saw him, and crying out joyfully, "Ah, Father, I knew you would come by this path, and something told me you were near!" she sprang forward, and sank on her knees before him, bowing her head for his blessing. In silence he laid his hands on her brow. It would not have been easy for him to speak to her at that first moment. She looked to the devout old monk, as she sprang through the cloud of golden flowers, the sun falling on her bared head, her cheeks flushed, her eyes shining, more like an apparition of an angel or saint, than like the flesh-and-blood maiden whom he had carried in his arms when she was a babe.

"We have been waiting, waiting, oh, so long for you, Father!" she said, rising. "We began to fear that you might be ill. The shearers have been sent for, and will be here tonight, and that was the reason I felt so sure you would come. I knew the Virgin would bring you in time for mass in the chapel on the first morning."

The monk smiled half sadly. "Would there were more with such faith as yours, daughter," he said. "Are all well on the place?"

"Yes, Father, all well," she answered. "Felipe has been ill with a fever; but he is out now, these ten days, and fretting for—for your coming."

Ramona had like to have said the literal truth,—"fretting for the sheep-shearing," but recollected herself in time.

"And the Señora" said the Father.

"She is well," answered Ramona, gently, but with a slight change of tone,—so slight as to be almost imperceptible; but an acute observer would have always detected it in the girl's tone whenever she spoke of the Señora Moreno. "And you,—are you well yourself, Father?" she asked affectionately, noting with her quick, loving eye how feebly the old man walked, and that he carried what she had never before seen in his hand,—a stout staff to steady his steps. "You must be very tired with the long journey on foot."

"Ay, Ramona, I am tired," he replied. "Old age is conquering me. It will not be many times more that I shall see this place."

"Oh, do not say that, Father," cried Ramona; "you can ride, when it tires you too much to walk. The Señora said, only the other day, that she wished you would let her give you a horse; that it was not right for you to take these long journeys on foot. You know we have hundreds of horses. It is nothing, one horse," she added, seeing the Father slowly shake his head.

"No," he said; "it is not that. I could not refuse anything at the hands of the Señora. But it was the rule of our order to go on foot. We must deny the flesh. Look at our beloved master in this land, Father Junipero, when he was past eighty, walking from San Diego to Monterey, and all the while a running ulcer in one of his legs, for which most men would have taken to a bed, to be healed. It is a sinful fashion that is coming in, for monks to take their ease doing God's work. I can no longer walk swiftly, but I must walk all the more diligently."

While they were talking they had been slowly moving forward, Ramona slightly in advance, gracefully bending the mustard branches, and holding them down till the Father had followed in her steps. As they came out from the thicket, she exclaimed, laughing, "There is Felipe, in the willows. I told him I was coming to meet you, and he laughed at me. Now he will see I was right."

Astonished enough, Felipe, hearing voices, looked up, and saw Ramona and the Father approaching. Throwing down the knife with which he had been cutting the willows, he hastened to meet them, and dropped on his knees, as Ramona had done, for the monk's blessing. As he knelt there, the wind blowing his hair loosely off his brow, his large brown eyes lifted in gentle reverence to the Father's face, and his face full of affectionate welcome, Ramona thought to herself, as she had thought hundreds of times since she became a woman, "How beautiful Felipe is! No wonder the Señora loves him so much! If I had been beautiful like that she would have liked me better." Never was a little child more unconscious of her own beauty than Ramona still was. All the admiration which was expressed to her in word and look she took for simple kindness and good-will. Her face, as she herself saw it in her glass, did not please her. She compared her straight, massive black eye-brows with Felipe's, arched and delicately pencilled, and found her own ugly. The expression of gentle repose which her countenance wore, seemed to her an expression of stupidity. "Felipe looks so bright!" she thought, as she noted his mobile changing face, never for two successive seconds the same. "There is nobody like Felipe." And when his brown eyes were fixed on her, as they so often were, in a long, lingering gaze, she looked steadily back into their velvet depths with an abstracted sort of intensity which profoundly puzzled Felipe. It was this look, more than any other one thing, which had for two years held Felipe's tongue in leash, as it were, and made it impossible for him to say to Ramona any of the loving things of which his heart had been full ever since he could remember. The boy had spoken them unhesitatingly, unconsciously; but the man found himself suddenly afraid. "What is it she thinks when she looks into my eyes so?" he wondered. If he had known that the thing she was usually thinking was simply, "How much handsomer brown eyes are than blue! I wish my eyes were the color of Felipe's," he would have perceived, perhaps, what would have saved him sorrow, if he had known it, that a girl who looked at a man thus, would be hard to win to look at him as a lover.

But being a lover, he could not see this. He saw only enough to perplex and deter him.

At the sheep-shearing sheds and pens all was stir and bustle. The shearing shed was a huge caricature of a summer-house,—a long, narrow structure, sixty feet long by twenty or thirty wide, all roof and pillars; no walls; the supports, slender rough posts, as far apart as was safe, for the upholding the roof, which was of rough planks loosely laid from beam to beam. On three sides of this were the sheep-pens filled with sheep and lambs.

A few rods away stood the booths in which the shearers' food was to be cooked and the shearers fed. These were mere temporary affairs, roofed only by willow boughs with the leaves left on. Near these, the Indians had already arranged their camp; a hut or two of green boughs had been built, but for the most part they would sleep rolled up in their blankets, on the ground. There was a brisk wind, and the gay-colored wings of the windmill blew furiously round and round, pumping out into the tank below a stream of water so swift and strong, that as the men crowded around, wetting and sharpening their knives, they got well spattered, and had much merriment, pushing and elbowing each other into the spray.

A high four-posted frame stood close to the shed; in this, swung from the four corners, hung one of the great sacking bags in which the fleeces were to be packed. A big pile of these bags lay on the ground at foot of the posts. Juan Can eyed them with a chuckle. "We'll fill more than those before night, Señor Felipe," he said. He was in his element, Juan Can, at shearing times. Then came his reward for the somewhat monotonous and stupid year's work. The world held no better feast for his eyes than the sight of a long row of big bales of fleece, tied, stamped with the Moreno brand, ready to be drawn away to the mills. "Now, there is something substantial," he thought; "no chance of wool going amiss in market!"

If a year's crop were good, Juan's happiness was assured for the next six months. If it proved poor, he turned devout immediately, and spent the next six months calling on the saints for better luck, and redoubling his exertions with the sheep.

On one of the posts of the shed, short projecting slats were nailed, like half-rounds of a ladder. Lightly as a rope-walker Felipe ran up these, to the roof, and took his stand there, ready to take the fleeces and pack them in the bag as fast as they should be tossed up from below. Luigo, with a big leathern wallet fastened in front of him, filled with five-cent pieces, took his stand in the centre of the shed. The thirty shearers, running into the nearest pen, dragged each his sheep into the shed, in a twinkling of an eye had the creature between his knees, helpless, immovable, and the sharp sound of the shears set in. The sheep-shearing had begun. No rest now. Not a second's silence from the bleating, baa-ing, opening and shutting, clicking, sharpening of shears, flying of fleeces through the air to the roof, pressing and stamping them down in the bales; not a second's intermission, except the hour of rest at noon, from sunrise till sunset, till the whole eight thousand of the Señora Moreno's sheep were shorn. It was a dramatic spectacle. As soon as a sheep was shorn, the shearer ran with the fleece in his hand to Luigo, threw it down on a table, received his five-cent piece, dropped it in his pocket, ran to the pen, dragged out another sheep, and in less than five minutes was back again with a second fleece. The shorn sheep, released, bounded off into another pen, where, light in the head no doubt from being three to five pounds lighter on their legs, they trotted round bewilderedly for a moment, then flung up their heels and capered for joy.

When they rode down into the valley, the whole village was astir. The vintage-time had nearly passed; everywhere were to be seen large, flat baskets of grapes drying in the sun. Old women and children were turning these, or pounding acorns in the deep stone bowl; others were beating the yucca-stalks, and putting them to soak in water; the oldest women were sitting on the ground, weaving baskets. There were not many men in the village now; two large bands were away at work,—one at the autumn sheep-shearing, and one working on a large irrigating ditch at San Bernardino.

In different directions from the village slow-moving herds of goats or of cattle could be seen, being driven to pasture on the hills; some men were ploughing; several groups were at work building houses of bundles of the tule reeds.

"These are some of the Temecula people," said Alessandro; "they are building themselves new houses here. See those piles of bundles darker colored than the rest. Those are their old roofs they brought from Temecula. There, there comes Ysidro!" he cried joyfully, as a man, well-mounted, who had been riding from point to point in the village, came galloping towards them. As soon as Ysidro recognized Alessandro, he flung himself from his horse. Alessandro did the same, and both running swiftly towards each other till they met, they embraced silently. Ramona, riding up, held out her hand, saying, as she did so, "Ysidro?"

Pleased, yet surprised, at this confident and assured greeting, Ysidro saluted her, and turning to Alessandro, said in their own tongue, "Who is this woman whom you bring, that has heard my name?"

"My wife!" answered Alessandro, in the same tongue. "We were married last night by Father Gaspara. She comes from the house of the Señora Moreno. We will live in San Pasquale, if you have land for me, as you have said."

Whatever astonishment Ysidro felt, he showed none. Only a grave and courteous welcome was in his face and in his words as he said, "It is well. There is room. You are welcome." But when he heard the soft Spanish syllables in which Ramona spoke to Alessandro, and Alessandro, translating her words to him, said "Majel speaks only in the Spanish tongue, but she will learn ours," a look of disquiet passed over his countenance. His heart feared for Alessandro, and he said, "Is she, then, not Indian? Whence got she the name of Majel?"

A look of swift intelligence from Alessandro reassured him. "Indian on the mother's side!" said Alessandro, "and she belongs in heart to our people. She is alone, save for me. She is one blessed of the Virgin, Ysidro. She will help us. The name Majel I have given her, for she is like the wood-dove; and she is glad to lay her old name down forever, to bear this new name in our tongue."

And this was Ramona's introduction to the Indian village,— this and her smile; perhaps the smile did most. Even the little children were not afraid of her. The women, though shy, in the beginning, at sight of her noble bearing, and her clothes of a kind and quality they associated only with superiors, soon felt her friendliness, and, what was more, saw by her every word, tone, look, that she was Alessandro's. If Alessandro's, theirs. She was one of them. Ramona would have been profoundly impressed and touched, could she have heard them speaking among themselves about her; wondering how it had come about that she, so beautiful, and nurtured in the Moreno house, of which they all knew, should be Alessandro's loving wife. It must be, they thought in their simplicity, that the saints had sent it as an omen of good to the Indian people. Towards night they came, bringing in a hand-barrow the most aged woman in the village to look at her. She wished to see the beautiful stranger before the sun went down, they said, because she was now so old she believed each night that before morning her time would come to die. They also wished to hear the old woman's verdict on her. When Alessandro saw them coming, he understood, and made haste to explain it to Ramona. While he was yet speaking, the procession arrived, and the aged woman in her strange litter was placed silently on the ground in front of Ramona, who was sitting under Ysidro's great fig-tree. Those who had borne her withdrew, and seated themselves a few paces off. Alessandro spoke first. In a few words he told the old woman of Ramona's birth, of their marriage, and of her new name of adoption; then he said, "Take her hand, dear Majella, if you feel no fear."

There was something scarcely human in the shrivelled arm and hand outstretched in greeting; but Ramona took it in hers with tender reverence; "Say to her for me, Alessandro," she said "that I bow down to her great age with reverence, and that I hope, if it is the will of God that I live on the earth so long as she has, I may be worthy of such reverence as these people all feel for her."

Alessandro turned a grateful look on Ramona as he translated this speech, so in unison with Indian modes of thought and feeling. A murmur of pleasure arose from the group of women sitting by. The aged woman made no reply; her eyes still studied Ramona's face, and she still held her hand

"Tell her," continued Ramona, "that I ask if there is anything I can do for her. Say I will be her daughter if she will let me."

"It must be the Virgin herself that is teaching Majella

what to say," thought Alessandro, as he repeated this in the San Luisene tongue.

Again the women murmured pleasure, but the old woman spoke not. "And say that you will be her son," added Ramona.

Alessandro said it. It was perhaps for this that the old woman had waited. Lifting up her arm, like a sibyl, she said: "It is well: I am your mother. The winds of the valley shall love you, and the grass shall dance when you come. The daughter looks on her mother's face each day. I will go," and making a sign to her bearers, she was lifted, and carried to her house.

The scene affected Ramona deeply. The simplest acts of these people seemed to her marvelously profound in their meanings. She was not herself sufficiently educated or versed in life to know why she was so moved,—to know that such utterances, such symbolisms as these, among primitive peoples, are thus impressive because they are truly and grandly dramatic; but she was none the less stirred by them, because she could not analyze or explain them.

"I will go and see her every day," she said; "she shall be like my mother, whom I never saw."

"We must both go each day," said Alessandro. "What we have said is a solemn promise among my people; it would not be possible to break it."

Ysidro's home was in the centre of the village, on a slightly rising ground; it was a picturesque group of four small houses, three of tule reeds and one of adobe,—the latter a comfortable little house of two rooms, with a floor and a shingled roof, both luxuries in San Pasquale. The great fig-tree whose luxuriance and size were noted far and near throughout the country, stood half-way down the slope; but its boughs shaded all three of the tule houses. On one of its lower branches was fastened a dove-cote, ingeniously made of willow wands, plastered with adobe, and containing so many rooms that the whole tree seemed sometimes a-flutter with doves and dovelings. Here and there, between the houses, were huge baskets, larger than barrels, woven of twigs, as the eagle weaves its nest, only tighter and thicker. These were the outdoor granaries; in these were kept acorns, barley, wheat, and corn. Ramona thought them, as well she might, the prettiest thing she ever saw.

"Are they hard to make?" she asked. "Can you make them, Alessandro? I shall want many."

"All you want, my Majella," replied Alessandro. "We will go together to get the twigs; I can, I dare say, buy some in the village. It is only two days to make a large one."

"No. Do not buy one," she exclaimed. "I wish everything in our house to be made by ourselves." In which, again, Ramona was unconsciously striking one of the keynotes of pleasure in the primitive harmonies of existence.

It did not take many words to tell the story. Alessandro had not been ploughing more than an hour, when, hearing a strange sound, he looked up and saw a man unloading lumber a few rods off. Alessandro stopped midway in the furrow and watched him. The man also watched Alessandro. Presently he came towards him, and said roughly, "Look here! Be off, will you? This is my land. I'm going to build a house here."

Alessandro had replied, "This was my land yesterday. How comes it yours today?"

Something in the wording of this answer, or something in Alessandro's tone and bearing, smote the man's conscience or heart, or what stood to him in the place of conscience and heart, and he said: "Come, now, my good fellow, you look like a reasonable kind of a fellow; you just clear out, will you, and not make me any trouble. You see the land's mine. I've got all this land round here," and he waved his arm, describing a circle; "three hundred and twenty acres, me and my brother together, and we're coming in here to settle. We got our papers from Washington last week. It's all right, and you may just as well go peaceably, as make a fuss about it. Don't you see?"

Yes, Alessandro saw. He had been seeing this precise thing for months. Many times, in his dreams and in his waking thoughts, he had lived over scenes similar to this. An almost preternatural calm and wisdom seemed to be given him now.

"Yes, I see, Señor," he said. "I am not surprised. I knew it would come; but I hoped it would not be till after harvest. I will not give you any trouble, Señor, because I cannot. If I could, I would. But I have heard all about the new law which gives all the Indians' lands to the Americans. We cannot help ourselves. But it is very hard, Señor." He paused.

The man, confused and embarrassed, astonished beyond expression at being met in this way by an Indian, did not find words come ready to his tongue. "Of course, I know it does seem a little rough on fellows like you, that are industrious, and have done some work on the land. But you see the land's in the market; I've paid my money for it."

"The Señor is going to build a house?" asked Alessandro.

"Yes," the man answered. "I've got my family in San Diego, and I want to get them settled as soon as I can. My wife won't feel comfortable till she's in her own house. We're from the States, and she's been used to having everything comfortable."

"I have a wife and child, Señor," said Alessandro, still in the same calm, deliberate tone; "and we have a very good house of two rooms. It would save the Señor's building, if he would buy mine."

"How far is it?" said the man. "I can't tell exactly where the boundaries of my land are, for the stakes we set have been pulled up."

"Yes, Señor, I pulled them up and burned them. They were on my land," replied Alessandro. "My house is farther west than your stakes; and I have large wheat-fields there, too,—many acres, Señor, all planted."

Here was a chance, indeed. The man's eyes gleamed. He would do the handsome thing. He would give this fellow something for his house and wheat-crops. First, he would see the house, however; and it was for that purpose he had walked back with Alessandro. When he saw the neat whitewashed adobe, with its broad veranda, the sheds and corrals all in good order, he instantly resolved to get possession of them by fair means or foul.

"There will be three hundred dollars' worth of wheat in July, Señor, you can see for yourself, and a house so good as that, you cannot build for less than one hundred dollars. What will you give me for them?

"I suppose I can have them without paying you for them, if I choose," said the man, insolently.

"No, Señor," replied Alessandro.

"What's to hinder then, I'd like to know!" in a brutal sneer. "You haven't got any rights here, whatever, according to law."

"I shall hinder, Señor," replied Alessandro. "I shall burn down the sheds and corrals, tear down the house; and before a blade of wheat is reaped, I will burn that." Still in the same calm tone.

"What'll you take?" said the man, sullenly.

"Two hundred dollars," replied Alessandro.

"Well, leave your plough and wagon, and I'll give it to you," said the man; "and a big fool I am, too. Well laughed at, I'll be, do you know it, for buying out an Indian!"

"The wagon, Señor, cost me one hundred and thirty dollars in San Diego. You cannot buy one so good for less. I will not sell it. I need it to take away my things in. The plough you may have. That is worth twenty.

"I'll do it," said the man; and pulling out a heavy buckskin pouch, he counted out into Alessandro's hand two hundred dollars in gold.

"Is that all right?" he said, as he put down the last piece.

"That is the sum I said, Señor," replied Alessandro. "To-morrow, at noon, you can come into the house."

"Where will you go?" asked the man, again slightly touched by Alessandro's manner. "Why don't you stay round here? I expect you could get work enough; there are a lot of farmers coming in here; they'll want hands."

A fierce torrent of words sprang to Alessandro's lips, but he choked them back. "I do not know where I shall go, but I will not stay here," he said; and that ended the interview.

"I don't know as I blame him a mite for feeling that way," thought the man from the States, as he walked slowly back to his pile of lumber. "I expect I should feel just so myself."

Almost before Alessandro had finished this tale, he began to move about the room, taking down, folding up, opening and shutting lids; his restlessness was terrible to see. "By sunrise I would like to be off," he said, "It is like death to be in the house which is no longer ours." Ramona had spoken no word since her first cry on hearing that terrible laugh. She was like one stricken dumb. The shock was greater to her than to Alessandro. He had lived with it ever present in his thoughts for a year. She had always hoped. But far more dreadful than the loss of her home was the anguish of seeing, hearing, the changed face, changed voice, of Alessandro. Almost this swallowed up the other. She obeyed him mechanically, working faster and faster as he grew more and more feverish in his haste. Before sundown the little house was dismantled; everything, except the bed and the stove, packed in the big wagon.

"Now, we must cook food for the journey," said Alessandro.

"Where are we going?" said the weeping Ramona.

"Where?" ejaculated Alessandro, so scornfully that it sounded like impatience with Ramona, and made her tears flow afresh. "Where? I know not, Majella! Into the mountains, where the white men come not! At sunrise we will start."

—*Helen Hunt Jackson.*

DESCRIPTION OF ILLUSTRATIONS

IN PART X

Busy Street at the Nijni Novgorod Fair.

Nijni means *lower*, and this place is called Lower Novgorod to distinguish it from Novgorod, the much larger town.

In Nijni Novgorod is held each year a great Russian Fair which lasts for two months. It is conveniently situated on the Volga—"Mother Volga," the Russians affectionately call this valuable stream—and the Volga leads directly to the Caspian Sea. The prices obtaining here control the prices for the whole Russian Empire, and every merchant of considerable wealth keeps a branch shop here. During the busy summer season there are sometimes as many as 200,000 people on these grounds in one day, and during the two months the Fair lasts, $200,000,000 changes hands. In Mediaeval times there were many of these fairs. This is one of the few continuing to our day and it is an experience never to be forgotten to visit the various quarters of the nationalities convened here and to examine the wares exhibited.

Four Thousand Sheep in Australia.

The resources of Australia are only now becoming well understood. The interior of the country is a desert inhabited by primitive tribes. It may be noted in passing that men are studying these tribes of Central Australia today for the purpose of gaining a better understanding of primitive humanity in whatever age or clime.

Great herds of cattle and vast flocks of sheep are raised on the large ranches. Here four thousand sheep are being changed from one pasture to another.

Indian Girls Weaving Baskets—Hopi Reservation.

Year by year the reservations set aside by the government for the use of the Indians have grown smaller and smaller throughout the country. Only a few large reservations are found today—these being for the most part in the west. In Arizona and New Mexico one may see Indians living today much as they lived long ago. They are more peaceable and quiet, having been held in order for years; again, the schools are educating Indian children and the old war-like spirit is dying out. Besides, these southwestern tribes were never actuated with the ferocity of the northern tribes.

With the rapid change from uncivilized to civilized living, mortality is great among these people. For this reason it is likely that in no remote future baskets such as these will no longer be obtainable.

Columbus' First Landing Place—Porto Rica.

It was while Henry VII. sat upon the English throne that Columbus made his successful voyage across the Atlantic and opened a new world to an astonished world. This is a picture of Aguadilla, his first landing place on the island of Porto Rica as it looks today.

DESCRIPTION OF ILLUSTRATIONS. 513

SMITHSONIAN INSTITUTE.

Perhaps only comparatively few who visit this national museum stop to inquire into its origin. James Smithson, son of Sir Hugh Smithson, Duke of Northumberland, died in Genoa in 1829. He left his fortune to a nephew, stipulating that should this nephew die leaving no children, the property should be left to the United States "for the purpose of founding an institution at Washington, to be called the Smithsonian Institute, for the increase and diffusion of knowledge among men." The nephew died without heirs, in 1835, and over one-half million was paid into the United States treasury for the above mentioned purpose. By 1846 this had increased to $750,000. The government donated the land and with part of this sum a building was erected. It was built to provide for library, museum and art gallery. The National Museum here should be of interest to all citizens of this country, for it contains much that is closely interwoven with our history.

HYDAH INDIANS—ALASKA.

The Indians of the north are wholly different from those of the south. The totem pole before the house records the lineage of the chief who dwells there. Totem poles served three purposes; to mark the burial place of the dead, to give the genealogy of the chiefs, or to commemorate a place of victory. In the National Park in Sitka one may see many totem poles. To be sure, these are now resplendent in new paint and have been gathered here from many places. Nevertheless, this was the site of a battle once waged between Russians and Indians; the Indians were victorious and raised totem poles to publish their triumph.

HELEN HUNT FALLS.

Helen Hunt Jackson endeared herself to the American people as a whole, but particularly to the people of the west. Here she lived and wrote her stories, notably Ramona, in which she roused sympathy for the Indians. Many years of her life were spent in Colorado, and in accordance with her wish she was buried high up on a mountain-side. This spot became such a mecca for tourists that the remains were finally brought down again and re-interred. These Falls, a short distance from Colorado Springs, are named for her.

OLD FAITHFUL—YELLOWSTONE.

This is the most famous geyser in the world. Every hour, or sometimes with intervals of one hour and fifteen minutes, it bursts forth with a stream of boiling water. Between its eruptions, which last for about five minutes, one may examine the mound of geyserite, oblong, about 145 by 215 feet in size. This is streaked with rose, saffron, orange, brown and gray—in proportion as the water has carried various minerals in solution. When the stream bursts forth it rises in a nearly perpendicular height, while the breeze blows the cloud of steam above in the air—a "pillar of cloud by day." It is estimated that 33,000,000 gallons of water are thrown out every twenty-four hours.

ROTUNDA GALLERY—CONGRESSIONAL LIBRARY.

This wonderful library was begun in 1889 and completed in 1897, costing $6,000,000. The exterior of the building is built of New Hampshire marble; the interior is finished in marbles brought from all parts of the world, and is dazzling in brilliancy.

The Library of Congress has had several backsets. In 1814 the British burned the library that had already been accumulated. Congress soon after bought Jefferson's private library of 7,000 volumes and made that a nucleus around which to collect their books. In 1851 the library was again destroyed by fire, only 20,000 out of 55,000 volumes being saved. The final home of the Congressional library is planned to withstand the storm and stress of centuries.

Looking Down from Inspiration Point.

This view down the Grand Cañon is one of the most inspiring in the world. No river has ever cut down a more remarkable channel than the Colorado, the cañon of which defies description. The rocks reflect the light of the sun and produce a sight seldom seen anywhere. Every year this section of our country is visited by many foreigners, as well as by large numbers of Americans.

A Mexican Cathedral.

Soon after the discovery of a new world, Spanish explorers reached out in every direction to ascertain the nature of recently discovered lands. They were accompanied almost from the first by brave-hearted men who wished to carry the Christian religion to the furthermost parts of the earth. Jesuits were later followed by Franciscan monks, who from Mexico came up into California and the Coast regions to teach and preach.

The Catholic Church has always found it useful to teach by symbol and painting, and especially where the masses are ignorant, all means of illustrating religious stories are eagerly embraced.

INDEX OF ART AND ARCHITECTURE

Abbey, Edwin A., x. 223, 237.
Adoration of the Mystic Lamb, ix. 48.
Alexander, John W., x. 240.
American Art—
  See Expositions, General.
  Early American Painters, x. 207.
  Recent American Painters, x. 214.
  Mural Painting, x. 235.
  Galleries, x. 225.
American Art Centers—
  New York, x. 225.
  Philadelphia, x. 227.
  Washington, x. 231.
  Boston, x. 230.
  Chicago, x. 234.
American Institutes of Archæology ii. 47.
Anatomy Lesson, Rembrandt, ix. 58.
Andalusian Art, ix. 72.
Angelico, Fra, ix. 25, 112, 115.
Angelus, Millet, ix. 90.
Angelo Michael, ii. 157; ix. 32, 122.
Antwerp, Art of, ix. 49.
Architecture—
  Babylonian, i. 300.
  Greek, iii. 341.
  Roman, iv. 380.
Antiquities—
  Egyptian ix. 184.
  Classical, ix. 184.
Apollo Belvedere, ix. 128.
Art—
  Beginnings, i. 225.
  Of Ancients, i. 15.
  Hebrew, ii. 9.
Art Galleries, American—
  Metropolitan, x. 225.
  Pennsylvania Academy, x. 227.
  Boston Museum, x. 230.
  Corcoran, x. 231.
  Chicago, x. 234.
Art Galleries, European—
  Florence—
    Academy, ix. 110.
    Uffizi, ix. 112.
    Pitti Palace, ix. 117.
  Rome—
    Vatican, ix. 120.
  Venice—
    Academy, ix. 129.
  Milan—
    Brera, ix. 136.
  Belgium—
    Bruges Academy, ix. 138.
    Antwerp Gallery, ix. 139.
  Netherlands—
    The Hague Royal Museum, ix. 142.
    Rotterdam, ix. 144.
    Amsterdam, ix. 145.
  Spain—
    Prado, ix. 147.
    Seville, ix. 150.
  Germany—
    Dresden, ix. 151.
    Berlin, ix. 154.
    Munich, ix. 156.
  France—
    Louvre, ix. 158.
  London—
    National, ix. 169.
    Tate, ix. 173.
Assumption of the Virgin, ix. 45.
Aurora, ii. 84, 126.

Bachelier, ix. 82.
Barbizon School, ix. 85.
Basilica, ix. 16.
Bellini, ix. 129.
Biblical Pictures, ix. 12, 23, 122.
Blashfield, x. 240.
Bol, Ferdinand, ix. 143.
Bonheur, Rosa, ix. 92.
Book—
  Of Kells, ix. 104.
  Of Durrow, ix. 104.
  Of Hours, ix. 107.
Boecklin, ix. 154, 156.
Bordone, ix. 133.
Botticelli, ix. 29, 113.
Boucher, ix. 161.
Bruges, Art of, ix. 46.
Brussels, Art of, ix. 48.
Burne-Jones, ix. 174; x. 219.
Byzantine Art, ix. 15.

Calumny, Botticelli, ix. 30.
Capanna, Puccio, ix. 24.

Carnegie Institute, x. 241.
Carrara Marble, ix. 34.
Carpaccio, ix. 130.
Castilian Art, ix. 72.
Catacomb Pictures, ix. 10.
Cathedral of Ghent, ix. 48.
Celtic Illumination, ix. 104.
Chardin, ix. 82, 162.
Chase, William M., x. 224.
Chiaroscuro, ix. 39.
Churches, Early, ix. 16.
Church—
  Of Assisi, ix. 23.
  Of St. Apollinare Nuove, ix. 19.
  Of St. Bavon, ix. 48.
  Of Santa Croce, ix. 119.
  Of Santa Marie Novella, ix. 119.
  Of the Sepulcher, ii. 61.
  Of the Nativity, ii. 65.
Christian Art, ix. 9.
Christian Symbols, ix. 10.
Cimabue, ix. 22.
Claude (Lorrain), ix. 80.
Classical Art, ix. 81.
Clouet, Jean, ix. 80.

Dance of Death, ix. 65.
Daubigny, ix. 165.
David, Gheeraert, ix. 49.
David, Jean Louis, ix. 83.
Decorative Art, Egypt, i. 135.
De Hoogh, ix. 59.
Delacroix, ix. 85.
Diaz, ix. 92, 165.
Dome of the Rock, ii. 61.
Doughty, Thomas, x. 211.
Doric Architecture, iii. 342.
Dou Gerard, ix. 59.
Ducal Palace, ix. 134.
Duomo, Florence, ix. 24.
Dupre, ix. 92, 165.
Dutch Art, ix. 62, 153.
Dürer, ix. 44, 66, 115.

Egyptian Art, i. 42.
Elgin, Marbles. iii. 349; ix. 184.
El Greco, ix. 73, 147.
Exultet, ix. 108.

Fappa, Vincenzo, ix. 136.
Filippo Lippi, ix. 27, 112.
Flemish Art, ix. 46.
Flora, Titian, ix. 44.
Foreshortening, ix. 39.
French Academy, ix. 80.
French Art, ix. 79.
  Modern, ix. 85.

Gaddi, Taddeo, ix. 24.
Gainsborough, ix. 96, 171.
Genre Painting, ix. 59.
German Art, ix. 64, 153.
Ghirlandajo, ix. 8.
Giotto, ix. 22.
Giottoesques, ix. 24.
Giottino, ix. 24.
Giorgione, ix. 118.
Gleaners, The, ix. 90.
Goya, ix. 77, 150.

Hals Frans, ix. 55, 145.
Harley, Robert, ix. 179.
Heene, David de, ix. 63.
Hermes, Praxiteles, iii. 357, 368.
Herrera, ix. 72.
Hide Pictures, i. 27.
History of Art—
  Pleasure of Art Study, ix. 1.
  Early Christian, ix. 9.
  Byzantine, ix. 15.
  Mosaics, ix. 17.
  Early Italian Painting, ix. 22.
  Angelico, ix. 25.
  Filippo Lippi, ix. 27.
  Realistic, ix. 29.
  Botticelli, ix. 29.
  Angelo, ix. 33.
  Correggio, ix. 39.
  Titian, ix. 41.
  Flemish, ix. 46.
  Dutch, ix. 53.
  German, ix. 64.
  Spanish, ix. 70.
  French, ix. 79.
  English, ix. 94.
  Illumination, ix. 101.
  American, x. 207.
Hobbema, ix. 62, 144.
Hogarth, ix. 94, 169.
Holbein, ix. 64, 94.
Homer Winslow, x. 216.
Horse Fair, The, ix. 93.
Houses—see General.
Hudson River School, x. 211.

Iconoclastic Movement, ix. 18.
Illumination, ix. 46, 101.
Ingres, ix. 163.
Inness, x. 212.
Interior Decoration—
  Babylonian, i. 302.
  Assyrian, i. 321.
Ionic Column, iii. 342.
Italian Art, ix. 22.
Israels, Joseph, ix. 63, 146.

Kells, Book of, ix. 104.

La Farge, x. 218, 235, 244.
Landseer, ix. 98, 175.
Landscape Painting, ix. 61.
Laocoön ix. 128.
Last Judgment, Angelo, ix. 36.
Last Supper, Leonardo, ix. 31.
Lebrun, Charles, ix. 81.
Lebrun, Madame, ix. 83.
Leighton, ix. 175.
Leonardo da Vinci, ix. 30, 34, 79, 136.
Le Sueur, ix. 161.
Leyden, Lucas van, ix. 54.
Lion Gate, iii. 348.
Lotti Lorenzo, ix. 119.
Louis XIV, Art of, ix. 80.
Louis XV, Art of, ix. 82.
Luini, ix. 136.

Mabuse, ix. 49.
Madonas—
  Cimabue, ix. 21.
  Angelico, ix. 25.
  Filippo Lippi, ix. 27.
  Raphael, ix. 37, 117, 151.
  Correggio, ix. 39.
  Dutch, ix. 55.
  German, ix. 64.
  Spanish, ix. 72.
Magi, ix. 115.
Manuscripts Illuminated, ix. 102, 182.
Mars, Nicholas, ix. 59.
Masaccio, ix. 26, 112.
Massys, Quentin, ix. 49.
Mauve, ix. 63, 146.
McEwen, Walter, x. 240.
Medici—
  Cosimo de, ix. 27, 112.
  Lorenzo de, ix. 33.
  Marie de, ix. 80.
Meister Wilhelm, ix. 64.
Melon Eaters, Murillo, ix. 76.
Memlinc, ix. 49, 139.
Millet, ix. 85, 88, 166.
Millet, F. D., x. 243.
Millais, ix. 99, 173.
Miniatures, ix. 46.
Mona Lisa, ix. 32, 166.
Mosaics, ii. 46; ix. 17.
Mural Painting—
  Boston Museum, x. 236.
  Congressional Library, x. 239.
  Carnegie Institute, x. 240.
  Appellates Courts, x. 243.
  Ponce de Leon Hotel, x. 243.
  Capitol of Minnesota, x. 244.
Murillo, ix. 74, 159.

Museums—
  Alexandria, i. 181.
  Athens, iii. 371.
  Berlin, ii. 240; ix. 154.
  British, i. 187, 207; ii. 277; iii. 349; ix. 179.
  Cairo, i. 146, 185.
  Constantinople, i. 210; ii. 373.
  Delphi, iii. 373.
  Louvre, i. 187; ii. 143; ix. 158, 184.
  Naples, iv. 391.
  Olympian, iii. 368.
  Palermo, iv. 389.
  Seville, ix. 150.
Museums—American—
  Boston, ix. 98.
  Metropolitan, i. 187; ix. 93; x. 225.
  University of Pennsylvania, i. 210.
Mycenæan Art, iii. 348.

Nativity—
  Corregio, ix. 41, 151.
  Ghirlandajo, ix. 3.
Nave, ix. 16, 19.
Napoleonic Art, ix. 83, 158, 163.
Night Watch, ix. 58.
Nimbus, ix. 13.

Oxen Ploughing, ix. 93.

Pacheco, ix. 72, 148.
Painting—
  Egyptian, i. 133.
  Greek, iii. 347, 351.
Parthenon, ii. 121, 319; iii. 343, 349.
Peale, Charles W., x. 210.
Pearce, Chas. S. x. 239.
Pediments, iii. 349.
Perugimo, ix. 37, 112.
Phidias, ii. 104, 110, 121, 233, 307, 319; iii. 348.
Physician of Parma, Titian ix. 44.
Pitti Palace, ix. 117.
Polyclitus, ii. 110.
Polynotas, iii. 352.
Pompey's Pillar, i. 182.
Portrait Painters, ix. 55, 65, 95.
Potter, Paul, ix. 62, 143.
Pottery, Egyptian, i. 105.
Poussin, iv. 80, 161.
Prado, The, ix. 147.
Praxiteles, ix. 28; iii. 350; iv. 392.
Pre-Raphaelites, ix. 99.
Presentation in the Temple, ix. 44, 131.
Puis de Chavannes, x. 236.
Pyle, Howard, x. 244.

Raphael, ix. 34, 37, 113.
Raphael, Loggie, ix. 126.
Raphael Stanze ix. 127.
Ravenna, Mosaics of, ix. 19.
Rembrandt, ix. 42, 56, 143.
Reynolds, ix. 94, 171.
Ribalta, ix. 73, 147.
Ribera, ix. 73, 147.
Romano ix. 119.
Romney ix. 171.
Rossetti, ix. 99, 175; x. 219.
Rousseau, ix. 88, 164.
Royal Academy, ix. 96.
Rubens, ix. 3, 50, 73, 141.
Ruisdael, ix. 62, 144.

San Marco ix. 25, 112, 119.
Sargent, John Singe:, x. 223, 238.
Sarto, Andrea del, ix. 29, 79, 114.
Schongauer ix. 64.
Scrolls—
  Egyptian, i. 135.
Sculpture—
  Egyptian, i. 134
  Greek, ii. 422; iii. 346, 356.
Siddons, Sarah, ix. 95.
Sistine Chapel, ix. 35, 38, 121.
Sistine Tapestries, ix. 124.
Six Collection, ix. 146.
Slave Ship, ix. 98.
Sloane, Sir Hans, ix. 180.
Spanish Art, ix. 70.
Spring, Botticelli, ix. 30, 110.
St. Catherine, ix. 40.
St. Paul's, viii. 34.
St. Ursula, ix. 64, 137.
Steen, Jan, ix. 60, 144.
Stuart, Gilbert, x. 210.
Statuary—
  David, Angelo, ix. 34, 110.
  Moses, Angelo, ix. 35.
  Day and Night, ix. 36.
  Twilight and Dawn, ix. 36.
  Apollo Belvedere, ix. 128.
  Laocoön, ix. 128.
  Sleeping Endymion, ix. 185.
Surrender of Breda, ix. 148.
Swabian Art, ix. 64.
Symbolism, Christian, ix. 10.

Tabernacle Madonna, ix. 25.
Tadema, Laurence Alma-, ix. 52.
Tapestry Weavers, ix. 149.
Temeraire, ix. 98, 175.

Temples—
  Karnak, i. 69, 159.
  Abu Simbel, i. 78.
  Egyptian, i. 125.
  Babylonian, i. 300, 312.
  Ziggurats, i. 300.
  Solomon's, ii. 9, 61.
  Jupiter's, ii. 105.
  Artemis, ii. 133.
  Greek, ii. 422; iii. 341.
Three Ages of Man, ix. 44.
Tintoretto, ix. 74, 132.
Titian, ix. 41, 67, 114, 130, 153.
Tomb Pictures i. 100, 133.
Tribute Money, Titian, ix. 43.
Trojan, ix. 165.
Trumbull, x. 211, 235.
Turner, ix. 97, 172.

Uffizi Gallery, ix. 112.

Van Dyck, ix. 51, 94.
Van Eyck, ix. 47.
Van Goyen, ix. 61.
Van der Velde, ix. 62.
Van der Weyden, ix. 48, 139.
Varges, Luis de, ix. 72.
Vase Painting, ii. 385.
Vasari, ix. 116.
Vatican, ix. 34, 120.
Vedder, Elihu, x. 214, 240.
Velasquez, ix. 4, 72, 73, 148.
Venus de Milo, ii. 84, 143.
Ver Meer, ix. 160, 143.
Veronese, Paul, ix. 132, 134, 159.
Volk, Douglas, x. 244.
Votives, iii. 346.
Vulgate, ix. 104.

Walker, Henry O., x. 239.
Watteau, ix. 82, 161.
Watts, Geo. F., ix. 174.
Weenix, Jan, ix. 63.
West, Benjamin, x. 207.
Westphalian Art, ix. 64.
Whistler, James McNeill, x. 220.
White Mountain School, x. 211.
Wilson, Richard, ix. 172.
Woodcuts, ix. 65, 67.
Wren, Sir Christopher, viii. 34.
Wyant, x. 210.

Ziggurats, i. 300.
Zurbara, ix. 72.

DRAMA AND MUSIC

Actors—
  Women, vii. 25, 43.
  Early English, vii. 68, 188.
  Early English actresses, vii. 191.
Æschylus, ii. 265, 299; iii. 4, 29, 84; vii. 12.
Agamemnon, iii. 5.
Aïda, v. 327.
Ajax, iii. 29.
Alchemist, The, vii. 150.
Andromache, iii. 45.
Annunzio, vii. 284.
Anthem—
  Origin, v. 253.
Antigone, iii. 29.
Aristophanes, ii. 265.
  Plays of, iii. 63.
Arraignment of Paris, vii. 91.

Bacchæ, iii. 45.
Bach, Johann Sebastian—
  Life, v. 255.
  Compositions, v. 257.
Ballads, v. 307.
Barber of Seville, opera, v. 323.
Bayreuth, v. 358.
Beaumont and Fletcher, vii. 154.
Beethoven, Ludwig Van—
  Life, v. 279.
  Opera, v. 286.
  Sonatas, v. 284.
  Symphonies, v. 285.
Before Dawn, vii. 380.
Betterton, Thomas, vii. 189.
Berlioz, Hector—
  Life, v. 309.
  Symphonies, v. 311.
Birds, The, iii. 63.
Bizet, George, v. 347.
Blackfriars, vii. 68.
Blue Bird, vii. 269.
Brocco, Robt., vii. 286.
Burbage, James, vii. 68.
Burbage, Richard, vii. 68, 188.
Buskins, vii. 15.

Campaspe, Play of, vii. 75.
Cantata, v. 260.
Carmen, v. 347.
Cavalleria Rusticana, v. 328.

Chanticleer, vii. 274.
Chants—
  Gregorian, v. 233.
  Anglican, v. 253.
Cherubini, v. 337.
Choephori, iii. 5.
Chopin, Frederic—
  Life, v. 305.
  Compositions, v. 307.
Chorale, v. 249.
Chorus, vii. 16.
Cid, The, vii. 219.
Citta Morta, La, vii. 285.
Clouds, The, iii. 63, 70.
Cockpit, The, vii. 69.
Comedy, Greek, iii. 62.
Comedy, Italian, vii. 39.
Comedy of Errors, vii. 110.
Commedia dell'Arte, vii. 468; vii. 29.
Composers, Musical—
  Early German, v. 255.
  Classical, v. 255.
  Romantic, v. 289.
Congreve, vii. 168.
Corneille, vii. 215, 217.
Corpus Christi, Play, vii. 28.
Counterpoint, v. 238.
Curtain, The, vii. 68.
Cyrano de Bergerac, vii. 275.

Das Rheingold, v. 366.
David and Bethsabe, vii. 91.
Der Freischütz, v. 291.
Die Walküre, v. 369.
Die Zauberflöte, v. 351.
Dionysia, Greater, ii. 425; iii. 1; vii. 13.
Dionysia, Lesser, ii, 425; iii. 2; vii. 13.
Doll's House, The, vii. 297.
Don Giovanni, v. 276.
Double Dealer, vii. 169.
Drama—
  Hebrew, ii. 23.
  Greek, ii. 315; iii. 1; vii. 12.
  Greek, decline of, iii. 84.
  Roman, iv. 94, 145; vii. 15.
  General Survey, vii. 1.
  Beginnings of, vii. 9.
  Mediæval, vii. 20.

Interludes, vii. 44.
Masques, vii. 55.
Elizabethan, vii. 73.
Shakespearean, vii. 107.
Restoration vii, 166.
Recent English, vii. 195.
French, vii. 215.
French, modern, vii. 266.
Italian, vii. 283.
Norwegian, vii. 297.
German, vii. 317.
German, recent, vii. 371.
Drolls, vii. 166.
Dryden, vii. 168.

Egmont, vii. 333.
Electra, iii. 29, 45.
Elijah, oratoria, v. 303.
Eumenides, iii. 5.
Euripides, ii. 265; iii. 41.
 Plays, iii. 45, 84; vii. 13.
Euryanthe, v. 291.
Every Man in his Humor, vii. 149.

Faust, opera, v. 342; vii. 341.
Faust, play, vii. 337.
Faustus, Dr., vii. 97.
Fidelio, opera, v. 286.
Fletcher, vii. 154.
Flying Dutchman, opera, v. 361.
Folk music, v. 219, 240.
—— German, v. 247.
Fortune, The, vii. 68.
Four P's, vii. 47.
Francesca da Rimini, vii. 284.
Freischütz, Der, v. 291.
Friar Bacon and Friar Bungay, vii. 84.

Garrick, vii. 190.
Getting Married, play, vii. 206.
Gioconda, La, vii. 285.
Globe, The, vii. 68, 71.
Gluck, Christoph—
 Life, v. 335.
 Operas, v. 336.
Goethe, vii. 331.
Goetz, Herman, v. 352.
Goldmark, Karl, v. 352.
Gounod, Charles, v. 341.
Greene, Playwright, vii. 74, 83.
Guilds, Plays given by, vii. 24.
Guillaume Tell, v. 323.

Hamlet, vii. 3.
Handel, George Frederic—
 Life, v. 261.
 Operas, v. 263.
 Oratorios, v. 265.

Hansel and Gretel, v. 354.
Harmony, v. 239.
Hauptmann, vii. 371, 380.
Haydn, Joseph—
 Life, v. 268.
 Sonatas, v. 271.
Henry IV. and V., vii. 110.
Herman and Dorothea, vii. 334.
Heywood, John, vii. 47.
Hippolytus, iii. 45.
Huguenots, Leo, v. 339.
Humperdinck, Ingelbert, v. 354.
Hymns—
 Origin, v. 248.
 Protestant, v. 249.

Ibsen, vii. 297.
Il Trovatore, v. 326.
Improvised comedy, vii. 40.
Instruments, musical—
 Early Church, v. 229.
Interludes, vii. 44.
Ion, play, iii. 45.
Iphigenia, iii. 56.
Irving, Henry, vii. 193.

Jew of Malta, vii. 98.
Job, Book of, vii. 340.
Joy of Living, play, vii. 374.
Jonson, Ben, Masques, vii. 56, 149.
Julius Cæsar, vii. 3.

Kean, actor, vii. 193.
Kemble, actor, vii. 193.
Kennedy, vii. 212.
King John, vii. 110.
King Lear, vii. 112.
Kyd, vii. 74.

La Tosca, opera, v. 329.
Lenæa, The iii. 2, 62; vii. 13.
Lessing, vii. 317.
Leid—German, v. 293.
Liszt, Franz—
 Life, v. 312.
 Concert work, v. 313.
 Compositions, 314.
Liturgical Music, v. 229.
 Western Church, v. 230.
 Anglican, v. 252.
Lohengrin, opera, v. 362.
Love's Labor Lost, vii. 110.
Lyly, playwright, vii. 75.

Macklin, vii. 191.
Madrigal, v. 237.
Maeterlinck, vii. 263, 267.
Magic Flute, v. 276.

Manon, opera, v. 348.
Mansfield, Richard, vii. 193.
Marlowe, vii. 74, 97, 338.
Marriage of Figaro, v. 276.
Masks, Greek, vii. 14.
Masques, vii. 55.
Mass, v. 229, 231.
  Bach, v. 260.
  Haydn, v. 271.
  Mozart, v. 276.
Master-singers, v. 241.
  Nuremberg, v. 361.
Massenet, Jules, v. 348.
Mazurka, v. 307.
Medea, iii, 45, 51.
Melody, v. 236.
Menander, iii. 63, 82.
Mendelssohn, Felix—
  Life, v. 301.
  Compositions, v. 303; vii. 317.
Merry Wives of Windsor, vii. 3.
Merchant of Venice, vii. 122.
Meyerbeer, v. 338.
Mignon, opera, v. 345.
Midsummer Night's Dream, vii. 73, 110.
Minna von Barnhelm, vii. 318.
Mimes, vii. 15.
Minnesingers, v. 241.
Minstrels, ii. 430; v. 101, 241.
Miracle Plays, vii. 20, 73.
Molière, vii. 215, 238.
Montevede, v. 319.
Morality Plays, vii. 27.
Motifs, musical, v. 359.
Mozart, Wolfgang—
  Life, v. 272.
  Concert work, v. 273.
  Operas, v. 275.
  Requiem mass, v. 276.
Music—
  Egyptian, i. 98.
  Greek, ii. 403.
  Origin of, v. 218, 225.
  Ancient, v. 225, 234; ii. 277.
  Early Church, v. 226.
  Catholic, v. 228.
  Eastern Church, v. 230.
  Mediæval, v. 236.
  Dutch, v. 239.
  Protestant, v. 248.
  Romantic, v. 289.
  Programme, v. 308.
  Music-Dramas, v. 357.
  Mystery Plays, vii. 20.

Nathan der Weise, vii. 317.
Nell Gwynne, actress, vii. 189.
New Bach Society, v. 260.
Notation, Musical, v. 236.

Oberon, opera, v. 291.
Œdipus the King, iii. 29, 34.
Œdipus at Colonus, iii. 29.
Opera—
  Handel, v. 263.
  Beethoven, v. 286.
  Romantic, v. 289.
  Weber, v. 291.
  Origin of, v. 317.
  Grand, v. 318.
  Comique, v. 318.
  Italian, v. 319, 321.
  French, v. 351.
  German, v. 355.
  Wagner, v. 357.
Oratorio—
  Origin, v. 265.
  Handel, v. 265.
  Mendelssohn, v. 303.
Orchestra, vii. 69.
Orpheus and Eurydice, v. 335.
Othello, vii. 3.

Pageants, vii. 24.
Pantomines, vii. 15.
Parsifal, opera, v. 361.
Passion, Music—
  Origin, v. 260.
  Bach's, v. 261.
Peele, vii. 74, 91.
Persians, The, iii. 5.
Philaster's Jealousy, vii. 156.
Philemon, iii. 63, 83.
Piano, v. 296.
Pinero, vii. 197.
Plain-song, v. 233.
Plautus, iv. 146; vii. 15, 74.
Playwrights, Italian, vi. 468.
Polonaise, v. 307.
Programme Music, v. 308, 315.
Prometheus Bound, iii. 5, 20.
Proserpine, opera, v. 343.
Puritan Opposition to Plays, vii. 67.

Queen of Sheba, opera, v. 352.

Racine, vii. 215, 227.
Red Bull, vii. 68.
Reformation—
  Puritan, ii. 31.
Restoration Drama, vii. 166.
Richard III., vii. 110.
Rienzi, opera, v. 361.
Rimini, Francesca da, vii. 287.
Ring, The Nibelung, v. 361.
Rivals, The, vii. 168, 178.
Romantic School of Music, v. 289.

Rose, The, vii. 68.
Rossini, v. 322.
Rostand, vii. 274.

Saint-Saëns Camile, v. 343.
Samson and Delila, v. 344.
Scale-system, v. 226.
Scarlatti, v. 320.
Scenery, Theatrical, vii. 26
Scherzo, v. 307.
Schiller, vii. 331, 354.
School for Scandal, vii. 168.
Schubert, v. 293.
   Songs, v. 295.
Schumann, Robert—
   Life, v. 298.
   Compositions, v. 299.
Scribe, vii. 216.
Seneca, vii. 74.
Seven against Thebes, iii. 5.
Shakespeare—
   Forerunners of, vii. 73.
   Life, vii. 108.
   Plays, vii. 110.
Shaw, Bernard, vii. 204.
She Stoops to Conquer, vii. 168, viii. 190.
Sheridan, vii. 176.
Siddons, vii. 192.
Siegfried, v. 375.
Singing Schools, v. 235.
Singspiel, v. 351.
Sir Thomas Moore, play, vii. 44.
Sonata—
   Form of, v. 270.
   Haydn, v. 271.
   Beethoven, v. 284.
Songspiel, v. 291.
Sophocles, ii. 265; iii. 3, 28, 34, 43, 84; vii. 13.
Spanish Tragedy, vii. 110.
Stage, Greek, vii. 16.
Stage, English, vii. 70.
St. Paul, oratorio, v. 303.
Strauss, Richard, v. 355.
Sudermann, vii. 371.
Sunken Bell, The, vii. 380.
Suppliants, The, iii. 5, 45.

Swan, The, vii. 68.
Symbolism vii. 267.
Symphony—
   Form of, v. 270.
   Haydn, v. 270.
   Beethoven, v. 285.
   Schumann, v. 300.
   Berlioz, v. 310.

Tamburlaine, vii. 97.
Tannhauser, v. 361.
Tell, Wilhelm, vii. 364.
Tempest, The. vii. 3, 137.
Terence, iv. 173; vii. 15, 74.
Theatre, The, vii. 68.
   Roman iv. 94; vii. 16.
   Greek, vii. 14.
   Elizabethan, vii. 64.
Theatre de l'Opera—comique, v. 334.
Thespis, iii. 2.
Thomas, Charles A., v. 345—
   Operas. v. 346.
Three Maries, The, vii. 32.
Titus Andronicus, vii. 110.
Transcriptions, v. 314.
Tristan and Isolde, v. 361.
Troubadours, v. 241.
Twilight of the Gods, v. 379.
Two Gentlemen of Verona, vii. 110.

Verdi, Giuseppe—
   Life, v. 325.
   Operas, v. 326.

Wagner, Richard—
   Life, v. 357.
   Writings, v. 358, 384.
   Orchestra leader, v. 360.
   Operas, v. 361.
Wasps, The, iii. 63.
Water Carriers, opera, v. 338.
Weavers, The, vii. 380.
Weber, Carl von, v. 290.
Wilhelm, Meister, opera, v. 345
Woffington, Peg, vii. 191.

HISTORICAL INDEX

Abelard, iv. 473; vi. 13.
Abraham, i. 434.
Academy, ii. 406.
Achaea, ii. 233.
Achaean League, iii. 456.
Achilles, ii. 247.
Acropolis, ii. 307, 375; iii. 348, 371.
Actium, iii. 485.
Adams, John, x. 28.
Adams, John Quincy, x. 32.
Adrianople, iv. 49.
Aetolian League, iii. 456.
Agamemnon, ii. 247.
Ages, Rough, Smooth Stone, i. xvii.
Agincourt, viii. 21.
Agora, ii. 376; iv. 380.
Agricola, iv. 26; viii. 5.
Ahmos, i. 54.
Alaric, iv. 50.
Alaska Purchase, x. 42, 196.
Albigenses, v. 105.
Alcibiades, ii. 338.
Alcuin, iv. 412.
Alexander the Great, i. 181, 345, 351;
  ii. 3, 358, 366; iii. 455.
Alfred the Great, v. 70, 79; viii. 8.
Alien and Sedition Laws, x. 29.
Alpheus, ii. 233.
Amenemhet I, i. 46.
Amenemhet III, i. 47.
Amenhotep IV, i. 68.
America—
  Discovery of, i. 18.
  Exploration of, x. 30.
  Colonial, x. 39.
  Independence of, x. 40.
American Colonies, x. 12.
American School of Archæology, ii. 47.
Ammonites, i. 435, 446.
Amon, Priests of, i. 81.
Amphictyonic League, iii. 101.
Ancus Martius, iii. 390.
Angles, iv. 56; viii. 6.
Anne Boleyn, viii. 25.
Anne, Queen, viii. 35.
Anti-Federalists, x. 27.
Antoninus Pius, iv. 31.
Anthony, Mark, iii. 482.
Apella, ii. 271.
Appian Way, iv. 394.
Arcadia, ii. 232.

Areopagus, ii. 136, 305.
Aristides, ii. 296, 309.
Aristotle, ii. 262.
Argolis, ii. 232.
Artaxerxes, ii. 306.
Articles of Confederation, x. 21.
Aryans, ii. 267.
Asia Minor, ii. 234.
Asshurbanipal, i. 259.
  Library, i. 208, 283, 291, 324.
Assyria—
  Settlement, i. 226.
  Conquers Babylonia, i. 241.
  Fall of, i. 330.
Assyrians—
  Religion of, i. 310.
  Palaces, i. 321.
  Influence, i. 359.
Astyages, i. 336.
Athens, ii. 275.
  Constitution, ii. 277, 345.
  Empire, ii. 302.
  Beautifying of, ii. 318.
  Fall of, ii. 337.
  Modern, iii. 370.
Attila, iv. 51.
Attica, ii. 232.
Augustine, v. 67.
Augustine in Britain, viii. 7.
Augustus, iv. 1; Deeds of, iv. 7.
Aurelius, Marcus, iv. 31.
Austrian Succession, viii. 38.
Austro-Prussian War, viii. 470.

Babylon, i. 232.
  Conquest of, i. 250.
  Rebuilding, i. 256.
  Wonders of, i. 267.
  Fall of, i. 269.
  Walls of, i. 304.
  Hanging Gardens, i. 305.
Babylonia—
  Antiquity of, i. 202.
  Excavations, i. 205.
  Language of, i. 207.
  Physiography, i. 212.
  Products, i. 216.
  City-states, i. 227.
  Assyrian Conquest of, i. 241.
  Revolt of, i. 260.
  People of, i. 270.

Babylonia Social Life—
  Houses, i. 272.
  Family Life, i. 274.
  Literature, i. 283.
  Learning, i. 287.
  Dress, i. 293.
  Religion, i. 307.
  Temples, i. 312.
  Labor, i. 317.
  Professions, i. 322.
  Military Life, i. 324.
  Influence, i. 357.
  Historical Sources for, i. 211.
Balboa, x. 6.
Bathsheba, i. 463.
Bastile, Fall of, viii. 446.
Becket, Thomas à, viii. 17.
Belshazzar, i. 268, 319.
Bethlehem, ii. 4.
Bernard of Clairvaux, iv. 423.
Boetia, ii. 232, 331.
Berosus, Priest, i. 211.
Bismarck, viii. 470.
Black Plague, viii. 20.
Boadicea, Queen, viii. 5.
Boule, ii. 407.
Braddock, Gen., x. 17.
Brazil, x. 7.
Bucephalus, ii. 366.
Burgundians, iv. 56.
Byzantine—See Literature and Art.
Byzantium, iv. 37.

Cabot, John, viii. 23; x. 7.
Cabot, Sebastian, viii. 23; x. 7.
Caesar, Julius, ii. 3; iii. 400, 480; iv. 121; viii. 4.
Caesar, Octavius, iii. 483.
Cairo, i. 182.
Calais, viii. 20.
Caledonians, viii. 5.
Calhoun, x. 29, 34.
Caligula, iv. 18.
Cambyses, i. 340, 385.
Canaanites, i. 437; ii. 7.
Canterbury, Bishop of, viii. 17.
Campagna, iii. 382.
Campus, Martius, ii. 136.
Capet, House of, viii. 434.
Capitoline, iii. 384.
Carbinari, vi. 372.
Carthage, i. 340, 391; iii. 438.
Cartier, x. 6.
Cassander, ii. 371.
Catacombs, iv. 394; ix. 9.
Catiline, iv. 181.
Cavour, vi. 373.
Caxton, ix. 41.
Catholic Emancipation, viii. 47.

Celts, viii. 4.
Chalcidice, ii. 326.
Chaldea, i. 201.
  Prehistoric, i. 218.
  Religion, i. 219.
  Empire of, i. 264.
Charlemagne, iv. 55, 411, 414; v. 91; vi. 365; viii. 432; ix. 104.
Charles Martel, iv. 57, 409; ix. 70.
Charles I, viii. 31; ix. 50.
Charles II, viii. 33.
Charles VI, viii. 21.
Charles VII, viii. 21.
Charters—
  Henry I, viii. 13.
  Magna Charta, viii. 19.
Chivalry, v. 1.
Christianity, Early, iv. 40, 47, 418; ix. 10.
  Christ, birth of, ii. 4; iv. 40.
  Christians, iv. 45.
  Church of the Sepulchre, ii. 61.
Cinon, ii. 303, 313.
Circus Maximus, iv. 95, 112.
Civil War in America, x. 38.
Claudius, iv. 19; viii. 5.
Clarendon, viii. 17.
Cleon, ii. 337.
Cleopatra, iii. 484.
Cleveland, Grover, x. 33.
Clisthenes, ii. 286.
Cloth of Gold, viii. 24.
Clovis, iv. 56.
Cnidus, ii. 347.
Cnut, viii. 9.
Codrus, ii. 277, 348.
Colbert, viii. 439.
Colonna, Vittoria, ix. 36.
Commons, House of, viii. 21.
Columba, St., viii. 7.
Columbus, i. 18; ii. 79; viii. 23; ix. 42; x. 3.
Condottieri, vi. 13.
Confederacy of Delos, ii. 302.
Congress of Vienna, iv. 372; viii. 462, 468; x. 31.
Conon, ii. 347.
Constantine, iv. 35; ix. 15.
Constantius, iv. 34.
Constitutions of Clarendon, viii. 17.
Constitution Convention, x. 21.
Constitution of the United States, x. 25.
Corcyra, ii. 323.
Coriolanus, iii. 412.
Corinth, ii. 323; iii. 456.
Cortez, x. 5.
Council—
  of Constantinople, ix. 14.
  of Nicaea, ix. 18.

HISTORICAL INDEX.

Courts—
  Ecclesiastical, viii. 16.
  Star Chamber, viii. 23.
Crassus, ii. 3, 292; iii. 477.
Crecy, viii. 20.
Crœsus, i. 337.
Cromwell, viii. 33.
Crusades, ii. 60; iv. 451; iv. 456; v. 105.
Custer, Gen., x. 43.
Cynaxa, ii. 346.
Cyrus the Great, i. 335; ii. 2, 292.

Damascus, i. 376; ii. 58.
Danes, viii. 7.
Darius, i. 342; ii. 293, 296.
David, i. 455; ii. 19.
Deborah, i. 442.
Delphi, oracle, i. 337; ii. 93, 128, 135, 348; iii. 372.
Demosthenes, ii. 265, 361.
Descent of Ishtar, i. 287.
Diocletian, i. 182; iv. 34.
Dionysia—See Drama Index.
District of Columbia, x. 26.
Dodona, ii. 102, 232.
Doge, vi. 26.
Dome of the Rock, ii. 61.
Domitian, iv. 25.
Dorians, ii. 270, 292.
Draco, ii. 279.
Dress—
  Primitive, i. 24.
  Egyptian, i. 93.
  Babylonian, i. 293.
  Greek, ii. 382.
  Roman, iv. 73.
Druids, viii. 4.
Drusus, iv. 4.
Dutch Colonies, x. 13.

Edict of Nantes, viii. 439.
Edomites, i, 435.
Edward I, viii. 19.
Edward II, viii. 20.
Edward III, viii. 20.
Edward VI, viii. 25.
Edward VII, viii. 43.
Edward the Confessor, viii. 9.
Egypt, i. 15.
  Antiquity of, i. 20.
  Physiography of, i. 23.
  Topography of, i. 26.
  Prehistoric, i. 28.
  Unification of, i. 37.
  Descriptions of, i. 153.
  Modern, i. 181.

Egyptian History—
  Sources of, i. 31.
  Pyramid Age, i. 37.
  Old Empire, i. 37.
  Middle Empire, i. 44.
  Shepherd Kings, i. 51.
  New Empire, i. 54.
  Earliest Queen, i. 57.
  Expedition to Punt, i. 59.
Egyptians—Social Life of—
  Houses, i. 86.
  Gardens, i. 88.
  Furniture, i. 90.
  Food, i. 90.
  Family Life, i. 91.
  Dress, i. 93.
  Sports, i. 96.
  Banquets, i. 98.
  Occupation, i. 100.
  Crafts, i. 103.
  Markets, i. 106.
  Military Service, i. 108.
  Education, i. 113.
  Literature, i. 115; v. 31.
  Religion, i. 119.
  Religious Ceremonies, i. 128.
  Art, i. 133.
  Tombs, i. 138.
  Burials, i. 139.
Egyptian Exploration Fund, i. 145.
Egyptian Research Account, i. 145.
Eleusinian Mysteries, iii. 371.
Elis, ii. 233.
Elizabeth, Queen, viii. 26.
English History—
  Prehistoric, viii. 3.
  Roman Period, viii. 4.
  Norman Conquest, viii. 11.
  English Nationality, viii. 16.
  Tudors, viii. 23.
  Stuarts, viii. 29.
  Civil War, viii. 33.
  Restoration, viii. 34.
  Hanover Kings, viii. 37.
Epidamnus, ii. 322.
Epaminondas, ii. 349.
Epirus, ii. 231.
Eretria, ii. 294.
Esarhaddon, i. 256.
Etruscans, iii. 381.
Excavations—
  Egyptian, i. 144, 149; ix. 169; i. 150.
  Babylonian, i. 204.
  Assyrian, i. 208.
  Susa, i. 276.
  Nippur, i. 301.
  Palestine, i. 432; ii. 45.
  Troy, ii. 238.
  Mycenae, ii. 241.

Elis, iii. 356.
Corinth, iii. 366.
Marathon, iii. 372.
Delphi, iii. 373.

Fayoum, i. 48, 149.
Feudal System, iv. 442.
Florence, Modern, iv. 395.
Florence, Descriptions of, vi. 15, 147.
Forum, Roman, iv. 28, 112, 380, 392.
Franco-Prussian War, viii. 472.
Franks, iv. 56; viii. 431.
Frederic William I, viii. 466.
Frederick the Great, viii. 466.
French History—
  Formation of France, viii. 431.
  House of Valois, viii. 434.
  House of Bourbon, viii. 438.
  Revolution, x. 28; viii. 442, 448.
  The Directory, viii. 455.
French in America, x. 13.
French and Indian War, x. 27.

Galba, iv. 20.
Galileo, ii. 79.
Garibaldi, vi. 372.
Genet, x. 28.
George I, viii. 37.
George II, viii. 38.
George III, viii. 39; x. 19.
George IV, viii. 40.
George V, viii. 43.
German Palestine Society, ii. 45.
German Unity, viii. 466.
Germanic Peoples, iv. 49.
Gerousia, ii. 271.
Ghibillines, vi. 11.
Godfrey of Bouillon, iv. 454.
Golden Book, vi. 27.
Goths, iv. 49.
Gracchi, iii. 468.
Greece, ii. 229.
Greece—Social Life—
  Cities, ii. 375.
  Houses, ii. 377.
  Dress, ii. 382.
  Food, ii. 387.
  Position of Women, ii. 394.
  Education, ii. 396, 401.
  Civic Training, ii. 406.
  Sports, ii. 410.
  Occupations, ii. 414.
  Religion, ii. 421.
  Spartan Life, ii. 426.
  Festivals, iii. 357.
Greek Church, ix. 21.
Greek Cities, revolt of, i. 343.

Greek History—
  Sources of, ii. 262.
  Migrations, ii. 265.
  Sparta, ii. 269.
  Athens, ii. 275.
  City-States, ii. 288.
  Persian War, ii. 292.
  Athenian Empire, ii. 302.
  Pelopennesian War, ii. 322.
  Fall of Athens, ii. 337.
  Spartan Supremacy, ii. 345.
  Theban Supremacy, ii. 347.
Gregory the Great, v. 67.
Guelfs, vi. 11.
Guilds, vi. 16; vii. 25.
Gunpowder Plot, viii. 30.

Hadrian, iv. 30.
Halicarnassus, ii. 262.
Hall of Pillars, i. 70.
Hamilton, Alexander, x. 24.
Hammurabi, i. 232.
  Code of, i. 276, 317.
Hamilcar, iii. 445.
Hannibal, i. 392; iii. 446.
Hapi, i. 123.
Harold, viii. 11.
Hastings, battle of, viii. 11.
Hatshepsut, i. 58, 70.
Hayne, x. 35, 51.
Hebrews—
  Taboos, i. 29.
  Exodus, i. 453.
Hebrew History—
  Sources of, i. 426.
  Era of Judges, i. 441.
  Morality, i. 448.
  Kingdom, i. 453.
  Babylonian Exile, ii. 1.
  Later History, ii. 3.
Hebrew Social Life, ii. 7.
Helen of Troy, ii. 142.
Hellas, ii. 87.
Hellenizing of Ancient World, ii. 370.
Hengist, viii. 6.
Henry I, viii. 13.
Henry II, viii. 16.
Henry III, viii. 19.
Henry VII, viii. 23.
Henry VIII, viii. 24.
Henry, Patrick, x. 19, 45.
Heracleopolis, i. 44.
Herculaneum, iv. 25, 391.
Herod, ii. 3.
Herodotus, i. 22, 31, 34, 200, 212, 262, 328, 336, 341; iii. 149.
Hesiod, ii. 86.
Hezekiah, i. 248, 479.

Hipparchus, ii 286.
Hippias, ii. 286.
Hiram, i. 382.
Historical Addresses—
  Call to Arms, x. 45.
  Boston's Place in History, x. 48.
  Hayne-Webster Debate, x. 51.
  Gettysburg Speech, x. 73.
  Lincoln's Second Inaugural Address, x. 74.
  The Martyr President, x. 76.
  The New South, x. 79.
Hittites, i. 374.
Hohenstaufen Rulers, vi. 367.
Holstein, viii. 470.
Homer, ii. 86, 94.
Homeric Women, ii. 395.
Honorius, iv. 50.
Horatius, iii. 411.
Horizon of Solar Disk, i. 146, 235.
Horsa, viii. 6.
Horsea, i. 473.
Huguenots, viii. 436, 439.
Humanists, vi. 8; ix. 65.
Hundred Years War, v. 2; viii. 16, 20. 434.
Huns, iv. 51.

Iconoclasm, vi. 364; ix. 18.
Indians, i. 18, 25; x. 15.
Ionians, ii. 233.
Ionic Cities, ii. 294.
Irene, iv. 58.
Isabella of Castile, x. 3.
Isocrates, ii. 359.
Italy, iii. 378; iv. 387; vi. 363, 370.

Jackson, Andrew, x. 33.
Jacobius, viii. 450.
Jahweh, i. 436.
James I. viii. 29.
James II, viii. 34.
Jamestown, x. 10, 184.
Janiculum, iii. 390.
Jay, John, x. 28.
Jefferson, Thomas, x. 24, 30.
Jephthah, i. 446; ii. 14.
Jericho, i. 437.
Jerusalem, siege of, i. 266, 460, 477.
  Fall of, i. 481.
  Rebuilt, ii. 2.
  Destruction, ii. 4.
Jews, ii. 6.
Joan of Arc, viii. 20.
John, King, viii. 18.
Jonathan, i. 455.
Joppa, ii. 60.

Jordan, i. 412.
Joseph, story of, i. 20.
Judah, Revolt, i. 247.
Judea, i. 411.
Julius, ii. 9, 34.
Julian the Apostate, iv. 47.
Justinian, iv. 54.
Jutes, iv. 56.

Karnak, i. 69, 159.
Kentucky Resolutions, x. 29.
Khufu, i. 39.
King George's War, x. 15.
King William's War, x. 15.
Knighthood—See Chivalry.
Knights Templars, viii. 434.
Koran, i. 181.

Labyrinth, i. 48, 151.
Laconians, ii. 325.
Lake Regillus, iii. 422.
Lancaster, House of, viii. 16.
Lars Porsena, iii. 410.
Laurium, ii. 310.
League of Augsburg, viii. 439.
Lebanon, i. 379.
Legion of Honor, ix. 93.
Leo X, ix. 35.
Lepidus, iii. 476, 482.
Leonidas, ii. 297.
Leuctra, ii. 349.
Lincoln, Abraham, x. 37, 73.
Lombards, iv. 56; vi. 363.
London, viii. 42.
Lotus, i. 136.
Louis XIII, viii. 438.
Louis XIV, viii. 439.
Louis XV, viii. 440.
Louis XVI, viii. 444.
Louis Philippe, viii. 463.
Louisiana, x. 16.
Louisiana Purchase, x. 30, 160.
Luxor, i. 73.
Lyceum, ii. 406.
Lycurgus, ii. 270.
Lydia, i. 292, 337.
Lysander, ii. 346.

Maccabees, ii. 3.
Macedonia—
  Rise of, 354.
  Phalanx, ii. 357.
Mafia, vi. 376.
Magna Græcia, iii. 429.
Mamertine Prison, iv. 392.
Manetho, i. 32, 37.

Marathon, ii. 295, 310; iii. 154, 372.
Marco Polo, v. 21.
Marius, iii. 472.
Matilda, Countess, vi. 15.
Matilda, Queen, viii. 14.
Marie Antoinette, viii. 450.
Mary, Queen, viii. 26.
Maryland, x. 12.
Maximilian, ix. 67.
Mayflower, x. 11.
Mazarin, viii. 439.
Mecca, i. 184; ii. 62; iv. 56.
Medes—
 History, i. 328.
 Palaces, i. 329.
 Religion, i. 331.
Megaron, ii. 377.
Melos, ii. 338.
Memphis—
 Founding, i. 37.
 Description, i. 161.
Menelaus, ii. 142.
Menes, i. 37; i. 38.
Merovingian Kings, viii. 432.
Mesopotamia, i. 202, 214.
Metternick, viii. 462, 469.
Middle Ages, iv. 408.
 Institutions of, iv. 476.
 Chivalry, v. 1.
 Stories of, v. 61.
Midianites, i. 436.
Miltiades, ii. 295.
Missouri Compromise, x. 36.
Mithridates, iii. 475; iv. 183.
Moabites, i. 435, 446.
Mohammed, iv. 56.
Monasteries, ix. 21.
Monasticism, iv. 422.
Mohammedans, ix. 70.
Montfort, Simon de, viii. 19.
Monroe Doctrine, x. 31.
Monroe, James, x. 31.
Moors, v. 126; ix. 70; x. 5.
Moses, i. 80, 436, 452.
Mount of Olives, ii. 59.
Mycenae, ii. 233, 238.

Nabopolasser, i. 265.
Napoleon, vi. 372; viii. 39, 455; x. 161.
 Defeat of, viii. 462.
National Assembly, viii. 445
Naxos, ii. 305.
Nebuchadnezzar, i. 236, 306, 384, 481; ii. 1.
Neccho, i. 399.
Necker, viii. 444.
Necropolis, i. 82, 139.
Nelson, viii. 39.

Nemea, ii. 233.
Neolithic, i. 17.
Nero, Golden House of, iv. 71, 269.
Nerva, iv. 27.
New England, x. 11.
New Forest Laws, viii. 12.
New France, x. 16.
Nicias, ii. 338.
Nile, i. 23.
 Rise of, i. 25.
 Worship of, i. 121.
Nineveh, i. 203.
Norman Conquest, viii 11, 14.
Nullification, x. 29, 34.
Numa Pompilius, iii. 390; iv. 381.

Odeum, ii. 320.
Olympian Games, i. 32; ii. 105, 290; iii. 347, 356, 369.
Ordeals, iv. 451, 464.
Ornaments—
 Egyptian, i. 104.
 Prehistoric, i. 25.
 Greek, ii. 383.
 Roman, iv. 75.
Ostracism, ii. 312.
Ostrogoths, iv. 49, 56; vi. 363.

Palatine, iii. 384.
Paleolithic Age, i. 16.
Palestine, i. 408.
 Modern, ii. 58.
Palestine Exploration Fund, ii. 45.
Papacy, iv. 420.
Papyrus, Harris, i. 81.
Paris, ii. 141.
Parliament, viii. 19.
Parthenon ii. 121, 319; iii. 349.
Parthians, iv. 30.
Parsis, i. 352.
Pater Familias, iv. 59.
Patricians, iii. 395.
Pausanians, ii. 233, 264, 303.
Peace of God, iv. 452.
Pelasgians, ii. 354.
Pelopidus, ii. 349.
Peloponnesus, ii. 232.
Peloponnesian War, ii. 263, 322.
Perdiccas, ii. 355, 369.
Pericles, ii. 305, 314, 399.
Perioeci, ii. 304.
Persia, i. 332.
 History, i. 333.
 Religion, i. 350.
Persian War, ii. 292.
Peru, x. 8.
Phidias, ii. 104, 110, 121, 232, 307, 319; iii. 384.

HISTORICAL INDEX

Philip II of Macedonia, ii. 355; iii. 211.
Philip the Fair, vi. 368; viii. 433.
Philippii iii. 484.
Philistines, i. 250, 437, 453; ii. 7.
Phoenicia, i. 341, 378.
  Religion, i. 405.
  Learning, ii. 293.
Phoenician Ships, viii. 2.
Picts, viii. 4.
Pilgrimages, iv. 453.
Pippin, vi. 365; viii. 482.
Piræus, ii. 320, 375; iii. 362.
Pisa, vi. 20.
Pisistratus, ii. 284.
Plantagenets, viii. 16.
Platæa, ii. 295, 299, 331, 337.
Plebeians, iii. 395.
Pliny the Elder, i. 400.
Poitiers, viii. 20.
Polo, Marco, x. 3.
Pompadour, Madame, ix. 161.
Pompey, ii. 3; iii. 476.
Ponce de Leon, x. 6.
Potidaea, ii. 326.
Prehistoric Man, i. 28.
Prehistoric Period, i. 14.
Pretorian Guards, iv. 17, 22, 30, 34.
Principate, iv. 1.
Prussia, viii. 466.
Ptolemy, ii. 3, 370; iii. 480.
Pyramids, i. 39.
Pyramids, Battle of, viii. 456.

Rameses the Great, i. 74.
Rameses III, i. 80.
Raymond of Toulouse, iv. 455.
Reformation, ii. 31; viii. 24, 436; ix. 53.
Rehoboam, i. 469.
Renaissance, vi. 1.
  Italian, vi. 10.
Revolution, French, viii. 442.
Revolution, American, x. 20.
Richard the Lion-Hearted, vii. 18; x. 2.
Richelieu, viii. 338.
Rienzi, vi. 370.
Roanoke, x. 9.
Robert of Normandy, iv. 454.
Rome, History of—
  Founding of, iii. 383.
  Kingdom, iii. 386.
  Republic, iii. 399.
  Decemvirs, iii. 403.
  Laws, iii. 404.
  Conquest of, 410.
  Conquest of Italy, iii. 426.
  Government, iii. 432.

Punic Wars, iii. 438.
  Eastern Conquests, iii. 455.
  Social War, iii. 473.
  Principate, iv. 1.
  Decline of Principate, iv. 27.
  Fall of, iv, 47.
Rome, Social Life of—
  Family, iv. 59.
  Weddings, iv. 61.
  Houses, iv. 66.
  Dress, iv. 73.
  Meals, iv. 77.
  Childhood, iv. 83.
  Toys, iv. 85.
  Education, iv. 87.
  Literature, iv. 102.
  Occupations, iv. 106.
  Slavery, iv. 103.
  Army, iv. 121.
  Burial Customs, iv. 125.
Roses, War of, viii. 12, 21.

Salamis, i. 343; ii. 298.
Samaria, i. 411.
Samuel, i. 454.
Sardis, ii. 294.
Sargon, i. 230.
Saul, i. 454.
Savonarola, ix. 25.
Saxons, iv. 56; viii. 6.
Scarabs, i. 141.
Schleswig, viii. 470.
Scipio, iii. 452.
Schliemann, ii. 236; iii. 365.
Segesta, ii. 341.
Sejanus, iv. 17.
Seleucidae, ii. 370.
Seleucus, ii. 369.
Semitic Invasions, i. 52, 224.
Sennacherib, i. 249.
  Palace of, i. 302, 477.
Servius, Tullius, iii. 391.
Seti, i. 70.
Seven Years War, viii. 39.
Sharon, Plain of, i. 409, 446.
Shay's Rebellion, x. 21.
Sicilian Expedition, ii. 339.
Sicily, iv. 389.
Sidon, i. 380.
Sixtus, ix. 121.
Slavery, x. 35.
Smerdis, i. 341.
Smith, John, x. 4, 10.
Solar Disk, i. 68.
Solomon, i. 382, 463.
Solon, ii. 277.
South Sea Company, viii. 37.
Spain, x. 4, 8.
Spanish Armada, viii. 27.

HISTORICAL INDEX.

Sparta, ii. 233, 269, 304, 323, 337, 345, 348.
  Modern, iii. 369.
Spartans i. 343; ii. 426.
Sphinx, i. 130.
Spoil System, x. 33.
Spurius Cassius, iii. 402.
St. Benedict, iv. 434.
St. Bernard, viii. 394; ix. 26.
St. Bruno, ix. 161.
St. Francis, v. 14; vii. 394; ix. 23.
St. Mark, vi. 26.
St. Peter, iv. 393; vi. 26.
St. Theodore, vi. 26.
Stamp Act, x. 18.
State Sovereignty, x. 29, 34.
States General, viii. 444.
Stephen, viii. 14.
Stilicho, iv. 50.
Stone Age, i. 17.
Strabo, i. 48, 264.
Suez Canal, i. 187.
Sulla, iii. 473.
Syria, i. 372.

Taboo, i. 29, 312.
Tel-el Amarna Letters, i. 145, 202, 235, 373; ii. 47.
Temples—
  Egyptian, i. 125.
  Solomon's, ii. 9.
Teutons, iv. 409.
Texas, x. 36.
Thebes, i. 45; ii. 330.
  Description, i. 70.
  Ascendency, ii. 347.
  Supremacy, ii. 348.
Themistocles, ii. 296, 303, 309.
Theodoric, iv. 54.
Theodorius, iv. 49.
Thermopylae, i. 343; ii. 297.
Thessaly, ii. 231.
Thirty Tyrants, ii. 346.
Thirty Year Truce, ii. 318.
Thucydides, ii. 263, 273, 322, 327, 340.
Thutmose I, i. 55.
Thutmose III, i. 62, 237.
Tiber, iii. 387.
Tiberius, iv. 4, 15.
Tiglath Pileser I, i. 238.
Tiglath Pileser III, i. 245, 475.
Tiryus, ii. 258.
Titus, ii. 6.
Tiy, Queen, i. 67.
Tournament—See Chivalry.
Tours, iv. 57; v. 3; ix. 70.
Trafalgar, viii. 39.
Trajan, iv. 27.
Treaties—
  Wedmore, v. 67, 81; viii. 8.
  Aix la Chapelle, viii. 38.

Truce of God, iv. 452.
Tudor, House of, viii. 23.
Tuileries, viii. 451.
Tullus Hostilius, iii. 390; iv. 382.
Turgot, viii. 444.
Tyler, Wat, viii. 22.
Tyre, Siege of, i. 257, 380; i. 403.

Ulysses, ii. 176, 185, 259.
United States, ii. 304.
United States History—
  Discovery and Exploration, x. 2.
  Age of Settlement, x. 8.
  Colonies, x. 12.
  Beginnings of a Nation, x. 15.
  Articles of Confederation, x. 21.
  Adoption of Constitution, x. 24.
  The Republic, x. 26.
  War of 1812, x. 30.
  From Jackson to Lincoln, x. 33.
  Cival War, x. 38.
  Reconstruction Period, x. 39.
Utica, i. 390.
Ur Dynasty, i. 230.

Valens, iv. 49.
Valois, House of, viii. 434.
Vandals, iv. 51, 56.
Vatican, iv. 393; ix. 34, 120.
Venice, vi. 24.
  Description, vi. 156.
  Grand Canal, vi. 163.
Vespasian, ii. 4.
Vespucci, Amerigo, x. 7.
Vesuvius, Eruption of, iv. 25.
Via Sacra, ii. 6; iv. 112, 381.
Victor Emmanuel, vi. 373.
Victoria, viii. 40.
Virginia, x. 10.
Virginian Resolutions, x. 29.
Visigoths, iv. 49, 56.

Walpole, viii. 38.
Washington, George, x. 17, 26.
Waterloo, viii. 39.
Webster, Daniel, x. 35, 59.
William IV, viii. 40.
William the Norman, viii. 11, 433.
William of Orange, viii. 35.
William I of Prussia, viii. 470.
William Rufus, viii. 13.
Witan, viii. 9, 12.

Xenophon, i. 328, 336; ii. 263, 346, 415; iii. 159, 174.
Xerxes, i. 343; iii. 296.

York, viii. 16.

Zoroaster, i. 341.

INDEX OF LITERATURE

Abou Ben Adhem, viii. 248.
Achitophel, viii. 156.
Addison, viii. 382.
Adventures of the Exile Sanehat, i. 171.
Aeneid, iv. 234, 255.
Aeschines, iii. 202.
Aeschylus, ii. 265, 299; iii. 2.
Aesop, iii. 145.
Aesop, poem, iii. 148.
Agamemnon, play, iii. 11.
Alcaeus, ii. 477; iii. 225.
Aldrich, Thos. B., x. 438.
Alexander's Feast, viii. 159.
Alfieri, vi. 479.
A Little Journey in the World, x. 473.
Allegories, v. 103.
Amandis di Gaula, vi. 233.
Ambitious Guest, The, x. 324.
American Fiction—
  Bret Harte, x. 489.
  Charles Dudley Warner, x. 473.
  Helen Hunt Jackson, x. 498.
  Henry James, x. 482.
  James Fenimore Cooper, x. 304.
  Nathaniel Hawthorne, x. 322.
  Washington Irving, x. 279.
  W. D. Howells, x. 466.
American Literature—
  General Survey, x. 247.
  Colonial Literature, x. 255.
  Benj. Franklin, x. 270.
  Washington Irving, x. 279.
  James Fenimore Cooper, x. 304.
  Nathaniel Hawthorne, x. 322.
  Ralph Waldo Emerson, x. 348.
  American Fiction, x. 466.
  American Poetry, x. 363.
American Poetry—
  William Cullen Bryant, x. 363.
  Henry W. Longfellow, x. 372.
  James Russell Lowell, x. 396.
  Oliver Wendell Holmes, x. 408
  Edgar Allen Poe, x. 412.
  John G. Whittier, x. 421.
  Thos. Bailey Aldrich, x. 438.
  Bayard Taylor, x. 441.
  Edwin Markham, x. 445.
  Eugene Field, x. 447.
  Joaquin Miller, x. 450.
  Walt Whitman, x. 452.
  E. Clarence Stedman, x. 458.
  Sidney Lanier, x. 460.
  James Whitcomb Riley, x. 462.
  Sam Weller Foss, x. 463.
  Emily Dickinson, x. 465.
Amis and Amile, vi. 174.
Amos, i. 472; ii. 43.
Anabasis, iii. 159.
Anacreon, ii. 477; iii. 243.
Ancient Mariner, viii. 257, 263.
Angelo, Michael, vi. 128.
Anglo-Saxon, v. 67.
Annunzio, vii. 284.
Apocalypse, ix. 19.
Apocryphal Books, ii. 39.
Archilochus, ii. 474.
Areopagitica, viii. 34.
Ariosto, vi. 380.
Aristopheus, ii. 265; iii. 63.
Aristotle, ii. 227, 285; iii. 111.
Arnold, Mathew, viii. 320.
At Nijnii-Novgorod, x. 439.
Atys, iv. 211.
Aucassin et Nicolete, v. 5, 201.
Aurelius, Marcus, iii. 318; iv. 31.
Aurora Leigh, viii. 331.
Austen, Jane, ix. 225.
Autumn, viii. 179.

Bacchae, play, iii. 45.
Bacon, Francis, viii. 366.
Balaam, Story of, ii. 14.
Balder, Death of, v. 194.
Ballad of East and West, viii. 352.
Ballads, viii. 99.
Balzac, ix. 443.
Bandello, vi. 430.
Bardi Circle, vi. 447.
Barker's Luck, x. 489.
Beaumont, vii. 154.
Beauty of Life, viii. 408.
Bede, The Venerable, v. 69.
Beowulf, ii. 431; v. 61.
Berkeley, Bishop, x. 266.
Berkeley, Robert x. 255.
Bible, i. 426; ii, 12.
Bion, iii. 259.
Blessed Damozel, The, viii. 325.
Boccaccio, vi. 7, 67.
Boiardo, vi. 112.
Book of the Dead, i. 115, 142, 168.

Bostonians, The, x. 482.
Bradstreet, Mrs. Anne, x. 256, 262.
Break, Break, Break, viii. 292.
Brotherhood, x. 446.
Browning, Elizabeth, viii. 331.
Browning, Robt., viii. 294; v. 477.
Bryant, x. 250, 363.
Bulwer-Lytton, ix. 318.
Bunyan, viii. 34, 360.
Burdette, Robt., x. 246.
Burns, viii. 196.
Butterfly, The, x. 446.
Byron, viii. 208.
By the Balboa Seas, x. 451.

Caedmon, v. 69.
Caesar, iv. 185, 222.
Callimachus, iii. 265.
Callinus, poet, ii. 470.
Canadian Boat Song, viii. 252.
Canterbury Tales, viii. 61.
Captive, The, iv. 146.
Carlyle, viii. 389.
Castiglione, vi. 121; vii. 55.
Catullus, iv. 182, 204.
Cavalier Tunes, viii. 309.
Cellini, vi. 135, 145.
Centennial Hymn, x. 99.
Centennial, The, x. 90.
Cervantes, vi. 240.
Chambered Nautilus, x. 410.
Chant of the Arval Brothers, iv. 137, 143.
Chanson de Roland, v. 93.
Chansons de Geste, v. 93.
Chaucer, viii. 14, 22, 57.
Chaucer, poem, x. 377.
Chesterfield, Lord, v. 402.
Chevy Chase, viii. 99.
Chiabrera, vi. 448.
Childe Harold, viii. 209.
Cicero, iv. 183, 191.
Cid, The, v. 128, 131.
Cinthio, vi. 397.
Clarissa Harlowe, ix. 197.
Cleanthes, iii. 277.
Cloister and the Hearth ix. 47, 309.
Cloud, The, a poem, viii. 230.
Clouds, The, play, iii. 70.
Coleridge, viii. 255.
Colonna, Vittoria, vi. 126.
Columbian Ode, x. 100.
Comus, ii. 126; viii. 137.
Congreve, vii. 168.
Contentment, x. 411.
Cooper, James F., x. 249, 304.
Corneille, vii. 215.
Cotter's Saturday Night, viii. 200.

Courtier, The, vi. 121.
Courts of Love, v. 110.
Crossing the Bar, viii. 293.
Cry of the Children, viii. 338.
Cyclopean Walls, poem, ii. 246.
Cynewulf, v. 78.

Dante, vi. 5, 30, 368.
Daphnis and Chloe, v. 49.
Darwin, vii. 443.
David's Lament, i. 457.
Death of the Flowers, The, x. 367.
Decameron, vi. 78.
Deer Slayer, The, x. 306.
DeFoe, viii. 34; ix. 186.
Deluge, Chaldean Acc. of, i. 284, 291, 361.
De Monarchi, vi. 368.
Demosthenes, ii. 265, 361; iii. 161, 209.
Derelict, The, viii. 351.
Descent of Ishtar, i. 287.
Deserted Village, viii. 191.
Destruction of Sennacherib, i. 478.
Diana of the Crossways, ix. 335.
Dickens, Charles, ix. 250.
Dickinson, Emily, x. 465.
Dinias and Dercyllis, v. 49.
Divine Comedy, vi. 21, 40.
Don Quixote, vi. 240.
Doni, vi. 441.
Dostoievsky, ix. 502.
Drinking Song, ii. 165.
Dryden, vii. 153, 168.
Dumas, ix. 431.

Ecclesiasticus, ii. 41.
Eclogues, iv. 233, 244.
Eddas, v. 177, 187.
Edgeworth, Maria, ix. 225.
Edwards, Jonathan, x. 257.
Egyptian Literature, i. 117; v. 31.
Egyptian Princess, An, i. 154, 156.
Elegy in a Country Churchyard, viii. 185.
Eliot, George, ix. 283.
Emerson, Ralph W., v. 440; x. 348.
Endymion, ii. 133.
English Literature—
  General Survey, viii. 49.
  Chaucer, viii. 57.
  Spenser, viii. 106.
  Milton, viii. 127.
  Dryden, viii. 153.
  Pope, viii. 164.
  Thomson, viii. 173.
  Goldsmith, viii. 189.

Byron, viii, 208.
Shelley, viii, 225.
Keats, viii. 236.
Coleridge, viii. 255.
Wordsworth, viii. 263.
Tennyson, viii. 276.
Browning, viii. 294.
Swinburne, viii. 315.
Arnold, viii. 320.
Minor 18th Century Poets, viii. 331.
Prose Writers, viii. 360.
Later Prose Writers, viii. 389.
Ennius Quintus, iv. 139, 143.
Epicurus, iv. 189.
Epictetus, iii. 316.
Essay on Man, viii. 171.
Essays, Bacon, viii. 373.
Esther, ii. 36.
Eupheus, vii. 75.
Euripides, ii. 265, 399.
Evangeline, x. 384.
Ezekiel, i. 393.
Fabliaux, v. 117.
Faerie Queene, viii. 116, 173.
Faust, vii, 337.
Federalist, The, x. 269.
Fiction, Egyptian, v. 31.
Fiction, English—
  Beginning of, ix. 186.
  Richardson, ix. 196.
  Fielding, ix. 206.
  Austen, ix. 225.
  Historical Novel, ix. 226
19th Century—
  Dickens, ix. 249.
  Thackeray, ix. 269.
  Eliot, ix. 283.
  Reade, ix. 308.
Recent Fiction—
  Meredith, ix. 334.
  Hardy, ix. 345.
  Stevenson, ix. 363.
Fiction, French, v. 100.
  Beginnings of, ix. 375.
18th Century—
  Prevost, ix. 382.
  Voltaire, ix. 393.
  Rousseau, ix. 403.
  Hugo, ix. 409.
  Dumas, ix. 431.
  Balzac, ix. 443.
Fiction, Greek, v. 49.
Fiction, Polish—
  Early Polish Fiction, ix. 461.
  Sienkiewicz, ix. 463.
Fiction, Renaissance, vi. 67.
Fiction, Russian—
  19th Century, ix. 476.
  Gogol, ix. 482.

Turgenieff, ix. 488.
Tolstoy, ix. 510.
Fiction, Spanish, vi. 231.
Field, Eugene, x. 447.
Fielding, ix. 196, 206.
Filicaja, vi. 454.
Finding of the Lyre, ii. 153.
Fiorentino, vi. 103.
Fishing Party, The, x. 461.
Flamenca, v. 113.
Fletcher, vii. 154.
Folk-lore, ii. 32.
Forest Children, iv. 398.
Foscalo, vi. 496.
Foss, Sam Weller, x. 463.
Founding of Thebes, ii. 351.
Fra Lippo Lippi, viii. 298.
Franklin, Benj., x. 248, 269, 270.
French Revolution, viii. 392.
Froissart, v. 2, 13, 216; vi. 184.

Garden of Persephone, ii. 189.
Garden of Roses, The, v. 161.
Gaskell Elizabeth, ix. 310.
German Literature, viii. 474.
Georgics, The, iv. 233.
Gil Blas, ix. 375.
Gilgamish Epic, i. 361.
Goblin La Laugh, The, x. 447.
Gods of Greece, poem, ii. 74.
Goethe, vii. 331.
Gogol, ix. 482.
Goldoni, vi. 468.
Goldsmith, viii. 189; ix. 197.
Gower, viii. 96.
Gracchi, iv. 140.
Grave by the Lake, x. 424.
Gray, viii. 184.
Grecian Urn, viii. 237.
Greek Literature—
  Beginning of, ii. 429.
  Homeric, ii. 437.
  Lyric, ii. 469.
  Early Prose, iii. 145.
  Later Prose, iii. 159.
  Orations, iii. 197.
  Byzantine, iii. 324.
  Romances, iii. 327.
Greene, Robert, vii. 83.
Gudron, v. 160.
Gulliver's Travels, ix. 187.
Gyges and Asshurbanipal, i. 372.

Hardy, Thos., ix. 345.
Harp that Once through Tara's Hall, viii. 252.
Harte, Bret, x. 489.
Hauptmann, vii. 371, 380.
Hawthorne, x. 322.

INDEX OF LITERATURE.

Hebe, poem, ii. 113.
Hebrew Drama, ii. 23.
Hebrew Fiction, ii. 30.
Hebrew Philosophy, ii. 39.
Hebrew Poetry, ii. 12.
Heine, viii. 485.
Helen at the Loom, iii. 359.
Heliodorus, v. 49.
Hellas, poem, ii. 374.
Henley, viii. 346.
Henry, Patrick, x. 269.
Hermesianax, iii. 279.
Herondas, iii. 281.
Hesiod, ii. 262, 384, 431, 464.
Heywood, vii. 47.
Holmes, Oliver W., x. 90, 408.
Holy Grail, v. 117.
Homeric Poems, ii. 247, 387, 437.
Horace, iv. 236, 242, 261.
Horatius, poem, iii. 416.
House of Seven Gables, x. 332.
Howells, William D., x. 466.
Hugo, Victor, ix. 409.
Human Life, viii. 323.
Hundred Ancient Tales, vi. 71.
Hunt, Leigh, viii. 245.
Hymn of Apollo, ii. 123.

Ibsen, vii. 297.
I Stood Tip Toe upon a Hill, viii. 239.
Iliad, ii. 136, 236, 247, 387, 431, 440.
Il Penseroso, viii. 127.
In All, Myself, x. 453.
Ingelow, Jean, viii. 341.
In Memoriam, viii. 287.
In Poppy Fields, x. 447.
Intimations of Immortality, viii. 268.
Iphigenia, iii. 56.
Iris, poem, ii. 111.
Irish Melodies, viii. 249.
Irving, Washington, x. 249, 279, 283.
Ishtar's Descent to Hades, i. 367.
Isles of the Blest, ii. 194.
Isocrates, ii. 359; iii. 161, 197.
Italian Literature, Modern, vi. 379.
Ivanhoe, ix. 229.

Jackson, Helen Hunt, x. 498.
James, Henry, x. 482.
Jasher, i. 438; ii. 13.
Jerusalem Delivered, vi. 416.
Job, Book of, ii. 23.
Jonah, ii. 36.
Jonson, Ben, vii. 56, 149.
Josephus, i. 431, 453; ii. 4; iii. 287.
Joshua, Book of, ii. 12.

Judges, Book of, i. 441.
Judith, v. 70.
Juvenal, iv. 272, 367.

Keats, viii. 236.
Kenilworth, ix. 228, 237.
King Arthur, Legends of, v. 117; viii. 278.
Kingsley, iv. 398, 425; ix. 310.
Kipling, Rudyard, v. 497; viii. 1. 350; ix. 364.
Knight's Tale, viii. 74.

Lalla Rookh, viii. 251.
L'Allegro, viii. 127, 130.
Langland, viii. 87.
Lanier, Sidney, x. 460.
Last Days of Pompeii, ix. 319.
L'Envoi, v. 497.
Le Gallienne, ix. 371.
Le Sage, ix. 375.
Lessing, vii. 317.
Les Miserables, ix. 409.
Libanius, iii. 337.
Little Boy Blue, x. 448.
Livy, iii. 386; iv. 238, 296.
Longfellow, x. 372.
Longus, v. 49.
Lorelei, ii. 177.
Lost Leader, The, viii. 297.
Love Among the Ruins, viii. 312.
Lowell James R., vii. 424; x. 396.
Louis XIV, Age of, vii. 237.
Love's Young Dream, viii. 250.
Lucan, iv. 337.
Lucian, iii. 310.
Lucilius, iv. 140.
Lucretius, iv. 141, 186.
Lyly, John, vii. 75.
Lyric, ii. 469.

Machiavelli, vi. 107.
Maeterlinck, vii. 268.
Maffei, vi. 459.
Mandelay, viii. 352.
Manzoni, vi. 503.
Marlowe, vii. 97, 338.
Marriage of Cupid and Psyche, ii. 147.
Martial, iv. 270, 361.
Martin Chuzzlewit, ix. 258.
Mather, Cotton, x. 256, 265.
Medea, play, iii. 51.
Medea, Seneca, iv. 332.
Meleager, iii. 298.
Memorabilia, iii. 160, 190.

Menander, iii. 63, 82.
Meredith, George, ix. 334.
Metamorphoses, iv. 237.
Metastasio, vi. 461.
Miller, Joaquin, x. 450.
Mill on the Floss, ix. 285.
Milton, John, ii. 126, 137; viii. 34, 127.
Mimnermus, ii. 472.
Minnesingers, v. 163.
Miracles, poem, x. 463.
Molière, vii. 215, 238.
Monk as a Civilizer, iv. 425.
Monroe, Harriet, x. 102.
Montaigne, vi. 210.
Moore, Thomas, viii. 249.
Moorish Ballads, vi. 226.
Morot, vi. 219.
Morris, William, viii. 408.
Moschus, iii. 262.
Mountain Glory, viii. 403.
Müller, viii, 493.
My Lost Youth, x. 375.

Naevius, iv, 139.
Napoleon at Gotha, poem, x. 442.
Narcissus, poem, ii. 107.
New Atlantis, viii. 370.
Newcomes, The, ix. 275.
New England, poem, x, 261.

Ode to a Grecian Urn, viii. 237.
Odes, Horace, iv. 264.
Odium Theolgicum, x. 462.
Odyssey, ii. 185, 236, 247, 387, 431, 454; iii. 362; iv. 138.
Œdipus the King, play, iii. 34.
Oh, Captain! My Captain! x. 457.
Old Curiosity Shop, ix. 264.
Old Testament, ii. 12.
One's Self I Sing, poem, x. 456.
Open Window, The, x. 374.
Origin of the Harp, viii. 259.
Orlando, vi. 383.
Ovid, iv, 236, 275.

Pæan of Joy, poem, x. 454.
Palestine, poem, ii. 8.
Pamela, ix. 196.
Paradise Lost, viii. 127, 132.
Parcival, v. 121.
Parini, vi. 476.
Paul Revere's Ride, x. 378.
Peele, George, vii. 91.
Pellico, vi. 499.
Pentaur's Poem, i. 75.

Pericles, ii. 333; iii. 166.
Persephone, poem, ii. 160.
Petrarch, vi. 6, 58.
Petronius, iv. 345.
Phaedon, iii. 134.
Phaedrus, iv. 322.
Phidias to Pericles, iii. 353.
Philemon, iii. 63, 83.
Philosophy, Greek, iii. 87.
Pickwick Papers, ix. 253.
Pictor, Quintus Fabius, iv. 140.
Piers Plowman, viii. 87.
Pierre Vidal, v. 111.
Pilgrim's Progress, viii. 361.
Pilot, The, x. 304.
Pindar, ii. 264, 478; iii. 233.
Pioneers, The, x. 304.
Pippa Passes, v. 477.
Plautus, iv. 139, 160.
Plato, ii. 415; iii. 95, 106.
Pliny the Elder, iv. 71, 103, 271, 354.
Pliny the Younger, iv. 271, 365.
Plowman's Creed, The, viii. 95.
Plutarch, ii. 263; iii. 305.
Poet's Song, The, viii. 285.
Polybius, ii. 263; iii. 456.
Pope, Alexander, viii. 164.
Porto, vi. 122.
Portrait, A, viii. 265.
Portrait, The, poem, viii. 332.
Praise of Famous Men, ii. 54.
Precepts of Ptah-hotep i, 117, 164.
Princess, The, viii. 279.
Prisoner of Chillon, viii. 215.
Prometheus, ii. 98; iii, 6.
Propertius, iv. 236, 294.
Prophets, Hebrew, ii. 42.
Provost, ix. 382.
Psalms, ii. 16.
Put Yourself in His Place, ix. 311.

Queen of the Air, ii. 116.

Rabelais, vi. 193.
Racine, vii. 215, 227.
Rape of the Lock, viii. 167.
Reade, Charles, ix. 308, 311.
Recessional, The, viii. 359.
Renaissance—
  Italian, vi. 30.
  French, vi. 170.
  Spanish, vi. 222.
Republic, The, iii. 116.
Republic, The, iv. 200.
Reynard the Fox, v. 125.
Richardson, ix. 196.
Richter, viii. 474.

Riley, James Whitcomb, x. 462.
Rip Van Winkle, x. 286.
Rise of Silas Lapham, x. 466.
Robinson Crusoe, ix. 187.
Roland, Song of, v. 3, 91.
Romance of the Rose, v. 103; vi. 171.
Romance of the Swan's Nest, viii. 335.
Romances, Greek, v. 49.
Romans, iv. 130
  Early, iv. 137.
  Age of Cicero, iv. 183.
  Age of Augustine, iv. 233.
  Later Writings, iv. 269.
Rome, poem, iii. 377.
Romolo, ix. 284, 291.
Romona, x. 498.
Rossetti, viii. 325
Rostand, vii. 274.
Rousseau, viii. 443; ix. 403.
Rubaiyat, x. 215.
Ruskin, ii. 171, 175; viii. 396.
Ruth, ii. 35, 48.

Sacchetti, vi. 97.
Sallust, iv. 216.
Sand, George, ix. 423.
Sappho, ii. 475; iv. 182.
Saxon Chronicle, v. 84.
Sayings of the Seer, ii. 40.
Schiller, vii. 331, 354.
Scott, Sir Walter, ix. 26.
Seafarer, The, v. 65.
Sea Limits, The, viii. 329.
Seasons, The, viii. 173.
Seneca, iv. 269, 328; v. 411; vi. 353.
Sensitive Plant, viii. 233.
Septuagint, ii. 3.
Shakespeare, vii. 108.
Shelley, viii. 225.
Shepherd's Calendar, viii. 106.
Sheridan, vii. 176.
She Stoops to Conquer, viii. 190.
Siegfried, v. 151.
Sienkiewicz, ix. 463.
Silas Marner, ix. 287, 297.
Simonides, ii. 474.
Simonides of Ceos, iii. 232.
Skylark, To a, viii. 227.
Smith, John, x. 255, 258.
Smollett, ix. 196.
Snow-Bound, x. 427.
Socrates, iii. 95, 134.
Solomon and the Bees, poem. i. 465.
Song of the Flowers, vii. 481.
Song of the Harper, i. 179.
Song of Roland, v. 3, 91.

Song of Solomon, ii. 21, 55.
Song of the Sirens, ii. 177.
Song of Seven, viii. 341.
Sonnets, Milton, viii. 136.
Sonnets, The, vi. 63.
Sophocles, ii. 265; iii. 2, 28.
Spanish Literature, v. 126.
Spectator, The, viii. 377.
Spring, viii. 174.
Stedman, Clarence, x. 458.
Steele, Richard, viii. 376.
Sterne, ix. 197.
Stevenson, ix. 363.
Straparola, vi. 405.
Sudermann, vii. 371.
Suetonnies, iv. 374.
Summer, poem, viii. 177.
Sunflower, The, ii. 129.
Swift, Dean, ix. 187.
Swinburne, viii. 315.
Symbolism, vii. 267.
Symphony, The, x. 459.
Symposium, iii. 122.

Tacitus, iv. 271, 313.
Tales of the Magicians, v. 31, 31.
Talmud, i. 431.
Tam o' Shanter, viii. 203.
Tantalos, poem, ii. 192.
Tasso, vi. 379, 412.
Tassoni, vi. 451.
Taylor, Bayard, x. 441.
Tears, Idle Tears, viii. 280.
Tempest, play, viii. 28.
Tennyson, viii. 276.
Terence, iv. 139, 173.
Tertullian, vii. 17.
Tess of the D'Urbervilles, ix. 345.
Thackeray, ix. 269.
Thanatopsis, x. 365.
Theagenes and Chariclea, v. 49.
The Ambitious Scholar, x. 350.
The Battlefield, poem, x. 370.
The Bells, x. 414.
The Raven, x. 417.
Theocritus, iii. 251.
Theogony, ii. 432.
Theognis, iii. 226.
The Seasons, viii. 174.
Thespis, iii. 2.
The Rain, x. 461.
There Was a Child, poem, x. 454.
Thomson, viii. 173.
Thoreau, vii. 483.
Thucydides, ii. 322, 327, 340; iii. 152.
Tibullus, iv. 291.
Tieck, viii. 482.

Tintern Abbey, viii. 272.
'Tis Sweet to Think, viii. 253.
To a Greek Girl, poem, iii. 376.
Tolstoy, ix. 510.
Tom Jones, ix. 206.
To the Winds, ii. 182.
Toujours Amour, x. 458.
Trollope, ix. 309, 310.
Troubadours, v. 104.
Turgenieff, ix. 488.
Twilight, x. 382.
Two Brothers, The, v. 32, 39.
Two Moods, x. 438.
Tyrtaeus ii. 471; iii. 219.

Undiscovered Country, The—Aldrich, x. 440.
Undiscovered Country — Stedman, x. 458.

Vanity Fair, ix, 271.
Vasari, vi. 132.
Vicar of Wakefield, viii, 190; ix, 197.

Vision of Sir Launfal, x. 398.
Vita Nuova, vi. 31, 34.
Voltaire, viii. 443; ix. 393.

Waiting by the Gate, x. 368.
Walter von der Vogelweid, v. 166; x. 380.
Warner, Charles D., x. 473.
Waverley Novels, ix. 227.
Welcome to Alexandria, viii. 286.
Whitman, Walt, x. 251, 452.
Whittier, John G., x. 99, 421.
Wigglesworth, x. 256, 264.
William of Poitiers, v. 106.
Winter, viii. 182.
Wolfram von Eschenback, v. 168.
Wordsworth, viii. 263.
Works and Days, ii. 262, 432.
Worship of Nature, x. 423.

Zenda—Vesta, i. 351.
Zoroaster's Prayer, i. 371.
Zola, ix. 453.

INDEX OF MYTHOLOGY

Acheron, ii. 190.
Achilles, ii. 247.
Adonis, ii. 142.
Aeacus, ii. 190.
Aeneas, ii. 191, iii. 387.
Aeolus, God of Wind, ii. 183.
Aether, ii. 88.
Agamemnon, ii. 247.
Amazons. ii. 215.
Amphitrite, ii. 174.
Ana, Chaldean deity, i. 219.
Anu, i. 309.
Anthaeus, ii. 221.
Anthiope, ii. 103.
Aphrodite, ii. 140, 247.
Apollo, ii. 124, 148.
Aquilo, ii. 185.
Arcadian Stag, ii. 209.
Areopagus, ii. 136.
Ares, God of War, ii. 135.
Argo, ii. 175, 196.
Argus, ii. 104, 151, 175.
Ariadne, ii. 166.
Arion, ii. 175.
Artemis, Goddess of the Chase, ii. 124, 130.
Artemisia, Festival of, ii. 133.
Asshur, i. 310.
Astoreth, Moon-Goddess, i. 405.
Athena, Goddess of Wisdom. ii. 115; her contest with Arachne, 118; with Poseidon, 116.
Atlas, ii. 180, 221.
Atropos, ii. 157.
Anchises, ii. 191.
Augean Stables, ii. 213.
Aura, ii. 185.
Aurora, Goddess of Dawn, ii. 183.

Babylonian Deities, i. 227.
Bacchus, *see* Dionysus.
Bael, God of Sun, i. 405.
Bag of Winds, ii. 185.
Battle of the Giants, ii. 93.
Bel, i. 308.
Beowulf, ii. 225.
Boreas, ii. 185.

Cadmus, ii. 348.
Caduceus, ii. 150.

Calliope, Muse of Poetry, ii. 156, 195.
Cave of Sleep, ii. 197.
Cecrops, ii. 276.
Centaurs, ii. 212.
Cerberus, ii. 188.
Ceres, *see* Demeter.
Ceyx, ii. 187, 201.
Chaos, ii. 88.
Chiron, ii. 212.
Chloris, *see* Flora.
Clio, Muse of History, ii. 156.
Clotho, ii. 157.
Clytie, ii. 125.
Cocytus, ii. 191.
Corus, ii. 185.
Creation Legends, i. 285.
Cretan Bulls, ii. 214.
Crocodile-Myth. i. 116.
Cronus. Age of, ii. 91.
Cupid, ii. 143.
Cyclops, ii. 91, 241.

Dagon, Philistine God, i. 453.
Danaë, ii. 103, 178.
Daphne, ii. 125.
Deluge Legend, i. 209. 287, 291.
Demeter. Goddess of Harvest, ii. 92, 158.
Deucalion, ii. 99.
Diana, *see* Artemis.
Diana of Ephesus, ii. 133.
Diomedes, ii. 214.
Dionysus, God of Wine, ii. 163; festivals of, iii. 10.
Discord, ii. 141: apple of, 141.
Dolphins, ii. 164.

Ea, i. 308.
Echo, Story of, ii. 106.
Egyptian Myths, i. 116.
Elysian Fields, ii. 143, 191.
Endymion, ii. 132.
Epimetheus. ii. 91.
Erebus, ii. 88.
Eros, ii. 88.
Erymanthian Boar, ii. 211.
Eurus, ii. 185.
Eurydice, ii. 196.
Eurystheus. ii. 207.

Fates, The, ii. 156.
Flora, ii. 185, 398.

Gades, ii. 217.
Gaea, ii. 88.
Geryon, ii. 217.
Gilgamesh, i. 287.
Golden Fleece, ii. 175.
Golden Touch, ii. 164.
Gorgons, ii. 87, 178.
Grey Sisters, ii. 179.
Greek Mythology—
  Greek attitude toward, ii. 78; Nature myths, 80; in English Literature, 82; in Art, 84; Golden Age, 91; Silver Age, 93.

Hades, ii. 188.
Halcyone, ii. 187, 201.
Hapi, i. 123.
Harpies, ii. 87, 186.
Hebe, ii. 113, 224.
Hebrew Myths, ii. 33.
Hecate, ii. 203.
Helen of Troy, ii. 247.
Helicon, Mount, ii. 156.
Hephaestus, ii. 137.
Hera, Queen of Heaven, ii. 92, 105, 163.
Herae, The, ii. 110.
Hercules, Labors of, ii. 206, 208.
Hermes, Messenger of gods, ii. 95, 148.
Hesperides, ii. 87; apples of, 218.
Hestia, Goddess of Hearth, ii. 92, 154, iv. 157.
Hippolyte, ii. 215.
Horus, i. 116, 120.
Hyacinthus, ii. 124.
Hydra, Lernean, ii. 208.
Hyperboreans, ii. 87, 124.

Io, ii. 103, 151.
Iris, ii. 110, 201.
Ishtar, i. 309.
Isles of the Blessed, ii. 87.
Isis, i. 116.

Janus, iii. 397, iv. 157.
Jason, ii. 175, 196.
Jove, *see* Zeus.
Juno, *see* Hera.

Lachesis, ii. 157.
Lethe, ii. 190.
Leto, ii. 124, 131.
Liber, God of Wine, iii. 398.
Lorelei, ii. 177.
Luna, *see* Artemis.

Maia, ii. 148.
Marduk, Babylonian God, i. 236, 237, 247.
Mars, *see* Ares.
Mat, i. 120.
Medea, ii. 175.
Medusa, ii. 178.
Memnon, ii. 184.
Menelaus, King, ii. 142, 247.
Mercury, *see* Hermes.
Mermer, Wind-God, i. 220.
Midas, King, ii. 164, 170.
Minerva, ii. 122.
Mines, ii. 190.
Minos, King, ii. 165.
Minotaur, i. 407.
Morpheus, ii. 199.
Mors, ii. 197.
Muses, ii. 156.
Mythology, Greek, ii. 78.

Narcissus, ii. 107.
Nemean lion, ii. 208.
Nemesis, ii. 204.
Nereides, ii. 176.
Nereus, ii. 196, 220.
Niobe, story of, ii. 131, 204.
Noah, ii. 99.
Norse Mythology, v. 267, 278, 293.
Nox, ii. 88, 198.
Nut, i. 116.
Nymphs, ii. 219.

Oannes, Man-Fish, i. 285.
Oceanus, ii. 86.
Olympus, ii. 94, 173.
Oracles, of Dodona, ii. 102.
Oreads, ii. 171.
Orion, ii. 131.
Orithyria, ii. 185.
Orpheus, ii. 177, 195.
Osiris, i. 116.

Pan, God of Nature, ii. 169.
Panathenaea, the, ii. 121, 138.
Pandora, ii. 95, 138.

Paris, ii. 141.
Persephone, ii. 158.
Perseus, ii. 178.
Phaëton, ii. 126.
Phlegethus, ii. 191.
Pomona, iii. 398.
Pontus, ii. 88.
Poppies, ii. 198.
Poseidon, God of Ocean, ii. 92, 136, 173.
Pygmalion, ii. 140.
Pygmies, ii. 87, 221.
Pyrrha, ii. 99.
Pythian Games, ii. 128.

Qeb, i. 120.

Ra, i. 120.
Rhadamanthus, ii. 190.
Rhea, ii. 92.
Romulus and Remus, ii. 136, 388.

Sabine Women, iii. 389.
Samele, ii. 163.
Samson, ii. 225.
Saturn, iv. 157.
Saturnus, iii. 397.
Seb, i. 116.
Set, i. 116.
Selene, see Artemis.
Shamash, i. 309.
Silenus, ii. 163.

Sirens, ii. 87, 176.
Somnus, ii. 197.
Stymphalian Birds, ii. 214.
Styx, ii. 191.
Syrinx, ii. 169.

Tamman, i. 309.
Tartarus, ii. 89, 191.
Terminus, iii. 398.
Theophane, ii. 175.
Theseus, i. 407, ii. 165, 276.
Thetis, ii. 141.
Tithonus, ii. 183.
Titans, ii. 88.
Triton, ii. 174.
Troy, Walls of, ii. 174.
Tun, i. 120.

Ulysses, ii. 176, 185.
Uranus, ii. 88.

Venus, see Aphrodite.
Venus de Milo, ii. 143.
Vesta, see Hestia.
Vulcan, see Hephaestus.

Zephyrus, ii. 185.
Zeus, Ruler of Heaven, ii. 92, 100; powers of, 101; love affairs of, 103; in Art, 104.

GENERAL INDEX

Abbey, Edwin A., x. 223, 237.
Abraham, i. 434.
Academy, ii. 406.
Acropolis, see Historical.
Actors, see Drama.
Addams, Miss Jane, x. 113, 134.
Agriculture in Egypt, i. 100.
Almond, origin, i. xxiii.
Alaska Purchase, x. 42, 196.
Alaska-Yukon Exposition, x. 196.
Alexander the Great, i. 345, 351; ii. 3, 358, 366; iii. 455.
Alexandria, i. 181.
Amalfi, iv. 391.
American Flag, x. 1.
American School of Archaeology, ii. 47.
American School of Classical Studies, iii. 366.
Ammonites, i. 435, 446.
Amon, i. 59, 69, 81.
Amsterdam, ix. 57.
Annunzio, vii. 284.
Anti-Slavery Society, x. 36.
Anthony, Susan B., x. 112.
Antwerp, ix. 49.
Anulets, i. 141.
Apis Ball, i. 120, 341.
Aqueducts, iv. 19, 69.
Aristippus, iii. 138.
Assisi, Church of, ix. 23.
Assyria, see Historical.
Australia, Tribes of, i. xxx.

Babel, Tower of, i. 201.
Babylonia, see Historical.
Balboa, Panama, x. 205.
Basle, ix. 65.
Beecher, Henry Ward, x. 76.
Bell Telephone, x. 94.
Belshazzar, i. 268, 319.
Beyreuth, v. 358.
Bible, i. 426; ii. 12.
Biremes, i. 397.
Bismarck, viii. 470.
Blashfield, Edwin, x. 240.
Blue Bird, The, vii. 269.
Boecklin, ix. 154, 156.
Book of the Dead, i. 115, 142.
Book of Kells, ix. 104.

Book of Durrow, ix. 104.
Book of Hours, ix. 107.
Books, iv. 102; ix. 101.
Booth, Maude Ballington, x. 113, 138.
Boston Library, x. 236.
Botta, i. 205.
British Isles, see Historical.
British Museum, ix. 179, also see Art.
Buffalo, x. 153.
Burroughs, John, vii. 425.
Buskins, vii. 15.

Cabbage, origin of, i. xxiii.
Cadore, ix. 42.
Caesar, Julius, ii. 3.
Cairo, i. 182.
Campagna, iv. 391.
Canaanites, see Historical.
Cape of Good Hope, i. 182.
Capri, iv. 391.
Carnegie Institute, x. 241.
Caravans, i. 394.
Carrara, ix. 34.
Carthage, i. 340, 391; iv. 113.
Catacombs, i. 182; iv. 394; ix. 9.
Cathay, x. 3.
Caxton, ix. 41.
Centennial, The, x. 91.
Central Park, ii. 58.
Chanticleer, vii. 274.
Chagres River, x. 204.
Chariot Races, iv. 96.
Charters, see Historical.
Chase, William M., x. 224.
Chicago Fair, x. 104.
Christianity, see Historical.
Christmas, v. 470.
Cities, Greek, ii. 375.
Civil Service, x. 34.
Coal Mines, English, viii. 44.
Co-education, v. 391.
Code of Alfred, viii. 9.
Code of Hammurabi, viii. 9.
Cologne, ix. 64.
Colon, x. 203.
Colonna, Vittoria, ix. 36.
Columbus, viii. 23.
Comedy, see Drama.

Conduct of Life, v. 390.
  Manners, v. 393, 400, 407.
  Good Breeding, v. 402.
  Happiness, v. 410, 416, 418.
  Tact, v. 428.
  Friendship, v. 433.
  Simple Life, v. 455.
  Simplicity, v. 463.
  Right Living, v. 468.
Congress of Women, x. 112.
Congresses, World, x. 111.
Congressional Library, x. 216.
Contracts, Babylonian, i. 277, 290.
Convent La Rabida, x. 109.
Conversation—
  Art of, vi. 329.
  Principles of, vi. 330.
  If You Can Talk Well, vi. 342.
  Culture by Conversation, vi. 348.
  Rules for Conversation, vi. 350.
  Reflections on Conversation, vi. 350.
  Happiness through Conversation, vi. 355.
  Conversation and Courtesy, vi. 361.
Corfu, iii. 362.
Corinth, iii. 366.
Cox, Kenyon, x. 241.
Crocodile, Worship of, i. 121.
Crusades, see Historical.
Croesus, i. 337.
Crystal Palace, x. 84.
Columbian Exposition, x. 103.
Culebra Cut, x. 204.
Cuneiform writing, i. 208.
Curfew, viii. 13.
Custer, General, x. 43.
Cynics, iii. 139.
Cyrenaics, iii. 138.
Cyrus the Great, i. 335; ii. 2, 292.

Damascus, i. 376.
Danes, viii. 7.
Darwin, i. xv, vii. 443.
David, see Historical.
Dead Sea, i. 413.
Delphi, i. 337; ii. 93, 128, 135, 348; iii. 372.
Democritus, iii. 94.
Demotic Writing, i. 33.
District of Columbia, x. 26.
Doll's House, The, vii. 297.
Dome of the Rock, ii. 61.
Domestic Service, x. 134.
Dreams, i. xxviii.
Dress, History of, see Historical.
Druids, viii. 4.
Duomo, Florence, ix. 24.

Easter, ii. 65.
Edomites, i. 435.
Education, History of—
  Egyptian, i. 113.
  Babylonian, i. 288.
  Medes, i. 330.
  Persians, i. 334, 347.
  Greece, ii. 396, 401.
  Aristotle on, iii. 112.
  Roman, iv. 87.
  Middle Ages, iv. 469.
Education, vi. 269.
  Present Day, vi. 271.
  Schools and Education, vi. 273.
  Education and Development, vi. 276.
  Child's Education, vi. 280.
  Education in Life, vi. 282.
  The Common School, vi. 285.
  Physical Education, vi. 286.
  Citizenship and Schools, vi. 288.
  Democratic Society and the School, vi. 295.
  Ethics in Schools, vi. 303.
  Efficiency of Schools, vi. 310.
  Creative Education, vi. 314.
  Drama and Education, vi. 323.
Educated Women, x. 113.
Elgin, Lord, i. 185.
Elgin Marbles, iii. 349; ix. 184.
Embalming, i. 138.
Empedocles, iii. 93.
England, see Historical.
Epicurus, iii. 141.
Esdraelon, i. 414.
Euphrates, i. 202, 214.
Excavations, see Historical.
Expositions—
  Early Fairs, x. 83.
  London 1853, x. 84.
  Paris, 1867, x. 86.
  Vienna, 1873, x. 88.
  Centennial, x. 91.
  Columbian, x. 103.
  Pan-American, x. 152.
  Louisiana Purchase, x. 160.
  Lewis and Clark, x. 168.
  Jamestown, x. 184.
  Alaska-Yukon, x. 196.
  Panama-Pacific, x. viii. 201.
Factory Laws, viii. 41.
Fairs, Early, x. 83.
Fayoum, i. 48, 149.
Fellah, in Egypt, i. 90.
Festivals, Greek, iii. 357.
Festivals, Roman, iv. 92.
Field, Cyrus W., x. 88.
Field, Marshall, x. 110.
Field Museum, x. 110.

Fire, Discovery of, i. xviii.
Flag, The, x. 1.
Florence, iv. 395, *also see* Historical; see Art.
Flowers in Egypt, i. 88, 136.
Flowers in Palestine, i. 409.
Flowers, Mythical Origins of, ii. 124.
Food of Primitive People, i. xxi.
  Egyptians, i. 90.
  Babylonians, i. 295.
  Greeks, ii. 387.
  Romans, iv. 77.
French Archaeological School, iii. 373.
Friendship, v. 440, 443, 451.

Garnsey, Elmer E., x. 236.
Garrick, vii. 190.
Gatun Dam, x. 204.
Gatun Lake, x. 203.
Gatun Locks, x. 203.
Genre, *see* Art.
Geology, i. xiv.
Genoa, iv. 397.
German Archæological Institute, iii. 368.
Glaciers, vii. 407.
Gladiatorial Combats, iv. 97.
Globe Theatre, vii. 68, 71.
Gondolas, ix. 43.
Grains, Cultivation of, i. xxix.
Greece, *see* Historical.
Greek Archæological Society, iii. 371.
Greek Church, ix. 21.

Haarlem, ix. 55.
Hale, Edward Everett, x. 48.
Half-Moon, x. 12.
Hall of Pillars, *see* Historical.
Hampton Roads, x. 184.
Hanging Gardens, i. 305.
Hannibal, i. 392.
Harley, Robert, ix. 179.
Hauptmann, vii. 371, 380.
Heracleistus, iii. 92.
Heracleopolis, i. 44.
Herculaneum, iv. 391.
Herod, ii. 3.
Herodotus, i. 32, 34, 328, 336, 341.
Hieroglyphics, i. 33.
Hittites, i. 374.
Houses, Primitive, i. xx.
  African, i. xxi.
  Egyptian, i. 86.
  Babylonian, i. 272.
  Greek, ii. 377.
  Roman, iv. 66.

Howe, Julia Ward, x. 112, 129.
Hudson-Fulton Celebration, x. 12.
Hudson, Henry, x. 12.

Ibsen, vii. 297.
Incest, i. 91.
Iona Monastery, viii. 7.
Ionian Islands, iii. 362.
Irrigation, i. xxii.
Irving, Henry, vii. 193.
Ismail, i. 182.
Ithaca, iii. 365.

Jackson Park, x. 106.
Jamestown Exposition, x. 184.
Jerusalem, *see* Historical.
Jews, *see* Historical.
Joppa, ii. 60.
Jordan, i. 412.
Josephus, i. 431, 453; ii. 4.
Judaea, i. 411.
Justinian Code, iv. 55.

Kells, Book of, ix. 104.
Kells Monastery, ix. 104.
Kennedy, Charles, vii. 212.
Kindergarten, x. 94, 115.
Koran, i. 181.
Ku Klux Klan, x. 41.

Labyrinth, Egyptian, i. 48, 151.
Laplander, Houses of, i. xxi.
Laws, Babylonian, i. 276, 317.
  Roman, iii. 404.
  Sumptuary, iv. 4, 237.
  Justinian Code, iv. 55.
Layard, i. 206.
Lebanon, i. 378.
Legion of Honor, ix. 93.
Lepers, v. 17.
Letters, iv. 103.
Lewis and Clark Exposition, x. 168.
Libraries—
  Alexandrian, i. 181; ii. 372.
  Babylonian, i. 283.
  Asshurbanipal, i. 291.
  Roman, iv. 102.
  Vatican, ix. 120.
  Boston Public, ix. 98.
  British Museum, ix. 179.
  Congressional, x. 216.
Loftus, i. 207.
Lotus, i. 136.
Lucippus, iii. 94.
Luxor, i. 73.
Lydia, i. 337.

Maccabees, ii. 3.
Madonas, see Art.
Madrid, ix. 73.
Mansfield, Richard, vii. 193.
Marathon. see Historical.
Marco Polo, v. 21.
Mariette, i. 185
Markets, Egyptian, i. 106.
Marlowe, Julia, x. 112.
Marriage, x. 131.
Masks, Greek, vii. 14.
Maspero, i. 106, 147, 186, 231, 296.
McCormick Harvester, x. 88.
McEwen, Walter, x. 240.
Mecca, i. 184; ii. 62; ix. 56.
Medes, see Historical.
Memphis, see Historical.
Mesopotamia, see Historical.
Midway Plaisance, x. 109.
Military Life, i. 108.
  Babylonian, i. 324.
  Persian, i. 346.
  Roman, iv. 121.
Moabites, i. 435, 446.
Modena, ix. 39.
Modjeska, Madame, x. 112, 144.
Mohamet Ali, i. 182.
Mohammedans, i. 40; see History.
Morgan, J. Pierpont, x. 225.
Morris, Clara, x. 112.
Mosaics, ii. 46; ix. 17.
Moses, i. 80, 436, 452.
Mount Athos Monastery, ix. 20.
Mount Vernon, x. 28.
Muir, John, vii. 397.
Mummies, i. 103.
Museums, see Art Index.
Music, see Music Index.

Naples, iv. 389.
Nature Study, vii. 393.
  Forests, vii. 398.
  Fountains and Streams, vii. 402.
  Glaciers, vii. 407.
  Winter, vii. 415.
  Birds, vii. 426.
  Herbs, vii. 434.
  Wild Flowers, vii. 435.
  Deserts, vii. 457.
  The Sea, vii. 466.
  The Sky, vii. 469.
  Pond Life, vii. 477.
  Solitude, vii. 488.
Natural Selection, vii. 443.
Nebuchadnezzar, i. 236, 306, 384, 481; ii. 1.
Necropolis, i. 82, 139.
Neith, Feast of, i. 154.
Neo-Platonists, iv. 47.
Nero, iv. 20.

New Bach Society, v. 260.
New York Fair, x. 92.
Niagara Falls, x. 155.
Nijnii-Novgorod, x. 83.
Nile, i. 22, 24, 121.
Nilometer, i. 25.
Nina, x. 3.
Nuremberg, ix. 66.

Old Testament, ii. 12.
Olympian Games, i. 32; ii. 105, 290; iii. 347, 356, 369.
Opera, see Music.
Oratorio, see Music.

Palestine, i. 408; ii. 58.
Palmer, Mrs. Potter, x. 113.
Panama Canal, x. 201.
Panama-Pacific Exposition, x. viii. 201.
Panama Republic, x. 202.
Pan-American Exposition, x. 152.
Papyrus, Harris, i. 81, 118.
Paris Exposition of 1867, x. 86.
Parma, ix. 39.
Parsis, i. 352.
Patroons, x. 13.
Peach, Origin of, i. xxiii.
Pearce, Charles S., x. 239.
Pedro Miguel Locks, x. 205.
Persecution, see Christians, in Historical Index.
Peter the Great, ix. 479.
Petrie, i. 145.
Philadelphia, x. 12, 92.
Philosophy, see Literature.
Phoenicia, see Historical.
Pinta, x. 3.
Pisa, iv. 394.
Pittsburg, x. 242.
Plato, iii. 95, 106.
Plague, ii. 334.
Plants, Cultivation of, i. xxii.
Pliny the Elder, i. 400.
Point Toro, x. 203.
Polish Women, x. 144.
Polygamy, i. 91, 451; iv. 60; v. 391.
Pompeii, iv. 99, 391.
Pompey's Pillar, i. 182.
Portland, x. 171.
Potato, Origin of, i. xxiii.
Pottery, x. 142.
Precious Stones, i. 104.
Prison Reform, viii. 41.
Psychologists, i. 13.
Pyle, Howard, x. 244.
Pyramids, i. 39.
Pythagoras, i. xxix.

Ramadan, Feast of, i. 184.
Rameses the Great, i. 74.

Ravenna, ix. 19.
Religion, Pre-historic, i. xxviii.
  Ancestral Worship, i. xxix.
  Solar Disk, i. 68.
  Egyptian, i. 119.
  Babylonian, i. 307.
  Median, i. 331.
  Persians, i. 350.
  Phoenicians, i. 405.
  Jahweh, i. 436.
Rome, see Historical.
Roosevelt, x. 195.
Rosetta Stone, i. 33, 208.
Rostand, vii. 274.
Rotterdam, ix. 56.
Rubaiyat, x. 215.

Sahara, i. 25; ii. 128.
Saïd, Viceroy, i. 182, 187.
Salamis, i. 343.
Salvation Army, x. 138.
Samaria, see Historical.
Samuel, i. 454.
San Marco, ix. 25, 112, 119.
Santa Maria, x. 3.
Saul, i. 454.
Savonarola, ix. 25.
Scarabs, i. 141.
Schliemann, ii. 236.
Seattle, x. 197.
Seneca, iii. 141.
Sennacherib, i. 302.
Shaw, Anna, x. 131.
Shaw, George Bernard, vii. 204.
Sidon, i. 380, 403.
Siena, iv. 394.
Sistine Chapel, ix. 35.
Slavery, iv. 113; x. 35.
Socrates, iii. 95, 134.
Solomon, i. 382, 463.
Sophists, iii. 94.
Smith, George, i. 209.
Sparta, see Historical.
Sphinx, i. 130.
Spoils System, x. 33.
Sports—
  Egyptian, i. 96.
  Babylonian, i. 295.
  Persian, i. 349.
  Greek, ii. 128, 410; iii. 357.
  Roman, iv. 93.
Stadium, iii. 358.
Stage, The, and its Women, x. 140.
Stanton, Elizabeth Cady, x. 112, 121.
Stoicism, iii. 140; iv. 31, 269.
Store Cities, i. 21.
Strabo, i. 48.
Sudermann, vii. 371.
Suez Canal, i. 187, 191.
Sunken Bell, The, vii. 380.

Symposium, ii. 410; iii. 122.
Syria, see Historical.

Tablets, i. 209, 283.
Taboos, i. xxix. i. 312.
Talmud, i. 431.
Telautograph, x. 116.
Telegraphone, x. 167.
Temples, Egyptian, i. 125, see Art.
Thales, iii. 92.
Theaters, see Drama.
Thebes, i. 45, 73.
Thermae, iv. 101.
Thermopylae, i. 343.
Thoreau, vii. 483.
Tiber, see Historical.
Tigris, i. 202, 214.
Titus, ii. 6; iv. 25.
Tombs, Egyptian, i. 124, 138, 140.
Tombs, Roman, iv. 125.
Totem, i. xxx.
Toys, Egyptian, i. 92, 152.
Toys, Greek, ii. 402.
Toys, Roman, iv. 85.
Trans-Atlantic Cable, x. 38.
Triremes, i. 397.
Troubadours, v. 101, 241.
Tyre, i. 380, 403.

Union Jack, viii. 35.
United States, see Historical.

Vatican, ix. 34.
Vatican Library, ix. 120.
Vegetables, Cultivation of, i. xxix.
Venice, iv. 396; ix. 41.
Vespasian, iv. 22.
Vienna Exposition of 1873, x. 88.
Volk, Douglas, x. 244.

Wagner, Richard, see Drama.
Walker, Henry O. x. 239.
Weavers, The, vii. 380.
Weimar, vii. 331.
Whitehall, ix. 50.
Willard, Frances, x. 112.
Woman's Suffrage, x. 120, 123, 125.
Women—
  Educated Women, x. 113.
  Women and Politics, x. 118.
  Women and Moral Initiative, x. 129.
  Women and Marriage, x. 131.
  Women and the Stage, x. 140.
  Polish Women, x. 144.
  Women in Spain, x. 147.
World's Fair Congresses, x. 111.
Yosemite, vii. 402.
Yuma, x. 172.
Zeno, iii. 94.
Zoroaster, i. 341.

PRONOUNCING VOCABULARY

Abelard (ab'e-lärd)
Acheron (ăk'e-ron)
Achilles (a-kĭl'ēz)
Acropolis (a-krŏp'ō-lis)
Adonis (a-dō'nis)
Aeacus (ē'a-kus)
Aeneas (ē-nē'as)
Aeneid (ē-nē'id)
Aeolus (ē'ō-lus)
Aeschines (ēs'ki-nēz)
Aeschylus (es'ki-lus)
Aesop (ē'sop)
Agamemnon (ag-a-mĕm'non)
Agincourt (āzh-an-kör')
Agora (ăg'ō-rā)
Agricola (a-grĭk'ō-lā)
Ahmos (ā'mos)
Aix la Chapelle (āks-lā-shā-pel')
Alaric (ăl'a-rik)
Albigenses (al-bi-jen'sēz)
Alcibiades (al-si-bī'a-dēz)
Alexander (al-eg-zan'der)
Alpheus (al-fē'us)
Amenemhat (ā-men-em'hāt)
Amenhotep (ā-men-hō'tep)
Ammonites (am'on'ītes)
Amphictyonic (ām-fĭk-ti-ŏn'ĭk)
Anabasis (a-nab'a-sis)
Anacreon (a-nak'rē-on)
Anaxagoras (an-ak-sag'ō-ras)
Anaximander (an-aks-i-man'der)
Anaximenes (an-aks-ĭm'e-nēz)
Anchises (an-kī'sēz)
Andalusian (an-da-loo'zi-an)
Andrea del Sarto (ăn-drā-yā-del-sär'to)
Andromache (ăn-drom'a-ke)
Annunzio (ān-nun'tzi-ō)
Antigone (an-tig'o-nē)
Antiope (an-tī'ō-pē)
Aphrodite (af-rō-dī'tē)
Apocalypse (a-pŏk'a-lips)
Areopagus (ā-rē-ōp'a-gus)
Areopagitica (ar'ē-ō-pa-git'i-ka)
Ariadne (ar-i-ad'nē)
Aristippus (ar-is-tĭp'us)
Aristides (ar-is-tī'dēz)
Aristophanes (ar-is-tŏf'a-nēz)
Aristotle (ar'is-totl)
Artaxerxes (ār-taks-erks'ēz)
Artemis (ār'tē-mis)

Artemisia (ār-tē-mish'iā)
Aryan (ār'yan)
Assisi (ā-sē'sē)
Atropos (at'rō-pōs)
Attica (at'i-kā)
Attila (at'i-lā)
Asshurbanipal (ash-er-bän'i-pal)
Astyages (as-tī'a-jez)
Aucassin (o-ka-sān')
Aurelius (a-rē'li-us)

Babel (bā'bel)
Babylon (bab'i-lon)
Babylonia (bāb-i-lō'ni-a)
Bacchae (băk'ē)
Bach (bäch)
Balder (băl'der)
Barbizon (bär-bi-son')
Bathsheba (bath-shē'ba)
Bayreuth (bī-roit)
Beaumont (bō'mont)
Beethoven (bā'tō-ven)
Bellini (bel-lē'nē)
Belshazzar (bel-shaz'ar)
Beowulf (bā'ō-wulf)
Berlioz (bär-lē-ōz')
Bernard of Clairvaux (ber'närd of klär-vō')
Boecklin (beck'lin)
Boadicea (bō-a-di-sē'a)
Boccaccio (bok-kā'chō)
Boeotia (bē-ō'shia)
Bol (böl)
Bonheur (bo-ner')
Boreas (bō'rē-as)
Botticelli (bot-tē-chel'lē)
Brera (brā'rā)
Bucephalus (bū-sef'a-lus)
Byzantium (bi-zān'tium)
Byzantine (bi'zān-tine)

Caedmon (kăd'mon)
Cairo (kī'rō)
Calais (kā-lā')
Caligula (ka-lĕg'ū-lā)
Caledonian (kal-e-dō'ni-an)
Callinus (ka-li'nus)
Calliope (ka-lī'ō-pe)
Cambyses (kam-bi'sēz)

546

Canaanites (kā'nan-īts)
Carbonari (kär-bō-nä'ri)
Carpaccio (kär-pä'chō)
Cartier (kär-ty-ā')
Carthage (kär'thaj)
Castiglione (käs-tēl-yō'ne)
Cathay (ka-thā')
Catullus (ka-tul'us)
Cavour (kä-vör')
Cellini (chel-lē'nē)
Cerberus (ser'be-rus)
Cervantes (ser-van'tēz)
Ceyx (sē'iks)
Chalcidice (kal-sĭd'i-sē)
Chaldea (kal-dē'ä)
Chardin (shär'dan)
Charlemagne (chär'le-mān)
Charon (kā'ron)
Chaucer (chā'ser)
Chillon (shē-yōn')
Chiron (kī'ron)
Choephori (kō-ef'ō-rē)
Chopin (shō-pan')
Cimabue (chē-mä-bō'a)
Cleopatra (klē-ō-pä'tra)
Clisthenes (klĭs'the-nēz)
Clotho (klō'thō)
Clouet (klö-ā')
Clovis (klō'vis)
Cnidus (nī'dus)
Cnut (knoot)
Cocytus (kō-sē'tus)
Colbert (kōl-bār')
Colonna (kō-lon'nä)
Columba kō-lum'bä)
Comus (kō'mus)
Corcyra (kor-sī'rä)
Corfu (kor-foo')
Coriolanus kō-ri-o-lā'nus)
Corneille (kor-nāy')
Corot (kō-rō')
Correggio (kor-red'jō)
Cortez (kór-tās')
Condottieri (kon-dot-te-er'ē)
Cousin (kö-zan')
Crecy (krā'sē)
Croesus (krē'sus)
Cunaxa (kū-nak'sä)
Cnyp (kojp)
Cyclops (sī'klops)
Cyclopean (sī-clō-pē'an)
Cyrano de Bergerac (sē-rä-nō' de-barzh-sāk')
Cyrenaic (sī-rē-nā'ik)
Cynewulf (kin'e-wulf)

Damascus (da-mas'kus)
Dante (dän'te)
Darius (dā-rī'us)

Daubigny (dō-bēn-ji')
Decameron (de-kam'e-ron)
De Hoogh (de-hōg')
Delacroix (de-lä-krwä')
Delphi (del'fī)
Delphian (del'fi-an)
Democritus (de-mok'ri-tus)
Demeter (de-mē'ter)
Demosthenes (dē-mos'thē-nēz)
Deucalion (dū-kā'lī-on)
Diaz (dē'äth)
Diocletian (dĭ-ō-klē'shian)
Diomedes (dĭ-ō-mē'dēz)
Dionysia (dĭ-ō-nis'i-ä)
Dionysus (dī-ō-nī'sus)
Domitian (dō-mish'ian)
Don Quixote (dōn-kē-hō'tē)
Dostoievsky (dos-tō-yef'skē)
Druids (droo-idz)
Duomo (dwō'mō)
Dupré (dü-prā')
Dürer (dü'rer)

Edomites (ē'dom-ītes)
Eisdraelon (es-drā'ē-lon)
Electra (e-lek'trä)
El Greco (el-grĕck'ō)
Empedocles (em-ped'ō-klēz)
Endymion (en-dĭm'i-on)
Epaminondas (e-pam-i-non'das)
Ephraim (ē'fra-im)
Epicurus (ep-i-kū'rus)
Epictetus (ep-ik-tē'tus)
Epidamnus (ep-i-dam'nus)
Epimetheus (ep-i-mē'thŭs)
Epirus (ē-pī'rus)
Esarhaddon (e-sär-had'on)
Etruscans (ē-trus'kanz)
Eumenidas (ū-men'i-dēz)
Eupheus (ū'fes)
Euphrates (ū-frā'tēz)
Eurotas (ū-rō'tas)
Euripides (ū-rĭp'i-dēz)
Eurydice (ū-rid'i-sē)
Eurystheus (ū-riz'thŭs)
Euterpe (ū-ter'pē)
Ezekiel (e-zē'ki-el)

Fabliaux (fäb'li-ō)
Fayoum (fi-oom')
Fiesole (fē-ä'sō-le)
Filippo Lippi (fē-lĭp'pō lēp'pi)
Fra Angelico (frä än-gēl'ī-kō)
Frans Hals (fränz häls)
Froissart (froj'särt)

Garibaldi (gä-rē-bäl'dē)
Genet (zhe-nā')

Ghibilline (gib'e-lin)
Ghirlandajo (gēr-län-dä'yō)
Gilgamish (gĭl-gam'ısh)
Giotto (zjŏt'tō)
Giottoesque (zjŏt-to-esque')
Giottino (zjot-ti'no)
Giorgione (zjor-jō'nē)
Gluck (glook)
Goethe (gē'te)
Gounod (goo-nō')
Goya (gō'ya)
Gower (gou'er)
Gracchi (grak'kī)
Gregorian (greg-ō'rıan)
Guelfs (gwĕlfs)
Guido Reni (gwē-do rā'nē)

Hadrian (hă'dri-an)
Halcyone (hăl'sē-on)
Halicarnassus (hal-i-kär-năs'sus)
Hammurabi (häm-mö-rä'bē)
Handel (han'del)
Hannibal (han'i-bal)
Hapi (hä'pé)
Hatshepsut (hāt-chep'set)
Haydn (hā'dn)
Hauptmann (houpt'män)
Hecate (hek'ā-tē)
Heliodorus (he-li-ō-dō'rus)
Hengist (heng'gist)
Hephaestus (he-fes'tus)
Hera (hē'rä)
Heracleitus (her-a-klī-tus)
Heracleopolis (her-ak-le-ŏp'o-lis)
Hercules (her'kŭ-lēz)
Herculaneum (her-kŭ-lā'nē-um)
Hernes (her'nēz)
Herodotus (he-rŏd'ō-tus)
Herrera (er-rā'rä)
Hesiod (hē'si-od)
Hesperides (hes-pēr'i-dēz)
Hezekiah (hez-ē-kī'ä)
Hittite (hit'īt)
Hippias (hĭp'i-as)
Hipparchus (hi-pär'kus)
Hippolytus (hi-pŏl'i-tus)
Hippolyte (hi-pol'i-tē)
Hobbema (hob'be-mä)
Hogarth (hō'gärth)
Hohenstaufen (hō-en-stou'fen)
Holbein (hol'bīn)
Honorius (ho-nō'ri-us)
Horsa (hór-sä)
Huguenots (hū'ge-nots)
Humperdinck (höm'per-dingk)
Hyacinthus (hī-a-sin'thus)
Hyksos (hik'sōz)
Hyperboreans (hi-per-bō'rē-anz)
Hypnos (hip'nos)

Ibsen (ĭb'sen)
Iconoclast (ī-kon'ō-klast)
Iliad (il'i-ad)
Il Penseroso (ēl-pen-se-rō'sō)
Ion (i'on)
Ionian (i-ō'ni-an)
Iphigenia (if-i-je-nī'ä)
Isagoras (ī-säg'o-ras)
Ishtar (ish'tär)
Isocrates (ī-sŏk'rā-tēs)

Jahweh (jä'va)
Janiculum (ja-nik'ū-lum)
Jephthah (jĕf'thä)
Joppa (jŏp'pä)
Jordan (jòr'dan)
Judaea (jū-dē'a)

Karnak (kär'nak)
Keats (kēts)
Khufu (kö'fö)
Khafra (khäf'rä)
Koran (kō'ran)

Lachesis (lăk'e-sis)
Laconians (lā-cō'ni-ans)
L'Allegro (lä-lä'grō)
Laocoön (lā-ŏk'ō-on)
Lares (lā'rēz)
La Rabida (lä-răb'i-da)
Lebanon (lĕb'a-non)
Lebrun (le-brun')
Lenaea (le-nē'ä)
Leonidas (lē-ŏn'i-das)
Lethe (lē'thē)
Leonardo da Vinci (le-o-när'dc dä vin'che)
Le Sueur (le-sü-er')
Liszt (list)
Lohengrin (lō'en-grin)
Loki (lō'kē)
Lorelei (lō're-li)
Louis Philippe (lö-ē fil-lēp')
Louvre (lövr)
Lucippus (lū-cĭp'pus)
Luini (lō-ē'nē)
Luxor (lŏk'sor)

Macedonia (mas-ē-dō'ni-ä)
Machiavelli (mak-i-a-vĕl'li)
Madrigal (mäd-rē-gäl')
Maeterlinck (mä'ter-lingk)
Mafia (mä-fē'ä)
Manetho (măn'e-thō)
Marathon (mar'a-thon)
Marduk (mär'duk)
Masaccio (mä-sät'chō)
Maspero (mäs-pe-rō')
Massenet (mäs-nā')

Massys (mäs-sīs')
Mauve (mōv)
Mazarin (măz'a-rin)
Media (mē'di-ä)
Medes (mēdz)
Medici (mĕd'ē-chē)
Memlinc (mĕm'ling)
Menander (me-nan'der)
Menes (mē'nēz)
Menelaus (men-e-lā'us)
Mesopotamia (mes-ō-pō-tā'mi-ä)
Metternich (mĕt'ter-nich)
Midianites (mĭd'i-an-ītes)
Mignon (mēn-yon')
Milan (mi-län')
Millais (mĭl-lā')
Millet (mē-yā')
Miltiades (mĭl-tī'a-dēz)
Mimnermus (mĭm-ner'mus)
Minnesingers (min'e-sing-ers)
Mithradates or Mithridates (mith-ra-dā'tēz)
Moabites (mō'ab-īts)
Molière (mō-lyär')
Mona Lisa (mō-nä lē'sä)
Montaigne (mon-täny')
Morpheus (môr-fūs)
Mozart (mō'zärt)
Murillo (mö-rēl'yō)
Mycenae (mī-sē'nē)
Mycenaean (mī-sē-nē'an)

Nabopolasser (na-bō-pōlas'sar)
Nantes (nants)
Naxos (nak'sos)
Nebuchadnezzar (neb-ū-kad-nez'är)
Neccho (nē-kō)
Necropolis (nē-crŏp'o-lis)
Nemesis (nĕm'e-sis)
Neolithic (nē-ō-lĭth'ic)
Nibelungenlied (nē'be-lung-en-lēd)
Nicaea (nī-sē'ä)
Nicias (nĭsh'i-as)
Nicolete (nē'kō-let)
Nijni Novgorod (nēzh-ni nŏv'go rod)
Nilometer (nē-lom'e-ter)
Nineveh (nĭn'e-ve)
Niobe (nī'ō-bē)

Odin (ŏ'din)
Oedipus (ĕd'i-pus)
Odyssey (ō-dis'ūs)
Orithyia (ôr-ith'ya)
Orpheus (ôr'fūs)
Osiris (ō-sī'ris)

Pacheco (pä-chä'kō)
Paleolithic (păl-ē-ō-lĭth'ic)

Palestine (pal'es-tine)
Panathenaea (pan-ăth-ē-nē'ä)
Parsis (pär'sēz)
Parthenon (pär'the-non)
Pausanias (pa-sā'ni-as)
Pelasgians (pē-las'ji-ans)
Pelopidas (pe-lŏp'i-das)
Peloponnesus (pel-ō-pō-nē'sus)
Penates (pē-nā'tēz)
Pentaur (pen'taur)
Perdiccas (per-dik'as)
Pericles (per'i-klēz)
Persephone (per-sĕf'o-nē)
Perugino (pā-ro-jē'nō)
Petronius (pē-trŏ'ni-us)
Phantasos (fan'tä-sos)
Phidias (fīd'i-as)
Philemon (fi-lē'mon)
Phlegethus (flej'e-thus)
Phoenician (fe-nĭsh'an)
Pinero (pē-ner'ō)
Piraeus (pī-rē'us)
Pitti (pit'ti)
Pisa (pē'sä)
Pisistratus (pi-sis'trä-tus)
Plantagenets (plan-taj'e-net)
Plataea (pla-tē'ä)
Pleiades (plī'a-dēz)
Poitiers (pwä-tyā')
Polybius (po-lĭb'i-us)
Polyclitus (pol-i-klī'tus)
Polynotus (pol-ig-nō'tus)
Polyhymnia (pol-i-hĭm'ni-ä)
Poseidon (pō-sī'don)
Potidaea (pot-i-dē'ä)
Poussin (pō-san')
Ponce de Leon (pōn-thä dä lā-ōn')
Prado (prä'thō)
Praxitiles (praks-it'e-lēz)
Princepate (prĭn'ke-pät)
Prometheus (prō-mē'thūs)
Propertius (pro-per'shius)
Psyche (sī'kē)
Ptah (ptä)
Ptolomey (tŏl'e-mi)
Pythagorus (pi-thag'ō-ras)
Pyrrha (pir'ä)
Pyrrhus (pir'us)

Ra (rä)
Racine (ra-sēn')
Ramadan (rä-mä-dän')
Ramses (ram'sēz)
Raphael (räf-ā-ĕl)
Ravenna (ra-vĕn'ä)
Rehoboam (rē-hō-bō'am)
Rembrandt (rem'bränt)
Renaissance (re-na-säns')
Ribalta (rē-bäl'tä)

Ribera (rē-bä′rä)
Richelieu (rēsh′lye)
Rienzi (rē-en′zē)
Rosetta (rō-zet′tä)
Rossini (ros-sē′nē)
Rossetti (ros-sĕt′tē)
Rostand (ros-tän′)
Rousseau (rō-sō′)
Rubens (rö′benz)
Ruisdael (rois′däl)

Said (sä-ēd′)
Salamis (sal′a-mis)
Samaria (sa-mā′ri-a)
Sargon (sär′gon)
Savonarola (sä-vō-nä-rō′la)
Schliemaun (shlē′män)
Schubert (shö′bert)
Schumann (shö-män)
Seleucus (se-lū′kus)
Selencidae (se-lū′si-dē)
Segesta (se-jes′tä)
Semitic (sē-mit′ic)
Sennacherib (se-năk′e-rib)
Seti (sē′ti)
Seville (sĕv′il)
Shephelah (shef′e-la)
Sidon (sī′don)
Sienkievicz (syen-kyē′vich)
Simonides (sī-mon′i-dēz)
Sisyphus (sis′i-fus)
Smerdis (smer′dis)
Socrates (sok′ra-tēz)
Solomon (sol′ō-mon)
Somnus (som′nus)
Sophocles (sŏf′ō-klĕz)
Sparta (spär′tä)
Stilicho (stil′i-kō)
Strabo (strā′bō)
Sudermann (zö′der-män)
Suetonius (swē-tō′ni-us)

Taddeo Gaddi (tad′dē-ō gäd′de)
Tadema (tä′de-mä)
Talmud (tal′mud)
Tannhauser (tän′hoi-zer)
Tantalus (tăn′ta-lus)
Tartarus (tär′ta-rus)
Temeraire (tā-mā-rār′)
Terpsichore (terp-sik′ō-rē)
Tertullian (ter-tul′yan)
Thales (thā′lēz)
Thanatos (than′a-tos)
Themistocles (the-mis′to-klēz)
Theodoric (thē-od′ō-rik)
Theodosius (thē-ō-dō′shius)

Theocritus (thē-ok′ri-tus)
Thermopylae (ther-mop′i-lē)
Thespis (thes′pis)
Thor (tor)
Thoreau (thō′rō)
Thucydides (thū-sid′i-dēz)
Thutmose (thut′mōs)
Tiglathpileser (tig-lath-pi-lē′zer)
Tintoretto (tĕn-tō-ret′tō)
Tiryns (tī′rinz)
Titian (tīsh′an)
Trafalgar (traf-al-gär′)
Trollope (trŏl′up)
Troyen (trō′yen)
Tuileries (twē′le-riz)
Turgenieff (tor-gän′yef)
Turgot (tur-gō′)
Tyre (tīr)
Tyrtaeus (ter-tē′us)

Uarda (ö-är′dä)
Uffize (öf-fēt′sē)

Van der Weyden (văn der vī′den)
Van Eyck (van īk′)
Van Goyan (van gō′yen)
Valois (väl-wä)
Vargas (vär′gäs)
Vasari (vä-sä′rē)
Velazquez (vă-läs′keth)
Verdi (ver′dī)
Veronese (vā-rō-nä′ze)
Vespasian (ves-pā′shian)
Vespucci (Amerigo) (ves-pö′chē)
Vesuvius (ve-sū′vi-us)
Via Sacra (vī-ä-säk′rä)
Vittoria Colonna (vē-tō-rē-ä kō-lon′nä)
Voltaire (vol-tär′)

Wagner (väg′ner)
Watteau (vä-tō′)
Weber (vä′ber)
Weenix (vē′nix)

Xerxes (zerk′sēz)
Xenophon (zen′ō-fon)

Yosemite (yō-sem′i-tē)

Zenda Vesta (sendä ves′tä)
Zoroaster (zō-rō-äs′ter)
Zurbaran (thör-bä-rän′)

AMERICAN HISTORY

We do not read even of the discovery of this continent, without feeling something of a personal interest in the event; without being reminded how much it has affected our own fortunes and our own existence. It would be still more unnatural for us, therefore, than for others, to contemplate with unaffected minds that interesting, I may say that most touching and pathetic scene, when the great discoverer of America stood on the deck of his shattered bark, the shades of night falling on the sea, yet no man sleeping; tossed on the billows of an unknown ocean, yet the stronger billows of alternate hope and despair tossing his own troubled thoughts: extending forward his harassed frame, straining westward his anxious and eager eyes, till Heaven at last granted him a moment of rapture and ecstasy, in blessing his vision with the sight of the unknown world.

Nearer to our times, more closely connected with our fates, and therefore still more interesting to our feelings and affections, is the settlement of our own country by colonists from England. We cherish every memorial of these worthy ancestors; we celebrate their patience and fortitude; we admire their daring enterprise; we teach our children to venerate their piety; and we are justly proud of being descended from men who have set the world an example of founding civil institutions on the great and united principles of human freedom and human knowledge. To us, their children, the story of their labors and sufferings can never be without interest. We shall not stand unmoved on the shore of Plymouth, while the sea continues to wash it . . . .No vigor of youth, no maturity of manhood, will lead the nation to forget the spots where its infancy was cradled and defended . . . .

Our history and our condition, all that is gone before us, and all that surrounds, authorize the belief that popular governments, though subject to occasional variations, in form perhaps not always for the better, may yet, in their general character, be as durable and permanent as other systems. We know, indeed, that in our country any other is impossible. The principle of free government adheres to the American soil. It is bedded in it, immovable as its mountains.

The great trust now descends to new hands. Let us apply ourselves to that which is presented to us, as our appropriate object.... Our proper business is improvement. Let our age be an age of improvement. In a day of peace, let us advance the arts of peace and the works of peace. Let us develop the resources of our land, call forth its powers, build up its institutions, promote all its great interests, and see whether we also, in our day and generation, may not perform something worthy to be remembered.

–Daniel Webster: Bunker Hill Oration

I. AGE OF DISCOVERY

1. What conditions in the fifteenth century made it desirable to find a new route to the Orient? 2

2. What writings gave zest to the desire? 3.

3. With what conviction did Columbus set said from Spain? 3

4. How to you account for the neglect which overtook Columbus before his death? 4

5. Was the true situation concerning the New World understood at once? 4

6. What part did Spain take in exploring the new continent? 5

7. What motives prompted this? 6

8. What parts of the present United States did Spaniards explore? 6

9. The French attempted exploration where? 6 The English? 7

10. How happened it that our continent was called by its present name? 7

II. AGE OF SETTLEMENT

1. What were the first permanent settlements to be made in our country? 8

2. Did Spain continue to hold her own? 8

3. Did the defeat of the Spanish Armada have any effect in the part England afterwards played in America? 9

4. What was the general character of those who were sent out by the London Company to people Virginia? 10

5. In what respects was the political organization of Virginia a result of natural conditions prevailing there? 10

6. When was the first legislative assembly ever convened in America?

7. Compare the settlement of Plymouth and Virginia. 11

8. What was the situation in England in the seventeenth century when so many English flocked to the New England shores? 12

9. What other nations planted colonies in the New World? 12

III. THE BEGINNINGS OF A NATION

A. Colonial Times

1. On what occasions did European wars lead to wars in America? 15 Is it plain why this came about?

2. Is it true that struggles between colonists and Indians fill many a page in our history? 15

3. Note that the French and Indian War was a keen struggle between France and England for predominance. 16

4. What differences in colonial policy is noted with regard to either country? 16

5. How were the English colonies hampered by trade restrictions? Why were these imposed? 18

B. The Articles of Confederation

6. Was it well that the states having "sea-to-sea" grants were required to cede lands west of the mountains to the general government? 21

7. How do you account for the fact that for years feeling in the United States was local rather than general? 22

8. What were the glaring defects of the government under the Articles of Confederation? 22

9. What was the real situation here at the time? 23 Do you understand why this is known as the critical period of United States history?

10. What was the attitude of foreign powers toward the young Republic? 23

11. What difficult problems confronted the Constitution Convention? 24

12. Why did many patriotic men, such as Henry and Samuel Adams, oppose the new constitution? 25

IV. AFTER THE ADOPTION OF THE CONSTITUTION

1. In what ways was it fortunate that Washington could remain at the head of the new government for eight years? 26 Would it have been well for him to have staid longer?

2. Why did the Sedition law call forth such opposition? 29

3. For what reason did the Kentucky Resolutions cause alarm? 29

4. How extensive was the land included in the Louisiana Purchase? 30

5. What was the situation under which the Monroe doctrine was promulgated? 31 Have we ourselves continued to hold to it?

6. Why do you think it was that the Spoils System fell gradually into disfavor? 33

7. Why have tariff bills in this country frequently been hard upon the South? 34

8. Note the rise and progress of the slavery question in America 35

9. Why was Lincoln's death a serious blow to the South? 39 Was this understood at the time as it is today?

10. Note the unparalleled industrial progress in the United States during the last forty years. 43

BOOKS FOR FURTHER READING

History of the American People, 5 vol. Woodrow Wilson

History of the United States, 1801-1817, Henry Adams

The American Nation–A History, ed. Hart

Discover of America, etc. 11 vol. John Fiske

American Commonwealths, states individually, ed. Scudder

American History Series, 1492-1875

American History Told by Contemporaries, ed. Hart

English Colonies in America, 5 vol. Doyle

Rise of Republic of United States, Frothingham

History of the United States, Hildreth

History of the People of the U.S., McMaster

PROSE LITERATURE IN AMERICA

"As we go back in history, language becomes more picturesque, until its infancy, when it is all poetry; or all spiritual facts are represented by natural symbols. The same symbols are found to make the original elements of all languages. It has moreover been observed that the idioms of all languages approach each other in passages of the greatest eloquence and power. And as this is the first language, so is it the last. This immediate dependence of language upon nature, this conversion of an outward phenomenon into a type of somewhat in human life, never loses its power to affect us. It is this which gives that piquancy to the conversation of a strong-natured farmer or backwoodsman which all men relish.

"A man's power to connect his thoughts with its proper symbol, and so to utter it, depends on the simplicity of his character; that is, upon his love of truth and his desire to communicate it without loss. The corruption of man is followed by the corruption of language. When simplicity of character and the sovereignty of ideas is broken up by the prevalence of secondary desires, the desire of riches, of pleasure, of power, and of praise–the duplicity and falsehood takes the place of simplicity and truth, the power over Nature, as an interpreter of the will, is in a degree lost; new imagery ceases to be created and old words are perverted to stand for things which are not; a paper currency is employed when there is no bullion in the vaults. In due time the fraud is manifest, and words lose all power to stimulate the understanding or the affetions. Hundreds of writers may be found in every long-civilized nation, who for a short time believe, and make others believe, that they see and utter truths, who do not of themselves clothe one thought in its natural garment, but who feed unconsciously on the language created by the primary writers of the country, those, namely, who hold primarily on Nature . . . .

"The poet, the orator, bred in the woods, whose senses have been nourished by their fair and appeasing changes year after year, without design and without heed, shall not lose their lesson altogether in the roar of cities or the broil of politics. Long hereafter, amidst agitation and terror in national councils, in the hour of revolution, these solemn images shall reappear in their morning lustre as fit symbols and words of the thoughts which the passing event shall awaken. At the call of a noble sentiment, again the woods save, the pines murmur, the river rolls and shines, and the cattle low upon the mountains as he saw and heard them in his infancy. And with these forms, the spells of persuasion, the keys of power are put into his hands."

–Language: Emerson

I. BEGINNINGS OF AMERICAN LITERATURE

A. Colonial Writings

1. It should be noted that the exigencies of early years in America precluded any chance for literature, properly so-called, to develop. A certain degree of leisure and relief from cure must precede literary effort. Such writings as survive were letters sent to friends in England describing life in the New World; diaries, wherein were chronicled events of interest; pamphlets, etc. 255

2. Note that Captain John Smith wrote a history of Virginia. 255, 259

3. Cotton Mather belonged to a strong, intellectual family. He wrote many pamphlets. 256, 265

4. Who were some of the religious writers of this epoch? 256

5. Would we regard the literature of this age as absorbing if we were obliged to depend largely upon it for diversion today?

B. Revolutionary Writers

6. Note that writings now took the form of printed orations, political pamphlets, etc . 268

7. Who was the greatest writer of this period? 248, 270

8. How do you account for the popularity of Poor Richard's Almanac? 272

9. Do you enjoy reading Franklin's writings?

10. It might be noted in passing that to great armies of school children, who have been compelled to read his Autobiography in school, the very name of Benjamin Franklin stands for much that is dry and uninteresting.

II. FIRST HALF OF THE NINETEENTH CENTURY

A. Washington Irving

1. Washington Irving is remembered today as an essayist and writer of descriptions and sketches. While he also wrote histories and biographies, these are little read at the present time. 279

2. What is said of his life? 283

3. Note that he once represented our country in Spain–this sojourn leading him to write The Alhambra. 284

4. The story of Rip Van Winkle will be long a favorite—as it has been for years past. 286

5. Who immortalized this play on the stage?

6. Are there still to be found schoolhouses like the one Irving describes on p. 300.

B. James Fenimore Cooper

7. Cooper was the novelist of adventure. He practically created the sea-tale, and never was more at ease than when describing a ship in the storm. 304

8. Like Irving, Cooper was a loyal patriot, but he had a less happy way with men, making plenty of enemies at home and abroad. He became involved in broils that embittered his life and were of small importance after all.

9. To what European writer has he been compared? 305

10. The Pilot is one of Cooper's best stories. 304

11. The Deerslayer turns largely upon the death of an Indian chief. 306

III. NINETEENTH CENTURY WRITERS–CONTINUED

C. Nathaniel Hawthorne

1. Hawthorne's private life was delightful. However, he never moved with ease among men. 322

2. For the principal events of his life, see p. 322

3. What books did he write? 323

4. The Scarlet Letter is one of the most extraordinary books ever produced in America. It has been translated into many foreign languages.

5. The Marble Faun is a story centering around the Faun of the Vatican and one who was thought to resemble it. 323

6. Tanglewood Tales and the Wonder Book remain special favorites among young readers. In them Hawthorne relates stories of Greek gods and heroes most charmingly.

7. What is said of Ralph Waldo Emerson? 348

BOOKS FOR FURTHER READING

American Literature, Bronson

History of American Literature, Trent

Literary History of America, Wendell

American Literary Masters, Vincent

American Men of Letters, ed. Warner

Bryant, Cooper, Curtis, Emerson, Franklin, Irving, Poe, Taylor, Thoreau, Hawthorne, Longfellow, Parkman, Prescott, Whittier.

AMERICAN POETS AND POETRY

He is the poet who can stoop to read

The secret hidden in a wayside weed;

Whom June's warm breath with child-like rapture fills,

Whose spirit 'dances with the daffodils.'

  –Holmes

The Way to Sing

The birds must know. Who wisely sings

Will sing as they;

The common air has generous wings,

Songs make their way.

No messenger to run before,

Devising plan;

No mention of the place or hour

To any man;

No waiting till some sound betrays

A listening ear;

No different voice, no new delays,

If steps draw near.

'What bird is that? Its song is good.'

And eager eyes

Go peering through the dusky wood,

In glad surprise.

Then late at night, when by his fire

The traveller sits,

Watching the flame grow brighter, higher,

The sweet song flits

By snatches through his weary brain

To help him rest;

When next he goes that road agian,

An empty nest

On leafless bough will make him sigh,

'Ah me! Last spring

Just here I heard, in passing by,

That rare bird sing!'

But while he sighs, remembering

How sweet the song,

The little bird on tireless wing,

Is borne along

In other air, and other men

With weary feet,

On other roads, the simple strain

Are finding sweet.

The birds must know. Who wisely sings

Will sing as they;

The common air has generous wings,

Songs make their way.

–Helen Hunt Jackson

I. EARLY WRITERS OF VERSE

"All good poets, epic, as well as lyric, compose their beautiful poems, not as works of art, but because they are inspired or possessed." –Plato

1. Bryant grew up in western Massachusetts where the scenery is not unlike that of the Lake district in England. Unquestionably he was influenced by the general picturesque surroundings amid which he lived. 363

2. In general, what was the trend of his life? 364

3. Thanatopsis was written before he was eighteen, but it should be remembered that only a youth with his environment and inheritances could thus have written. 365

4. What frequently supplied the theme of his poems? 365

II. BEST KNOWN AMERICAN POETS

A. Longfellow

1. Note the principal events in Longfellow's life. 372

2. Why is he sometimes called the people's poet? 372

3. In what field was he most at home? 372

4. See what a picture he paints in his Twilight 382

5. Several of his shorter poems are here given. 374

B. Lowell

1. What do you know of Lowell's life? 396

2. What general qualities may be found in his poems? 396

6. Why has Lowell been called our "representative writer"? 396

7. What political issues called forth many of his poems? 396

8. The Vision of Sir Launfal is one of the most beautiful of American productions. It repays one for careful study. 398

9. Do you feel that this poem has a purpose? If so, what is it?

10. Which of its several descriptions seems to you most remarkable?

C. Holmes

1. What do you know of Holmes' life? 408

2. It is difficult to grasp the full significance of the Chambered Nautilus unless one has seen the nautilus shell. 410

4. This poem should be memorized by all.

5. The quiet fun of Contentment is characteristic of Holmes. 411

III. LATER AMERICAN POETS

1. By different people Walt Whitman is differently estimated. Many are devoted to him; others do not find him tolerable. 452

2. Note that Whitman served as a hospital nurse during the Civil War and under the strain lost his health, which he never recovered. 453

3. Democracy, the brotherhood of man and fraternal spirit inspired many of Whitman's poems. Science fascinated him, but he was prone to drag into the full light of day whatever theme he touched upon-forgetting that twilight, dawn and even pitch darkness fill each a purpose. 453

4. What kind of poems did Field write? 447

5. Little Boy Blue and Wynken, Blynken and Nod are great favorites. 448, 449

6. To what section of our land do most of Joaquin Miller's poems belong? 450

7. Perhaps he never wrote anything nobler than his Columbus. 450

"A musical thought is one spoken by a mind that has penetrated into the inmost heart of the thing; detected the inmost mystery of it, named the melody that lies hidden in it, the inward harmony of coherence which is its soul, whereby it exists and has a right to be here in the world."

–Carlyle

BOOKS FOR FURTHER READING

Study of English and American Poets, Clark

American Literature, Bronson

Poets of America, Stedman

Poems of American History, Stevenson

American Anthology, Stedman

Pen Pictures of Modern Authors, Walsh

Homes of American Authors, Curtis

Builders of American Literature, Underwood

Men and Letters, Scudder

Introduction to American Literature, Matthews

Made in the USA
Middletown, DE
06 April 2024